Destruction of Cultural Heritage in 19th-century France

Heritage and Identity

ISSUES IN CULTURAL HERITAGE PROTECTION

Edited by

Joris D. Kila
James A. Zeidler

Editorial Board

Charles Garraway (*UK*)
Patrick Boylan (*UK*)
Karl von Habsburg (*Austria*)
Laurie W. Rush (*USA*)
Thomas Schuler (*Germany*)

VOLUME 4

The titles published in this series are listed at *brill.com/ichp*

Destruction of Cultural Heritage in 19th-century France

Old Stones versus Modern Identities

By

Michael Greenhalgh

BRILL

LEIDEN | BOSTON

Cover illustration: Périgueux, Tour de Vésone, with the railway cutting through this important archaeological site. Tourists could view the surviving remains of the temple complex without leaving their train seat.

Library of Congress Cataloging-in-Publication Data

Greenhalgh, Michael.
  Destruction of cultural heritage in 19th-century France : old stones versus modern identities / by Michael Greenhalgh.
    pages cm. — (Heritage and identity : issues in cultural heritage protection, ISSN 2211-7369 ; volume 4)
  Includes bibliographical references and index.
  ISBN 978-90-04-28920-8 (hardback : acid-free paper) — ISBN 978-90-04-29371-7 (e-book) 1. France—Antiquities. 2. France—Antiquities, Roman. 3. Cultural property—Protection—France—History—19th century. 4. Cultural property—Destruction and pillage—France—History—19th century. 5. Historic buildings—Conservation and restoration—France—History—19th century. 6. Architecture—Conservation and restoration—France—History—19th century. 7. Monuments—Conservation and restoration—France—History—19th century. 8. Landscape protection—France—History—19th century. 9. France—Cultural policy—History—19th century. 10. Social change—France—History—19th century. I. Title.

  DC20.3.G73 2015
  363.6'9094409034—dc23

2015025381

This publication has been typeset in the multilingual 'Brill' typeface. With over 5,100 characters covering Latin, IPA, Greek, and Cyrillic, this typeface is especially suitable for use in the humanities.
For more information, please see www.brill.com/brill-typeface.

ISSN 2211-7369
ISBN 978-90-04-28920-8 (hardback)
ISBN 978-90-04-29371-7 (e-book)

Copyright 2015 by Koninklijke Brill NV, Leiden, The Netherlands.
Koninklijke Brill NV incorporates the imprints Brill, Brill Hes & De Graaf, Brill Nijhoff, Brill Rodopi and Hotei Publishing.
All rights reserved. No part of this publication may be reproduced, translated, stored in a retrieval system, or transmitted in any form or by any means, electronic, mechanical, photocopying, recording or otherwise, without prior written permission from the publisher.
Authorization to photocopy items for internal or personal use is granted by Koninklijke Brill NV provided that the appropriate fees are paid directly to The Copyright Clearance Center, 222 Rosewood Drive, Suite 910, Danvers, MA 01923, USA. Fees are subject to change.

This book is printed on acid-free paper.

Contents

Preface   IX
Map of France   XIII

Introduction: Heritage and Identity in 19th Century France   1
   The Changing Face of 19th Century France   1
   Heritage, Identity, Memory   10
   Creating and Destroying Heritage   15
   Etymology   19
      Heritage, Identity, Patrimony   19
      Antiquarian, Archaeology/Archaeologist   22

1 The Early Architecture of France   29
   Spolia and the Persistence of Re-use   29
      Reuse and the Tower of Hanoi   33
   Prehistoric Antiquities   34
   Roman Sites in France   38
   Rome in Imperial Decline   40
      Theatres and Amphitheatres   43
      Baths and Aqueducts   45
      Villas, Mosaics and Sculpture   47
      Marble Veneer   53
      Cemeteries   53
   After Antiquity   55
      Merovingian Antiquities   57
      Later Religious Architecture   59
      Civic Architecture: Châteaux   68
   Conclusion: Preventable Destruction   69

2 The Defence of France   76
   The Enceintes of Late Antiquity   76
   Old Fortifications Cannot Satisfy New Requirements   78
   New Requirements: Barracks   81
   Le génie de la destruction: The French Military and the Defence of France   83
   Servitude et grandeur militaires – and boulevards   91
   The Génie in North Africa   93
   Conclusion: The Fate of Town Walls and Monuments   95

3 Technology and Change: Improved Communications 101

Railways 102
Map-making Military and Civil 108
    The Carte de France 109
Roads, Canals and Bridges 113
Photography 116
Tourism 117
Conclusion 118

4 Vandalism, Ignorance, Scholarship, Museums 121

Heritage and Destruction 121
Vandalism 122
Preservation, Conservation, Restoration: The Dilemma 123
Destruction, Resurrection and Vandalism 128
Ignorance: Workmen, Administrators, Proprietors 133
Administration and Destruction 134
The Persistence of Vandalism 138
Money, Speculators, Scholars 141
Conclusion 144

5 The Organisation of Scholarship and Museums 148

Archaeology and Archaeologists 148
    Education 151
    Restoration Alternatives 153
    Initiatives on the Ground: The Gard 154
    Museums and International Prestige 155
    Museums in Provincial France 158
    Façadism Nourishes Museums 165
Cataloguing the Past: Censuses of Antiquities 167
    The Commission des Monuments Historiques (CMH)
    and its Origins 170
    Census Problems 172
    Cataloguing Dilemmas 175
    Different Owners, Different Problems 177
    Laws for Monument Protection 179
Conclusion 181

CONTENTS   VII

6 **Modernity and its Architectural Consequences**   185
    Modernity   186
    Communications and Industry   190
    Modernisation and Destruction   191
        Promenades   193
        Alignment and the Picturesque: The New and the Old
        (*or, Périsse l'art plutôt que la ligne droite*)   194
        Dismantling Enceintes to Achieve Modernity   197
        The Declassification Movement   199
    Bordeaux and Paris: Leaders of the Pack   202
        Bordeaux   202
        Paris   208
    Conclusion   212

7 **The Île de France and Champagne**   217
    Beauvais 218, Évreux 219, Reims 221, Laon 222, Sens 223, Soissons 225
    Conclusion   228

8 **Normandy, the North, Burgundy and Points East**   231
    Normandy and The Loire   231
        Rouen 231, *Le Mans* 235, *Jublains* 235, *Tours* 235, *Angers* 236,
        Blois 237
    The North   237
        Amiens 237, *Arlon* 238
    The East   239
        Langres (Haute-Marne) 239, *Nancy* 242, *Metz* 242
    Burgundy (plus Points East and the Upper Rhône Valley)   243
        Autun 244, *Beaune* 246, *Dijon (Côte-d'Or)* 246, *Lyon* 248, *Valence* 251,
        Vienne (Isère) 252
    Conclusion   254
9 **Centre and West**   259
    Bourges 259, Auxerre 260, Orléans 261, Limoges 262, Clermont
    Ferrand 262, Périgueux 263, Poitiers 266, Saintes 269, Toulouse 273
    Conclusion   275

VIII   CONTENTS

10   Centuries of Destruction: Narbonne and Nîmes   278

       Narbonne   278

         Introduction   278

         Narbonne from Roman Times to Mediaeval Walls   280

         Dilapidated Mediaeval Walls   284

         The Capitol   287

         The Palace   289

         The François Ier enceinte   291

         Availability of Antiquities   293

         From Open-Air Museum to Notre-Dame de la Mourgier   296

         Conclusion   300

         Ensérune   301

       Nîmes   302

         Nîmes in Earlier Centuries   302

         The Amphitheatre   305

         The Maison Carrée   307

         The Town Walls   309

         The Discovery and Display of Antiquities   311

         Conclusion   313

11   Provence and the South: Monumental Losses   318

       Arles   318

         Introduction   318

         Town Walls   323

         Amphitheatre and Theatre   325

         Cemeteries and Roads   327

         Other Ancient Monuments   330

         Civic Pride and the Monuments   332

         The Downside of Civic Pride   333

         Aix-en-Provence 335, Avignon 336, Dax 338, St-Lizier 340, Béziers 341, Perpignan 341, Fréjus – Cannes – Antibes – Villefranche 342, Orange 345, Vaison-la-Romaine 346

         Conclusion   348

Conclusion: Heritage? What Heritage? The Transformation of Townscape and Landscape   353

Appendix   357

Bibliography: Sources   375

Bibliography: Modern Scholars   397

Index   418

Illustrations

Preface

> Apart from sanitation, medicine, education, wine, public order, irrigation, roads, a fresh water system, public health and peace, what have the Romans ever done for us?[1]

The dilemma of what to do with solidly built but outdated building stock is with us today with greater acuity than in previous centuries, because population and space demands are themselves so much greater. This is due to a range of triggers, generally connected: the backwash from industrialisation; movements of population and of factories; improved technologies; Europe-wide decline in church attendance. The destruction of buildings might be considered along a spectrum from active planned demolition to appropriation, reuse, and benign neglect, with the same building often showing evidence of several different processes at different periods. These trends are magnified today for the reasons stated: churches and chapels, and rural railway stations, are turned into housing, apartments, social centres, museums or even clubs. Indeed, the factories of the Industrial Revolution proclaim their uselessness by becoming museums hymning their "heritage." Even bigger buildings, including skyscrapers, are now routinely demolished to make way for something better or more profitable. Aficionados touring modern architecture in Japan should check that what they wish to worship actually survives. Destruction and modernisation are, as we shall see, two sides of the same coin, with museums as the safeguard – or, as the British pound coin has it, "Decus Et Tutamen."

What follows examines the fate of the historical building stock and prominent ruins in France during the 19th century, supported by contemporary documentation and archival material, largely provided through the numerous local historical and archaeological associations which sprang up all over the country, usually publishing their proceedings at least annually. These charted, sometimes in great detail, the architectural and archaeological treasures lost to modernisation. By France is meant the area from the Rhine to the Pyrenees, since the history of her monuments must include present-day France, but not necessarily the whole of "Gaul," "Gallia," "Francia," which stretched as far as towns such as Cologne and Aachen, as demonstrated by a glance at Espérandieu's *Recueil général des bas-reliefs de la Gaule romaine* (11 vols, 1907–1938). Town fortresses in France went out of fashion during the 19th century and sometimes earlier, as this book will demonstrate; but fashion, or indeed

---

1 The People's Liberation Front of Judea (not to be confused with the Judean People's Front), in *Monty Python's Life of Brian*, 1979.

modernisation, did not affect some elements of the French army, which persisted in believing in fixed fortifications much longer than Prussia (in the new German state), in spite of the lessons offered in 1870–1.

Although something similar to this book could be written for Italian towns, France is unique in Northern Europe in having a large collection of Gallo-Roman town walls and antiquities which part-survived into the 19th century. It was a country ruled over in recent centuries (apart from various wars) by a central authority directing a large regular army (by 1914 there were 44 active divisions of c.18,000 men each) headquartered in geographical districts throughout the country. Some towns in Belgium and around the Rhine (Arlon, Luxemburg, Cologne, Mainz) had similar walls and antiquities; but the German States were anything but unified or centrally controlled. Nor is there anything similar in Britain, where Roman town walls had long been replaced by mediaeval walls, also in ruins; and where a small army entailed no concept of that army controlling the country district by district, as was the case in France. Indeed, Britain was an island fortress, protected by sea forts, and the Royal Navy.

This book follows logically from my broad 1989 survey of *The Survival of Roman Antiquities in the Middle Ages* (London 1989), and from *Constantinople to Córdoba: Dismantling ancient architecture in the East, North Africa and Islamic Spain*, (Leiden 2012). But like *From the Romans to the Railways. The Fate of Antiquities in Asia Minor* (Leiden 2014), it concentrates on a specific territory, and is even narrower in the time-span covered. This is because the parameters of knowledge and writing are different: for locally-generated documentation 1500-1900 in Asia Minor is sparse, and bulked out only by European travellers. In France, however, from the Renaissance onwards town and regional structures and a few enthusiastic scholars studied and wrote about local antiquities, often to glorify again their once-famous towns, often with a literary dimension, and often with reference to Rome itself.[2] Some, in periods of town expansion and improvement, railed against the damage to and destruction of that glorious past; and in the 19th century local and departmental historical and archaeological societies documented landscape and townscape change in great detail. Thus whereas knowledge of mediaeval alteration or reuse of earlier architecture generally relies on sparse and tight-lipped documents (such as charters) which mention any changes in passing, Renaissance and later scholars, including foreigners,[3] sometimes describe standing monuments in detail, and say what happened to them, and when.

---

2 McGowan 2000; Cooper 2013.

3 Lemerle 2011 for foreign accounts of Gallic antiquities 1494–1520 – i.e. deals with foreigners such as Jerome Munzer and Hubert Thomas Leodius, then Cardinal d'Aragon, in travel account by his secretary Antonio de Beatis.

PREFACE   XI

The theme of this book is important for three reasons. Firstly, the extent of the destruction of monuments needs to be charted, as an antidote to the triumphalism and concomitant amnesia which present the 19th century as one of concern for the past (recall destruction and modernisation as the two sides of the same coin). Such assessment will allow us to set "progress" in the saner context of change, by measuring the consequences for French townscapes. Secondly, destruction (especially of the Roman and then the Romanesque past) radically affected, with some admixture of developing nationalism, the choice of architectural models the French used. These were not often from Roman buildings in France, but from Italy and then Greece,[4] so that there was little sense of continuing traditions of a national heritage, let alone a continuous and specifically French identity in architecture, and plenty of evidence that such an identity was continually reinvented, often relying on earlier architecture.[5] And finally, the destruction of the French past affected the development of the disciplines of Art History and Archaeology in France because it obscured for scholars any perception of what the past was really like, and downplayed the contribution of monuments in France.[6] This is to be seen in their tardy appreciation of Roman and late antique art and architecture – which in its turn affected attitudes to antiquities in North Africa (the subject of my last book *The Military and Colonial Destruction of the Roman Landscape of North Africa, 1830–1914*, Leiden 2014). We might add that archaeology is not necessarily helpful, since it can often pin down change only over centuries, not decades.[7]

To survey the building stock, this book will deal with a selection of themes, treated chronologically. It is necessary to treat the material thematically, since the fate of the building stock depends upon the nature of the monuments, and their usefulness (or otherwise) at various periods: defensive walls are a very different proposition from baths, or aqueducts. The themes surveyed include fortresses and defensive walls, temples and churches, baths and theatres, water-distribution systems, road, canals, factories, barracks and, eventually, railways. A mention of the département accompanies any first significant

---

4 Hellmann 1982 for French architects studying in Rome and Greece.

5 Citron 2008, ch.8: La Nation; ch.9: L'historiographie du XIXe siècle en questions. 307–8: Une histoire plurielle pour une France à réinventer; Andrieux 2011 for the integration of old styles into the century's identity – i.e. the mechanics of identity formation.

6 Bonnet 2010 has papers on Egyptology, French schools in Athens and Rome, the Enciclopedia Italiana, Afghanistan, Carthage and Spain – but little on archaeology in France; the same applies to Barbanera 2011, where Italy holds the spotlight, even though the book is about a French artist.

7 Esmonde Cleary 2013, 7 for Braudel, the Annales approach, and archaeology, which "is much better adapted to recognition of more drawn-out change in the moyenne durée, the medium term measured in centuries."

mention of minor, but not of major towns. Modern scholarship appears page by page in the footnotes. An important feature of the book is the extensive endnotes, which will provide chapter-and-verse on archival, printed material up to circa 1900, plus a few extensive quotations from modern scholars. The printed book will only have author-date-page references to this source material (keyed to the Bibliography), while the electronic version will contain full citations, amounting to some 400,000 extra words of quotes from the sources. The full endnotes are available at http://dx.doi.org/10.6084/m9.figshare.1494729.

My thanks to all those librarians and archivists who have helped and advised me during the research for this book, to the several websites storing 19th-century documents (especially archive.org and gallica), and to the many scholars who have illuminated some of the themes of this book, especially Richard Hingley and Michael Wolfe.

Map of France

Introduction: Heritage and Identity in 19th Century France

The Changing Face of 19th-century France

The necessary first task, even before examining the topics of heritage and identity, is to sketch a broad overview of what France looked like at the beginning and end of the 19th century, and to emphasise just how unsettled (in comparison with across the Channel) was the tenor of French life between 1789 and 1871, with no fewer than three revolutions, five coups d'état, and two definitive and crushing military defeats. The country was also much poorer than Britain.[1] And was France to be a monarchy, a republic or an empire?[1] We know the eventual answer, but the birth-pains during the process explain the prominence of the Army throughout this book. If the population's concerns and horizons changed radically between 1789 and 1900 so also did the townscapes and landscapes wherever modernity took hold and the old was jettisoned. The title of Robb's *The discovery of France* (2007) alludes largely to the discovery of the country by the French themselves, for improved communications, especially from the 1840s, allowed them to visit its distant parts, while the Revolution's remodelling of the country into départements[2] had the opposite effect of contrasting the modernity of Paris with the quaint provincials (including their learned societies)[3] and primitive peasants of what is still called *la France profonde*. But this transformation was much slower than that in the United Kingdom, struggling against market and transportation problems, and other structural deficiencies, until the development of the railway system.[4] What we know today as French was not the language of much of the country, for well into the 20th century most people spoke a dialect or patois

---

1   Seigel 2012, chap. 2: Precocious integration: England; chap. 3: Monarchical centralization, privilege, and conflict: France.

2   Weber 1976, 4, in the Drôme: "where in 1857 a colonel expressed the hope that railways might improve the lot of "populations two or three centuries behind their fellows" and eliminate "the savage instincts born of isolation and of misery." Pertué 1998, 3–14; 15–26 for the impact of posts and telegraph services.

3   Chaline 1995, 197–220: Provincialisme et centralisation; 47–67: Une géographie de la France "savante" with maps showing their growing numbers for 1810, 1846 and 1902; 91–129 Le milieu érudit, including a 1902 map showing the "population savante" per department; Parsis-Barubé 2011, chap. 6: Antiquaires en sociétés.

4   Horn 2015, 241.

2 INTRODUCTION: HERITAGE AND IDENTITY IN 19TH CENTURY FRANCE

unintelligible to other regions.[2] This was a particular problem for the army, recruits in the mid-19th century and even as late as 1914 (for all the improved communications, newspapers and primary education) not necessarily understanding commands in French.[5]

Towns in France had once possessed walls, with gates closed at night, "en sorte que les habitants de ces villes étaient prisonniers de guerre en temps de paix."[3] But by 1800, several towns had already modernised; others had ruinous walls, and were in the process of demolishing them and substituting promenades and new streets. Some rings of walls dated from Late Antiquity, others were mediaeval, often rebuilt or improved on earlier foundations, and ripe for change.[6] Their upkeep and manning was usually a local or regional responsibility, and a substantial burden,[4] given that fortification needed to change over the years, requiring expensive changes, to accommodate gunpowder weapons and new theories.[7] Bribery and cash payments were sometimes required so that citizens would perform such onerous tasks.[8] Indeed, from the later 14th century many towns had to take on the task of defending themselves, with "un véritable délire obsidional collectif qui justifie l'énormité des masses de terre déplacées par corvée."[9] This same century saw a declining population, but the need for more fortifications because of the Hundred Years' War, although little material evidence remains today.[10] The Wars of Religion, and the King's continuing need to secure the population, also led to new forts. Financing town development, including the maintenance of walls, often relied on excise taxes

---

5   For the development of the French army from the later 19th century, see Elizabeth Greenhalgh 2014, 7–36: The Pre-War Army.

6   Saupin 2002, 48–59: Un héritage médiéval à transformer, viz, Murailles et structuration de l'espace, Densification et nouvelles constructions.

7   Buisseret 2000 49, table 1 for the enormous cost of fortifications for 1600–10 alone; Salamagne 2001, 32–61 for the work needed at Douai; Parisel 1999 for the changes at Perpignan, but with no mention of anything earlier than the 13th century.

8   Benedict 1989, 18: "Rights of municipal government were still being extended in the late fifteenth and early sixteenth century – to Angers in 1475, for instance, as Louis XI sought to gain the loyalty of this great stronghold within what had formerly been an independent apanage, or to Etampes in 1514, in return for a cash payment, or to Langres on several occasions in the sixteenth century in order to encourage the commitment of this border town's inhabitants to its defense and the upkeep of its walls."

9   Faucherre 1996, 67; see also 76–87, Le temps des citadelles, namely un château urbain retranché dans la ville pour y assurer une fonction de police autant que de dernier réduit.

10   Salch 1978, 6: De ce gigantesque effort militaire, échelonné sur un millénaire, il ne subsiste aujourd'hui que bien peu de chose, par suite des destructions massives, volontaires ou accidentelles, survenues depuis quatre siècles.

INTRODUCTION: HERITAGE AND IDENTITY IN 19TH CENTURY FRANCE

and efforts to secure crown permission not to remit royal taxes collected locally. It was thus a process of negotiation and occasional coercion, especially with forced loans. The frontiers of the country also changed, and threats along with them, so that towns came into or left the spotlight for refurbishing,[11] just as their inhabitants were dragooned to dismantle châteaux or town walls, as at La Ferté-Milon[5] and Lunéville.[6] Yet any changes left many towns still fortified, especially to the North,[12] and also to the East,[13] whereas towns in the interior often left believed that they could dispense with their defences.[14]

By the 17th century, fortifications (such as those associated with Vauban (and, in the later 18th century, with Montalembert)[15] could be very elaborate,[16] if not necessarily better built than Roman defences.[7] These were often star-shaped, covering large areas of ground outside the original town walls, and inevitably destroying large quantities of ancient funerary monuments (plus extra-mural churches and abbeys) in the process. To the best of my knowledge, nothing is known of any antiquities retrieved during such works. Because of later modernisation which often banished fortification altogether and allowed towns to expand over what were once defences, few such complexes survive on the ground today. Expensive to build, such fortifications were also costly to dismantle, but with the gleaming bonus of profit from new building once the land had been cleared. Frequently portrayed in triumphalist battle paintings, tapestries and prints of the period, such bastioned and star-shaped fortifications are best seen in the models preserved in the Musée des Plans-Reliefs in

---

11   Potter 2008, 157–161 Fortification of the frontier. This included Vauban's strengthening of a network begun in the later 15th century and 16th century: Sainte-Menehould; Châlons-sur-Marne; Saint-Dizier; Vitry-le-François; Chaumont; Is-sur-Tille; Auxonne: ramparts (Vauban) surviving in 1835 and in use as public promenades; Seurre; Chalon-sur-Saône; Mâcon; Briançon; Bayonne (late antique walls); Dax.

12   Dolphin 2007, 136–40 for maps showing the various types of ville fort between Leiden and Amiens.

13   Zeller 1928 for details underlining the effort and expense of such extensive fortification work from the 16th century onwards.

14   Saupin 2002, 49, since Louis XIV il convient de distinguer les villes de l'intérieur, vouées à la démilitarisation, et les villes de la frontière ... dans le cadre de la ceinture de fer de Vauban.

15   Prost 1996 for an overview.

16   Langins 2004, ch.14: The conservative art of military engineering in Old Régime France; Faucherre 2011, 59–63 for the disturbance Vauban's works produced for existing towns, and of course not only within existing walls.

the Musée de la Guerre in Paris, which give a good idea of the expense and desperate seriousness of the endeavour to keep the country safe.[17]

However, the 19th-century rush to modernise, and especially to pull down town walls, encountered two problems. In this, as in earlier periods of ambitious building projects, the first was the continuing thirst for stone which, combined with the high costs of quarrying, cutting to shape and transporting, meant that blocks liberated from earlier walls, including figured reliefs, were often promptly reused yet again. They were sometimes recut (we can never know the extent of such recycling) by unsympathetic masons who probably had little knowledge of or interest in antiquities, and were under pressure from the cost-conscious entrepreneurs who employed them.

The second problem stemmed from the sheer quantities of antiquities such old walls could contain. The walls of Narbonne may have been exceptionally rich, but by 1890 her museum contained 684 inscriptions, and 1229 sculptured pieces.[18] Where were municipalities to house such treasures, most of which did not exactly match in esteem those trophies of French looting, the *Venus de Milo* or the *Winged Victory*? As we shall see, a continuing irony was that the development of museums provided something of an alibi for the destruction of archaeological sites, because – surely? – everything of interest had been retrieved, housed and labelled. Hence the effort to preserve France's "heritage" from destruction proved to be extremely destructive in the long run, because new streets, roads and railways and their stations destroyed archaeological sites in the name of modernity and progress. In this age before heritage management and the flow of tourists upon which it depended, where were scholars to explain the part of such local monuments in the creation of French identity? And, above all, where was the money to come from for such new museums, which were to be storehouses of heritage?

The emergence of an educated middle class from long before the 19th century provided many of the antiquarians who were to deplore some of the results of the French Revolution. This unintentionally marked the triumph of the bourgeoisie, and scholars like Thiers and Sainte-Beuve saw it as "as the embodiment of an unstoppable collective mass bearing within it the ineluctable arrival of modernity."[19] In its bid to change society by breaking links with established religion, the Revolution targeted many churches, abbeys and mon-

---

17   Faucherre 2007, 6–7 for map of sites, plus map of N & NE frontiers 1643–1715.; 22–3 Bayonne, 26–9 Tournai, 30–32 Auxonne, 34–9 Besançon.

18   Ouzoulias 2010, 202–3 & fig. 6 for the quantities of inscriptions retrieved throughout Gaul, c. 21,500 in 2,324 locations. The Narbonnaise alone yielded 1,537.

19   Prendergast 2007, 216.

INTRODUCTION: HERITAGE AND IDENTITY IN 19TH CENTURY FRANCE

asteries, stripping their contents, and destroying or selling them off,[20] since they were considered state property.[21] Some religious institutions had immense holdings, and occupied large tracts of land with often prestigious stone buildings, in both towns and the countryside. As a result speculators got rich by buying and then selling off the structures or their materials, fuelling something of a building boom. This was especially the case around the periphery of those towns demolishing their walls and the adjacent areas ("servitudes"), and it was not uncommon for speculators to undertake new construction (with demolished walls providing stone) in municipalities which could not afford the large costs involved in reworking their towns. Equally, towns were often left with the problem of what to do with all those empty buildings. Storage, schools and museums were eventually to be three possibilities, with the Army taking its usual predatory interest in barracks for troops, hospitals, and parks for artillery and cavalry (and, as we shall see, helping vandalise or destroy many good buildings in the process). The other downside of surviving buildings which had lost their purpose (apart from occupation by the Army) was a continuing lack of maintenance for some very important structures, and throughout the century we will find local societies and annual congresses bemoaning not only the ruinous condition of some structures, but also the unfortunate "restoration" to which some of them were subjected.

A characteristic of accounts of the past is to dwell on change as both harbinger and proof of progress, so that the growth of towns and the development of new architecture is privileged at the inevitable expense of whatever it replaced. Indeed, such replacement therapy usually included forgetting all about the old, let alone describing it accurately. As a result, we are often badly informed about destruction: descriptions can be vague or non-existent, as can drawn representations. Of course, change (to our minds) is inevitable, the new seeming better than the old, which is largely forgotten because it has disappeared.

A persistent theme throughout this book is that destruction (whether complete dismantling, part-reuse, or simply neglect to ruination) continues throughout the 19th century, and even increases, when we might have expected public sentiment to have developed to prevent it. This is generally given the name "vandalism," a term invented in France, and popularised by the Abbé Grégoire in 1794, who was the first (but far from the last) to attempt to halt

---

20   Hermant 1978.
21   Hurley 2013, 149–185. The Dilemma of Destruction.

6 INTRODUCTION: HERITAGE AND IDENTITY IN 19TH CENTURY FRANCE

such destruction by legislation.[22] Indeed, its French practitioners were to be credited with more devastation than their eponymous forbears. It continues to be a serious problem.[23] The term is an emotive one, and frequently invoked in 19th-century France, expressing one point of view about demolition, a practice which others might see as part of salutary town improvement, or simply the replacement of something old and decayed with new structures. Vandalism is therefore what *you* do, destructive and nihilistic; whereas what *I* do is build for the sparkling future – and small pity about the eggs broken in making the new omelette. For this reason of perspective, therefore, vandalism is not a very useful term in describing the fate of French architecture. "Behold, I make all things new," hears John in Revelation 21, vouchsafing that New Jerusalem which, in a minor form, was the vision of modern town planners. Vandals or prophets, now that the former things have passed away?

The progress of the middle classes from long before the Revolution (many of whom were antiquarians) was evident in various towns throughout France as they made their mark and emphasised their status by building. These were people without the heritage or identity of the gradually sidelined nobility, and crucially the movers and shakers on town councils, overwhelmingly interested in modernising their environment, and leaving their own mark on it. This went directly contrary to the existing complexion of most towns, which were walled, and with a maze-like layout with large quantities of old, wooden houses in narrow, winding and insanitary streets; plague was sometimes the result.[8] Even the areas around churches were often crowded with housing, so designed squares did not often exist, except for those created in the 17th century at Bordeaux,[9] which opened up the city,[10] and then in Pierre Patte's 1765 compilation of the monuments which formed their centrepiece and raison-d'être.[24]

In the course of the 19th century, under pressure to expand and improve, towns changed because many old fortifications were seen to be redundant, and most inhabitants were in favour of knocking them down, thereby sanitising their environment with fresh air and beautifying the town with drains, lighting and new architecture. Modernisation looked to the future, to improved com-

---

22 Loew 1998, 27 Abbé Grégoire: His campaign led to the first measures of protection against uncontrolled demolition: a decree of 1793 threatened those who mutilated monuments with two years in prison; inventories of art objects and monuments were established in a number of départements in order to stop their destruction.

23 Gamboni 1997.

24 Gravagnuolo 1994, 8–11: Il piano di Patte e l'esperienza delle «places royales» in Francia; 18–22 Dalla città-monumento alla città-servizio: la transizione sulla soglia del XIX secolo; 22–27 for Haussmann and 27–31 for emulation elsewhere in Europe.

INTRODUCTION: HERITAGE AND IDENTITY IN 19TH CENTURY FRANCE 7

munications, trade and industry, and saw the buildings of the past variously as restrictive, quaint, uninteresting, old-fashioned, ruinous, insanitary – and, in any case, incapable of providing, let alone sustaining, the requirements of modern life. Hence within three generations the French saw their landscapes (and with them, their townscapes) made new, with speedy roads, railways and telegraphs, plus the development of industry and expansion of commerce which these brought.[11] Mock-military architecture does not seem to have formed part of 18th-century landscape design, as it did in England.[25]

Another theme of this book is therefore the difficulty of reconciling the survival of the past, in the face of often intractable opposition from the modernisers, and the insistent introduction of new buildings which meant the destruction of old ones. Thus scholars and their learned societies,[26] as well as those concerned government ministers or municipalities who actually set policies and provided finance, had an uphill struggle persuading the majority that there was any interest at all to be found in old buildings, let alone any need to preserve them. What follows will also demonstrate the importance of such societies: it has been estimated that by 1900 there were some 120,000 people in provincial France belonging to such societies which, by 1885, had published over 84,000 articles, and helped found over 200 museums (not necessarily well guarded or maintained) by 1848.[27]

Scholars sought to mold public opinion by letter-writing, congress attendance and site visits (usually by omnibus and railway!), but preservation and modernisation were simply irreconcilable opposites. Romanticism, with its interest in ruins (the parameters for which had been set in Renaissance Italy),[28] the past, and an anti-modern nostalgia,[29] was indeed an important literary movement, but insufficient to impinge much on public consciousness. The result was an extended dialogue of the deaf between would-be preservers and much more powerful commercial interests, probably supported by the majority of citizens and go-ahead municipalities. Today's aesthetics wish for some balance between the inevitable new and the prestigious old; but the 19th century sought no such balance – out with the old, in with the new. Hence 19th-century France lost a large quantity of important monuments, and her museums contain far less than the upheavals of that century could have

---

25 Tatlioglu 2008 for the impact of militarism on landscape, but only in England.

26 Chaline 1995, 257–261 for an index of several hundred; 230–232: Des Sociétés savantes pour quoi faire? – quoting from their statutes.

27 Dyson 2006, 55–56.

28 Forero-Mendoza 2002.

29 Brown 2010 for a survey of various antidotes to modernity

8 INTRODUCTION: HERITAGE AND IDENTITY IN 19TH CENTURY FRANCE

delivered. Even Espérandieu's *Recueil* is now being re-done, taking account of materials which have disappeared since its volumes were published.[30]

Memory is now considered by some (but not others)[31] a necessary concept for the well-equipped historian, but it is a mystery to some (including the present author) how such an all-encompassing term can be crafted into a useful historical tool with which to manipulate the past.[32] For how was such manipulation to be accomplished? Millin perhaps began the focus with his *Antiquités Nationales* of 1790ff, and with the subtitle *Pour servir à l'Histoire générale et particulière de l'Empire François, tels que Tombeaux, Inscriptions, Statues, Vitraux, Fresques, etc.; tirés des Abbayes, Monastères, Châteaux et autres lieux devenus Domaines Nationaux.* This is a very strange work, and nowhere uses the term *archéologie.* Not one of the many illustrations amongst the five volumes is of a Roman monument, the term *romains* (often used of the Romanesque) does not appear frequently, and never to designate an ancient monument; so we must assume that he did not see Roman monuments as forming part of national antiquities, although this was to become a commonplace in 19th-century Europe.[33] It has no introduction whatever, simply launching into his first monument (the Bastille) and ditto for the other four volumes – straight into the monuments, with no rationale whatever, except the intention that his work should be a follow-on to the (well illustrated) compendia of Guattani and Caylus.

If modernisation means destruction, then so is forgetfulness the fellow of memory – an attitude that has obliterated much of the story of the destruction that modernisation entailed. The purpose of this book, while incidentally noticing how a few now-famous monuments survived by the skin of their teeth, is to explain and document those processes which left France monumentally – physically and spiritually – short-changed on both her heritage and

---

30 Lavagne 2009, 819–821. This will be called Nesp, and add all material found since 1959 (when Raymond Lantier's additions stop; he was working 1947–1965): lorsque les oeuvres ont disparu ou ont été mutilées depuis l'époque d'E – they'll keep E's illustrations, otherwise re-photograph the lot. For the databases: cf. sites.univ-provence.fr/ccj or nesp.mmsh. univ-aix.fr

31 Heers 2006, 9: Ce que nous appelons la Mémoire n'a que peu de commun avec l'Histoire. Ce sont deux démarches différentes, parfois contradictoires, en tout cas incompatibles.

32 Hurley 2011, 118, on Millin: Le monument sert donc de lieu de réconciliation [viz after the revolution] entre les divers moments de l'histoire de la France... lieux de mémoire qui mettent le visuel au service d'une histoire proprement nationale.

33 MacGregor 1998.

INTRODUCTION: HERITAGE AND IDENTITY IN 19TH CENTURY FRANCE 9

her identity. Could it be that the widespread optimistic assessment of France's conservation achievements is overblown?[34]

What were the sources of the urge to investigate the past? In the most general terms we could go back at least to the Renaissance, and then to the great compilers of the 18th century, Mabillon, Montfaucon and Caylus, to name only some French candidates, and institutions such as the Académie des Inscriptions et Belles-Lettres (AIBL).[35] But 19th-century Frenchmen, Caumont influential amongst them,[36] believed that the impulse came largely during their own century, following the destruction of the 18th century and the Revolution, and influenced by the vigorous British growth of scholarly societies dealing with monuments.[12] For Caumont, it is "les recherches rélatives à notre histoire et à nos monumens nationaux"[13] which are important. He is admirably open-minded about the antiquities to be studied amongst "ces débris de trente siècles entassés confusément sur notre propre sol," from classical material and mediaeval churches, to fortifications and "pierres druidiques."[14] Naturally, French scholars such as Prosper Mérimée (Inspector-general of historical monuments, 1834–52)[37] were anxious to underline just how much better funded were museums and collections across the Channel,[15] not to mention the German efforts in finishing Cologne Cathedral.[16] Naturally, they also flew the flag at international exhibitions, such as Vienna in 1873,[17] praising and showcasing the work of the Commission des Monuments Historiques (the CMH), which "a puissamment et énergiquement contribué à la conservation des précieux monuments des siècles passés appartenant à toutes les écoles d'architecture, qui sont une des gloires de notre pays et composent, dans leur

---

34 Glendinning 2013, 77: "France, which exploited its strong administrative tradition to create the world's first fully fledged conservation bureaucracy;" 86–89: Restoration France: the First Government Heritage Service. And 90 for the partnership of modernisation and restoration in France.

35 Hurley 2013, 233–290 for the 18th century milieu; Barret-Kriegel 1988 19–167 for the Benedictines; 169–321 for the AIBL, founded 1663, 211–2 for the list of subjects for the Durey de Noinville prize in ancient history, 1735–94, not one of which deals with France; the named prize in the history of France, 1733–81, produced no archaeological or monumental submissions; explained 221: il ne faisait pas bon s'aventurer trop audacieusement sur les chemins des antiquités nationales.

36 Lagarde 1979, 31–53: Arcisse de Caumont; Bercé 1986; Parsis-Barubé 2011, chap. 2: Les appels de l'inventaire et le retour aux antiquités.

37 Gannier 2003 for overview of his attitudes to ruins and restoration, his preference for Gothic, and his interest in earlier periods; Poisson 2008 for his interest in monumental architecture – he ordered books from England. Lagarde 1979, 103–139: Prosper Mérimée ou la naissance d'une administration.

ensemble, la véritable histoire de notre art national."[18] And by the 1830s, religious architecture was back in fashion: the country should also preserve "nos antiques sanctuaires, afin qu ils transmettent aux siècles à venir ce que peut le génie inspiré par la religion."[19]

Heritage, Identity, Memory

The series in which this book appears aims to discuss amongst other topics "the social value of cultural heritage as collective memory and identity...how the past is or was represented in history...the role of military forces," and this book does indeed examine how France catalogued, valued and preserved her monuments. However, the contemporary popularity of such terms, readily agreed to be slippery,[38] can lead to confusing, vague and inclusive claims that see heritage everywhere,[39] thereby surely nullifying standard 19th-century connections with national identity. Memory is an insidious term when linked to any of the devastating massacres of the 20th century, especially when cut loose from any rigorous historical basis. What follows will demonstrate that the implied ligature between heritage and identity can be misleading, because they are not necessarily chains binding people together, let alone offering one focussed entity, understood and accepted, fruitful for all, and a heart-warming narrative of shared nationhood. On the contrary 19th-century France, with her several periods of political and social instability, not to mention her disastrous wars, shows deep cultural divisions echoing political and social ones – a phenomenon also to be seen in Late Antiquity.[40] Large sections of the educated population eschew the heritage of the past in favour of the benefits of industrial revolution and modernity. These included roads and railways, efficient and airy towns and housing, newspapers and magazines, and the delights of nascent consumerism. In the competition between the past and the future,

---

38 McDowell 2008 for an overview; Graham & Howard 2008, 1: "slippery and ambiguous – yet dynamically important concepts, heritage and identity," with heritage referring (2) "to the ways in which very selective past material artefacts, natural landscapes, mythologies, memories and traditions become cultural, political and economic resources for the present."

39 Preface by Series Editor, in Butler 2007, on the Library at Alexandria, 11: "outlining and creating new agendas within cultural heritage discourse...an alignment with a wider scholarship committed to disrupting the 'Eurocentrism' that continues to underpin cultural heritage theory." Just how a library of Graeco-Roman books could help this wider aim is unclear.

40 Cf. Drinkwater & Elton 1992.

much of old France was wiped out, to the satisfaction of the majority of the population if not of the cognoscenti. Unsurprisingly, here as elsewhere, archaeology took on a political dimension, dubbed by one commentator as "la guerre des ruines,"[41] but equally such remains were considered to form part of a national heritage, and not just in France, and archaeology was enlisted to provide content.[42] Indeed, culture frequently has a political dimension, with implications for both heritage and identity,[43] tamed through the soothing messages provided by museums.[44] "Public utility," claimed Martin in 1841, "is not a purely material thing; national traditions, history, art itself, are they not in truth matters of public utility, just as much as bridges and arsenals and roads?"[20]

There is indeed plentiful evidence that in 19th-century France identity is provided not by the monuments of the illustrious past, but by the other side of the coin, by modernisation, especially the roads and railways which helped make modern France into one country out of a scattered collection of dissimilar areas which often shared but few characteristics, opinions or even language.[45] It was apparent to all that physically binding the areas together entailed enormous changes to landscape and townscape, and that identity would be strengthened only by the destruction of monuments that stood both actually and metaphorically in the way of progress. Indeed, to think in terms of one France is to deny the focus on local identity confirmed in the 83 initial départements and over 40,000 communes formed from existing entities in 1790, as well as the continuing existence of "la France profonde." These figures put into perspective De Gaulle's despair at uniting a country with 265 different cheeses. Today, over two centuries after the Revolution, we might think of "France" as an entity, linked by road, rail and air into some kind of like-thinking unity. But it is crucial to realise that in the earlier 19th century vast regions of the country were virtually unknown to each other, difficult or dangerous to traverse, devoid of detailed maps, "connected" by atrocious roads, if sometimes by rivers and canals. We have been taught about the centralised administration

---

41 Payot 2010.

42 Glendinning 2013, 65–115: International revolutions and National Heritages, 1789–1850; Castillo 1994; Schnapp 1996.

43 Chaitlin 2008: Culture, Politics and National Identity, Internal Xenophobia: Culture Wars during the Third Republic.

44 Rigby 1991, 14: No longer is popular culture a living, sometimes subversive culture. It is now a 'heritage' ['un patrimoine'] and can be safely assimilated into the comforting setting of a museum.

45 Robb 2007, chapter 1, The Undiscovered Continent; chapters 2 & 3: The Tribes of France.

12   INTRODUCTION: HERITAGE AND IDENTITY IN 19TH CENTURY FRANCE

of the French state; and we shall encounter the predatory nature of central government, whether republican or monarchical, when antiquities were "presented" to Paris, thus depriving towns like Arles[21] or Fréjus of their plums.[22] Yet even in the 19th century administrative control from Paris or even from each departmental centre could be fitful.[46] Developmental change depended on local initiative, and towns and their regions were autonomous to the extent that their complexion could not be controlled effectively by the first well-run national entity, namely the army, and certainly not by the structure of ministries, legislature, départements, their prefects and mayors.[47] The other well-run entity was the Republican educational system, with its emphasis on Latin and Greek; this serviced scholars as well as soldier-officers, and such knowledge equipped them the better to understand what they were destroying, scholarship and publication perhaps to be seen as a substitute for preservation. There is surely an ironic link between greater reverence for classical scholarship encouraged through the democratization of education, and the attempt to associate France more thoroughly with a classical past, in part to differentiate it from Teutonic Germany whose ancestors wore animal skins and sang Wagner. The irony is more clearly drawn that scholarship, nationalism, and destruction went hand in hand. Germany had less to preserve, but performed the task better, and catalogued the remains better.

As we shall see, cultural heritage is decidedly not collective, but distinctly partial – a fight by an educated few to preserve the past, effectively countered by the inertia, nonchalance, administrative lack of interest, energetic modernisation or vandalism of the many. Heritage might well be construed as the gift of the past, and developments in education and textbooks did eventually (but not much before the 20th century) help foster an agreed (or at least officially promoted) collective memory and identity, as did the cataclysm that was the First World War. But that would be the subject of a different book.

There are of course political and religious dimensions to destruction, as admirably expounded in Louis Réau's *Histoire du Vandalisme*, to which readers are referred for chapter and verse; therein it is amply demonstrated that the French state of today is as competent and merciless in its destructiveness as any of its predecessors. In certain times, indeed, destruction was targeted, just as it has been in modern Iraq. Mnemocide ("the murder of cultural memory"), both negligent and deliberate, is the term coined to describe the

---

46   Burdeau 1996, 188–252, La résistance de la centralisation.

47   Ozouf-Marignier 1992, 79: Le département était donc une petite république qui s'administrait librement; and cites the Comte de Luçay in 1895 that la Constituante faisait...la centralisation administrative.

INTRODUCTION: HERITAGE AND IDENTITY IN 19TH CENTURY FRANCE 13

act,[48] accompanied by a commercial market in antiquities – the commodification of the past, as well as the advertising of antiquities to sell services.[49] In many instances, however, vandalism outside the few periods of red-hot political or religious revolution was (to use an inappropriate term) even-handed, with Gallo-Roman walls disappearing just as readily as Christian sculptures or seigneurial properties. We should always bear in mind that it is the materials which are generally more important than the use to which they were put; and that it is ancient monuments, churches and châteaux that were the most solidly and sometimes splendidly constructed, and therefore most at risk.

Memory and identity can certainly be welded together by monuments. "Memory" can mean "an historical account," the act of remembering, the ability to recall, while "monument" derives from the Latin *monere*, to warn, or to remind. Tombs are indeed monuments, erected for the living to be reminded of the dead. But "monument" also carries the broader meaning of a great structure exuding the grandeur of the past. General acknowledgment of which structures are indeed monuments (the 19th century made lists of them, as we shall see) therefore helps promote a sense of shared identity (Latin *idem* = the same). Terminology is important, the more so since meanings change over time, and will be discussed further below, under Etymology. One defence in 1844 made by the inhabitants of a gate at Saint-Riquier noted that "leurs ancêtres s'étaient défendus du haut de cette porte," and that it should be preserved, "comme on réclame le drapeau qui vous a mené au combat."[23] Two years later Mérimée on behalf of the Commission des Monuments Historiques named "la conservation des grands souvenirs" as a national duty.[24] On similar lines, at Dijon in 1853 it was protested that by destroying the Renaissance frontispiece of the Chambre des Comptes, "l'on a détruit ainsi le souvenir,"[25] just as was to happen to a Christian monument near Nantes in 1867.[26] Even the Génie (the Army Engineers) got into the act, proposing in 1858 the restoration of a tower at Aigues-Mortes "en raison non de l'utilité du monument comme ouvrage défensif, mais des souvenirs historiques qui s'y rattachent."[27] Memories abounded when old Orléans was destroyed in the 1880s, "ces tristes restes d'un passé plein de souvenirs;"[28] whereas, at Saint-Gaudens, a remaining section of the old ramparts "serait toujours un témoin du passé"[29] and those demolished at Carentan "rappelaient à tous un passé militaire dont les habitants ont quelque droit d'être fiers."[30] Indeed, this "culte des souvenirs" – which

---

48   Al-Tikriti 2010.

49   Lowenthal 1998, 185: A Lascaux cave painting in a 1995 France Telecom ad adds persistence to priority: "20,000 years ago we were on the cutting edge of communications. And we've been there ever since." The French got there first and are still the best.

14   INTRODUCTION: HERITAGE AND IDENTITY IN 19TH CENTURY FRANCE

"s'est presque élevé en lui à la hauteur d'une religion"[31] – was viewed in 1875 as a duty to be engendered by "le goût des études archéologiques"[32] because, of course, it would help the preservation of threatened monuments.

So destroying monuments destroyed memory, as Lafont had already remarked in 18th-century Narbonne, where a sculpor who took and reworked blocks was worse than the Goths and Sarrasins, who only buried Roman antiquities

> "pour ôter au peuple dudit Narbonne la mémoire qu'ils avoient des Romains; mais le premier au contraire les rompt à martelle pour en effacer entièrement leur mémoire et les mettre dans l'oubli pour jamais . . . [Such destruction should be prevented by the Magistrates] afin de conserver à leur patrie tant de belles inscriptions, qui marquent l'antiquité et la renomée dudit Narbonne.[33]

Heritage and identity come together in French appreciation of the past through its monuments, one scholar proclaiming in 1805 that the time had come "d'inventorier l'héritage précieux de la langue et des monumens de nos ancêtres,"[34] another in 1852 that "abandonner le culte des anciens souvenirs, c'est briser la chaîne des temps, c'est renier un héritage de gloire, c'est profaner la mémoire de nos aïeux,"[35] and a mayor in 1898 prompting scholars "de veiller sur ce qui reste."[36] The population of 19th-century France fell relative to that of other European powers,[37] but town populations expanded, leaving some centres bursting at the seams[50] and desiring to pull down their old walls. The coming of the railway was generally a trigger for expansion.[51] But what was to be the fate of monuments if towns could no longer house them? Transport to Carpentras and Avignon, as happened to inscriptions at Vaison in the later 18th century.[38]

---

50   Urban Population Trends, 1550 & 1790, from Benedict 1989, Table 1.2: Paris 250,000 660,000; Rouen 75,000 73,000; Lyon 37,500 146,000; Toulouse 50,000 53,000; Orléans 47,000 48,500; Bordeaux 33,000 111,000; Marseille 30,000 110,000; Amiens 28,000 44,000; Angers 17,500 32,000; Nantes 17,000 80,000; Reims 22,500@1600 32,000; Metz 19,000@1600 36,500; Bourges 16,000 18,500; Poitiers 15,000 21,500; Chartres 12,500 13,000; Dijon 12,500 22,000; Montpellier 12,500 32,000; Auxerre 7,500@1500 10,500; Nîmes 6,000@1500 50,000; Grenoble 6,000 24,000; Auch 4,000@1600 8,500; Lisieux 9000@1600 11,000; Valence 6,500 9,500. Cf ibid., Table 1.1 "Statement [for 1538] of the Cities of This Kingdom which the King Expects to Aid Him."

51   Philip 2008, 30–35 for Fréjus, where the railway arrived in 1863, and the population expanded: 1911, 4,000; 1926, 9,000; 1962, 24,000; 1982, 50,000.

Creating and Destroying Heritage

> Les anciens monuments, élevés par la main de nos pères, révèlent souvent aux villes des titres de gloire qu'elles peuvent montrer avec un juste et légitime orgueil... Aussi voyons-nous partout les amis de nos antiquités nationales, qui sont aussi les amis de la gloire et de l'honneur de leur pays, veiller avec un soin religieux à la conservation de nos monuments historiques... et lutter avec force contre le mauvais génie de ces hommes qui s'enrichissent de leur vandalisme et trafiquent même des monuments pleins de souvenirs que le temps a respectés.[39] [1862]

What towns make of their architectural fabric depends greatly on the acumen and vision of their rulers and administrators. The Great Fire of London produced some well-regulated and glorious architecture, but this was not repeated following the opportunity presented by the Luftwaffe in 1940. Paris, once with substantial Roman remains and mediaeval churches, suffered mightily from modernisation in the 19th century (the Grands Boulevards) and several not-so-Grands Projets in the 20th century. Unfortunately, other towns also modernised in Luftwaffe-like fashion, Paris being only the most conspicuous in her response to new social, industrial and indeed military conventions and requirements. For we should bear in mind that the protection of France herself through her fortresses, town walls and ports was often at the forefront of modernising concerns. This could often entail the demolition of mediaeval curtain walls, and their replacement by styles of fortification imported from Italy in the 16th century – the *trace italienne* style.

If progress necessarily promotes destruction, is the desire for preservation and even restoration mere necrophilia, or a version of romantic nostalgia, against the "spirit of the age"? Is Viollet-le-Duc, who had studied so conscientiously in Italy,[40] the saviour of French mediaeval (and earlier) architecture,[41] or its nemesis? Or, more awkwardly, both?[52] "Omnipotent et exclusif," and accused "d'avoir détruit bien des choses curieuses qui avaient échappé à la Révolution, pour y substituer des pastiches secs et laids,"[42] a wrong-headed defender argued that "on lui refuse toute espèce de qualité d'invention et d'originalité"[43] – yet these are precisely the qualities he employed, aided by large grants which might have been better spent elsewhere, in his destruction of the mediaeval past.

---

52 Bercé 2013a, 174–184: Fortunes et infortunes critiques; Lagarde 1979, 140–168: Viollet-le-Duc ou une certaine idée de la restauration.

16   INTRODUCTION: HERITAGE AND IDENTITY IN 19TH CENTURY FRANCE

Although the term "identity" as a route to copying or emulation, or collective experience, was not invoked in anything resembling current usage, many publishing scholars were interested in architectural heritage, and could consider France as a unity growing stronger, and its architecture more French, as time passed.[44] Their interests were broad, from megaliths and the Romans to mediaeval churches and Renaissance buildings, as we can tell from the various (and ever-lengthening) lists of important structures scheduled for preservation and/or restoration. But there was no general agreement on what to preserve, what it would cost, or what to destroy. In the course of the 19th century the concept of heritage did become associated with the destruction and survival of monuments underlined by the establishment and growth of museums, a cultural innovation largely of the previous century. But art history, a discipline admired for its ability to set aesthetic priorities, was still in its infancy, as was professional history.[53]

Most people were never much interested in the past or its products, the uncertainties of their own lives being sufficient to demand all their attention. This fact was well known, Sommerand noting in 1876 that the previous two centuries had been so indifferent to old buildings that many disappeared.[45] They still stood while they were useful, and were destroyed when something better came along. The aesthetics of architecture touched few except some scholars and, on the evidence of most locations, town councils least of all, packed as many were by go-ahead businessmen and entrepreneurs. This book will not plot the development of various kinds of historical consciousness, except incidentally as an aid to explaining the changing fate of architecture over the century of the present survey. Of many structures, of course, we have by definition no knowledge at all, since they were destroyed before any accounts of them were written down. Although some structures discussed are in the countryside, most attention is focussed on towns and their immediate vicinity, and where feasible attention is given to the whole fabric of structures that make up the town, not just its plums.

What follows is largely a survey of destruction, and the processes involved, which for understandable reasons is frequently overlooked in favour of narrating the progress of architecture via its surviving buildings, and the changed society which brought it about. As already noted, what was destroyed in the process usually gets conveniently forgotten, just one more example of the pliant uses of "memory." Yet, even admitting that monuments must sometimes be destroyed to make the future, any dispassionate assessment of the past and of the engines and perpetrators of change must try to look at both sides of

---

53   Keylor 1975.

the balance sheet, to determine whether change really is progress, identifying those instances where both important monuments from the past, and some good architecture – that enhancement of living – have fallen prey to insouciance, neglect or vandalism.

The aim of French archaeologists in the 19th century was to compensate for the lack of written documents (which begin with charters c. 600) or, to quote the prophet Habbakuk, "La pierre parlera du haut de la muraille, et le bois qui fait la jointure des édifices répondra à ceux qui l'interrogent."[46] Their investigations were, in one dispensation, to form a national search,[54] not simply a Parisian one, and therefore against the French tendency toward centralisation. The provincials resented Parisian scholars, "eux qui croient assez facilement qu'il suffit d'avoir étudié à Paris pour trancher toutes les questions, même les questions locales."[47] The effort was to be exerted throughout France with, as De Caumont warned in 1849, the Société française d'Archéologie voting against Parisian domination: "Plus de cette suzeraineté de Paris, le temps de la féodalité est passé: que Messieurs de Paris le sachent bien et qu'ils en prennent leur parti."[48] He was the archaeologists' tutelary deity, invoked for his skill in writing of vandalistic dangers.[49] Many instances appear below of the resentment felt by mere provincials at the supremacy of Paris,[55] not least as the gold standard for modernisation, but also as the home of those scholars who operated the levers of power.[50]

But not everyone thought France and its patrimony (an emotional term like "patrie," which both developed during the 19th century) should be the focus of archaeological effort. The enormously influential (and well-placed) Charles Lenormant, for example, writing in 1844, clearly saw classical lands and Egypt as the true aim and quality standard for scholarship and imitation, and penned a definition of the discipline which did not mention archaeology on the French mainland at all, let alone the opportunities in Roman archaeology, offered in Algeria.[51] For him, classical archaeology meant Greece, not Rome, surely another reason for the neglect of the monuments and excavation possibilities offered by his homeland.[56] For him, India and China had pasts which should be explored.[52] Already in 1778 Charles-Louis Clérisseau had questioned the concentration of interest on monuments abroad, at the expense of home-grown ones: "Pourquoi négligerions-nous les monuments de la France, qui, par

---

54 Thomas 2004, 108–1111 for 19th-century nationalism and archaeology, 96–118, Nation-States; Poulot 2008, 19–29: Une culture d'amateurs.

55 Parsis-Barubé 2011, 172–192: L'antiquarisme provincial à l'épreuve du centralisme culturel.

56 Dyson 2006, 50–51 for Charles, founder of the *Revue Archéologique*, and his son (1837–83).

leur proximité et leur perfection, doivent intéresser les Amateurs éclairés?"[57] Given the strong interest in French antiquities from the 16th century onwards, we might suspect that at least a part of such arguments was intended to attract funding for preservation and restoration at home, rather than funding schools and students abroad.

Yet what makes an archaeologist? For Lenormant, it is an interest in architecture abroad, especially Greece and Italy. The history of art is the key,[53] which allows him to belittle Winckelmann (against Caylus) for his failings in philology,[54] a continuing fault.[55] Furthermore, to emphasise the superiority of good archaeologists, he gilds the lily by stipulating a range of desirable languages in addition to the essential Greek and Latin.[56] Architecture he maintains to be a discrete branch of the discipline, and all the names he cites are of practising architects, plus students at the Ecole Française in Rome.[57]

Just how popular French archaeology was for 19th-century intellectuals is difficult to determine, unless journal subscriptions provide any guide. In 1872, the Société française d'Archéologie could show only 160 advance subscriptions, and lectured its members on the large numbers the English societies attracted, and how each of their members should try and attract two or three new subscriptions each year.[58] Awards were another way of encouraging good work: for the Commission des Antiquités de la France, in the Académie des Inscriptions et Belles-Lettres, three medals were awarded each year for reports received, and Caumont's *Histoire de l'art dans l'ouest de la France* received a medal, with the comment (among others) of "Qui ne sait avec quel zèle M. De Caumont a propagé dans toute la France l'étude de nos monuments?"[59] This propagation included enthusiastic followers, to whom a poem was addressed in 1886 including the lines

> Vous écoutez d'où vient le bruit sourd de la hache,
> Ou de la pioche aveugle; et marchant sans relâche
> Vous arrêtez soudain le destructeur surpris.[60]

But the problem, as Lenormant's 1844 report reveals, was a lack of productive digs, while "On verra souvent des trésors inappréciables surgir à la surface du sol, et se disperser aussitôt entre des mains ignorantes et cupides."[61] One remedy was for local commissions themselves to collect antiquities, as happened at Dijon in the 1860s,[62] and Touraine in the 1880s, when they described their aim as the

---

57   Pinon 2013, 210; Landes 2009 for amateurs and learned societies.

INTRODUCTION: HERITAGE AND IDENTITY IN 19TH CENTURY FRANCE   19

découverte, collection, conservation et publication des monuments matériels et des monuments écrits, compilations vastes et méthodiques, thèses brillantes mettant en relief les points obscurs de notre histoire locale, enfin vulgarisation de ces résultats et initiation du grand public à les goûter.[63]

Etymology

Heritage, Identity, Patrimony

Precision of language is important if exact meanings are to be understood, the more so because meanings vary over time. For example, *culture* in 19th-century French means husbandry of the fields, *héritage* generally means a legal inheritance (items handed down into new ownership from a previous generation), rather than anything like cultural heritage. Thus concepts one might have imagined to be popular such as Celtic or Roman heritage do not often occur. Because of its legal dimension, heritage is often identical with patrimony (see below). What was handed down could be money, moveable goods such as furniture or artworks, property and land,[64] style of various kinds,[65] or other notions such as titles. In more general terms, heritage can describe intangible (supposedly transmissible) tastes, assets and attitudes passed down to individuals, groups or countries[66] such as love of beauty, of justice, of personal glory, of liberty – or conversely of debts, bad luck, malevolence and the rest. Such inheritances are personal, strictly defined and circumscribed, and, as legal entities, go to named individuals. Tangible heritage (an author's written work,[67] or a group of buildings,[68] an architectural style,[69] land,[70] or the country itself)[71] can also be transmitted. Legal inheritance of course survives, and underlines the peculiarity of hitching identity to heritage. The legal version is targeted – tailored, as it were – to one individual, whose identity cannot legally be in question. On the other hand, the broad conjunction defines heritage by diktat, and specifies that it forms part of everyone's identity. Tradition is another frequent term, similar to heritage (Latin traditio = handing on).[72]

The conjunction of the terms "heritage" and "identity" in the title of this book's series might suggest to some that the latter is in some way defined or augmented by the former. This is not the case, because neither emerges naturally like a spring of fresh water: both have to be deliberately constructed or excavated.[58] Thus the term "identity" has been used to construct completely

---

58   Rigby 1991, 8: France's national identity and cultural unity were themselves not a natural given but needed to be constructed. Historians have suggested that it was particularly in

INTRODUCTION: HERITAGE AND IDENTITY IN 19TH CENTURY FRANCE

new narratives,[59] even enthusiastically tracing European integration into the EU from Antiquity onwards,[60] although many scholars consider the whole notion a myth with highly political spin-offs.[61] Equally, "heritage" today has sometimes become a feel-good term (based on nebulous marketing slogans) cut loose from its essential legal meaning, of some thing or characteristic inherited from forebears. The problem (and attraction) of such a broad usage is that, rather than a transmission from individual to individual, it forms a kind of mystical grail to be imbibed by anyone for cultural sustenance; without its nourishment, the very land itself remains barren, as it does in the Grail legend itself. In contemporary usage, heritage comprehends buildings,[73] ideas and attitudes, and promoters of the concept understand it as the gift of the past to the present and future, often enshrined in museum objects and historical buildings.

But whether such broad usage actually encapsulates any specific meaning is doubtful – which is part of its attraction, as already noted. To state that identity is partly defined by heritage is easy, and the terminology is evidently scalable from individual and village right up to World Heritage sites, which we may understand as belonging to everyone, at least those of the highest importance; or, for cynics, shared out so that even small and monument-poor countries might attract a piece of the tourist cake. The cynics (who see the whole notion as a fabrication)[62] may suspect that a terminology first developed by nation states has now burst national borders. But if this is the case, then identity is just as broad, and equally vague in meaning:

---

the late nineteenth century that national identity and cultural unity were forged on the basis of myths and symbols drawn from history and disseminated through the curriculum of the national educational system.

59   Anheier & Raj Isar 2011 for today's preoccupations; Graham & Howard 2008, 5: identity indicates "the ways in which markers such as: heritage; language; religion; ethnicity; nationalis; and shared interpretations of the past, are used to construct narratives of inclusion and esclusion that define communities."

60   O'Byrne 1997.

61   Meyran 2009 for copious scepticism, noting Sarkozy's 2007 creation of a Ministère de l'Immigration, de l'Intégration, de l'Identité nationale et du Codéveloppement, then re-named Ministère de l'Immigration, de l'Intégration, de l'Identité nationale et du Développement solidaire. Abolished 2010. Its aim was not to offer national identity, but rather to eject sans-papiers at an estimated cost of EUR27,000 per person.

62   Lowenthal 1998; sections of Poulot 1998 such as Inventions du patrimoine (211–263) and Patrimoine et immatériel (267–307), leading to the conclusion that anything can be erected into patrimony if people are so persuaded.

INTRODUCTION: HERITAGE AND IDENTITY IN 19TH CENTURY FRANCE 21

> le champ de définition du patrimoine s'est ... ouvert, conduisant les plus pragmatiques des analystes à défendre l'idée selon laquelle est patrimoine ce qui est défini comme tel par un collectif d'acteurs sociaux.

– that is, which does not necessarily exist as an objective entity.[63]

Just as today, "patrimony" was used in the 19th century as a portmanteau term.[64] It could indicate all the monuments of France,[74] or the collective of assets in a town, including shops,[75] but more usually the monuments in a town,[76] or just a section of them,[77] targeted for protection by scholarly societies.[78] Today it is sometimes seen as a 19th-century invention, and even as a substitute for what the new industrialised world has destroyed.[65] Similarly, tradition had to be invented.[66] Early in that century, action against vandalism was described as "pas les plus heureux résultats de cette vive émulation nationale,"[79] By mid-century, the conservation of buildings could be considered a patriotic act;[80] and by the 1880s, even the work of the societies was acclaimed as patrimonial,[81] the works of art as a sacred national patrimony,[82] and a disturbed eye cast abroad because "La plupart des États de l'Europe nous avaient devancés dans les mesures de sauvegarde du patrimoine national."[83] Indeed, the upbeat version of the past is that "Le XIXᵉ siècle, siècle de l'Histoire,

---

63 Fournier 2012, 7; hence 10: Le fait de mixer les perspectives disciplinaires et d'aborder des objets volontairement très divers évite de souscrire à une vision fixiste des identités et conduit à entériner la vision large du patrimoine.

64 Poulot 1998, 9–10 for a definition, and 23–35: La Révolution, le vandalisme et l'invention de la culture moderne du patrimoine, a paper surveying 18–19th century developing consciousness of history, patrimony and museum; Desvallées 1998 for the origins of the term; Fournier 2012 for an overview; Frangne 2011 for various definitions of patrimoine, identité, and culture. See also 277–280: Identité et patrimoine entre mémoire et histoire. Andrieux 1997 9–27, Du mot à l'object, with quotes from Quatremère, Michelet and the Commission to Chastel, Nora etc., plus (23) six definitions from dictionaries 1694–1992; 103–144 Monuments et patrimoine – on the ways in which monuments were rescued, restored and classified in the 19th century.

65 Cabanel 2011, 18–19: Ainsi le patrimoine serait-il non pas tout à fait ce qui reste, mais ce que l'on invente comme reste ou monument, une fois que l'on a tout perdu ou que l'on croit avoir tout perdu. De ce point de vue, l'Europe sécularisée, industrialisée, alphabétisée et mobile du XIXe siècle avait tout perdu, oublié ou saccagé, les dieux, la nature, l'innocence ... Elle a donc cherché à maintenir, retrouver, classer, collecter, enregistrer, muséifier, panthéoniser, patrimonialiser. In similar fashion, the popularity of philosophy in universities has been explained as a substitute for a lost religious faith.

66 Hobsbawm 1992, 271 for French Republic's invention of traditions: 1) primary education as "a secular equivalent of the church," with instituteurs as priests; 2) Public ceremonies, Bastille Day from 1880; 3) Mass-production of public monuments.

22   INTRODUCTION: HERITAGE AND IDENTITY IN 19TH CENTURY FRANCE

s'attacha à la conservation de ces témoignages," quoting the 1837 Minister of the Interior "où les vestiges… font partie du patrimoine nationale et du trésor intellectuel de la France."[67] And like memory, patrimony can be assumed like new clothing, to suit new states such as Jordan.[68] It can even encompass enthusiasm for those few military structures in France that survived the declassification movement.[69]

Antiquarian, Archaeology/Archaeologist[70]

The period covered by this study is also that of Renaissance and Enlightenment, one of the characteristics of which is an interest in and study of the past. This is prosecuted through its remains both literary and physical – history, antiquarianism, archaeology – so that the picture of the past comes into closer focus as its artefacts continue to disappear. Hence consciousness of losses becomes the more documented as yet more monuments disappear, scholars in a sense plugging the gap, writing books and papers replacing the monuments themselves.[71]

But again the terminology is a moveable feast, for the terms *archéologue* and *antiquaire*[72] are often used interchangeably in the 19th century,[84] many times together for one individual,[85] even if the subject is sometimes defined as the "science de l'antiquité,"[86] with a move toward built monuments.[73] Thus the *Bulletin Archéologique* for 1887 refers to various members of the *Société des Antiquaires de France*, writing that "Ces archéologues ont constaté"; or the *Bulletin Archéologique d'Arles* of 1889, which refers to the death of Claure Terrin

---

67   Durand 2000, 7; cf. Goudineau & Guilaine 1991, 284–305 for Roman architecture and life; since the book divides by type (agriculture, settlements, death, art, etc.) it is easier to concentrate on survival, and to give the impression of an adundance of finds. But the emphasis on modern digs (all shown in colour) leaves in the dark what happened *before*.

68   Maffi 2004, 57–157: L'Etat: historiographie officielle, construction du patrimoine, et muséographie.

69   Meynen 2010, 10: Ce questionnement sur l'identité, l'héritage et la mémoire commune. A broad set of papers, mostly on French sites; how much more would have been available for study had so much 19th-century demolition been resisted.

70   Pinon 1991 for a fundamental overview of the topic. Gran-Aymerich 1998 for a survey of the origins of archaeology.

71   Barret-Kriegel 1988, 221–64: Antiquaires et historiens. Le redéploiement des études antiques et orientalistes à l'Académie des Inscriptions.

72   Krings & Valenti 2010, 8–10 for a discussion of Momigliano's "Ancient History and the Antiquarian" of 1950; Schnapp 2010 for similarities and differences, some of the former laying the foundations for modern archaeology.

73   Parsis-Barubé 2013, 69: move from earlier 19th century notion of "antiquities:" On assiste ainsi à un découplage définitif dans "antiquités" et de l'Antiquité.

INTRODUCTION: HERITAGE AND IDENTITY IN 19TH CENTURY FRANCE 23

in 1710, "célèbre antiquaire (on dirait aujourd'hui archéologue)." The *Grande Encyclopédie*, s.v. Archéologie, tries to make a delicate distinction:

> Les deux mots d'antiquaire et d'archéologue sont encore employés concurrémment, mais avec une nuance assez délicate dans le sens. Un antiquaire est plutôt celui qui recueille les monuments de l'antiquité que celui qui les comprend.

This article, by Charles Lenormant, whom we have already encountered, originated in the *Encyclopédie du XIXe siècle*, and was also reprinted in the *Revue Archéologique* 1844–1845, 1–17.[74] The *Dictionnaire Biographique* of 1888 lists Auguste-Emile Braun (1809–1856) as *archéologue et antiquaire*, just as it does Pignoria (1571–1631). The distinctions made in Momigliano's famous paper on "Ancient History and the Antiquarian" were therefore not necessarily recognised in the 19th century.[75]

Concern by some for the preservation and the study of the past are 19th-century preoccupations, joined by a new interest in ruins which was, however, far from general. This is an important point: if, for some, ruins were romantic, picturesque and evocative, for many they were simply inchoate masses of potential building materials. Eighteenth-century antiquarianism we might categorise (wrongly) with stamp collecting (as do some 19th-century scholars),[87] noting that the terms *archéologue* and *archéologie* simply do not appear in that Enlightenment behemoth, the D'Alembert/Diderot *Encyclopédie*, the entry for Antiquaire (written by Abbé Mallet, who wrote the entries on theology, ancient and modern history, and much of literature as well) reading:

> *Antiquaire* est une personne qui s'occupe de la recherche & de l'étude des monumens de l'antiquité, comme les anciennes médailles, les livres, les statues, les sculptures, les inscriptions, en un mot ce qui peut lui donner des lumières à ce sujet. Voyez Antiquité, voyez aussi Monument, Médaille, Inscription, Sculpture, Statue, &c.

---

74 Dyson 2006, 53 for the foundation of the *Archäologische Zeitung* and the *Archaeological Journal* in London, both in 1843, and the *Revue archéologique* in 1844: "Lenormant distinguished the new scientific archaeologists from the ancient historians by their knowledge of the figural monuments, and from the antiquarians by their wider perspective, which was based on their mastery of critical techniques, especially those of art history."

75 Miller 2007.

As for *Antiquité* itself, this gets less than one column, with the statement "On se sert de ce terme pour désigner les siècles passés." For Thomas, the development from antiquarianism to archaeology is bound up with nation states, and with the kick-start to excavation provided by the Industrial Revolution.[76] Evidently the *Encyclopédie* had other priorities, and is a curious work, patchy in its coverage of things past. For example, Nîmes does quite well for space, but Arles attracts only the following: "Arles, (Géog. anc. & mod.) ville de France dans le gouvernement de Provence; elle est sur le Rhône. Long. 22. 18. lat. 43. 40. 33." The Pont du Gard gets nearly half a column, while Langres attracts over two columns, and Narbonne (with its canal) three columns. In 1890 some scholars were still calling themselves antiquarians, noting that their main task was the publication of "travaux d'archéologie,"[88] a similar conjunction to that seen three decades earlier.[89]

Again digging, which we associate with the discovery of antiquities, and a prime task of archaeologists today and for the past century, was not a priority for 17th and 18th century scholars who, in holy orders, noble, or well-connected, conducted voluminous correspondance instead, relying on the usually chance finds reported by workmen or, like Caylus, commissioning engineers to be on the alert for sites and discoveries, and to make drawings. But once found, the market in antiquities was well organised, with finds going abroad even from the 16th century. Archaeology was prosecuted from an armchair or at a desk, or in the case of the really dedicated, overlooking a trench, but not wielding a shovel: digging was for workmen, who might uncover objects that could be traded. "Monuments" were of course structures standing above ground, so other procedures were needed for the archaeologist which entailed digging. It was soon recognised that digging could produce further wonders; but although supervisors sometimes contributed finds to local museums, it was inevitable that most workmen would simply loot anything valuable, breaking anything that stood in their way.[90] Small objects such as coins and statuettes, which could easily be concealed, provided income for workmen in the 19th century, especially as tourism increased. Heavy columns, statues or bas-reliefs were left alone, unless they were deemed suitable for extraction as trophies to Paris.

---

76 Thomas 2004 2 for Industrial Revolution and modernity; 7: "Antiquarianism at once fed off the growing importance of intellectual activity, and helped to provide a temporal grounding for the European nation-states;" 109–110: "Broadly speaking, the rise of nationalism in Europe coincided with the transformation of antiquarianism into archaeology. The development of a discipline with a more rigorous methodology was at least in part a consequence of the greater weight of public expectation and curiosity now vested in the study of the past."

INTRODUCTION: HERITAGE AND IDENTITY IN 19TH CENTURY FRANCE

For Caylus (1692–1765; his *Recueil d'antiquités* 1752–1767),[77] for example, no attention is given to actually going out and digging things up himself (this was not a pursuit for a gentleman, except well into the 19th century), although he visited digs during his 1714–15 travels in Italy. In later life, he is happy to receive information and drawings from others, and then delights in publishing them for the pleasure of connoisseurs,[91] including finds from Paris.[92] The advantage of drawings is that they can be engraved to illustrate (and profusely) his *Recueil*; but the problems are that their quality remains independently unchecked, and they are uniform neither in scale nor in detailing. In vol IV Caylus frankly admits such difficulties with drawings he has received of Roman ruins in Barcelona:

> Je dois au moins avertir que je n'ai d'autre autorité sur les monumens que je vais rapporter, que celle qu'il est possible de prendre sur des desseins: j'ai lieu de les croire très-exacts; cependant leur détail pourroit être encore plus satisfaisant. Quelques-uns m'ont été envoyés sans échelle ou sans distinction de matières: quels qu'ils soient, je m'estime heureux de les posséder.[93]

His interest is restricted to such reports and drawings, and to what can go in a packing case, opening which is akin to Christmas: "Dans l'instant où ses trésors arrivent, il ouvre avec une douce inquiétude, mêlée d'espérances, les caisses qui les renferment: il se flatte d'y trouver des choses rares & inconnues."[94] The best cases came from abroad, and it was not until the publication in 1759 of volume III of his *Recueil d'antiquités egyptiennes, étrusques, grecques et romaines* that the additional *et gauloises* was tacked onto the end of the title. He clearly did not expect to get much of use from his compatriots, naming the Italians in volume II (1766) as the likely source of most information, enlightened as they were by the classical and Egyptian past: "Ils habitent une région fortunée, où les Arts fugitifs de l'Egypte & de la Grèce, cherchèrent autrefois un azyle, se fixèrent long-temps leur séjour."[95] For Caylus, then, Gallic and Roman antiquities are different, and he drifts into dealing with the Gauls because they are on French soil, demonstrating conventional disdain for their debased Roman art; thus he apologises for the vignette he uses for Gallic Antiquities, but "Le goût du tems dans lequel on a coulé ce plomb n'étoit pas bon; mais il faut songer à quelle distance de Rome la Ville de Metz étoit placée."[96] Hence it is his interest

---

77 Barret-Kriegel 1988, 245, for his Recueil with 826 plates and 3,000 objects: Ne craignant pas de concevoir de nombreux dessins ou de les confier à des ingénieurs ou à des architectes lorsqu'il s'agit de monuments, il a fait incontestablement faire de très grands progrès à la connaissance des arts et à celle des techniques anciennes.

in less debased (that is, earlier) Roman remains in France which predominates: "j'ai dessein de ramasser, avec encore plus d'exacitude, toutes les Antiquités que la France peut produire. On en trouve même un assez grand nombre dans cette Classe consacrée aux Romains,"[97] one instance being material retrieved from the Fontaine de Diane at Nîmes.[98]

This stay-at-home attitude changed during the course of the 19th century, when physical changes to the landscape meant that any serious archaeologists either had to dig themselves, or at least get workmen to dig on their behalf. Thus Napoleon III, who had a particular interest in Julius Caesar and his battles in France, studied ancient weaponry, and pressed for the creation of a map of Roman Gaul in the Cassini tradition.[99] It is from his reign that some institutions were founded which anchored the study of the past in French life.[78] One reason for change was that much more soil was being turned over during the 19th century than previously, as towns modernised, and new roads and especially railways were built.

In what follows, how are we to deal with the terms patrimony, heritage and identity, discussed above? By citing them when they appear (if rarely) in 19th-century accounts, but always keeping in mind that they are modern terms applied to the past, and to be treated as slippery and protean constructions which allow some of us today to make sense of the past by categorising it, and others of us to delve deeper into the complexities of the past. We shall discover that 19th-century France was a fragmented society, imprisoned in far-flung regions which only talked to each other as communications improved; and that, while patrimony was often comprehensively destroyed, ignorance and confusion about Celts, Gauls and Romans meant that neither heritage nor identity could easily be pinned down, even with the new data supplied by the new "science" of archaeology. Gallic identity was part-myth, part archaeological speculation,[79] with a literary dimension provided by, for example, Sainte-Beuve.[80]

Our investigation deals with the reuse of monuments and buildings, and their survival in sufficient quantities for antiquarians and archaeologists (see

---

78   Den Boer 2011, 192: "In 1858 a committee was created for the study of the topography of Gaul and a new chair for Latin epigraphy was created at the College de France. An archaeological museum for national (Celtic and Gallo-Roman) antiquities was opened in 1867 in Saint-Germain-en-Laye. In spite of clerical opposition, even a special room for 'pre-historical' finds was created. Prehistory was considered by the church as a dangerous discipline, creating uncertainty and doubts about biblical wisdom."

79   Gran-Aymerich 1988 for "Visions de la Gaule indépendante au XIXᵉ siècle. Mythe historique et réalité archéologique."

80   Prendergast 2007, chap. 7: Romans, Gauls, and Franks.

INTRODUCTION: HERITAGE AND IDENTITY IN 19TH CENTURY FRANCE

Chapter Four for definitions) to rediscover and study them. When we study the past, we search for patterns, for influence, and hence for meaning – no more so than when we study the reuse of the past. This book proceeds chronologically, examining monuments and then the consequences of 19th-century attitudes to them. Following this Introduction, which has discussed the themes of preservation and destruction, Chapter One surveys the early architecture of France from Prehistory onwards, and Chapter Two examines the Defence of France, and treats what was in store for millennial towns and their walls and antiquities when, through the course of the 19th century, town walls were considered indefensible and some were replaced by complexes of forts. Change was predicated on improved technologies and communications, the subject of Chapter Three. Chapter Four, on Vandalism, Ignorance, Scholarship and Museums, surveys what happened to monuments because of rapid change, and Chapter Five surveys Modernity and its Architectural Consequences, charting the enormous scope of the problem, and examining two leaders of modernising change, Bordeaux and Paris. The remaining chapters, forming a kind of gazeteer, offer an overview of the impact of modernity on erstwhile Roman towns throughout France.

[1] Dutens_I_1829_XXV

[2] AD_Centre_(Limousin)_ 1903_49–50

[3] Déclassement_ Narbonne_1888_15

[4] Babeau_1894_125

[5] SG_LIV_Soissons_ 1887_209

[6] Guibert_IV_1845_548

[7] Carnot_1812_467

[8] Ménard_III_1832_14

[9] Caumont_1838_346–347

[10] Murray_1848_267

[11] BSA_Seine-et-Marne_ III_1864_89

[12] Caumont_1830_5

[13] Caumont_1830_3–4

[14] Caumont_1830_6

[15] Mérimée_1843_12–13

[16] Sommerard_1876_345

[17] Sommerard_1876

[18] Sommerard_1876_1

[19] Bonnald_1839_229

[20] Brown_1905_74

[21] Estrangin_1837_5–6

[22] Garcin_I_1835_452–453

[23] AA_I_1844_91

[24] BM_XII_1846_385

[25] Mém_Côte_d'Or_III_ 1853_367

[26] BSA_Nantes_VII_ 1867_132

[27] Lenthéric_1879_514

[28] BSA_Orléanais_VIII_ 1883–1886_215B

[29] Revue_Comminges_ IX_1894_268

[30] Annuaire_Normandie_ LXII_1896_5

[31] SG_XX_Troyes_1853_292

[32] BSA_Nantes_XIV_1875_15

[33] Lafont_1739_fol_57

[34] Cambry_1805_384

[35] Migne_1852_972

[36] SG_LXIII_Morlaix_ 1898_22–23

[37] Bertillon_1911_43

[38] Carpentras_BM_Ms_ 1721_105

[39] SG_XXIX_Saumur_ 1862_638

[40] Paté_1900_19–20

[41] Hunnewell_1898_63–64

[42] SG_XXXIV_Paris_1867_ 175–176

[43] Année_Artistique_ II_1879_496

[44] BM_I_1834_125–126

[45] Sommerard_1876_3

[46] SAH_Charente_1870_ 516–520

[47] Annuaire_Archéologie_ Français_I_1877_164

[48] Caumont, BM_XV_1849_ III–IV

[49] SG_XVIII_Laon_1851_52

[50] Brown_1905_82

[51] Lenormant_1844B_1–17

[52] Lenormant_1844_7

[53] Lenormant_1844_3

[54] Lenormant_1844_4

[55] Lenormant_1844_6

[56] Lenormant_1844_13–14

[57] Lenormant_1844_15

[58] SG_XXXIX_Vendôme_1872_XLI–XLIII

[59] Lenormant_1844B_368

[60] SG_LIII_Nantes_1886_77–78

[61] Lenormant_1844B_373–374

[62] Mém_Côte_d'Or_VI_1861–1864_LXXXX

[63] BSA_Touraine_1882_413–428

[64] AMPF_XV_1901_206–207

[65] AMPF_XIX_1906_24

[66] Mém_Lyon_1879–81_14

[67] Franklin_1877_399

[68] Goze_1854_27

[69] Mém_Picardie_VII_1844_137

[70] Jousselin_1850

[71] Dussieux_1843_ii

[72] Réunion_BA_XIV_1890_20

[73] Enlart_I_1902_3

[74] Paté_1900_5

[75] Dictionnaire_Universel_III_1771_333

[76] BA_Arles_I_1889_19

[77] Jullian_II_1890_310

[78] BA_Comité_Bibliographie_1909–1910_XI

[79] Bottin_1821_122

[80] Mém_Picardie_X_1850_54

[81] BA_Comité_Bibliographie_1887_343

[82] Vaux_1888_51

[83] Réunion_BA_IV_1890_17

[84] SG_XIII_Metz_1846_200

[85] Estrangin_1838_379

[86] Scheler_1888

[87] Lenormant_1844_1

[88] MSA_Ouest_XIII_1890_XLIX

[89] BM_XXII_1856_179

[90] Bonnin_1857_342

[91] Caylus_II_1766_I

[92] Caylus_II_1766_367–392

[93] Caylus_IV_1761_358ff

[94] Caylus_II_1766_ii

[95] Caylus_II_1766_iii

[96] Caylus_IV_1761_xix

[97] Caylus_II_1766_272

[98] Caylus_II_1766_339–366

[99] PV_Seine-Inférieure_II_1849–1866_91

CHAPTER 1

The Early Architecture of France

Travellers to France today often remark how close together and plentiful are her civic, military and ecclesiastical monuments (in comparison, for example, with Spain or even parts of Italy). This book shows that they were once much more plentiful, and that the survivals have often been mangled by 19th-century restoration. Even if ecclesiastical architecture remains plentiful, large quantities have been destroyed, many by the occupation of the French army, as we shall see. As for Roman architecture, the following chapters will demonstrate how false is the common notion that the Romans only really built anything in Provence, by detailing the inexorable march of modernisation, open towns and railways which destroyed large quantities of antique structures in the rest of the country, and continues that task almost to the present day. But what about laws against such destruction, and the protection provided to some monuments? With aggressive prefects (such as Baron Haussmann) and local administrations, plus litigious property owners, and the imperative of new roads and railways, it is a miracle that as much survived as it did.

Spolia and the Persistence of Re-use

Throughout the Middle Ages, and indeed to our own day, we have contemporary accounts which express enthusiasm for the prestigious materials of antiquity, especially marble (which could exude and express "power"), in the shape of columns, and squared building-blocks, some of large dimensions – an enthusiasm for the heroic age, and the older the better (perhaps), similar to Pausanias' attitude to his material. Modern studies are also plentiful.[1] Such spolia, a term referring to the systematic or casual re-use of material from previous structures, were useful over the centuries, because they might be reused again and again in a variety of locations and for a wide range of purposes.[1] Columns were attractive to the Middle Ages for a host of reasons. Not only were they almost a trademark of classical architecture, but they were easy to get at and easy to transport, because they could be rolled like logs, or given wheels, when they formed an improvised axle. Usually of marble or granite, but sometimes of limestone, they were (when monolithic) long and strong,

---

1 Pinon 1978 & 1985 for re-use of theatres, amphitheatres etc. in France.

© KONINKLIJKE BRILL NV, LEIDEN, 2015 | DOI 10.1163/9789004293717_003

30   CHAPTER 1

and beautiful as well, gleaming because highly polished. In at least one 12th-century French account of rebuilding of the Abbey at Ardres, near Boulogne, c. 1172 by the Abbot Peter, the spolia may be antique, but taken from a ruined church.[2] The Romans themselves reused materials, and so, routinely, did the early Church. Thus it is not surprising that the Middle Ages in the West, France included, shared Cassiodorus' enthusiasm about the qualities of spolia.[3] Today, the market for spolia continues unabated.[2]

Marble reliefs and veneers, and large building blocks, were also prized in later centuries, and like columns became the building elements of much long-lasting mediaeval religious architecture, as well as of that of later centuries. Louis XIV did make efforts to quarry marble at S. Béat, but getting it thither to Paris and Versailles was tedious, and digging for spolia very much easier, some of it imported on French vessels from around the Mediterranean. Of course, there was so much building activity during the Middle Ages and later, civil, ecclesiastical as well as military, that quarrying was essential,[3] and sometimes took place under the town itself, as at Bourges (Cher).[4] But if ruins were available, as at Vaison, they were used. In the later 18th century the Abbé de Saint-Véran comments on the locals' desire for materials, the local château being treated

> à peu près par eux comme le fut autrefois le collissée de Rome. C'est un inconvénient auquel notre police pouvoit bien aisément remedier, en punissant avec sévérité ces destructeurs d'ouvrages publics.[4]

And one look at the town shows why the château went before the Roman ruins: it was at the top of the hill, so blocks were easily rolled down from it – whereas plundering the Roman ruins would have required lifting equipment.

Because of the enormous costs of quarrying and (especially) transporting new stone, a large proportion of architecture anywhere is based on reuse. Technological competence through the centuries was also variable.[5] The build-

---

2 Il Messagero, Monday 12 February 1996, 4: a porphyry column shaft weighing five tons was stolen from the Baths of Caracalla. This was obviously for slicing into table tops, for the going rate for Corinthian capitals (Hellenistic, Roman, or Byzantine) for use as table pedestals was up to 10m lire.

3 Bayrou 2013, 28–9 for quarrying at Peyrepertuse in 1250; 137–148 for repair work at Carcassonne in 1120 etc.; 167–171 for the Palais Vieux at Narbonne, newly built and renamed in the 14th century, and much reworked in 17–18th century.

4 Narboux 2003, 45–68: Un sous-sol gallo-romain, including the walls, and quarries.

5 Scheidegger 1991 I, 132–140 for Techniques 400-Romanesque

THE EARLY ARCHITECTURE OF FRANCE   31

ing of enceintes in Late Antiquity was more of a farewell to the past than a continuation of it.[6] The Ottomans guarded the Dardanelles with cannonballs recut from ancient sculpted blocks,[5] as did mediaeval armies in North Africa[6] and European settlers during the 19th century.[7] Later walls at Saint-Bertrand-de-Comminges included such marble blocks[7] as did, in much larger quantities, town walls that feature throughout this book. Because they contained so many reusable stones, whole sections of Roman walls could disappear, as happened in part at Nîmes.[8] The Middle Ages reused marble with enthusiasm, for church structures as well as for sarcophagi and altars. Cures obtained from marble dust scratched by pilgrims were one of S. Martin's many miracles.[9] Dismantling or excavating ancient structures could be dangerous (collapse of columns),[10] or pointless if what was found was stolen;[11] but it was essential for showcases for ancient columns and marble such as S. Trophîme at Arles,[12] or the similar and equally prestigious S. Gilles du Gard. The 19th century was alert to the practice, even suggesting that the arch at Cavaillon was built from earlier monuments.[13] Nor was it only marble from Roman structures that was reused: any kind of useful stone, from any period, was susceptible,[8] and little is known about (for example) earlier versions of churches on the same site because the later (often larger) structure would routinely reuse its materials. It is also likely that many pieces were reused more than once, but their history generally cannot be traced, because they were recut.

Reuse of monuments allows us to trace the afterlife of classical art and architecture (or, in different contexts, of Phoenician, or cyclopean architecture; or mediaeval architecture in Britain after the Dissolution of the Monasteries). Recycling generally reflects diminished population levels, whilst the quantity employed underlines the large scale of many classical cities. Sometimes there is an aesthetic component in reuse, so that classical *gloria* survives, as if reuse were a thermometer of a continuing classical tradition. But without documentary evidence, or abundant comparanda, there are manifold problems. Does display mean pride in one's own or an adopted past? Or can use be equated simply with nonchalance or convenience? To the practical and aesthetic reasons for such reuse, we may add the interest of later generations in linking with

---

6   Frye 2003, 186: Thus, well before the fall of the Western Empire, the psychological link between Gaul and the Imperial culture had demonstrably weakened. City life had once embodied the very essence of Romanitas. In dismantling the urban monuments, the wall builders of Late Antiquity had broken irrevocably with the past.

7   Esmonde Cleary & Wood, 2006, 231–261.

8   Salamagne 2001, 144–145: Une politique de réemploi at Douai, but nothing on any Roman materials.

their own past, or of invaders in constructing a local identity. Whether antique spolia would be suitable would of course depend on the nature of the stone: at Amiens in 1468, for example, parishioners asked for the materials from a tower in the walls which was being demolished, and there is evidence of pilfering. They were rebuffed, because the blocks were to go into new fortifications; but a 19th century commentator remarked that in any case such old stones can degrade quickly, especially when recut, and that "Aujourd'hui, les architectes, plus instruits, réservent les pierres provenant des démolitions, comme moëllons, pour remplissages et fondations."[14] We may assume that earlier entrepreneurs also knew all about stone, and were equally alert to the savings to be had from reusing stone and wood.[9]

Not, of course, that reuse of spolia is restricted to Greek or Roman materials, or indeed to the Middle Ages or later. There are plentiful examples of pre-mediaeval use; at Rome, the 3rd century BC Temple of Apollo Sosias used 5th century BC spolia to make a coherent monument with reference to the older antique. Nor is it unusual in Greece to find megalithic spolia in Christian churches, presumably with some meaning to be attached to the effort or the result;[10] and it has been argued that the history of monument construction and reuse in Messenia (SW Greece) specifically refers back to the Heroic Age.[11]

Gallo-Roman architecture was frequently transformed into something else, as later chapters will demonstrate. Although some housing in Nîmes (and also at Aix-en-Provence) seems to have been in decline from the later 2ndC, there is evidence for the survival into the 4th century of sumptuous housing at Bordeaux, Saint-Bertrand-des-Comminges and Périgueux but, thus far, nowhere else, in part perhaps because of the problems of urban excavation. Even posing these questions suggests the murky status of our knowledge of architecture between late antique times and the Romanesque, which was indeed in part such a transformation. For example, the amphitheatres at both Périgueux and Tours were incorporated in later enceintes, but were they still used for games? This is unlikely, since such enceintes did not incorporate more than a section of the old towns.[12] Did Limoges, Poitiers and Saintes also shrink

---

9 Bernardi 2008 for a wide-ranging and abundantly referenced survey, including Table 2 for relative costs of eight jobs undertaken 1376–1697.

10 Hadjiminaglou 1994; cf. plates 1–3, fig. 16 for reuse from prehistoric megalithic blocks to sculptured bas-reliefs and capitals.

11 Spencer 1995.

12 Halsall 2007, 83–84: "Gallic towns received defensive circuits after the final quarter of the third century. Tours' amphitheatre became a bastion (a phenomenon encountered across Gaul, at for example Périgueux) and enclosed only about a quarter of the early city … The

THE EARLY ARCHITECTURE OF FRANCE

in population? How about the "Grand Amphithéâtre" at Metz? Was there any similar survival at Bordeaux or Saintes?[13] Indeed, the enceintes were of greatly varying dimensions.[14] In many cases, ancient structures were dismantled, and the stones left around, gradually being stolen. It may have been a deliberate ploy on the part of entrepreneurs down the centuries to allow monuments to degrade to the point where they could be declared eyesores, and then dismantled to the benefit of something up-to-date such as, at Reims, the railway in the 1860s.[15]

Occasionally, we know about monuments' state at various periods, because ruins were occasionally drawn as early as the 16th century, sometimes accurately. For example, at Lisieux, at the end of the 18th century, where an entrepreneur found a temple, baths and a theatre; in this case the monuments were drawn before destruction:

> M. Hubert dressa un plan des substructions qu'il découvrit et qu'il fut forcé de détruire; il rédigea un rapport dont prit, plus tard, connaissance l'Académie des Inscriptions et Belles-Lettres.[16]

It is pointless to enquire why such monuments, recognisable as such, had to be destroyed. Worse even than "conservation" was destruction of antiquities without description let alone explanation. At the end of the 17th century, a "panthéon romain" in Clermont-Ferrand was destroyed, apparently near-perfect, but no full descriptions of it survive.[17]

Reuse and the Tower of Hanoi

The Tower of Hanoi is a puzzle invented by the French mathematician Édouard Lucas in 1883, requiring the displacement of disks from one of three rods. This must be done one at a time, and no disk is to be placed over a smaller one as the player reconstructs the original layout, with the largest disks at the bottom, and the smallest at the top. Architects wishing to reuse a spolia-rich old wall, or re-erect blocks from a monument, faced an engineering version of this

---

extreme example of the phenomenon, however, appears to be Bavay in the far north, where the fortifications enclosed only the forum."

13　Esmonde Cleary 2013, 137, 147.

14　Coulon & Golvin 2011, 44 for length of town enceintes: Arles 1.6km; Autun 6; Fréjus 3.7; Nîmes 6; Orange 3.5; Toulouse 3; Vienne 7.2. For castra in area: Amiens 20ha; Beauvais 10; Bordeaux 32; Bourges 40; Chalon-sur-Saône 15; Dax 3.5; Dijon 10; Évreux 9; le Mans 9; Metz 70; Nantes 18; Orléans 30; Poitiers 50; Reims 35; Rennes 10; Rouen 18; Saintes 16; Senlis 7; Sens 25; Soissons 12; Tours 8.

puzzle, usually needing lifting equipment, namely where to store blocks in an appropriate order? The largest blocks would be in the foundations, but what to do with the lesser stones above them?

The problem suggests reasons for some of the ways in which such antiquities were handled, and which we shall encounter throughout this book. The first is that reaching foundation blocks meant dealing somehow with what lay above them, and storing the materials somewhere, or recutting and reusing them. This helps explain why so many late antique wall foundations survived into the 19th century: they were simply too unwieldy to deal with, in centuries when few were interested in their decorated blocks, and appropriate machinery may not have been available. The second explains why decorated blocks displayed in later walls (such as Narbonne) are not necessarily there exclusively because of antiquarian interest. Rather, rebuilding a new wall by dismantling an old one would necessarily entail reusing the upper courses first, so the decorated blocks in the old foundations would naturally be retrieved after the new foundation had been built – and hence be built into the upper courses. The third helps explain the rapidity and ease with which promenades would be constructed atop town walls because (to coin a phrase) the foundation building blocks were already in place: leave them there, reuse the upper courses elsewhere, and plant trees on what was left, which was essentially a viewing platform surrounding the town, just as the town walls themselves had been, only a little lower. The fourth explains the relative ease with which boulevards could be constructed: pull down all the walls, reuse the materials in expanding the town, and line trees along the free-fire zones, which in many cases would later become the inner ring-roads. The boulevards could also make large gardens, providing breathing-space from the suffocating town for the élite, conspicuously the high clergy.[18]

The Tower of Hanoi puzzle also helps us understand why the dismantling of town walls and the creation of promenades and boulevards would be contemporaneous with redevelopment inside the walls, because under such plans their materials had necessarily to be disposed of, most conveniently recut and reused in new buildings and stone-paved streets.

Prehistoric Antiquities[19]

Voilà ce qui se passe en France au xixe siècle: voilà comme les monuments sont détruits sans que qui que ce soit le remarque ou le signale. Il est urgent qu'ils soient mis sous la protection spéciale du gouvernement ou d'une société.[20] [1837]

THE EARLY ARCHITECTURE OF FRANCE   35

In the 19th century the age of megalithic monuments was not known, any more than was that of axes in stone or metal, let alone the distinction and date-ranges between Druids, Gauls and Celts. Such monuments were often called "Celtic," a term which sufficed even for monuments of the more recent past, and especially for tombs the grave-goods of which were clearly not Roman, and sometimes included objects in metal. The Académie Celtique, founded in 1805, studied and published accounts of the monuments of the Gauls, including illustrations,[15] and was reorganised into the Société des Antiquaires de France in 1814. By mid-century some metal grave-goods were entering museums instead of being melted down, but most other antiquities were recycled.[21]

During the increased building cadence of the 19th century, many standing prehistoric stone antiquities (some already dealt with long before by Montfaucon)[22] were broken up to provide construction material, such as dolmens in the Vendômois,[23] and Mérimée had been alarmed at the extent of their reuse as road metal.[24] And not just roads, for dolmens were also destroyed to build canal locks.[25] The fact that such destruction was so frequently mentioned is an index of the growing realisation of the importance of prehistoric material in charting the past. Dolmens, menhirs, cromlechs and the like were widely scattered across France (more so than Roman sites?), and studied by scholars of wide interests.[16] Their stone would often have been much easier to deal with than the marble or limestone in Roman structures, which often required tackle and skill to dismantle. We cannot know just what quantities of prehistoric monuments were destroyed for their materials, but the journals abound with descriptions of large monuments, for example in Poitou.[26] As one scholar lamented in 1866, "Combien de monuments romains ont servi de carrière à nos ingénieurs!... Qui reconstruira tant de dolmens convertis en macadam?"[27] Brittany had many stones in alignments,[28] which were depleted casually over the years. Here the systematic destruction of both tumuli and megaliths was also noted, and rather fancifully attributed to Julius Caesar himself.[29]

Large prehistoric structures or alignments got in the way of farming, and their re-use as anything from building-stone to macadam was easy.[30] In one instance the Romans themselves knocked several down when they built a

---

15   Pomian 1996, 29.

16   Coffyn 1990 for François Daleau, studying megaliths and the paleolithic as well as ethnography and modern history; but the title includes the term "origines," and Daleau's first publication is 1874. Laming-Emperaire 1964 for a survey of the origins of prehistoric archaeology in France.

camp, but apparently did not reuse them.[31] Scholars were already searching for and cataloguing such antiquities by 1821,[32] and by 1837 Caumont was exhorting engineers from the Ponts et Chaussées (the civil engineers, founded in 1716) to map them, and underline their importance to their sub-contractors, who otherwise broke them up "faute de les connaître."[33] This was over-generous, because two years later passage-graves at Briquebec (Manche) were destroyed in a State Forest, "en présence et sans doute avec la permission des employés forestiers qui dépendent du ministère des finances."[34] Nor could local administrations be trusted any more than the Ponts et Chaussées, let alone the Génie, said to be responsible for destruction at Toulinguet (Finistère).[35] Road-building reigned supreme, responsible for the destruction of whole complexes, from the Neolithic onwards.[36] In the early 20th century, such monuments were still being openly destroyed "en dépit de toutes les défenses officielles et officieuses."[37] Even castra such as Gergovia were being destroyed for road gravel until recently.[17] Prehistoric stone tools fared better than mega-liths because they were of no use except as curiosities: the Byzantines sent one as a gift in 1081, and in 1730 Mahudel lectured on them to the AIBL, and illus-trated them.[38] Sites were also being excavated by interested scholars, such as Moreau at Fère-en-Tardenois (Aisne), whence he retrieved 24,000 stone tools over two years.[39]

Equally misguided was the optimistic assertion in 1843 that it was often strangers (read: the English!), not proprietors, who were whittling away the alignments at Carnac and Locmariaquer (variously spelled), and indeed using them as quarries.[40] Customs officers (who had been taught their importance) could not protect the stones, and one individual arrested for defacing a sculpted stone had been acquitted.[41] Prehistoric monuments had been recycled since Neolithic times, but there was much destruction from the Middle Ages onward;[18] this may have increased by the 19th century, or simply been more extensively reported. It was emphatically land-owners who destroyed most such antiquities, although a few protected them (see below). Near Cognac in 1859, an owner who wished to destroy a monument because visitors kept tram-pling his crops to visit it, was dissuaded by the locals, who affirmed that it was

---

17 Eychart 1994, 8: Un site exceptionnel que l'on transforme en granulat pour empierrer les routes ... Il faut que chacun sache ce qu'on dynamite à deux pas de Clermont. 7, and in bold: Elle est un site national classé et protégé. The quarry closed in 2004, and not every-one agrees this was the site of Gergovia; cf. Goudineau 2007, 171–173.

18 Patton 1993, 56: menhirs pulled down and reused in Neolithic passage graves; 104–5, 114 for the alignments at Carnac and St-Just, and their depletion by quarrymen, "so that the original extent of many alignments cannot now be ascertained."

THE EARLY ARCHITECTURE OF FRANCE   37

"un titre appartenant au pays."[42] Such monuments (sometimes with names similar to La Roche du Géant / aux Fées) were powerful foci for local superstition. One mound near Carnac displayed light at night, and conversations were overheard, unfortunately in Latin;[43] elsewhere, they were the loci for pilgrimage, or therapeutic healing.[44] In the Channel Islands, a house burned down after the owner started to break up a monument, which impressed the locals, so that "désormais l'antiquaire est rassuré sur le sort de ces vénérables ruines."[45] But not always: in 1843 a dolmen in Seine-et-Marne disappeared without even the dimensions being known,[46] and in 1846 another in the Loire-Inférieure was destroyed to make a dairy.[47] In 1879 in the Aisne, men looking for road-core found a passage grave, but by the time a scholar arrived, alerted by a farmer, half the monument had gone.[48] In 1882, in the Lyonnais, a finger was even pointed at the Ponts et Chaussées for destroying a cromlech for the same purpose.[49] And all this in spite of the 1879 creation of a Sous-Commission des Monuments mégalithiques, for monuments continued to be destroyed.[50] However, many remained, Le Rouzic classifying 117 of them (individuals or groupings) by 1938.[19]

Indeed, given the apparent scale of destruction outside Brittany (and Atlantic Europe, as one characterisation has it), just how many dolmens etc. once existed? In 1830, Caumont reckoned nearly 40 dolmens near Saumur had been destroyed for road metal.[51] In 1851 Angers called for a departmental listing for Maine-et-Loire, "pour que les autorités locales veillent à ce qu'ils soient désormais respectés de tous les entrepreneurs de travaux publics, auxquels il serait formellement interdit de se servir de matériaux provenant de la destruction de ces monuments primitifs."[52] This followed the 1843 Congress where one of the several probing questions concerned prehistoric monuments.[53] In 1853 one scholar made a list of twenty-three for the Aube, many of them damaged, some recently destroyed.[54] Monuments in the Auvergne[55] and the Limousin[56] were also described. It was agreed by mid-century that dolmens were tombs, and it was suggested that they had once spread over the whole of France, and been destroyed.[57] Certainly, this was believed in Maine-et-Loire, where owners had mined them and blown them up.[58] Continuing destruction made counting difficult, as Cartailhac recognised in 1903.[59]

Greater attention, therefore, did not mean more preservation as the century progressed. In 1863 a proprietor in the Aisne, in spite of protests, destroyed

---

19 Le Rouzic 1939, 234, acknowledging the demage done by treasure hunting: "De tout temps on a fouillé les dolmens pour chercher l'or qui se trouvait dans quelques-uns d'entre eux... [and in the 19th century] une foule de chercheurs de trésors s'était jetée sur ces monuments, quelques uns même falsaient sauter les tables de recouvrement à la mine."

38   CHAPTER 1

for flooring material four-metre-high monolithic menhirs.[60] Near Péronne in
1865, the locals told the scholars of attempts thirty years previously to break up
the Menhir de Doingt.[61] A dolmen in Loir-et-Cher was saved from the same
fate in 1863 because another landowner bought it;[62] and a tumulus in Loire-
Inférieure was similarly protected.[63] In the Morbihan in 1891 a local even
bought, moved, and re-erected part of a tumulus in the village square.[64] But
when scholars wished to examine a tumulus at Carnac, the landowner did not
even reply to the request, so they had to find another one.[65] Perhaps the owners or lessees at Carnac were especially difficult: in 1877 one stipulated that any
stones uncovered during excavation should be removed from his fields.[66] But
at least such monuments were targeted in the 1879 Comité, mentioned above,
as part of the Commission des monuments historiques.[67] This was indeed
necessary, one scholar exclaiming in 1881 that "Les monuments mégalithiques
qui couvraient le vaste territoire de nos Gaules disparaissent insensiblement,
et, si l'on n'y veille, bientôt il n'en restera plus qu'un souvenir qui ne tardera pas
à s'effacer."[68]

Roman Sites in France

Chose à remarquer, ce sont les barbares qui, en ruinant la Gaule, en for-
çant nos pères à élever en toute hâte des fortifications autour des villes, à
employer à cette fin les matériaux des édifices placés en-dehors de la
nouvelle enceinte; ce sont eux, dis-je, qui ont été ainsi la cause de cette
accumulation de richesses architectoniques et épigraphiques qui nous
restent encore dans quelques villes. Ces pierres, si elles étaient demeurées au jour, auraient été probablement taillées et retaillées plusieurs fois
pour entrer dans des constructions diverses. Les archéologues pourront
donc profiter de ce que nous ont laissé les barbares. C'est peut-être un
motif d'étre un peu indulgent pour le souvenir de leurs ravages.[69] [1861]

Pour que l'existence d'édifices souvent considérables, et même de
villes gallo-romaines nous soit révélée, il faut que des circonstances accidentelles amènent des fouilles profondes qui déplacent une grande
quantité de terre.[70] [1854]

The French of course knew about Roman monuments within and near towns,
but they were also familiar with many Roman military camps. Such castra were
recognised near several modern towns,[71] and several of the many in France
were published by Caylus and others. They were often named Camps de César
(following an enduring desire to connect sites with famous names), and some

THE EARLY ARCHITECTURE OF FRANCE

scholars wished to dig them.[72] And they were also well aware of such camps in much better condition than the (generally) jumble of grass-covered mounds to be found in France, because their army re-established and reoccupied many in Algeria from 1830 onwards.[73] Probably as much was soon known about that country's Roman remains as about those of metropolitan France, whence so much had already disappeared.[74] Their attraction to archaeologists was their country location, offering excavation possibilities without modern buildings obscuring them, which usually made excavation in towns impossible. Way-stations between them, on the Roman roads, were also plentiful in France, and waiting to be investigated.[75] "Camps" was a generic name, and many sites so-called were probably those of villas or sanctuaries, with worked blocks, bas-reliefs, columns and capitals to be unearthed, at first usually by the landowner, as happened at Champlieu (Oise) in 1850,[76] sometimes by the Génie,[77] and also near Bagnols,[78] which had yielded antiquities since time immemorial.[79] Military itineraries were an important source of information, and conspicuous antiquities were always marked,[20] an indication of just how many roads in France had a Roman origin, flanked by ruins of buildings. Some towns, large today, probably began as small settlements which then became fortresses. For example, the walls of Arras were built in the late 3rd century, enclosing only some 8ha, and built partly right over a religious complex. By the late 4th century, this was an important fortress. The town yielded antiquities throughout the 19th century, and not only on the site of the castrum,[80] although Vauban's extensive outworks might well have produced more.[21]

Many Roman sites continued to be used by locals as quarries,[81] and destroyed. Amongst them, standing here as one example from many, is Saint-Paul-Trois-Châteaux (Drôme), down the Rhône near Pierrelatte, on the Via Domitia (which the locals called "lou camin ferra, le chemin ferré"), in an area rich in ancient walls.[82] It was important enough to boast a fine Romanesque church, and to be the seat of a bishopric. Antiquities were collected there in the 1780s,[83] the area within the walls (and using some of them) part-occupied by a Dominican monastery, where broken columns abounded in 1837.[84] The site attracted scholarly attention in 1864 when, as well as statues, the "imposing" remains of circus, amphitheatre, forum and aqueduct were noted: "Il n'y a pas longtemps encore, deux de ses portes étaient appelées, l'une, Fanjoux (Fanum Jovis), à cause du temple de Jupiter qui se trouvait dans cette partie de

---

20   Itineraries: habitually carried out by the army in France, for foot soldiers as well as for artillery. e.g. in the archives of the Service Historique de la Défense (SHD): any of the MR series for "Intérieur de la France," such as MR1247 through to MR1301, Allier to Yonne.

21   Bernard 1993, 70–82 for mediaeval ramparts; 83–122 for le système bastionné, and Vauban.

la ville; et l'autre, Puy-Jou, de Podium Jovis."[85] By the 1870s little was left "grâce à l'esprit de destruction et à l'insouciance" except for a fragmentary altar and a few inscriptions,[86] plus another altar and a section of frieze found in the walls, and destroyed.[87] In 1884 a mosaic was carted off to the museum in Avignon (Vaucluse).[88] And another was discovered in 1894 when the local railway line was cut, plus an important bronze candelabrum which was taken for restoration to Saint-Germain, and stayed there.[89] More railway work uncovered a villa 2.5m down,[90] so that the Abbé Fillet could comment in 1908 that "Assez peu d'autres villes de France nous en offrent une collection aussi curieuse et aussi variée."[91]

Very close to Saint-Paul was the Roman Senomagus, identified by the curé of Saint-Pierre-de-Senos, its modern name, in 1883, marked by numerous sarcophagi which hindered local agriculture and were therefore destroyed, but also by tombstones flanking the Roman road and, one metre deep, "des fragments de colonne, des chapitaux ornés de feuillages de l'ordre corinthien, des mosaïques et autres débris de tout genre."[92]

Rome in Imperial Decline

> Tous les jours, nous faisons des découvertes importantes. Si César n'avait qu'à frapper du pied la terre, pour en faire sortir des légions, ici nous n'avons qu'à fouiller le sol pour en exhumer des richesses.[93] [1894]

As this congressist boasted at Saintes, the soil of France was indeed rich in Roman antiquities, and there was extensive knowledge of the complexion of late Roman town walls.[94] Some suggested that it was the Saracen threat that saw walls built,[95] perhaps influenced by mediaeval toponomy which often named them.[96] France had once been much richer in monuments, as the numbers of ruined theatres and amphitheatres (some little more than depressions and mounds)[97] made plain.[98] Scholarly knowledge of Roman Gaul was predicated on two types of evidence, the first largely literary and inscriptional, the second archaeological. "External military threat, internal dynastic instability and financial turbulence" form the first category, and the second, for which there is also plenty of evidence,

> massive changes to the form and fabric of the major cities along with a decline in the largely urban phenomenon of setting up inscriptions; the (near) disappearance of lesser urban centres; the abandonment of villas; the atrophying of the long-distance trade networks with the

THE EARLY ARCHITECTURE OF FRANCE 41

Mediterranean and of some of the major industries, particularly ceramics, associated with these networks; and spates of coin hoarding.[22]

The change is generally agreed to have come during the 3rd and 4th century, after which in any case long-distance communications contracted. To which should then be added the weakness of the Roman military, which concentrated in strengthened and militarised towns, mainly to protect communications routes.[23]

"Decline" is an emotive term, well known in Antiquity,[99] and today sometimes expunged by the more sensitive for the term "transformation," a term more likely to attract funding. Townscapes certainly changed: for large structures, upkeep replaced construction, and important building work was eventually confined to town walls, many built from earlier monuments, including inscriptions.[24] This happened not only in France, but also in Spain, where Kulikowski, noting the "very liberal attitude toward the reuse of old materials," is properly suspicious about the old verities such as barbarian invasion, and the dating of walls, of which fewer than half can confidently be dated to the 3rd or 4th century. He suggests control over territory, prestige, status and display as better reasons for such wall-building than decline or invasion-panic. We can follow Kulikowski and accept for France his affirmation that

> town walls, regardless of the practical ends they may also have served, belong to the same world of civic display and construction as the old monuments of the early empire. But they were a new fashion in monumentalism, appropriate to an age that already possessed a full complement of the monuments that had accompanied the early years of romanization.[25]

Monumental they certainly were, and required machinery and great technical skill to erect – as the French army found to their cost in Algeria, where the Génie, often given the task of their repair or even relocation, was sometimes not equal to the task.[26] We are also left near-rudderless by a shortage of materials for study in subsequent centuries: "in terms of the material culture of the towns and the countryside alike, it is unquestionable that the archaeological remains of the Early Medieval period are harder to find, and materially much

---

22 Esmonde Cleary 2013, 19, 25.

23 Ibid., 72, 75.

24 Lavan 2003 for neglect and redevelopment in the late antique city.

25 Kulikowski 2004, 101–109: "The walling of cities in late antiquity." Quotes 106, 110.

26 Greenhalgh 2014, 192 5.

simpler when one finds them."[27] So the 19th century knew well from the plentiful evidence that late antique fortifications were often built from splendid monuments, and that later enceintes regularly followed on exactly the same foundations.[100] Apparently, however, prosperity did not decline everywhere at once: Ausonius (c. 310–395; consul in 379), the owner of some seven estates, gives details of his 653-acre estate near Bazas, not far from Bordeaux, implying that it is fully functioning – and this supposedly in a period of decline. His view of rural reality might have been a poetic one, but his distaste for degraded towns is clear.[28] In any case, Gaul offers for late antiquity the best range of narrative sources across the whole of the Mediterranean, patchy of course, from the 5th century to about 800.[29]

The foundation models for some later French architecture were the Roman monuments erected on French soil – Gallo-Roman architecture. They suffered extensive demolition and stone-robbing in later centuries (as did buildings in Britain),[30] for they offered a near-effortless source of sturdy and long-lasting materials for later structures for those who did not wish to make use of wood. Some monuments (such as mausolea at Avenches-en-Chaplix, Switzerland, near a large villa suburbana) were evidently demolished over many years, and needing a crane to complete the work.[31] Some today tend (incorrectly, of course) to think of Provence as the natural and only home of Roman architecture in France, and this continues in some books.[32] Certainly, the urban network in the south was well established in Antiquity, and any urban growth took the form of new towns or bastides after the 11th century. But this is a geographical fluke for two associated reasons: earlier and greater prosperity further north

---

27   Wickham 2003, 387; Wickham 2005, 398–406 for the Île de France, its estates and economy; ibid., 505–514 for settlement patterns in Francia; and ibid., 674–681 for northern Francia and urbanism in the 8th century.

28   Frye 2003, 188: In his *Order of Famous Cities*, Ausonius troubles himself with Gallic cities only long enough to praise their commerce...What else could he say of Gallic cities? Toulouse spews forth people. Narbonne had once had a nice temple. Only Bordeaux is, to Ausonius, a pretty place, with straight boulevards and a fountain.

29   Wickham 2005, 41; 42–43 for the historiography of the region.

30   Gerrard 2008 179–182 for the demolition of the Temple of Sulis Minerva in Bath, of the Principia at York, and the demolition and re-use (184–190) of materials from two villas.

31   Flutsch & Hauser 2006, tombs dated between 25/40 AD. 9/10ths of the blocks have gone: the S. monument had 220.35 cubic metres, and 23.71 remain; of the N. monument's 204.5 cubic metres, 11.72 remain. Calculations such as these would be most useful for a whole range of monuments.

32   Sautel & Imbert 1929, with no hint in the Introduction that other parts of France also used to house large collections of Roman monuments.

THE EARLY ARCHITECTURE OF FRANCE

saw many ancient buildings demolished in centuries before scholars got some grip on the preservation/destruction merry-go-round in the 19th century; and the southern regions of inland France were poorer and thus less concerned with town development than communities further north, so that survival in some cases stemmed from poverty rather than from a solicitous pride in the past. This may be one reason why so many megaliths survive in Brittany. If, in the north, some new towns grew up around existing castles, many others had Roman origins.

The conversion of pagan structures into Christian monuments will be dealt with below, but what about the usefulness or otherwise of civic structures such as baths, theatres, amphitheatres and fora? Some of these provided housing or fortresses for a shrunken population, and we can assume that such structures survive longer because they were reused, although there is no archaeological evidence to register when such reuse began. Extensive abandonment of baths by the end of the third century[33] suggests a decline of skills, population to maintain them, or interest in bathing itself. Just how much population shrank is impossible to determine, simply because archaeology cannot sensibly register non-existence without remains to excavate; hence figures for town populations in the later Empire sometimes come from ancient authors or, in the case of Gaul, from guessing.[34]

Theatres and Amphitheatres

Many more theatres than amphitheatres survived in France, in whole or in part; but many of these have vanished, used for building materials.[35] They are

---

33 Esmonde Cleary 2013, 115: "in the south-east there was abandonment and demolition of public baths by the end of the third century at Arles, Fréjus, Nîmes, Vaison-la-Romaine and Vienne (Saint-Romain-en-Gal)."

34 Bowman & Wilson 2011, 188–189: "For Gaul and Germany I have used lists of cities from Pliny's Natural History and in Bekker-Nielsen 1989, and have simply guessed populations to give a profile with, on the whole, smaller city populations than for North Africa and Asia Minor (see Table 7.12)."

35 Sear 2006 for vanished theatres. 200 Limoges, mentioned in life of St Martial and in drawings of 1593; ruins still visible in 17th century; 200 Salles-la-Source: stone footings of first 11 rows of seats survive; no trace of scene; 203 Saintes: fine frieze and theatrical mask found in late Roman walls; 207 Soissons: excavated between 1840 and 1848; nothing now visible; 218 Mainz: completely destroyed; 220 Lyon: excavated in 1691; mostly destroyed in 1825–35; outer wall still survived in 1905; now buried; 228 Orléans: excavated in 1821; destroyed soon after; parts which remained under houses untouched; 239 Évreux: excavated in 1843, later destroyed by owner of property; 244 Antibes: theatre demolished (in 1592); amphitheatre demolished (in 1691), 249 Narbonne. many monuments, including

the easiest structures to assess, because they are strong. In effect, an amphitheatre is a solidly supported oval wall, with the buttressing (the ranked seats) in the inside; and a theatre is more-or-less the same structure in a half oval closed by the proscenium wall. They were arcaded annular structures, perhaps with some decoration on the exterior, and the seating, if of worked stone, was easily removable for convenient rebuilding, because all the seats in each rank would have identical dimensions. In those cases where (like some amphitheatres) they were not built into gulleys or hillsides, theatres also stood well on their own because of similar ranked seating-cum-buttressing. Such structures contained immense quantities of stone. At Grohan, a convent was established in the amphitheatre in 1632,[101] and in 1698 stones were being sold off at Orléans by the administrators of the Hôtel-Dieu.[102] Centuries earlier, at Limoges[103] and Reims,[104] stones were also sold off. For decoration, they might contain inscriptions, as at Autun.[105] And these were more festive structures, with their scenae frons designed in marble for more-or-less extravagant display, with columns, veneers and often statues; these never survived intact, usually being stripped for reuse, with perhaps some fragments fallen to the ground. If, as local scholars maintained, the amphitheatre at Vienne was nearly intact in the 16th century, then similar sell-offs occurred there,[106] as they did at Tintignac.[107] Baluze drew it in the 1660s, but the stones were subsequently robbed, presumably reused in local villages. Yet in 1849 a Ponts et Chaussées engineer could not understand why this and other antiquities had not been properly explored.[108] Even Mérimée (who deserves credit for his interest in archaeology),[36] who did not believe Baluze had seen as much as he drew (fanciful elaboration is a perennial problem with drawings of antique structures), nevertheless thought that a dig should be undertaken.[109] This does not appear to have happened, for by 1835 wall remnants were only at ground level,[110] and sculptures (if not many in number) continued to be collected in the local fields. At Grand, the large amphitheatre had lost its seats by 1850, and antiquities removed in a dig early that century.[111] Some villas, for example at Nérac,[112] even had their own small amphitheatre.

Amphitheatres and theatres at Nîmes, Arles and Orange, and theatres at Saint-Bertrand-de-Comminges and Toulouse, appear to have been used for

---

theatre, still lie under medieval city; 250 Toulouse: lowest seats and substructures of cavea (H 2.50 m above orchestra level); no remains of scene building.

36   Pailler 2008 for overview; Bercé 2008, 155–6 points out that the 10% of antiquities on the 1840 Monuments Historiques list was a high figure, and due in large part to Mérimée. 162: in 1845 he obtained 420,000fr. for the amphitheatre at Arles – the usual annual sum for *all* the Monuments historiques.

THE EARLY ARCHITECTURE OF FRANCE 45

their original purpose throughout the 4th century, but thereafter (though when, is unknown) their high and sturdy walls and easily blocked entrances made them ideal for reuse as secure walled villages, even fortresses, and it was for this reason that so many of them survived, and not just in France (cf. Lucca, Dugga). So useful were the amphitheatres at Nîmes and Arles, and the theatres of Arles and Orange that, after various vicissitudes, they have survived to this day, precisely because of the security they provided through uncertain times, and because the houses therein were privately owned. If sections were indeed dismantled and the structure remained standing (as in the amphitheatre at Arles, which also had chapels)[113] that demonstrates how sturdy they were.

By the mid-19th century some unoccupied amphitheatres were still being degraded. Lillebonne was sold during the Revolution and its stones sold off for 15 years, before being excavated between 1819 and 1840;[114] it was still being damaged in 1874.[115] But most remaining structures were too conspicuous for quarrying, and attention turned to their preservation and reuse. In 1883 Senlis set up a lottery "à la restitution de l'amphithéâtre gallo-romain et au nivellement de l'arène jusqu'au sol primitif."[116] It was recognised that utility (if a different utility from housing) was the key to preserving ancient structures from further damage.[117] Thus the theatre at Orange, restored by 1894 and designated a théâtre national, hosted performances every August, including by the Comédie Française. Saintes knew of their success, and a local scholar suggested they should do likewise, and offered to "s'occuper de cette affaire à Paris."[118] This, however, was wishful thinking, for calling the remains at Saintes "superbes arènes" did not make them anything more than heaps of hard core and rubble.

Baths and Aqueducts

Bathing was a popular pursuit in Gaul,[37] and bath structures well known to 19th-century scholars.[119] They are useful as a cultural thermometer, the decline of the practice indicating a loss of tradition, and the fate of bath buildings by the end of the 3rdC confirming this. Some were demolished to build defensive walls (Bordeaux), others for unknown purposes (Arles, Fréjus, Nîmes, Vaison-la-Romaine, Vienne), and only a few surviving thereafter, as at Saint-Bertrand-de-Comminges and Marseille.[38] Dismantling usually meant stripping marble veneers and other useful blocks, and leaving a concrete core and surviving water provision in place, for which reason baths are so frequently re-occupied

---

37   Chevallier 1992.

38   Esmonde Cleary 2013, 115–116; 418: Saint-Bertrand had a house decorated with mosaics in the 5th century, and a church constructed nearby.

by Christian baptisteries. This might have been the case with the site and structures of Saint-Pierre-aux-Nonnains, at Metz.[39] Exotic marbles seem to have been common in French baths, and were enthusiastically listed in 1838 in the Franche Comté, at Sequanie[120] and Mandeure.[121]

Many remains of aqueducts survived from Antiquity, and some supplies were tapped during the Middle Ages.[40] These fed household water, but also baths, and both were in danger of destruction. However, longevity into the 19th century was at least in part because some concrete-core constructions were practically indestructible;[122] for example at Metz,[123] Nîmes,[124] and Lyon.[125] ("Roman cement" was advertised widely in the 19th century.)[126] At Nîmes, there was evidently enough water provided by the Temple de Diane complex that the supply via the Pont du Gard was not needed; indeed, although some stone was taken from this famous aqueduct-bridge, most of it so that carts could cross it, there appear to have been no plans for its re-establishment.[127] At Lyon a bylaw was required in 1808 to safeguard the aqueducts;[128] at Saintes in 1820 an attempt was made to buy the baths in order to preserve them,[129] and at Paris in 1831 the Salle des Thermes was bought by the municipality.[130] For the archaeologists, baths were seen as prime targets for digging, because of the known richness of their decoration. Samples of this were discovered at Vienne in 1829,[131] and at Die in 1846,[132] although there was little left at Autun,[133] and at Vienne the connecting aqueduct pipes were already destroyed.[134] Mining at the base of the structure (simple sapping, not using gunpowder) was done at Cahors,[135] presumably to bring reusable materials more easily to the ground. The discovery of hypocausts and marble was a sure indication of bath remains,[136] sometimes at once-sumptuous villas.[137] But large bath-sites had too many tempting materials to be left to archaeologists and preservationists. Thus by 1852 the complex at Feysin (Isère) was stripped by the owner to improve agriculture, and to provide road-core for the Marseille road; he also sold off 4,800 cubic metres of stone for building, which was scarce thereabouts.[138]

With the extension of the road (and then rail) network, sites which flourished included the Roman monuments of Provence, and also refurbished Roman baths, for curative bathing was very popular in 19th-century Europe. Néris-les-Bains,[139] Evaux-les-Bains, Aix-les-Bains, and Vichy-les-Bains (Aquae Calidae on the Peutinger Table) were popular locations, advertised widely.[140] Amélie-les-Bains (originally Arles-les-Bains, 5km from Arles, Pyrénées-

---

39 Escher 2013, 94–102.

40 Esperou 2009, 15: mediaeval millers knew the aqueduct feeding Béziers (36.3km in length), and avaient bâti la branche nord/sud en se raccordant sur une galerie romaine existante. Figs 189–193 for photos of other aqueducts in France.

THE EARLY ARCHITECTURE OF FRANCE   47

Orientales) had a military hospital by the 1850s, on the site of the ancient baths, where some of the ancient facilities were in use,[141] and where further excavation was carried out in the 1860s. Just as amphitheatres and theatres could be preserved by being turned into something useful, so also could baths associated with springs, of which there were plenty throughout some regions of France, still marked by Roman structures. At Évaux, in the Creuse, in 1852, enough works were retrieved to form a museum.[142] On the site of the Roman baths there were two hotels by 1852, decorated (apparently badly) from such retrieved artefacts, and some 3km from the railway station,[143] the aim being to attract "baigneurs touristes" by erecting a large sign.[144] The enterprise was a success, and its expansion in 1854 led to the discovery of further ruins.[145]

Such commercialisation could be a curse as well as a blessing, as was seen at the antique curative springs of Bourbon-L'Archambault (Allier) and Bourbon-Lancy (Saône-et-Loire). Connected with the Bourbons, of course, the latter's name was changed to Bellevue-les-Bains during the Revolution. Bourbon-l'Archambault perhaps had functioning baths in the 13th century,[146] and certainly in the 17th century. The Sainte-Chapelle at its château, finished in 1508 and presumably part-built from marble on the site, was sold off during the Revolution,[147] yet in 1821 the area was still known as rich in antiquities,[148] in spite of the quantities reused in the previous two centuries,[149] as was nearby Montfeu, with the ruins of an amphitheatre.[150] At the end of the century, elements of a temple were unearthed, as well as mosaics, columns and medals.[151] Bourbon-Lancy[152] was dug on several occasions in the 16th and 17th centuries,[153] with twelve statues going to Richelieu (to keep Michelangelo's *Slaves* company?) and others to Paris and Mâcon,[154] as well as to Autun, which was still receiving antiquities from this site in the 1890s.[155] There was a modern bath building here from 1838, preparations for which uncovered antiquities.[156] At Luxeuil in 1857, while preparing the modern bath, sections of the original structures were blown up.[157] It would be interesting to make a census of how many local museums still hold the items from baths unearthed in the 19th century and, from earlier catalogues, establish just what proportion survive.

Villas, Mosaics and Sculpture

Evidence survives that some Roman villas in Gaul were exceptionally rich, and this even into the 5th century, especially if we assume Sidonius' description of his own villa was not make-believe.[41] Between the Loire and the Seine, some villas survived that long, but by the 4th century and sometimes much earlier,

---

41   Frye 2003, 190: "an elegant Roman villa ... inscriptions in Latin verse ... massive swimming pool ... columned portico and a connected cryptoportico ... an array of dining and living

48 CHAPTER 1

many villas in northern and central Gaul – perhaps as many as half[42] – had already been abandoned, and those remaining declined in quality.[43] This probably left some establishments simply as working farms,[44] and a few of these arguably had a very long life.[158] Some were known in the Middle Ages,[159] no doubt with their materials reused. Further south, surveys have shown "the persistence of the villa as an important, structuring element of the rural settlement hierarchy, even if there had been numerical decline since the later second-century peak," and there have been some impressive post-19th-century discoveries.[45] But just why villas fizzle out (by 350–450 in the north, and in the 6th century and 7th century further south) is a puzzle. As Wickham observes, this is a cultural shift, with aristocrats abandoning bath houses and heating, and apparently not erecting anything monumental except for fortresses, and these much later: "the signs are that architectural display had become rather less important for the aristocracies of post-Roman Gaul."[160] Nevertheless, some villa elements and mosaics seem to have survived into Merovingian times.[46]

Villas were as well known to 19th-century scholars as houses in towns, of which there were also plentiful remains, usually to be found in the cellars of later housing.[161] There were so many villas throughout France, many uncovered by ploughing, road- or railway-building in the days before aerial photography, that accounts by scholars are frequent. However, spectacular retrievals are few.[47] Villas generally lay on private property, hence destruction of their

---

areas." Ibid., 190–191 for villas at Palat de Saint-Emilion (with a gallery, large ornamental basin and mosaics), at Montmaurin, Plassac, Seviac and Saint-Julian-les-Martiques.

42 Halsall 2007, 83 for N. Gaul; between 1/3rd and 1/2 of villas abandoned by 4th century; "Many sites in the countryside were now clearly fortified, or at least defensible." Wickham 2005, 475–481 for dating the end of the villa in various regions.

43 Esmonde Cleary 2013, 94.

44 Wickham 2005, 280–293 for discussion of estates in Francia, 600–800.

45 Esmonde Cleary 2013, 187, 248–249, perhaps not known in 19th century: Seviac, Loupian, Nérac, Pont d'Orly, Saint-André-de-Codols, La Ramière, Palat and Lalonquette; known: Montmaurin, Lescar, Valentine, and Bapteste/Moncrabeau. Naturally, the grand villas attracted digging and attention: "It must be recognised that because of the concentration of archaeological work on the grand villas of this region, particularly on the residential areas, we are woefully ignorant of the other forms of rural settlement, be they lesser villas or 'farmsteads', so our overall picture of rural settlement in the region must be very skewed."

46 Blanchard-Lemée 1982.

47 Anderson 2013, 220: "Surprisingly little evidence for country villas and farms has been found to date in Gallia Narbonensis."

THE EARLY ARCHITECTURE OF FRANCE

ruins usually distant from the attention of town-dwellers could often go unreported as the ruins were somehow reused or the materials sold off. Caumont visited one in 1829, dug to obtain material for a barn; he drew a plan "de ce qu'on voyait encore, pour conserver le souvenir d'une découverte qui serait demeurée inconnue, si je ne l'avais signalée dans le temps à la Société des Antiquaires."[162] One was uncovered in 1830 at Autun, while a farmer was looking for stone,[163] and a rich one near the same town in 1831: "La prodigieuse quantité de marbres rares et précieux qui surgissent des ruines était tous les jours un objet d'étonnement et d'admiration pour les étrangers qui visitaient ces fouilles."[164] In the Limousin, the Villa d'Antone was excavated by scholars short of money, hoping to get help from the Génie, and navigating the attitudes of proprietors father and son.[165] Toponymy could help discovery. The 1830 Autun find was next to a field called "le Champ des Orfèvres," and in 1846 a rich villa with later structures was found near Lyon in a place called

> Palais, en latin Palatium, emprunté à un vieil édifice détruit depuis bien longtemps, mais dont on retrouve encore chaque jour de riches débris, malgré les circonstances qui semblaient s'être réunies pour en faire disparaître toute trace.

This was a site so splendid, with baths, that one commentator concluded that it had been "la résidence du premier magistrat de la province ségusiave."[166]

The most spectacular villa (of nearly 3ha) not only in France, but in the whole of Europe,[167] for the quantity and quality of its sculpture,[168] was excavated at Chiragan,[48] near Martres-Tolosane, in 1826, 1840 and 1890,[169] with spectacular sculptures uncovered.[49] It was far from extravagant to compare the complex with Pompeii,[170] and its splendour makes one wonder just how many similar ones existed but were obliterated, some in the same area,[171] with sculptures retrieved.[50] Caseau suggests the retrieved statues were heirlooms, or obtained from temples; so that a taste for such work survived even after large-scale production had ceased.[51] As well as architectural blocks, 160 statues, figurines and bas-reliefs, plus 73 portrait-busts and "trois grands

---

48 http://www.villa.culture.fr/accessible/fr/annexe/carte_08-8.

49 Lehmann 2007: late antique but *not* from Aphrodisias.

50 Stirling 2005, chap. 3: Late Antique Villas in Southwest Gaul and Their Sculptural Collections.

51 Esmonde Cleary_2013, 228–229; Caseau 2011, 490: "At this time [5th century], the production of statues had almost completely stopped, and landowners had to buy ancient statues if they wanted to adorn their house in the traditional way."

ensembles décoratifs et trois séries de masques scéniques et bacchiques" were recovered.[172] It appears on neither the 1840 nor the 1862 list of protected monuments, despite already having yielded the most important collection of antique sculpture ever to be found in France, some showing strong links with productions from Aphrodisias, in Asia Minor. Evidence that the finds were not publicised as they deserved is to be found in the AJA for 1899, reporting the discovery of the villa, rather than renewed excavation.[173] The 1826 dig certainly excited the locals, and the floor of the mairie at Martres-Tolosane groaned under their weight.[174] The excavator, du Mège, was apparently known as a forger, but too many antiquities came to light during his time and later to be his work,[175] so by the 1890s scholars were sure of their originality,[176] and they formed in the Augustins at Toulouse "la plus grande partie de notre trésor."[177]

If such sculptures were still displayed in the 5th century, how many other complexes might once have existed in Gaul, their owners collecting artwork from previous centuries with which to decorate them? The same valley that held Chiragan was rich in remains: three kilometres north of Chiragan was the villa of Sana, excavated in 1898, uncovering mosaics. Two others stood in the same plain, at Bordier and Coulieu; and the villa at St-Georges-de-Montagne, near Bordeaux, thought to belong to Ausonius, also had a large collection of sculptures.[178]

Lebègue's 1891 dig at Chiragan was criticised as "surtout une chasse aux objets de musée" – that is, the commodification of antiquities not for sale, but for local prestige. The question here was, "n'aurait-il pas trouvé profit à diriger une portion de cette équipe sur quelque autre point où, en terrain vierge, elle aurait travaillé à saisir l'arrangement de quelqu'un des édifices de l'établissement romain?"[179] This was valid, for the actual architecture was neglected: as so often during the 19th century, the object of digging was indeed treasure-hunting, whether for sale or for stocking museums, rather than the investigation of ancient architecture and life. Thus for the villa at Antone (Limousin) in 1862, it was thought (as already mentioned) that the Génie would do the digging;[180] but this did not happen, so the local society provided the funds, paid the workmen, and had a case of interesting finds delivered.[181] Museum-quality objects and photographs were sometimes the only result of a dig, as at Soulosse in the Vosges in 1889.[182] Even worse occurred at Serquigny, in the Eure, the demolition of which began 1773–1780; here the proprietor destroyed the walls of a large room, "situé à couchant du four à chaux actuel," and put statue fragments on his windowsill; they disappeared.[183] As for the remains of three villas near Clermont-Ferrand, one of them was revealed during the building of the Artillery School, with frescoed walls "dont les fragments ont été recueillis par des particuliers ou transportés au Musée de la ville." More of the complex was unearthed in the cutting for the Orléans railway.[184] Not all ruins could be

THE EARLY ARCHITECTURE OF FRANCE

51

so firmly identified, for example the 1849 discovery during the Sens-Langres railway work, because "Les premières fouilles ont été faites avec assez peu de soin par les ouvriers, qui n'avaient intérêt qu'à déblayer au mètre cube et ce avec le plus de célérité possible." But by inference the ruins probably were a villa, because "sur toute la ligne du chemin de fer, dans la partie qui avoisine les routes romaines, on fait de semblables découvertes, plus ou moins complètes, plus ou moins intéressantes."[185]

Ancient wall frescoes were also recognised and published, but few survived except in fragments, generally because such wall coverings had crumbled and fallen off, although techniques for removing frescoes whole had been known since Napoleon I (who supposedly intended to bring the frescoed walls of the Stanza della Segnatura back to Paris). At Tauroentum (Bouches-du-Rhône) the cellars of a villa were uncovered, along with "les débris de revêtement recouverts de peinture qui se trouvaient dans les déblais;"[186] these were not investigated, any more than were "des murs d'un grand appareil ornés de peinture, des tronçons de colonnes, des marbres de toute espèce" at a villa near Soissons,[187] where even a mosaic was destroyed. At Chiragan, walls stood several metres high at the beginning of the 19th century, but it is not even known whether they were frescoed.[188]

Mosaics fared better than frescoes, not only because they were usually flat to the ground, but because there were so many of them, and some found their way into later religious buildings,[189] or had a religious building erected on top of them.[190] Some were extracted for reuse, as at Vaison in 1774, when one was taken from the Quartier de Puymin to the château of M. de Vérone.[191] Unfortunately many discoveries soon vanished, doubly unfortunate since their existence in the countryside indicated villas (as with a find near Montbéliard in 1764),[192] which would likewise usually be lost without any archaeological dig.[193] Some scholars even wondered whether the medium might be incorporated in contemporary architecture,[194] though without any contemplation of reusing antique floors. Their tesserae were picked up by children at Vieil-Évreux, who used them as dice;[195] but unfortunately tourists also "collected" fragments of mosaic pavements as the most accessible of ancient remains. Hence even uncovered and supposedly preserved floors were not safe, for it was

> la rapacité des visiteurs, qui, pour emporter un souvenir pris sur les lieux qu'ils admirent, n'oublient jamais d'enlever quelques fragments comme indemnité de la faible rétribution que demande le gardien des ruines.[196]

Are there heritage and identity implications in the collecting by tourists of what would be called "souvenirs" – memories or reminders of the past? Whichever was the case, a curé at Dieppe got part of a mosaic (which had been covered with earth for protection) moved to his church, because tourists wished to see it.[197] In later years, mediaeval mosaics were also reused, for example in the Friedenskirche at Potsdam.[52]

With road and rail available to carry visitors, some archaeological sites were popular by mid-century, because they often had mosaics to display. But this left scholars in a quandry: should mosaics be left in place, or moved to a museum?[198] Left in place, as Caumont complained in 1861, they were doomed to disappear through lack of surveillance, or the nonchalance of guards. Indeed, when large sculptured blocks could disappear without trace (as happened at Grenoble),[199] could a mosaic ever survive, even on a site with other ruins, "dans une localité où les archéologues font défaut"?[200] At one site near Châteaudun, "on laisse emporter à chaque visiteur une poignée de cubes, et qu'on les frotte avec le balai le plus dur que l'on ait sous la main pour démolir plus vite le tableau."[201] Little surprise, then, when marbles simply disappeared from the local museum.[202] Peasants and farmers also destroyed mosaic floors: in 1833 a mosaic of marine divinities was found at Saint-Rustice, near Toulouse, but large sections quickly disappeared because of agricultural work,[203] as also did another floor at Chazeaux, near Meursault (Côte-d'Or), which was broken and planted over with vines.[204] In many cases, as with a floor of the baths at Feysin (Isère), workmen destroyed the remains, and simply described them to the archaeologists.[205] A large compartmented floor in a villa at Pompogne (Lot-et-Garonne), said to stand comparison with examples in Italy, disappeared without trace.[206] In the Comminges in 1885, a mosaic had to be taken to a secure location, because sections of it were disappearing every night.[207] Three mosaics were retrieved near the amphitheatre in Arles in 1851, underneath later houses.[208] On the western side of the Rhône at Vienne, there were so many mosaics to be seen at Sainte-Colombe and Saint-Romain-en-Gal, unearthed from the 17th century onwards, that substantial quantities survive today.[209] Some were saved by Schneyder, and placed in his Drawing School,[210] while some of his drawings were catalogued by Millin.[211]

Mosaics were also to be found inside towns, but these had even less chance of survival than those in the country. One was found near the railway station at Reims in 1853, "qui fut détruite en quelques jours, attendu que l'on ne jugea pas à propos de la conserver."[212] The "mosaïque des promenades" at Reims, one of several which had been found about the town,[213] was uncovered in 1860 during work between the railway station and the public promenade which had taken the place of the ramparts.[214] At Lyon, Monfalcon complained that it was only mosaics which relayed anything about the early state of art there.[215]

---

52   Bellanca 2008.

THE EARLY ARCHITECTURE OF FRANCE

Unfortunately, the toll on mosaics from visitors and modernisation was large: of 1,674 mosaics listed 1909 (not all of them antique), some 251 had already been destroyed.[216]

Marble Veneer

Many Roman structures were built with a rubble and concrete core, then decorated with fresco or marble veneer inside, and sometimes veneer outside, the solution being cheaper than using solid, structural marble blocks. Few such structures remain in their original state because veneer was prized down the centuries for its luxurious effect, hence was removed, leaving the characteristic core. Baths in France often had marble wall veneer and pavements,[217] as did civic buildings and some houses. Nor were only French marbles used, but imports as well: at Avenches, near Geneva, cipollino and rosso antico were found;[218] jaspers and alabasters at Saint-Quentin;[219] Egyptian at Murviel, near Montpellier;[220] and probably exotics in Vienne,[221] given those at the Palais du Miroir. There were also largely exotic marbles in the baths at Vieux,[222] and presumably also at Autun, if the baths were the source of those donated to the museum.[223] Here the Abbey of S. Martin boasted veneers "des marbres de Grèce et d'Asie."[224] Clearly, mediaeval builders knew which marbles were prestigious, witness how the exotic ones at S-Gilles-du-Gard were placed in prominent positions.[225]

It is difficult to determine the period when most veneer was stripped from structures such as the theatre at Arles,[226] although much went during the Middle Ages, to decorate churches. We reach documented operations under Louis XIV who, as well as re-opening the quarries at Saint-Béat,[227] decorated Versailles and the Grand Trianon with marbles from Barca,[228] as well as keeping records of "des états du prix des marbres de Gènes, des Pyrénées, du Languedoc et de Hollande,"[229] of which the last named might have been spolia, imported for resale on Dutch ships. Not all available sources were tapped, presumably because others were easier, or they were underground. This was perhaps the case with parts of the Tour de Vésone at Périgueux,[230] or those sections of the "Palais des Proconsuls" at Cherchel, excavated in 1849 by the Génie for new buildings, wherein were found veneers "de blanc veiné, brèche violette, bleu turquin, jaune antique, rouge et plusieurs autres dont le nom m'est inconnu."[231]

Cemeteries

Cemeteries were often used (and their vessels reused) over several centuries, even including adjacent housing,[232] and 19th-century references to their rediscovery rarely attempt anything except a general dating. A few standing funerary monuments survived, such as the Pierre de Couhard near Autun[233] but, like Italy, France also had streets of tombs outside her towns. These have disappeared, with scholars believing that the street of tombs on the Lyon-Vienne road was largely intact in the Middle Ages, but then went into bridge-work.[234] Some ancient monuments were given funerary use during the Middle Ages, for example in Normandy.[53] Plenty of relicts from such streets of tombs survived, including civilian and soldiers' monuments, which often turned up in later town walls.[235] One conspicuous Roman mausoleum (among what must have been a common type)[54] was at Lanuejols, in the Gévaudan (Lozère), which was apparently reused as housing.[236] It was cleared in 1814,[237] and survived, although large parts of its structure had been scattered around the houses of the village.[238] In the Middle Ages, especially during church construction, cemeteries (pagan and also Christian) would have been discovered routinely, a documented example being that of Guilbert of Nogent at Nogent-sur-Coucy.[239]

The most prestigious survivals were marble or stone sarcophagi, some believed to have been made of foreign marbles.[240] They were common at Arles, and plentiful at Narbonne.[241] Mérimée was shown one in a private house at Beaucaire in 1835,[242] and saw marble fragments in the cathedral of Nantes.[243] Nantes was a town with plentiful antiquities,[244] some of its walls still in place in the 1870s;[245] Gregory of Tours reports one with a lid that needed six oxen to shift it,[246] and another equally heavy at S. Bénigne, Dijon.[247] At Reims one was claimed for an illustrious native of the town;[248] and at Le Puy (a region rich in antiquities),[249] equally, for a 7th-century bishop, the lid later used as a water trough.[250] Here the cathedral incorporated figured antiquities in its structure, and Roman columns inside.[251] Some of the sarcophagi discovered throughout France were identified as Merovingian.[252] Even fragments were considered valuable, witness their reuse in the façade of S. Just at Valcabrère, presumably from a nearby cemetery,[55] or even from the walls of the town,[253] which could have provided the spolia used in the nave.[254] But such vessels (at least conveniently placed – they were too heavy to move far) were in short supply, and improvisation was needed, such as recutting a column near Valognes[255] or in the Nivernais[256] or, as time passed, poorer quality stone.[257] Later burials also sought Roman spolia, such as milestones, for example at Bayeux[258] and Poitiers,[259] but also architectural blocks,[260]

---

53   Le Maho 1994.

54   Goudineau & Guilaine 1991, 410–413.

55   C. Deroo, M. Durliat & M. Scelles, Recueil général des monuments sculptés en France pendant le haut moyen age (IV–X siècles), Paris 1987, IV: Haute-Garonne. Valcabrère, 144ff.

THE EARLY ARCHITECTURE OF FRANCE

and indeterminate pieces such as the "une longue pierre sculptée placée en manière de linteau" at Tours.[261]

By mid-century, old cemeteries were being carefully dug for museum-quality contents. Vases were retrieved from one in Seine-Inférieure in 1857, "assez près de la ligne du chemin de fer,"[262] and presumably uncovered when the track was laid. Such fruitful contiguity was common: near Lyon 10 tomb-bases were discovered in 1885 whilst digging the railway from Saint-Just to Vaugneray.[263] At Arras in 1886 it was the Génie rather than the railway that provided the help,[264] as they did for the retrieval of part of a monument at Grenoble in 1879;[265] and, at Nancy in 1895, it was road levelling that produced Merovingian funerary antiquities.[266]

After Antiquity

In early mediaeval Gaul the epicentre of settlement sometimes shifted away from Roman towns, which probably implies some shrinkage of population, if not necessarily contempt for the Roman way of life. Ennen cites the cases of Bonn, where the legionary oppidum remained outside the mediaeval walls; and of Neuss (near Cologne), where the mediaeval settlement grew up around a civilian settlement at S. Quirinus, instead of inside the legionary headquarters.[56] Throughout the countryside oppida, Gallic as well as Roman,[57] disappeared under the plough.[267] Similarly, some Roman cities were enclosed within newer, smaller enceintes: this happened at Trier where, although the mediaeval city occupied little more than half the ancient one (which boasted 285 hectares under Gratian), the only important building left outside the new walls was the amphitheatre, and the kings owned land and vineyards within the Roman wall.[58] Elsewhere, Roman suburbs contained many important buildings.[59] But then, it was not unusual for such structures to be some distance from the houses. In the case of Tours, two centres seem to have grown

---

56   Ennen 1979, 28–9.

57   Fichtl 2012m 3–10 for history of research from Caylus & Napoleon III to Déchelette; 25–42: architecture des remparts; 43–50: L'urbanisme des villes gauloises; 87–92 for development into Roman towns, such as Besançon, Bourges, Chartres, Langres, Metz, Orléans & Poitiers, Reims. Pierrevelcin 2012, but nothing on 19th-century scholarship. Cf www.oppida.org for a list keyed to map, each site with description, chronology and bibliography.

58   Roslanowski 1965, 97, and fig. 1; Westermann-Angerhausen 1987 for spolia in Trier.

59   Goodman 2007 concentrates on Gaul.

up at either end of the Roman city, with most of the intervening parts documented in the tenth century as being covered with vines.[60] Some villa sites probably survived as villages, but such matters are outside the scope of this book.

The position of Provence as a "front-line" buffer between the Franks and their successors to the North, and the Visigoths and Arabs to the South, was instrumental in regulating the fate of many of her antiquities. In broad terms, monuments (including sculpture) survived where they were of immediate and continuing use, and the rest suffered in the various waves of sieges, sackings and burnings: one of the most terrible of these was neither Visigothic nor Saracen (the latter not concerned with destroying monuments),[268] but Christian, namely the devastation caused by Charles Martel in 737: then, for example, the thriving city of Maguelonne (with a Roman milestone as a lintel in its cathedral) was ruined because it was a nest of Saracens, to be rebuilt (and then only partially) in the eleventh century by Arnaud, its Bishop.[269] "Saracen" remained an everyday term of abuse in 19th-century France.

Exactly why so many towns in Europe should contemporaneously destroy the monuments which had arguably been the civic pride for centuries (the stone manifestation of charters of liberties?) is still not clear. Barrière offers a likely range of possibilities.[61] One was that the wall-builders were making the future secure with monuments of only the recent past, some of which was probably in any case still unfinished. Another was that several towns had already been sacked and burned by barbarians, probably leaving the monuments in a sorry state, and fit for little else. The other two arguments are ethnic and social: the first is that the gleaming marble and stone buildings were the work of foreigners from Italy, and were therefore out of tune with Gallic aspirations; the second that, in any case, they represented not a plebeian but an aristocratic culture, and were therefore unworthy to survive. All of these arguments could be opposed on many fronts, not least because there is no more than speculation in support of any of them.

As Mazauric remarks, it was finding a new use that ensured the survival of some monuments.[62] By comparison, in the Middle Ages Rome was almost a backwater yet, with the other Roman cities of Italy, led a more stable existence. Perhaps the main problem with the cities studied below is that, in terms of economic prosperity, they "peaked" very early, and were insufficiently strong (whether because of natural disasters, or war) to compete against younger and

---

60   Galinié 1978, fig. 7.

61   Barrière 1930, 171f.

62   Mazauric 1934, 5.

THE EARLY ARCHITECTURE OF FRANCE   57

more dynamic settlements such as Montpellier, Aigues Mortes or Avignon. Perhaps the title of Charles Lenthéric's book (*Les Villes Mortes du Golfe de Lyon*, 2nd ed., Paris 1876) is a little too definitive, linking as it does the still-breathing towns of Arles and Narbonne with the dead settlement of Maguelonne, but his dictum on Arles is explanatory and memorable: "Arles, avec sa population remuante de plus de vingt-cinq mille âmes, n'est pas une ville morte; mais c'est une reine déchue."

Merovingian Antiquities

The history of our area as Gaul becomes France is complicated, and this is exemplified not just in the changes wrought in the cities,[63] but also in church architecture, early examples of which are very thin on the ground, although cemeteries are plentiful.[64] Suffice it to say that Clovis I (481–510), the vanquisher with his sons of the Visigoths, was baptised in 497; and religious architecture, some of it in stone to become a staple of the Middle Ages. There were plenty of quarries exploited in Roman Gaul, and some of them presumably continued in use.[270] Charlemagne, founder of a veritable empire, died in 814, his territory split between his three sons at the Treaty of Verdun in 843. Lothar gained the strip between East and West Francia, but also much of Lombardy and Italy as far as the Duchy of Benevento. Charles the Bald wrested all of West Francia by 875, including the Duchy of Vienne, with Vienne and Arles. Within the several areas listed above, where is the continuity of Gallo-Roman architecture, especially that of churches and monasteries built in stone?

Few temples were converted immediately into churches, and this only underlines a large problem with church architecture. We know that Christian structures existed in great numbers, thanks to authors such as Gregory of Tours who, as an important landowner,[65] also knew of Spanish buildings set up on ancient materials.[271] But we have little idea what they looked like, or even of the materials of which they were made, for authors' mentions of them rarely extend to construction details. Dates are always uncertain, and what happened after the 5th century is usually a blank. Without eschewing textual evidence, historians of architecture like to see actual buildings, and these are very scarce

---

63   Dey 2015, 127–220, "Dark Ages" and the Afterlife of the Roman City. 160–178 for Merovingian Gaul.

64   Escher 2013, 15 for listing of 12 Merovingian sites, of which 6 are foundations only; 6 v–vi^e churches are listed; 16–17 for Carolingian sites; 43–7 for Civaux, Vienne, with sarcophagi lids serving as the cemetery wall.

65   Wickham 2005, 160–165, 168–203 for powerful landed aristocrats in their context, including Gregory of Tours.

58 CHAPTER 1

in Gaul. Nineteenth-century treatments of the period described as "archaeological" might be thought to help, but generally these deal with topics such as cemeteries, grave goods, dress, ethnicity, identity.[272]

Churches were the rock of Christianity, and church councils were held in most of the towns of interest to us.[66] then what architecture of the Merovingian Franks (5th century–8th century), including monasteries, could 19th century scholars identify? Not much, for scholars well knew of the dearth of Merovingian architecture throughout France,[273] and were also well aware that later and much larger churches had obliterated Merovingian structures subsumed completely in a later and larger structure by reusing even their very foundations. Cemeteries were easy, and burials were plentiful, because of grave-goods and sarcophagi (some of the latter found within later churches, often during restoration), and generally bespoke a nearby pre-existing church. Although some sculptures and capitals survived in later structures,[274] including reused sarcophagi,[275] decorated bricks[276] and the occasional altar,[277] and were even featured on façades,[278] standing Merovingian monuments were very rare, or mangled, such as the Baptistery at Riez, which in 1818 suffered "une restauration détestable."[279] Nor were Meroginvian survivals prized for what they were, since imitations of Roman elements were recognised, but not admired.[280]

An index of the destruction of early French religious architecture (of which not one stone stands upon another, writes Enlart)[281] is the survival of only one furnished 7th-century crypt, with reused marbles,[282] namely in Saint-Paul at Jouarre, near Meaux.[67] This was altered in the 17th century, but details are lacking. Caumont says he was responsible for noticing this structure (perhaps in the 1820s).[283] The crypt was "consolidated" (perhaps in the early 1840s)[284] and was discussed in the 1871 Congress[285] and again in 1875, when Roman and Italian influences were detailed.[286] This is the most important Merovingian survival, but we have no illustrations of its state before "restoration." However, it was already highlighted in 1847 for what was described as the reworking of the tombs and the capitals which the Commission had carried out; what a pity, it being "bien mieux de dormir et de laisser aux contribuables les huit cent mille francs qu'elle dépense annuellement pour détruire ou gâter nos plus illustres ou nos plus précieux monuments."[287] Merovingian material also came to light during landscaping work from 1853 at Lillebonne, when

---

66   E.g. Arles, Beauvais, Chalon-sur-Saône, Clermont, Lyon, Macon, Nîmes, Orange, Orléans, Paris, Riez, Reims, Soissons, Tours, Vaison, Valence. Moore 2011, 377–380 for a complete list.

67   Périn 1973; Escher 2013, 73–79.

the owner of land on which a church had been demolished in 1823 found capitals.[288] Of the decoration of other crypts we know only scraps, but they were prime sites for the reuse of marble, for example in the companion but later crypt at Jouarre,[289] at S. Honorat in the Champs Elysées at Arles, at S. Seurin in Bordeaux, and at S. Bénigne, Dijon.[290] That at S. Laurent, Grenoble was restored, but the results "laissent à désirer."[291]

Merovingian and Carolingian cemeteries had long been destroyed in the search for building materials.[292] Merovingian sarcophagi, some of them highly decorated, abound in France.[293] Their cemeteries, some of them huge, were common, as already noted, and other tombs, sometimes built from antique columns,[294] were investigated for their contents, and sites sometimes scoured for road-building material.[295] Frédéric Moreau, who is noticed elsewhere in this book for his industrious speed, dug the necropolis of Caranda and Fère-en-Tardenois (both Aisne) from the 1870s, aided by sand extraction from the latter site.[296] Over 20 years, he excavated over 15,000 Merovingian tombs, this being a record and, at an average of two each day, likely to remain so. He was praised for the achievement by the Artillery, to whose museum he donated some of the arms he had collected.[297] He drew at least some of his finds, but what happened to what must have totalled many hundreds of objects?

Later Religious Architecture

There are three intertwined reasons for the dearth of information on Merovingian architecture. The first is that much later religious architecture derives from models to be found in Italy, especially Old S. Peter's. The second is that, as already noted, earlier structures on the same site were usually swallowed without a trace remaining (except for the few archaeological digs), as outmoded churches were dismantled to help satisfy the continuing thirst for huge quantities of stone, recut as necessary. Cemeteries, sarcophagi (in plaster as well as stone), tombstones, grave goods and coins represent the majority of the material from which to determine continuity (in itself often a difficult proposition) or otherwise. The third response is that early excavators did not find what they did not search for, although they could recognise capitals, reliquaries, altars, and even baptisteries that were not Roman. Probably there was not much in the way of monumental domestic architecture to find, since the Merovingian lords apparently built palaces in wood as well as in stone, and none have survived.[68] Until the later Middle Ages, the development of civic architecture is almost a closed book because so little is known, and it is easily

---

68   Wickham 2005, 506–507: "But for further understanding of this issue we shall have to look to the excavations of the future." Samson 1987 for Merovingian housing.

60 CHAPTER 1

demonstrated that technological experimentation and vast amounts of money were focussed on church building, often by communities evidently in competition with one another.

There is little mystery about why the 19th century looked askance at much mediaeval architecture: it was grossly decorated, civil buildings usually in wood, so different from the modern enlightened environment:

> Dans les villes les maisons étaient sombres et mal distribuées; de petits escaliers obscurs et tournant sur eux-mêmes conduisaient à de vastes et incommodes appartemens... Il n'y avait que des rues étroites, sales et tortueuses. En général on paraissait ignorer les plus simples règles de l'hygiène publique et de l'assainissement, de même que l'on semblait dédaigner tout ce qui embellit aujourd'hui nos relations sociales et tout ce qui donne du charme à nos habitudes domestiques.[298]

Church architecture was in stone and, fortunately, there survive enough unrestored or lightly tainted Romanesque churches and Gothic cathedrals for us to be able usually to distinguish the original from the restored. But this is not the case with earlier buildings, which were scarce. Characteristically, it was the 19th century which caused the most damage, although they could certainly have profited from knowledge of such early architecture, even against the protestations of scholars. Thus the Carolingian church at Germigny des Prés, listed as an Historical Monument in 1840, was "restored" by Juste Lisch between 1867 and 1896, during which it lost much of its plan, frescoes and marble cladding, having already had missing pieces of the mosaic replaced in porcelain.[69] Outrage at vandalism was already well-developed by 1830, when De Caumont, in his lectures, requested protection for monuments:

> On renverse impitoyablement tout ce qui peut rendre la patrie grande et intéressante. Nous faisons chez nous ce que les Vandales ne faisaient que chez leurs ennemis!... Employons donc toute notre influence pour neutraliser les efforts des modernes Vandales.[299]

The following year, Victor Hugo pitched in with several examples from Paris, railing against entrepreneurs and the anti-clericalism that destroyed churches: "Quelquefois on sauve une admirable église en écrivant dessus: mairie."[300] De Caumont's 1830 expression of industrious confidence in the future of archaeology was translated into his popular and detailed books, but unfortunately

---

69   Soraluce Blond 2008, 240 for Germigny des Prés.

THE EARLY ARCHITECTURE OF FRANCE 61

it did not go hand-in-hand with any conservation movement, legally defined or enforceable. Monuments continued to disappear in their thousands, one example being his "pierres druidiques" in the alignments at Carnac, where over 12,000 menhirs had supposedly been counted in the 16th century, and of which only a few thousand remained, and were still in danger in 1875.[301] Everything was at risk, from forests and churches to châteaux and public monuments, in the rage to obliterate the past: "On dirait qu'ils veulent se persuader que le monde est né d'hier et qu'il doit finir demain, tant ils ont hâte d'anéantir tout ce qui semble dépasser une vie d'homme."[302]

France is unusual in the dearth of comparanda to help assess the relationship between Gallo-Roman and later architecture, and just what was borrowed from the one by the other. In Italy, North Africa and the Middle East, in contrast, evidence survives of temples (and baths) being turned into churches, just as churches were subsequently to be converted into mosques. Some evidence survives of converted temples in France,[303] but this seems in some cases to have happened after a period of abandonment lasting several centuries, no temples being constructed later than the third century, and even the literary evidence being equivocal.[70] One hint might be in Vergnolle's observation[71] that the taste for using regular blocks grows in 1040–50, citing the deambulatory of the crypt at Tournus and of that at Auxerre, whereas the use of squared blocks in most buildings of this period was "parsimonious."

Could the taste for squared blocks (often mentioned in contemporary documents as *quadratis lapidibus*) derive from an interest in reusing the stones from antique building? The question is important because it provides some measure of the longevity and continuing usefulness of converted pagan structures, some of which were violently destroyed, but whether by barbarians or Christians is unknown. And as one scholar has remarked, some temples did survive, conspicuously the Maison Carrée at Nîmes (where the monuments clearly did influence later structures),[72] the Temple of Augustus and Livia at Vienne (a church by the 11th century – but this scarcely helps us), and the Tour de Vésone at Périgueux – "but what purpose(s) they served and at what point they ceased

---

70   Goodman 2011, 181: "Sulpicius' words (*'ubi fana ... ibi aut ecclesias aut monasteria'*) do not necessarily imply a direct reuse of the site. They could equally mean that a church was built in the same village or region." 167: "In part, the drop-off may be accounted for by saturation: people concentrated on rebuilding and embellishing existing temples." 168 for rebuildings and embellishments after 350.

71   Vergnolle 1996.

72   Lassalle 2013.

62   CHAPTER 1

to be used for the worship for which they had been built are entirely obscure."[73] As for the preservation of the first two, "this might be explained partly by local pride in the monuments, especially given their political relevance as centres of the imperial cult," while laws allowed and then commanded the destruction of pagan complexes.[74] Percentage calculations can help, Goodman relaying that of 226 temple sites, there were 15, 34, 57 and then 120 abandoned in the 1st, 2nd, 3rd and 4th centuries, and only 17 remaining active into the 5th century.[75] This accords with what is known of church dedications, with Aix-en-Provence, Fréjus, Marseille and Riez all being 5th century.[76]

Churches and abbeys were especially vulnerable in the 19th century:

> Les amis de l'art chrétien doivent donc se hâter de saisir dès maintenant tous les moyens qui sont en leur pouvoir de conserver les monuments du moyen-âge que le temps et le vandalisme ont épargnés.[304] [1868]

At first this was because of the damage and destruction wrought by the Revolution (which often plundered and stripped structures),[305] then because of changes demanded by modernisation amongst those citizens whose knowledge of and interest in architecture was minimal.[306] Many important religious structures were at least part-destroyed during the 19th century, either sold off by the State during the Revolution, or sacrificed to modernisation, the churches of Paris suffering badly.[307] A few were bought by proprietors, and rescued.[308] At Soissons, S. Pierre became a gymnasium, but a bylaw required that the new owner must "laisser visiter ce précieux spécimen de l'art du xve siècle."[309] Alignment and modernisation affected churches just as much as they did other old structures, because the modern impulse was to clear away "clutter" (for example by sanitising church squares of anything old, wooden and picturesque) without asking whether thus denuding large structures improved appearances. Rossignol, inspector for the Société française d'archéologie thought not, stating in 1861 that "L'ennui naquit un jour de l'uniformité," and that towns should be preserving monuments, not destroying them: as he noted, the impulse for such clearances came from the top, and they were contagious and expensive.[310] Saint-Macaire, near Bordeaux, was thus infected; the area around her church was cleared, and one scholar warned

---

73 Esmonde Cleary 2013, 120; 191 for the enormous temple complex at Ribemont-sur-Ancre, near Amiens, rebuilt in the 3th century and functioning in the 4th century.

74 Goodman 2011, 174; 173 for laws of 397, 399 and 425.

75 Goodman 2011, 169.

76 Esmonde Cleary 2013, 174: textual evidence dates Narbonne Cathedral to 445.

THE EARLY ARCHITECTURE OF FRANCE

in 1860 that "Si elle rase ses fortifications, comble ses fossés, démolit ses portes, elle cessera d'être ville et passera dans la catégorie des vilains villages," and fall in prosperity even below nearby Langon,[311] which did indeed happen. A common complaint from towns which lost walls was that thereby they lost their very standing and credibility. They must have been well aware of the symbolism of town walls prior to demands for their demolition, since these had been an acknowleged indication of prestige since ancient times.

Vandalism occurred not only by destruction (such as the walls of Poitiers, or the Château de Pujols), but also by restoration and reconstruction. Many voices were raised against the disfiguration of important churches. Some dubbed the process of unsuitable modern tarting-up as "la vanité de clocher"[312] – not quite the French version of *campanilismo*. This happened at Auch, and also at Moissac (Tarn-et-Garonne), where "La municipalité s'est emparée de ce cloître et en a fait scier les admirables colonnes une à une pour construire une halle."[313] Many instances from the later Middle Ages onward could be cited for petty pilfering from ruinous buildings, building sites, and town walls themselves, some of them owned by the towns themselves, not the King.[77]

Abbeys were specially at risk because, once denuded of their inhabitants, large complexes occupying a lot of land, such as the Jacobins in Paris,[314] produced large returns when the materials were sold off. Occasionally, abbeys were destroyed but their church survived.[315] Mérimée, asked by Guizot to assess the state of the building,[316] explained in 1836 what had happened to the Abbey of Charroux (Vienne): only a few walls and a tower remained, the property of Mme de Grandmaison, who fought off masons wishing to reuse its materials, speculators wishing to enlarge the fairground, and police concerned at the danger of its shedding stones.[317] This was a Royal Abbey founded by Charlemagne, and possessed a fragment of the True Cross, so the rescued tower inevitably received the name of Tour Charlemagne. Fairgrounds and markets were important, of course, and were often placed in deconsecrated churches: a scholar complained in 1859 that the church cloister at Larroumieu (Gers) was in use for the weekly market: "Espérons qu'une administration vigilante et conservatrice arrêtera désormais cette lente destruction d'un monument trop longtemps délaissé, et dont se ferait honneur plus d'une grande ville."[318] The

---

77 Benedict 1989, 18: Rights of municipal government were still being extended in the late fifteenth and early sixteenth century – to Angers in 1475, for instance, as Louis XI sought to gain the loyalty of this great stronghold within what had formerly been an independent apanage, or to Etampes in 1514, in return for a cash payment, or to Langres on several occasions in the sixteenth century in order to encourage the commitment of this border town's inhabitants to its defense and the upkeep of its walls.

64   CHAPTER 1

Abbey of Beaulieu (Tarn-et-Garonne) was also threatened in 1872 with being sold off,[319] and in 1879 it was still "vouée à l'abandon et à là ruine," although by then classified as a monument historique.[320] But then, so many once-splendid structures were by mid-century no more than "des ombres et des fantômes,"[321] many too ruined ever to be included in the lists of the Monuments Historiques.[322] Even tombstones were in grave danger,[323] being turned over and reused as paving, sawn into usable slabs, or broken up by the workmen.[324] Calling on memory – "le culte des souvenirs" – to achieve preservation was useless[325] because, as one cleric writes in 1845, "les magnifiques monuments qu'avait élevés la foi de nos pères étaient considérés avec une froide indifférence."[326]

The dependence of church structure, decoration and furnishing on earlier monuments was evident not only from motifs[78] but also from the frequent reuse of ancient materials (this continued in Turkey into the late 19th century),[327] which may have been in part prompted by respect for the past.[328] Many mediaeval churches were built incorporating spolia.[329] "Ce fut une condition pieuse d'avoir pour pierre fondamentale un débris profane," writes one commentator,[330] but it is more likely that they were incorporated to add solidity and stability (for example, large blocks).[331] In the 19th century, survivals in churches were studied throughout France, for example at Bayeux,[332] Béziers,[333] Blagnac,[334] Chartres,[335] Fontenelle,[336] Jublains,[337] Le Mans,[338] Loches,[339] Marseille,[340] Nantes (cathedral[341] and S. Similien),[342] Orléans,[343] Reims,[344] Senlis,[345] Soissons,[346] St-Quentin[347] Toulouse,[348] Tours,[349] Vienne[350] and many more. The point of this enumeration is to underline the fact that, excluding Astérix' village, all of France was once Roman, with markers in churches the surviving reflection of a much richer presence, reflected also in the Romanesque propensity for imitation and adaptation of antique forms, for example in Autun and Langres,[351] and in Burgundy.[352] Evidence showed that "Le romain et le roman se heurtent et se confondent."[353]

By the 19th century, however, the stability of many churches, some of which had not been repaired for centuries, was often in doubt. For example Saint-Denis' north tower was struck by lightening in 1837, and disassembled as unsafe,

---

78   Lemerle 1996, Arles, Doric entablature of the theatre: very unusual, in that it offers metopes (with bull protomes!) and triglyphs and a running frieze above, which is against the vitruvian canon, following some Hellenistic relaxation of rules. But the device is very popular, for example in the jubé of Bordeaux Cathedral (begun 1529; destroyed), the chateau d'Uzès, a Renaissance house in Beaucaire, the chateau of Bournazel in the Aveyron, and several houses in Arles itself.

THE EARLY ARCHITECTURE OF FRANCE

65

an 1845 report to the Minister affirming that from this accident "quelques personnes étrangères à la pratique de l'architecture ont pris un argument pour soutenir que les édifices du moyen-âge ont fait leur temps, et que désormais leur ruine est devenue inévitable."[354] The cathedral survived, but was entered on the Monuments Historiques list only in 1862, not in 1840. Yet even as early as the 1850s, few were happy with restoration efforts, for "ces monuments ne seront plus eux-mêmes quand on les aura démolis pour les reconstruire."[355] Workmen degraded structures even as they sought to restore them;[356] money was wasted over fifteen years at St-Maximin (Var), and repairs were already coming adrift by 1845.[357] The Abbey of Preuilly, part-ruined under the Revolution, had its west porch sold off forty years later, when "le vandalisme a toisé ces œuvres de sculpture et les a vendues aux habitants du pays comme matériaux bons à construire des granges et des étables."[358] Such devastation continued, wrote one scholar in 1860, who had seen capitals and colonettes broken up for road rubble.[359] On another occasion, breaking down all abbey buildings to make a factory seemed unlikely since, given the difficulty of dismantling some of the masonry, the necessary work would cost too much.[360] An interesting thesis by an economic historian with archival interests could be written on just what guided decisions and outcomes in the business of restoration and dismantling.

Mediaeval wall frescoes in churches were numerous but were often plastered over,[361] and we know little about them because their survival rate was so low: "la racle des débadigeonneurs n'avait dépouillé pour jamais un grand nombre de nos édifices de leur antique parure."[362] (Badigeon: "masse, pâte, matière adhérente mise en une masse et comme pétrie ensemble.")[363] How much more would be known "si des mémoires avaient été rédigés immédiatement et si les plans de chaque fouille avaient été dressés," lamented a critic at Vienne in 1841.[364] Again, at Bourges little was known of frescoes because "la plupart de ces monuments intéressants ont disparu sous la brosse des plâtriers ou des maçons."[365] As well as being heavily plastered over, many old frescoes were removed during church modernisation programs, or even destroyed. The secularised Cordeliers at Chalon with a painted façade was one such church. In 1846 "Messieurs du génie militaire daignaient le laisser debout," but then "croyant avoir mal fait de ne pas avoir été plus vandales que 1793, ils viennent de le démolir."[366] Modern re-painting commissioned by ignorant clergy was also a problem, so that the congressists at Albi in 1863 were asked as one of their annual questions: "Exposer le système de peintures murales employé depuis quelques années dans la région; en signaler les abus."[367] Church furniture was similarly in danger, both through destruction[368] and "du zèle restaurateur mal dirigé."[369]

66   CHAPTER 1

Neither Cluny (Saône-et-Loire) nor Jumièges (Seine-Inférieure) was on the
Monuments Historiques list in 1840, but both appeared in 1862 – too late, of
course. The fate of Cluny was destruction,[79] in spite of the protests of the town
mayor in 1800.[370] The municipality had tried to preserve one of the defence
towers by renting it out in 1743 to a merchant; but nothing survives of it
today.[371] Much of the building went beginning in 1800, coverted into lime and
rubble, plus large blocks; gunpowder was not used here only because the danger to nearby houses.[372] But so huge was the building that even incomplete
demolition took fifteen years, over continuing local protests from some,[373]
but to the benefit of others: from 1810 to 1830, several houses were built from
the Abbey's materials, as well as some roads.[374] The town boasted a large
number of mediaeval houses but then, in the 1850s, "fatigués d'une immobilité
de sept siècles," the locals caught modernism, and the aspect of the streets
changed completely.[375] Jumièges was sold in 1795, and dismantling continued until stopped in 1824 when the Abbey was purchased again, and a park
made amongst the ruins.[376] The Abbey of La Grande Sauve, near Bordeaux,
which appears on the 1840 list, had also been sold off, and fell "sous le marteau
démolisseur du vandalisme et de l'ignorance." Its nave, decorated columns and
capitals disappeared,[377] some of the materials used (as at Cluny) to build the
few houses which constituted the village, the rest carted off elsewhere,[378]
some reportedly as road-metal.[379] There were enough ruins left in 1893 to be
visited by congressists, and part of them had become a Jesuit school.[380]

Four further examples will show that structures, once classified, were not
always safe, as they should have been, since this was the point of classifying
them in the first place. Not far from Jumièges is Saint-Wandrille (Orne), an
important and extensive abbey. But "vu son peu d'importance au point de vue
général,"[381] this was actually declassified in 1879, entailing "la destruction
d'une abside romane considérée comme un bijou par M. l'abbé Cochet," who
was responsible for much consciousness-raising about French archaeology.[80]
Bureacrats would sleep soundly knowing that "il n'en est pas moins juste de
reconnaître que les formalités ont été observées et que tout s'est régulièrement
passé,"[382] scholars knowing that at least some ruins survive. But why was such
an important structure declassified? Because of modernisation, of course:
that of Saint-Wandrille was "demandé afin de faciliter les constructions qu'on
exécute en ce moment, et dont le premier résultat a été la destruction d'une
abside romane."[383] At Reims, S. Rémi was on the list from 1840, but this did
not stop the destruction of her enceinte, "dont les dernières traces ont disparu

---

79   Montclos 1992, 22–37.
80   Hubert 1978; Flavigny 1992, including a description of his collection and digs.

seulement de nos jours" late in the century.[384] At Moissac (on the 1840 list), most of what was until the 19th century a fortified monastery was destroyed after its suppression in 1790; elements of fortification survived in 1865, when they were visited by congressists.[385] The church and a cloister survive – but the latter was apparently the smaller of two cloisters,[386] and so comprehensively was the other one destroyed that (except for the fact that it had colonettes in marble) little is known about it. Indeed, in about 1830 it was proposed to turn the gallery of the larger cloister into a market. The surviving cloister had already been bought by a public-minded citizen, but this nearly disappeared under the tracks of the Bordeaux-Toulouse Railway[387] – not that the latest "history" of the abbey mentions the losses.[81] But as the information plaque at Moissac today has it: "1845: Une importante mobilisation permit au cloître d'échapper à la démolition qu'imposait la construction de la ligne de chemin de fer... Le réfectoire seul fut détruit" – again to accommodate the railway tracks.[388] At Marseille, Saint-Maximin suffered "des désastres occasionés par la main des barbares qui ont ainsi consommé les actes du vandalisme le plus révoltant et du plus manifeste gaspillage de fonds."[389]

Instead of reducing, then, destruction increased during the 19th century, not just on account of the Revolution, but because of industry, "cette puissance de notre époque,"[390] or because of "tant de dépravation dans le goût et le sentiment des arts."[391] So industry, street-widening, and speculation were the "nécessités impérieuses" indicated by the Prefect who condemned a church in Rouen in 1861, adding "qu'on a pris tous les moyens possibles pour en conserver une partie et que M. Pollier s'empresse de recueillir les fragments les plus remarquables."[392] In the same town, the destruction of the church of Bonne-Nouvelle and rebuilding of the eponymous barracks produced a lot of rubble, but also four columns and "quelques fragments de sculptures récoltées çà et là par les ouvriers."[393] As a substitute for conservation, this was the continuing story of "put the useless bits in a museum," which was echoed all over, for example at Reims, where the fittings of Saint Niçaise went at the Revolution, the débris seen all over town, "épaves précieuses qu'il convient de recueillir avec soin et dont il faudrait assurer la conservation en les réunissant toutes dans un même musée."[394] It is paralleled by the impulse to make plans of ramparts (as at Beauvais) as they are pulled down.[395]

---

81   Fraïsse 2006, 90, for six lines on the sale of the abbey. The author is Conservateur au Centre d'Art roman de Moissac, and teaches at Bordeaux.

Civic Architecture: Châteaux

Long before they became the benign bijoux of the Loire Valley, châteaux were fortified houses, sometimes miniature towns, and hence down the centuries could represent a military threat to local or central powers. France was full of them,[396] and the consensus was that several naturally dated back to Roman fortified positions,[397] as did mediaeval building strategies: "jamais les traditions romaines ne furent tout-à-fait oubliées par les architectes militaires du moyen-âge."[398] Material was sometimes scavenged between châteaux, as for example between Montélimar and Narbonne,[399] and several structures reveal not only ancient forms as a model,[400] but also Roman material in their walls,[401] such as Argenton (Indre),[402] Pons, near Saintes,[403] S. Privat, near the Pont du Gard,[404] Beaucaire (Gard),[405] Prény (Meurthe-et-Moselle),[406] St-Paulien (Haute Loire),[407] perhaps Cassel, near Dunkirk (Nord),[408] as well as Roman dolia for storage.[409]

Just as with town walls, the centuries saw the ruination and demolition of many châteaux,[82] the remains of which could be used for further building or rebuilding, such as for the reconstruction of the church façade of Parthenay.[410] Since early châteaux were, just like so many towns, built at strong-points, it is not surprising to find their ruins surviving into the 19th century, or as complexes constructed inside older structures, the most famous being the Château des Arènes (the amphitheatre) at Nîmes, and the theatre at Orange.[411] Real châteaux also survived, as at Limoise,[412] and also yielded earlier antiquities. The threat they posed well into the 19th century was evident by devastation visited on such buildings in earlier centuries, commented on even to English visitors.[413]

The annual Congrès Archéologique, held each year in a different location, posed a series of pressing questions each year in an attempt to gather information on important topics. They continued to ask for research on "les monuments de l'architecture militaire en France aux diverses époques du moyen âge."[414] These were routinely destroyed during and after wars and insurrections, especially by Richelieu[415] and his successors, for such feudal nests represented for French kings "un souvenir d'insultes souvent demeurées impunies."[416] Whole areas of defences were denuded,[417] including towns such as Marseille,[418] where Colbert initiated an extensive re-design of the city for naval and trade purposes, including wide boulevards.[83]

---

82   Montclos 1992, passim.

83   Takeda 2011, 25: By June 1666, the Crown had given the developer François Roustan permission to demolish the old walls and to collect taxes to support the project.

THE EARLY ARCHITECTURE OF FRANCE   69

Such destruction hindered a good knowledge of such buildings, and "l'archéologue lui [Richelieu] pardonnera difficilement d'avoir accumulé tant de ruines sur son chemin pour arriver à établir en France le régime politique du despotisme."[419] Poetic justice ensured that his own château at Richelieu was destroyed after 1805, and disappeared completely: "Pendant vingt ans, de la base au faîte, c'est comme une mine que l'on exploite."[420] Nor was his the only one for, as a congressist noted in 1846, "la Touraine, qui jadis, couverte de superbes châteaux, les a vu disparaitre insensiblement, soit par le fait du vandalisme moderne, soit par suite d'une coupable incurie."[421]

Lords did not build or dismantle their own fortresses, whether châteaux or towns, for local people were usually rounded up for the task, to form a corvée, which could last several months.[422] In the case of the Château-du-Marché at Châlons-sur-Marne, a lime kiln was placed in one of the towers, and rented out for three years; other towers later became private houses.[423] It took very large numbers of workers when dealing with siege works, or providing waggons.[424] In many cases, such as Lyon, the citizens were taxed to pay for defences.[425] So it is not too fanciful to imagine that mere inhabitants could feel proprietorial about the walls they had erected (guarded, as at Narbonne,[426] and perhaps helped pay for in the case of towns such as Nîmes),[427] or pulled down. So when it came to demolition, proprietors might sell stone off cheaply,[428] as at part of Montaigu,[429] or locals be employed to do the work, as at Ferté-Milon (Aisne) in 1594.[430] If the locals "owned" such châteaux, they could also dismantle them such that no trace of decoration remained, as was the case at Coulommiers.[431]

Conclusion: Preventable Destruction

When considering the destruction of archaeological sites (there are plentiful examples throughout this book) we should bear in mind that the anchoring of any retrieved object to where it was found is a 20th-century preoccupation quite correctly deemed essential by archaeological methodology. But this was not how objects were viewed in earlier centuries. If some conspicuous treasures gained prestige from their source (Athens, Ephesus, or Rome, perhaps) and were so labelled in their museum, most small objects, as a perusal of Montfaucon or Caylus will show, were lucky to be attributed to a country or a region within a country. "Don't touch an object unless you know its provenance" is a concept unknown to 19th-century scholars or museums, but a watchword with which to attack museums today. Vandalism in the 18th and 19th centuries was indeed a significant impediment to preservation, but was

70   CHAPTER 1

usually part of a quest for cheap building materials. Archaeological sites were
not often destroyed in an effort to extract and sell their antiquities; rather,
it was the objects themselves which were seen as worthy of study and –
evidently – the sites themselves which were expendable. Efforts to protect such
sites were few, and the usual trajectory was discovery and digging by farmer or
builder, then a report of finds in one of the scholarly periodicals; these might
go to a museum, but the site was generally on private land, and many disappeared as their materials were re-used. This neglect of sites can be seen in the
choices of the Commission des Monuments Historiques (see Chapter Four)
which, as the name indicates, concentrate on monumental buildings. In the
1840 listing, for example, at Arles the Église Saint-Honorat is protected (but
not the Alyscamps in which it stands); at Fréjus only the amphitheatre; the
only whole Gallo-Roman sites protected are those at Tintignac (Corrèze) and
Jublains (Mayenne), and to these was added Bavay in the 1862 list. In a sense
these listings avoid the issue because, as we shall see, it was modernism in the
towns that saw the discovery of so many remains; but discoveries which today
would have a excavation order slapped on them before one could say "underground car-park" might well be reported but were almost never protected,
because they were on private property.

[1] Devic_&_Vaissete_
    XV_1892_814.698
[2] Mortet_1911_I_391
[3] Migne_PL_
    LXIX_1865_547–8
[4] Carpentras_BM_
    Ms_1721_127
[5] Pingaud_1887_84
[6] Piesse_1862_252
[7] BA_Comité_1908_400
[8] Mém_Nîmes_
    XXXI_1908_275
[9] Gregory_of_Tours_
    II_1860_13
[10] Gregory_of_
    Tours_I_1857_183
[11] RA_XXVII_1874_359
[12] Labande_1904_40–41
[13] RA_V_1848–9_223
[14] Goze_1854_54–55
[15] BSA_Soissons_
    IX_1860_156

[16] Vasseur_1860_315–316
[17] Laporte_1897_167–168
[18] Babeau_1880_249
[19] Cartailhac_1903_1–27
[20] BM_III_1837_144
[21] SG_XXIII_
    Nantes_1856_341
[22] Momméja_1898
[23] Sorbonne_1869_18
[24] Cartailhac_1903_175–176
[25] CS_France_II_1834_
    Poitiers_174
[26] Roach_Smith_1855_23
[27] Journal_des_
    Sçavans_1866_403
[28] Le_Rouzic_1908
[29] BSA_Nantes
    XXI_1882_38–39
[30] Cartailhac_1903_208
[31] MSA_Ouest_II_1883_488
[32] Bottin_1821_16
[33] BM_III_1837_61

[34] BM_V_1839_366
[35] ASA_Château-
    Thierry_1895_134–135
[36] BSA_Provence_II_1908–
    1914_119
[37] Cartailhac_1903_201
[38] Cartailhac_1903_4
[39] BSA_Soissons_
    VII_1872_110
[40] BM_VI_1840_424
[41] BM_IX_1843_652–653
[42] BSA_Limousin_
    IX_1859_21
[43] Miln_1877_7
[44] BSA_Nantes_
    XXI_1882_102–103
[45] BM_XI_1845_326–327
[46] BM_XIII_1847_380
[47] MSA_France_
    VIII_1846_281
[48] BSA_Soissons_X_1879_
    258

THE EARLY ARCHITECTURE OF FRANCE

[49] Mém_Lyon_1882_LXVI

[50] Paté_1900_26

[51] Caumont_1830_79

[52] Mém_Angers_1851_578

[53] CS_France_XI_1843_
Angers_24–5

[54] SG_XX_Troyes_1853_30

[55] Michel_III_1847_172

[56] BSA_Limousin_
LV_1905_615

[57] BM_XXX_1864_425

[58] SG_XXXVIII_
Angers_1871_59–60

[59] Cartailhac_1903_203

[60] BSH_Soissons_
XVII_1863_356

[61] Mém_Picardie_X_1865_
344–345

[62] RA_VII_1863_206

[63] BSA_Nantes XI 1872, 35

[64] BA_Comité_1891_492

[65] SG_XLVIII_Vannes_
1881_350

[66] Miln_1877_12

[67] Cartailhac_1903_178

[68] Mém_Pontoise_
III_1881_13–14

[69] BM_XXVII_1861_206

[70] BSA_Soissons_VIII_
1854_29

[71] SG_XXIX_Saumur_1862_
529–530

[72] BCA_Seine-Inférieure_
VIII_1888–1890_159–160

[73] JDPL_17_September_1850

[74] Blanchet_1908_6

[75] Roach_Smith_1855_5–6

[76] BSA_Soissons_
XII_1868_147–148

[77] Espérandieu_XIV_
1955_41

[78] CS_France_XII_1844_
Nîmes_258

[79] CS_France_XIV_1846_
Marseille_32–3

[80] Terninck_1879_25

[81] BA_Comité_1894_L

[82] RA_II_1845_562

[83] Bull_Acad_Delphinale_
I_1856–1860_341

[84] BSA_Drôme XLII 1908,
455–456

[85] SG_XXXI_Fontenay_
1864_399–400

[86] BSA_Drôme VIII 1874,
348

[87] BSA_Drôme_VIII_1874_
348

[88] BSA_Drôme_XVII_1883_
445

[89] Corresp_Hist_Archéol_I_
1894_151

[90] BSA_Drôme_XLII_1908_
461

[91] BSA_Drôme_XLII_1908_
457

[92] BSA_Drôme_XLII_1908_
338–339

[93] SG_LXI_Saintes_1894_
22–23

[94] BM_XXVI_1860_317–318

[95] Goussard_1861_28

[96] Blanchet_1907_60

[97] Mémoires_Franche-
Comté_I_1838_69–71

[98] Hunnewell_1898_7

[99] Ausonius_I_1919_159

[100] Revue_Génie_Militaire_
IV_1890_411–414

[101] Lachèse_1843_6–7

[102] Lottin_1837_248

[103] Ducourtieux_1884_51

[104] Bazin_1900_28 Reims

[105] Millin_I_1807_322

[106] Charvet_1869_65

[107] Mém_AIBL_1863_407

[108] MDANE_IX_1849_393–
394

[109] Mérimée_1838_129

[110] Hugo_1835_III__265

[111] CS_France_XVII_1850_
Nancy_150–1

[112] SG_LXI_Saintes_1894_57

[113] Estrangin_1838_29

[114] Espérandieu_IV_1911_182

[115] BCA_Seine-Inférieure_
IV_1879_229

[116] ASA_Château-Thierry_
1883_8

[117] Annuaire_archéologie_
français_I_1877_127

[118] Recueil_Comm_
Charente-Inférieure_
XVII_1905–1907_353

[119] Bottin_1821_56–60

[120] Mémoires_Franche-
Comté_I_1838_54

[121] Mémoires_Franche-
Comté_I_1838_117

[122] SG_XXIV_Mende_
1857_118

[123] Piganiol_XII_1754_497

[124] BM_III_1837_154

[125] Allmer_&_Dissard_II_
1889_274ff

[126] Bertrand_1903_79

[127] Devic_&_Vaissete_I_
1872_309

[128] Millin_II_1808_516

[129] Chaudruc_de_
Cazannes_1820_47–48

[130] RA_1844_21

[131] BSH_XI_Paris_1829_
50–51

[132] Greppo_1846_188–189

[133] Secrétaires_Autun_
1848_47

[134] Charvet_1869_65B

[135] SG_XXXII_Montauban_
1866_375

[136] MSA_Ouest_II_1883_321

[137] BA_Tarn-et-Garonne_
II_1872_59–60

[138] CS_France_XIX_1852_
Toulouse_440–1

[139] Bonnard_1908_432–433

[140] AD_Limousin_1903

[141] BM_XXVIII_1862_124–125

[142] BSA_Limousin_IV_1852_260

[143] BSA_Limousin_IV_1852_255

[144] BSA_Limousin_IV_1852_256

[145] BSA_Limousin_V_1854_255

[146] Bonnard_1908_107

[147] Dumas_1841_154–155

[148] MDANE_III_1821_59

[149] Greppo_1846_26–27

[150] SG_XXI_Moulins_1854_42

[151] AMPF_IX_1895_138

[152] Pan_Pitt_France_II_1839_24

[153] Greppo_1846_52

[154] Greppo_1846_53–54

[155] BA_Comité_1892_254

[156] BA_Comité_1892_254–255

[157] Cochet_1866_401

[158] BM_LV_Paris_1889_110

[159] Mortet_1911_53–55

[160] Wickham 2005, 201

[161] BA_Comité_1894_41

[162] Caumont_II_1850_176

[163] Thomas_1846_177

[164] Thomas_1846_179

[165] BSA_Limousin_XII_1862_292

[166] MSA_France_XVIII_1846_392–393

[167] BSA_Midi_XXII_1898_142

[168] Espérandieu_II_1908_29

[169] RA_1891_121

[170] AMPF_XIII_1899_50

[171] Joulin_1901

[172] Annales_Midi_XIV_1902_120

[173] AJA_III_1899_83

[174] Espérandieu_II_1908_29_Note_2

[175] Lahondès_1920_304

[176] Lebègue_1891_396

[177] AMPF_X_1896_7

[178] Espérandieu_II_1908_220ff.

[179] Perrot_1891_67–68

[180] BSAH_Limousin_XII_1862_292

[181] BSAH_Limousin_XIII_1863_260

[182] BA_Comité 1889, 163

[183] Mém_Normandie_1831_190

[184] SG_LXII_Clermont-Ferrand_1895_172

[185] BSS_Yonne_IV_1850_4–5

[186] BSA_Provence_I_1904–1907_71

[187] BSA_Soissons_XVI_1861_28

[188] Perrot_1891_66

[189] Soc_Borda_XVI_1891_12

[190] Rev_Comminges_XIX_1904_116–117

[191] Carpentras_BM_Ms_1721_107

[192] Mémoires_Franche-Comté_I_1838_182

[193] SG_XXXVII_Lisieux_1870_63

[194] CS_France_X_1842_Strasbourg_54

[195] Rever_1827_45

[196] SG_XXVIII_Reims_1861_39

[197] PV_Comm_Seine-Inférieure_II_1849–1866_19

[198] SG_XXVIII_Reims_1861_39B

[199] SG_XXIV_Mende_1857_360–368

[200] BCA_Seine-Inférieure_1870_II_27

[201] BM_XXVI_1860_455

[202] BS_Dunoise_I_1864–1869_33

[203] Acad_Toulouse_IV_1834–36_45

[204] Mém_Côte_d'Or_1847_76

[205] CS_France_XIX_1852_Toulouse_448

[206] CS_France_XIX_1852_Toulouse_169

[207] Rev_Comminges_I_1885_7

[208] BA_Comité_1912_CLXXIII

[209] BA_Comité_1909_194–208

[210] Millin_II_1807_19

[211] Millin_II_1807_11–16

[212] Histoire_Reims_1864_174

[213] Loriquet_1862_VIII-X

[214] Loriquet_1862_32

[215] Monfalcon_1857_227–228

[216] Lafaye_&_Blanchet_I_1909

[217] Bonnard_1908_507

[218] BM_IV_1838_443

[219] BSA_Laon_VII_1858_208–209

[220] RA_VII_1863_158

[221] Schneyder_1880_72–73

[222] Sorbonne_1861

[223] Mém_Éduenne_XII_1883_430

[224] Mém_Beaune_1904_65

[225] Hartmann-Virnich_2000_288–290

[226] Lenthéric_1878_240

THE EARLY ARCHITECTURE OF FRANCE

[227] Revue_Comminges_XIII_1898_283

[228] Dezobry_&_Bachelet_Dictionnaire_1888_230

[229] Clément_V_1868_363

[230] CHA_I_1894_374

[231] RA_V_1849_348

[232] BSAH_Limousin_XL_1892_786

[233] Stendhal_1891_I_65B

[234] Allmer_&_Dissard_II_1889_321

[235] BA_1887_213-223

[236] SG_XXIV_Mende_1857_17-18

[237] Espérandieu_II_1908_472

[238] SG_XXIV_Mende_1857_23

[239] Mortet_1911_318

[240] SG_XXXV_Carcassonne_1868_251

[241] BCA_Narbonne_1892_405-406

[242] Mérimée_1835_358

[243] Mérimée, Prosper_1836_286

[244] SG_LX_Abbeville_1893_86

[245] BSA_Nantes_XVII_1878_28

[246] Gregory_of_Tours_II_1860_373-375

[247] Gregory_of_Tours_I_1857_149

[248] Espérandieu_V_1913_3677

[249] Annales_du_Midi_XI_1899_535

[250] Michel_III_1847_161

[251] CS_France_XXII_1856_Le_Puy_387

[252] Bull_Soc_Hist_Paris_IV_1877_74

[253] Mège_1835_54

[254] AD_Pyrénées_Centrale_1922_14-15

[255] BM_XXVI_1860_145

[256] SG_XL_Chateauroux_1873_256-257

[257] BA_Comité_1887_299

[258] SG_XXIII_Nantes_1856_128-129

[259] SG_XXIII_Nantes_1856_120-121

[260] BSA_Drôme_X_1871_215

[261] BSA_Touraine_XXI_1871_543

[262] Cochet_1871_348

[263] Allmer_&_Dissard_III_1890_I_28-39

[264] BA_Comité_1886_325

[265] SG_XLVI_Vienne_1879_323-4

[266] AMPF_IX_1895_248-249

[267] Revue_Génie_Militaire_II_1888_680

[268] V-le-Duc_VIII_1875_216

[269] Lentheric 1876, 333ff.

[270] Jullian_1902_135

[271] Gregory_of_Tours_I_1857_65

[272] Esmonde_Cleary_2013_3

[273] Enlart_I_1902_92

[274] AJA_I_1885_403

[275] BA_Comité_1888_208

[276] AMPF_IX_1895_292

[277] MSA_Ouest_1883_26

[278] CHA_III_1896_201

[279] Enlart_I_1902_195

[280] BA_Comité_1893_9

[281] Enlart_I_1902_114

[282] SG_XXXVIII_Angers_1871_365

[283] BM_IX_1843_182-193

[284] RA_1844-5_550

[285] SG_XXXVIII_Angers_1871_186

[286] BSA_Seine-et-Marne_VII_1875_LVI

[287] AA_IX_1849_60, 61 Jouarre

[288] Cochet_1866_414

[289] SG_XXXVIII_Angers_1871_366

[290] Mém_Côte_d'Or_IV_1856_IX

[291] SG_XXIV_Mende_1858

[292] BM_XXXVI_1870_160-161

[293] SG_XXXII_Montauban_1865_98

[294] BCA_Seine-Inférieure_1867_401

[295] SG_LIX_Orléans_1892_188-189

[296] RA_XXX_1875_122

[297] Revue_d'Artillerie_XXIII_1895_551

[298] Fabre_II_1834_155

[299] Caumont_IV_1831_360-361

[300] Hugo_1832_614

[301] SAH_Charente IX_1873-1874_394-395

[302] Montalembert_1839_7

[303] Millin_III_1808_196

[304] Mém_Picardie_II_1868_76

[305] Saint-Fergeux_1836_293

[306] CS_France_XVIII_1851_Orléans_27

[307] BSH_Paris_XXXV_1908_221

[308] Mém_Lorraine_IX_1867_251-252

[309] ASA_Château-Thierry_1886_141

[310] BM_XXVII_1861_264-265

[311] BM_XXVI_1860_749-750

[312] AMPF_I_1886–1887_50–51

[313] BM_XXVIII_1862_730–747

[314] AA_IX_1849_122

[315] Murray_1848_56

[316] BA_Comité_II_1886_47

[317] Mérimée_1836_400

[318] Revue_Aquitaine_III_1859_287

[319] BA_Tarn-et-Garonne_II_1872_379

[320] BA_Tarn-et-Garonne_VII_1879_116

[321] Revue_Aquitaine_I_1857_537

[322] BSA_Drôme_XXXI_1897_179

[323] Bourassé_1841_244–245

[324] Murcier_1855_69

[325] Mém_Picardie_X_1850_118

[326] Bull_Soc_Nivernaise_XI_1883_XII–XIII

[327] RA_V_1885_98

[328] Enlart_I_1902_80–81

[329] Enlart_I_1902_80–81

[330] Michel_III_1847_70

[331] Mérimée_1835_216

[332] BM_XIX_1853_417–418

[333] Bonnet_1905_176

[334] Revue_Aquitaine_X_1866_424

[335] BSA_Eure-et-Loire_I_1858_305–318

[336] Cochet_1866_483

[337] SG_XLV_Le_Mans_1878_540

[338] BM_VI_1840_215

[339] SG_XXXVI_Loches_1870_28

[340] Panorama_Pittoresque_II_1839

[341] MSA_France_1840_xxxiii–xxxiv

[342] AMPF_IX_1895_237–238

[343] BM_XVIII_1852_232–233

[344] Tarbé_1844_477

[345] SG_XXXIII_Senlis_1866_121

[346] BSA_Soissons_V_1875_345

[347] BM_XXXVI_1870_202

[348] Acad_Toulouse_IV_1837

[349] Grandmaison_1879_66

[350] Charvet_1869_127

[351] Foisset_&_Simonnet_1872_LII–LIII

[352] Foisset_&_Simonnet_1872_XLIX-L

[353] SG_LXIII_Morlaix_1896_179–217

[354] BM_XI_1845_389

[355] SA_Bordeaux_III_1876_87

[356] BM_XVII_1851_551

[357] BM_XI_1845_536–537

[358] MSA_France_XXIII_1857_380

[359] AA_XX_1860_229

[360] BM_III_1837_336

[361] Réunion_BA_XVI_1892_516

[362] SG_XXI_Moulins_1854_179

[363] Scheler_1888_s.v. badigeon

[364] SG_XLVI_Vienne_1879_17–18

[365] Gembloux_1840_101–102

[366] AA_IV_1846_190–191

[367] SG_XXX_Rodez_1863_460

[368] BM_XXVIII_1862_328

[369] SG_XXX_Rodez_1863_15

[370] Penjon_1884_162–163

[371] Penjon_1884_12

[372] Millénaire_1910_II_314–315

[373] Millénaire_1910_I_XCVIII

[374] Penjon_1884_98

[375] Penjon_1884_53

[376] AJA_I_1885_136

[377] Malte-Brun_II_1881_30

[378] SA_Bordeaux_XVII_1892_71

[379] SA_Bordeaux_XIX_1894_7

[380] SA_Bordeaux_XVIII_1893_XXXIV

[381] BCA_Seine-Inférieure_V_1882_305

[382] BCA_Seine-Inférieure_V_1882_303–305

[383] BCA_Seine-Inférieure_V_1882_303

[384] BA_1892_386

[385] SG_XXXI_Montauban_1865_489

[386] Rupin_1897_200–201

[387] Rupin_1897_199–200

[388] Viollet-le-Duc_Dictionnaire_I_1876_261

[389] CS_France_XIV_1846_Marseille_111

[390] BSA_Nantes_IV_1864_182

[391] SG_XXIV_Mende_1857_137–138

[392] PV_Seine-Inférieure_II_1849–1866_182

[393] BCA_Seine-Inférieure_VII_1885–1887_287

[394] BA_Comité_1884_123

[395] Mém_Picardie_IX_1848_26

[396] Moncaut_1857_83

[397] Mém_AIBL_1863_392–393

[398] SG_XVIII_Laon_1852_286

[399] BSA_Drôme_XXX_1896_123

[400] SG_XXIX_Saumur_1862_278

[401] Bulliot_1856_203

[402] SG_XL_Chateauroux_1873_692

[403] SG_LXI_Saintes_1894_61–62

[404] SG_LXIV_Nîmes_1897_268

[405] Mérimée_1835_355–356

[406] SG_XIII_Metz_1846_125

[407] Michel_III_1847_69

[408] SG_XXVII_Dunkerque_1861_53–54

[409] BSA_Provence I 1904–1907, 36

[410] Babeau_1880_251

[411] Mérimée_1835_168

[412] SG_XXI_Moulins_1854_29–30

[413] La Scava_1818_112–113

[414] BA_Comité_1888_33

[415] Annales_du_Midi_XIV_1902_517

[416] V-le-Duc_IX_1885_189

[417] Germain_1869_152

[418] Réunion_BA_1893_XVII_1893_215–36

[419] Normand, Charles, AMPF_XIV_1901_84

[420] BSA_Touraine_VII_1886–1888_247–341

[421] CS_France_XIV_1846_Marseille_328

[422] Babeau_1878_233

[423] Grignon_1889_10-16-20–21

[424] Babeau_1889_284

[425] Boitel_1843_II_488ff

[426] Mouynès_1872_469

[427] Puech_1884_10

[428] SG_XXXII_Montauban_1866_101

[429] Panorama_Pittoresque_II_1839_22

[430] Panorama_Pittoresque_V_1839_15

[431] BM_XIX_1853_610

CHAPTER 2

The Defence of France

The Enceintes of Late Antiquity

The enceintes of Late Antiquity in Gaul had characteristics well-known to 19th-century scholars,[1] and often described in detail.[2] They were also familiar with the general features of late antique collapse.[1] A few believed that religious structures were placed carefully in the late walls in order to protect them,[3] but most were clear that they were simply intended to protect a civilian population, erected with whatever blocks came conveniently to hand.[4] But were some enceintes just military garrisons? We have no firm information on this matter, save for the inference from the enormous effort (manpower and machinery) required to set in place such defences with foundations of large stone blocks.[2] But if such construction capabilities were in place, they were evidently not employed to erect new civic buildings, let alone new villas out of re-used blocks, for there is no evidence whatever of this. Some earlier villas survived, degrading gently (indeed, as was the whole environment),[3] and some were eventually turned into cemeteries. As for the period of such decline, and shrinkage within new walls, dating tends naturally to be associated with finds from within such walls when they were demolished.[4] Many inscriptions were recovered, and the great majority of these were dated or dateable; however, the Achilles' heel of such an apparently cut-and-dried result is that the output of inscriptions declines steeply from the 3rdC, questioning if not exactly invalidating the common dating of such enceintes to the 3rdC itself, "proved" by the recovered inscriptions. Another spanner in the works is Halsall's suggestion

---

1   Liebeschuetz 1992.
2   Garmy & Maurin 1996, 10 for list of enceintes certain from archaeology or texts. Bedon 1988 I, 101–17; ibid. 11 for an A–Z atlas of towns Agen-Xanten; Henigfeld & Masquilier 495–512 for 97 enceintes in Lorraine, only a few (Metz, Toul, Verdun, Deneuvre) from Antiquity; Massy 1997.
3   Frye 2003, 186: In many ways, Ausonius and Sidonius represented an aristocracy vainly attempting to emulate the perceived lifestyle of the past, while at the same time struggling to deal with a contemporary urban environment that differed both physically and culturally from classical models.
4   Esmonde Cleary 2013, 107: "Further south, into Provence, a similar pattern can be detected with a certain amount of evidence that shrinkage was already under way from the early third century, well before the construction of wall circuits. The best evidence comes from a series of cities in southern Gaul, in particular Aix-en-Provence, Arles, Nîmes and Vienne."

© KONINKLIJKE BRILL NV, LEIDEN, 2015 | DOI 10.1163/9789004293717_004

that such enceintes were small because of a disinclination to spend money on such public building;[5] this, if accepted, throws out any idea of even crudely measurable population shrinkage.

Other structures could also become forts, such as La Turbie, near Monte Carlo. This victory monument (the Tropaea – hence Turbie – Augusti) to the Roman conquest of local tribes in an area not yet a Mediterranean playground, was fortified in the 16th or 17th century, and by the 20th century the location was almost a suburb of Monaco. Some of its sculptural elements were to be found in surrounding walls in 1800[5] and also in the adjacent fortress,[6] to which the monument was "utilisé comme motte d'un donjon."[7] By 1866 some pieces apparently decorated the palace of the Governor General at Monaco,[8] although by that date it was classified as a monument historique.[9] In the early 20th century excavation produced some more fragments of sculpture and inscriptions.[10]

If given the known decline of long-distance trade some towns shrank in extent to become fortresses, who and what might they have been protecting in addition to their inhabitants? In other words, how was the countryside of Late Antiquity farmed, and the population fed?[6] If the population declined, where is the evidence, apart from shrunken town walls? Were forts constructed to protect farmers, or perhaps as military way-stations, as they were in North Africa? We simply know that several towns, such as Arles, Nîmes, Béziers, Narbonne and Carcassonne, and then Avignon, Die, and Grenoble, had late antique fortifications. Whereas at other likely sites (Valence, Orange, Vienne) there are no remaining signs of them above ground.[7] At certain sites, such as

---

5   Halsall 2007, 84: "The shortness of the walled circuits, adduced to suggest hasty construction and the decline in the cities' size, needs further consideration. It is perhaps not unlikely that the scale of their construction reflected the general late antique unwillingness to spend money on public building."

6   Buffat 2010 for the explosion of archaeology in the countryside in the past 25 years, mostly from rescue archaeology.

7   Esmonde Cleary 2013, 134–135; 68–69 for Bavai (Belgium), "with one of the more remarkable wall circuits of the Late Empire." Forum and antiquities were known to 19th century, including inscriptions which presumably came from the enceinte; 62 for enceintes between Rhine and Loire; Trier and Cologne had their walls extended; 125: "walls in Gaul which could be 5m and more in thickness and more than 10 m in height, requiring a considerably greater volume of material and of labour than the monuments of the High Empire. So the central and northern Gaulish defences fit into the discussion on urban monumentality in the Late Empire, showing that whoever commissioned them, civic authorities, the army or the state acting through either of these, still appreciated the need to present the site in the approved monumental vocabulary."

Béziers, it is indeed only inscriptions in the walls which give evidence of her Roman monuments,[11] partly perhaps because the enceinte was reduced and rebuilt in 1289. Arguments about some continuing interest in town structure and monumental impressiveness should be treated with care, evenly balanced between the grandeur of new walls (monumentality!) and the destruction of other prestigious markers demolished in order to construct them.

Some enceintes took a long time to destroy. Sections of those at Angoulême surviving to 1930,[12] having been remodelled for artillery in the 17th century.[8] Promenades were created there in 1699, because "l'extension et l'aération des villes imposaient la démolition partielle des murailles." But the gates were retained to mark the town limits, and control entry; clearly of no further use by the 19th century, some gates and stretches of wall went in 1820, and others in 1859–60, and 1888.[9]

Old Fortifications Cannot Satisfy New Requirements

If ancient fortifications could sometimes still serve during the Middle Ages,[10] and form the foundations for later walls, to everyone with eyes and some knowledge of changes in fortification since the Renaissance in Italy and especially in France since Louis XIV, it was obvious that old defences were of no use whatever against gunpowder weaponry. They were often not worth rebuilding yet again because towns had expanded beyond them, or wished to do so. And just as late antique fortifications were rebuilt, for example at Agen,[13] and mediaeval ones superceded, as at Bayonne,[14] so mediaeval fortifications in large numbers[15] also survived as useless ornaments in settlements now too somnolent to require dismantling. What is more, the days of siting cannon directly in front of town walls and blasting away were long over, replaced since Vauban with outlying and intricate defensive structures. In addition, detached forts in advance of main defences also made siege more difficult, and were added to strategic points such as Paris, Lyon[16] and Grenoble (from 1830), and in the 18th century at Montalembert. Besançon is a good example of a town with

---

8   Moreau 1997, 8–10; 2–3: the late antique enceinte ne disparut jamais compètement mais servit de base à diverses reconstructions.

9   Moreau 1997, 10–12.

10   Wolfe 2009, Part I: The walls go up (900–1325), 3–53, including 3–19, Urban Legacies and Medieval Trends up to 1100, with (4) a map of walled towns in Roman Gaul. But brief on years up to 900.

THE DEFENCE OF FRANCE 79

detached forts as well as a citadel. She lost her ancient monuments[11] except for one arch, probably in part through 17th-century fortification work; baths were uncovered in the 1780s,[17] and others had been found in the late 16th century.[18] Then modernisation took its toll. The remains of a temple were uncovered in 1840, and other débris during sewer construction in 1850 and 1863,[19] but these disappeared. And as late as the 1870s the remains of amphitheatre, theatre and capitol were still visible[20] along with a conspicuous aqueduct.[21]

One continuing controversy questioned whether guns should be permanently sited, or moveable, but this paled before the 19th-century development of more accurate and powerful guns equipped with high explosive. As any of the multitude of gunnery manuals from the Renaissance onwards will relate, gunpowder cannon could throw balls over fortifications, if at first from relatively close to them. Later weaponry with high trajectories could drop projectiles well behind fixed fortifications. Modern howitzers designed for this task had a range of up to 7km., rendering useless old-fashioned walls clinging near the town; and such firepower could even nullify external rings of forts, as Petitjean pointed out for Paris in 1895.[22] To cope with such technology, detached forts would be sited between 4km and 9km from the main defended site, as the fortifications in the Île-de-France during the 19th century demonstrate.[12] These caused yet more building and, as we shall discover, yet more destruction of defensible sites of archaeological interest.

The Germans generally avoided laying sieges during the Franco-Prussian War (1870–1871), the extensive, recently built fortifications of Paris proved largely useless,[23] and the Génie outraged Parisian property owners by the demolitions they carried out in the name of defence.[24] Instead, the Germans assaulted Paris with guns, from a distance, rather than by storming the walls.[25] The fact that the Germans won the war signalled time for a re-think of defence throughout France, the results of which were have a great impact on French landscape and townscape alike as rings of fortifications expanded: "La mélinite et les canons à longue portée ont montré que le génie militaire, nouveau Juif errant, doit toujours marcher."[26]

The French mis-step over the importance of fortifications echoed in German assessments after the war, remarking that defences received more attention in France than in Germany, and that the French should be concentrating on attack, not defence,[27] looking at the use of railways, and fortifying as few towns as possible.[28] Germany continued to maintain fortifications in

---

11   Frézouls 1988, 137–54.
12   Barros 2005, 15–31 for defence of Paris to 1830; 33–75 for programs 1820–50; 197–209 for long list of forts around the capital.

80 CHAPTER 2

Metz, Strasbourg and Thionville post-1871. It gradually abandoned fortifying Rhine crossings from the 1880s because it judged that Belgium was not a threat. Some fortifications were also seen as pivots of maneuver, as with the Schlieffen Plan of 1914. But, as a commentator pointed out for Toul in 1874: "On croyait si peu, dans ces dernières années, à une guerre défensive, que ce complément de fortifications, si souvent réclamé par les officiers du génie, n'avait jamais reçu même un commencement d'exécution."[29] Why was this? Mobility was the answer, for it was the railway which helped the Prussian victory – the railway, the antithesis of fixed fortifications, plus mobile artillery.[13] And when Marshal Achille Bazaine could have stopped the Germans with the huge fortifications of Metz (while that town was still French territory), and perhaps helped prove the efficacy of rings of forts, he simply bungled the task. In the reckoning after this great disaster, the Génie was rightly blamed:

> Entourons, au plus vite, nos places de guerre de forts détachés, placés à de grandes distances; (le génie militaire a persisté trop longtemps à ne tenir aucun compte de l'immense portée des nouveaux engins).[30]

We need not pursue the re-think, but instead concede that the French army retained a love of chains of forts extending to the Maginot Line, and concentrate on the fact that many towns were still classified by the military in the 19th century as "places de guerre," with military needs taking precedence over civilian desires. In any case, the Army was (mentally) a conservative institution, and "What we have we hold" would have been a suitable motto for their attitude even to superannuated town walls, as well as to the extensive fire zones outside them which, as "servitudes militaires," (see below) they guarded jealously. This dog-in-a-fort attitude clashed with the pretentions of modernist town planners, for whom the dismantling of such fortifications presented great opportunities for beautification, industrial development, and profit.

By the end of the 19th century, some of the great towns of France still had fortifications, or additional defences consisting of a ring of forts, such as Metz (a German possession after 1871) or Paris. Several of these were naturally

---

13   Wawro 2003, 47 von Moltke: "To facilitate deployments, he diverted military spending from fortresses to railways and steadily brought even private railway companies under military control. In practice, this meant that state and private railways were constructed in militarily useful regions and provided with rolling stock." Ibid., 59: " 'Artillery masses' were dynamic; they were independent batteries of guns that massed where needed, poured in gouts of fire, then limbered up and massed somewhere else, either with the same group of batteries, or with others."

THE DEFENCE OF FRANCE   81

strengthened after the disastrous Franco-Prussian war,[31] because for some theorists (German as well as French) fortresses were still very much in vogue,[32] "plus que jamais considérées comme indispensables,"[33] together with the large numbers of troops required to man them.[34] But when some fortresses were declassified, other towns could point to them and ask for the same permission to dismantle. Thus the replacement of fortifications by boulevards at the Croix-Rousse in Lyon in 1887[35] was cited by Narbonne the following year, where the doubled population and the fact that "la ville de Narbonne ne fut jamais un objectif pour l'ennemi" were used as pressing arguments to build anew and to open the town up to the air.[36] Various laws were passed to free up towns no longer useful, those of 1853–1889 leading "à de nombreux déclassements portant plus particulièrement sur les anciennes places à simple enceinte."[37]

Because of military alerts and sensitive locations, however, several of the towns in which we are interested were still defended fortresses at the beginning of the 20th century: if Narbonne had been de-classified, Langres is still described in Baedeker's Northern France (1909) as a "fortress of the first class." The new fortifications were separate from those provided by the town walls, but it is not known whether antiquities were destroyed to build them.

New Requirements: Barracks

On both sides of the town, and of the entrance to the harbour, old fortifications are being replaced with new forts of the most modern type, some facing the Mediterranean, others protecting the town, the harbour, and the lake. Barracks are being built for the reception of several thousand troops, and in every way it is clear, as French writers themselves avow, that Bizerta is intended to be one of the strongest fortresses in the world.[38] [1908]

If town walls guarded by local militia were no longer effective, whence came defence? The answer, as at Bizerta, was garrisoned troops, which many towns would naturally request.[39] And universal conscription, introduced in 1798, plus population growth, fueled huge military building needs. Barracks were therefore needed, already decreed by Louis XIV on or near frontiers; and these were also built in inland towns from the 18th century (where soldiery had previously lodged in private houses). Such barracks were built at Nîmes, Montpellier and Béziers; at Vienne they date from 1712. With such arrangements, with the Army in residence, "les habitants des villes de l'intérieur purent respirer à l'aise, démanteler leurs murailles et déposer les armes que leurs pères avaient portées pour en assurer la défense."[40] Not surprisingly, antiquities from demolished town walls were consumed into such new structures, but the new building also uncovered blocks in and around the excavations at the Caserne de la Cité, Paris, in 1863, and around the caserne at Langres. At Besançon, it was the château which was turned into barracks and mutilated in the process.[41]

In metropolitan France barracking troops was already a burden in the 16th century,[42] and depradations stretched back into the 17th century (for example at Avignon),[43] into the 18th century,[44] and right through the 19th century, the Army being over half-a-million strong by 1800.[45] Tours had difficulty providing barracks, and also a militia.[14] Orléans groaned under their weight.[46] In 1866 there were difficult negotiations at Nîmes about barracks;[47] at the same date an abbey at Vernaison (Rhône) had the same use,[48] while in nearby Valence a 17th-century convent was similarly occupied.[49] The historic Maison Cujas in Bourges was a gendarmerie barracks,[50] having been bought for that purpose by the municipality in 1835.[51] Beauvais boasted two religious buildings turned into barracks,[52] and was glad to have them for the commerce they provided,[53] likewise Châlons-sur-Marne, where their loss would have ruined trade.[15] The English would have done things better, moaned the French following destruction and conversion at Caen, Le Mans and Angers.[54]

As more and more towns lost their now-ineffective walls, so the 19th-century extended the fashion for barracks, but there was a new twist: given the attacks of the Revolution against organised religion, and its structures, namely abbeys and churches, there survived much building stock disconnected from its original use. Hence many structures (including châteaux, as at Bayonne)[55] were given over to military use, for barracks, hospitals, or storage. Selling them off when they became superfluous could bring towns some funds, as at Nîmes in 1870.[56] At Caen, a convent became a barracks, and a church a provision store.[57] The Franco-Prussian war provided an impulse to build yet more barracks for a bigger army, and to train healthy soldiers in a modern environment.[16] Once again, surviving elements of the ancient world fall before aggressive campaigns of modernisation.

There was so much barrack construction that archaeological finds were almost an automatic spin-off, as at Metz in 1841 where a headless statue was unearthed while digging for the cavalry barracks, and again in 1842.[58] In the

---

14   Baumier 2007, 263–277: L'alourdissement de l'aide militaire.

15   Clause & Ravaux 1983, 211–27 for the High Command's consideration of the area, following the 1840 crisis, for a large camp for defending the NE frontiers.

16   Chanet 2006.

THE DEFENCE OF FRANCE 83

same year, while building foundations for bomb-proof barracks, an honorific column was excavated at Marsal (Meurthe),[59] and its pedestal then extricated and carefully preserved.[60] At Nîmes in 1877 an inscription was found in the grounds of the artillery barracks.[61] In 1879 the engineers also uncovered no fewer than 90 tombs at Poitiers.[62] A well full of amphorae came to light at Foiral (Aveyron) in 1887,[63] a mithraeum at Sarrebourg (Meurthe) in 1895,[64] and an ossuary at Toulouse in 1897.[65] In 1902, antiquities were still in danger from such activities. Thus at Périgueux, the ancient Tour de Vésone was in danger from a projected barracks until the local society kicked up a fuss.[66] Ruined buildings were also at risk. At Saint-Martory (Haute-Garonne) a romanesque church façade was saved, but the remainder went to build a barracks.[67] Nowadays, even military installations are called patrimony, and are frequently re-converted into something else.[17]

Le génie de la destruction: The French Military and the Defence of France

Livré au Génie militaire, qui est le génie de la destruction, à chaque fois que le marteau entre dans son enceinte [Château de Blois], les colonnes, les chapiteaux, les sculptures, les cheminées, les galeries disparaissent, et l'édifice ne présentera bientôt plus, au-dehors comme au-dedans, que des murailles éntièrement nues. Il est impossible de remédier à cet état de choses: les autorités locales n'y peuvent rien; le Génie militaire est là.[68] [1834]

Le génie militaire fait obstacle aux vœux et aux besoins des populations; qu'il maintient en temps de paix, contre nos administrations municipales, contre les habitants des villes de guerre, les vieilles murailles de nos petites cités, avec autant d'énergie et de ténacité qu'il les défendrait certainement en temps de guerre contre l'ennemi.[69] [1865, in the Chamber]

With few exceptions, the Génie appeared to French townspeople as a law unto themselves, charlatans careless or even destructive of monuments, outdated in their knowledge of fortification, dog-in-the-manger over their retention of assets they no longer needed, generally bloody-minded, and a brake on

---

17 Godet 2007, 12–31 for survey, admitting the problems surrounding military installations; e.g. 238 La caserne Villars à Moulins a été malmenée au cours des ans – and is now a museum.

84   CHAPTER 2

any kind of modernity and (as Stendhal complained in 1837 for Le Havre)[70] town development. It was understandable, then, that they were sometimes described as "le génie de la barbarie et du vandalisme."[71] Of course, since their task (and their alibi for all their actions) was the defence of France,[72] they were well-funded. One of their continuing concerns was that the frontiers of France could always change, so nothing should be destroyed without due consideration.[73] In this they were supported by Article 510 of the Code Napoléon, from which the reader could conclude that military defences would be guarded more jealously than national monuments.[74] The law was the law, and the spirit of an article of 1791 protecting *places de guerre* was still in force in 1869,[75] bolstered by the law of 1851.[76] Citizens in favour of dismantling town walls met the obvious retort, for they claimed in 1791 that the Génie "leur ont fait le reproche de compromettre la liberté publique" although this was denied.[77]

The French, some maintained in the 19th century, had a genius for destruction, the Génie in this case being a malevolent spirit with human-like propensities which made monuments disappear, both ancient[78] and Christian,[79] and which we have already encountered going about its destructive business. It was the task of the archaeological societies, declared a scholar in 1840, to dethrone the pest,[80] described the previous year as "ce besoin de détruire, ou même de dégrader en restaurant, qui n'est que trop souvent le partage de l'administration elle-même."[81] It was not just the bad luck of the military engineers to be called the Génie, and formed in 1766,[82] but the general perception throughout metropolitan France and North Africa that the pest had not disappeared, and was as powerful as ever. If a common comment was that the French destroyed more than the Vandals, so also was the opinion that the Génie destroyed more than the Jacobins, although they were only one of the entities to reuse buildings declared by the Revolution to be surplus to requirements.[18] This was not just a 19th-century, let alone a French problem, for armies are still destroying antiquities today.[19]

The explanation for such a persistent pest was easy to discover. If government aims and administrative actions changed with bewildering frequency during the 19th century (and, by the very nature of administrative DNA,

---

18   Léon 1917, 139–195, L'utilisation des monuments, including (172 etc) problems with army occupation.

19   Rush 2010: all WWII and after, including ways of instilling in soldiers a sense of cultural heritage and how they can protect it.

THE DEFENCE OF FRANCE

continued to expand),[20] the French army was one perpetual national institution of practised bureaucratic in-fighters, and of vital importance to the maintenance of central government, equipped as it was with guns and overwhelming force. They based their right and duty to control on laws which designated certain towns and forts as necessary for defence, and strictly enforced regulations dealing with military areas – "servitudes militaires." They occupied prestigious sites for their administration, and often degraded or destroyed them.[83] Such "servitudes," when understood as defining "des restrictions apportées, dans l'intérêt de la défense du territoire national, aux droits de jouissance des propriétaires des terrains voisins des places fortes et autres ouvrages militaires,"[84] obviously designate severe restrictions on the use and especially development of property anywhere near military fortifications.

There is some evidence that the Génie was not always competent in the work it did. In 1880 the report by two entrepreneurs, made the previous year, was discussed in the Chambre des Députés:

> L'administration du Génie a engagé les travaux sans études suffisantes, et, dès le début, les plus graves imprévisions se sont produites sur la nature du sol, sur l'existence et la provision des matériaux... Le Génie veut se couvrir d'autant en niant ce qu'il doit. De là sa résistance à toute vérification indépendante.

and the entrepreneurs had been hurried along in 1875 because of renewed fears of war.[85] This was not an isolated incident, since their work in Algeria often left much to be desired.

The Army kept a tight grip on any fortifications it believed to be useful for defence, and altered them where it was thought necessary. Paris still had fortifications in 1895, but one commentator (even after the experiences of 1870) thought their retention for defence to be counter-productive.[86] For some towns, they simply held on to outdated walls, as at Boulogne, where in 1892 following declassification of the 13th-century (!) enceinte, "la municipalité a racheté ces vénérables restes, jusque-là jalousement gardés par l'administration du Génie." The Roman ramparts were found to contain antiquities.[87] The municipality preserved them, and discovered old artefacts in the process; yet the ramparts and boulevards had to be wrested from the Génie although, according to the scholars, these were simply the "vestiges d'un art militaire démodé."[88] The town had certainly been rich in antiquities: perhaps a Roman temple found

---

20   Burdeau 1996, 108–187, L'expansionisme administratif.

86 CHAPTER 2

during excavation for new crypts under the cathedral,[89] which sat on top of the castrum.[90] And an ex-Minister of War was still arguing in 1902 for the retention of the walls of Langres.[91]

The lists of defensible "places de guerre" in 19th-century France is long,[92] and includes the servitudes to be covered by the guns, and hence even cemeteries. Regulations were strict, prohibiting many kinds of building within the range of the defending guns and fortifications.[93] Even towns whose walls had fallen, such as Saumur, were controlled.[94] In other words, the Génie hung on to fortifications well past their use-by date, and could thereby be seen as a force against modernisation.

For those sites destroyed in earlier centuries by the Génie, we cannot know how much was lost. In 1561 the forerunner of the Génie demolished parts of the walls of Metz, offering blocks *au choix* to the inhabitants, reusing the rest – the rejects – on the foundations of a new enceinte. The location was surely very rich in antiquities, for the rue des Murs was still yielding stelai in the 1930s.[95] At Vienne, productive excavations on army property in 1864 had to be abandoned, force majeure being cited.[96] Granted, townspeople were not necessarily easy to deal with, witness the problems with locals filching blocks from the walls of Langres in 1816 – a town the army had to defend.[97] This problem existed in part because it was not always clear whether (as at Laon) it was the army or the town which owned the walls – possession often being a grey area which led to much petty squabbling.[98] Châteaux such as Blois also fell to their hammer, as Vergnaud-Romagnési, Inspecteur des Monuments du Loiret, could complain in the 1834 quote that starts this section.

The declassification movement (discussed in Chapter Five) seemingly meant little to the Army; there was no agreement as to what enceintes might safely fall; and, sweeping aside any local administrative opposition, they fought all the way to maintain their prestige by building new barracks, stores and parade-grounds, and destroying untold quantities of antiquities in the process. A spin-off of the "servitudes militaires" which kept towns bottled up within their circuit of walls was a dearth of building immediately outside most of them, and hence potential treasure for archaeologists in land largely untouched in previous centuries.

Mérimée[21] was in an excellent position to assess the awkward truculence, incompetence and vandalism of the Génie, making a short list in 1850: at Soissons, digging a bastion, refusal to continue digging after fragments of the Niobid group were found; refusal to accept architectural guidance when taking over buildings for military purposes, as at Vincennes; mangling historic

---

21 Andrieux 1997, 219–227 for Mérimée's reports to the Commission, 1838–1851.

architecture, in the Palais des Papes at Avignon, and at the Château de Blois,[99] still noted in 1910 as having been "indignement saccagé par le génie militaire."[100] Nor did he appreciate the octagonal observatory erected on top of the remains of Vézelay's left tower by the Génie officers working on the Carte de France.[101] And although he did acknowledge the knowledge and the courage of the Génie, nevertheless "toutes nos provinces attestent qu'ils s'entendent beaucoup mieux à renverser des forteresses qu'à conserver des monuments."[102] There were plenty of examples, not necessary of dismantling. At Dax, following the age-old maxim "if it doesn't move, paint it," the Army made alternations to the Roman walls and then lime-washed them, making them appear at night like a crouched spectre in a white shirt, enough to make any enemy take fright.[103]

Mérimée was far from the only one complaining about the Army. At Saintes the municipality was condemned at the end of the century for ruining the triumphal arch, and the army for mangling a church they had turned into barracks.[104] At Soissons in 1860, more of the Niobid group was found, and sent to the Louvre, but the site itself ("le Château d'Albâtre") was evidently completely destroyed.[105] Soissons certainly need defensible fortifications, being bombarded by the Germans for four days in 1870; so at this site force majeure did indeed operate. Hence again at Soissons in 1875, the Génie were still endangering standing monuments,[106] but five years later were praised for the "intelligent collaboration" they rendered in the retrieval of antiquities.[107] Was this simply that army manpower proved useful in excavations the army needed in any case to complete? Or were scholars just being polite to a powerful entity that had already proved disruptive and that could blight archaeology at Soissons for decades to come? Probably the latter explanation is the likely one, given the Army's conversion of the cloister of Saint-Jean-des-Vignes into an artillery park. Vitet wrote and complained direct to the Minister in 1876, suggesting that this was done through brutal insistance:

> Je sais que, si le besoin du service militaire l'exigeait impérieusement, il faudrait se résigner à voir abattre ces galeries, fussent-elles encore plus élégantes et mieux sculptées; mais j'ai lieu de croire que ce n'est nullement par nécessité et seulement par goût de propreté, par envie de faire place nette et faute de savoir la valeur de ces ruines, que MM. les officiers du génie ont formé le projet de les abattre.[108]

"La liberté publique" was certainly what townspeople sought, just as scholars sought an end to destruction of monuments. The development of Montpellier was held back because the Génie insisted on retaining the citadel for

88 CHAPTER 2

troops;[109] in 1837 (not a time of war) Stendhal could not enter Grenoble after 10.00pm because the Génie closed the gates.[110] Part of Autun's ancient walls were demolished in 1838 because the Génie wished it so;[111] and Montalembert affirmed in 1839 that "la ruine et le mépris des souvenirs historiques sont encore à l'ordre du jour."[112]

Even historic fortifications (presumably distant from concerns with contemporary defence) did not interest the Army, as they proved throughout the century. In the Roussillon, they mutilated the splendid jewel-like Renaissance fortress of Salses.[113] In 1837, they destroyed part of the Roman wall at Tours;[114] in 1862 the Château de Chambéry was partly torn down and inferior walls put up instead;[115] an old tower at Verdun was maltreated.[116] The Porte Notre-Dame at Cambrai was threatened,[117] but was saved, unlike the 800 houses earlier demolished for materials to build fortifications,[118] let alone the Cathedral.[22] The Army continued Richelieu's work for him, albeit a little tardily. Richelieu had targeted the Château de St-Maixent for destruction in 1626, and the Génie began their destruction in 1880, dismantling two towers of the enceinte,[119] including work put in place by Louis VIII.[120] The château was indeed demolished. At Chaumont, both château and town walls were being demolished by the mid-19th century,[121] while antiquities were removed from the enceinte and château at Meaux.[122] In 1841 the Génie were accused of destroying Roman aqueducts and using the material to build forts,[123] and much the same at Lyon the following year, including mining mosaics and rooms of a bath.[124] They degraded Carcassonne[125] where Viollet-le-Duc had to grapple with the Génie,[126] at a site where it was surely ludicrous to suggest that the ruined fortress (and it was indeed ruined before it got "restored") retained any military worth.[127]

With their growing need for accommodation, the Génie frequently reused and maltreated churches, convents and abbeys, of which there was a surplus after the Revolution. Just like the Grim Reaper, it was remarked in 1874, "il fauche églises, châteaux, remparts, rien ne lui échappe."[128] They turned a church at Chartres into a forage store;[129] at Vendôme (Loir-et-Cher) another into stables,[130] and then built barracks there which were still in place in 1910.[131] A convent at St-Valéry-en-Caux (Seine-Inférieure) became a store,[132] and the cloister of St-Jean-des-Vignes at Soissons (discussed in Chapter Seven) was destroyed.[133] They demolished an apparently Roman tower at Laon in 1853[134] and, what is more, blew it up because the concrete was so tough.[135] The Augustins at Toulouse (which, had it been in Italy, would have attracted all tourists) was mangled in various ways,[136] and they went on to cause much

---

22 Montclos 1992, 54–62.

THE DEFENCE OF FRANCE

damage in the same city.[137] At Dijon the Carmelites held a barracks and a military prison.[138] At Avesnes (Nord), tombstones were used in their building on the site of the Pères Récollets.[139]

At Narbonne, however, the Génie met their match in the shape of a determined and well-organised citizenry, supported in parliament, as the second quote at the beginning of this section makes clear. In 1870, good news! When the Génie ceded the church of Notre Dame de L Mourgier (there are diverse spellings) as a store for a large number of blocks retrieved from the town walls;[140] but by 1874 the Génie wanted the church for a barracks;[141] then, "dans l'impossibilité d'offrir au service militaire un autre local" (which beggars belief) the Génie was ceded part of the site as a food-store.[142] Some dog; some manger.

The examples above demonstrate that whenever possible the Génie never let go. At Abbeville, where in 1849 they cleared out a late 18th-century cemetery to make a *champ de manoeuvres*,[143] they still retained their offices well after the town's declassification as a place de guerre.[144] At Algiers, they would not let go of the ramparts, described in 1887 as a "ceinture inutile et coûteuse que le génie militaire ne veut pas sacrifier et qui empêche le développement régulier de la ville."[145] But then it was routine in North Africa for the Génie to dismantle ancient structures and reuse their materials to build new ones,[23] for example at Onellaba,[146] so they evidently felt proprietorial about the walls of Algiers, which they had helped strengthen. But then their métier and that of the whole Army in Africa was destruction, colonists being said in 1875 to prefer locusts to a visit from the zouaves.[147] At Avignon (their depradations will be described in Chapter Ten), they destroyed frescoes in Saint-Pierre de Luxembourg, using a chapel as a meat store and then building latrines for their prison.[148] The gendarmerie likewise destroyed frescoes in the Carmelite Convent at Caen.[149]

Not all members of the Génie were always destructive (only those giving the orders?). Indeed, one puzzling aspect of the Génie's involvment with antiquities is the long tradition of military report-writing (best seen in the archives in Vincennes concerning the monuments of Algeria) which required all reports on requests for military construction, destruction or extension to include an historical section placing any monuments involved in their context. Hence it is impossible to believe that at least the central military authorities were not perfectly well aware of any ancient monuments encountered in their surveys. Cosying up to the Engineers held several attractions for archaeologists: they knew about digging and had the necessary equipment; they were experienced in stone types, soil types and reading trenches; and they could

---

23   Greenhalgh 2014, passim.

probably date the walls they were intent on demolishing. Just as the Army sometimes destroyed architecture (such as the old fortress at Étretat, Seine-Inférieure, in 1870),[150] so also its own building work could reveal antiquities. This happened at Soissons in 1854 as the Génie was digging new courtines.[151] Indeed, many Génie officers were members of archaeological societies, not necessarily following the adage to keep your friends close but your enemies closer. Some practised archaeology with distinction,[152] and sometimes surprised sceptics who believed the corps "ennemi mortel jusqu'à présent de l'archéologie chrétienne."[153] Because of the unique opportunities their work gave them (the rule of law, access to earth-moving resources, usually human ones) an interesting thesis should be written examining how they developed and implemented their interest in archaeology in their plentiful letters, memoirs, or memoranda. There were already details and drawings of the monuments of Nîmes, with estimates for repair, in the Génie archives in 1692 and later;[154] in 1734 details were entered of the amphitheatre at Besançon, the ancient walls at Valence, and the need to remove houses from the defences at Colmar.[155] Even La Turbie was drawn in 1705, although not its reliefs,[156] which were perhaps already scattered.

Attitudes to antiquities naturally depended on the interests of local commanders. The state of affairs described above, however, was not universal. At Narbonne in 1831–1833, for example, an attempt via the Captain of Engineers in command there failed to wrest antiquities for Toulouse, the mayor writing that "les habitants de Narbonne sont tous jaloux de conserver ces objets précieux d'antiquité qu'ils ne céderaient peut-être pas pour les restes les plus curieux de la Grèce et de Rome."[157] In those many cases when scholars encountered "des maires peu instruits ou peu soucieux de la conservation des restes archéologiques," recourse to the government was necessary.[158]

Examples of the Génie's helpfulness are frequent in scholarly periodicals, perhaps because the exception proved the rule. At Arras in 1879, Terninck discovered 3rd-century houses by the fortifications, helped by Captain Dutilleux;[159] but of course this happened only because the Génie were carrying out work, and the scholar tagged along.[160] Much the same happened to effect the discovery of cemeteries outside the walls of Rome,[161] this benefit balanced, however, by the damage done by the Génie to S. Sabina, on the Aventine.[162] So the officer could also turn into a scholar, as did Alexandre Du Mège, a member of several learned societies, in charge of an expedition on the archaeology of the Pyrenees, and a prolific author.[163]

The 19th century was one of progress, nowhere more so than in the science of fortification, but here again even the new defences erected by the Génie attracted criticism, for they not only imposed a boring uniformity on once

THE DEFENCE OF FRANCE 91

picturesque sites, but also destroyed large quantities of antiquities during their construction. At Langres, the local historians complained in 1858 about the work and its effects: the Génie

> ont successivement enlevé à la vieille enceinte murale de cette ville son aspect si pittoresque. Ses fortifications si variées, qui rappelaient les différents siècles auxquels elles avaient été élevées, et où l'on pouvait étudier les modifications apportées à l'architecture militaire depuis l'époque romaine jusqu'aux temps modernes, ont généralement disparu sous une enveloppe de maçonnerie uniforme, et les parties conservées ont subi de nombreuses modifications.[164]

By that date, indeed, the Génie in attempts to improve the fortifications had already managed to destroy a north gate, perhaps a triumphal arch to Constantine Chlorus, but now gone so impossible to study, as was lamented in 1830:

> Nous regrettons ces vieilles murailles de notre ville natale qui disparissent, car c'était l'histoire encore vivante qu'elles rappelaient...Vains regrets! Langres est devenue place de guerre, la science moderne militaire l'a décidé.[165]

Servitude et grandeur militaires – and boulevards

The 19th century was one of new technologies, and this applied not only to factories and railways but to matters military as well, not only to increasingly sophisticated guns and projectiles, but also to the art of defence against them – namely fortification, the nature of which had to change in accommodation, as it did (for example) with the spectacular defence works of Vauban (1633–1707) at Neuf-Breisach or Saarlouis. Keeping such servitudes and boulevards in good condition often occasioned the discovery of antiquities, as at Nîmes in about 1820.[166] But one area in which the defence of France coincides with modernisation is in the dismantling of inland fortresses or defensive walls protecting towns. Alfred de Vigny, an army officer 1814–1827, wrote his *Servitude et grandeur militaires* in 1835 – "servitude" meaning (in the author's double-entendre) not only his own military service but also, as we have seen, the area served by the guns. Such servitudes militaires, which were closely regulated,[24] naturally

---

24   Sardain 2014.

took up a great deal of space, necessarily open (or sometimes with allowed structures in wood that had to be easy to knock down), so the guns could bear on attacks. Thus at Nice, a site we do not today associate with its earlier frontier responsibilities,[25] was besieged by the French in 1691, defended by 1,400 men, and "la défense est bien assurée, grâce surtout à une batterie nouvelle, appelée l'Impériale, de douze canons, renforcés au-dessus par les boulevards qui regardent la citadelle."[167] In many European towns we can still "reconstruct" such fire-zones, because it was the walls which disappeared and the fire-zones which survived in a peacible dispensation, leaving boulevards and railway lines in their place.

The alternative name for such areas evokes the cannonballs that ensured their protection – the area of the "boulevards," in one extrapolation from "boules," the projectiles themselves. These bowling alleys, or boulevards, are often tree-lined, and often now form the inner ring-road of a once-fortified town: the French Wikipedia entry has: "un boulevard est donc une *"promenade plantée d'arbres sur l'emplacement d'anciens remparts"* (définition donnée en 1803)." Their conversion to traffic and leisure spaces was already under way in some towns, starting in the 17th century. The term "boulevard" can also used for "balouart/balouard" meaning "bulwark," the original meaning from 15th century German boolwerk = rampart,[168] describing for example Narbonne[169] or Toulon.[170] We also think today of an esplanade as being a peaceful, open expanse, but it was a technical term which designated the open space between defensive walls and the houses of the town – in effect a military term for an open free-fire area outside defences.[171] Both esplanades and bastions were frequently converted into promenades.[172]

Accounts of various towns to appear in later pages will feature boulevards appearing as peacable, tree-lined and flower-rich promenades, after each town had struggled with the local or regional army administration to release the town walls for redevelopment. At Chartres, an important antique town,[26] some of the walls were pulled down in 1835, producing "un boulevard riant et coquet;"[173] Pontarlier also made the change early,[174] and Caen even earlier, on long-destroyed 15th-century battlements,[175] and following a devastating fire in the mid-18th century. At Cahors little was known of the Roman walls, but the town had the remains of a theatre,[176] and part of what had been the ancient walls were reformed into boulevards to make the town modern.[177] Antiquities were still lying around the town into the 1880s.[178]

---

25   Bouiron 2013 17–24 for digs at the site, early 19th century to present day; 77–87: La fortification de la ville haute; Barelli 2013 for 16th-17th-century accounts of the fortification.

26   Frézouls 1997, 175–268.

THE DEFENCE OF FRANCE

The expansion of Paris meant several changes well before the 19th century, and these and their effects are well documented,[179] as are the the attempts of strolling citizens to take them over.[180] Any siege, such as during the Franco-Prussian War, combined with ramparts, meant that building had to be upward, not outward.[181] New fortifications had been built only in the 1840s under Thiers, for Paris had been essentially an open city since Louis XIV had the enceinte torn down nearly two centuries earlier. Although the reuse of old boulevards could be profitable, the construction, in the sacred name of Modernity, of new boulevards (with their new meaning of grand avenues) could also destroy the city fabric, as happened conspicuously in Paris, with the building of barracks and the sacrificing of religious institutions.[182] Nearby communities also petitioned to re-attribute boulevards to civil construction, as at Saint-Mandé on the eastern outskirts. By 1890 the municipality owed its prosperity to the Army, at nearby Vincennes, with its fortifications and the railway;[183] but it nevertheless petitioned in 1913 to have the walls pulled down and boulevards substituted.[184] A crucial point to bear in mind is that Paris developed her boulevards inside the city well before the destruction of her for-tifications; indeed, as late as 1895 Petitjean was calculating how much material and land could profitably be milked from their destruction – but he was also suggesting the erection of another, larger set of walls.[185]

The Génie in North Africa

Algeria was a part of France, and the fate of her antiquities is another mea-sure of the insouciance of the Génie, and a further example of why antiquities in the hexagon were unlikely to survive their attentions. We learn about their depradations from the accounts of local scholarly societies in North Africa, with the added spice of the increasing numbers of colonists, often cast with-out help upon some deserted plain and told to get on with it – which they frequently did, reusing any antiquities they could scavenge.

The French invaded Algeria in 1830, and sought to colonise that country (and then Tunisia) with Europeans, using the Génie and then the settlers them-selves to build forts, barracks, houses and churches.[27] There were few standing structures considered suitable for Europeans and, although some Roman and Byzantine fortresses were reused, and mosques converted, much new building was needed. It was impractical to convoy building materials from metropolitan

---

27 Greenhalgh 2014. Some commentators wondered why funds were poured into Africa, when Brittany needed cultivating, and the Limousin needed railways. cf. Weber 1976, 489.

France, so the ancient monuments suffered exponentially. If some 1,400 years were needed to destroy much of Roman France, the Génie accomplished the same task in North Africa in well under a century, with antiquities used for everything from sheep-pens,[186] bridges[187] and fountains[188] to houses, barracks and hospitals.

Egypt had recently suffered from the French – not just Cairo, but also as far south as Aswan.[189] Algeria was to present to the traveller only bits and pieces which for whatever reason "le génie militaire, destructeur plus impitoyable que la guerre," had left alone.[190] What they found when digging they certainly did not leave alone, and we are asked to believe that they unearthed the first bronze bust in the whole of North Africa only in 1844.[191] This is unlikely, and we may surely assume that many discoveries were melted down for their metal. This assumption is fortified from their work at Cherchel in the 1840s, where they found six marble statues, and destroyed them all.[192] At this same once-important city, much of the theatre – the best in Africa, wrote a settler[193] – went into their new barracks,[194] and Roman defences were brought back into use for fortified watchtowers.[195] Nor was Cherchel's museum favoured, since important and suitable material was taken to Algiers instead[196] – an echo of what had been happening for centuries to antiquites in Provence.

The Génie altered existing towns so much that by mid-century, at Blidah, only one old street survived: speculators had bought properties from the locals, and the rest had been modernised, for "Partout ailleurs s'élèvent de larges rues tirées au cordeau et des maisons de deux ou trois étages."[197] Their arrogance was painfully evident at Philippeville where, claiming their approach was better, they laid out the town ignoring the Roman grid, which had taken the lie of the land into account. This was modernisation, but "L'amour des lignes droites et des angles droits, avec le défaut d'études pratiques, ont produit de bien mauvais résultats dans les créations françaises!"[198] For their building work, they stripped the amphitheatre down to the ground.[199] At Miliana also, an important monument fell before street-alignment.[200] Bard stated the obvious in 1854, that all the Génie's buildings "portent l'empreinte de la solidité romaine"[201] – not by chance, since so many Roman structures had been vandalised to build them. Even when they unearthed antiquities, these were sometimes sold off to entrepreneurs,[202] because the Army was always short of funds. Parts of some ancient towns outside the main settlement areas, such as Tebessa, survived only because they were too extensive to be completed destroyed.[203] But the abundant Roman antiquities of Constantine were largely obliterated.[204] Even new discoveries, such as those found in 1882 at Toukria, were often lost for, "suivant l'usage, les pierres de taille et les principaux débris ont disparu dans les constructions du génie militaire."[205]

THE DEFENCE OF FRANCE

As the population and communications of the country expanded, the destruction simply got worse, as indeed it did in Turkey, where population expansion also won over ruins, as at Pompeiopolis.[206] In Algeria, for example, the remains of a "vaste édifice romain," mosaic and columns went at Philippeville[207] and elsewhere, with monuments "en voie de destruction rapide, à cause des progrès de la colonisation."[208] Consequently, by the 1870s Tissot could estimate the needs of road and rail construction at 100,000 cubic metres, with the Roman ruins used as quarries,[209] and complete monuments disappearing "sans que les agents du Gouvernement aient pris la moindre mesure préservatrice."[210] Something similar happened at Medjerda.[211] Local administrations, just like their fellows in metropolitan France, also seem to have acted as building entrepreneurs, one critic stating as a fact that Algiers held lists of ruins suitable for exploitation as quarries.[212] Even Carthage, for all its erstwhile fame, had little to show: "Quand donc nous déciderons-nous à arrêter cet odieux trafic, à conserver ces vestiges splendides, qui sont le domaine du monde entier, non celui d'avides particuliers, pour le compte de l'État?" wrote Postel in 1885.[213] There was a poor museum, and a school for the courtyard of which a temple had been demolished.[214]

Conclusion: the Fate of Town Walls and Monuments

The first duty of towns, ports and France herself was to protect citizens and their activities. Stone-built defences were solid, but not necessarily long-lasting, as changes in population levels meant that towns shrank behind new and smaller walls, or spread beyond existing enceintes and required new and more elaborate defences. Later, seigneurial castles also form part of the story, because for several centuries they were the only structures apart from some churches which were built of stone – often of stone reused from earlier structures, as we have seen. In many instances, it was the vicissitudes of peace and war which occasioned reuse, sometimes following the deliberate dismantling of an existing structure or of a complete fortified complex – a *place* – which was a common ploy in order, as it were, to *debellare superbos*, by putting down noble rebellious subjects. In the Middle Ages and later, all settlements above a certain size stood behind walls, late antique or newly constructed, with many older towns enlarging their defences in the 11th–13th century.[215] Many of the the strongest were built on ancient foundations.[28] Rather than a

---

28   Salch 1978, 5, 13: Les cités les plus solidement et les plus anciennement fortifiées au moyen âge sont celles qui ont profité de remparts antiques – and noted in the book's entries; 56–9

96   CHAPTER 2

panicky response to invasion, such solid enceintes are better seen as expressions of social solidarity and skill.[29] Nevertheless, many people lived in small settlements only a little larger than villages.[30]

A large number of towns in France survived into the Renaissance and later with all or part of their gallo-roman enceintes (or at least their foundation levels with mostly later superstructures) intact.[31] Although solidly built, their usefulness varied according to their original size, fluctuating population levels, local industry or fecklessness, and strategic location. Many walls must always have looked messy, because they were overlaid with later accretions of new buildings and bastions. They thus formed part of an ever changing composite ensemble altered to meet changing town horizons until yet more needs (such as railways) argued for their removal.

Some towns wanted the military to stay, to provide continuing income. Luxembourg feared it would decline when the Army and garrison abandoned the site and the fortifications were dismantled; but this did not happen, and the only bugbear was the position the railway station, "que les exigences du génie militaire avaient éloignée de l'ancienne ville."[216] At others, such as Aigues Mortes,[217] the Army did leave, "abandoning" the fortifications, and provoking calls for the State to pay for the conservation[218] of this, the most remarkable 13th-century enceinte in France. The idea that it could be defensible against a 19th-century army is preposterous. Fortunately, the archaeologists managed to save Aigues-Mortes,[219] although its prosperity had long since receded together with its access to the sea.

Before considering the accounts of towns in the gazetteer which forms Chapters Six to Eleven, and which lost their walls during the 19th century,

---

  Langres, 65–75 Carcassonne, 113–18 Bordeaux, 181–3 Laon, 191–2 Le Mans, 220–4 Strasburg
  with castrum and walls, 284–5 Arles, 441–3 Fréjus, 452–5 Poitiers, 456–9 Auxerre.

29 Lange 1988, 71: l'utilisation des immenses blocs de pierre n'est pas simplement une exhibition formelle; elle représente symboliquement la capacité de travail, le témoignage concret d'une communauté et la forte cohésion qui animait les rapports en son sein, puisque la mise en place des grandes masses dégrossies exigeait la collaboration harmonieuse de nombreux hommes. This argument is the same used for the social context of the construction of megalithic monuments.

30 Benedict 1989, 9: "Small towns were numerous and their importance deserves underscoring. In 1809, the first date for which reliable information exists, 498 of 722 communities of more than two thousand inhabitants housed under five thousand people, together accounting for 30 per cent of the urban population."

31 These include Angers, Angoulême, Autun, Bayonne, Beauvais, Bordeaux, Bourges, Brazay-en-Plaine, Brest, Carcassonne, Chalon-sur-Saône, Dax, Doué, Évreux, Fréjus, Le Mans, Nantes, Péran, Périgueux, Poitiers, Narbonne, Rennes, Rouen, Senlis, Sens, Tours, Troyes.

THE DEFENCE OF FRANCE 97

we should remember locations today largely devoid of antiquities, because stripped in previous years for town improvement, or for military purposes. Some of these losses will be considered in detail in later chapters, but here is an overview. Fréjus shrank in the 16th century, and a new shorter wall was erected, rendering much of the earlier enceinte useless and hence expendable.[220] At Rennes, where there were successive rings of walls,[221] the opposite occurred, the town expanded in the 14th century, and parts of the earlier enceintes survived to be studied in the 19th century,[222] especially around the citadel;[223] In 1896 these rendered some important inscriptions,[224] although some materials then noted did not survive the century.[32] At Antibes (Antipolis),[33] the walls were donated to the citizens by Henri IV in 1608.[225] At Auch, its 11th-century walls (now gone) were built in part with Roman antiquities,[226] but only a few blocks survived in the town's later buildings.[227] Beaune lost its Gallo-Roman walls in the 18th century,[228] and Carpentras lost her 1357–79 walls "pour des raisons d'urbanisme plus que discutables."[229] These contained spolia,[230] were judged competitors for those of Avignon and Carcassonne,[231] and were demolished toward 1840.[232] Clermont lost its walls under Louis XIV, but Mérimée, surprised to find so few antiquities there, nevertheless found the remains of Roman walls.[233] At Grenoble, the course of the Gallo-Roman walls was still traceable in 1842, and had been "parfaitement reconnaissable avant le dernier agrandissement de la ville."[234]

The obvious conclusion, to be confirmed in detail in later chapters, is that the majority of French administrators, townspeople and army were enthusiastic about the benefits promised by modernisation, and perfectly happy to have their old towns ripped up for drains, sewers and new streets. But they were insufficiently interested in the remains of the past to make a place for them as the walls came down and the land within them was eviscerated. Losses were numerous, and by the nature of building work we know nothing about them unless local scholars kept watch over trenches as they were dug. Boulevards and promenades were a favourite way of dealing with old walls, as we shall see in Chapter 6. This is because town walls necessarily provided sight lines for the military, and the townspeople, eager for picturesque views for their promenades, simply took over. All that needed to be dismantled in such cases was superstructure. Why move the foundations? These often exposed

---

32   Pouille 2008, 39–85; 47: blocks taken from the walls, but neither studied nor catalogued, and known only from photos; 55–6: le poids des ans, discussing what has disappeared; 50–2 for the monument in the rue de l'Hôtel Dieu: ici encore, on ne dispose que de descriptions généralement très sommaires non accompagnées de relevés ou de plans.

33   Froissard 2002.

antiquities, and we might guess that these would be left in place less as exhibits of municipal pride than as great blocks of stone that it was impractical to move. Completely dismantling old walls was a gargantuan task, best left alone if it could be avoided – hence, of course, the survival of so many spolia in the foundations of surviving late antique walls with later superstructures. It soon became clear even to the most enthusiastic of 19th-century antiquarians that transferring everything into the local museum (if there was one) would be impossible for lack of space. It was only as towns expanded that such walls and most of their antiquities were almost completely obliterated.

[1] Montaiglon_1881_6–7
[2] Revue_Maine_IX_1881_124–125
[3] BSA_Midi_1893_35
[4] Jullian_1902_156–159
[5] Millin_II_1807_580
[6] SG_XXXIV_Paris_1867_365
[7] Enlart_II_1904_559
[8] SG_XXXIII_Senlis_1866_411
[9] SG_XXXIII_Senlis_1866_397
[10] BSA_Provence_I_1907_147
[11] BSA_Béziers_IV_1841_36
[12] Le_Temps_15_January_1930
[13] Mosaïque_du_Midi_IV_1840_135
[14] Moncaut_1857_95
[15] Bonnet_1905_532–533
[16] Guilbert_1844_402
[17] Mémoires_Franche-Comté_I_1838_117
[18] SG_LVIII_Dôle_1891_121–224
[19] Sorbonne_1869_60–61
[20] RA_XXXIII_1877_373
[21] Laporte_1897_170
[22] Petitjean_1895_29
[23] Petitjean_1895_26–27
[24] Zônes_militaires_Paris_1872

[25] Lehugeur_1884_204–205
[26] AD_Banlieue_parisienne_1921_166–167
[27] Revue_Génie_Militaire_I_1887_61–81
[28] Revue_Génie_Militaire_I_1887_61–81
[29] Lacombe_1874_6–7
[30] Campagne_du_nord_1873_159–160
[31] EB_1910_France, 796
[32] Revue_d'Artillerie_XXIX_1887_515
[33] Réunion-des-Officiers_1873_5
[34] Revue_d'Artillerie_XXIX_1886_433
[35] Ville_de_Narbonne_1888_10
[36] Ville_de_Narbonne_1888_3–5
[37] Cf. Grande_Encyclopédie, s.v. Place
[38] Cook_1908_377
[39] Mém_Doubs_1867–1868_479
[40] Babeau_1880_317
[41] SG_LVIII_Dôle_1891_110
[42] BSA_Touraine_VII_1886_188
[43] Cat_MSS_Carpentras_III_1862
[44] Mém_Lyon_1879–81_82

[45] Jablonski_II_1891_393
[46] Vergnaud_Romagnési_1830_283–292
[47] Pieyre_II_1887_359
[48] BSA_Drôme_IV_1869_463
[49] BSA_Drôme_VI_1871_109
[50] BM_XXXIV_1868_224
[51] France_Pittoresque_I_1835_281
[52] Pihan_1885_124
[53] Doyen_1842_479
[54] SG_XXIX_Saumur_1862_197
[55] Moncaut_1857_95B
[56] Pieyre_III_1888_45
[57] BM_XXXIII_1867_590
[58] SG_1842_Caen_198
[59] B_Lorraine_I_1849_20
[60] Mém_Inst_France_XVI_1846_383–384
[61] Espérandieu_IV_1911_3160
[62] BA_Tarn-et-Garonne_VII_1879_244
[63] Mém_Soc_l'Aveyron_XV_1894–1899_418
[64] Espérandieu_VI_1915_28
[65] BSA_Midi_1896–1897_10
[66] BSA_Limousin_LI_1902_380
[67] Malte-Brun_II_1881_52–53

[68] BM_I_1834_315–316

[69] Déclassement_Narbonne_13

[70] Stendhal_II_1891_75

[71] Revue_Art_Chrétien_I_1857_310

[72] Hugo_1835_I_33ff

[73] Mém_Doubs_1866_277

[74] Breuillac_1870_159

[75] Blanche_1869_112

[76] Blanche_1869_129

[77] Bureaux-Pusy_1791_9

[78] Sorbonne_1865_128

[79] Revue_Art_Chrétien_I_1857_393

[80] Mém_Picardie_III_1840_24–25

[81] BM_V_1839_223–224

[82] Jablonski_II_1891_141–142

[83] Inventaire_général_1883

[84] Grande_Encyclopédie_Servitudes

[85] Candas_&_Yveri_1881_24

[86] Petitjean_1895_28

[87] Schuermans_1888_77–78

[88] AMPF_X_1896_121

[89] SG_XXVII_Dunkerque_1861_55–56

[90] BM_XXVIII_1862_271

[91] Revue_d'Artillerie_XXXI_1903_CXXXVII

[92] Blanche_1869_7–9.

[93] Laferrière_1860_659

[94] Pinkney_1809_149

[95] SA_Bordeaux_VIII_1881_18

[96] BM_XXX_1864_340

[97] SHD_Artillerie_XE.512

[98] SHD_Artillerie_XE343

[99] Sommerard_1876_363–364

[100] AD_Touraine_Anjou_1910_27

[101] Mérimée_1835_30

[102] Sommerard_1876_364–365

[103] Merson_1865_42

[104] AD_Centre-Ouest_1898_237–238

[105] BSA_Soissons_XV_1860_166

[106] BSA_Soissons_V_1875_357

[107] BSA_Soissons_XI_1880_272

[108] Sommerard_1876_328

[109] Renaud_de_Vilback_1825_305–306

[110] Stendhal_1891_II_131–132

[111] BM_IV_1838_280

[112] Montalembert_1839_214

[113] Lenthéric_1879_169

[114] Blanchet_1907_40

[115] Mém_Savoisienne_VI_1862_122

[116] SG_XLII_Châlons-sur-Marne_1875_177

[117] MSA_France_1881_181

[118] Tastu_1846_482

[119] Ministère_Répertoire_I_1882_66–67

[120] BSA_Ouest_II_1880–1882_153

[121] BM_XVII_1851_313

[122] Espérandieu_IV_1911_3212

[123] SG_VIII_Caen_1841_215

[124] SG_IX_Bordeaux_1842_209

[125] Annales_archéologiques_I_1844_448–458

[126] Exp_Universelle_Vienne_1873_Paris_1876

[127] Sommerand_1876_221

[128] SA_Bordeaux_I_1874_121

[129] AA_IV_1846_59

[130] BM_XXXIV_1868_84

[131] AD_Touraine_Anjou_1910_71–72

[132] BM_XXVII_1861_698–9

[133] BSA_Soissons_XII_1881_141–142

[134] BSA_Laon_IV_1855_152–153

[135] BSA_Laon_VI_1857_190

[136] BM_XXVII_1861_461–462

[137] APC_VIII_1878_182–183

[138] Goussard_1861_219

[139] MSA_Avesnes_V_1877–1886_254

[140] SG_XXXVII_Lisieux_1870_68

[141] BSA_France_1874_111

[142] BCA_Narbonne_I_1876–1877_554–555

[143] Prarond_II_1880_125

[144] Prarond_1880_175

[145] Baudel_1887_152

[146] BA_Comité_1887_468

[147] Villacrose_1875_41

[148] Réunion_BA_XIII_1889_151

[149] BM_XIII_1847_460–461

[150] BCA_Seine-Inférieure_1870_14

[151] BSA_Soissons_VIII_1854_48

[152] BA_Comité_1888_223

[153] AA_VIII_1848_338

[154] SHD_Génie_Art_8.1_Nîmes

[155] SHD_MR976_III

[156] SHD_Génie_Art_8_PA_La_Turbie

[157] BCA_Narbonne_1892_150

[158] BSAH_Limousin_XXXVI_1888_461

[159] Terninck_1879_16

[160] Bull_Arch_1886_325

[161] RA_XXXVI_1878_82
[162] BM_XXXVI_1870_98–99
[163] Archives_Missions_Scientifiques_X_1890
[164] MSHA_Langres_1847
[165] Mém_Langres_I_1847_135–141
[166] Veaugeois_1821_384
[167] ASL_Alpes-Maritimes_XX_1907_400
[168] Malte-Brun_II_1881_21
[169] Panorama_Pittoresque_II_1839_20
[170] BA_Tarn-et-Garonne_XXIV_1896_1
[171] Blanche_1869_166
[172] Malte-Brun_II_1881_26
[173] BSA_Eure-et-Loire_IV_1867_44
[174] Guilbert_1848_266 Pontarlier
[175] Revue_Maine_III_1878_302
[176] SG_IX_Bordeaux_1842_80
[177] Revue_d'Aquitaine_X_1866_207
[178] Malinowski_1880
[179] CHA_I_1894_198–199
[180] Labédollière_1860_4
[181] Merruau_1875_329
[182] Du_Camp_1875_IV_197
[183] BSH_Paris_XVII_1890_55
[184] Déclassemen_Saint-Mandé_1913

[185] Petitjean_1895_36–37
[186] Bull_Tvx_1886_104
[187] BA_Comité_1887_456
[188] Cherbonneau_1857_14
[189] Bull_Sciences_Historiques_XI_1829_261
[190] L'Illustration_X_Sept–Dec_1847_&_Jan–Feb_1848_203
[191] RA_1844–45_68–69
[192] RA_V_1848–9_348
[193] L'Illustration_4_June_1850_343
[194] RA_V_1848–9_345
[195] RA_V_1849_344
[196] BM_XXVI_1860_151
[197] L'Illustration_IX_21_August_1847_594
[198] Lestiboudois_1853_238
[199] Gsell_1901_201
[200] Piesse_1862_113–114
[201] Bard_1854_37
[202] BA_Comité_1901_CLXXX
[203] Barbier_1855_178
[204] Cherbonneau_1857_14
[205] Rép_Tvx_Historiques_III_1883_632
[206] RA_V_1885_97
[207] BA_Comité_1886_370
[208] BA_Comité_1891_207–208
[209] Année_Archéologique_1879_126
[210] BA_Comité_1882_143
[211] BCA_III_1885_251

[212] BCA_III 1885_194
[213] Postel_1885_32
[214] Hérisson_1881_103
[215] Blanchet_1907_249
[216] STA_Reims_CIII_1899_175–176
[217] SG_LVI_Évreux_1889_434–6
[218] SG_LVI_Évreux_1889_125
[219] SG_LVI_Évreux_1889_435
[220] SG_XXXIII_Senlis_1866_350–351
[221] CS_France_XVI_1849_Rennes_178
[222] BM_XV_1849_347–348
[223] Decombe_1882_13–14
[224] CHA_1896_382
[225] SG_L_Caen_1883_27–28
[226] Revue_Aquitaine_V_1861_570
[227] Lafforgue_1851_205–206
[228] Foisset_&_Simonnet_1872_Col_146
[229] Dubled_1975_11ff
[230] Cottier_1782_vii–viii
[231] AA_I_1844_91B
[232] Tastu_1846_121
[233] Mérimée_1838_311–312
[234] SG_XXIV_Mende_1857_360–368

CHAPTER 3

Technology and Change: Improved Communications

One result of the industrialisation necessary to feed French and international commerce was the development of new types of building which catered to such needs and their many spinoffs. Earlier townscapes featured churches, town hall and inns, perhaps a market hall, slaughterhouses, police stations and jails, and law courts. But from the 19th century we find banks and museums, and larger factories, shops and theatres, as well as railway stations. Frequently these new structures not only made earlier townscapes obsolete, but also destroyed them.

A country growing in prosperity (a quality to be measured in part by culture),[1] population and opportunities for trade also required improved communications to move people and goods around from point-of-production to point-of-sale, or indeed for export. Factories, although not a new invention, were a device for gathering workers together under one roof, often with housing nearby, to benefit from motive power and closer organisation. The building of roads as well as railways (including trams) was essential for such a process, as were canals (in the construction of which France was a pioneer),[2] which could carry larger and heavier loads than could carts, and were speedier for goods transport than roads – until the railways arrived. However, when they did, canal companies felt insecure about the competition, and in Britain many sold out to railway companies.[3]

France's developing commercial and industrial economy needed an army and navy to protect her interests at home and abroad. Garrisons were strategically sited near frontiers; trade through ports (a mechanism whereby countries acquired the pretension of empire or at least of a goodly slice of international commerce) meant that harbours had to be protected by walls and fortresses. Communications – road, canal, river, sea – augmented by semaphore, then electric telegraph and railways, were essential to development. As we have seen, the development of a more efficient infrastructure was already well under way in the 18th century, provided by the Ponts et Chaussées, as well as by the Génie.

© KONINKLIJKE BRILL NV, LEIDEN, 2015 | DOI 10.1163/9789004293717_005

Railways[1]

La commission, M. le Ministre, n'hésitera jamais à s'élever de toutes ses forces contre les projets qui sacrifieraient à de prétendues nécessités publiques des monuments anciens et vénérés.[4] [1846]

On a introduit le gaz dans nos églises; avant peu, nous y verrons le chemin de fer. Quand une fois une paroisse a pris goût aux innovations, il n'est point de folies ni d'indignes tentatives qu'elle n'entreprenne.[5] [1850]

It was not only Mérimée and clergymen such as the Abbé above who felt justifiably threatened by railways. This new, quick, cheap method of transport was introduced into France (using English locomotives) in 1832,[6] and was often called in French "railway" rather than "chemin de fer." This was, after all, a technology "que l'on doit aux Anglais."[7] By 1843 Great Britain had over four times the length of completed canals and railways than France, and that for a smaller population.[8] But France strove hard to catch up, with one eye on the advantages for industry,[9] and for the prosperity of towns on the main lines, such as Dijon,[10] even if the walls suffered, as they did at Reims.[11] The developing network was about to do for the interior what steamships had done for French seaside towns,[12] for example at Dellys in Algeria.[13] By the 1857, communications by rail down the Rhône valley were fast, Paris-Aix in 16 hours, Lyon-Aix in seven hours.[14] However, they were not a life-giving transfusion for the whole or France, but rather "created by urban capital, went where the interests of capital and of urban industries took them, not where people actually lived."[2] What is more, many were undertaken by companies that had not the resources to complete them, so the State had to take several of them over,[15] making the government rather than the entrpreneurs responsible for much of the devastation visited upon antiquities in the areas where they were constructed.

By late in the 19th century, transport prices had lowered considerably,[16] Paris was inevitably the centre of the network,[17] and its use was compared in 1882 to mediaeval pilgrimages[18] – secular ones, of course, to visit towns and monuments. Already by mid-century long-distance travel was possible and efficient only by rail, and some basked in the glory of the achievement. For example, with the help of gunpowder, the Paris-Lyon railway was considered by some to match the grandiose projects of the Romans themselves.[19]

---

1 Weber 1976; Robb 2007 ch. 13 Colonization – of France, in the sense of cultivation (Latin "colere"), namely efforts to weld France into a unity via railways and roads.

2 Weber 1976, 197; ibid., 205–206 for the extent and reach of railways by the 1880s onwards, and how communities without a station suffered.

TECHNOLOGY AND CHANGE: IMPROVED COMMUNICATIONS

Baedeker, as usual, says it all: by 1884, "Le touriste qui visite les principales curiosités de la France, n'y voyage plus guère qu'en chemin de fer, du moins dans le Nord;"[20] and in 1898, alert to up-to-date gamesmanship: "The tourist should carefully consult the railway timetables in order to guard against detention at uninteresting junctions."[21] Tourism by railway was by now a powerful force, even for scholars.

Entrepreneurs built not only houses but also railways, since the State could not always afford the cost, and the investment could be attractive. Monopolies (albeit under tight if variable government control)[22] could give railways a higher rate of return than other commercial activities,[23] in several cases erecting a question-mark over the viability of the canal system.[24] So it was little wonder that they were popular, and spread quickly – funds going in their direction rather than to the maintenance of cathedrals,[25] since it was now mercantilism that was in charge.[26] Their spin-off for new building was unstoppable, and since stone could now be transported much more cheaply than by carting it along dubious roads,[27] this made the old brick-and-wood houses of many towns (such as Rouen)[3] look even more old-fashioned, although reusing old blocks of course still provided price-savings.[4] The growth of railways was unstoppable, regulations being developed in 1844 giving them some of the privileges of the country's main roads,[28] described as "un pur sacrifice imposé aux particuliers dans un but d'intérêt général."[29] This privilege allowed expropriation for the public good – the same manoeuvre available but rarely invoked to protect monuments on private property. An example of this is seen in the agreement between the State and the Compagnie du Chemin de Fer du Nord, concerning the enlargement of the station of Aire-sur-la-Lys in 1897, which required working the land of the old fortifications:

> L'État cède à la compagnie du chemin de fer du Nord, avec les matériaux et les plantations qui peuvent s'y trouver, la compagnie se substituant purement et simplement aux droits appartenant à l'État et à toute charge ou servitude pouvant lui incomber, les terrains des anciennes fortifications ... ainsi que les terrains non encore occupés par elle.[30]

Ceding of rubble to builders is found in late medieval building contracts, as another way to keep costs down. Not surprisingly the Génie, the most powerful monopoly of all, soon got into the act, and introduced their own level

---

3 Mollat 1979, 88–95.

4 Weber 1976, 160 for travel broading the concept of possible building materials, so that "What is lost in picturesqueness is gained in health."

of regulations.[31] Naturally, the military recognised the strategic potential of railways[32] but, as usual, wished to control where they went, as at Besançon, where in 1906, and surely shortsightedly, "le génie militaire n'admettait pas une gare dans l'enceinte du corps de place."[33]

The railways presented scholars with difficult problems. One was the sheer pace at which railway entrenchment proceeded, so that discoveries during the construction of the Grand-Central line revealed ruins "découverts dans un espace de quelques centaines de mètres carrés, dans des fouilles faites avec la rapidité imprimée aux travaux du chemin de fer."[34] So scavenging archaeologists had to be on-site, and quick. Again, such gigantic projects as long-distance railways destroyed many antiquities, but by the 1840s scholars were well aware of how railway work and modernising work in towns could also bring large quantities of antiquities to light.[35] This happened while digging for track ballast near Abbeville in 1878, which revealed "un nombre invraisemblable de pierres taillées, particulièrement des haches,"[36] and also when retrieving Roman inscriptions and bas-reliefs at Melun.[37] Indeed, the cubic metres of ground turned over to build the railways (much deeper than ordinary ploughing) was the greatest upheaval to French soil since the Romans. Geologists liked railway construction because of such upheaval, which of course caused their nascent profession no difficulties, for the work got their trenches dug for them.[38] And some archaeologists did gain dubious benefits from railway track all over the country: for once a large railway network was in place, materials for building (such as those needed after the Franco-Prussian War) could be stored centrally instead of scavenged locally,[39] and this might have saved various antiquities.

Scholars recognised the importance of railways for the development of industry, for easy participation with colleagues in Paris,[40] and for the ease they offered of holding congresses in the provinces;[41] they exulted in the granting of cheap tickets for attendance at conferences,[42] although they were still struggling for some concessions in the 1860s.[43] A prime example of the importance of railways is presented by Bazin's 1900 illustrated book on Reims, where the very start of the Introduction shows the railway track and station, and the very first words are not about monuments, but rather about ease of access:

> A quarante lieues de la Capitale, à laquelle trois lignes de chemin de fer la rattachent, et dont elle est éloignée de deux heures à peine, la ville de Reims peut justement être aujourd'hui considérée comme étant de la grande banlieue de Paris.

Such gains were to be set against losses, such as that at Champtier-des-Cercueils (the very name is a giveaway) at Marboué (Eure-et-Loir), where railway work

TECHNOLOGY AND CHANGE: IMPROVED COMMUNICATIONS

wrecked a large number of sarcophagi.[44] This simply kept up the tradition of allowing visitors to a nearby site to walk away with handfuls of mosaic tesserae – and this in "notre France qui était, pour l'archéologie, le plus riche pays du monde il y a deux siècles!"[45] "Destroy the monuments to build the railways" might have been one motto for the antique blocks used in the foundations of a restaurant in the Aisne built to cater for the nearby railway station,[46] for that was progress! Down the Cher in 1889, the railway traveller could see the old routes of road ("sur laquelle les modernes véhicules ont remplacé les chariots des Romains") and river to either side: "Impossible d'imaginer une plus satisfai-sante rencontre du passé et de l'avenir dans une plus radieuse journée d'été."[47]

But again, while scholars recognised that France should not be left behind the rest of the continent,[48] they recorded plentiful examples of the destruc-tion they caused. The railway took the scholar to the monument – "C'est un service immense, réel, dont on aurait tout à fait tort de ne pas profiter"[49] – but how many monuments did railway construction destroy? For although rail-way engineers often presented antiquities to museums (see below), they were frequntly called vandals for wishing to bring the lines as close as possible to the towns and their population, so that antiquities were threatened, such as the Alyscamps of Arles and the town walls of Avignon. What was needed was "une sainte ligue contre le vandalisme administratif,"[50] but this was whistling against the wind of popularity and modernity that the railways encouraged. Who (except for Cambridge colleges) was going to sanction a railway station distant from the town centre?

The problem was further exacerbated because the railways brought tourists, and tourists brought destruction, just as did catering for them.[5] In 1892 one commentator noted that bringing railway stations into Paris would destroy the very sights the tourists came to see: "Nul doute qu'on ne nous propose un de ces jours de démolir le Louvre pour qu'un chemin de fer permette d'y péné-trer plus facilement."[51] And the eventual conversion of the Gare d'Orsay into the Musée d'Orsay merely softened the insult of driving the lines into the cen-tre of the city, whilst proving the lack of adequate forward planning for the capital's transport. Indeed, the railway, like road-widening, could be used as a strong argument for museums distributed throughout France. And in 1863 one scholar complained that a mosaic from Tyre was to go outside the capital: "Qui va et qui ira jamais à Saint-Germain-en-Laye?" The answer: wait a while, and the railway (and now the RER) will take you there.[52]

---

5 An English cartoon from the 1970s has a developer exhorting: "Gentlemen! Let us get out pri-orities right! Historic buildings must not be allowed to stand in the way of expensive accom-modation for the tourists who come to see these historic buildings!"

Vandalism during railway construction was extensive, because railway workmen did not bother with the niceties of antiquities,[53] and survivals were often a matter of pure chance.[54] Fréjus lost a section of her ramparts to the Toulon-Nice line.[55] The famous cemetery at Arles, the Alyscamps[6] (a corruption of *Champs Élysées*, supposedly containing the tombs of Charlemagne's knights), was devastated by the railway by 1845, attracting the sarcastic comment that "Il faut employer les moyens les plus rapides et les plus puissants de locomotion, pour doubler le temps si court de la vie humaine."[56] The next year, Mérimée was already railing against the proposed intrusion of the railway into Avignon, because this would destroy large swathes of the mediaeval walls, largely intact in his day.[57] The railway and station were in fact sited outside the walls to the south, but large sections of the walls were to disappear in succeeding decades, as we shall see in Chapter Eleven. Unfortunately, the railways' thirst for building materials was insatiable, and many antiquities no doubt disappeared into the track without a nod or a wink. Occasionally, the scholarly societies could warn of coming danger, as when in 1883 the château of Châtillon en Vendelais was threatened with sale as track ballast.[58] This was a common occurrence: thus in 1871 the 12th-century château at Neufmarché (Seine Inférieure) was being stripped for road hardcore and track ballast.[59]

Ironically, just as the railways were destroying monuments, so also they were necessary to get quickly to new explosions of vandalism: "prenez le chemin de fer et courez à Orléans," was one 1845 recommendation, to see the Hôtel-Dieu being destroyed and the cathedral mangled – but hurry![60] Why was it destroyed? In order, writes one scholar, to free the view of the cathedral's nave.[61] At this same town in 1859, the local society protested against setting up public toilets in two arcades of the Roman walls;[62] by 1885, a better suggestion was "de contraindre les propriétaires à placer dans leurs maisons des cabinets avec tous les perfectionnements que la science moderne comporte."[63] And at Toulouse, unspecified "monuments d'utilité publique" were made possible by knocking down part of the walls.[64] "Freeing up" monuments seems to have been in vogue, witness what happened to the Hôtel de Ville in Paris,[65] where enlarging public squares had a similar effect on old monuments.[66] At Reims, the triumphal arch was a "grand embarras pour les démolisseurs" but, generously, it was decided that the railway should detour around it.[67]

Every cloud, then, had a silver lining. Without government assistance (rarely forthcoming), archaeologists simply could not afford to dig for themselves, so "terrassement" work for the railways should be closely watched, to see what antiquities were turned up,[68] including inscriptions at Narbonne[69]

---

6   Escher 2013, 22–26.

TECHNOLOGY AND CHANGE: IMPROVED COMMUNICATIONS   107

and Lyon,[70] and cemeteries.[71] Archaeologists, in other words, had to swallow their pride and cultivate the very vandals against whom they protested so loudly – a humiliation dealt with in detail in my recent book on Algeria.[7] When they did so cultivate, the finds were reported to local or national societies,[72] or scholars followed such excavations like birds followed the plough.[73] But vigilance was required, one correspondant in 1858 noting that he could visit only parts of the long Bordeaux-Sète line, so that "il est hors de doute que beaucoup d'objets ont dû échapper à ses investigations."[74]

Yet when antiquities were unearthed, what was to happen to them? Would the engineers lend lifting equipment? Would anyone stop their destruction, and was any museum waiting to welcome such finds? The easiest was to draw the find "sur la place avec l'exactitude la plus rigoureuse," as happened near Nîmes in 1840.[75] In 1895 it was the railway engineer who provided the archaeologists with the drawing of a 27-square-metre mosaic from a villa discovered at Saint-Paul-Trois-Châteaux (Drôme);[76] but presumably this was destroyed (along with the villa itself) because it was impossible either to lift it or satisfactorily display it in the museum at Saint-Germain, where the engineer suggested it be sent.

As the century progressed, as antiquities became more popular along with museums to house them, finds stood a better chance of survival. In 1882, railway work around the Roman roads Lillebonne-Lisieux and Rouen-Le Mans uncovered a Frankish cemetery, and the mayor of Pont-Audemer (Eure) claimed them for his museum. The Ministry stepped in, eventually assessing the finds as unworthy of a national museum, so the finds did indeed go to Pont-Audemer, but the cemetery was destroyed.[77] Sometimes the engineers themselves reported antiquities, as in the Vienne in 1847.[78] The same engineer also in 1847 thought to be saving a tower in the ramparts of Poitiers by rerouting the track,[79] although he perhaps did so because the ground was marshy; and indeed, Murray's *Handbook* of 1848 reported that the town walls were "now almost entirely swept away by town-council improvements." A cynic might suggest that finds useless for railway material were punctiliously reported, such as kilns and pots on the banks of the Vienne in 1883,[80] or objects (unspecified) to the museum of Boulogne in 1848; the Société des Antiquaires de Picardie were delighted.[81] Something similar may have happened at Fréjus in 1864, when bricks and pottery were unearthed[82] – but nothing is said of building stone.

Sometimes workmen retrieved antiquities, as happened at Boulogne in 1848,[83] or near Orléans in 1846, when they took an inscribed stone back to their landlady's house; on two occasions the very same stone nearly got re-cut

---

7   Greenhalgh 2014, chap. 5.

108   CHAPTER 3

but, seventeen years later, Dufaur de Pibrac described its heroic rescue, and its importance.[84] In 1849, railway work near Melun uncovered part of a large cemetery, and the engineer collected together some antiquities from it.[85] At Évreux in 1853 a Roman cemetery yielded a stone sarcophagus, as well as "des morceaux de corniches, de frises d'une très-grande proportion,"[86] presumably all destroyed, as were the majority of finds at other cemeteries in the area in the 1880s. By 1892, a railway company actually promoted a monograph on the Merovingian cemetery uncovered during work on the Paris-Mantes stretch of track,[87] so perhaps it was unfavourable publicity that attracted such an egregious piece of PR-spin.

The railway provided yet another lazy wrinkle to growing tourism, namely admiration for whatever could be seen from the train window, without necessarily descending. By the 1850s, English clergymen were making excursions into France to view mediaeval architecture, some organising their tour railway to railway,[88] while others were pointing out that the beaten (railway) track had to be abandoned if the antiquities of France were to be properly examined.[89] At Nîmes, only the Tour Magne, high on a hill, could be seen from the train:[90] one had to leave the train to view the rest. In Calvados in 1868, railway work required moving a stone cross, but a commentator complained that it was scarcely visible from the track in its new location, and in danger of being knocked about by carts.[91] But most tourists alighted, so that in 1857 Sopwith could attribute a new café and hotel at Nîmes to the influx of tourists.[92] Short-distance archaeological sight-seeing could be catered by writing targeted books, such as Z-J. Piérart's *Guide complet du touriste et de l'archéologue sur le chemin de fer de Saint-Quentin à Maubeuge* (2nd edn, Paris 1897).

Map-making Military and Civil

Just as good maps were essential both for the construction of railways and for the accurate location of antiquities, so an outline of the importance of map-making for the 19th-century fits well between military and civil concerns, since maps not only underlined just how much of France remained to be discovered and charted,[8] but their making required large resources and smooth organisation. Railway companies and the Army had these, but archaeologists did not. And since it was the military which had the greater need for knowledge of

---

8 Robb 2007 chap. 9: Maps, Delambre and Méchain mapping in the late 18th century: "Instead of reducing the country to the size of a map and a table of logarithms, they had shown how much of France remained to be discovered."

TECHNOLOGY AND CHANGE: IMPROVED COMMUNICATIONS

terrain, it is not surprising that accurate work percolated from the military to the civilian arena, as did the Ordnance Survey in the UK.

But if the scholars were to pinpoint antiquities on maps, what did they know and learn about the layout of Roman occupation, which would surely help them? Centuriation was a method used by the Romans for the regular division of newly occupied land. Its imprint was recognised in part of Britain[93] and, by the end of the century, in Tunisia as well as Italy.[94] But there seem to be no references to such layouts recognised in France, although the French were familiar with cadastres, which were land surveys usually for tax purposes (Latin *capistratum*, poll register), for they employed them from the Middle Ages onwards.[95] Reports of archaeological finds are frequently given according to cadastre locations, the format explained in 1886 as useful to archaeologists, and providing "une mine inépuisable pour l'histoire locale et l'ancienne topographie d'une commune."[96] There were even archaeological maps,[97] created specifically for relaying archaeological information, as at Rouen in 1907, when one was suggested for museum or archives,

> qui enregistrerait avec précision, au fur et à mesure des données fournies par le hasard des excavations, et les rares débris de l'antique Rotomagus, et les vestiges qui peuvent éclairer les origines gallo-romaines, franques et mérovingiennes de la cité actuelle.[98]

But this is the creation of a new cadastre, not any recognition on the ground of any Roman ones, although they knew that the Romans did cadastrate. Indeed, they referred to its existence in France[99] but, as was remarked in 1867, "l'on ne connaît pas bien le système."[100] Archaeologists were therefore certainly interested in maps, and saw their use for publication as well as for museum displays: we might say they were alert to monuments in the landscape. So it is strange that scholars did not seem to recognise those parts of the country that the Romans also centuriated as well as cadastrated. Since centuriation was indeed regular, this would have helped them in their hunt for new sites in regular relation to those visible or even dug.

The Carte de France

The Cassini maps of 1744–1787 (in 185 sheets) were monumental, but maps need to be updated continuously, because both requirements and mapping technologies change. Politics and finance also altered the approach: the Corps des Ingénieurs Géographes (often accompanied by artists who drew monuments in addition to battlefields) was suppressed in 1791, and the Bureaux Topographiques set up only five years later.[101] The Carte de Cassini was purchased by the State, in fact by the Dépôt de la Guerre, and a reduction in 24 sheets published in 1816–1821.[102] Begun in 1817 after the Napoleonic wars, following various other preliminary work, the new map enterprise naturally used much Cassini material in its preparation.[103] This, the Carte de l'État Major, sometimes called the Carte du Dépôt de la Guerre, took until 1880 to complete.[104] The schedule for data collection was written according to pre-determined chapter headings, and instructions were given to include, where possible, information on Roman roads, no doubt because the army prized and needed such viability. The data for each area were to be arranged logi-cally, including information such as physical description, statistics and history, in an ordering very similar to that adopted for military engineering projects. This section often started with political events, and then went on to summarise the archaeology. Beginning with generalities, monuments were then listed by period and date. Some entries surviving in the Army archives are probably valu-able, because they quote from Mémoires which may not have been printed or published,[105] the more so since the trawl included "dolmens" and "monuments druidiques" of which a fair proportion probably subsequently disappeared.

Reports vary according to the assiduity and knowledge of the officers. Captain Blondat has several pages of information about antiquities in his "Mémoire" on Poitiers. Equally interesting in the reporting is Section 2 of Chapitre 5, which always deals with the military history of the area. Occasionally, drawings of antiquities are included, such as the pencil drawings (careful, with measure-ments) of the Dolmen de Vaon, in the section for Trois Moutiers, Vienne.[106] Nor was reporting restricted to standing antiquities: thus Commandant Saint-Hippolyte, Chef de la 3e Subdivision Topographique, also prepared a "Mémoire d'ensemble descriptif et militaire" for Poitiers. This is 328 pages in length, 17 of which are devoted to archaeology, and of these two to "documents histo-riques." Prominence is given to what the author calls "Celtic" antiquities such as dolmens,[107] but conceivably at least sometimes because these immense and immoveable stones were useful trig-points or markers for map-making, as indeed were standing Roman remains such as theatres.[108] Roman roads were also useful markers; some were important in French history, such as that from Alésia;[109] but many, together with mediaeval byways, seem to have been omitted from earlier maps.[110] Châteaux of the Loire also appear in map mak-ers' reports, providing earlyish accounts of their condition.[111] For the study of Caesar's campaigns, the detailed work done by the Génie, and deposited in the Dépôt de la Guerre, provided crucial information for research.[112] Some of this could be decidedly problematic, one investigator suggesting that the number of villages with the name –igny –ogny on the Cassini map was evidence for Gallic telegraphy, using fire signals to send messages.[113]

TECHNOLOGY AND CHANGE: IMPROVED COMMUNICATIONS 111

Already, by the 1860s, the new mapping was helping historical studies. Guizot's edition of Gregory of Tours (2 vols, Paris 1862, rev. Jacobs, Alfred), makes many references to the help afforded him by the "carte de France publiée par le Dépôt de la guerre," and also by the Carte Cassini. Hence new sheets of the Dépôt map were eagerly awaited by scholars, for example when in 1871 two map sheets were delivered by Baron de Chabaud-la-Tour, général de division du génie and also a member of the Académie du Gard.[114] In Provence it was quickly realised how useful the information on new maps could be for the study of ancient monuments: "Une carte monumentale... des études dirigées dans ce sens de la part des hommes qui se vouent au culte des choses du passé, auraient un grand résultat pour la géographie historique de notre pays."[115] An earlier suggestion, of 1825, had been to add discoveries of Roman antiquities to the Carte de Cassini,[116] which remained an essential reference for decades, providing yet another instance of the reliance of archaeologists on the Génie. Thus in the one year of 1859, the Mémoires de la Société des Antiquaires de Picardie referred to that map no fewer than 65 times.

The desire to augment the representation of antiquities on local maps, and to invent local systems of conventional signs, was widespread, and one might wonder whether the agenda contained some unstated requirements about local identity. Thus in 1836 a scholar making a map of the diocese of Le Mans in the Middle Ages intended to add "l'indication par signes particuliers des anciens monuments du pays, comme dolmens, peulvans, tombelles, voies romaines, aqueducs, enceintes de camp, etc."[117] Indeed, already in 1826 an engineer had proposed lithographing a map of the antiquities of the Haute-Vienne;[118] and plenty of do-it-yourself suggestions followed, such as that to congressists in 1866, "qu'il soit préparé une carte sur laquelle l'assemblée relèvera tous les monuments celtiques ou gaulois bien constatés," together with relevant mémoires.[119] In 1843 scholars were thinking of how to represent antiquities on maps.[120] By 1851 a proposal was made for colour-coding sections of monuments (churches are the example given) according to date.[121] And in a congress in 1873 Elie de Beaufort received praise:

> Ce savant a recueilli avec un soin minutieux les antiquités, les a représentées sur une carte bien faite, et a envoyé un relevé de la voie romaine qui traverse son arrondissement, sur une grande échelle, d'après le cadastre, et avec de tels détails que l'étude de son mémoire vaut presque l'exploration les lieux; éloge que l'on ne saurait adresser que bien rarement.[122]

This does not seem to have been an idea based on the Army map; nevertheless, so valuable was the Carte du Dépôt de la Guerre deemed to be for study, that in 1866 it was proposed that the Société Archéologique de Seine-et-Marne should purchase a relevant sheet, with the help of which "on éviterait bien des erreurs aux archéologues futurs."[123] But the production of a complete Carte Archéologique de la France was a long time coming, and still being anticipated and in process in 1904.[124]

But how detailed should any additions be? In 1851 a commission reported that the Cassini method of indicating antiquities should be continued, and that

> Pour l'époque gallo-romaine, votre commission n'a pas cru non plus devoir adopter pour les cirques, les théâtres, les amphithéâtres, les arènes, les temples, les autels votifs, les arcs de triomphe, les naumachies, les bains, les bornes milliaires, et enfin la statuaire en général, des signes spéciaux pour tous ces monuments. Ces signes eussent été trop nombreux et trop difficiles à dessiner sur une carte.[125]

This is an indication of the information overload that was flooding in as societies reported new finds and digs. Enthusiasm tended to run away with judgment, some scholars asking for conventional signs on maps for "camps des Sarrasins," druidic monuments, aqueducts, and mediaeval battle sites.[126] No, replied others: information overload was one thing, but brain/memory overload was especially dangerous.[127] The selection of items to represent on maps was always going to be a problem. One scholar in 1866, exploring the Roman ruins of Fréjus and its vicinity, confessed to "la déception que nous avons éprouvée en consultant les beaux dessins-minutes du Dépôt de la guerre," and wanted to know why 100-metre-long stretches of Roman aqueduct were not recorded:

> Nous avons vivement regretté que les ruines imposantes de ce grandiose édifice n'aient pas été assimilées à la plus chétive maison isolée qui, elle, a le droit d'être indiquée sur les cartes cadastrales. Espérons, lorsque les cartes du Dépôt de la guerre seront remises entre les mains des graveurs, que l'on fera en faveur de l'aqueduc de Fréjus ce que l'on a fait avec tant de soin pour les voies gallo-romaines.[128]

Small-scale mapping could also be useful to archaeologists. Soissons was praised in 1868 for having a plan in its museum "au moyen de teintes différentes, le plan de la ville ancienne et son état actuel, et permettant de reconnaître d'une manière précise la position des édifices détruits" together with a large-scale map of the circumscription whereon new discoveries could be marked – two innovations which should be encouraged in all area museums.[129]

Roads, Canals and Bridges

If the railway was to be the transport miracle of the later 19th century, canals and roads were preceding requirements, and still necessary in the later decades but (in Weber's phrase) "in the same relation to France as the Nile to Egypt: fertilising only a narrow strip along their course."9 Both were expensive to build, and there was neither time nor expertise nor funding to reproduce Roman roads, of which plentiful examples survived, some too tough even to be broken up,[130] and estimated to be some 15,000km in total.[131] They were often visible and some were well-known since the Middle Ages, sometimes named "chemin de César"[132] or a variant. These included Chemin des Romains, Chemin Chaussée or Haussée,[133] le Vieux Chemin; or something equally informative, such as being named after a saint; or villages named after its characteristics, such as via strata giving l'Estrade.[134] And if a road or path was called "chemin de César," it was a sure bet, given the built solidity of such roads, that useful materials were to be found along it.[135] When wheeled vehicles became popular from the end of the 16th century, maintaining such earlier roads (if this happened) was insufficient, and new roads were built or old ones refurbished.[136] This was necessary, the English as well as the French complaining about the quality of the roads in towns as well as the countryside.[137] In the process many Roman roads, some of them traceable in their entirety (such as from Sens to Orléans in 1830)[138] had their materials reused,[139] and milestones as well.[140] For some Roman roads the only paved stretches remaining were in the woods,[141] and for road-building ruined churches and graveyards suffered as well, stripped for their materials.[142] Roads also needed infill, so that in the 1770s Lisieux, for example, provided 500 cartloads for the road to Caen, while over 300 cubic metres of brick and débris were taken from Évreux.[143] The law stated that materials could be taken from private property if they were needed for road-building[144] because, as with railway construction, this was expropriation for the public good.

The opening of new roads also brought antiquities to light, such as near Narbonne in 1783.[145] And since the route for roads so often depended on the lie of the land, it was not unusual (but exceedingly convenient) to find remains of Roman roads while preparing the ground for new French ones, which so often followed a similar route.[146] Scholars were well aware of the importance

---

9 Weber 1976, 196: "The same was true of the first railway lines, which fanned out in the 1840's and especially the 1850's and left aside vast areas where the old way of life survived untouched."

of Roman roads and, in 1839 in the four départements of Picardy, they began plotting them, together with "l'emplacement des camps, stations militaires, champs de bataille, et sur celui des villes, bourgs, villages, châteaux, etc., ruinés, dont les traditions locales, ou des titres conserveraient le souvenir."[147] The environs of Roman roads, which of course were built to service adjacent settlements, were also valuable to archaeologists, since examining their environs almost inevitably led to markers such as a "mine probable d'antiquités à explorer,"[148] and then to actual finds. This happened on a road near Autun in 1848, at a site which yielded altars (but only one medal since the workmen had spirited away the rest) where further excavation was counselled;[149] at a villa near the Le Mans–Chartres road in 1872;[150] or when trenches opened up for road-work at Nantes in 1877.[151] In 1888 even a Gallo-Roman mason's workshop was unearthed in the process of searching for road-building stone.[152] Again, investigation near a road at Venouse (near Auxerre) in 1867 yielded "des fûts de colonnes cannelées de 50 centimètres de diamètre, un chapiteau d'ordre dorique, des pierres de taille de grand appareil reliées par des crampons et des ferrements à double queue d'aronde, de larges tuiles à rebord, etc."[153]

Rescue digs over the past decades have underlined just how much was lost during the 19th century. Thus a 20km ring-road deviation south of Bayeux in our century generated 13 rescue digs, including two Bronze Age farms, three Gallic farms (one "aristocratic"), two Gallo-Roman farms, and a coin hoard of 908 items.[10]

Inevitably, however, most archaeological finds went for building materials, as near Sens in 1840,[154] or in the area adjacent to the Orléans-Sens road in 1854: "on aperçoit encore à fleur de terre une grande quantité de fondations de murs, et chaque jour les propriétaires de ces champs en font extraire des pierres propres à bâtir."[155] Inscriptions, on flat slabs, were especially vulnerable[156] and sometimes nothing or only a few lines of them could be retrieved.[157] The Prefect of the Moselle was warned in 1841 of the likely disastrous effect on old roads of current road-building,[158] but to what effect is not known – although in 1846 the Ministère des Travaux Publics was careful to blame the scholars (not, of course, its own officials) for a lack of vigilance in the matter.[159] Even standing monuments went for hardcore, such as in 1847 a 2.5-metre-high monument by the Roman road near Sancoins.[160] In the 1860s in Chénérailles (Creuse) an old monument known as "Le Boisseau" was destroyed simply to provide road-metal for the area where it stood.[161] And at Petit-Mars (Loire-Inférieure) in 1885, a local showed a Roman road to a visiting scholar, and spoke of ruins, "m'énumérant parfaitement toutes les transformations qu'avait subies la

---

10   Billard 2002.

TECHNOLOGY AND CHANGE: IMPROVED COMMUNICATIONS 115

contrée depuis un demi-siècle, mais se déclarant incapable de me montrer un mur debout."[162] As a report to the Académie Royale des Sciences of Berlin noted in 1882, "Les maçons et les entrepreneurs de chemins publics sont les ennemis jurés de l'antiquité." The report concerned Algeria, and Reinach confirmed this in 1890, also for North Africa where, without Roman ruins, "les entrepreneurs de routes modernes seraient souvent bien embarrassés."[163] The identical conclusion was also valid for mainland France.[164] Later buildings also went for hardcore, such as the 13th-century ramparts of the Bastide de Vianne (Lot-et-Garonne),[165] a Cistercian abbey near Orléans in 1862, a victim to "l'amour du lucre" and the Ponts et Chaussées.[166] Although entrepreneurs are frequently recorded as giving unearthed objects (which were of no use to them) to the local museum, in essence the scholarly interests and culture of archaeologists were antithetical to the down-to-earth (and into the earth!) public mandate from which entrepreneurs derived their authority.

Canals were perceived as able to carry large loads more cheaply and easily than roads, so under the Restoration it was planned to achieve a network of nearly 4,000km, although only 2,071 had been built by 1837,[167] soon to be outdistanced by competition from the arrival of the railways, which provided greater speed. In France by mid-century, canals were known to be much less costly than railways,[168] and it was believed that "la rapidité des transports sur les chemins de fer, quoique très-utile et très-avantageuse sans contredit, ne compense pas cette économie dans la plupart des cas."[169]

Bridges go with canals and rivers, and some Roman bridges survived, as at Sommière (Gard).[170] Mediaeval bridges were sometimes built with Roman materials, as at Lyon[171] where some of the blocks from the earlier bridge were still to be seen in the river,[172] or Limoges.[173] Many of those built before the 17th century were ruined or in bad condition.[174] Survival of ancient bridges was precarious:

> ils doivent leur durée plutôt à leur solidité, qu'aux soins que l'on a pris de leur conservation: les autres n'ont pu résister aux ravages du tems et à l'abandon funeste auquel ils ont été livrés.[175]

Unfortunately, their survival was in danger from modern roadwork, hence the 1856 Congès question, "comment doit-on étudier ces curieux monuments de la civilisation ancienne que respecte si peu le vandalisme moderne?"[176] A survey of 1812 (by no less than the Secretary of the Ponts et Chaussées) noted that most bridges were of pierre de taille, and one wonders whether some of the stone came from old monuments, as the account does not note quarries, let alone any recycling by civil engineers.[177] We might also note that modern

116　　　　　　　　　　　　　　　　　　　　　　　　　　　　　　　　　　CHAPTER 3

technology brought the two banks of the Rhone together in the 19th century: between Lyon and Avignon there were at least 21 suspension bridges, the earliest built near Tain l'Hermitage in 1825.

Photography

Photography was of growing importance as the 19th century developed, eventually to take over from engraving and other reproduction techniques in books and periodicals. Photography is often in the background to academic journals, bolstering annual congresses and archaeological books, and it is also used as a reaction to record monuments, if not exactly as an excuse alleviating the pain of their demolition. It was also an instrument of the Commission des Monuments Historiques who, in summer and autumn 1851, sent five photographers already known for their work on architecture (Baldus, Bayard, le Gray, Mestral, Le Secq) throughout 47 departments of France. Of their work, 258 negatives or prints survive.[11] As the century developed, so the picture postcard grew in popularity, and helped fuel tourism to towns and monuments pictured thereupon.

In 1866 a series of photographs was made of the dismantled Cathedral of Gap, and "elles conserveront ainsi le souvenir des détails architectoniques d'un monument disparu,"[178] as would photographs of the dismantled Cordeliers at Cahors in 1896.[179] In 1875 one scholar, observing how many churches were being altered, suggested photographs pre-change "soient déposées dans un musée, soit diocésain, soit départemental."[180] Even Viollet-le-Duc, responsible for so much irresponsibility, and who found artists overwhelmed by "les restes si nombreux et si précieux de nos édifices anciens," suggested photography be used to create "en quelques années un inventaire fidèle de tous ces débris."[181] The dismantling of several enceintes could also be recorded in photographs, underlining once again the huge amount of work this often entailed.[12] In some cases photography therefore became a sustitute for the (destroyed) monument – a kind of valuable alibi. Witness the politician who, on compli-

---

11　　Méaux 2003; cf. Mondenard, A. de, Le fonds de photos du musée des Monuments français; mémoire de recherche de l'École du Louvre, Paris 1996.

12　　Capelle 1994 for Bergues, Bouchain (declass. 1877, dismantled 1893–5), Cambrai (dismantled 1892), Condé sur l'Escaut (declass. 1901, dismantled 1923), Douai (declass.1892, dismantled in 4 years) & Le Quesnoy (declassified at the beginning of the 20th century, but not dismantled).

TECHNOLOGY AND CHANGE: IMPROVED COMMUNICATIONS

menting a mother on her child, received the reply, "That's nothing – you should see his photo!"

Tourism

Tourism appears in this chapter because its spread depended on the technology of road and rail to deliver customers to the sights and sites, which included museums as a draw-card.[13] The railways marked the beginning of mass tourism and the nascent leisure industry, whereas in the previous century only grandees, travelling privately, could absorb the education provided by the Grand Tour. University degrees in tourism management were in the distant future, but the realisation that old monuments could indeed attract tourism and hence money was frequently expressed from the 1850s, when journals such as *L'Illustration* were already promoting railway excursions with long text accounts and accompanying pictures. This was a Parisian journal that began publication in 1843 (the *Illustrated London News* began the previous year), devoted much space to the development of railways, and followed this up with profusely illustrated accounts of sights to see, accessible by rail. Excursions promoted in the 1840s were in the environs of Paris – naturally so, since road and rail connections were developed here much earlier than in the rest of France. The rail network, and hence tourism, grew slowly: lists were compiled of completed track, such as 340km around Paris, 165km around Lyon, 159km Strasburg-Bâle, 45km in the Nord, and 168km in the Gard and the Hérault.[182] Excitement about the completion the Paris-Avignon railway was at full pitch by 1850.[183] The section Dijon-Châlon was projected for completion in 1847; the Paris-Bordeaux railway inaugurated Paris-Tours in March 1846; Avignon-Marseilles inaugurated 9 January 1848. In November 1845 steam ships Lyon-Avignon and Marseille were still being advertised. Early guide books naturally highlighted information on monuments, picturesque towns, and of course the ease of getting there by rail, thereby indeed "guiding" potential visitors, as was their evident purpose, to sites their authors thought noteworthy. Here there was an economic calculation (how much do we spend, and how much do we recoup from tourism?) that is still important today.[14]

But what about towns which had been modernised? In several cases, such as Guérande (Loire-Inférieure), they were thought to have lost any attraction for tourists, as was protested in 1855:

---

13   Cf Gucht 2006, *Ecce Homo Touristicus* charting what he calls the muséalisation du monde.

14   Lazzeretti & Cinti 2001, 24–28; *La rilevanza economica dei beni culturali.*

Guérande moins ses murailles, moins ses fossés et ses boulevards, sera la dernière des petites villes et parfaitement oubliée des étrangers, qui se rendront désormais au Croisic par un chemin direct, laissant Guérande au nord. Espérons donc que l'Autorité saura repousser l'idée d'un projet [the demolition] si défavorable aux intérêts du pays.[184]

Conclusion

The destruction of much of old France through the transformation of her towns, the main theme of this book, to be treated at length in later chapters, was considered essential to satisfy the demands of modern life. There are three ironies associated with such radical changes to town and countryside. The first is that only when the changes were in progress did action trigger the administrative and legal resources that would provide some protection, indicating that devastating losses are necessary to initiate preservation. The second is that as roads and railways opened France up to tourism, what travellers especially wished to see were monuments and picturesque towns. But these were precisely the ensembles that such new arteries had helped destroy in such large quantities. The third is the ever-growing esteem which museums have attracted, when so many of the 19th-century foundations were little more than storehouses for the débris from destroyed archaeological sites.

In just a few cases, modernisation aided the recovery of antiquities. Road construction all over the Mediterranean turned them up, a good example being the curious experience by the German engineer Humann at Pergamon, in Asia Minor. He had been engaged to build a road to a railway station,[185] but also interested himself in the classical past. Here again, the road-building comes first, and the antiquities which he discovered on the acropolis at Pergamum, now the pride of Berlin, could not have reached the sea and Germany without Humann's new road. One might say the same for the roads and railways of France, which allowed the transport of antiquities into museums. But might they have been better preserved (and contextualised) had they been left on site?

TECHNOLOGY AND CHANGE: IMPROVED COMMUNICATIONS

[1] CS_France_v_1837_Metz_176

[2] EB_V_1910_sv_Canal_168

[3] EB_V_1910_canals, 171

[4] BM_XII_1846_386

[5] AA_X_1850_218

[6] Levasseur_1912_190

[7] Gerstner_1827_1–2

[8] L'Illustration_9_29_avril_1843

[9] L'Illustration_10_6_mai_1843

[10] Goussard_1861_153

[11] Anon_Reims_1864_149

[12] Ann_Normandie_v_1839_46

[13] BA_Comité_1895_132

[14] CS_France_XXIV_1857_Grenoble_596–7

[15] EB_X_1910_sv_France_786

[16] Guillaumot_1899_35

[17] Guillaumot_1899_7

[18] BA_Comité_1882_157

[19] L'Illustration_10_6_mai_1843

[20] Baedeker_1884_XIV

[21] Baedeker_1898_XII

[22] Kirkman_1894_322–325

[23] Recueil_Actes_Acad_Impériale_XIX_1857_419–420

[24] BSS_Yonne_VI_1852_294

[25] AA_XI_1851_187

[26] AHL_Nord_III_1833_121

[27] Picard_1918_225

[28] Guillaumot_1899_69–70

[29] Guillaumot_1899_74

[30] APC_VII_1897_277

[31] APC_II_1852_51

[32] Spectateur_Militaire_XXXIV_1859_198

[33] Acad_Besançon_1906_208

[34] CS_France_XXII_1856_Le_Puy_646

[35] AA_I_1844_154

[36] BSA_Abbeville_1886–1887_92–93

[37] BSA_Seine-et-Marne_1864_175

[38] CS_France_XVII_1850_Nancy_302

[39] Revue_Génie_Militaire_I_1887_372

[40] BM_XVI_1850_313

[41] AA_XVIII_1858_256

[42] BSA_Nantes_III_1863_158

[43] BM_XXX_1864_484

[44] BS_Dunoise_I_1864–1869_33B

[45] BM_XXVI_1860_455

[46] BSA_Vervins_I_1873_22

[47] BSA_Touraine_VIII_1889–91_145

[48] Séances_Tvx_Acad_Reims_XI_1849–1850_111

[49] AA_XXVI_1869_287

[50] AA_III_1845_242

[51] AMPF_VI_1892_103–104

[52] AA_XXIII_1863_279

[53] BCA_Seine-Inférieure_V_1897–1881_517

[54] BA_Comité_1892_XXIV

[55] Aubenas_1881_630

[56] Caumont in BM_XI_1845_113

[57] Sommerard_1876_358–359

[58] BM_XLIX_1883_747

[59] Cochet_1871_220

[60] AA_III_1845_293

[61] AA_XIX_1859_267

[62] MSA_Orléanais_III_1859–1861_105

[63] Ann_Acad_Mâcon_v_1885_94

[64] SG_XXX_Rodez_1863_406–407

[65] Merruau_1875_157

[66] RA_XXXVIII_1879_87–88

[67] Anon_Reims_1864_150

[68] MSA_Ouest_1847_27

[69] Devic_&_Vaissete_XV_1892_13.33

[70] Bazin_1891_370

[71] BM_XXVI_1860_139

[72] BSA_Soissons_XX_1846_105

[73] BCA_Seine-Inférieure_II_1870_368

[74] Acad_Toulouse_XI_1858_103

[75] Perrot_1840_379

[76] BA_1895_XXXVIII–XXXIX

[77] BA_comité_1888_4

[78] MSA_Ouest_1847_92

[79] MSA_Ouest_1847_383

[80] BSA_Touraine_v_1880–1883_285

[81] Mém_Picardie_IX_1848_42

[82] BM_Collection_Mémoires_1864_569–612

[83] Mém_Picardie_IX_1848_42

[84] BSA_Orléanais_IV_1870_235–236

[85] MDANE_IX_1849_159–160

[86] BM_XIX_1853_664

[87] BA_Comité_1892_XXXIX

[88] AJ_IX_1852_59–68_&_141–150

[89] Roach_Smith_1855_1

[90] BM_XXXVI_1870_500

[91] BM_XXXIV_1868_133_135

[92] Sopwith_1857_48

[93] AR_II_1889_333

[94] BA_Comité_1902_129–173

[95] Daremberg_&_Saglio_census_cadastre

[96] BA_Comité_1886_317–318

[97] CHA_I_1894_388

[98] BCA_Seine-Inférieure_XIV_1907_157

[99] SG_LXVI_Macon_1899_175

[100] SG_XXXIV_Paris_1867_147

[101] BCA_Narbonne_VI_1900_140

[102] Bull_Soc_Géographie_XV_1858_184

[103] CHA_V–VI_1899_370

[104] EB_XVII_1911_650

[105] SHD_MR1298_26–7

[106] SHD_MR1298_13–16

[107] SHD_MR1298_52–59

[108] SAH_Charente_1870_317

[109] BM_XIX_1855_99

[110] BM_XVII_1851_118

[111] SHD_MR_1145–58

[112] Mém_Côte_d'Or_IV_1853–1856_216

[113] Gembloux_1840_84

[114] Procès-Verbaux_Gard_1871_45

[115] BM_XIX_1853_488–501

[116] Mém_Normandie_1825_XVII–XVIII

[117] CS_France_IV_1836_Blois_188

[118] MDANE_VII_1826_CLXIV

[119] SG_XXXIII_Senlis_1866_434–435

[120] P-V_Comm_Seine-Inférieure_I_1818–1848_339

[121] SG_XVIII_Laon_1851_213

[122] SG_XL_Chateauroux_1873_14

[123] BSA_Seine-et-Marne_III_1866_18

[124] BSA_Provence_I_1904–1907,_65

[125] BM_XVII_1851

[126] BM_XVII_1851_121–122

[127] BM_XVII_1851_120

[128] SG_XXXIII_Senlis_1866_370

[129] BM_XXXIV_1868_455

[130] Jullian_1920_108

[131] Lucas_1873_6

[132] Sorbonne_1861_61

[133] Annuaire_Normandie_LXXVIII_1908_94

[134] AMPF_X_1896_287–288

[135] BSA_Orléanais_1872_313–314

[136] Babeau_1894_170–171

[137] Hughes_1803_5–6

[138] Mém_Aube_XXXIII_1830_17–18

[139] BSS_Yonne_XVIII_1864_31–32

[140] RA_XXVII_1874_4–5

[141] BSA_Orléanais_VII_1878–1882_337

[142] SG_XXX_Rodez_1863_43

[143] Caumont_Cours_II.2_1831_157–158

[144] Ann_ss_Indre-et-Loire_XXXVIII_1860

[145] Bosquet_1783_III_305ff

[146] SG_XL_Chateauroux_1873_271

[147] Mém_Picardie_II_1839_69

[148] BSS_Yonne_VI_1852_267

[149] BSS_Yonne_II_1848_367–368

[150] SG_XXXIX_Vendôme_1872_92

[151] SA_Nantes_XVI_1877_12–13

[152] Mém_Éduenne_1888_216

[153] BSA_Sens_IX_1867_360

[154] BM_VI_1840_234

[155] BSA_Orléanais_I_1854_207

[156] Mém_Senlis_V_1879_28

[157] SG_XXIII_Nantes_1856_122

[158] SG_VIII_Caen_1841_70

[159] AA_IV_1846_54

[160] SG_XVIII_Laon_1851_131

[161] Bull_Arch_1886_252–255

[162] Maître_1885_58

[163] Reinach_1890_8–9

[164] BCA_I_1882_399

[165] SG_XLI_Agen_1874_186

[166] BSA_Orléanais_III_1862_148

[167] Levasseur_1912_188

[168] Chevalier_1838_149–150

[169] Ministère_canaux_1840_42

[170] Lenthéric_1879_220

[171] Boitel_1843_II_439–45

[172] Mém_AIBL_XXIII_1868_28

[173] AA_XX_1860_101

[174] Lucas_1873_10

[175] Courtin_1812_89

[176] BM_XXII_1856_595

[177] Courtin_1812

[178] SG_XXXIII_Senlis_1866_231

[179] AMPF_X_1896_105

[180] SG_XLII_Châlons-sur-Marne_1875_261

[181] V-le-Duc_I_1876_VII

[182] L'Illustration_I_22_April_1843

[183] L'Illustration_XV_13_April_1850

[184] BSA_Nantes_III_1863

[185] RA_XXXVIII_1879_317

CHAPTER 4

Vandalism, Ignorance, Scholarship, Museums

Heritage and Destruction

Nous avons beau nous enorgueillir, et nous défendre contre les périls qui assiégèrent le Bas-Empire, par le spectacle des belles formes de notre liberté moderne. Hélas! cette liberté elle-même, universelle, indéfinie, sans nom et sans aïeux, mal comprise, plus mal pratiquée, sans souvenirs et sans point d'appui, quelles racines a-t-elle dans nos esprits, dans nos mœurs? ... Comment veut-on que le travail de nivellement, qui use et décompose notre pays depuis tant de siècles, laisse encore comprendre ce qu'il y avait de fort et de beau dans les diverses institutions qui couvraient autrefois notre territoire? ... L'esprit des masses est séparé par mille siècles de nos souvenirs nationaux.[1] [1845]

In the above quotation Lorain is writing about the destruction of the Abbey of Cluny, but he makes it clear that his condemnation is general, and that Cluny is but one manifestation of the broad disease, with symptoms including "modern liberty" on top of centuries of destruction, accepted by a population most of which is indifferent to any sense of national memory. Is it possible that such sentiments were rooted in the anti-republican and anti-modernist ideology on the right wing of politics?

It was indeed a minority of cognoscenti who appreciated the remains of the past. Protesting against the demolition of the late antique walls of modernising and expanding towns was generally a non-starter, because the preponderance of public opinion was strongly in favour of opening up towns, rationalising their layout, and improving their services. Of course, nobody (except the Army) could argue that more-than-millennial walls continued to be of any use. Any scholars wishing to study the contents of such walls were nearly always short of funds and manpower for digging – and dismantling often required specialised equipment, always assuming they could sort out the legal ownership of the walls and their adjacent structures. The solution was to complain long and hard about the vandalism of unfeeling municipal administrations which did the actual hard work – and then reap the benefits deriving from the uncovered antiquities.

© KONINKLIJKE BRILL NV, LEIDEN, 2015 | DOI 10.1163/9789004293717_006

Vandalism

> On seeing sculptures decorating a house at Le Mans being sawed up, the man was asked: "Mais vous êtes donc un Vandale?" Celui-ci, sans comprendre, lui répondit tranquillement: "Non, Monsieur, je suis épicier à Mayenne."[2] [exchange c. 1830]

References to vandalism (the perpetual cry of the antiquarians against the modernists, and effortlessly linked with restoration)[3] occur throughout this book, because the old is frequently compared with the new, the relative honours depending on the point of view, and destruction being perennial.[1] The topic also made good newspaper and journal copy, with plentiful space dedicated year after year to the latest outrages.[4] Caumont was one of the first to recognise, in 1834, that the problem was so large it needed the whole population to take a hand in preventing it.[5]

Much went during the Revolution, in senseless acts of anti-monarchical fervour which "ont privé le pays d'une foule de titres précieux et de monuments qui attestaient son amour des arts et le recommandaient à l'attention des étrangers."[6] At Rouen, Hughes complained in 1803 that "while churches and convents of superlative elegance and beauty have been destroyed with vandal wantonness, whatever was cumbersome, awkward, ugly, has been preserved with a sort of pious care."[7] Not so antiquities: at Sens in 1837, bas-reliefs retrieved from the walls and stored on the promenade (there was no museum) were re-cut for new building work, and few were saved.[8] At the end of the century, something similar happened at Algiers – but this time with material extracted from the town's museum.[9] In 1844, a priest from the Besançon diocese catalogued "plusieurs actes récents de vandalisme et contre certains projets de restauration dont on menace nos plus remarquables et nos plus chers monuments."[10] At Château-Thierry in 1847, a correspondent felt himself surrounded by vandals, preaching in the desert, while the very monuments "tremblent à l'approche de ces destructeurs; ils sont l'effroi des souvenirs historiques."[11] Unsightly construction was as bad as destruction and, asked one outraged observer at the Hôpital de Beaune in 1852, "Voilà pour quelles futilités on autorise des additions déplorables! Que font donc les commissions archéologiques!!!!"[12]

---

1 Léon 1951, 255–306 for cultural vandalism, including reuse for barracks, prisons, administration.

Preservation, Conservation, Restoration: The Dilemma[2]

Themes throughout the century associated with the Commission des Monuments Historiques (CMH) and similar enterprises were expertise, funding, coverage, and preservation, conservation and destruction, all of which of course had a long history.[3] By preservation, we understand the maintenance of a monument in the state in which it currently exists, without the addition or removal of any of its elements. Conservation entails the intervention of a curator, who "looks after" the monument (the meaning of the term) and, in the 19th century, may well alter it in some way, perhaps by removing later additions, to present it clearly and museum-like to the visiting public. Restoration implies work on a structure to rebuild or reveal earlier (perhaps original) characteristics. This should obviously be performed by an architect knowledgeable about the history of architecture, and approved by commissioners who know in advance what the end result will look like. But whereas preservation and conservation imply care (and, at least today, restraint), restoration often produced outrage in the 19th century because performed by the ignorant, the slap-dash or the over-confident. Much the same "restoration tragedy" was enacted in the United Kingdom during the same period.[4]

With any monument, then, the dilemma was just how much intervention was required to keep it standing and secure from collapse. "Expert advice before restoration" was the motto promoted from the 1820s by local societies (in effect pressure groups offering recommendations) as well as the CMH itself, with an era of restoration supposedly succeeding one of blind vandalism.[13] Thus the Société des Antiquaires de Normandie put it in their Statutes to lobby prefects, and through them mayors, "à ne faire faire aucune reconstruction, ni démolition, ni regratage des ornements architectoniques ou autres monuments remarquables de leur département" without advice.[14] This was necessary to counteract those such as Viollet-le-Duc who

> coined "restoration" as a practice that upholds the stylistic and structural integrity of architecture above and beyond the historicity of a given building. Having studied the system that underlies the constructional logic of

---

2 Bercé 2000, 35ff: Restaurer ou reconstruire sous la Monarchie de Juillet et le Second Empire; Bercé 2001 passim for Mérimée's ideas on these matters, including funding such work; Bercé 2013 for an overview; Glendinning 2013, 35–62 for Antiquarian Antecedents, 17th & 18th centuries.

3 Léon 1917, 123, Léon 1951, 15–62: La conservation des monuments avant la Révolution.

4 Fawcett 1976.

124 CHAPTER 4

a monument, the 19th century restorer often redesigned the building in an ideal form, which it had never had in history.[5]

Viollet-le-Duc claimed that architects chosen to restore buildings were experienced,[15] but the evidence points elsewhere, and by the late 1840s scholars were questioning the qualifications and experience even of those sitting on the various commissions, and merrily eviscerating reputations.[16]

What was the alternative to "restoration"? At Nîmes, in 1835, the commission archéologique would allow no work unless it was demonstrated to be essential;[17] at Poitiers in 1832, the restoration-destruction involved in preparing S. Jean to be a museum was simply halted by Vitet, the inspector.[18] At Château-Thierry in 1878 the local society set its face against "unity of style" for Saint-Crépin, preferring to leave in place "l'embellissement de ces églises où ils ont vécu et passé avant nous."[19]

Again, restoration to what?[6] Were standing monuments to be simply preserved as they were? (Yes, some maintained.)[20] Or should know-it-all architects, feeding anti-modernist nostalgia for a past that never was, create a new make-believe?[7] Caumont labels such over-confident restorers as doctors, for

> il y a encore des médecins architectes qui ont inventé un autre système le nec plus ultra de la médicamentation, c'est de démolir de fond-encomble les édifices pour avoir le plaisir de les refaire.[21]

At the same period the medical professions were also organizing and asserting primacy through licensing requirements, so doctors and architects all form part of broader trends in the rise of experts. The tension was between archaeologists (lovers of old stones) and architects who often wished really to rebuild rather than just to secure and clean what was already there.[22] Advice in 1906 was that "il convient, lorsque l'occasion s'en présente, de louer un architecte qui, ayant à restaurer des ruines, n'a pas entrepris de les reconstruire à neuf,"[23]

---

5 Bilsel 2003, 7: "Correcting" the stylistic or structural "mistakes" of the original builders was an important task of restoration. The restorer also erased systematically the traces of later historic additions—for instance, depriving the medieval cathedrals of their Baroque additions, hence, forcing the building into a structural and stylistic purity."

6 Jokilehto 1999, 137–156 for "stylistic restoration" in France, with examples of modern de-restoration. Pevsner 1976 for the scrape versus anti-scrape bettles across the Channel.

7 Cf Lady to JMW Turner: "But I've never seen a sunset like that, Mr. Turner!" "No, Madam," was the reply, "but don't you wish you had?"

VANDALISM, IGNORANCE, SCHOLARSHIP, MUSEUMS

but this came too late to save many of France's most prestigious buildings, which had already been smothered by "cast-iron rigidity and sameness."[24]

But what was to be conserved and, by neglect or otherwise (including supposed conservation!) destroyed? At the beginning of the 19th century, some buildings were so badly damaged that the choice was a stark one between restoration and abandonment.[8] Much destruction took place, as we shall see; and when the CMH proposed, local authorities could dispose, especially those with modernising tendencies, as happened with a church at Creil in 1895.[25] One scholar, sniffing out the inevitable vested interests, commented in 1868 on "une foule de travaux regrettables dans plus de 30 départements":

> Mieux vaudrait mille fois qu'il n'existât pas de commissions départementales pour la conservation des monuments que d'en avoir qui se donnent pour mission de tout détruire; que d'en avoir, comme elles le sont presque partout, composées de personnes, dont l'intérêt est de démolir.[26]

Again, lack of maintenance could cause destruction, as when in 1906 part of the Narbonne church used as a museum collapsed, damaging monuments placed there for protection.[27] Nor can we judge today what needed restoration, or simply conservation, since earlier drawings and prints of monuments are not necessarily to be trusted.[9] But with the advent of photography, we can sometimes judge the devastating effects of "restoration" visited upon some monuments.[10]

Characteristically, the 19th-century architectural reform movement, faced with the problem of large numbers of dilapidated monuments (which was strong in the United Kingdom, as well as in Germany),[28] was fascinated by mediaeval churches, which they often wished to rebuild or restore. Unfortunately, architectural evangelists saw nothing of interest in antiquities reused in late antique structures, dismantling them or stripping them back as near as feasible to their antique appearance, without taking the opportunity provided by these veritable "time capsules" to study how mediaeval secular life might have been lived. This was probably because grand monuments were the rage, and the civic life and habitation of ordinary people of little interest.

---

8   Léon 1917, 352–3: but later Cet entretien vise beaucoup moins à exécuter qu'à éviter des travaux.

9   Durand 2000, 15–50: L'antiquité en images (XVIe–XIXe siècles), with accounts of the work of Montfaucon, Clérisseau, Millin, Laborde, and Taylor; 73–85: Le cadre réglementaire (1810–1887); 115–147: Les chantiers de restauration: laboratoires de la doctrine (1809–1904).

10   Léon 1951, 359–538, for a host of before-and-after photos.

126   CHAPTER 4

As a result we know little about centuries of ordinary life within the theatre at Orange or the amphitheatre at Arles. Much the same applies to large sections of mediaeval Rome, sanitised by Mussolini without any exploratory excavation (although the Via dei Fori Imperiali did time-capsule land around the fora of Trajan and Augustus). The tilt against the mediaeval would not have been serious had funding been abundant, but it was not; and few funds were allocated in the course of the century to archaeological digs, although the building surge of the Second Empire (such as Haussmann in Paris) released large sums of money for restoration, many of them mis-used by Viollet-le-Duc.[11] Scholars undermined the very notion of restoration to the earliest state of a building, pointing out the high proportions of monuments which would be damaged: "Laissez, croyez-nous, les monuments tels qu'ils sont, et les grilles rococo dans une église du xive siècle."[29] And speedy restoration on the cheap was no use, for it was good only to kill the patient.[30] Cleaning was also a problem. At Versailles, for example, it was predictably the Génie that "procède à un grattage général des bâtiments," which damaged the stone and made it crumble.[31]

Late antique walls were also a problem for preservation-conscious 19th-century antiquarians and archaeologists. On the one hand they were standing monuments of antiquity; but on the other they were often suspected, sometimes known and sometimes seen to contain antiquities which could be studied, published and preserved. For even if their upper courses were sometimes of semi-rubble ("petit appareil"), everyone knew that more substantial stones, often taken from earlier monuments, usually formed their foundations, footings and sometimes core, as happened at Sens and Bourges,[32] and also at Saintes.[33] Some walls, conspicuously Langres, were almost completely constructed from antiquities.[34] Such walls had provided building materials for several centuries, and fed museums and provoked scholarly activity during the 19th century.

Other useful elements of the ancient townscape that were sometimes preserved because of their continuing utility were entrance gates and arches, some of which had a triumphal air about them. All walled mediaeval towns needed gates, so it is not surprising that several ancient ones survived either until an increased population necessitated a larger set of walls, or until the walls themselves also vanished in the Great 19th-century Knockdown. At Fréjus, for example, an antique gate went at the mid-century, and the nearby walls were demolished to make way for the railway.[35] At Nîmes, the Porte d'Auguste

---

11   Den Boer 2011, 192: "His principles for restoring a complete neo-Gothic state, which probably had never existed, were also often very damaging. In any event, a growing amount of money was allocated for restoration and conservation."

VANDALISM, IGNORANCE, SCHOLARSHIP, MUSEUMS

survived by sheer luck concealed under mediaeval alterations, its four passage-ways reduced to one.[36] But many others were sooner or later destroyed, at Orléans,[37] Troyes,[38] Sens,[39] Senlis,[40] and Narbonne.[41] Or they were mutilated, for example at Tours.[42] At Orléans, a madcap 1794 scheme to build a revolutionary Sainte Montagne (which never got off the ground) would have got stone by dismantling walls and gates.[43] Few arches were saved: Besançon kept a gate when in 1894 the Army authorised the demolition of the walls;[44] and at Lille the Porte de Paris was eventually restored but in the face of counter-petitions seeking "de donner plus d'air au quartier et d'y faciliter les communications."[45]

The dilemma of what to do with conspicuous antiquities was resolved by Viollet-le-Duc at Carcassonne, his intervention bravely supported with weasel words by today's local exhibition.[12] The disaster is sometimes downplayed,[13] but aptly described as "a nineteenth-century architectural monument," created from 1855 by a man with no interest in urbanism, and

> aimed beyond the mere accuracy of an archeological reconstruction. Its ultimate purpose was rather to convey to the French nation its first monument of military architecture as a representation of the permanence of territorial occupation.[14]

Artillery had long made this fortress obsolete, and the 1659 Peace of the Pyrenees gave the Roussillon to France, placing it far from any military front line, whereupon it became a quarry for locals.[46] (In the same situation was Narbonne, yet this town was still listed as a place de guerre in 1865.) Before Viollet got there, Carcassonne was still occupied by Army barracks, and part-mangled by them,[47] although by mid-century acknowledged to be of no defensive use. As Viollet asked in 1849, recalling the demolition of the walls of Carpentras and Sens, and the dangers to Avignon, could not the ruins be drawn exactly? He had studied the ramparts, and

---

12 Carcassonne 2000, 28: Viollet-le-Duc a rebâti ces superstructures sans remanier la partie ancienne … dont l'authenticité est scrupuleusement conservé. Dans son travail de restitution, une partie est valablement déduite de l'analyse et de l'observation; une autre est une hypothèse, une autre encore est une création. L'important est, sans doute, la cohérence et l'unité de la pensée qui a présidée à l'entreprise: aujourd'hui, Carcassonne témoigne aussi de l'art de Viollet-le-Duc et de ce qu'était le XIXᵉ siècle. What an admission to have to make, as if Viollet-le-Duc were Zeus, and his thought made Carcassonne flesh!

13 Bercé 2013a, 103–111, and mostly illustrations, whereas the account of his architectural and restoration work is longer (32–88), as is that of his work as an architecte engagé (132–172).

14 Costa_Guix_1988_66, 3. Ibid., 38–49 for critical fortune of the restoration.

128   CHAPTER 4

> la conséquence d'un relevé complet de ces murailles me mettrait à
> même de découvrir bien des faits curieux et ignorés, car ces remparts,
> bâtis à différentes époques, donnent des exemples très-variés d'ouvrages
> militaires.[48]

There were indeed "curious and unknown facts" to be discovered, because elements were Roman, with seven standing towers and elegant masonry,[49] albeit with the village inside falling in ruins, in contrast to the adjacent Bourg-Neuf[50] which, as prosperity increased, built hôtels to replace its 13th-century houses.[51] The local archaeologist Gabriel Cros-Mayrevieille not only commissioned drawings of the fortress, but also went to Paris in 1843 to lobby the government for funds. The church of S. Nazaire was on the 1840 Monuments Historiques list but, as a result of such lobbying, the Cité appeared only the 1862 list, with funds released for restoration. With some houses clinging to the walls still to be removed in 1904,[52] the popular press in France welcomed the fortress' resurrection, coyly admitting that "Cela, il est vrai, est un peu une restitution."[53] Architects in Britain were much more critical,[54] while the French section of the 1873 Vienna Exposition account made a lot of the work, written up by Viollet-le-Duc himself, no doubt because so much money had been spent on it.[55] The final word should lie with Viollet's own comment, quoted from his Dictionnaire, but not followed by him when he was "pris d'un zèle trop artistique," as here, or when he mangled the façade of Notre Dame de Paris:

> il proclame que toute partie postérieure à d'autres, dans un ancien édifice, doit toujours être conservée ou fidèlement rétablie, si elle offre par elle-même un certain intérêt d'art ou d'originalité, si elle a entraîné elle-même des remaniements généraux dont il soit intéressant de maintenir la trace.[56]

Destruction, Resurrection and Vandalism

> Le vandalisme mérite de respirer à l'aise. Malheureusement, nous sommes encombrés de documents qui attestent la présence des vandales sur plusieurs points de la France; pour constater tous les actes de ces Bédouins de l'art, de ces Kabyles des monuments historiques, il faudrait un numéro entier, et nous ne pouvons disposer, à grande peine encore, que d'un seul article.[57] [1845]

Didron Ainé can find no greater insult than to compare French vandals with the largely blameless inhabitants of Algeria, but he documents plenti-

VANDALISM, IGNORANCE, SCHOLARSHIP, MUSEUMS 129

ful examples.[58] He was far from the first, and there are plentiful surveys.[15] We find Quatremère de Quincy on the attack in 1826: "il dénonce l'envie de l'architecte qui restaure, de se produire lui-même."[59] But evidently without any change of heart on the part of architects, since the same wish was being expressed in 1868: "En face d'un édifice ancien devenu insuffisant, l'architecte devra modérer son propre désir de faire du neuf, et le secret penchant de tout administrateur à fonder."[60] Yet Quatremère was not alone,[16] for from the 1830s we find Victor Hugo, Vitet, Montalembert[61] with his expertise in politics,[62] and others, directing fire "sur les vandales de tout genre, démolisseurs, restaurateurs, constructeurs."[63] Lack of care over the centuries meant that many structures were ruinous, as Mérimée remarked in 1843,[64] but

> Rien de ce qui a survécu à la destruction d'une grande cité ne doit échapper à nos investigations. Les églises, les beffrois, les hôtels-de-ville, sont la révélation de l'importance politique des villes qui les ont construits.[65]

Caumont suggested in 1853 that churches would survive in spite of mutilation and restoration, because "le respect qui les entoure les protège encore contre le vandalisme."[66] However, he was to be proved wrong many times by errors of restoration, one scholar complaining in 1857 that "les plus stupides profanations ont été accomplies; le nombre des œuvres d'art ainsi dégradées est innombrable; il surpasse beaucoup les actes de vandalisme de la révolution."[67]

Much wishful thinking informed scholarly journals, some suggesting vandalism must be a thing of the past. Thus Didron Aîné suggested in 1853 that "C'est donc la gloire de la France d'être à la tête de l'archéologie chrétienne en Europe, parce que cette archéologie y est plus militante qu'ailleurs."[68] Yet Montalembert, while deploring some restorations,[69] wrote in the past tense about how "Personne ne défendait notre art chrétien et national."[70] But destruction continued: the walls of Thouars (Deux-Sèvres) came down, by which act "le conseil municipal a déchiré les pages les plus intéressantes de son histoire."[71]

Although the large losses to the French patrimony have been described in outline-survey fashion,[17] the narrative adopted by historians in the past few decades describes not their destruction, but rather the saving and restoration of monuments (by Merimée, Viollet-le-Duc and others) and the development of museums. Aided by 19th-century guidebooks (such as Murray's Handbooks,

---

15 Erder 1986 118–140 for survey of destruction and conservation from 17th century to 1900.

16 Jokilehto 1999, 69–75 for an overview of conservation in France, including Quatremère de Quincy.

17 Réau 1959, brought up to date by a 1994 edition.

130   CHAPTER 4

which attribute destruction to the Calvinists and then the Revolution), this is an uplifting interpretation, relying on collective amnesia about what really happened, and concentrating instead on the development and expertise of French scholarship and the creation of museums, which the more cynical would rather view as an alibi excusing if not explaining the destruction that occurred. Such a positive attitude to the swathe of architectural destruction visited on France by her architects survives today.[18]

Rewriting the past included a focus on Provence as the domain of the majority of surviving Roman monuments; but this evades the fact of the large numbers of important Roman structures further north which have disappeared over the years, many of them during the 19th century; so that the tally of survivals is meagre indeed, although some towns guarded their antiquities jealously, as we shall see at Narbonne.[72] The scale of destruction is underlined by the listings of protected monuments[73] which contain more prehistoric monuments than Roman ones. Although a few of the former were retained for religio-superstitious reasons, presumably so many survived because of their very large numbers; some went into roads, but most must have stood distant from any area which needed roads; and Roman monuments provided ready-made or easily trimmed blocks for reuse – much preferable to some types of prehistoric stones, which would have needed extensive recutting.

The popular tendency has been to equate vandalism with the Wars of Religion, and the French Revolution, but 19th-century scholars (excluding the wishful thinkers mentioned above) were quite clear that it was increasing in their own time, helped by "la manie des innovations."[74] One cynic in 1844 even claimed that the new zeal for digging produced nearly as many monuments as were being destroyed, and "c'est un adoucissement au mal."[75] As we shall see below, societies were founded to counter the continuing threat, such as that at Langres in 1836.[76] If some monuments went because they were deemed useless, others were destroyed when they could have been repaired and put to use, such as a Roman aqueduct and reservoir at Lyon in 1846, or at Saint-Césaire (near Nîmes), where the villagers suffered a long trek down the hill for water, rather than refurbishing the Roman channels.[77] Scholars saw the possibilities for restoring such aqueducts, yet the administration of the Génie seemed blind

---

18   Glendinning 2013, 90: "France reaped the benefits of her precociously developed school of official conservation architects, able and eager to develop a consistent ethos and body of work over decades, aided by lavish government repair funds and the scientific rationalism of French architectural education." 91–97 for Viollet and Carcassonne, though the author acknowledges that radical "restoration" by Viollet and others "encountered increasing opposition."

VANDALISM, IGNORANCE, SCHOLARSHIP, MUSEUMS 131

to the possibilities. At Lyon, for example, they destroyed a reservoir by sapping, instead of moving the required gate a few metres.[78]

The sapping of monuments, and the use of explosives by mining, was a cheaper way of demolishing structures, especially those employing rock-hard cement (such as ancient walls), than using workmen. It may have been a 16th-century innovation, brought from Italy.[79] The ramparts of Château-Gaillard (Eure), following permission from Henri IV, were mined in 1603 for the use of "des révérends pères capucins d'Andely" after the structure had been stripped of useful items;[80] in 1759 the ancient fortress of the Motte-du-Ciar, near Sens, was blown up and the rubble used to build the Château de Nolon;[81] a quarter of the Château of Crussol, near Valence, was tumbled by an artillery mine in 1846.[82] Inevitably, such a technique, probably at first purely military, destroyed more than it preserved, but was also attractive to civilians, especially those wishing to clear their land for ploughing and sowing. Thus the proprietors at Sanxay (Vienne), an important Gallo-Roman site, brought pressure on the excavator in 1883 to "détruire par la dynamite les édifices qu'il a découverts, et à rendre à la place un sol nivelé et labourable."[83]

Destruction and resurrection are of course complementary elements in building cycles: Gothic cathedrals replace Romanesque replace Carolingian and Merovingian structures, and so on, re-using the various materials where possible – from the small, to the large, to the spectacular. Unfortunately, how-ever, most structures were destroyed for pedestrian re-use in ordinary struc-tures, in roads and eventually factories, forts and barracks. The spectactular (in size and materials) was thereby re-converted into the ordinary, where it didn't disappear altogether – unless one wishes to argue that these are quint-essential expressions of the modernist era, and thus in that sense "monumen-tal." Thus was much of the architectural heritage of Roman and mediaeval France frittered away. It was the realisation by Vitet, Mérimée, and others[19] – veritable heroes of the conservation movement in France[84] – just how fast the past was vanishing that fuelled the restoration movements,[85] and the origins of "heritage."[20] There was also a conservation movement in England,[21] and their opinion mattered to the French. English scholarship, for example,

---

19   Jokilehto 1999, 127–32 for the beginnings of state administration of historic monuments in France, with Vitet and Mérimée.

20   Den Boer 2011, 189: "Without any expertise but with great historical enthusiasm, Ludovic Vitet and Prosper Mérimée played important roles in the birth of heritage studies in France."

21   Gerrard 2008, 176: "the analysis of the destruction and demolition of Roman buildings has so far been superficial" with a distinction to be made between collapse and demolition.

132   CHAPTER 4

helped inspire Millin's history of France.[22] Not that the English necessarily admired French scholarship, one accusing Lenoir in 1809 of "presumptuous ignorance... a certain bragging nationality... His knowledge of architectural antiquities is apparently neither very extensive nor correct."[86] But the English were not ignorant about French art treasures, for they bought large quantities of them during the Revolution and the Napoleonic wars.

Foreign visitors early in the 19th century admired the French for preserving so many earlier buildings,[87] but opinions changed as much restoration work was seen to be of poor quality. New building there was a-plenty but, as was remarked in 1857,

> n'hésitons pas à le dire, jamais, à coup sûr, on n'a moins bien construit. Au lieu d'architecture, nous n'avons le plus souvent qu'une détestable maçonnerie, et avec l'argent qu'on a dépensé depuis cinquante ans à élever les ignobles édifices qui déshonorent l'aspect de nos villes ou de nos campagnes et témoignent de notre mauvais goût.[88]

Once monuments were catalogued (see below), there was then the problem of what to do with them. Restore them? But expertise was conspicuously lacking, given that the poor quality of "restoration" was a constant reproach from archaeologists and connoisseurs against administrators.[89] Resurrection of crumbling monuments often came at a high price, because many architects did not restore or recreate the past – they forged it. By 1844 even the high clergy were losing patience with the poor restorations of their priests: "Cette manie des restaurations prodigues et inintelligentes commence à fatiguer les plus hauts dignitaires ecclésiastiques."[90] Given the lack of any appreciation of the distinction between preservation and restoration, let alone of the properties of quarried or reused stone,[91] this was at least in part the obvious reaction to a lack of comparative models. But there was also general misunderstanding of how mediaeval buildings especially evolved and changed during the decades or even centuries it sometimes took to build them, there frequently being no perfect original form except in the imagination of the original architect(s). The same problems occurred also with Roman monuments, their restoration often meeting with opprobrium, such as that showered on Henri Revoil for his work at Nîmes, Arles and Orange, which necessarily included replacement of elements abstracted in previous centuries, as well as accommodation

---

191: "if we want to understand the end of Roman Britain, we need to understand the end of its buildings and develop an archaeological study of destruction and demolition."

22   Hurley 2013, 291–348: In Albion's Shadow.

VANDALISM, IGNORANCE, SCHOLARSHIP, MUSEUMS 133

for the modern use of the structures.[92] In any case, what price objectivity in the development of archaeology and its view of the past?[23] A respectable position, unfortunately rarely followed, was "laissez les ruines au temps qui les dévore; ne cherchez pas à ressaisir un passé dont nous ne nous soucions plus...soutenez, mais ne réparez rien" – and spend any funds on beautiful new buildings, leaving ruins to the painters.[93] Hence the motto for some was "De l'entretien partout; de la restauration nulle part!"[94]

Ignorance: Workmen, Administrators, Proprietors

An erroneous but persistent myth about the Vandals is not only that they hated what they destroyed, from Roman civilisation (and the sack of Rome) to Christian architecture, but that they were indeed great destroyers. The epithet "vandalism" is constantly invoked by 19th-century French scholars about their own times, but much more damage was done by ignorance than by intent. Levels of education no doubt governed different attitudes toward the built environment, from the ignorant to the highly sophisticated. At the bottom of the heap were the workmen who did the digging or demolition, and their destruction of the past (especially mosaics)[95] was probably constant over the centuries.[96] Generally workmen were not educated men, and several demo-lition/building schemes were instituted to give employment to the needy, such as soldiers at Arles,[97] so it is not surprising that they sold off whatever small antiquities they could find.[98] Important objects had also gone unrec-ognised and thus destroyed in earlier centuries, such as the tomb inscription of Maître Adam, of Reims Cathedral, "entre les mains indifférentes de maçons ou d'entrepreneurs peu soucieux d'en assurer la conservation."[99] All workers recognised the easy solution was to destroy antiquities, for example a 16th-century marble to make chimney panels at Arles in 1837,[100] and building a new house completely from antiquities, as did one mason at Archelles (Seine-Inférieure) in 1853.[101] However, some masons made their own collections of antiquities, and sold them on.[102]

Scholars usually arrived too late to rescue anything at the sites being worked for new building, railways, etc, especially those distant from towns, and mosaics and sarcophagi were frequently destroyed by the pick.[103] At Marseille in 1853, part of a Phoenician inscription did end up in the museum, but "bien d'autres pierres ouvrées," seen when it was uncovered, subsequently

---

23 Thomas 2004 224: "The demand that archaeology should create a disinterested and objec-tive understanding of the past has left it impoverished and etiolated."

134 CHAPTER 4

disappeared, because they could be useful.[104] The appearance of the city was not improved because funds were lacking even for the restoration of approved and classified buildings, such as S. Maximin in the early 1840s.[105] At Reims in 1843, some 16th-century panels were rescued by "un œil vigilant" just as the workman was attacking them.[106] Inscriptions, because they were on flat slabs, usually of marble, were particularly vulnerable, and often simply disappeared.[107] The problem with workmen was permanent, as Millin, the author of a series of essays on French antiquities,[24] noted in 1811. But there was also "la méchanceté, le besoin de nuire, de détruire" which degraded monuments.[108] In the countryside, monuments could survive untouched for centuries, but disappear when "les hommes civilisés" got to them,[109] for this was destruction caused by modern civilisation.[110] In the 1870s at Bordeaux, material from the walls was gathered under "une sorte de hangar," but it took "un partisan dévoué de nos antiquités locales, qui suivait attentivement les travaux" to get the agreement of both administration and entrepreneur "que les pierres monumentales fussent préalablement relevées au lieu d'être brisées sur place," which had of course made life so much easier for the workmen.[111]

Administration and Destruction

Ce bâtiment... a été malheureusement défiguré pour y établir les classes du collège royal sous l'administration de M. Caffarell, préfet du Calvados. L'ignoble mutilation que ce préfet a autorisée, montre à quels actes de vandalisme des fonctionnaires, d'ailleurs honorables, peuvent se laisser entraîner.[112] [1835, of part of S. Étienne, Caen]

If the Génie were an institution that the 19th century loved to hate, then so also were often those who administered France, from central government, prefects and mayors to town councils. Townspeople were to be prevented by law from filching antiquities for building materials, but they were lesser offenders than Officialdom itself:

---

24   Hurley 2011, 111: in his attempt to counter the Revolutionary belief that all to do with the feudal past must be destroyed, une suite de soixante et une dissertations individuelles consacrées à des bâtiments divers, villes, monuments de France, sans l'apparence d'aucun ordre.

il faudroit décerner des peines sévères contre ceux qui enlèvent des pierres des monumens antiques, et punir quelques infracteurs de ce règlement: il faudroit surtout que la commune ne donnât pas l'exemple de ces infractions.[113]

There is plentiful evidence that administrators often saw their task as town improvement, and wished to leave their mark in the form of new buildings, which involved destruction of antiquities, such as a gate at Domfrout (Orne).[114] It was the Assemblée Nationale that was responsible not only for triggering much of the destruction during and after the Revolution,[115] but also, in 1790, for dividing France into 83 départements, each with its own administrative apparatus, ruled over by a préfet. Their predecessors, the intendants, commissioners sent by the King and primarily responsible for finance, policing and justice, had often been responsible for 18th-century town developments,[116] often at the expense of earlier structures.[117] Each commune also had some level of administration, and there were some 36,000 of them throught France. Personnel were short, as the 1847 *Almanach* makes clear: 29 inspectors of travaux publics for the whole of France, and 5 for the railway network; 26 members of the Comité historique des arts et des monumens in Paris, and 11 in the provinces. But a host of tax-inspectors and lawyers.[118]

Make-believe suggested that high-ranking administrators and legislators in Paris were patriotically "jalouses de nos gloires nationales," as Mérimée wrote in 1842. This was sheer flannel,[119] because they were still the decision-making and funding authority – as indeed were the prefects, whom Guizot asked as early as 1830 to encourage and promote local learned societies.[120] Prefects were generally not much use, except in a few cases, such as the Sous-Préfet of the Aisne's help in preserving a fragment of the Abbey of Saint-Ursin.[121] The French Revolution was an excuse as malleable in the 19th century as is "war damage" in today's museums; and we might suspect that it was extensively used by modernising administrators early in the new century: "C'est peut-être alors que les plus grands ravages furent accomplis sous les yeux des préfets complaisants. La Restauration elle-même se soucia fort peu du culte des souvenirs."[122] Indeed it did, for more monuments may have gone under the Restoration than during the Revolution.[123] Equally make-believe were the part-hopeful, part realistic instructions which the prefect of the Creuze issued in 1874:

engager les habitants de votre commune à vous signaler les objets trouvés par eux et ayant une valeur archéologique, afin que vous puissiez immédiatement m'en informer... Quant aux découvertes qui ne sont pas transportables, telles que tombes gauloises, gallo-romaines ou franques, vestiges de voies romaines ou d'habitations, etc., les Directeurs du Musée se feront un devoir d'aller relever les plans et descriptions de ces monuments avant leur destruction complète nécessitée par les travaux.[124]

Administrators were in one sense similar to architects; so that "En face d'un édifice ancien devenu insuffisant, l'architecte devra modérer son propre désir de faire du neuf, et le secret penchant de tout administrateur à fonder."[125] The results could be disastrous, as at Rouen by 1860, where "ces belles maisons jadis innombrables" fell before bad taste, sacrificed "pour la plus grande gloire de la bureaucratie et des architectes municipaux."[126] Few indeed were the prefects to whom one might confidently write, "je sais qu'il suffira de vous signaler ce besoin pour qu'il soit immédiatement satisfait."[127] However, one scholarly tactic to try and minimise unfortunate developments and the destruction they entailed was to invite the high and mighty (prefects, bishops, mayors) as honorary members of scholarly societies.[128] This did not always work. If in 1841 the Prefect of Mayenne sought funds for digging the castellum of Jublains,[129] in 1835 the Prefect of Calvados authorised the mutilation of part of the Abbey of Saint-Étienne at Caen to contain a college;[130] although by 1860 Caumont was ready to acknowledge that there were "des administrations éclairées" here and there.[131] However, most prefects were simply not interested in old buildings, unable to distinguish good new buildings from bad ones, and all the work they approved was of course the result of watertight decision-making: "il n'y a pas de travaux déplorables et inutiles qui ne soient autorisés et préconisés même par les commissions départementales."[132]

Nonchalance was widespread because the administrators at national, regional and local level knew they had the control of building and destruction in their hands.[133] Apart from monuments in private hands, they "owned" the building stock. Hence Millin might rail in 1807 against the destruction of the enceinte at Autun, pointing out that pilferers of stones were pursued and fined, not through any desire to conserve the structures being nibbled away, but because "le droit de les détruire n'appartient qu'à la ville; c'est un vandalisme dont elle se réserve le privilège exclusif."[134] Wrong, wrote Normand when complaining about the destruction of the walls of Avignon: "les remparts d'Avignon ne sont pas la propriété de la ville, mais la propriété de l'État. Le ministre de l'Instruction publique ne saurait en disposer. Il faut une loi pour aliéner une partie, si minime soit-elle, du domaine public."[135] And did the Assemblée Nationale ever vote extra funding for conservation, as Mérimée suggested in 1850 that they might?[136]

VANDALISM, IGNORANCE, SCHOLARSHIP, MUSEUMS

As the conservation movement took hold, one might expect fewer rebuilding disasters but, instead, they increased – or was it perhaps just the added publicity they attracted now that the conservation movement was so much stronger? In 1880s Touraine the administrators were ignorant and lacking in taste, and entrusting monuments to their supervision "n'est pourtant pas toujours les placer à l'abri des dévastations."[137] Vulgar utilitarianism or ignorance damaged or destroyed many buildings. At Amiens in 1806 speculators spread the rumour that the cathedral was in danger of collapsing, squashed only by an engineer who published "un avertissement qui démentait cette sordide imposture."[138] Not to be outdone, a scare campaign was started about the onerous cost of upkeep of such a large building.[139] Such "vulgar utilitarianism" laced with ignorance was still being castigated at the end of the century, as an author at Valence complained in 1891.[140] Hence complaints about vandalistic administrators not only at Paris, but also Bordeaux, Auch, Évreux, right down to small settlements such as St-Nazaire-de-Valentane, in the Quercy. Administrative vandals also get their place in the index of the Bulletin Monumental.[141] At Auch, for example, the Cathedral was threatened with "restoration," the Cordeliers became a store for forage,[142] and a grain hall was built in the Abbey garden.[143]

But even if some prefects were conscientious, and interested in old monuments,[144] the local mayors ruled their own roost. In the Marne in 1853 the desire was that "l'administration surveille un peu plus l'entretien de nos monuments,"[145] and in Maine-et-Loire as late as 1864 the Préfet had to remind them of the law "dont la stricte observation devrait assurer, du moins en grande partie, la conservation des monuments appartenant aux administrations publiques et même aux particuliers."[146] One problem, indeed, had been enunciated in the 1858 Congress list of questions attendees should address: "Quelles sont les pertes faites, depuis quelques années, par la négligence des Administrations municipales, en ce qui touche à la conservation des fragments antiques?"[147] Losses continued, the inhabitants of Soulosse (Vosges) selling off what they could of their antique sculpture, and destroying the rest.[148]

Village priests often had almost as much executive power as some civilian administrators, ruling over their churches, and altering them, perhaps to accord with the modernising ideas of their parishioners. They removed stained-glass windows,[149] often considered old-fashioned, and put marble where it was not needed, as at Saint-Quentin.[150] Bishops (although they could send round-robins counselling conservation)[151] sometimes had as little influence as prefects:[152] pictures were sold off,[153] the majority of choir-screens were destroyed,[154] and an English visitor could complain in 1898 that "unmutilated

138   CHAPTER 4

abbeys are now very rare in France."[155] This was because, perhaps surprisingly, many scholars thought the Middle Ages (as opposed to Celtic, Greek and Roman material) undervalued; this would change one day, and "nos enfants les montreront avec orgueil aux étrangers, comme des témoins irrécusables de l'opulence de la cité [Rouen] et de la puissance de volonté de leurs aïeux."[156] The problem was destruction, and it was not revolutions or time which were the main culprits, but rather "le vandalisme et le mauvais goût moderne, aidés de l'ignorance et de la cupidité."[157]

Evidently, it was concluded in 1859, priests should learn something about art and learn to distinguish the good from the bad.[158] With other more modern styles now prized, and "ne pouvant démolir les églises ogivales qu'on leur avaient appris à dédaigner," some old churches were sometimes given a cosmetic make-over,[159] while others were completely destroyed.[160] Modernism could also help with memory: when the Abbey of Saint-Crépin-le-Grand at Soissons was pulled down in 1855, the municipality commemorated it with the invention of new street names, which a commentator in 1897 dubbed an anachronism and a new type of vandalism.[161] The Abbey was gone, surviving only as the Rue de Saint-Crépin-le-Grand.[162] Many important structures were destroyed because they were not classified by the Commission but, as an English visitor remarked, "in the case of private property, the State has no power to prevent destruction, however grievous the national loss."[163] English indignation at the way the French mistreated their monuments was widespread.[25]

The Persistence of Vandalism

By the 1830s it was clear the vandalism of the Revolutionaries (simply knocking things down) was no longer adequate to describe what was happening throughout France, because rebuilding could be just as destructive, and was now attributable to a wide range of parties:

1. Vandalisme Destructeur: Première catégorie. Le gouvernement. 2e Les maires et les conseils municipaux. 3e Les propriétaires. 4e Les conseils de fabriques et les curés. En 5e lieu, et à une très grande distance des précédans, l'émeute.
2. Vandalisme restaurateur. Première catégorie. Le clergé et les conseils de fabrique. 2e Le gouvernement. 3. Les conseils municipaux. 4e Les propriétaires.[164] [1839]

---

25   Léon 1951, 75–104 for their fate under Empire & Restoration.

Thus Montalembert ranked those responsible for vandalism, and matters had scarcely improved two decades later.[165] As already noted, rather than diminishing as the century progressed, vandalism actually increased, so that the 1897 Congress at Nîmes repeated (as it had done for years previously) Caumont's 1834 warning: "le vandalisme continue d'exercer ses ravages; de tous côtés l'affligeant spectacle de la destruction vient frapper les regards."[166] One response (suggested by Alexandre Lenoir in 1799) was to make casts of structures to be demolished;[167] but of course this was no real solution.

But why so much vandalism in this, the supposedly enlightened 19th century? After all, a law was in place from 1841 offering expropriation of notable structures (including megaliths) from recalcitrant private owners,[168] such as those occupying the theatres of Orange and Arles.[169] Again listings, laws and scholarly outrage and lobbying were supposed to eradicate the problem but, instead, it got much worse, so that "une loi vraiment protectrice des monuments historiques" was still being sought in 1886,[170] and Hunnewell was still offering up a prayer for preservation in 1898.[171] Materialism was the cause, compounded by an unenlightened government, wrote Caumont in 1835.[172] For Hugo, writing three years earlier, the destroyer was likened to a rat, nibbling away now at Vincennes, now at the "beaux remparts" of Toulouse, and simply replacing them with bad buildings.[173]

It should also be underlined that little difference is perceptible between Paris and the provinces. We might expect Paris to lead the charge of scholarly concern, and this it did;[174] but the various administrations provided the model of just how quickly and ruthlessly urban change could be effected and monuments destroyed. Paris may well have set the fashion in modernity, but the rest of France was eager to follow. The sorry story of the discovery and then further dismantling of the amphitheatre of Paris is a case in point, the destruction of which, according to Henri Martin, would rob Paris of her oldest surviving structure, and would be "une honte pour Paris aux yeux de toute l'Europe savante."[175]

Wars and revolutions were no longer the cause of vandalism, as Montalembert affirmed in 1839. He worried about the damage such destruction did to France's reputation, placing civil disturbance far behind the actions of government, mayors, town councils, curés and factory owners, of which he offered many examples.[176] Such an accusation in this, the age of increased trade and international exhibitions, should have disturbed successive governments, but their reaction to such charges was, generally, masterly inactivity spliced with nonchalance. History was of course to blame, not modern administrators: indeed, Caumont had already placed much blame on Richelieu, Louis XIV and Louis XV,[177] with their desire to make a clean sweep of rebels

140　　　　　　　　　　　　　　　　　　　　　　　　　　　　　　　　　　CHAPTER 4

and their fortifications.[26] Pointing to the usual suspects was one ministerial response. Thus Despois's 1868 tract on *Le vandalisme révolutionnaire* was distributed with a sticker on the front cover reading *Ouvrage approuvé par le Ministère de l'Instruction Publique pour les bibliothèques populaires & scolaires*; it deftly attempted to pin the blame for most vandalism on the Middle Ages and the French Revolution.[178] Despois shows the generator of Revolution-period reports on vandalism, the Abbé Grégoire,[27] as sometimes wrong.[179] But he was sometimes successful in his efforts (as at Reims).[180]

However, given developing and ever-increasing scholarly firepower, trying to deflect the blame could not work, even if some optimists suggested that vandalism was decreasing, and declared a new golden age of respect for the past.[181] Scholars throughout the century cherished the notion that all they had to do to trigger action for conservation was to accumulate more and more examples of vandalism. But from the early decades of the century this was to prove misguided. Rey, writing in 1839, noting that "enfin de tout ce qui, pouvant être détruit, l'a été par haine de nos institutions ou seulement par ignorance et par cupidité,"[182] did indeed enunciate the touching belief that the more evidence he accumulated, the sooner the powers that be would eschew vandalism[183] – although perhaps he wrote thus simply for effect. Nevertheless, he did rehearse the "miracle" that earlier centuries had still left monuments to be admired,[184] and proclaimed that Caumont had managed to replace a taste for destruction with one for conservation.[185] This was of course far from being the case, and Hugo was much more realistic about the continuing disaster, which was decidedly not dependent on any particular flavour of politics, declaring that there was not even one commune in France where a monument's destruction was not being contemplated or completed.[186] Other were, like Rey, more optimistic, Bourassé declaring in 1841 that public opinion would not allow such destruction, but also warning against the problem of unsuitable restoration[187] – so that now the term "vandalisme reconstructeur" became common. Paris, like the rest of the country, was losing monuments in even greater quantities at the end of the century, one such casualty described by Marmottan as a "triste conséquence d'une trop tardive intervention, ou d'une nonchalante insouciance, à tout jamais regrettable!"[188] Public opinion was also invoked in 1895 when, the commentator thought, systematic demolition was at an end – but

---

26　　Benedict 1989, 31: "The cities remained a political and military force to be bargained with ... His subsequent wars provided him with the occasion to requisition the artillery of all of the cities in the kingdom, thereby depriving them of one of the great symbols of their military importance."

27　　Tauber 2009, the reports with editor's commentaries.

VANDALISM, IGNORANCE, SCHOLARSHIP, MUSEUMS   141

Christian monuments, "chefs-d'oeuvre de la foi de nos pères," were still in great danger.[189] He was wrong about the focus: protests against the demolition of the walls of Antibes with dynamite, thereby damaging or destroying many of the inscriptions they contained, date from 1897.[190]

Money, Speculators, Scholars

Behind much of the vandalism outlined above, and of the best efforts of associations to counter it, was the matter of money. Funding was never adequate for either cataloguing or restoration, as an increasing number of monuments drew attention. The theatres at Orange and Arles were closely watched by scholars to check that the quality of conservation they received accorded with their "allocations considérables,"[191] and it was realised that entrepreneurs had to be watched to ensure what they did had been approved.[192] Money remained short, and Mérimée often lobbied for increased funds, needed as the extent of necessary conservation work was realised, for example for old houses in Orléans.[193] As everyone's list of worthy monuments expanded, coverage was seen as a problem, as was conservation: as Caumont wrote in 1860,

> ce qui manque, c'est la volonté de conserver: l'indifférence nous tue en archéologie comme en autre chose. Il n'y a pas plus d'esprit de conservation qu'il n'y a de véritable patriotisme, qu'il n'y a d'esprit public, qu'il n'y a de véritable amour du pays et de ses richesses artistiques.[194]

Neither the associations nor the government ever had sufficient funds, and they knew that antiquities were attractive to despoilers because they cost less than quarrying fresh stone. This applied to enceintes, for example at Thérouanne (Pas de Calais, where the Cathedral also disappeared).28 Here, as was observed in 1730, the town once had "diverses moyennes Tours rondes ou quarrées... mais le tout est si ruiné par la fouille qu'ont fait les peuples pour arracher les pierres des fondemens de ses murs."[195] Monuments were disappearing daily, and even to illustrate them would be expensive. As Caylus wrote in 1759, "il faudroit faire une dépense véritablement royale pour remplir cet objet; mais chaque instant de retardement diminue l'agrément de l'entreprise; les altérations & les destructions qui arrivent nécessairement."[196] Archives, the necessary basis for much historical research, were perenially underfunded.[197] Even digging up antiquities could be subject to price-fixing (as was found in

---

28   Montclos 1992, 38–53.

1821 when work was done on an ancient canal)[198] or to the sale of ancient metals for their bullion value alone.[199] Another thesis for an economic historian would be a study of the place and proportion of preservation/restoration funds within overall public budgets, and how they evolved over time.

Naturally, few were ever satisfied by how funds were distributed, and the *quis custodiet?* question was raised: "Il y a donc lieu de ... surveiller l'emploi de l'argent public, argent qui se distribue trop souvent sur des recommandations étrangères et même nuisibles à la conservation de nos grands édifices."[200] Why, asked one scholar in 1869, playing the jesting Pilate rôle, did the Government lavish money on scholarships to study monuments abroad, and neglect those in France?[201] Why indeed, except because schools in Athens and Rome were long-founded? Nor was it necessarily the case that more money (and the Government did commit large sums to monuments)[202] meant better exploration and preservation of monuments. At Chartres in 1867, for example, one scholar deplored thirty years' supply of too much money, and in some towns, "les plaintes des archéologues ont été incessantes, tant contre les démolisseurs sacrifiant le passé, que contre ceux qui encouragent et applaudissent ce goût moderne si désastreux." Whereas Chartres, luckily,

> n'a pas encore suivi cet engouement général de destruction, mais elle a suivi celui de déserter la vieille cité et sa rivière, pour aller créer de nouveaux quartiers extra-muros, dans la poussière![203]

But the converse was usually the case, for funds were often scarce. Évreux in 1870 had insufficient funds to deal with the finds from her walls,[204] and in 1875 its cathedral was wiped "du budget et de l'administration spéciale des monuments historiques."[205] At Sanxay in 1883, only the State could save the remaining structures in the face of predatory proprietors, and "Qu'est-ce qu'un crédit de 100,000 francs pour un budget de 3 milliards?"[206]

Large demolition jobs could raise revenue, and in some cases reduce town expenditure, and often uncover antiquities.[29] Henri III sold off sections of walls at Lyon in 1584,[207] as did Louis XIV at Château-Thierry in 1695.[208] The municipality petitioned the king in 1614 to allow the demolition of the citadel of Pirmil (Nantes); demolition began in 1626, but the remainder went only in 1839

---

29 It is interesting that several fortified cities (Langres; parts of Bordeaux) appear to have been ceded back to their citizens in 1816 (presumably when France was at a low), and the same walls dismantled and their stones sold off. This should be the time for some discoveries of spolia and, if so, they must be in newspapers, the transactions of local archaeological societies, and some departmental and town archives.

VANDALISM, IGNORANCE, SCHOLARSHIP, MUSEUMS

"pour l'élargissement de la place et l'établissement d'une cale descendant à la Loire."[209] Revenue-raising saw châteaux proposed for demolition before[210] or during the Revolution.[211] In other words, speculation for the profits to be made from demolishing old monuments was in force from 1790,[212] and a complaint in 1844 was that vandalism was greater in France than in Asia Minor, "régulièrement formée en association commerciale pour exploiter, comme carrières, nos monuments religieux, militaires et civils."[213] In 1869 the misreading an inscription suggested that a church in Vienne was the mausoleum of Pilate and contained treasure;[214] and early in the century speculators dug at Château-Gaillard expecting to locate treasure.[215] The Roman camp at Péran (Côtes-du-Nord) received similar attention.[216] A proprietor at Château-Thierry in 1763 gave permission to demolish ramparts on his land, but only if he could be compensated for costs he incurred; the mayor apparently outflanked him, selling off retrieved stones to an entrepreneur whose son-in-law used them for building work at his house[217] – such deals a common practice from the late Middle Ages onward. And of course, many monuments fell during the Revolution,[218] the revenue they could bring calculated to a nicety.[219]

In the 19th century, erstwhile military property could also generate revenue. The amount recouped would depend on the hectares freed up; but, for example, it was reported in 1890 that Coblenz was to declassify its fortifications, and that "L'étendue du terrain disponible pour les constructions va se trouver ainsi sextuplée."[220] Thus Nîmes sold off barracks in 1872; the money went into new roads, and into enlarging the railway station, "malgré les efforts des habitants pour s'y opposer."[221] And one of the arguments for declassification at Narbonne was the "ressources qu'on réaliserait par la vente des terrains et des bâtiments militaires."[222]

Large-scale demolition could also remind citizens, such as those of Troyes in 1853, of how much they had paid out for the now-demolished walls,[223] and archives listed large garrisoning and defence costs going back centuries.[224] At Romans (Drôme) in 1801, the site of antiquities,[225] the dangerous church (by then a storehouse for fodder) would have cost a large sum to restore, so it was sapped and brought down by fire, "et le vieil édifice s'écroula avec un épouvantable fracas."[226] Little more is known of the town's antiquities.[227] Certainly, monuments were a charge, Caumont instancing in 1870 the church of S. Pierre at Touques, near Lisieux, funded in the 1840s by the government, but which the town council now refused to maintain;[228] the council was still pleading poverty in 1895.[229] Many towns, of course, simply could not afford extensive excavations, Boulogne in 1896 unable to help because "une telle entreprise dépasserait de beaucoup les ressources dont la ville de Boulogne peut disposer,"[230] and Saint-Lizier being in such a state of decadence that her

144 CHAPTER 4

monuments crumbled.[231] Yet in this same decade, the tiny municipality of Martres-Tolosane (Haute Garonne) could commit 3,000fr to three years of new digging.[232]

In 1812 funds were allocated for the Porte de Mars at Reims, but an inadvisable restoration was abandoned.[233] In 1827 Lillebonne, on private land, was being dug by the municipality, the owner stipulating that "les matériaux, sans intérêt, lui seraient abandonnés" – a far from theological dodge.[234] By mid-century Saint-Martin-d'Angers was a wood store;[235] and the bell-tower at Valliquerville (Seine-Inférieure) had been ruined in spite of the large sums spent on it.[236] In 1856 it was suggested that the old walls of Laon, declassified in 1850, be left in place, and used for tax-collection,[237] but the proposal came up against the objections of owners of adjacent land.[238] And in 1861, Dijon invested 35,000fr in wall-building for the same purpose.[239] At Lyon in 1529, the councillors at Lyon defended their purchase of a bronze inscription by noting that the metal alone was worth 34 of the 58 écus they paid for it.[240] It was fixed on a prominent wall.[30]

Conclusion

This account of the place of money in the biography of French monuments leads directly to the plague of entrepreneurs and speculators, who of course appear throughout this book, and whose depradations had long ago been recognised by the Romans, who had legislated against their actions.[241] Hence some towns in the interior that began to cede their militarized peripheries for other purposes as early as the 17th century (for example, at La Rochelle after the 1629 siege). Part of their aim was to make money from destruction. This could involve the clearing of complete sites, such as the ancient baths of Alincourt (Seine-Inférieure, near Lillebonne) in 1880, where "pour préparer l'assise des maisons qui s'élèvent à vue d'œil sur toute l'étendue de l'enclos, la pioche heurte les entassements ou les maçonneries antiques à chaque pas."[242] Sometimes they followed the Génie around, as in North Africa, and profited from the disruption the Army had caused;[243] or took advantage of the age-old diggings at Carthage, by 1911 extracting and selling materials for a completely

---

30 Pelletier & Rossiaud 1990, 455, Lyon: the Tables de Claude placed on one of the walls of the Town Hall to, as Claude Bellieuvre said, "apprendre à nos filz à honorer nos pères les Romains, puissent-ils les imiter." According to Maurice Scève, the conseillers were descendents of ancient senators, and seemed to possess "l'antique générosité romaine."

VANDALISM, IGNORANCE, SCHOLARSHIP, MUSEUMS

new suburb.[244] At least archaeologists could profit from what entrepreneurs could not sell.[245]

If some entrepreneurs donated material they could not use to the local museum, as at Toulouse in 1888,[246] or at Narbonne in 1904,[247] the materials they could re-use were always in danger. In 1845 Sens solved the problem by paying on the nail for recovered antiquities, "la valeur matérielle de chacune de ces pierres aux propriétaires ou entrepreneurs concessionnaires et une indemnité aux ouvriers pour leur temps et leurs soins."[248] This would not work in Tunisia, because few quarries were open;[249] nor yet in Algeria, where there was so much new building.[250] Of course, time was money, and many monuments no doubt disappeared because new work could not be held up.[251]

[1] Lorain_1845_V–VI
[2] SG_XLV_Le_Mans_ 1878_372
[3] BCH_Nord_XVI_1883_9
[4] AA_I_1844_87–99
[5] CS_France_II_1834_ Poitiers_538
[6] Melleville_1846_335
[7] Hughes_1803_23
[8] BM_IV_1838_465
[9] BA_Comité_1892_107
[10] AA_I_1844_412
[11] BSA_Soissons_I_1847_34
[12] BM_XVIII_1852_258–259
[13] CS_France_XVII_1850_ Nancy_260
[14] Mém_Normandie_1824_ XXIV–XXV
[15] V-le-Duc_I_1876_II
[16] AA_VIII_1848_170–171
[17] Mérimée_1835_363
[18] MSA_France_XIII_ 1837_425–426
[19] ASA_Château-Thierry_1878_51
[20] Brown_1905_46–57
[21] BM_XV_1849_90
[22] Paté_1900_23–24
[23] AMPF_XIX_1906_161–167
[24] Brown_1905_82–83

[25] ASA_Château-Thierry_ 1895_118
[26] BM_XXXIV_1868_818
[27] BA_Comité_1906_CLIX
[28] Clemen_1898
[29] AA_IV_1846_48–49
[30] Archives_Nord_de_la_ France_1842_260–261
[31] AMPF_XVIII_1904_141
[32] SG_XVI_Bourges_1849_ 119–120
[33] Moreau_1841_118
[34] Migneret_1835_46
[35] SG_XXXIII_Senlis_ 1866_327–328
[36] Mém_Gard_1847–1848_ 43–66
[37] BM_III_1837_195
[38] Mém_Aube_ XVIII_1854_196
[39] Vaudin_1882_222, Tonnere
[40] Mém_Senlis_1869–871_ 1872_XLVI
[41] Favatier_1903_251–252
[42] SAH_Charente_III_ 1863_184–185
[43] Réunion_BA_XX_ 1896_521
[44] BA_Comité_1894_XIX

[45] Réunion_BA_ XV_1891_162–177
[46] Boyer_1884_28
[47] Boyer_1884_42
[48] Summerand_1876_ 219–220
[49] Acad_Toulouse_I_ 1827_53
[50] Mérimée_1835_137
[51] SG_LVIII_Dôle_1891_262
[52] AD_Haut-Languedoc_ 1904_141
[53] AD_Haut-Languedoc_ 1904_132
[54] RIBA_Transactions_ 1866_140–148
[55] Sommerard_1876_ 188–224
[56] Saint-Paul_1881_32
[57] AA_III_1845_291–292
[58] AA_IV_1846_40–67
[59] Schneider_1910_22
[60] Mém_Doubs_IV_1868_ 15–200
[61] AA_XXI_1861_254
[62] AA_XXI_1861_252
[63] AA_XIII_1853_160–161
[64] Mérimée_1843_21
[65] MSA_Somme_I_1838_18
[66] Caumont_I_1853_488

[67] CS_France_XXIV_1857_
Grenoble_531
[68] AA_XIII_1853_161
[69] AA_XIII_1853_162
[70] AA_XIII_1853_161–162
[71] AA IX 1849, 242
[72] Direction_des_Beaux-
Arts_1889
[73] Direction_des_Beaux-
Arts_1889
[74] AA_I_1844_201
[75] AA_I_1844_317
[76] Réunion_BA_1877_13
[77] Garcin_I_1835_294
[78] SG_XXIX_Saumur_
1862_461
[79] V-le-Duc_I_1876_449
[80] Guilmeth_1849_69
[81] Rép_Archéol_
Yonne_1868_204
[82] BSA_Drôme_II_1888_
68–82
[83] BCA_Seine-Inférieure_
VI_1883_301–302
[84] Sommerard_1876_16
[85] Mérimée_1843_17
[86] Whittington_1809_169
[87] MSA_Rambouillet_
XII_1897_58
[88] CS_France_XXIV_1857_
Grenoble_529
[89] Paté_1900_19
[90] AA_I_1844_235
[91] Goze_1854_54–55
[92] Mém_Acad_Nîmes_
XXIX_1906_10
[93] Frossard_1854_27–28
[94] AMPF_XVIII_1905_375
[95] BSA_Orléanais_I_
1848–1853_302
[96] Mém_Comm_Côte-
d'Or_IV_1856_264
[97] Clair_1837_25
[98] Tarbé_1844_143

[99] BA_Comité_1898_41
[100] Clair_1837_140
[101] Cochet_1866_248–249
[102] CS_France_X_1842_
Strasbourg_350
[103] RA_XXX_1875_122
[104] Tvx_Soc_Stat_Marseille_
XVI_1853_344–345
[105] CS_XIV_1846_
Marseille_110
[106] Ann_Acad_Reims_
1843–1844_267–268
[107] Caumont_I_1846_182
[108] Millin_IV_1811_130–131
[109] MSA_Midi_de_la_
France_IV_1840–41_3–4
[110] SG_XII_Lille_1845_12–13
[111] SA_Bordeaux_III_1876_
75–91
[112] Caumont_1835_431–432
[113] Millin_I_1807_347–348
[114] SG_VIII_Caen_1841_189
[115] Mège_1835_184–185
[116] Babeau_1894_183
[117] Babeau_1880_529–530
[118] Almanach_Royal_et_
National_1847_175–177
[119] Mérimée_1842_14
[120] SG_XLII_Châlons-sur-
Marne_1875_528
[121] BM_XXXIV_1868_221
[122] BSA_Midi_XXV–XXVI_
1899–1900_51
[123] Brown_1905_75
[124] RA_XXVII_1874_271
[125] Mém_Doubs_IV_1868_
15–200
[126] BM_XXVI_1860_
382–383
[127] BSA_Seine-
Inférieure_1867_282
[128] BSA_
Orléanais_V_1868_18
[129] SG_VIII_Caen_1841_85

[130] Caumont_Cours_V_
1835_431–432
[131] Caumont_1860_35
[132] BM_XXXV_1869_82
[133] Brown_1905_73–96
[134] Millin_I_1807_310
[135] Corresp_Hist_Arch_
VII_1900_210
[136] Sommerard_1876_367
[137] BSA_Touraine_V_
1884_421bis
[138] Dusevel_1848_517
[139] Dusevel_1848_436
[140] BSA_Drôme_XXV_
1891_29
[141] BM_Table_générale_
1873_10
[142] BM_XXVIII_1862_
730–747
[143] Revue_Aquitaine_
II_1857_53
[144] SG_XIII_Metz_1846_95
[145] BM_XIX_1853_276
[146] Rép_Arch_Anjou_1864_
50–51
[147] Annuaire_Provinces_
Cong_Sc_XI_1859_
427–441
[148] Espérandieu_VI_
1915_172
[149] BM_XV_1849_371
[150] SA_Saint-Quentin_
XXXIII_1858_90
[151] Bonnald_1839_231–232
[152] SG_XX_Troyes_1853_
189
[153] PV_Comm_Archéol_
Narbonne_1842–1889_166
[154] Bourassé_1841_240–241
[155] Hunnewell_1898_51
[156] Tvx_Acad_Rouen_
1859_325
[157] AA_I_1844_197
[158] AA_XIX_1859_321

VANDALISM, IGNORANCE, SCHOLARSHIP, MUSEUMS

[159] Revue_Aquitaine_III_
1859_524
[160] Despois_1868_267
[161] BSA_Soissons_VII_
1897_III
[162] BSA_Soissons_XI_
1867_68
[163] Barker_1893_79
[164] Montalembert_1839_11
[165] AA_XXI_1861_254
[166] SG_LXIV_Nîmes_
1897_VI
[167] Inventaire_général_
1883_142
[168] BA_Comité_1888_28
[169] Mérimée_1843_7
[170] SG_LIII_Nantes_1886_35
[171] Hunnewell_1898_253
[172] Caumont_V_1835_381
[173] Hugo_1832_614
[174] AMPF_VI_1892_106
[175] BM_XXXVI_1870_
327–328
[176] Montalembert_1839_4
[177] Caumont_V_1835_
380–381
[178] Despois_1868_184–197
[179] Despois_1868_229–244
[180] Réunion_BA_
XIII_1889_755
[181] AA_IV_1846_189
[182] Rey_1839_226
[183] Rey_1839_224
[184] Rey_1839_225
[185] Rey_1839_223
[186] Hugo_1832_607–608
[187] Bourassé_1841_306–307
[188] Marmottan_1891_20
[189] ASA_Château-
Thierry_1895_234
[190] SG_LXIV_Nîmes_1897_
39–40
[191] BM_IX_1843_357–358
[192] Bull_Comités_
Historiques_1849_132

[193] BM_XI_1845_381
[194] BM_XXVI_1860_456–457
[195] Massé_1730_5
[196] Caylus_III_1759_
322–323
[197] Montalembert_1839_213
[198] Acad_Toulouse_II_
1830_237–238
[199] Mège_1835_71–72
[200] AA_I_1844_I
[201] BSA_Nantes_IX_
1869_171–172
[202] AA_XIII_1853_163–164
[203] BSA_Eure-et-Loire_
IV_1867_44
[204] BM_XXXVI_1870_
362–363
[205] SG_XLII_Châlons-sur-
Marne_1875_384–5
[206] AHA_Château-Thierry_
1883_38–39
[207] Boitel_1843_II_496
[208] AHA_Château-
Thierry_1883_89
[209] BSA_Nantes_VI_
1866_242
[210] BCA_Seine-Inférieure_
XII_1903_353
[211] Revue_Maine_
XIX_1886_271–272
[212] Mège_1835_8–9
[213] AA_I_1844_184–185
[214] Charvet_1869_40
[215] BM_IX_1843_107
[216] BM_XII_1846_484
[217] ASA_Château-
Thierry_1869_59–60
[218] Terninck_1879_305
[219] STA_Reims_
LXXI_1883_79–80
[220] Revue_Génie_Militaire_
IV_1890_549
[221] Pieyre_III_1888_161–62
[222] Déclassement_
Narbonne_1888_11

[223] SG_XX_Troyes_1853_
293–294
[224] Flammermon_1881_126
[225] Dochier_1812
[226] BSA_Drôme_III_
1868_34
[227] Dochier_1812
[228] SG_XXXVII_Lisieux_
1870_325–326
[229] Revue_Comminges_X_
1895_18–19
[230] AMPFX_1896_122
[231] Reclus_1903_28
[232] BSA_Midi_1897_82
[233] Tarbé_1844_210
[234] PV_Seine-Inférieure_I_
1818–1848_229–230
[235] AA_IX_1849_59
[236] PV_Seine-Inférieure_
II_1849–1866_147–148
[237] Demilly_1860_3–4
[238] Demilly_1860_16
[239] Goussard_1861_249
[240] Allmer_&_Dissard_I_
1888_2–3
[241] AMPF_X_1896_56
[242] BCA_Seine-Inférieure_
V_1879–1881_440
[243] BA_Comité_1901_
CLXXX–CLXXXI
[244] BA_Comité_1911_
158–158
[245] BCA_Seine-Inférieure_
V_1879–1881_279
[246] BSA_Midi_1888_52
[247] BCA_Narbonne_
VIII_1904_XLV
[248] Espérandieu_IV_1911_3
[249] Trumet_de_
Fontarce_1896_115
[250] Moliner-
Violle_1891_45–46
[251] BSA_Touraine_
XIII_1901–1902_274

CHAPTER 5

The Organisation of Scholarship and Museums

Archaeology and Archaeologists

De toutes parts, il se fit comme une levée en masse, sous l'influence de l'état à qui on est redevable de ces premières tentatives. Bientôt on organisa des comités officiels; on créa des commissions; on fonda des sociétés. Ecrivains, journalistes, prêtres, laïcs, chacun se fit archéologue, comme autrefois on se faisait soldat. Et en ce moment, une correspondance active, partie du ministère de l'instruction publique, centre de toutes les communications archéologiques, lie entre eux tous les hommes de nos départements qui se vouent à ce genre de recherches; des publications nombreuses nourrissent leur zèle, et répandent partout le goût des études sérieuses et l'amour des choses d'autrefois. / Grâce à cette révolution aussi heureuse qu'inopinée, tous les monuments entassés sur notre sol, et qui ont survécu à tous nos bouleversements, quel que soit du reste, leur âge, leur destination, furent environnés de respect, et l'on étendit sur leur vieillesse décrépite ou prématurée comme un manteau de charité qui prolongera leur existence ou du moins honorera leurs derniers moments.[1] [1847]

M. Décamp, a mover and shaker at Soissons, editor of the *Journal de Soissons*, and instrumental in the creation of the local museum, provides above a well-judged and ironical creation myth for the universal sweetness and light that flooded French archaeology, for which of course the previous century had been a preparation.[1] We have already seen from the examples above that this was indeed a myth, and just how fragile, slow and faltering were the various processes involved. Today such myths are still in place, being dismantled by the sceptical.[2]

---

1 Grell 1995, 3–106 for education; 107–191 for academic institutions, and 192–280 for L'étude des vestiges (including 222–231 les antiquités nationales); Schnitzler 1998 43–71 for soceties, celtomania and publications; 73–104 Le temps des antiquités nationales.

2 Demoule 2012, 86–110: Nos ancêtres les Gaulois? Including La construction d'un mythe consolateur, followed by 111–129 Les Romains: nos civilisateurs? and 130–161: Le Moyen Âge: une longue nuit? Grell 1995, 1113–1135: Gaulois et Romains, le mythe des Gaulous, le problème de la conquête romaine.

© KONINKLIJKE BRILL NV, LEIDEN, 2015 | DOI 10.1163/9789004293717_007

THE ORGANISATION OF SCHOLARSHIP AND MUSEUMS

149

> La science de l'archéologie et de l'histoire est, au surplus, une science éducatrice par excellence: elle élargit et élève l'esprit; elle excite et entretient l'amour de la petite patrie et, avec lui, le dévouement à la grande.[2]
> [1902]

But if the public could be educated in archaeology, what about the archaeologists themselves? According to J-A Brutails, member of the Académie Française, and archivist of the Gironde, these were indeed a mixed bunch, often lacking in any sense of historical method,[3] with a tendency to neglect facts for fanciful opinions[4] in what was "moins une science positive qu'une longue initiation, une éducation de l'œil et de l'esprit."[5] Indeed, unlike the exact sciences, archaeology required no lengthy studies but, as an 1878 congressist declared to his fellows about to go on an excursion, and with no sense of irony, the discipline

> a cela de précieux pour l'homme du monde, qu'il peut s'en occuper, presque sans autre initiation que quelques lectures attentives, quelques excursions qui sont pour lui plutôt un plaisir qu'une fatigue.[6]

And not just archaeologists, but architects as well: "M. Viollet-le-Duc me permettra de lui rappeler que depuis cinquante ans, les archéologues ont plusieurs fois obtenu la conservation de monuments que les architectes voulaient détruire."[7]

The task of archaeologists, we are assured in 1838, was "de dérober à la faulx du temps et au marteau des démolisseurs, en les réparant, ou en les reproduisant par le dessin ou par des descriptions fidèles, les monuments antiques que possède notre contrée, et de fouiller les archives et les bibliothèques."[8] The definition does not suggest, let us note, that archaeologists dug anywhere other than in libraries and archives; and of course antiquarians had been collecting artefacts in their cabinets for centuries.[9] This mission statement was followed by the creation of a national society,[10] and praise for Caumont and the problems he had faced in promoting the subject: "Qui pourrait dire les obstacles, les mécomptes, les dégoûts de tout genre contre lesquels il a dû lutter pendant cette laborieuse croisade de vingt-cinq années?"[11] The Society was also in the forefront of mitigating problems with architects: "Elle a de plus fourni des modèles d'architecture de différents siècles aux architectes chargés de restaurer d'anciennes basiliques, et qui ont reclamé ses conseils."[12] By 1853, "L'art chrétien et national a été successivement retrouvé, célébré, enseigné et pratiqué."[13] Archaeologists were credited with having helped against the vandalism of religious architecture[14] and as agents in the development of nationalism,[15] especially with the encouragement of a Gallic identity.[3] Added to this, most finds and excavations were largely fortuitous.[4] As one scholar remarked, writing of a speculators' project to dismantle the cloisters at Condom (thankfully blocked), ruining monuments was as bad as pulling families apart, "car dans ce premier cas on appauvrit la nation comme dans le second les individus."[16]

By 1858, "fouiller" could indeed mean digging, and missing opportunities to dig could be reproved.[17] For now the archaeologist's task was to reveal the life and genius of a people: "c'est là tout l'intérêt d'une fouille pour l'archéologue qui va déchiffrer une nouvelle page de l'histoire du passé dérobée à la main du temps."[18] This was indeed exciting work: "l'œil de l'archéologue, à qui les palpitantes jouissances de la fouille sont réservées,"[19] with hints of the necessity for professional competence then following.[20] At the same period the idea gains ground of an "archéologue de profession,"[21] and whatever precisely the term means, it is distinguished from an amateur,[22] emphasising thereby the importance of establishing professional legitimacy and thus authority. Naturally, by the 1880s digging archaeologists are being praised,[23] and they were the ones who were (for example) going to "sauver Sanxay d'une ruine prochaine, qui serait une honte pour l'archéologie française."[24]

Whether such scholars always told the truth about their work and the cadence of finds is another matter. One example is René Cagnat's 1896 Candide-visits-Algeria version of uplifting research there. He restricts his survey to the past fifteen years, which is cunning because so much had already gone; but it is a direct lie (as Cagnat was in a good position to know) to write of "des fouilles heureuses, le ministère de l'Instruction publique y subventionnait les recherches d'officiers, d'administrateurs, de colons même" when all had been complicit in raping the country for decades.[25] Dishonesty also invaded the discovery of finds. The level of expertise of some scholars, and the thirst for antiquities, is illustrated by a man named Chrétin at Nérac (Lot-et-Garonne), who was certainly selling marbles and other antiquities, but where did he get them, and were some of them his forgeries? In 1835 the mayor of Nérac complained about his activies, Chrétin's house was sealed, and an inquest begun, Chrétin explaining where he had got various of the antiquities he sold.[26] The criticism then widened to his having sold real antiquities, but illegally,[27] and probably "improved" actual antiquities from Nérac.[28] He died in 1856 without admitting fraud. Either the skill or the inclination to prove him a forger was not

---

3   Diaz-Andreu & Champion 1996; Dietler 1994, 587–593 for French Nationalism and Celtic Identity.

4   Pinon 2009 surveying XVI–XIX centuries.

THE ORGANISATION OF SCHOLARSHIP AND MUSEUMS

forthcoming. In fact, forgery had long been a common practice, since at least the sixteenth century.

Education

Il faut avant tout populariser la science archéologique; que le meilleur moyen serait d'engager les institutions, tant ecclésiastiques que laïques, à faire suivre aux enfants un Cours d'archéologie, comme cela se fait pour l'histoire naturelle.[29] [1839]

Although its full exploration would require another book, this is the place to flag the importance of education (together with increasing mobility)[5] in the attitudes of both scholars and citizens to the past and the present. France was behind Britain in educational provision, just as Britain was behind the German states, which in the 19th century were developing curricula and methodologies the rest of Europe would emulate. Scholars such as Millin, who networked internationally,[30] were well aware of the happenings in other countries. But some early textbooks were written in France, such as Crosnier's 1835 *Éléments d'archéologie,*[31] still being used twenty years later,[32] as was Caumont's six-volume 1830–1841 *Cours d'antiquités monumentales: histoire de l'art dans l'Ouest de la France, depuis les temps les plus reculés jusqu'au XVIIe siècle, professé à Caen.* What is more, some textbooks were targeted at seminaries as well as colleges,[33] because a continual complaint at archaeological congresses and in societies' journals was the damage caused to churches by well-meaning but ignorant clergy who decided to repair or beautify them. In addition, many universities and other scientific institutions were resistent to the acceptance of archaeology as a discipline.[6] Although Jean-Antoine Letronne held chairs of history (1831) and archaeology (1838) at the College de France, then became

---

5 Robb 2007 ch. 8 Migrants and commuters: "The advent of compulsory education, industrial investment, canals, railways and roads that remained open for most of the year produced changes so dramatic that the older France seems by comparison to have been almost entirely inert, waiting in its mud-clogged villages and unmapped wastes for administrators, doctors, teachers and busybodies to hack their way through the thicket and release it from an ancient spell."

6 Perrin-Saminadayar 2001. Díaz-Andreu_2007_109: "In France the German-inspired reform of the universities during the early years of the Third Republic (1871–1940) encouraged the creation of new chairs of archaeology at the Sorbonne and several provincial universities, these usually being taken by former members of the French School at Athens and Rome." See also Albanese 2008, 64: "By transforming this system into an instrument of social integration, [policy makers] aimed to promote the ideal of national unity and, to this end, elaborated a

152   CHAPTER 5

Director of the National Archives (1840), his scholarly focus was on Greek and Latin inscriptions in Egypt, not France.[7] Hence textbooks are late: Camille Jullian began working on his *Histoire de la Gaule* only in 1896.[8]

By mid-century, however, "Archaeology is there [France] especially fostered and encouraged by the bishops and higher orders of the clergy."[34] It was suggested that primary-school teachers should also help, the idea prompted by a Congrès question in 1869: "Quels services les instituteurs primaires peuvent-ils rendre à l'archéologie? Moyen d'utiliser leur concours pour l'exploration et la conservation des anciens édifices."[35] Well-taught children would grow up with sound ideas, and

> Plus tard ils combattront, si l'on y pense encore, aux conseils de la mairie ou de la fabrique, les destructions inintelligentes, les distractions illégales, les restaurations sans goût, les démolitions maladroites.[36]

Teachers could contact local archaeological societies, which were also concerned to educate the public, the Indre even proposing an archaeological manual specifically for that département.[37] Architects would do likewise for advice on restoration, just as was suggested in mid-century in the Netherlands.[38] But there was still a pull abroad, to the glories of Greece and Rome: in 1880 Jules Ferry, Minister of Public Education projected organising holiday excursions for students at the école normale, to study "historical monuments, relics of archaeology, picturesque views, topographical peculiarities, natural phenomena, the products of industry and agriculture, local traditions, customs, and languages"; but this came seven years after the establishment of a course on archaeology in Rome,[39] while in Greece "les études archéologiques y sont poussées avec autant d'activité que de bonheur,"[40] though not without plenty of destruction at Athens, as at Olympia and Pergamon.[41]

Equally important for our theme, but with space here to be mentioned only in passing, are libraries and archives, repositories of collective memory and identity, "ruines d'où l'on retire encore quelques lambeaux de notre héritage historique."[42] They were often handled brutally by the Revolution, and on occasions considered of little account. Thus the library at Argentan (Orne), it was claimed in 1816, no longer existed whereas, in fact, the designated room was turned into a ballroom the following year.[43] About 1849, most of the

---

  consensual discourse capable of reconciling various elements of diversity such as regional
  particularisms and class differences which threatened to destroy the social fabric."
7 Feyel 2001.
8 Van Andringa 2001.

THE ORGANISATION OF SCHOLARSHIP AND MUSEUMS 153

archives of Saint-Maclou at Pontoise (Seine-et-Oise) were sold off to a local grocer-shop for wrapping material.[44]

Restoration Alternatives[9]

There were plenty of architects who built with few or no qualifications,[45] and were responsible for the recognised and growing problem of barbaric destruction, when important elements could be lost,[46] and equally barbaric restoration, helped by "l'ignorance profonde du clergé des campagnes en matière d'art et d'archéologie chrétienne."[47] When a member of the Dutch Institut Royal suggested in 1857 that it was better to allow old monuments to fall down to give young architects the opportunity to build new, he was fortunately shouted down.[48] This was where archaeology could help since, as was explained in 1844, architects had taken

> une fausse direction, l'ignorance des arts et des procédés anciens pouvaient entraîner les artistes, chargés de restaurations, dans des erreurs déplorables, plus fatales à nos monuments que l'indifférence et l'oubli.[49]

– not all architects, of course, one of whom was even described as "un habile architecte, un savant archéologue, un ingénieur de mérite."[50] Yet the difficulty of restoring a monument to its "physionomie primitive" was still being stated as an aim in 1884,[51] by which time many churches, for example, had been "restored."[52] Indeed, there seemed to be plenty of blame to spread around, one scholar railing in 1847 against "le déplorable mépris des architectes modernes . . . ce triple anathème, d'écrivains injustes, de maçons ignorants et de démolisseurs passionnés."[53]

As a result of several well-publicised "restorations," by 1845, therefore, the practice was frequently viewed as vandalism.[54] This was easily computed at Saintes in 1844, where it was the fifth man down the chain of competence who was really in charge of dealing with the triumphal arch, the Parisian architect having dashed off elsewhere[55] – so much work, so little supervision! At Vendôme the church of S. Martin, already damaged by the Génie, the "restoration led to the collapse of much of the structure with noise like an earthquake, leaving only the tower surviving."[56] Thus the alarm was justified, as was the opprobrium, for many of France's buildings were ruined by arrogant know-alls – presumably archaeologists as well, since one scholar suggested that no dig should be undertaken without the help of an architect,[57] and the

---

9 Léon 1917, 245-347.

well-equipped were even described as "architecte archéologues."[58] Nor was straight reproduction to be encouraged, because such "solutions" "blessent à la fois l'art, l'archéologie et l'histoire."[59] Archaeologists were learning all the time, especially about the Middle Ages, and had written and thereby taught the public: "Ces cours, ces manuels et ces monographies, le public les a achetés, lus, étudiés; il les a comparés à son tour avec les monuments dont il a approfondi la structure et l'ornementation."[60] But architects were often ignorant of archaeology, wrote Champollion-Figeac in 1833.[61] Inevitably that great panjandrum, Viollet-le-Duc, was attacked for his pig-headed tabula rasa approach:

> cet architecte s'est tracé certains préceptes qui n'appartiennent qu'à lui, qu'il suit obstinément, et qui le conduisent à détruire toute œuvre d'art, toute ornementation qui ne remonte pas à la fondation première de nos églises du moyen-âge.[62]

Equally inevitably, he had his supporters: "il a su rétablir avec une ingénieuse fidélité les œuvres des siècles passés,"[63] at the same time supposedly restraining "le zèle restaurateur de ses confrères" by having them consult archaeologists, erstwhile enemies hostile to their "restoration" work,[64] as well as to the vandalistic intentions of prelates.[65]

Initiatives on the Ground: The Gard

The consequence of attempts at restoration would be that surviving antiquities were largely stripped of later accretions and restored, often ruthlessly, with no account being taken of their post-antique history. The attempt to have such work done voluntarily would inevitably mean tensions between preservation on the one hand, and re-use on the other. This problem of the conceptual distance between the preservers and the re-users is, of course, age-old, and can be illustrated by a report from A. N. Meusnier, the architect commissioned to conserve the antique monuments of Nîmes. He found pieces of a marble inscription at the site where the new Palais de Justice was being built and, on enquiry, found that the workmen had already built a similar piece into a new wall: they found it, copied out the inscription, and left it in place. The previous year, Meusnier complained to the prefect that the workmen refused his order to take antique pieces out of the same excavations, protesting that he did not have the necessary authority. Nevertheless, by 13 July 1808, permission was given to transport the remains of a monument found on the Beaucaire road to the Temple de Diane, and on 15 July 1809 Paris authorised a dig in the well on the site of the Maison Carrée, in which it was hoped to find antiquities – alas, in vain.[66]

THE ORGANISATION OF SCHOLARSHIP AND MUSEUMS

As a result of the 1819 circular, the Commission pour la Recherche et la Description des Monuments antiques du Gard was established on the 3 December 1819. This was not a success, as M. Grangent, Ingénieur en Chef des Ponts et Chaussées, made clear in a letter to the Prefect of 19 February 1821, for not only was the task enormous, but it was unpaid. For our purposes, the initiative is important for what it omits as much as for what it includes. In the Gard, for example, the city of Nîmes was excluded from the survey because of work already published. And although it indicates a willingness to uncover and study monuments, the emphasis is (perhaps naturally) on Gallic, Roman and then post-mediaeval material.

The work of the Commission for the Département du Gard had also to fight casual damage done to the monuments, including the carting away of their stones. On 19 June 1821, for example, a decree was published protecting the monuments:

> Considérant que ce serait en vain que la munificance royale et les efforts généreux du Conseil de ce Département n'auraient rien épargné pour assurer la restoration et la durée des Monuments qui font la gloire de cette contrée, si leur conservation ne devenait l'objet d'une surveillance spéciale et assidue...La Maison Carrée et tous les matériaux destinés aux réparations de ce précieux Monument, sont placés sous la sauve-garde des citoyens et sous la surveillance des autorités municipales."[67]

It was forbidden to mutilate this or any of the monuments of the Gard, and the Decree was to be posted on the outside and inside of all monuments, as well as in the villages and post-relays near to the Pont du Gard. Indeed, it may be that the Pont du Gard had suffered particularly badly; in the Middle Ages it had, according to Mazauric,[10] furnished materials for the three Nîmes-area churches of Bezonce, Saint-Gervasy and Saint-Hilaire,[68] a nearby chapel,[69] and also coffin-lids for sarcophagi at the necropolis of Saint-Baudile-hors-les-Murs at Nîmes.[70] Later constructions in the surrounding countryside are also partly built from its remains.

Museums and International Prestige

Progress is generally incompatible with the survival of earlier landscapes and townscapes, but museums at first sight fit the new dispensation, preserving for admiration small trophies of the past, because generally it is only the smaller objects which survive. They are the alibi for continuing destruction

---

10   Mazauric 1934, 4.

156 CHAPTER 5

and vandalism, storage-barns for the tattered ruins of the past and (some hoped) their contents veritable models for contemporary and future good taste; memory has so often been replaced by amnesia. This is not a book centrally focussed on museums, but we must briefly inspect their origins and purpose in order to assess their impact in 19th-century conservation. Since it was the 19th century that rivetted in place the understanding of what museums were for, it is important to highlight what they might have been – but were not. This is a counter-factual procedure, but the brief account below should underline that museums could have been very different, had other priorities and choices prevailed.

The great early museums were not repositories for local antiquities, but for grand pieces given, bought, smuggled or stolen from abroad, first Rome, and then Greece and the Middle East. Their purpose was to complement aesthetic knowledge, and (for some optimists) to improve and direct artistic production by offering suitable models. During the Revolution, the Louvre (whose complexion already had political overtones)[11] was indeed named the Muséum National, because it contained national property – the relicts of royal collecting. But it was not a museum which targeted French productions, and Lenoir's Musée des Monuments Français (the name itself a new idea, according to Léon)[12] came into existence to house the orphans of the Revolution,[71] not because there was any direct move away from foreign and toward French objects. Díaz-Andreu suggests that the 19th century saw a new focus on national antiquities, on prehistoric remains, and on an historical methodology that "sanctioned the entry into the university curriculum of the fields of epigraphy, numismatics and history of art, all three using material retrieved through archaeology."[13] All true, but France came late to the game: it was the Germans to the forefront for education, as Díaz-Andreu relates, and the British for national antiquities, including prehistory. The rivalry between France and Germany, especially after the Franco-Prussian War (a disaster which, it is claimed, helped cement French identity),[14] derived from French knowledge that they were behind: most

---

11 McClellan 1994.

12 Léon 1917, 31.

13 Díaz-Andreu 2007, 318–319, of Lenoir's museum, in a section on national archaeology in Europe: "the objects it exhibited, together with the political difficulties it faced and its ultimate closure, provide a good example of the way in which the balance between the antiquity of the Great Civilizations and a national past was still weighted towards the former."

14 Lowenthal 1998, 64: "Misfortune continued to cement French unity. Defeat by Germany in 1870 impelled pedagogues to promote French language unity as patrimony. Regional dialects and other local legacies succumbed to nationalist mystique. "The fatherland is

THE ORGANISATION OF SCHOLARSHIP AND MUSEUMS

scholarship flowed from Germany to France, thanks to her far superior educational system (an object of envy for the British as well), and that in spite of France's long and distinguished record of commissions, lists of monuments, congresses and publications, which we shall consider below. Was the Pergamon Altar in Berlin, a victory monument, intended as a celebration of Germany's victory in the war?[15]

International competition for antiquities was fierce in the 19th century, as it had been already for two centuries, with ambassadors and consuls in Britain and France understanding monument acquisition as part of their job description.[16] There is plentiful material for a different book, but the fact is mentioned here only in passing, because France never seems to have considered that she might gain points by focussing more on her own Roman antiquities rather than continuing to plunder Italy and points east. What we might call the Elgin Defence was still being evoked in 1870s, France self-consciously excusing her continuing depradation of foreign antiquities. It was indeed a race, and France was conscious that since the Revolution that she was losing her artefacts abroad.[72] Thus in 1838 the paucity of survival at Nîmes was contrasted with the numbers of her antiquities enriching various European museums.[73] A. W. Franks, Keeper at the British Museum, spoke in 1850 of "two Roman fibulae, recently obtained in France,"[74] and in 1857 he bought the eponymous Franks Casket (a unique Anglo-Saxon artefact) in Paris, later presenting it to the British Musem. A Roman silver situla, retrieved at Vienne in 1842, also reached England.[75] The Prussian consul in Smyrna, outwitted in acquiring an antique prize, wrote wearily that "l'homme propose et les Anglais disposent."[76] It is an index of her insecure monuments legislation[77] as well as a general nonchalance that France continued to lose portable objects abroad.

In 1876, Sommerand observed that several countries were now following France in establishing such commissions,[78] but does not name them. Mérimée complained in 1843 of the riches in German and English museums, some of them exported from France because French purchasers were not to be found.[79] England was certainly ahead in modernisation (especially as measured by kilometres of railway track), and its track-record in preserving

---

like a great family," exhorted an 1878 directive. It "is not your village, your province, it is all of France," its whole chronicle thus sanctified."

15 Bilsel 2003, 125, the Pergamon Altar: "even though we cannot establish whether the original altar was intended to celebrate Eumenes II's victory over the Celts, there is little doubt that fin-de-siècle Germany embraced the monument as one that crowned the Prussian victory over France."

16 Omont 1902, passim.

antiquities was not spotless.[80] Nevertheless some scholars believed that in England "L'état de démolisseur était inconnu."[81] This was untrue: "restoration" was an equally contentious problem across the Channel,[82] as was vandalism,[83] narrated with glee by the French for India (where they had lost nearly all their own colonies).[84] In 1787–9, for example Young noticed the many wooden houses in Abbeville – "their brethren in England have been long ago demolished."[85] Nor were the English slow in seeing the possibilities in French vandalism: in 1817 the Prince of Wales wanted to take the Fontevrault statues back home; he might have been influenced by the dilapidation of the the the monastery (which was a prison from 1804 to 1963). However, the Prefect pointed out to him that the figures represented were counts of Anjou as well as kings of England, and that "les monuments qui rappellent ces grands souvenirs historiques appartiennent essentiellement au sol français."[86] That this was a lesson some Frenchmen had yet to learn speaks volumes for their conflicted historical consciousness, as they reacted to the tensions between a future, modernist orientation and the backward, nostalgic one so often at work. Just how little was known by some about conditions in England is reflected in the curious notion that England was still in the 1880s "par excellence la terre classique des vieilles coutumes," while conceding that these were exhibited "au milieu des innovations les plus raffinées de la civilisation moderne."[87] Nevertheless, in 1847 there was strong opinion against placing the statues in a museum, and in favour of replacing them at Fontevrault or in some other religious environment.[88]

Museums in Provincial France[17]

Il est évident pour tout le monde qu'il y a une très-grande utilité à créer des musées d'antiquités, d'abord pour la conservation des objets antiques et ensuite en raison des avantages qu'ils peuvent procurer, pour l'étude des arts, de l'histoire, de la topographie et des usages de la région dans laquelle ces précieux monuments sont découverts. [1873][89]

Why were museums instituted? For education, certainly, as we have seen; and the destruction caused during the Revolution left a lot of waifs and strays which could be collected together.[90] Their gathering would be beneficial:

---

17 Poulot 2008, 185: En deux siècles les musées se sont inscrits dans le mémoire culturelle française – and developed an administration (46–62) which helped parameters for the Commission des Monuments. Seigel 2012, chap. 12: Public places, private spaces. The transformation of culture: an outline.

THE ORGANISATION OF SCHOLARSHIP AND MUSEUMS

"c'est s'enrichir soi-même par un acte généreux, profitable à l'instruction de tous; c'est prévenir une destruction inconsciente des monuments à conserver de notre vie publique et privée,"[91] and perhaps attract visitors from outside the region.[92] One thrust was for the creation of regional museums,[93] and especially local museums, defined by Reinach in 1890 as "un local convenablement approprié où les antiquités régionales sont déposées et soigneusement tenues en état."[94] This did not often happen. As was remarked of Nancy in 1837, finds were "jeté pêle-mêle dans une salle, et ne peut être examiné, encore moins dessiné."[95] Guizot had made the same point in 1833: "une foule de dépôts, surtout dans les départements, où les pièces les plus anciennes s'égarent ou deviennent indéchiffrables, faute des soins nécessaires à leur entretien."[96] Some museums, such as Bourges,[97] seemed interested in reconstructing retrieved monuments. But Quatremère de Quincy had already disputed the utility of museums, writing in 1815 that "depuis qu'on a fait des Musées pour créer des chefs-d'œuvre, il ne s'est plus fait de chefs-d'œuvre pour remplir les Musées,"[98] and describing them as more-or-less useless ragbags, as "ces réceptacles de ruines factices qu'on ne semble vouloir dérober à l'action du temps, que pour les livrer à l'oubli."[99] To his mind, as expressed in 1791, antiquities should be left on-site,[100] for "le vrai Musée c'est leur pays, leur cité,"[101] and "Quatremère nous exhorte à remuer notre Grèce ou notre Italie, la Provence, dont l'amphithéâtre de Nîmes serait le musée adéquat. 'Le reste, c'est la convoitise de Verres.' "[102]

Provincial museums are generally small-scale entities, and spolia from even a small ring of walls would fill several of them. As for rebuilding any of the monuments of which such walls were constructed, this was rarely considered. This is a pity, for the raw materials were sometimes available, as at Langres, for a funerary monument,[103] putative sculptures and inscriptions from a triumphal arch[104] and, albeit in the 17th century, a "palace."[105] Leaving the walls in place preserved historicity and the picturesque, and might attract tourists. But then again tourists would inevitably arrive and stay seduced by the attractions of modernity – a railway station, clean streets, no beggars,[106] recognisable monuments, and hotels. An additional conundrum was that cleaning up old and picturesque sites (such as collections of wooden houses) could entail the destruction of some of the very monuments which made them attractive and, in the case of ancient remains, the crumbling concrete cores of Roman ruins long stripped of any interesting features would attract few except the experts. Museums and technology were the answer: worthy elements from destroyed houses at Rouen went into the museum,[107] as did the débris found during road-building, as at Nantes (and also from houses near the old walls),[108] together with photographs of what was to be destroyed.[109] Hence museums

160   CHAPTER 5

often acted as small-scale storage for what remained from dismembered sites, as at the destruction of Saint-Evremont at Creil (Oise) in 1890 in favour of a porcelain factory. Here "nos collègues de Senlis ont pu toutefois obtenir des administrateurs de la manufacture quelques-uns des motifs les plus intéressants, des corniches, des fenêtres; et ils pourront ainsi conserver dans leur musée un souvenir de cet intéressant monument roman."[110]

Several museums were formed from earlier piecemeal collections (although many of these were subsequently dispersed and their contents lost).[111] At Rennes (Île-et-Vilaine) in 1845 the archaeological society angled for "quelques-uns des objets curieux enfouis depuis long-temps dans les combles de la mairie ou du palais de Justice;"[112] but apparently did not manage to preserve much of what was found.[18] At Bourges blocks spent twenty years in a pile, and open to the air, in the garden of the Archbishop's Palace;[113] a similar location housed those at Reims,[114] and material from the Cathedral would also come to the museum, which had yet to find a site.[115] At Nantes, there were slim pickings for the museum, for most material had already been reused in later buildings.[116] To create a museum was clearly an honour amongst scholars but, if we believe Alexandre du Mège, the Société Archéologique falsely claimed parentage for the Museum at Toulouse, although it had not actually been founded when the Museum opened.[117] Other towns surveyed in 1874 uncovered monuments mouldering away: while the tiny town of Sault (Vaucluse) could mount and curate a decent collection:

> à Orange, aussi bien qu'à Vaison, l'on a tout vendu ou laissé perdre; qu'à Carpentras les inscriptions sont remisées dans un cellier humide... Saint-Paul-Trois-Châteaux n'a pas le moindre débris à montrer en preuve de son antique importance... Valence ne parvient pas à trouver une place pour les siennes... Grenoble... enfouit la plupart et les plus intéressantes des siennes dans une cave, une sorte d'oubliette interdite au public.[118]

Belgium faced similar problems, for example at Arlon, where multitudes of blocks were retrieved from the ramparts. Before a museum was formed, they went into a cellar where, "ensevelies dans une obscurité crépusculaire, les vieilles pierres... n'éveillèrent plus que la curiosité de quelques archéologues de profession. Le public les ignorait ou les dédaignait."[119]

---

18   Pouille 2008, 24–30 for Historique des recherches: l'abondance de la moisson de mobilier archéologique effectuée... permettent également de prendre conscience de l'ampleur des destructions de vestiges archéologiques ayant eu lieu à cette époque.

THE ORGANISATION OF SCHOLARSHIP AND MUSEUMS

161

Indeed, should towns have museums? Some were all in favour of knocking down the past and modernising, "Mais un abri pour de vieilles pierres, de vieux pots presque toujours cassés, d'antiques ferrailles, à quoi bon? de quelle utilité cela peut-il être?"[120] Then again, where were museums to be housed? The existence of overflow was recognised early, when Lenoir's Musée[19] was praised for its contents, but criticised in 1809 for being obviously too small,[121] as well as for being a collection of fragments.[20] Redundant churches were one possibility, as at Narbonne (which by 1900 counted well over 1,500 decorated blocks),[122] or Béziers,[123] while at Dijon one was sought from 1803 but took time to be instituted.[124] Historic buildings in danger of demolition, or protected ancient monuments, were an obvious answer. The Hôtel-Dieu at Chartres was suggested for a musée lapidaire in 1867, but the structure was destroyed;[125] at Poitiers they were housed in the Baptistery of S. Jean for a while, before moving elsewhere.[126] By late in the century, scholars were suggesting that antiquities "doivent être conservées le plus près possible de leur lieu d'origine."[127] This was hardly original since, as already noted, in 1796 Quatremère de Quincy had suggested using standing ancient monuments to house retrievals.[128] Although museums were often located in disestablished churches, the strangest suggestion was for Narbonne, namely fixing three or four thousand blocks to the façade of the Cathedral: "Là, ce colossal mémento de la civilisation antique, accolé à ces palpables souvenirs du moyen-âge, se dresserait en face de cette création qui symbolise la civilisation moderne."[129] This was suggested in the knowledge that the designated storage site was clearly too small.[130]

Another problem concerned the attitudes and aspirations of the towns themselves, for in the course of the 19th century, and Paris excepted (where Haussmann transformed the city), they did not develop what we would call today an urban development plan, designating what was to be preserved, updated, or built anew. The storage problem has still not been solved; a 1995 publication of some of the Roman blocks from Saintes notes that the town

---

19   Lagarde 1979, 13–30: Alexandre Lenoir ou l'idée de monument historique.

20   Bilsel 2003, 20: "Lenoir's "depot" was to become an ambitious museum of Gothic architecture – the first of its kind – which intended a historical and didactic presentation of the architecture of the nation... It suffices to recall Quatremere de Quincy's relentless campaign against the Museum of French Monuments, which ultimately succeeded in establishing that a museum of fragments, which displaced "originals" from their context, was an unacceptable transgression of the Neoclassical canon."

museum is a tip, just like that at Narbonne.[21] It is a mixture of new research and town upheavals generating the books which put order into the blocks, not the museums.[22] This was not a new development, since 19th-century publications by scholars such as Millin[23] produced paper museums which in some respects paralleled Lenoir's physical collection of waifs from the Revolution.

Another aspect of museums which impacts on our main theme, and which is considered below, is what museums decided to collect. Beginning as Cabinets of Curiosities, small and easily transported objects were the norm, although the 19th century sometimes beat its technological breast by importing large sculptures and reliefs. Except for displays of capitals, bases, pediment sections and the like, architecture was generally off the agenda. The Pergamon Museum in Berlin is a conspicuous exception in its erection of some architectural elements to full height from base to entablature, such as temple and gate sections from Miletus, the Pergamon Altar, the Ishtar Gate from Babylon, and a section of the "desert fortress" from Mschatta. In this category of biggest-is-best, for the classical world at least, neither the British Museum nor the Louvre can really compete, although the French attempted to muscle in on the glories of Pergamon with various publications.[24]

Outside London, Paris and Berlin, small-object collections became the staple of 19th-century museums, and the evident lack of interest in architecture condemned many earlier structures in France to mouldering decay or demolition. If this seems an extreme statement, consider the technological advances of that century, which allowed the erection of large buildings, and especially in iron – engine sheds and railway stations. Had the will been there, more structures could have been saved either on site or after transportation to an

---

21   Tardy 1995, 5: l'un des musées lapidaires les plus riches de l'Europe. Des centaines de fragments provenant de portiques, de temples, de maisons ou de tombeaux s'y entassent en un désordre pittoresque qui n'est pas sans rappelelr celui du Musée Lamourgier de Narbonne.

22   Tardy 1989, 11: Les recherches qui se sont développées ces vingt dernières années ... sur l'archéologie gallo-romaine, liées aux profonds bouleversements qui ont affecté le cœur des villes ... suscité la publication de nouvelles monographies urbaines.

23   Hurley 2013, passim.

24   Bilsel 2003, 129: "The French response to the Pergamon Panorama of 1886 [a reconstruction of the city] came more than a decade later with the monumental publication of Pergame by the historian Maxime Collignon and the architect Emmanuel Pontremoli. Alarmed by the German appropriation of major archaeological sites in the Eastern Mediterranean, the French Ministry of Education sponsored a number of archaeological publications, which brought together a prize-winning architect of the Beaux Arts academy with a historian of antiquity, usually a member of the French School in Athens."

THE ORGANISATION OF SCHOLARSHIP AND MUSEUMS 163

iron-frame, railway-station-like museum complex, perhaps something like Paxton's structure for the 1851 Great Exhibition. This did not happen for three reasons: lack of any continuing, coherent central policy about the conservation and protection of artefacts; a propensity to prefer Greece before Rome, with an appreciation of mediaeval monuments which grew only slowly amongst the populace (the commissions were way ahead); and local preferences for things new, which relegated the protection of the past much further down the list for financial assistance than all-mod-cons modernity. Feeding museums with objects and publishing an annual set of papers was only part of what scholarly associations should accomplish: new research and more members were essential.[131] As one scholar insisted, museums were useful, because "de même à la vue des objets qui composent un musée, à l'aspect des monuments qui décorent nos villes, on peut apprécier les transformations sociales des peuples."[132] Municipalities did not necessarily agree, witness the accommodation problems faced at Nîmes in 1883, where "Ils ne tardèrent pas à considérer comme sans utilité ce musée lapidaire dont ils ne saisissaient pas assurément les enseignements historiques."[133]

Another consequence of the small-objects policy was that nearly every site was stripped of "significant" finds, because on-site museums had not been invented, nor a sufficiency of tourism to feed them. Sites were therefore left without much meaning, for the objects that provided it had been removed. This is a criticism of the very ethos of museums which, vampire-like, suck out the blood of context. In spite of the continuing plundering of sites abroad, some French scholars, as we have seen, thought antiquities should remain in place. English cannon captured in the 15th century at Mont-Saint-Michel should stay there, wrote one, because "ce glorieux trophée, éloigné de la place qui résista si courageusement aux efforts de l'ennemi, n'aurait plus aucun mérite."[134] But cannon are just about indestructible, so what about other antiquities? But what antiquities? The problem in the 1840s was the dearth of proper museum catalogues, so discovering what was available would be a difficult task.[135] Even in the 1860s, works in some museums, such as Évreux, were mouldering away in inchoate heaps,[136] and for others municipalities could not find enough funding.[137]

A more reasoned suggestion than decorating a cathedral with antique bas-reliefs was that intact monuments should be left in place, but that museums should not be raided to send objects back to their source (citing problems of cost, vandalism, and degradation). But this was condemned in 1849 as

vandalisme réfléchi... c'est, il faut l'avouer, un culte archéolâtrique poussé jusqu'au fanatisme le plus extravagant; c'est une impéritie aveugle,

164 CHAPTER 5

déguisée sous les formes trompeuses et séduisantes d'une science trans-
cendante et d'un patriotisme épuré.[138]

Fortunately, few scholars could be accused of such archeolatry, for they knew
all too well that funding, security and, above all, interest on the part of the
general public were lacking. The suggestion might have met with approval
after 1900, when mass tourism was coming on stream; but by then even fewer
sites were available for such treatment, and scholars restricted themselves to
arguing that finds from one site be kept together, in the face of the Ministry's
propensity to spread objects amongst several museums.[139] But archaeolatry
was indeed to be found in the scholarly congresses, when sermons to the converted, veritable flights of fancy, assured them that

> sous l'habile main de l'Archéologue, chaque morceau de pierre ... et tout
> ce monument détruit depuis tant de siècles ... se reconstruisent dans
> leur forme, leur caractère, leur signification; on assiste, enfin, à une résur-
> rection monumentale opérée à la voix de la science et du génie.[140]

Like Tertullian, they believed because it was impossible. Of course, out in the
countryside, and even today, very few sites can be preserved "intact." Towns are
another matter, and their monuments can be divided into ecclesiastical and
civil. Although many churches were lost in the 19th century, those saved had
an immediate and obvious re-use value. But this was not the case with housing
from centuries past, perhaps (horror!) of wood rather than of dressed stone,
and by various definitions old-fashioned. Thousands such properties were
swept away in modernisation, by street widening or alignment.

If the above strictures are accepted, then museums were far from being the
obvious the solution to preserving the past. Instead, we might argue that they
accelerated destruction by appearing as a panacea for the abandonment of the
sites themselves, the alibi being their neat labelling and (eventual) cataloguing
of artefacts, while the sites mouldered away, or were simply stripped for their
materials. This was indeed the result, if not the intention. When in 1904 the
achievements of Arcisse de Caumont and Montalembert were reviewed and
praised, along with the Comité des monuments historiques, as a crusade, it
was not the survival of sites that was counted a success, but rather "gravure sur
cuivre, gravure sur bois, lithographie, photographie."[141]

Museums were an arm of education, but even in 1903 they were described
as "encore trop rares dans nos provinces."[142] The main problem for scholars
of antiquity was one which haunted other centres such as Narbonne, and may

THE ORGANISATION OF SCHOLARSHIP AND MUSEUMS

be briefly stated as a question: if large quantities of antiquities from Roman monuments formed the walls, what was to be done with them if they were indeed retrieved? Leaving the walls in place was of little use for most centres, where the blocks were buried in the foundations, or revealed, but with the sculpture or inscriptions inward-facing. Nîmes was told by the Minister of the Interior in 1840 that it did not need a museum because "Votre ville est un musée."[143] Not to be fobbed off, Nîmes nevertheless initiated a musée lapidaire.[144] Arles, for a variety of reasons, lost many moveable antiquities, some of them abroad.[145] Dijon had two museums by 1860, and many pieces displayed in houses about the town.[146] Museum creation naturally depended on local initiative; thus even tiny Lectoure (Gers) had one by 1871.[147] Single-focus museums, depending on a single monument, were the most manageable: for example, in 1844 a museum of items from the church was formed at Saint-Gilles-du-Gard, and also incorporated eight stone sarcophagi and other pieces found around this small town.[148] A mosaic from the church had already gone to Fontainebleau during the reign of François Ier in 1545, "qu'encor pourtant ie n'y ay ueu employé."[149]

Façadism Nourishes Museums

Once museums were formed, the race was on to fill them, and has now become a marketing exercise.[25] And it does indeed seem to have been a race, with approval given to quantity, presumably because numbers helped balance-sheets and publications. This process may be loosely described as façadism, because the objects were merely the débris from the structures left behind or already destroyed, such as wooden houses, where typically only small façade ornaments would be preserved and the structures destroyed. This was a pity. The Japanese have been relocating large wooden temples since at least the 6th century, and moving whole collections of houses into museums today is routine. But apparently nobody in 19th century France considered such easy rearrangement as a way of accommodating the old in a new location, while still building the new.

Confirmation of the heave-it-don't-keep-it attitude to old architecture surfaces frequently during town road-widening and alignment schemes, when scholars make noise about destroying significant houses. Generally, the houses are destroyed, but sometimes their façades enter the local museum. Thus when a gothic house at Saint-Yrieix (Haute-Vienne) was demolished in 1844, its façade was preserved and taken to the museum at Limoges.[150] At Vendôme,

---

25   Choay 2009, XXXVI–XLIV, Muséification et marchandisation du patrimoine.

with an important wooden house, it was too expensive "de faire figurer ce vieux débris dans notre Musée;"[151] but at Valence it was demolishing houses which uncovered some inscriptions for the museum,[152] whereas the gothic "Maison des Têtes" missed the museum, and was a ruin by 1907.[153] At Orléans in mid-century, the citizens were said to be proud of their restorations,[154] but by 1882 they were knocking down old houses and preserving only façades, the administration asking a commission "de lui indiquer les façades qui, par leur mérite et leur conservation, pourraient être transportées sur d'autres points de notre ville moderne."[155] At Rouen scholars also fought battles with improvers ("la rigidité des alignements, le vandalisme et l'ignorance") to save old houses,[156] hoping in 1859 that "les entrepreneurs soient tenus de rendre à la ville les façades des maisons historiques."[157] Locals also sacrificed to the god of alignment: in Nîmes in 1908 a tradesman in the rue des Lombards demolished his façade (Roman inscription included) "pour la mettre sur l'alignement réglementaire."[158] Such negligent destruction had, of course, been going on for centuries, as we know from inscriptions reused in later buildings. Today, preservation orders make complete demolition difficult or impossible, so retaining just the façades is a widely-used dodge for dealing with an inconvenient past.[26]

Acknowledging the division between a thorough knowledge of site structures and their contents (in a sense, between digging and museums) has spin-offs for the development of archaeology, for collecting objects takes preference over the thorough examination of the sites themselves. Granted that 19th-century excavation techniques left much to be desired, the quantity of retrievals could be staggering. One famous excavator, Frédéric Moreau, digging from the 1870s, is celebrated in 1888 for the quantity of what he uncovered, listed tantalisingly as "300 mosaïques, marbres et peintures à fresques; 29 vases gaulois; 46 vases gallo-romains; 30 vases en verre; 19 monnaies gauloises et romaines; 154 objets en bronze, or et argent; 105 objets en fer, armes, etc.," the commentary being that "tout éloge serait froid devant cet immense travail, et l'énorme quantité d'objets qu'il a révélés."[159] The same man went through Merovingian cemeteries like the Angel of Death, discovering and excavating over 20 years an average of 750 tombs a year in one département.[160] His best-known dig was at Caranda in 1873–90, with the finds going to St-Germain-en-Laye.[161] However, unusually for the period, he published and illustrated some of what he unearthed.

---

26   Loyer & Schmuckle-Molard 2001 for good, wide-ranging papers on this 20th-century, and continuing, phenomenon.

THE ORGANISATION OF SCHOLARSHIP AND MUSEUMS

Cataloguing the Past: Censuses of Antiquities[27]

Depuis l'origine de la Société Française [1834], les questions suivantes ont servi, dans les séances publiques, de base aux enquêtes archéologiques qui ont été dirigées par M. de Caumont. L'année dernière, la Société réunie à Amiens, a demandé que ces questions fussent imprimées et envoyées à tous les membres de la Société, afin que chacun pût y répondre pour le pays qu'il habite. En conséquence, le conseil de la Société invite tous les membres qui recevront cette série de questions à vouloir bien les appliquer au pays ou au canton qu'ils habitent, et à faire parvenir leurs réponses au directeur de la Société, en rappelant les nos. sous lesquels sont classées les questions auxquelles s'appliqueront leurs réponses.[162] [1840]

Caumont was a powerhouse, not simply talking about the work needing to be done, but exemplifying it with much publication, with influential positions in learned societies,[163] and travels around France to search for monuments he could draw. He continued his inventory of monuments, and wrote in 1831 of "des catalogues d'édifices classés chronologiquement."[164] In 1834 Guizot, ministre de l'instruction publique, set up a commission "à faire dresser un inventaire complet, un catalogue descriptif et raisonné des monuments de tous les genres et de toutes les époques qui ont existé ou qui existent encore sur le sol de la France," and this drew breath in 1837 as the Comité des Arts et Monuments.[165] Guizot was praised appropriately in the *Archaeological Journal* in 1845, which remarked on the commission's issuing of

popular treatises on different branches of archaeology in the form of instructions for the use of its numerous correspondents. These instructions, at first brief and incomplete, have by degrees grown into learned treatises.[166]

Conservation was Caumont's first concern, and in 1834 he proposed a Société pour la conservation [et la description] des monumens historiques,[167] and presented the statutes to colleagues at the Poitiers Congress that year. Local archaeological commissions should be formed, and museums, the earlier creation of which he believed would have prevented "la perte de tant de morceaux précieux" because there was nowhere to house them.[168] He knew who he wanted inside the organisation, which would hold sessions tacked on

---

27   Parsis-Barubé 2011, 95–113: L'inventaire comme dressage de la curiosité antiquaire.

168   CHAPTER 5

to the annual congresses,[169] because some attendees were members of both organisations.[170] Monuments should be regularly inspected:

> VI. Les ministres d'état, l'inspecteur général des monumens nommé par le gouvernement, les membres du conseil supérieur des bâtimens, ceux de la deuxième classe de l'Institut, les préfets, les évêques et les recteurs d'académies sont de droit membres de la Société. XI. Les inspecteurs divisionnaires font annuellement des tournées dans leurs ressorts respectifs.[171]

Not everything went to plan, and the 1835 inception of a catalogue of inscriptions in Gaul was still unfinished half a century later, the report incorporating 50 pages of excuses.[172] Lack of manpower was the general reason, Charmes exclaiming in 1886 how silly it was to have expected Vitet alone to have acted as inspector of monuments; and then there were the pie-in-the-sky circulars, noting that one in 1832 "est remplie de bonnes intentions."[173] Similar doubts were expressed about English protective measures,[174] but across the Channel they were quite clear that legislation would work only if the monuments were public property,[175] which was a position never upheld in France. Again, the circulation of questionnaires (a large selection is given in the Appendix) and even learned treatises was all very well, but what happened to them? As Thierry wrote to the minister in 1838, "Votre appel comme le mien a nul pour eux; il n'en est sorti ni une lettre, ni un envoi, ni un indice quelconque. Dans beaucoup de préfectures, nos circulaires sont allées simplement grossir l'amas des papiers de rebut."[176] So if one 1839 correspondant could affirm that "L'histoire et les monuments de la France sont depuis quelque temps étudiés avec une ardente curiosité,"[177] the interest did not extend to many administrators.

We all know that energy can be neither created nor destroyed, but in nineteenth-century France it was certainly channeled hither and thither. The country was very rich in societies and commissions (with no real demarcation between the terminologies) dealing with history, archaeology, books, manuscripts, archives. These provided the scholars who generated the motive power to get monuments catalogued, listed and protected. They might be the work of one town (Narbonne, Angers, Arles), diocesan (Beauvais, Poitiers, Troyes), departmental (Côte-d'Or, Maine-et-Loire, Charente, Constantine), regional (the Midi, the Orléanais), or whole countries (Tunisia, Indo-China). They might deal with archaeology alone (Dijon, Narbonne, Soissons, Saintes, Compiègne), archaeology and history (Angoulême, Limoges, Mayenne), history (Nord, Gascogne, Cher, Paris), historical geography ("de l'ancienne France," "de la Gaule"), antiquities and arts (Seine-et-Oise) although allegiances and

THE ORGANISATION OF SCHOLARSHIP AND MUSEUMS

pairings varied over the years (Narbonne, for example, becoming literary as well as archaeological).[178] Of overarching importance is the Commission des Monuments Historiques, discussed below, and not to be confused with departmental and town versions with the same name (Pas-de-Calais, Sarthe, Côte-d'Or, Bordeaux). The historical dimension also came into play with the great shake-up of France into departments, in helping decide which towns should become chefs-lieux.[28] Some town walls, though decaying, were seen as not only useful for the octroi, but as a claim to chef lieu status, for the inhabitants liked them, and "lient aisément son existence à la préservation d'un patriotisme urbain."[29] Refining Caumont's ideas, the Congrès Scientifique de France set out in 1847 what cataloguing monuments should do:

> c'est les recommander à l'attention de ceux qui étudient, les désigner au respect de tous, c'est en prendre possession, pour ainsi dire, au nom de la science et les défendre contre l'impiété des démolisseurs cupides ou ignorants en les plaçant sous la sauvegarde de l'opinion publique et du bon goût.

All this had been successful, except for acts of vandalism by some towns bordering the Loire which good neighbourliness forbade the speaker to name.[179]

Local archaeological and historical societies provide an abundant overview of scholarly activity and actual digging during the 19th century, and they were roped in by Mérimée to help provide further information on classifiable monuments.[180] Their many Proceedings, often appearing several times a year, offer detailed accounts of their activities, but sometimes they appear to have been blind to opportunities for useful research, and missed taking some important initiatives. Near Saumur, for example, important dolmens went unprotected in the 1860s.[181] Then again, the Société Archéologique de la Touraine neglected an important Gallo-Roman find because of what we might call holier-that-thou "periodic snobbery." The Society was informed in 1895 of the discovery of Gallo-Roman blocks at Yzeures (Indre-et-Loire), where a new church was under construction. This was a site where by tradition S. Eustache had built a church (later much reworked) on top of a temple.[182] The contractor building the new church had found ten blocks, placed them in the

---

28 Ozouf-Marignier 1992, 202–3: Faire valoir l'ancienneté de son histoire est encore pour une ville un des meilleurs arguments . . . la ville se définit par ses possessions . . . le mythe de la ville éternelle; la ville hérité de la durée de ses titres: immémoriaux et inaltérables, ils la projettent hors de l'échelle du temps.

29 Saupin 2002, 49 51.

170   CHAPTER 5

presbytery garden, and the president of the Society did indeed come and look
at them. But he declared them "d'une mauvaise époque," and refused to pay for
the contractor to extract more of them from the earth. Charles Normand them
takes up the story, and recounts the eventual discovery of some 85 blocks, from
what he considers to have been a temple and its altar, plus two votive altars,
the most spectacular blocks forming a gigantomachy.[183]

To set the above census collection in context, and leaving out local and
departmental archaeological and historical commissions,[184] there are others
to lay beside them, perhaps as standard manifestations of any centralised state
with well-educated functionaries, the majority of whom would of course leave
the work to others. The following is merely a sampling:

> Commissions: des Antiquités nationales; archéologique de l'Afrique du
> Nord; archéologique de la Tunisie; arts et monuments historiques; biblio-
> thèques nationales et municipales; Égypte; études des enceintes préhis-
> toriques; fête nationale du 14 juillet; géographie historique de l'ancienne
> France; instruction publique; inventaire des richesses d'art de la France;
> monuments historiques; monuments mégalithiques; publication des
> documents économiques de la Révolution; publication des documents
> archéologiques de l'Afrique du Nord; recherche des chartes et documents
> historiques; topographie des Gaules; voyages et missions scientifiques.

The Commission des Monuments Historiques (CMH) and its Origins[30]

> Ce qui toujours a manqué à la France, c'est d'attacher à cette sorte de
> richesses l'importance qu'elle mérite, de veiller à sa conservation, et
> de chercher, sous le rapport de l'instruction et de l'histoire nationale, à
> en tirer parti. Il n'a jamais existé d'ouvrage méthodique qui présentât
> la nomenclature des monumens de tous les temps, à plus forte raison
> d'ouvrage destiné à en offrir la représentation.[185] [1824]

Caumont's admirable questioning over several decades forms a persistent
attempt to obtain uniform information from the very diverse regions of France,

---

30   Léon 1917, 47–59 for first inventory; 60–84 for classification; 85–98 for budget, 99–138 for
     personnel; Léon 1951, 107–252 for inventory, classification, budget & personnel; Costa_
     Guix_1988_24–26; Bercé 1979 for creation, rôle and budget, but no analysis of what they
     chose to target; This is provided in Bercé 2000, 11–50, including 24ff, Les Monuments
     Historiques: une affaire d'état, with discussion of how buildings were selected.

THE ORGANISATION OF SCHOLARSHIP AND MUSEUMS 171

concerning dolmens, tumuli, gallo-roman and finally mediaeval antiquities and monuments. His reaction to the growing tide of vandalism was to form the *Société française pour la conservation et la description des monuments historiques*, which published the *Bulletin Monumental* from 1834. Networking was a Caumont speciality, and the list of influential citizens and scholars who could propel the Society forward is a long one.[186] He was both energetic and prolific, as the 1873 Table Générale to the *Bulletin* entry under his name demonstrates:

> La suspension de la destruction du château de Montpeyroux...Quand donc les administrations locales auront-elles des idées raisonnables?... Une exploration des monuments celtiques du Finistère...fournit des documents sur l'état de l'art aux époques mérovingiennes et carlovingiennes, puisés dans des sépultures déposées dans plusieurs musées...Il signale aussi la nécessité de répandre les notions archéologiques et historiques parmi les instituteurs...Décentralisation. Qui veut la fin, veut les moyens. Sous ce titre M. de Caumont propose, comme moyen de décentralisation [revolution!], le transfert hors Paris des ministères de l'instruction publique, de l'agriculture et de l'intérieur...Anciennes notes sur quelques églises antérieures à l'an 1050.

For the monuments of France, the first task to be undertaken, the government believed, was conservation. It was for this purpose that the Commission des Monuments Historiques (the term "monument historique" is largely a 19th-century invention)[31] was founded in 1837,[187] requiring a listing and classification of vulnerable monuments.[188] (During this same period, parallel questions of classification and taxonomy were also well underway in the natural sciences, especially geology.) Mérimée was the secretary, and it had two archeologists (Auguste Leprévost and the Baron Taylor) and two architects (Augustin-Nicolas Caristie and Félix Duban). As already indicated, equally important for the development of "monument awareness" was Arcisse de Caumont (1802–1873), who was not only a teacher and author, but also initiated the idea of yearly congresses which, first held in Caen in 1833, migrated from region to region. This was a stroke of genius, because Caumont also initiated an annual questionnaire which, tailored to the region where the meeting was to be held, and completed by congressists, could give vital information not only about local monuments and their treatment, but also publicise recent discoveries. However, while classification could be applied to some important

---

31   Bercé 2013, for a well-illustrated overview, including "L'invention de la notion de Monument historique" (249–50), then Mérimée, then specific monuments at Nîmes.

172 CHAPTER 5

structures, disputes over ownership ensured many problems with maintenance, repair and even survival, particularly with private property. Not all monuments were the property of the state, and private owners could easily get their structures declassified.[189]

It was the unsatisfactory state of French monuments, and the very lack of consistent knowledge about them, that led to the eventual creation of a formal commission, the important names in the development of which were the historians François Guizot, Jules Michelet, and Augustin Thierry, and especially Arcisse de Caumont, Prosper Mérimée and Ludovic Vitet, who appear throughout this book. As outlined above, the Minister of the Interior in 1810, Montalivet, had tried to start a register of monuments, but funds for conservation were only made available in 1819. Guizot had filled the same post during the Revolution, and in 1830 he created especially for Vitet the post of inspector-general of historical monuments, an initiative which, given its range, necessarily spawned various committees, such as the Comité des documents inédits de l'histoire de France (1834), the Comité des arts et monuments (1835), the Comité des documents inédits de la littérature, de la philosophie, des sciences et des arts (1835), and the Commission des Édifices religieux (1848). The Société française d'archéologie was founded in 1834, the year Vitet resigned to start a political career, and was replaced by Mérimée, a veritable powerhouse in the post until 1852, travelling, writing reports, lobbying, and developing a network of correspondants from local archaeological societies.

Census Problems

So just what monuments did France possess, and how many were there? (This was the selfsame problem Britain had, although the question was posed there much later.[190]) Caumont's questionnaire had provided inspiration, but something formal was obviously required, following the great tradition of encyclopaedic lists developing since long before the Renaissance.

The Ministry's idea of having a general census of antiquities was that the Académie Royale des Inscriptions et Belles-Lettres should prepare archives for the whole of France; but they soon realised that the 1810 brief was far too narrow, and excluding material earlier than the Middle Ages, as was explained in a new circular numbered 18 and dated 8 April 1819. This instructed all Prefects to nominate "une personne habile et zélée qui puisse et veuille bien se charger de cet ouvrage, L'objet est important, et ne doit plus être abandonné." Attached to the letter was a memorandum explaining the rationale, but now in much fuller terms. This, together with other Ministry circulars, arranged by date, is given in the Appendix. The details requested were, of course, always impossibly ambitious, as well as vague, and a recipe for never-ending work: All the monuments?

THE ORGANISATION OF SCHOLARSHIP AND MUSEUMS 173

All the roads? All miscellaneous antiquities? Examine attentively? What about *criteria* for inclusion? Rejecting the notion that the framers of the questionnaire were mad, we must conclude that they simply did not realise the quantities of antiquities to be catalogued. This was a task which would take well over a century to bring to a semblance of completion, even accepting that the number of monuments classified would grow and grow over the years, thanks in part to the inevitability of state control.[32] In Antonin Proust's important 1887 list, Roman monuments would not even feature prominently in proportion to later (and earlier, megalithic) survivals.[191]

Yet instead of narrowing the task as a result of the 1819 circular, the 1824 report to the Minister by Walckenaer, Petit-Radel and Laborde asked for yet more cataloguing. The authors perhaps believed their assertion that for monuments "la révolution, plus habile encore que le temps, leur portoit un coup mortel," and that half of them were destroyed in that short period[192] – the "war damage" excuse in action. Information was to be gathered by departmental prefects, with these questions:

> Quels sont les châteaux intéressans, soit par des faits historiques ou des traditions populaires, soit par la forme de leur architecture?
> Dans quelles communes sont-ils situés? Quelles sont les anciennes abbayes qui existent encore dans le département? Où sont-elles situées? Dans quel état sont-elles? A quoi servent-elles maintenant? Que sont devenus, où ont été transportés les dessins, tombeaux, ornemens ou débris curieux qui existoient, au moment de la révolution, dans chacun des châteaux ou abbayes?
> Est-il, dans le département, quelque particulier avec lequel on puisse correspondre sur ces différens objets?[193]

However, no funding was provided for people with expertise to do the work, so naturally the results were poor.[194] Of the 86 departments, 41 provided "des renseignemens complets," 6 only a summary, and 39 sent nothing back,[195] the conclusion being that

> la brièveté des questions insérées dans la première circulaire, et le défaut d'explications sur la nature de ces questions, sont en partie cause que plusieurs des mémoires envoyés n'ont pas répondu au but qu'on s'étoit proposé.[196]

---

32   Léon 1917, 84: la permanence du contrôle de l'Etat, and leading to an increase in the numbers of classified buildings

174   CHAPTER 5

As might have been expected, the vagueness of the questions led to useless answers; so that, for example, the Prefect of the Gard tended to reply in two-line answers such as "an old tower with a more recent section."[197] Even the replies from contributing departments came in slowly.

The reader will see from a study of the Appendix that badly formulated, vague and over-ambitious questionnaires continued for decades, although we have no information about the mechanics of how these were put together, even though some sections were signed by more than one author. The continuing vagueness prompted the Academy, understanding what would be a continuing problem, to suggest delicately in the 1824 Report that census information should again be sought "avec invitation de vouloir bien donner suite aux excellentes intentions qu'il a manifestées par la remise des premiers mémoires,"[198] intention of course being very different from fulfilment. What is more, requirements were frequently revised, including an 1841 circular (see Appendix) which sent out lists of monuments in each department, and "invitait ces administrateurs à réviser la nomenclature qui avait été préparée à l'aide d'indications recueillies dans les bureaux, à la compléter, et à fournir, sur chaque édifice, une série de renseignements succincts."[199]

Equally problematical was the desire to catalogue just about everything. This was easy for scholars in Paris dreaming up the questions, but the result was that impossible targets were set. Of course, publicising the grandeur of French monuments and sites increased enthusiasm, and in a sense the 19th century was continuing the 18th-century encyclopaedic tradition of Montfaucon, Mabillon, caylus and Diderot/D'Alembert. Thus in 1856 the Ministry of Public Instruction decided on a *Recueil des inscriptions de la Gaule et de la France*, and sent out a list of instructions the impossible scope of which is reflected in the first in the list: "recueillir toutes les inscriptions connues, en quelque langue qu'elles soient exprimées, en grec, en latin, en hébreu, en français, ou quelqu'un de nos idiomes provinciaux," and then date, transcribe, and photograph them.[200] Even at a local level, expectations were inflated, with the parameters for a 1902 census of Roman material in the South-West[201] demonstrating how little had been learned about the yawning gap between the desirable and the possible, the gap confirmed by the detail in 20th-century publications.[33] Nevertheless, France seems to have been ahead of Britain in such census activity.[202]

---

33   E.g. Gaillard 1997, inventory by commune, with a level of detail the Commission was trying to extract 150 years previously. Since this volume needed the support of the Conseil Général de la Dordogne, could the whole of France yet be covered thus?

THE ORGANISATION OF SCHOLARSHIP AND MUSEUMS

175

Inscriptions are an important source of information about the ancient world, and a continuing problem for scholars was the propensity of the populace to destroy them, together of course with the imposing monuments on which they were generally located. This was the greater loss, since their production numbers also dipped through time, offering ever less information for identifying structures, people and chronologies. Thus in 1807 Millin maintained that there was only one ancient inscription remaining to be seen in Autun, and he suspected that many later inscriptions reused the verso of earlier ones.[203] In mediaeval France, no doubt inscriptions were devoured as they were in Greece in the 18th century, when Fourmont maintained that over 350 went into the construction of a new tower.[204] Inscriptions vanished in North Africa at a similar rate, in 1885 the AIBL asking the Ministre de l'Instruction Publique to formulate a law to stop the destruction.[205] Town walls were a source for many: by 1834, over 100 had been retrieved at Bordeaux, but only two were dated;[206] at Tours the walls still held visible inscriptions in 1873;[207] at Rennes, "important" inscriptions were retrieved in 1896,[208] several at Béziers,[209] while at Orléans only fragments survived.[210] But in many locations they were scattered around town, in house walls, as at Lyon,[211] Narbonne,[212] or Mirabeau.[213] Cemeteries were a rich source, for example at Cherchel,[214] as of course were churches,[215] because scholars collected later inscriptions as well as Roman ones.

Cataloguing Dilemmas

Cataloguing everything of historical worth in France (even if echoing parallel tasks of cataloguing manuscripts) was obviously to be a gigantic task, even assuming agreement on the types of monument and remains that should be listed. For nobody knew just what there was to be found in a France generally devoid of good roads and full of mysterious countrysides inhabited by sometimes dangerous peasants. The earliest recommendations, by Vitet in 1830, were narrow in scope – but then, he only examined some of the plums in five departments.[216] The Chef de Bureau of the Monuments Historiques in 1837 quickly laid out the real scale of the projected task. One man, he suggested, would need 130 years to deal with every department. He knew what he was talking about, having dealt only with Nancy and Toul: it took him 2.5 months to explore two arrondissements; six weeks hard work for drawings and notes – so four months in all for these, which "sont des moins riches dans la France archéologique." He listed 109 "points remarquables," then made 101 drawings at 48 localities. But he had to traverse 303 locations to find them. He covered 378 leagues [1,512km]; at 10 leagues/day, that is 38 days travelling. Hence on average 7/8 weeks were needed for each larger arrondissement. Weather and bad roads mean six months travelling, six months writing up and drawing: "Vous voyez, monsieur le Ministre, que je ne puis avoir la prétention de terminer seul ce travail."[217] One mitigating feature was that, naturally, the lists were to be compiled in part by reference to scholarly work already done, and it was recommended that mayors and priests be approached so that compilers might be pointed toward promising structures.[218]

Lists were therefore prepared, with attention paid first to threatened monuments, done, as already stated, by circulating questionnaires to the préfets of every département. The tasks of the national and local commissions were immense. The first step toward protecting a range of monuments was to discover what they were, in what quantity, and what needed to be done to protect them. The second was necessarily to set the basic parameters. What types of monuments? What dates? What to know about them? A characteristic of French 19th-century listings is the attention they pay (and which the scholarly societies echo) to mediaeval church architecture, of course because this forms a main glory of French architecture.[219] However, the emphasis is on the monuments themselves, and not on learning about everyday life in the Middle Ages or even later, as we can do today from the work of Le Roy Ladurie or Jacques Le Goff. Thus details of population levels, and of the occupation, use and reuse of earlier monuments, are almost always missing because of the regrettable tendency to leave much of the Middle Ages out of any archaeological investigations. Our modern concept of a monument developing and changing through time was not a preoccupation of the 19th century, because the main impulse was to take them back to their "original" form (whether antique theatres or mediaeval churches) as quickly and cleanly as possible. The French were simply doing what they and other nations did elsewhere, for example to the classical sites of Asia Minor and North Africa, or the Pharaonic and classical sites of Egypt.

Fortunately, efforts were better coordinated in 1841, when Mérimée enquired of prefects which monuments required conservation, and enclosed lists both of monuments already classified, and those already funded.[220] But every inspection, even if it knocked a few monuments off the list, added many more, so that the current list of 2,420 valued monuments was only a start, and restoration costs were going to rocket:

> les progrès des études archéologiques appellent chaque jour l'attention des autorités sur de nouveaux édifices dont on fait, pour ainsi dire, la découverte...Jusqu'à ce jour, 462 affaires seulement ont pu être suffisamment instruites pour que la Commission fût en état d'apprécier

THE ORGANISATION OF SCHOLARSHIP AND MUSEUMS

exactement le chiffre des dépenses qu'entraîneraient les réparations reconnues utiles et nécessaires.[221]

Since the 1836 conservation costs of 120,000 francs soon increased to 900,000 francs, protecting the patrimony was clearly going to be a very expensive business.[222]

Different Owners, Different Problems

By 1862, over 2,000 monuments throughout France had been listed, but if we think forward to Pevsner's *Buildings of England*, in whatever edition, it is clear that 2,000 items scarcely does more than catalogue the obvious. Adding together the 1840 and 1862 listings, few departments got beyond double figures,[34] perhaps some index of accessibility and local interest. The French clearly realised this, for the law of 30 March 1887 was to be a guarantee of conservation, maintenance and restoration.[223] Already in 1876, Ministry questionnaires had been circulated to local administrations with a view to expanding buildings for listing; and restoration without authorisation was forbidden.[224] In 1879 it was suggested that classified monuments should be labelled, giving

au classement une notoriété même locale qui lui manque trop souvent, d'attirer sur l'objet l'attention de la population, de le mettre pour ainsi dire sous la protection de tous, et peut-être même, à l'égard de certains, de leur en faire connaître la valeur.[225]

But establishing the mere existence of promising monuments was not the only problem with drawing up viable listings. Private ownership was an even greater hurdle because, from the very beginning, the State (wrongly and very inadvisedly) set its face against interference with monuments on private property, even conceding they be not classified if the owner was opposed:

La loi de 1887 pour la conservation des Monuments historiques touche à un très grand principe: le droit de propriété, et le respect de ce droit

---

34　Aube 23, Bas-Rhin 19, Bouches-du-Rhône 27, Calvados 39, Charente-Maritime 15, Côte-d'Or 22, Deux-Sèvres 15, Gironde 24, Haute Garonne 14, Haute-Loire 18, Indre-et-Loire 23, Loir-et-Cher 25, Loiret 24, Maine-et-Loire 26, Manche 22, Meurthe-et-Moselle 11, Nièvre 17, Oise 40, Paris 25, Pûy-de-Dôme 26, Seine-Maritime 43, Seine-et-Marne 18, Vaucluse 27, Vienne 20, Yonne 24. Comparisons call to mind the mischievous suggestion that all prehistoric sites within Germany were to be found within bicycling distance of a university.

explique la longue réserve du Gouvernement et des assemblées politiques.[226]

As will become clear, this was a mis-step of gigantic proportions for, without trying to answer Proudhon's 1840 question "Qu'est-ce que la propriété?"
it should have been well known to all that so many structures were built with
reused materials that ownership was customary rather than absolute. In 1877
an Englishman attempted to buy a plot of land near Carnac so he could excavate it more easily, but failed.[227] Indeed one account of attempts to acquire an
ancient monument for preservation noted that the postulant

> serait sage de se hâter, car la vieille sépulture, exposée à tous venants,
> peut disparaître d'un instant à l'autre, au bon plaisir du propriétaire, ou
> sur la désignation de ce terrain pierreux, non clos, comme lieu d'extrac-
> tion de matériaux pour l'entretien des routes et des chemins voisins.[228]

Thus mosaics could be destroyed with impunity,[229] and even church
towers.[230] Of course, ownership often redounded to the middle classes, rather
than the more moveable peasants, which is why the inhabitants of the monuments of Nîmes and Arles, not all of them poor, took decades to be cleared
out. Indeed, householders in ancient monuments knew how to stand firm
and call in the lawyers; so that as late as 1903 in Sens the Society had to compensate the owner of a stretch of the town walls if they wished to get antique
stones out of them – for the owner wished to build a house on top of such
firm foundations.[231] In 1874 one scholar bemoaned the fact that the concept
of "l'utilité publique" (which could be, and was, applied to expropriation for
building roads and railways) had never been defined in law, so that the prin-
ciple of the inalienability of private property generally stood firm.[232] Even
more contentious was the question of "public" ownership, and many were the
acrid tussles over whether a town council owned local monuments (and hence
the right to destroy or reuse them[233]), or whether that authority rested with
central government.[35] With proprietors, as late as 1900 it was still recognised
that forcible expropriation could be used only in exceptional circumstances,
for the method "offrait, dans l'exécution, trop de difficultés pour être considéré comme un moyen pratique."[234] Proprietors continued all-powerful, and

---

35 Potter 2008, 185: "The routine maintenance of fortifications was generally the responsibil-
    ity of town councils, usually financed by indirect taxes on merchandise, technically due
    to the King but more profitably employed locally, the *octrois*."

THE ORGANISATION OF SCHOLARSHIP AND MUSEUMS 179

across the Channel this was viewed with astonishment.[235] Certainly, examples are plentiful: one who wished to enlarge his courtyard announced in 1883 the destruction of a section of the walls of Tours,[236] and those like Truchet, near Constantine, who collected together antiquities they found on their land, were probably rare exceptions.[237]

Where the military got into the act, difficulties only increased. The château at Crest (Drôme) had been dismantled by Richelieu in 1627–33, but the donjon survived, given to the Département, and handed over to the army – yet as late as 1873 nothing could be done to restore it because ownership was unclear.[238] And in 1891 the remains of the Roman theatre at S.-André-sur-Cailly (Seine-Inférieure) were still in private hands, and the owner persisted in not wanting to cede the monument to the department.[239] The scholars did not need to bother with the ruins near Valogne (Manche), where the father of the 1820s owner of the baths "chercha à les détruire par la sappe et la mine; il fit casser en 1773, avec des masses de fer, la piscine et les petits fourneaux qui étaient dessous."[240] A monument at Vieux (Calvados) was a half-way-house by 1854, when one scholar had to guess that it was a theatre, because "on l'a détruit jusqu'aux fondements pour se procurer des matériaux."[241] Baths at Senon (Meuse) were hastily drawn two years earlier, just before the owner of the field "les ait entièrement détruits pour en utiliser les matériaux."[242] And at Saint-Porquier (Tarn-et-Garonne) in 1860 the dig at the newly-discovered villa could not be continued because of the dog-in-a-manger attitude of the land-owner; but luckily an ex-mayor of Bordeaux owned the adjacent Roman camp, so attention was turned there.[243] No such luck at Chassenon (Charente) in 1862, site of an important Roman town which was to be dug into the 20th century, where the owner had already moved one room's paving for reuse, and the workmen had destroyed that of another, believing the slabs to be gravestones, with treasure underneath.[244]

Laws for Monument Protection

Reconnaissant que les dispositions prises jusqu'à présent pour la conservation des monuments de l'antiquité, particulièrement dans l'Afrique française, sont restées inefficaces, parce qu'elles manquaient d'une sanction légale, émet le vœu que le gouvernement prenne auprès du Parlement l'initiative d'un projet de loi destiné à assurer la protection des monuments anciens dans toute l'étendue du territoire national et des possessions françaises, et charge son bureau de transmettre l'expression de ce vœu à M. le Ministre de l'Instruction Publique et des Beaux-Arts.[245]

180 CHAPTER 5

In 1882 the Société nationale des Antiquaires de France circulated the above resolution, and this must have been a general attack by societies, because La Société de l'Histoire de Paris et de l'Île-de-France uses identical wording in 1884.[246] In other words, the conclusion reached after years of nonchalant neglect and active vandalism, was that pressure alone could not conserve buildings: laws were needed. This final section underlines that recourse to law for monument protection was a counsel of despair, being the final step after persuasion and letter-writing by scholars, and a clear indication that destruction of the past did not attract much public opprobrium because so many people had a vested interest in dismantling the past in order to build the future. Of course laws need updating, but an index of legal helplessness was the number of times laws were declared to be in need of revision, as can be deduced from the following selection of date-markers:

1841: Law of 3 May provides for expropriation of privately owned classified monuments, a provision beginning in France with Art.545 of the Code Napoléon;[247]
1851: Ministère de la Guerre, Loi du 10 Juillet 1851 relative au classement des places de guerre etc etc.[36] Table has column for ouvrages détachés, now common at the more important sites. In the Ier série were Péronne, Soissons, Maubeuge, Langres citadelle (the town was in IIe série, as were Carcassonne and Narbonne). A separate table gives the classification for Algeria, divided into chefferies (such as Médéa and Alger) and IIe série. In all, 23 chefferies with over 40 centres to protect. Several of the articles of this law were abrogated only in 2004.
1880: Government should make a law "destiné à assurer la protection des monuments anciens dans toute l'etendue du territoire national et des possessions françaises;"[248]
1884: the Société nationale des Antiquaires de France repeats the plea;[249]
1886: Law dealing with conservation of monuments on public land, expanding the powers of the law of 3 May 1841;[250]
1887: Law declaring objects found in certain locations the property of the state – but immediately seen to be unworkable;[251]
1889: Parisian scholars were on the front line of modernisation, and were "frappé des insuffisances de la loi de protection des monuments historiques;"[252]
1906: when in doubt, form another commission;[253]
1909: Law needed to protect objects found in digs;[254]

---

36   Sardain 2014, 4–5.

THE ORGANISATION OF SCHOLARSHIP AND MUSEUMS

1911: the Société Archéologique de Provence writes in to support the 1909 proposal, regretting that pressure from learned societies has not persuaded the Government to move.[255]

Conclusion

In contradistinction to the often ineffective monument conservation laws, those involving the classification of towns as military posts ("places de guerre') were rigidly enforced, and often instituted by wars such as that of 1701,[256] with servitudes defined as rings flowing from the fortifications.[257] Public buildings were generally exempted from interference by the Military,[258] but these of course were well inside towns, not on the periphery near the walls. The laws also dealt with destruction, since it was the declassification of once-essential sites which allowed the dismantling of old walls, this action often triggering the expansion and modernisation of such towns, and then prompting yet more destruction of earlier monuments.

Since the need for so many laws proclaimed failure, how might matters have been better arranged? Certainly by government and its institutions paying greater attention to the scholarly societies which were so assiduous in their descriptions of monuments and in attempts to protect them. But, as Brown remarked in 1905, they were officially ignored. The rude provincials got their own back with "the criticisms freely lavished by provincial antiquaries and men of taste, on some of the restorations and other works carried out from Paris in the cities of the departments."[259]

[1] BSA_Soissons_I_ 1847_14–15
[2] BSA_Limousin_LI_1902_ 374
[3] Brutails_1900_viii–x
[4] Brutails_1900_143
[5] Brutails_1900_176
[6] ASA_Château-Thierry_1878_110–111
[7] SG_XLII_Châlons-sur-Marne_1875_440
[8] Mém_Picardie_I_1838_104
[9] Guilbert_1845_34
[10] AA_VIII_1848_238

[11] AA_XIII_1853_165
[12] CS_France_VI_1838_ Clermont_Ferrand_192–3
[13] AA_XIII_1853_163
[14] CS_France_VI_1838_ Clermont_Ferrand_119
[15] Shaw_2007_169
[16] Revue_Aquitaine_I_1857_ 147–148
[17] BSA_Laon_XIV_1864_ 27–28
[18] BSA_Laon_IX_1858_58
[19] SG_XXVII_Dunkerque_ 1860_290

[20] BSA_Nantes_XII_1873_ 110
[21] Recueil_Tvx_Soc_ Agriculture_Eure_IV_ 1856_342–343
[22] BSA_Touraine_VIII_ 1889–1891_233
[23] BCA_I_1882_225
[24] Comité_Archéol_Senlis_ VIII_1882–1883_LXXXIII
[25] AMPF_X_1896_268–283
[26] Samazeuilh_1865_269
[27] Samazeuilh_1865_266
[28] Samazeuilh_1865_263

[29] cs_France_VII_1839_Le_Mans_335

[30] Millin_1802

[31] Bull_Soc_Nivernaise_XI_1883_IX

[32] AA_XIX_1859_353

[33] AA_III_1845_567–568

[34] AJ_V_1848_353

[35] sg_XXXVI_Loches_1869_259–260

[36] sg_XXXVI_Loches_1869_257–258

[37] AA_I_1844_105

[38] AA_XIV_1854_51

[39] Circulars_Education_France_1881_56

[40] Année_Artistique_II_1879_387

[41] RA_V_1885_85

[42] BSA_Drôme_III_1868_40

[43] Sorbonne_1884_336

[44] Mém_Pontoise_V_1883_163

[45] Brutails_1900_177

[46] Perrot_1888_41

[47] AMPF_I_1885_51

[48] Revue_art_chrétien_I_1857_175

[49] AA_I_1844_335

[50] Réunion_BA_1877_243

[51] BSA_Touraine_V_1884_421

[52] sg_LXI_Saintes_1894_172

[53] BSA_Soissons_I_1847_13–14

[54] BM_XI_1845_401

[55] AA_I_1844_88–89

[56] BSA_Orléanais_II_1859_87–88

[57] RA_V_1885_86

[58] sg_LVI_Évreux_1889_78

[59] Saint-Paul_1881_33–34

[60] AA_XXIII_1863_187–188

[61] SA_Bordeaux_I_1874_8

[62] BCA_Seine-Inférieure_1867_I_183

[63] Saint-Paul_1881_22

[64] Saint-Paul_1881_31

[65] Ann_Acad_Reims_II_1843–1844_250–251

[66] ADG_8T250_No_12374

[67] ADG_8T250

[68] Goiffon_1881_52, 288f.

[69] MSA_France_1881_217

[70] Goiffon_1881_52_288f._257

[71] Courajod_I_1878_XVIII–XXIII

[72] Courajod_I_1878_XLIX–L

[73] Mém_Acad_Gard_1838–1839_108

[74] AJ_VII_1850_399

[75] PSA_London_III_1856_294

[76] RA_XXXI_1876_327

[77] Tétreau_1896

[78] Sommerard_1876_2

[79] Mérimée_1843_13

[80] Michaelis_1882_356–357

[81] BM_XXXV_1869_503

[82] BM_XXXV_1869_500

[83] BM_XV_1849_373

[84] Tour_du_Monde_XXIV_1872_184

[85] Young_1890_8

[86] BSH_Anjou_V_1858_50–51

[87] BSA_Nantes_XXII_1883_197

[88] cs_France_XV_1847_Tours_100

[89] sg_XL_Chateauroux_1873_614

[90] BSA_Soissons_XII_1881_188

[91] MSA_Ouest_1889_412

[92] BSA_Abbeville_1890_246

[93] CHA_I_1894_55

[94] Reinach_1890_224

[95] Grille_de_Beuzelin_1837_6

[96] Franklin_1877_107–108

[97] Bourges_Lapidaire_1873_2

[98] Quatremère_de_Quincy_1815_39–40

[99] Quatremère_de_Quincy_1815_55–56

[100] Schneider_1910_168

[101] Schneider_1910_195

[102] Schneider_1910_167–168

[103] Musée_Langres_1886

[104] Luquet_1838_168

[105] Vignier_1891_39

[106] MSA_Langres_1847_59

[107] Précis_Rouen_1864–1865_310

[108] Schuermans_1888_81

[109] BSA_Nantes_V_1865_17

[110] SH_Compiegne_Excursions_archéol_1875–1890_II_25

[111] sg_XXXIII_Senlis_1866_24–25

[112] BM_XI_1845_311

[113] Bourges_Lapidaire_1873_1–2

[114] Tarbé_1844_295

[115] BM_XI_1845_587

[116] sg_XXIII_Nantes_1856_100

[117] Mège_1862_76

[118] BSA_Drôme_VIII_1874_369

[119] Sibenaler_1905_128–129

[120] sg_XI_Chateauroux_1873_615–616

[121] Whittington_1809_163–164

[122] BCA_Narbonne_VI_1900_XXVIII

THE ORGANISATION OF SCHOLARSHIP AND MUSEUMS

[123] Espérandieu_I_1907_ 341

[124] Espérandieu_IV_1911_ 372

[125] SG_XXXIV_Paris_1867_ 54–55

[126] Réunion_BA_XIV_1890_ 339

[127] BCA_Seine-Inférieure_ IX_1894_87

[128] Schneider_1910_86

[129] SG_XXXV_ Carcassonne_1868_ 291–292

[130] BCA_Narbonne_I_ 1877_578

[131] Mém_Beaune_1899_18

[132] Mém_Angers_V_1842_ 386

[133] BM_XLIX_1883_382–383

[134] Annuaire_Normandie_ VI_1840_79

[135] RA_II_1845–6_390

[136] SG_XXXI_Évreux_ 1864_441

[137] BSA_Orléanais_III_ 1859–61_155

[138] BSA_Lorraine_I_1849_ 323–324

[139] BA_Comité_1902_CIX

[140] BSA_Seine-et-Marne_ I_1864_37–38

[141] Devic_&_Vaissete_XVI_ 1904_148

[142] Mém_Pontoine_XXV_ 1903_12

[143] Perrot_1840_289

[144] Mém_Gard_1847–1848_ 28

[145] Estrangin_1838_112–113

[146] Goussard_1861_12–13

[147] BA_Tarn-et-Garonne_ II_1872_373

[148] BM_X_1844_671

[149] Lafaye_&_Blanchet_ I_1909

[150] AA_I_1844_94

[151] BSA_Vendômois_XII_ 1873_240

[152] BSA_Drôme_XI_1877_ 452

[153] BSA_Drôme_XLI_1907_ 35

[154] BSA_Orléanais_II_1859_ 454

[155] BSA_Orléanais_VII_ 1882_52

[156] Précis_Rouen_1849_293

[157] PV_Seine-Inférieure_II_ 1849–1860_128

[158] Mém_Nîmes_XXXI_ 1908_280

[159] BSA_Soissons_XX_1889– 1890_97

[160] Revue_d'Artillerie_ XLVI_1895_551

[161] Murray_1904_II_164

[162] Bull_Mon_1840_80–85

[163] CS_France_X_1842_ Strasbourg_554

[164] Caumont_IV_1831_5–6

[165] Courajod_II_1880_14–15

[166] AJ_I_1845_72

[167] CS_France_II_1834_ Poitiers_175

[168] CS_France_II_1834_ Poitiers_541–2

[169] CS_France_IV_1836_ Blois_xxviii

[170] CS_France_VII_1839_ Le_Mans_376ff

[171] CS_France_II_1834_ Poitiers_539–40

[172] BA_Comité_1888_ 280–336

[173] Charmes_II_1886_CXCI

[174] Anderson_1888_186

[175] Anderson_1888_190

[176] Collection_ documents_1839_31–32

[177] Mém_Picardie_II_ 1839_22–23

[178] Réunion_BA_XVIII_ 1894_1570–1582

[179] CS_France_XV_1847_ Tours_231

[180] Sommerard_1876_4–5

[181] Merson_1865_11

[182] CHA_III_1896_25

[183] Normand_1896_294

[184] Bibliographie_ annuelle_1905

[185] Rapport_1824_8–9

[186] CS_France_VI_1838_ Clermont_Ferrand_191–2

[187] Proust_1887_1–10

[188] Paté_1900_9

[189] BCA_Seine-Inférieure_ IX_1891–1893_62

[190] Anderson_1888_190–191

[191] Proust_1887_18–119

[192] Rapport_1824_9

[193] Rapport_1824_9–10

[194] Rapport_1824_10–11

[195] Rapport_1824_12

[196] Rapport_1824_15

[197] ADG_8T_250

[198] Rapport_1824_16–17

[199] BSA_Limousin_XXII_ 1873_166

[200] AA_XVI_1856_179

[201] CHA_IX_1902_306–308

[202] Anderson_1888_191

[203] Millin_II_1807_48

[204] Omont_1902_I_610

[205] RA_V_1885_314

[206] BM_I_1834_378

[207] SG_XL_Chateauroux_ 1873_230

[208] CHA_III_1896_382

[209] BSA_Béziers_IV_1841_ 36

[210] BA_Comité_1886_320

[211] BM_XI_1845_357

[212] BCA_Narbonne_1892_ LXXXVII

[213] Mém_Comm_ Côte-d'Or_VI_1864_LI

[214] BM_XXVI_1860_149

[215] BCA_Seine-Inférieure_ 1870_40

[216] Sommerard_1876_ 306–335

[217] Grille_de_Beuzelin_ 1837_1–2

[218] Grille_de_Beuzelin_ 1837_3

[219] Mérimée_1843_8–9

[220] Mérimée_1843_25–30, 35–44

[221] Mérimée_1843_20

[222] Sommerard_1876_4

[223] Paté_1900_10

[224] Sommerard_1876_1–13

[225] BCA_Seine-Inférieure_ IV_1879_177

[226] Paté_1900_28–29

[227] Miln_1877_vi

[228] BSA_Seine-et-Marne_ V_1868_230

[229] BA_Comité_1884_151

[230] Précis_Rouen_ 1864–1865_298

[231] BA_Comité_1908_ CXLII

[232] SAH_Charente_IX_ 1873–1874_395

[233] Paté_1900_14

[234] Paté_1900_27

[235] Brown_1905_96

[236] BA_Comité_1883_124

[237] BA_Comité_1907_ CCXLII

[238] BSA_Drôme_VII_1873_ 340–341

[239] BCA_Seine-Inférieure_ IX_1891–1893_326–327

[240] Mém_Normandie_ 1820–1830_2–3

[241] BM_XX_1854_550

[242] BM_XVIII_1852_379

[243] BSA_Midi_VII_1860_319

[244] BM_XXVIII_1862_ 301–302

[245] BCA_Seine-Inférieure_ VI_1883_466–467

[246] BSH_Paris_XI_1884_162

[247] Peyronny_&_ Delamarre_1859

[248] BSA_Abbeville_ 1877–1880_71

[249] Mém_Lyon_1886_ LVIII–LIX

[250] BA_Comité_1888_30

[251] MSA_Ouest_ XIII_1890_101

[252] AMPF_IV_1890_15

[253] BSA_Drôme_XLII_ 1908_181

[254] BA_Comité_1909_XC

[255] BSA_Provence_II– 1908–1914_201

[256] Mém_Doubs_II_1866_ 278

[257] Breuillac_1870_168–169

[258] Breuillac_1870_271

[259] Brown_1905_78–79

CHAPTER 6

Modernity and its Architectural Consequences

Modernity has frequently and with justice been viewed in opposition to the old, its most persistent theatre being the *Querelle des Anciens et des Modernes* which, since the 17th century, argued for or against the dominance of the ancient world as a model for contemporary life, in art and architecture as well as in literature. The antithesis (for the poles were rarely seen as complementary) also exercised the 19th century, because the features of the battle were accentuated by the increased speed of modern life. Sainte-Beuve worried about the dichotomy, but knew the battle was lost,[1] Modernity had won the day, and the Querelle was now history, and could be kept in its cage by writing about it: for Hipppolyte Rigault published his *Histoire de la querelle des anciens et des modernes* in 1857.

But how to cope with radical change? By believing that the new could sit easily alongside the old. This was an illusion,[2] as quotations throughout this book make clear. Theoretically such conviviality was possible, but this rarely happened. The accounts of Bordeaux and Paris, two leaders of modernisation treated later in this chapter, demonstrate that the old simply gave way to the new. If two such large and important towns were modernising and prospering, why should the rest of France not do likewise?

Just like the witnesses in *Rashomon*, so the inhabitants living through the transformation of French towns told different accounts of what was happening and what it meant. For some, any up-to-date building in old towns was ipso facto vandalism.[1] Some could just block out the "inéluctables modernités," and admire old towers,[2] while the extensive series of turn-of-the-century guidebooks by Ardouin-Dumazet felt it necessary to point out which towns were modernism-free (such as Hyères),[3] and where the assaults of modernism were "vagues, bien vagues," as in Limoges.[4]

---

1 Prendergast 2007, 135–6: "Sainte-Beuve contemplates, with a melancholy foreboding verging at times on outright panic, the catastrophic prospect of the definitive loss of antiquity to modernity... In the conditions of 'modernity', it can no longer be a question of either imitating or competing with the Ancients, but rather of preserving a memory of what is otherwise at risk of disappearing into oblivion."

2 Rigby 1991, 30: "The politics of the heritage are ... based on the reassuring fantasy that change can be reconciled with continuity and that creating the new can be reconciled with conserving the old."

© KONINKLIJKE BRILL NV, LEIDEN, 2015 | DOI 10.1163/9789004293717_008

186   CHAPTER 6

This chapter and then chapters 7 to 11 demonstrate how the development of French towns under the impulsion of modernity threatened and often destroyed the heritage of monuments with which so many of them had once been adorned. They build on the accounts by concerned scholars discussed in Chapter 4. The information we have about towns varies, depending on the assiduity (or lack of it) of local scholars in promoting them, or that of the army and administrators in demolishing structures in the name of modernity. After an overview of the triggers and problems of modernity, the survey begins with Bordeaux and Paris, two towns which took the lead in demolition and modernisation, then considers towns in the Île de France (Ch. 7), Normandy, the North and Burgundy (Ch. 8), West and Centre (Ch. 9). Chapter 10 then looks in detail at two towns, Narbonne and Nîmes, which dealt well with their antiquities, before concluding with Provence and the South (Ch. 11), where many towns lost monuments for a variety of reasons. All these accounts underline just how much has been lost, and that the trend toward the obliteration of heritage in favour of modernity affected all of France, because all of France was once Roman, not just Provence. To that extent each town has a similar biography, but local interest and pride, energy and vision (or their lack) ensured that sufficient variety resulted to banish fears that modernism always meant a grey waste land of regimented uniformity. The towns studied were functioning in the 19th century; but we should also remember that some erstwhile Roman towns were by then mere ruin fields, ransacked by the locals for building materials, such as one near Sceaux,[5] one in the Nièvre,[6] and another once called Cosa, which featured on the Peutinger Table.[7]

Modernity[3]

> Il faut joindre aux causes de destruction qui ont à toutes les époques décimé le vieux Reims, le temps qui mine tout, la mode qui se lasse de tout, l'art qui souvent détruit sous prétexte de foire mieux, les nécessités de l'industrie qui ne respectent rien.[8] [1844]

In any period, being up-to-date ("modern") has generally involved at least the neglect and often the re-use or destruction of the old, which must be swept away to accommodate new technology and constructions, but include

---

3   Weber 1976 Part II passim: the agencies of change.

MODERNITY AND ITS ARCHITECTURAL CONSEQUENCES

patrimony where possible.[4] France, a country retaining even today many earlier buildings, nevertheless lost large quantities through modernisation, including some of her finest creations. From the Middle Ages to today, new towns, industries, population expansion and improved communications (road, canal and eventually railway building, motorways and airports) shook up what was left of the existing landscape, while barracks, fortress and factory construction obliterated large quantities of materials, many reused from the structures they helped destroy. Modernity is still a catchword today, even where it does not apply.[5] In the later 19th-century, some spurts of modernity were perhaps due to the spiritual and physical renewal of France after the disaster of the Franco-Prussian War but, as this book documents, radical change was under way in many towns well before 1870, some of it in competition with the technological developments viewed with envy across the Channel, especially railways and commerce.

New materials were also changing architecture, as Viollet-le-Duc made clear.[9] Railways encouraged tourist travel (beggars were to remain a problem),[10] and modernity was a selling-point for most visitors, far more than antiquities.[6] Others could put modernity on a level with dry rot and rats, and denigrated the attractions of modern Paris (which was to become the modern Athens[11]) against the achievements of the Romans as seen in Nîmes and Arles,[12] where old architecture was replaced daily by "des constructions modernes à la façade blanche."[13] Some scholars had even suggested that railways and gas lighting were impossible, and got laughed at for their pains.[14] But such lighting could be painful, as at Lourdes ("le modernisme aigu qui a fait entourer toutes les lignes architectoniques par des lampes électriques"),[15] and the quaintness of old towns where modernism had scarcely penetrated were publicised in tourist guides by the end of the century.[16] Such glimpses of the past were overwhelmed by the pace of change, which is reflected in Sageret's *Almanach et annuaire des bâtiments, des travaux publics et de l'industrie*, published from 1831, listing builders and associated trades, and costs of materials and manpower.[17]

In Paris, a town changing so much as to become unrecognisable even to those who had lived there only a few years before,[18] a sigh of relief was

---

4 Andrieux 1997, 63–102, Patrimoine et modernité, incl. 68–70 Le processus de "patrimonialisation."

5 Torrejon & Canet 2008, writing of urbanism at six bastides, but nowhere explaining how they might exemplify both the "patrimoine" and the "modernité" in their work's title.

6 Ward 1998 focusses on Britain, but see 39–41: French resort publicity.

breathed because cobblestones were no longer being wrenched up for insurrection, but simply to lay water and gas mains.[19] Heroic battles were nevertheless fought, for example over a barracks: as a sarcastic commentator pointed out, "l'autorité militaire se refuse à céder ladite caserne, la jugeant indispensable de par sa proximité même avec la gare Saint-Lazare."[20] Imitating Paris (where large parks were also landscaped)[21] was common: Laon not only had gas by 1841, but a Champs-Élysées by 1830.[22] Archaeology itself also has connections with modernity,[7] fuelled in part by the annual publication of construction accomplishments, divided by type: architecture, public baths, canals and rivers, bridges, ports, railways, stations, lighting, telegraph, and tunnels.[23] Were not the modern French the equal in achievement to the ancient Romans?

At Chartres, modernism nested in the plaster bas-reliefs in the choir;[24] at Toulouse, it was modern transport which perverted the traditional brick of the city;[25] at Angers, modern architecture was an invasion,[26] while plaster coated works of art, replacing them with modern decoration.[27] The result was banality.[28] Such architecture could not equal the buildings of antiquity,[29] and was destroying so much old stock that Caumont in 1853 suggested a campaign to record the large quantities likely to disappear within twenty years.[30] It was even suggested that only in a few (remote) parts of France survived "un religieux respect pour les reliques du passé."[31] At Orléans it was "les nécessités de la vie moderne" which had whittled away much of the best architecture;[32] at Nîmes in the early 19th century, it was lighting, clean and paved streets, water management, boulevards replacing ramparts – but also the restoration of the amphitheatre.[33] Condom by 1861 was making an effort to be modern, with some industry, a museum and library in gestation, and a subscription to the Gazette des Beaux-Arts.[34] At Bayonne, praise for the mayor (1856–1870) noted "des embellissements presque aussi considérables, comparativement, que ceux dont M. Haussmann a doté Paris."[35] Progress was everywhere, mentioned in every speech and casual conversation, and their grandparents' generation (lacking steam and telegraph) pitied for poor travel, inefficient killing weapons, and smallpox.[36]

But perhaps modernism and antiquity could sometimes live together. Bazin, writing of Rome, rather cunningly (because ignoring its very unusual history) reported in 1896 that it would surprise the tourist with its modernity, where "aux grands boulevards, aux larges avenues, où voitures, omnibus et tramways circulent avec une rapidité toute parisienne."[37] Yes and no, for these

---

7 Thomas 2004, 1–34: The emergence of modernity and the constitution of archaeology. Ibid., 54: "The case that I have made is that archaeology has been made possible by modernity, and also that it has contributed to the formation of the modern world."

MODERNITY AND ITS ARCHITECTURAL CONSEQUENCES

modernisms were over unoccupied areas of the ancient city, prepared for up-to-date living, and completely ignoring the riches awaiting discovery under the surface. Not everyone thought that the old and the new could exist together. Gillet, looking back on the transformations from 1934, and targeting Carpentras, wrote of the demolition of walls as an illusion, as "la forme où se déguise souvent la haine du passé," gaining in return for so much destruction only "une lâche ceinture de désolants boulevards."[38] "Chaque ville a, comme Paris, son Haussmann," concluded one commentator in 1883,[39] and some could gain an up-to-date look simply by plastering over the decoration on embarrassing old houses to make them look like modern, rendered walls, as happened at Chalon-sur-Saône,[40] a town which had suffered during the Revolution.[41] Antiquities were retrieved from the remains of the walls in the early 1880s,[42] including capitals and what appeared to be "un fragment de la frise d'un grand édifice,"[43] important enough for a photograph to be sent to the Comité.[44] Reims also suffered some modernisation: "une Haussmannisation rouennaise" took place, with the 1859 Plan Verdrel, very expensive because it destroyed 1,000 houses, and had 61,000 square metres of road to build or remodel.[8]

The disadvantages of destroying the old (in addition to leaving towns as rubbish-laden building-sites for years)[45] were easily recognised. One element was the reluctance of householders, who received only the value of the land if their building was demolished "pour cause de vétusté;"[46] another that rebuild plans were not always agreed, and disputes could drag on for decades.[47] At Verneuil (Eure-et-Loire) in 1856, it was seen as foolish to destroy the old town, for "ses nobles hôtels, ses belles façades historiques, ses curiosités architecturales" could bring tourists and therefore prosperity. Conversely, destroying churches and old houses would leave her without character – already the fate of several thousands of towns in France.[48] However, only a few communes swam against the trend, Trie-Château (Oise) in 1905 citing both archaeology and tourism as the reason for keeping their Gate:

> un acte de vandalisme préjudiciable à l'étude de notre archéologie nationale comme aux intérêts moraux et matériels de la commune, altérant l'ensemble curieux et pittoresque du monument qui attire aujourd'hui les touristes à Trie-Château.[49]

This is praiseworthy, the commune no doubt realising that modern change led to the disappearance of antiquities, as at Auch.[50]

---

8 Mollat 1979, 307–342: 1800–1914: Transformations urbaines et mutations économiques; 317 for Plan Verdrel.

Communications and Industry

Communications and their speed were continuing preoccupations.[9] "Dans l'état actuel de la France," wrote Pillet-Will in 1837, "toutes les questions d'économie publique sont intimement liées à la question des transports,"[51] canals and railways alike. Chevalier, in the following year, emphasised that France was behind both the US and the UK in rail and road, pointing out that the average European speed (the UK excepted) was 8km/hour in public vehicles, with la malle/poste attaining 14km/hour. France needed a railway, which would allow 24km/hour – three time the speed of diligences.[52] Henri IV's public coach services, instituted in 1594, to Rouen, Amiens and Orléans (none of them to the wild and woolly south) made 13/14 leagues/day, namely 52/56km.[53] A 1623 edict reckoned on 9 leagues a day,[54] which was optimistic, for in 1630 postal courriers from Paris reached the main towns throughout France, travelling at only 4km/hour in summer, and slower in winter.[55] But while the great roads of France might have been passable by the 18th century, lesser roads depended on local repairs, so their condition was a lottery.[56] For some, however, speedy transport meant that few really studied monuments, as they flashed past:

> car ce n'est pas voir que d'assister, impassible et inerte de corps et d'âme, au défilé rapide d'une série de tableaux dont on ne saisit ni l'ordre, ni l'origine, ni l'harmonie, qui n'éveillent dans le cœur aucune espérance et auxquels ne se rattache aucun souvenir.[57]

Industry was hampered by enclosed towns. St-Quentin got permission in 1810 "de briser la ceinture murée qui depuis longtemps arrêtait l'essor de son industrie;"[58] Luxemburg, with its walls down, could also "respire à pleins poumons, envahit sa banlieue qu'elle couvre d'usines et d'habitations somptueuses, agrandit ses places, créé des squares et des promenades."[59] But after such demolitions, there was often nothing to see: the Croix-Rousse at Lyon "ne peut offrir au voyageur aucun monument moderne ni aucune ruine intéressante; mais...le tic toc des métiers, les sifflements de la navette...lui rappellent pour quelle part immense le laborieux faubourg est dans les splendeurs de la métropole."[60] Nevertheless, architecture would have to change to fit industrial norms: "aux solutions qu'exigent les besoins modernes et que les progrès de l'industrie permettent d'aborder,"[61] although some trimmers believed a balance could be struck between the past and the present.[62] Others adopted

---

9   Robb 2007 ch. 12: Travelling in France II: the Hare and the Tortoise.

MODERNITY AND ITS ARCHITECTURAL CONSEQUENCES

the "horses for courses" measure, one at Marseille writing that "nous demandons un peu moins de modernisme, et, si possible, un peu plus de beauté."[63]

Yet communication produced its own problems, it even being suggested in 1903 that railways were responsible for introducing tuberculosis into the furthest corners of France,[64] just as by the middle of the previous century the railway was seen as noxious because it allowed lawyers to spread their influence far and wide.[65]

Modernisation and Destruction

Lorain's 1845 "modern liberty," cited at the start of Chapter Four, is clearly a two-edged sword. For although he was writing before any extensive industrialisation in France, he was well aware that the liberty to tear down was freely exercised: a church choir, interfering at Craon (Mayenne) with an inhabitant's building plans, was pulled down, some its materials used to build a house, the remainder lying around until 1853 when they were sold on to an entrepreneur.[66] Nor was this an isolated incident, but common practice: when Millin visited Autun at the beginning of the 19th century, he expected to find a rich harvest of antiquities, but the locals cleared everything out as soon as it was uncovered:

> Il faut que les insoucians Autunois aient une attention particulière de briser ou de vendre à des passans tout ce qui sort du sein de la terre; car on ne trouve dans leur ville qu'une seule inscription, qui a été déjà publiée.[67]

Even famous churches such as Vézelay had been manhandled, as Prosper Mérimée discovered in 1835, fearing also that the whole structure could well collapse.[68] But this was minor damage compared with what Viollet-le-Duc would eventually wreak.[10] Humbler churches had their windows reworked to let in more light, and interiors were tidied up[69] – again to make them more "modern."

Civic modernisation was to compete with the army for the destruction of the old France, as *places fortes* such as Perpignan lost their massive and extensive defences.[11] As one commentator wrote in 1863, the process began in the

---

10   Murphy 2000; Jokilehto 1999, 141–145.

11   Roux 1996, 223–250, La modernisation de la place forte et de la ville au milieu du XIXe siècle – i.e. changes instituted from 1820.

192 CHAPTER 6

teens of the 19th century, old stones were tarted up into new buildings, railways eviscerated the earth, yet

> Toutefois estimons-nous heureux si, par un reste de ménagement semi-religieux, on n'a pas converti tous les édifices de la foi de nos pères en auberges, en greniers à foin ou en casernes. Ce sont les besoins du temps qui l'exigeaient, disent les uns; c'est la marche des idées, ajoutent d'autres; c'est la civilisation enfin!

– so that soon not a vestige of the old France would remain.[70] In fact, the start is dated too late, since several towns, as we see throughout this book, had begun modernisation in the previous century.[12]

The loss of town walls certainly created fine promenades, as Malte-Brun noted in 1882 for Tarbes; but he pointed out that tourists searching for picturesque Basque costumes would be disappointed: these had disappeared twenty years before.[71] Even later at Arles, the locals certainly paraded along the promenades and in the Alyscamps – but it was the zouaves from the garrison who now provided the colour.[72] Other towns lost colour when they modernised: Autun gained "in light, healthiness, and convenience ... but when the last remnant of past times has disappeared forever the artists and archaeologists of the future will hear the name of Autun with regret."[73] This was a common complaint also made, for example, of Marseille in 1904: "Mais la science n'y triomphe-t-elle pas trop au detriment de l'art et n'est-il pas vrai que souvent un progres, s'il facilite notre vie, devore une parcelle de nos jouissances intellectuelles?"[74] For only sparse Roman relicts remained there, in the upper town.[75]

How were archaeologists to cope with such modernising? First, as retailed throughout this book, by protesting at the scale of destruction, a good example of which is Carthage which, in the early 20th century, was turned into a chic European suburb of Tunis.[76] One hopeful soul saw his discipline as unearthing ancient models for modern tools,[77] but most put their trust in regional academic associations which could be vigilant, and preserve Antiquity from the hammer, "sur les restes d'un monde presque écroulé."[78] One widely-used technique was to watch "town-improvement" excavations as they developed, and then try and rescue any antiquities which were turned up. This could

---

12   Baumier 2007, chap. VIII: L'urbanisme, une préoccupation nouvelle, including 386–8 partial dismantling of the walls, bastions rented out to kitchen gardeners from 1724 – a process accelerating in the 1770s and 1780s.

MODERNITY AND ITS ARCHITECTURAL CONSEQUENCES

sometimes work well, as we shall see; but there was no watertight legislation by 1863 to protect discoveries:

> Les monnaies, les médailles, armes, objets d'art ou d'antiquité, et tous autres effets trouvés dans les fouilles seront remis immédiatement au commissaire de police du quartier, qui devra constater cette remise, sans préjudice, s'il y a lieu, des droits attribués par la loi à l'auteur de la découverte.[79]

This was vague in the extreme. The workmen naturally took coins and medals where they could. Antique statues were of no interest to them, so these often survived, but good building stone (perhaps included in the ultra-vague "et tous autres effets" above) was too valuable to hand over without a struggle to the archaeologists.

Promenades

Promenades in French towns – for carriages as well as for strolling[13] – are often the result of the declassification and dismantling of town walls, sometimes long before the 19th century, and often indicated by street names.[80] In 1660, the King gave permission to dismantle the fortifications at Lombers, near Toulouse, including "la propriété des esplanades et terraces qu'occupaient les fortifications de la place avant la démolition de 1621."[81] At Cavaillon in the later 17th century, trees were planted "pour l'embellissement du pays et pour que leur ombre serve de refraîchissement des messieurs et demoiselles... Les fossés continuent à être comblés sur plusieurs points et transformés en prairies et jardins."[82] In 1753 the ramparts of Boulogne survived, but with "une très-belle promenade plantée d'ormes."[83] The promenade at Auxerre, which took the place of the town ditch in 1758, was destroyed in 1775 for road-building: "Grande rumeur parmi les habitants, qui, privés de leurs promenades, voulurent en avoir de nouvelles."[84] Hence pressure from the townspeople, who no longer feared a siege, wrested the necessary area from the King,[85] so another promenade was built in 1806–1817.[86] The walls of Marseille had fallen by 1808, and "à leur place on a fait des boulevarts magnifiques, qui forment, pour tous les

---

13 Benedict 1989, 34: "The spread of the carriage also stimulated the construction of broad *allées* and promenades on the edges of many towns for the fashionable to see and be seen – arenas for display whose influence in spreading fashion-conscious consumer behavior should not be underestimated... few towns of any significance did not see at least the construction of a few fashionable hôtels and such gradual modifications as the advance of stone houses at the expense of wood and of tile roofs at the expense of thatch."

quartiers, des promenades agréables."[87] The story is similar at Montpellier[88] and at Reims.[14] Mâcon also lost her ramparts to promenades,[89] and yielded antiquities from under later buildings; but the Roman enceinte, visible in some parts as late as 1850,[90] had gone by the end of the century.[91] Beauvais also lost her walls, one of the first acts of the new mayor in 1804 being to pull down the defences ("inutiles pour la défense du pays et genans pour la circulation") and convert them into promenades.[92] Châteaux also generated promenades when dismantled, and sometimes gardens as well.[93] Again, Monet's *La Terrasse à Saint-Adresse*, exhibited in 1879 (now New York, Metropolitan Museum) was perhaps painted on the embankment (terrasse = levée de terre) underneath the village's fort, which protected the great port, dominating the site at this date, and where there were also Roman remains. "Terrasse," in other words, can also be a military term.[94] Such conversion of military areas to leisure spaces for conspicuous display was surely one of the aims and results of bourgeois ascendancy.

Recognition that old walls were redundant was widespread, and they fell throughout the century. At La Ferté-Bernard (Sarthe), "paisible et désarmée" by 1845, the ramparts metamorphosed into gardens;[95] at Brussels when boulevards were built only one gate was retained "comme échantillon d'architecture militaire ancienne."[96] St-Macaire (Maine-et-Loire) lost her walls for promenades,[97] and so did Loches (Indre-et-Loire), in 1869.[98] Nangis (Seine-et-Marne) got her promenades in 1893.[99] Archaeologists wanted old walls preserved, of course, suggesting in 1900 that they should form part "d'une portion du square traité dans le style italo-français qui tirerait de ces bastions un élément de beauté, en même temps qu'il conserverait le monument historique."[100]

Alignment and the Picturesque: The New and the Old (or, Périsse l'art plutôt que la ligne droite)[101]

Autrefois l'alignement ne se dérangeait pas: il passait à travers les plus beaux édifices, et l'on abattait églises anciennes, hôpitaux du xiiie siècle, maisons du xiie, pour faire place au tout-puissant autocrate. Enfin le chef de la France vient de lui dire son fait en déclarant qu'il avait trop peu d'importance, lui et la fade régularité moderne, pour monter sur le dos, ou plutôt sur la ruine d'une pauvre maison, même de la Renaissance.[102] [1856]

---

14   Boussinesq & Laurent 1933, II, 206–210.

MODERNITY AND ITS ARCHITECTURAL CONSEQUENCES

A large contingent of commentators viewed progress as a lure for rural populations "vers les vaines jouissances des grandes cités." Certainly, migration to the towns was a feature of all 19th-century Western Europe, and intensified the pressure to expand, which in many towns translated into "la manie du déclassement."[103] The spin-offs for extending and altering towns were many.[15] The mania was an obsessive desire to have one's town freed from the Army's rule, with the varieties of servitudes overturned in various towns[104] so that fortifications could be dismantled, and the town breathe and expand. It encompassed a desire for straight streets, sweeping away the picturesque maeanderings of erstwhile mediaeval towns. A few towns, such as the old sections of Limoges, retained a non-modern layout,[105] and Vendôme balanced a picturesque old town with modern suburbs.[106] The tool was administrative imposition of alignment (often via legal expropriation),[107] whereby buildings which could not toe a newly drawn line were to be demolished, often over the protests of their owners,[108] unless they were named as historic monuments, in which case they were safe.[109] Such expropriation was to be only "pour cause d'utilité publique,"[110] but it was municipalities not house-owners who construed the meaning of the term. This was Lorain's modern liberty put to work for the public good. Modernity required straight streets, obeying the new building line. Along with town militias, the process begins in the 18th century,[111] but the same love of straight lines is also visible in the 17th century (not to mention the new towns of the later Middle Ages), and was encouraged by the central administration.[112] Nor were such grid-plans restricted to France, for towns such as Athens used such a plan to proclaim her smart newness, ignoring the monuments – "On en démolit tous les jours; car le plan d'alignement et les constructions nouvelles ont forcé de mettre la pioche dans ces monuments."[113]

Best known is what happened in Paris, before and after Haussmann,[16] where we encounter "l'implacable ligne droite, longue d'une lieue [4km], qui transperce Paris de la gare de l'Est à l'Observatoire."[114] The pitiless straight line was still rampant in the early 1890s, demolishing a house on the rue du Bac, to be replaced by a notice: "Ascenseur, gaz et eau à tous les étages."[115] The town's modernity was propagated in magazines such as *L'Illustration*, which is proclaimed as a Parisian publication by its weekly header of a view of the Seine with Louvre, Collège de France, and Notre-Dame in the background. Although the periodical does deal with the provinces, it is much more

---

15   Léon 1917, 196–244, Léon 1951, 307–357, L'entourage des villes, including roadwork, grid plans, and le dégagement des édifices. Early photos in both books.

16   Paquot 2010 for the context, and 211–227 for Haussmann.

interested (as perhaps were its provincial readers) in happenings in and around Paris, including theatre and musical performances. Thus there is a weekly article entitled *Le Courrier de Paris*, and a series on *Les promenades de Paris*. Activities abroad receive more attention than those in the French provinces. There is more on Algeria (e.g. experiences of colons at Cherchel) than there is on the rest of France. As we might expect, the magazine has a strong emphasis on modernisation – railways (with plenty of stations depicted), telegraph, shipping, mechanisation, factories, machinery, and new technologies. Almost every issue begins with something happening in Paris, or from Paris (Royal visits etc). And when monuments elsewhere in France are illustrated, these are usually as picturesque illustrations to train-excursions from Paris, such as vol. IX 20 March 1847 35–46 celebrating the railway from Paris to Le Havre.

Upheavals similar to those in Paris, and promoted if not propagated by smart, illustrated magazines, invaded the rest of France. For modernisers, "old" became a synonym for "past its time," "useless" or "inconvenient."[116] Hence in pursuit of "a desirable straight line" and of a "deadly indifference" to the past, monuments disappeared at Autun,[117] yet some of that mediaeval town survived because "there were no Improvement Acts, there was no Baron Haussmann."[118] In the face of the coming railway, walls and triumphal arch were targeted in Reims,[119] where new alignments produced squares;[17] while at Rouen in 1857 "la froide et roide monotonie qui nous envahit de toutes parts" was deplored.[120] A more reasonable attitude (at least from the point of view of scholars) was that it was the alignments that should cede place to the monuments: "Il semble que les édifices ne devraient pas reculer devant les routes, mais que les routes pourraient bien se déranger pour laisser passer les édifices."[121] At Auch, wrote one commentator in 1862, "on a tout sacrifié à l'amour de la ligne droite,"[122] while at Toulouse in the same year the only profit from such alignments (in this town of beautiful but unaligned streets)[123] was to be the antiquities uncovered as they were made.[124] At Compiègne the following year, the picturesque went by the board, as "l'aspect général de la ville devient d'une beauté uniforme, à la grande joie des amateurs de façades symétriques."[125] Unfortunately, archaeologists were apparently absent when streets were aligned at Marseille, and also during sewage works which "ont sillonné la ville dans presque toute son étendue, n'ont été suivis par aucun archéologue."[126] This was a pity, given that the regular grid-plans of Roman towns indicated building layout, and where to dig, as at Autun.[127]

The desire for straight streets impacted heavily on France's spectacular collection of wooden houses, some of them elaborately decorated. At Orléans the

---

17   Boussinesq & Laurent 1933, II, 181–206: Travaux d'alignement, Place Royale.

MODERNITY AND ITS ARCHITECTURAL CONSEQUENCES   197

Maison Dieu was replaced by a characterless promenade;[128] and here in 1859 the only monuments remaining were those "que les folies révolutionnaires, le culte de l'alignement et les intolérances de la voirie municipale ont laissé debout."[129] Many other towns were in danger. The typical scholars' reaction (there could be no other in the face of administrative intrasigence) was to draw them accurately before they were swept away[130] – or, as the century moved on, to photograph them.

Dismantling Enceintes to Achieve Modernity

The dismantling of ramparts affected towns all over France, whether or not these were Roman in origin. Indeed, any ramparts, and not just Roman ones, provided too much convenient stone to be ignored, and many were frittered away, as at Monségur (Gironde), where t.he walls were left to collapse, and robbed out,[131] and where all had gone by the time of the Revolution.[132] With the ground liberated, the bourgeoisie frequently took over, building large houses and, as walls began to grow outward in response to gunpowder weapons, leaving the old town interior still a maze of alleys and decaying housing, as at Bergerac (Dordogne).[133] At Angers, the old town was "eviscerated," and newly built suburbs crept up on the "admirables jardins qui font une verte ceinture à la cité."[134]

Mintzker sees defortification "as a metaphor for, or a parable about, the replacement of a whole older world by a new one that explains why, as it unfolded, defortification was everyone's business," a self-evident progression "demographic, socio-economic (industrialisation) or technological (military firepower)." In Germany, then, the transformation happened as it did in France, from a mix of military, political and social forces, with a surge at the turn of the 18th–19th century.[18]

Pulling down fortifications was hard work, and expensive; compact town walls were one thing, but the extensive outworks of the Vauban-type systems were quite another, and required years of effort.[19] Pressure for dismantling town walls for financial or military reasons may be nearly as old as the structures themselves. Senlis groaned in the 15th century under the burden of maintaining her walls[135] and dismantling nearby housing.[136] The States of Burgundy, "interprètes ordinaires des sentiments et des besoins du pays,"

---

18   Mintzker 2012, 4–5 for quote; 85–101: The Great Defortification Surge 1791–1815: Magnitude and General Characteristics; 93–6 for table of dates, from 1734 (Berlin); and 225–55: A Modern City, 1848–66.

19   Decamps & Guillemin 1992 for Maubeuge, with accounts; the rive gauche fortifications were classified in 1947.

lobbied in the late 16th century for the destruction of an enceinte no longer useful for frontier defence.[137] The Wars of Religion threw defensive capabilities into the spotlight,[138] as at Cuxac (Lot)[139] or Josselin (Île-et-Vilaine),[140] and large numbers of town walls and châteaux fell under Richelieu.[141]

The 19th-century taste for modernisation, with concerns for public health, and the provision of parks and promenades, inevitably included town improvements which, for the majority, required dismantling now-useless town walls which, like the quaint topsy-turvy streets inside, hindered wheeled traffic and trade, and restricted expansion. The 18th century had already developed a taste for grand buildings, according to one commentator, so that "Il n'y a presque pas une ville considérable où l'on ne veuille avoir une place, une statue en bronze du souverain, un hôtel de ville, une fontaine." Montpellier, Rennes (which yielded important Roman inscriptions in the early 1890s), Dijon and Rouen were embellished with squares and new roads, as walls were dismantled. A popular dismantling was that of the Paris Bastille, of which the entrepreneur made 83 models, one for each of the then départements of France.[142]

At Nîmes, dismantling work was already in hand by 1768, when the Conseil d'État ordered the demolition of the walls, including freeing the amphitheatre and building a new aqueduct.[143] This was to the displeasure of some residents, who did not wish to mix with the riff-raff in the suburbs,[144] but pleased archaeologists, for inscriptions noted in previous centuries and then lost were found once again in the ruins.[145] It was apparently the State which owned the walls of Nîmes, and of other towns.[146] In many towns, private houses had encroached on the ramparts. At Limoges in the mid-18th century, the King stated he owned the ramparts, and ordered supposed proprietors to produce their deeds; so that in 1773 a by-law charged the finance department of the town "de vendre aux enchères tous les terrains des fossés ou des remparts à ceux qui y avaient fait construire des maisons et échopes."[147] At Beaune, however, in 1844 "Le conseil municipal est dans l'heureuse impuissance de les détruire, parce que les anciens fossés creusés au pied des murs sont devenus des propriétés privées." The walls were eventually to be destroyed, for "néanmoins, rien ne serait plus populaire à Beaune que la destruction des murailles et des remparts, bien que ces remparts soient aujourd'hui de fort agréables promenades."[148] Troyes (Aube), lost its 16th-century enceinte in the course of the 19th century.[149] Roman antiquities were discovered during building work in the 1840s,[150] and the dismantled walls gave space for an abbatoir and revealed interesting antiquities in the process.[151] The town was one of the first towns to found its museum (in 1838) in the historic church of St-Loup.[152] At Reims, it was argued in 1884 that the demolition of the walls was inevitable because of their uselessness, the needs of circulation, and "l'intérêt des

MODERNITY AND ITS ARCHITECTURAL CONSEQUENCES

propriétaires des immeubles, intra et extra, qui longent le mur d'enceinte." The present octroi was susceptible to fraud, and it was suggested that 6,000 cubic metres of wall blocks at 8fr would yield 48,000fr of the overall cost of 70,000fr.[153] At Narbonne, old stone cost much less, presumably because there was so much of it.[154]

The Declassification Movement

One spinoff of the modernising of transport was that a comprehensive railway network lessened the strategic importance of town walls. This was recognised at Narbonne,[155] and also Strasburg, once considered "le boulevard de l'Alsace" (in the military sense), but by the 1880s all the enemy had to do to conquer was to "suivre la grande route et la voie ferrée de Paris sans se soucier de Strasbourg, qu'il laissait à plusieurs lieues sur sa gauche."[156] The railway also helped change the meaning of "boulevard," since these often now confronted the visitor emerging from the station, which was usually built where the town walls had once stood, as at Brive-la-Gaillarde.[157] And could not railways help the defence problem, by dispensing with walls? Petitjean's 1895 answer was a circular railway around Paris, carrying guns; plus strategic canals.[158]

As we have already seen (Chapter Two: The Defence of France) offensive weaponry developed in the 19th century in such a way as to make traditional fortifications useless. At the same time local citizenry developed a taste for modernisation – wide streets, boulevards and promenades incompatible with walled-in towns. The fly in the ointment was often the Army, and especially the arm which people loved to hate, namely the Génie, institutionally reluctant to cede their possessions to mere civilians and, of course, perenially claiming force majeure for leaving fortifications in place. But the push to modernity trumped even the Army, and occasionally made strange bedfellows, such as those in favour of preservation: at the sea-port of Granville (Manche) in 1837, Mérimée was cheering for the army because, if the inhabitants got their way, and the Génie "perd ses droits, la cupidité entassera les maisons laides et sales."[159] A problem in most towns was the costs of dismantling walls, and often of having to provide barracks for troops. If walls were indeed "intégrées dans la culture urbaine comme le symbole d'une identité spécifique," at the back of many minds must have been the enormous costs of dismantling them, some well known from town accounts which survive, for example, for Caen 1730–89, and exceeded only by the enormous burden of erecting barracks.[20]

---

20 Saupin 2002, 220 for quote. 222 for table of public works at Caen, in livres tournois – 30,631 for the walls, but 372,331 for the barracks.

Arguments in favour of dismantling walls were therefore plentiful, several predating the 19th century. Thus the walls of Limoges went in 1765–6 and 1785 to improve salubrity, and encourage the development of population and industry,[160] extended with the boost the railway would give to the porcelain industry.[161] At Valence in the 1860s, a street was named after the Deputy who "a si puissamment contribué au déclassement de la ville."[162] At Toulouse in 1897, the destroyed walls were marked in the rue de Metz by special paving stones,[163] harbinger of a popular tourist device of today. In 1873 at Trie-Château in the Oise, inhabitants and scholars objected to the proposed demolition of the fortified gate ("une valeur archéologique et historique incontestable") to obey new alignments, apparently supported by ministries;[164] by 1903, although the municipality wished to demolish this piece of private (!) property, they could do so only through expropriation.[165] The gate was demolished. At Angers, from 1808 it took nearly 30 years to get rid of the walls and gates, but it is difficult to determine whether this was because of opposition or simply a shortage of municipal funds.[166] The French also kept a weather eye on their (trade and industrial) competitors abroad. Joseph II ordered town walls in Belgium demolished, except for Antwerp and Luxemburg, and in 1784–1820 Brussels lost walls and gates (except for one which became a museum).[167]

Many town walls were dismantled over the centuries without any official sanction. At Amiens in 1478, land on the site of the old fortress, in course of demolition, was allotted as building plots to those who would clear and level the area, since the town itself lacked resources.[168] Useful blocks from the earlier enceinte must have made this proposition attractive.[21] Although a few towns (such as Abbeville, Péronne, Toulon and Saint-Quentin) were partly in military charge of their enceintes,[169] others had their walls demolished because of rebellion, such as la Rochelle (1628), Niort and Saintes; sections of the walls of Nîmes were demolished by the Connétable de Montmorency in 1622 and 1628 and, for the same reason (rebellion) Montauban in 1660.[170] In 1622, the walls of Montpellier were reinforced by the Protestants within, against the Royal artillery. At Nîmes sections of wall were rebuilt, apparently badly, according to a document of 1776, although this might have been special pleading in the effort to have them demolished once again. In many towns (as at Auxerre, Évreux, Caen, Epernay, and Clermont-Ferrand) lack of maintenance meant that the walls fell into ruins on their own, no doubt allowed to

---

21   Bayard & Massy 1983, 221–46: La ville fortifiée.

MODERNITY AND ITS ARCHITECTURAL CONSEQUENCES 201

do so in part because they were already recognised as useless for defence.[171] Encroachment was frequently a problem, residents building houses against the walls, thereby saving materials and getting some free stability.

The serpentine dance required to attain declassification of fortifications affected many towns, such as Arras (Pas-de-Calais), where 1871 negotiations with the State led to an agreed convention for demolition only in 1889.[22] The document trail of such difficulties is best seen at Narbonne, for in 1888 the town published a 181-page account of their travails with authority, beginning with their 1865 petition to Napoléon III. The Army seems to have taken little notice of the Ministerial dispatch of 1866 declassing the site, for the Mayor was asked to indicate "sur le plan ci-joint les parcelles de terrains et les bâtiments militaires (à aliéner) qu'il a l'intention de réclamer."[172] Two years later, Général Chauchard wrote to M. Peyrusse, Deputy and Mayor of Narbonne, informing him that the declassification request had been turned down. The latter, a loyal Frenchman in favour of useful defence, questioning the Army's position:

> comment le génie militaire a-t-il compris sa mission pendant les cin-quante années de paix que nous avons eues depuis 1815? Depuis cette époque, le régime des servitudes militaires a-t-il été moins lourd pour le pays? A-t-on cherché à diminuer cette charge pour nos populations ou au contraire s'est-elle augmentée?[173]

Letters flew between Peyrusse, the Minister of the Interior, and the Army Engineers until victory could be declared in October 1868. Part of the process involved Peyrusse undermining the Army's position by citing generals who thought there were too many places de guerre:

> Aussi l'honorable général de Girardin [Alexandre-Louis-Robert, comte de, 1776–1855] s'élève-t-il contre le trop grand nombre de places fortes, qui n'existent, dit-il, que nominalement. Il pense qu'il faudrait réduire le nombre de ces places, et faire disparaître celles de deuxième et de troi-sième classes, qui sont, dit-il, si généralement condamnées.[174]

---

22   Bernard 1993, 83–122.

202 CHAPTER 6

Bordeaux and Paris: Leaders of the Pack

Bordeaux
The Antique City and its Transformation

The walls of Bordeaux were mid-4th century or later, and built from antiquities (its gates as well)[175] that amazed 19th-century scholars by their freshness.[176] The enceinte, containing huge quantities of blocks,[23] left the forum outside, whereupon the river frontage (once supposedly faced with Parian marble)[177] became the defensible area, just as it was to be in the construction of post-mediaeval forts there. The amphitheatre may still have been in use in the 4th century, and sections of its structure, the "Palais Gallien," (named after the emperor Gallienus) much restored, survive today. Sold off during the Revolution, it contained housing in the early 19th century.[178] Such continuing use is echoed in the villas in the region, some of which were splendid indeed. Just how late the standing monuments named were maintained is, of course, difficult to determine. The "Piliers de Tutelle" were part of a temple on the forum, and formed one of the most famous standing monuments in France, measuring some 26m by 19m, and with 24 cannellated columns. It was destroyed under Louis XIV,[24] and some of the column drums turned up in 1826, for they had been used to construct the river quay by the Promenade des Quinconces,[179] as we shall see.

Bordeaux was an important port, and the King needed forts there to keep order. Although the town destroyed several important antique monuments, we know more about the spolia in her ancient walls than is the case anywhere else except Narbonne. This is because of the building of the two forts of Château Trompette and the Fort d'Hâ from antiquities, which acted as reservoirs of materials to be retrieved and understood later. In building them, of course, important structures, such as the Piliers de Tutelle, were destroyed. These are now discussed.

---

23 Garmy & Maurin 1996, for well-illustrated accounts, with plenty of references to the 19th century fieldwork. Only Périgueux really studied, Bordeaux being considered (11) comme une réserve de documents (surtout épigraphiques) sur la ville du Haut Empire. 35–49 tracé du rempart de Bordeaux. 62–68 her foundations of ramparts, all of spolia, estimated (67) at 64,800 cubic metres, with petit appareil above. 39 fig. 17 for Léo Drouyn's painting of demolition of a section of the ramparts during the Second Empire.

24 Montclos 1992, 16–21.

MODERNITY AND ITS ARCHITECTURAL CONSEQUENCES

Château Trompette and the Piliers de Tutelle

Bordeaux was surrounded by a "vieille muraille" bolstered by Renaissance fortifications, consisting of three old forts,[180] namely Château-Trompette (originally Fort Tropeyte, from the name of a suburb) and Château/Fort du Hâ or Haa (both 15th century, but much expanded under Louis XIV), and Fort Saint Louis (or de Sainte Croix, built 1676).[181] These were built partly from antiquities, including some very fresh-looking inscriptions,[182] as were many of the mediaeval and later structures, with some "enlevées jadis du mur d'enceinte par quelque entrepreneur désireux de ménager ses matériaux," suggests Jullian.[183] Antiquaries noted with care what materials were retrieved, and the fully-referenced diligence of Jullian in 1890 recorded both such earlier finds, and those uncovered in the course of the 19th century from the walls themselves and from the two forts.

Unfortunately, the Piliers de Tutelle, an elaborate temple, was pulled down and its columns incorporated in Château Trompette. Its construction as a small fort began along with the Château du Hâ in 1454 after Charles VII had subdued the town; but when turned in 1677 into a huge complex protecting the port, its expansion and the addition of a glacis entailed the destruction of that temple. This was "un des plus beaux édifices de la Gaule," writes Jullian,[184] which "dépassait en hauteur toutes les autres constructions de la ville."[185] Eighteen columns of the original 24 of the temple survived into the 17th century, which "Louis XIV fit impitoyablement abattre pour augmenter les fortifications du château Trompette."[186] This was indeed once a splendid monument, drawn by Perrault;[187] but its destruction was a crime, and a reflection of the city's indifference to antiquities in the 17th century. The only protest seems to have been a bad poem in 1702: "Il faut que leur orgueil cède à la Forteresse."[188] Caumont noted in 1834 that "c'est ainsi qu'une quantité considérable d'édifices de construction romaine ont disparu à diverses époques, et que les villes ont sacrifié ce qu'elles avaient de plus précieux, leurs monuments antiques."[189]

Construction of the fort was not without its problems: Colbert complained he was being charged for an agent "à la recherche des matériaux," surely in part reusable antiquities; and that he suspected the entrepreneur was loading the bill.[190] If some antiquities were retrieved when the fort was pulled down, the temple columns did not survive such reuse, and did not reappear on the same site, to grace the new theatre. This in its turn burned down in 1803, but during new building on the site in 1826 a seven-metre stretch of the town walls was dismantled, and this short section yielded no fewer than nearly 50 inscriptions.[191]

The demolition of Château Trompette was the largest 19th-century dismantling project in the town. Its destruction had been planned from the later

18th century,[192] and required the building of barracks in the city for the displaced troops. Sections of this fort's foundations were still being unearthed in 1903.[193] Arthur Young visited the city in the later 1780s, and remarked on the quartier called le Chapeau Rouge, adjacent to Château Trompette:

> This fort is bought of the king, by a company of speculators, who are now pulling it down with an intention of building a fine square and many new streets, to the amount of 1800 houses.[194]

Stendhal, travelling in 1837, thought it was the demolition of Château Trompette, "bonheur unique," which ensured that "Bordeaux est de bien loin aujourd'hui la plus belle ville de France."[195] This was at the cost of her older monuments, and against the advice of one deputy, who thought Trompette should be retained.[196]

The Fort du Hâ

Much smaller was the Fort du Hâ, but when this structure was demolished in order to build the Palais de Justice on the same site, large quantities of antiquities were uncovered, so presumably the fort had been built by taking materials from the Roman walls.[197] Tourny and his successors were well aware of the rising value of the real estate they would generate by dismantling the fortress. He had used funds received from selling off allotments to pay for new buildings, including the decoration of the new theatre,[198] which was standard practice for cash-strapped municipalities needing to generate funds for expensive building and planning work. The dismantling of the fortress took several decades. Apparently, the king sold the complex to a private company in 1785, but the sale was soon annulled, and the town authorised in 1816 to sell the materials and land "sous la seule condition de former des promenades, un quai, une place publique et des rues sur ceux de ces terrains dont la destination est spécialement indiquée."[199]

Early Modernisation

In modernising, Bordeaux is well ahead of any other town in France,[25] at least in part to accommodate the needs of merchants for better port facilities and to display the vast wealth acquired, especially from the West Indies. Prosperity more than doubled her population in the 18th century.[26] Much

---

25   Saupin 2002, 77–84, Bordeaux as the ville phare.

26   Horn 2015, 30.

MODERNITY AND ITS ARCHITECTURAL CONSEQUENCES

new town planning was completed in the second half of the 18th century, thanks to go-ahead intendants,[200] including "ces fameuses allées de Tourny, qui sont pour Bordeaux ce que sont les boulevards pour Paris, la Canebière pour Marseille."[201] Beautifying the city entailed much construction as well as destruction, during which other walls within the city were found to be built with spolia.[202] It was due in large part to the initiative of Monseigneur Louis-Urbain-Aubert de Tourny (1690–1760), Intendant of the Limousin under Louis XVI from 1730, and of Guyenne from 1743 – a grand panjandrum, indeed, with wide powers, described in one document as "intendant de justice, police et finance de la généralité de Bordeaux." The impetus for re-development he began had spinoffs. In 1757, a section of the Roman wall was discovered during house-building, two of its towers having recently been demolished.[203] then in 1775, when the Archevêché was demolished, columns, capitals and architraves were recovered, since the Roman wall backed onto the structure.[204]

Modernisation for commercial reasons meant that Bordeaux lost nearly all her ancient and later monuments and housing (some had already gone in earlier centuries), as well as three mediaeval sets of fortifications,[205] the re-naming of gates and streets being the only marker for some destructions.[206] The Altar of the Bituriges, seen in the enceinte of Château Trompette, and first published in the early 16th century by Hubert Thomas from Liège, was then rescued in the 1550s from the fort by a local scholar, Élie Vinet, with the help of the fort's captain, "pour l'amour de la ville de Bourdeaux, et reverence de l'antiquité." But it was placed on view in the Hôtel de Ville only in 1590.[207] So even in the 16th century, the French Renaissance, important inscriptions such as this were neglected instead of being show-cased,[208] although some antiquities were retrieved and carefully kept.[209]

19th-century Modernisation

> On n'a déjà que trop détruit dans notre département de ces vieux édifices qui formaient le type archéologique de la région pour y substituer des bâtisses dont le moindre défaut est l'uniformité.[210] [1876]

Care was exercised for at least some of the 18th–19th century dismantling of earlier structures, and her museum benefited, the objects recovered forming, writes Jullian, nine-tenths of the town's patrimony, the dismantling of the wall therefore being to the profit of knowledge.[211] What Tourny did in the 18th century, Pierre-Romain Blanc-Dutrouilh did in the 19th century, conserving antiquities from demolished fortifications.[212] But the 17th century was another matter: Perrault came and drew the Piliers de Tutelle, but there is no evidence he tried to prevent their destruction,[213] any more than that of the Renaissance hôtels, which also went under Louis XIV.[214]

Further town-planning developments in 1865 included the piercing of a broad road down to the Quai de Bourgogne, which entailed the demolition of houses near but not adjacent to the walls.[215] And because the line of new houses down the voie du Peugue followed the line of the wall, this provided a bonanza for the museum, which doubled its holdings from the venture.[216] The building of a main sewer was a main cause of the discoveries.[217] Since new finds were still being made from demolitions in 1868, it seems likely that many of the houses then demolished had made a practice of incorporating antiquities in their structure, presumably mostly for strength and solidity, and because the blocks in the town walls were conveniently near.[218] The 1845 listing of the Monuments historiques de la Gironde includes 13 churches in the town and, for monuments militaires, the two Portes Saint-Eloi and Royale de Calhau, plus "fragments de l'enceinte romaine."[219]

Retrieval of Antiquities 1600–1900

In the mid-19th century Bordeaux seemed especially indifferent to her monuments of all periods, "cet oubli dédaigneux" which left the tourists largely 18th-century buildings to admire.[220] Except, that is, for some scholars, who took numerous soundings on the line of the walls.[221] It was, inevitably, Caumont, who drew attention to the riches of the city in ancient tombs and inscriptions.[222] Unfortunately, however, antiquities were scattered all around the town, and more were being discovered during new building, many taken from the old walls. By the mid-19th century, although some sections had been plundered in earlier centuries for building material, inscriptions were still being unearthed.[223] There was evidently a fear that these and other antiquities would be frittered away as a convenient source of building stone, for in 1862 Léo Drouyn evinces the hope "que toutes les inscriptions, les statues, les cippes, etc., etc, trouvées dans ce mur soient laissées à la disposition du nouveau musée des antiques, établi dans un local spacieux et bien éclairé."[224]

Certainly, as a letter explained in 1881, many funerary monuments were to be retrieved from the late Roman walls,[225] and in 1890 high hopes were held for yet more material to be extracted from foundations.[226] Some vestiges of old houses and walls were indeed preserved, but only as photographs.[227] Yet by the end of the century it was still hoped that remains from the walls might be rebuilt into their original monuments.[228] This was not make-believe: for example, sufficient large blocks had been retrieved in 1865 from the Roman wall near the Tour Pey-Berland to suggest substantial sections of a monumental fountain.[229] Since these blocks were then adjudged "bien propres à faire

MODERNITY AND ITS ARCHITECTURAL CONSEQUENCES

connaître quelle devait être la splendeur de Bordeaux sous les commencements de la domination romaine," it is a pity nothing substantial was done with them.[230] Smaller antiquities such as bronzes and coins also mostly disappeared in the great rebuilding upheavals of the mid-19th century.[231]

By contrast, and in spite of the demolition and rebuilding in that period, no antiquities were recorded as retrieved from the walls between 1600 and 1740, evidently due to a lack of interest, rather than to a dearth of materials retrieved, as Jullian[232] and Espérandieu[233] conclude. Indeed, over 30% of known inscriptions have been lost, with discoveries in no great number before the later 19th century.[234] This is because the attention of most inhabitants was focussed on building the new town. Bernadau, writing in 1844, noted that "Dans ces derniers temps les alentours de la promenade des Quinconces se sont couverts de magnifiques édifices, qui attestent combien le goût de la belle architecture s'est propagé à Bordeaux."[235] Even those visitors, such as Montalembert in 1839, who were willing to list "des exemples déplorables de dévastation et de maladresse" conceded that the new town was architecturally good.[236] However, his assertion that restorations of old buildings were sound is contradicted by Rénouf in 1886, for

> le vandalisme qui détruit n'est pas un pire fléau que le vandalisme qui restaure ... le zèle malfaisant – j'allais dire impie – de ces restaurateurs à outrance qui, dans la Gironde comme ailleurs, ont dénaturé un trop grand nombre de monuments historiques.[237]

Since neither author specifies the buildings, we cannot judge who was correct. Filching such useful building materials was probably a continuing problem; as late as 1881 the president of the Archaeological Society confirms this, and also the difficulties of moving large blocks any distance through the town.[238] Indeed, as late as 1876 intervention with the mayor was needed to stop an entrepreneur's workmen, building a sewer, from simply chopping off any inconveniently large blocks they unearthed to fit in with the pipes they were laying.[239] Weight might have saved other blocks: Bernadau notes "plusieurs grandes pierres sculptées, formant des chapiteaux de colonnes, des fragmens de frontons, d'architraves" found during road construction in 1808. These had come from the walls, the section here demolished in 1795 – so had lain unused and unloved during those revolutionary times.[240]

By the mid 19th century, however, little of the previous town was left and, of the town's three successive sets of ramparts, "Il en reste plusieurs portes, comprises aujourd'hui dans l'intérieur de la ville, et formant à elles seules autant de petits monuments de l'effet le plus pittoresque."[241] Cries of vandalism

208   CHAPTER 6

were raised, citing the destruction of churches, including the Ministry of War's desire to retain the use of the Dominicans,[242] and by 1903 a Commission was being proposed to the mayor, to offer advice "préalablement à toutes fouilles et à toutes démolitions."[243] The local Society saw themselves as a brake on demolition.[244]

Paris

> Toi, que maître Villon célébrait, où souvent
> Sa muse s'enivrait, mélancolique et folle,
> Taverne des grands jours, où sous le vieil auvent
> L'enseigne aux gonds rouilles se balançait au vent,
> Hélas! qu'en ont-ils fait? Qu'ont-ils fait de ma ville?
> O noirs démolisseurs, tourbe exécrable et vile,
> Je ne vois que la place où Paris s'éleva![245] [1877]

In Paris, not only was the political and press focus constant, and we might expect innovation in the capital, but also because from mid-century the transformation was more consistent and more long-lasting than elsewhere and much more sweeping, and controlled by an administration with an iron grip.[246] Whereas many towns preserved an earlier core, with developments restricted to where the walls had been, and just outside them, in Paris much more was destroyed; and here, recycling material had been standard practice for centuries.[27] The evisceration of Paris probably happened because Paris (unlike communes throughout France) had no mayor, and was therefore administered by the departmental Prefect – Georges-Eugène Haussmann from 1853 to 1870. He carried out his remodelling under the direct commisssion of Napoleon III, with no municipal authorities to impede him. Had Paris been organised like the rest of France, there would have been around 50 municipalities (generally formed from parishes) to examine and deal with his plans. This short summary of what is a very well-known story is necessary in this book because Paris was to be a model for town aspirations elsewhere. It outlines what happened to Paris' old monuments, and the protests against their demolition. One tendency today is to continue protesting such demolition, pointing out how much

---

27 Carvais 2008, 531–2: la récupération de matériaux en vue de construire... devient une pratique courante voire systématique au point que l'on puisse parler de politique économique de récupération.

MODERNITY AND ITS ARCHITECTURAL CONSEQUENCES

good architecture went in the process, not least nearly all Ledoux' barrières.[28] Pillage continues today, of course, and not just within the city.[29]

Two aspects about the protests against destruction are striking. The first is just how late they were voiced, about half a century after plans were laid and devastation began, and the results were profusely illustrated in the press.[247] The second is that societies needed to be formed to voice support for preservation when, across the Channel, this was thought to be the duty of government and the law.[248] By the end of the century there were more than five societies[30] aiming to protect what remained.[249] Thus a "commission chargée de rechercher les vestiges du vieux Paris" was proposed in 1897,[250] by which time the only parts of Vieux Paris left to be treasured were mere fragments.[251]

Walls

Paris once had a gallo-roman enceinte which completely disappeared, but it was the one built under Philippe Auguste that was largely dismantled, with towers, in the mid-19th century under road extensions.[252] This was not the first occasion on which roads had been widened in Paris, and promenades inaugurated.[253] It would be interesting to catalogue the "moindres vestiges," of this wall, wrote a scholar in 1880, long after much had already gone;[254] and the destruction of the tower found near the Mont-de-Piété was inevitable.[255] Never mind, while Paris was being turned over, dig for victory! Alexandre Bertrand, the archaeologist, was given the task in the 1860s of digging in the Louvre courtyard:

> la ville lui a donné pour mission de scruter le sol parisien aussi bien que d'étudier les documents écrits. C'est le meilleur moyen, en effet, d'arriver à la vérité en contrôlant les renseignements que ces derniers fournissent par ce qui reste des monuments du passé.[256]

– except, of course, for the alternative of leaving old monuments standing. Is it cynical to suggest he was directed to the Louvre to keep him away from

---

28 Pinon 2011, 180–185: Faut-il sauver les arènes de Lutèce?; 204–211: restauration, destruction, reconstruction: le case des Tuileries; 299 engraving of demolition of Ledoux' barrières at the (now) Place de l'Étoile.

29 Flutsch & Fontannaz 2010, 166ff. not least with the Louvre's 2000/2003 acquisition of frescoes from a Theban tomb, photographed intact and in place in the 1970s.; naturally Egypt demanded them back.

30 Pinon 2011, 247–259: les sociétés de sauvegarde.

the numerous antiquities surely being destroyed in Haussmann's schemes throughout Paris?

Impelled perhaps by the heady mixture of modernisation and profiteering, but also by the knowledge that the Franco-Prussian War had proved that they were useless, inhabitants were sceptical about Paris' extensive and costly 19th-century walls, built in the 1840s. Some Prussian ideas were indeed adopted,[257] so that by 1895, critics were quoting the destructive power of modern artillery, and "avec une enceinte illusoire, sans forts imprenables," calling for the ramparts of Paris to fall.[258] The story of their servitudes, and eventual demolition, is long and complicated.[31] Scholars are now interested in the military patrimony, so much of it demolished over the past century.[32]

Arènes

The demolition and rebuilding work in Paris brought various antique structures to light, for example on Montmartre,[259] or a circus, perhaps still to be seen early in the century.[260] But the most interesting structure was the amphitheatre, preserved just like a corner of Pompei, and found in 1870 when "la Compagnie des Omnibus opérait des déblais pour y établir un de ses dépôts de voitures et de chevaux."[261] Scholars thought this could be saved by fixing ownership or by expropriation, and by using it for public meetings (utility being a strong argument against destruction),[262] because its destruction "serait une honte pour Paris aux yeux de toute l'Europe savante."[263] Cham used a cartoon to point to government, with one lad viewing the ruins and saying to his friend, "C'est ça les arènes? Encore une chambre de députés en vacances!" The Amis des Arènes was formed; they complained in 1892 that the structure had not been classified, and hinted at skulduggery in the Commission, "auteur du mal, était composée de gens incompétents pour la plupart, d'ailleurs mal disposés, non désintéressés."[264] It was also suggested that the town should acquire the site through the Prefect,[265] or should be left to private initiative, although most journals believed that the site should be sacrificed to the omnibus and its horses, and even the Emperor seemed uninterested in saving what was left.[266]

Vieux Paris

Concern for the fate of mediaeval Paris began before Haussmann's attack on the city, and even before Louis-Napoléon's innovations of 1848–52. Concern for the structures themselves was justified: multi-storey blocks using mediaeval construction techniques "were, by the late eighteenth century,

---

31   Sardain 2014, 10–15.

32   Pernot & Thomassin 2005, 43–82 Paris fortifié; 174–7 for the 1840–47 fortifications; 206–13 Paris militaire (1870 à 1914).

MODERNITY AND ITS ARCHITECTURAL CONSEQUENCES

considered fragile, unsanitary, and dilapidated, with cracks in walls and crumbling foundations forming the basis of common complaints."[33] Hôtels were already being destroyed in 1842, including the mediaeval Hôtel de la Trémouille.[267] By mid-century the alterations were named as vandalism, the finger pointed at the municipal administration,[268] and not pacified in 1869 by Haussmann's "heureuse idée de créer à l'Hôtel-de-Ville un bureau de travaux historiques destiné à recueillir tout ce qui intéresse l'histoire de la capitale de la France," and Hôtel Carnavalet as the museum for Paris' history.[269] Here is the quintessential idea seen in other towns: knock it down, but write it up, and put the débris in a museum, and of course photograph what went: "la résolution qui a été prise par l'administration municipale de faire photographier ou dessiner toutes les maisons, toutes les ruines qui seront atteintes par le marteau des démolisseurs."[270] However, some commentators were puzzled that, in the face of commissions and museums, and "nos innombrables administrations," parts of Paris' heritage were being lost abroad, perhaps to England or Russia: "C'est un morceau de la vieille France d'autrefois que nous a vendue la France d'aujourd'hui."[271] Posters were also now common throughout the city, many advertising aspects of modernity; and this may have been why one scholar railed against them: "De cette promiscuité malsaine avec la laideur et la barbarie naîtra l'indifférence du beau, et l'habitude la consacrera bientôt."[272] What is known about Roman housing in Paris, except from mediaeval texts?[273]

Vincennes

Vincennes often received a cold eye, because this royal fortress was so close to the righteous archaeologists in Paris. In 1844 Gothic fragments were discovered there, "ce qui prouve que le vandalisme n'est pas né d'hier;" and the demolition of the gate called the Tour-du-Diable was proposed. Luckily this, the mediaeval entrance to the fortress, facing the village, survived, but the attempt demonstrated that "l'administration de la guerre est l'ennemie la plus acharnée de la science archéologique."[274] Indeed it was, for at this date the Génie "qui jette à pleines mains sur le département de la Seine des bastions et des forts détachés" was playing dog-in-the-manger with Vincennes, with a donjon older than gunpowder.[275] But never mind: why not use the Sainte-Chapelle, rival for that of Paris, as a gunpowder store? "Adore ce que tu as brûlé" was one comment.[276] Such storage was blocked, but the Génie ("qui veut toujours avoir le dernier mot") got its revenge by knocking down a 17th-century portico (now back in

---

33 Potofsky 2009, 30: "After a mere 60 years, the typical Parisian apartment building of the eighteenth century needed a complete restoration, with just under half of the new work invested in masonry, indicating serious structural problems."

212   CHAPTER 6

place), as well as reducing (except for the donjon) the height of the towers, and lodging soldiers in the apartments of Anne of Austria and Louis xiv.[277]

Conclusion

Although today's zoning and protection laws have ensured the survival of some old buildings in middle of modern towns, previous centuries (including much of the 20th century) saw the demands of modernity as incompatible with the past, to the extent that any proportion of inhabitants cared about the matter. For the majority, the manifold benefits of broad streets, sewage, lighting, good communications and the trade and industry they encouraged simply proved that the new was better than the old. The results of this belief will be demonstrated in the following chapters.

Many people see Bordeaux as the most beautiful town in France, Baedeker writing of the splendid site, and of the buildings erected by the Marquis de Tourny as masterpieces. The destruction we have noted above, but the end result is elegance. Paris, on the other hand, we might wish to view as megalomaniac, with Haussmann's schemes destroying almost the whole of the old town. The desire for the grandiose both precedes and follows him, however, with constructions which break traditional town planning norms secure from Rome through to the 19th century (except of course for enormous cathedrals). The new structures defy building conventions in scale and size, and can do so by introducing wrought iron as a signature material, seen also in railway stations, factories, and the large shops and other buildings on Haussmann's boulevards. Road widths are increased in proportion, and railways viaducts can be long and immensely tall, thereby breaking up traditional townscape in both scale and extent.

These are excursions in modernity which many towns throughout France will attempt to rival, but can never equal in scale. Proof of this is provided by Paris' Arc de Triomphe de l'Étoile (commissioned in 1806 after Austerlitz, but not finished until the 1830s), and the Eiffel Tower, of 1889. Both are enormous. The Arch, at 50m high, trumps any antique arch, while the Tower (324m) was the tallest structure in the world until 1930. Modernity and industry are the key to both structures: the Arch crowned the Champs Élysées (originally created in 1667). This avenue is 70m wide, and was the setting for the 1855 Exposition Universelle. The Eiffel Tower was conceived as the entrance arch for the 1889 World's Fair. Their scale, construction technologies and materials, and their raison-d'être as key monuments in industrial fairs, proclaim French modernity and emphasise that the country is up-to-date and commercially

MODERNITY AND ITS ARCHITECTURAL CONSEQUENCES

important. They also underline the new landscape such monuments require and, for some, justify the evisceration of *le vieux Paris* under Haussmann. However, profiteering and modernisation did not make for a liveable city, as Abel Martin remarked in 1892:

> Quand il n'y aura plus dans Paris, que des rues, des gares et des cimetières, Paris sera devenu inhabitable. La conservation des places, jardins et esplanades de la capitale, dont l'administration est toujours tentée de calculer la valeur au mètre superficiel, afin de les vendre et d'en toucher le prix, sous une forme ou sous une autre, n'a jamais cessé d'entrer dans les préoccupations les plus vives du législateur français, sous tous les régimes politiques que nous avons traversés.[278]

[1] Revue_Bas-Poitou_IV_1891_144

[2] Mém_Acad_Marseille_1904–1905_484

[3] AD_Provence_Maritime_1898_207–208

[4] AD_Limousin_1903_60

[5] MSA_l'Orléanais_II_1853_479

[6] CS_France_VIII_1840_Besançon_128–9

[7] SG_XXXII_Montauban_1865_87

[8] Tarbé_1844_26

[9] V-le-Duc_IV_1868_146

[10] Merson_1865_15

[11] Kersaint_1792_45

[12] Pesquidoux_1857_279

[13] Mém_Acad_Gard_1838–1839_123

[14] Recueil_Actes_Acad_Impériale_XX_1858_95

[15] AD_Pyrénées_Centrales_1901_247–248

[16] AD_Provence_Maritime_1898_207–208

[17] Sageret_1841

[18] Labédollière_1860_1er-arrondissement

[19] Merruau_1875_496

[20] AMPF_XI_1897_297–298

[21] Malte-Brun_IV_1883_60

[22] BSA_Laon_VII_1858_153

[23] Nouvelles_Annales_Construction_I_1855

[24] AA_XIII_1853_351

[25] Roschach_1904_213–214

[26] Lachèse_1843_i

[27] Sorbonne_1864_16–17

[28] Bazin_1902_91–92

[29] MDANE_VII_1826_106

[30] Caumont_1853_175

[31] ASA_Château-Thierry_1864_15

[32] SG_LIX_Orléans_1894_20

[33] Trélis_1813_376–3777

[34] Revue_Aquitaine_V_1861_298

[35] Bitard_1886_172

[36] Ann_Départ_Yonne_XXVI_1862_102

[37] Bazin_1896_IV–V

[38] Gillet_1934_39–40

[39] BSA_Orléanais_VIII_1883–1886_215

[40] Chévrier_1883_53

[41] Chévrier_1883_27

[42] BA_Comité_1882_237

[43] BCH_Archéologie_1883_96

[44] BA_Comité_1883_84

[45] BM_XXVIII_1862_743

[46] Manuel_des_lois_1863_45

[47] APC_V_1885_49

[48] SG_XXIII_Nantes_1856_187–188

[49] AMPF_XVII_1905_152–156

[50] Lafforgue_1851_210–211

[51] Pillet-Will_1837_13

[52] Chevalier_1838_199

[53] Pigeonneau_II_1889_294

[54] Mém_Beaune_1878_52

[55] Pigeonneau_II_1889_400

[56] Babeau_1878_243

[57] Lenthéric_1878_5–6

[58] BSA_Laon_VII_1858_151

[59] BSH_Tarn-et-Garonne_VII_1879_162–163

[60] Malte-Brun_IV_1883_27

[61] Bazin_1902_278

[62] AMPF_XIX_1906_65–66

[63] MAS_Marseille_1904_352

[64] MSA_Orléans_III_1903_121

[65] cs_France_xxi_1854_Dijon_398–9

[66] sg_xlv_Le_Mans_1878_249–250

[67] Millin_i_1807_335

[68] Mérimée_1835_29–30

[69] Bonnald_1839_230–231

[70] Revue_Aquitaine_vii_1863_435–436

[71] Malte-Brun_iii_1882_16

[72] ad_Alpes_Provence_Maritimes_1897_108

[73] Hamerton_1897_213

[74] mas_Marseille_1904–1905_329

[75] Rép_Tvx_Soc_Stat_Marseille_xxvii_1864_103

[76] bsa_Midi_1907_95

[77] sg_xxxiii_Senlis_1866_266

[78] Revue_Aquitaine_i_1857_9

[79] Manuel_des_lois_1863_139

[80] Vergnaud_Romagnési_1830_146

[81] Devic_&_Vaissete_xiii_1876_390

[82] bm_Cavaillon_cc1_#17

[83] Piganiol_ii_1753_318

[84] bss_Yonne_viii_1854_140–141

[85] Chardon_1835_584

[86] Chardon_1835_490

[87] Millin_1808_iii_262

[88] Vilback_1825_296

[89] Mosaïque_du_Midi_iv_1840_282

[90] bm_xv_1849_261

[91] sg_lxvi_Mâcon_1899_184

[92] Doyen_1842_478

[93] ad_Touraine_Anjou_1910_348

[94] Piganiol_ix_1754_597

[95] Guilbert_ii_1845_398–399

[96] aa_iii_1845_70

[97] bm_xxvi_1860_553

[98] sg_xxxvi_Loches_1869_202

[99] Réunion_ba_xvii_1893_577

[100] ampf_xiv_1901_326

[101] bsa_Orléanais_1872_235

[102] aa_xvii_1856_305

[103] pv_Acad_Gard_1864_93

[104] Lalaure_1827

[105] bsah_Limousin_xliv_1895_lxv

[106] bsa_Touraine_xiii_1903_279

[107] bca_Seine-Inférieure_vi_1883_69

[108] apc_passim

[109] Hamerton_1897_209

[110] Favard_de_Langlade_iv_1825_225

[111] Babeau_1880_537

[112] Babeau_1880_361

[113] aa_i_1844_42

[114] ampf_ii_1888_104

[115] Réunion_ba_xvii_1893_297

[116] Schmit_1859_48

[117] Hamerton_1897_185–186

[118] Hamerton_1897_202

[119] bm_xx_Paris_1854

[120] Verdier_&_Cattois_ii_1857_132–133

[121] Charmes_iii_1886_572–573

[122] bm_xxviii_1862_743

[123] Devic_&_Vaissete_xiv_1872_cols_2210–2211

[124] Du_Mège_1862_256

[125] Sorbonne_1863_213

[126] bsa_Provence_ii_1908–1914_207

[127] Hamerton_1897_199–200

[128] Verdier_&_Cattois_ii_1857_151

[129] bsa_Orléanais_ii_1859_454B

[130] Verdier_&_Cattois_ii_1857_212

[131] sa_Bordeaux_xix_1894_5–6

[132] sa_Bordeaux_xix_1894_1–71

[133] ad_Bordelais-Périgord_1903_231

[134] ad_Touraine_Anjou_1910_352

[135] Flammermon_1881_124

[136] Flammermon_1881_120

[137] Mém_Côte_d'Or_iii_1847–52_270

[138] Babeau_1878_152

[139] bca_Narbonne_1890_139

[140] Guilbert_i_1844_86

[141] Babeau_1880_248

[142] Musée_Amiens_1845_86

[143] Babeau_1880_366–367

[144] Annales_du_Midi_xi_1899_523

[145] Devic_&_Vaissete_xv_1892_79

[146] Babeau_1880_245–246

[147] Ducourtieux_1884_127–128

[148] aa_i_1844_92–93

[149] Rép_Arch_Aube_1861_142

[150] Mém_Aube_xviii_1854_165

[151] ba_Comité_1884_151

[152] Mém_Aube_xli_1832_56

MODERNITY AND ITS ARCHITECTURAL CONSEQUENCES

[153] Appert_Allart_&_ Leclère_1884_3–4

[154] AM_Narbonne_H86_ Génie_Narbonne

[155] Tournal_1864_195, Narbonne

[156] Malte-Brun_V_1884_5

[157] AD_Limousin_1903_274

[158] Petitjean_1895_35

[159] Stendhal_II_1891_68

[160] Ducourtieux_1884_23

[161] CS_France_XXVI_1860_ Limoges_656

[162] BSA_Drôme_IV_1869_ 187

[163] BSA_Midi_XX_1897_35

[164] AMPF_XVII_1904_ 152–156

[165] Mém_Pontoise_XXV_ 1903_67

[166] Thorode_1897_4

[167] AA_III_1845_60–70

[168] Goze_1854_53

[169] Babeau_1880_242–243

[170] Babeau_1880_248–249

[171] Babeau_1880_249–250

[172] Ville_de_Narbonne_ 1888_83–84

[173] Ville_de_Narbonne_ 1888_19–20

[174] Ville_de_Narbonne_ 1888_24–25

[175] Viographe_Bordelais_ 1844_220–221

[176] SA_Bordeaux_III_1876_ 177

[177] Ausonius_I_1919_283

[178] Millin_IV_1811_624–625

[179] Caumont_1838_347

[180] Potter 2008, 161–162

[181] Piganiol_VII_1754_236

[182] Jullian_II_1890_281–282

[183] Jullian_II_1890_282–283

[184] Jullian_1902_7

[185] SA_Bordeaux_III_ 1876_193

[186] Marion_1852_38

[187] Viographe_Bordelais_ 1844_85–86

[188] RA_V_1885_231–232

[189] Caumont_Cours_III_ 1838_346–347

[190] Clément_V_1868_111–112

[191] Jullian_II_1890_317–318

[192] SHD_Génie_40/89

[193] SA_Bordeaux_XXIV_ 1903_60

[194] Young_1890_67, travelling 1787–9

[195] Stendhal_1891_II_365

[196] Corbun_18th century_4

[197] Jullian_II_1890_320

[198] Réunion_BA_XVII_1893

[199] Bernadau_1844_90–91

[200] Babeau_1894_183–184

[201] AD_Bordelais_ Périgord_1903_30

[202] SA_Bordeaux_V_ 1878_107–108

[203] Jullian_II_1890_313

[204] Jullian_II_1890_314

[205] Marion_1852_40

[206] Bernadau_1844_290

[207] SA_Bordeaux_XI_1886_ 11–12

[208] SA_Bordeaux_XI_1886_ 11

[209] Jullian_II_1890_ 310–311

[210] SA_Bordeaux_III_ 1876_163

[211] Jullian_II_1890_331–332

[212] SA_Bordeaux_XIV_1889_ 92

[213] Revue_Aquitaine_XIV_ 1869_575

[214] SA_Bordeaux_XXIV_ 1903_45

[215] SA_Bordeaux_IX_ 1882_45–48

[216] Jullian_II_1890_324

[217] Sansas_1878_123–130

[218] Sansas_1882_102–108

[219] SA_Bordeaux_XI_1886_ 62

[220] Marion_1852_37–38

[221] Caumont_I_1853_271

[222] Jullian_II_1890_400

[223] Jullian_II_1890_309–310

[224] Actes_Acad_Bordeaux_ 1862_34

[225] SA_Bordeaux_VIII_ 1881_154–155

[226] Jullian_II_1890_329

[227] SA_Bordeaux_XIX_ 1894_LXIV

[228] Société_Borda_Dax_ XVIII_1893_LXV

[229] Sansas_1874_56

[230] Soc_Arch_Bordeaux_ V_1878_171–172

[231] Jullian_1890_II_ 103–104

[232] Jullian_II_1890_332

[233] Espérandieu_II_1908_ 120–122

[234] Inscriptions_2010_ 116–146

[235] Bernadau_1844_15–16

[236] Montalembert_1839_ 53–54

[237] SA_Bordeaux_XI_1886_ XXI

[238] SA_Bordeaux_VIII_ 1881_156

[239] SA_Bordeaux_III_1876_ 76

[240] Jullian_II_1890_316–317

[241] Marion_1852_40

[242] AA_I_1844_97

[243] SA_Bordeaux_XXIV_ 1903_17

[244] SA_Bordeaux_XIV_1889_LIII–LIV

[245] BSA_Drôme_XI 1877_206

[246] Gravagnuolo_1994_18–19

[247] AMPF_XI_1897_64

[248] Brown_1905_93

[249] AMPF_XI_1897_195

[250] AMPF_XI_1897_49

[251] AMPF_II_1888_30

[252] RA_V_1848–9_255

[253] Panorama_Pittoresque_VI_1839_48

[254] Bull_Soc_Hist_Paris_VII_1880_91

[255] BSH_Paris_XI_1884_26

[256] RA_XIV_1866_361

[257] Réunion-des-Officiers_1873_13

[258] Petitjean_1895_30–31

[259] AA_I_1844_183

[260] AMPF_VIII_1894_55

[261] Normand_1894_72

[262] AMPF_IV_1890_18–19

[263] RA_XXI_1870_350

[264] AMPF_VI_1892_93

[265] AMPF_VI_1892_117

[266] AMPF_VI_1892_88–89

[267] Mérimée_1842_11

[268] BM_XVIII_1852_344

[269] Précis_Rouen_1869–1870_217

[270] BSH_Paris_XI_1884_71–72

[271] AMPF_I_1886–7_234

[272] AMPF_I_1886_130

[273] Labédollière_1860_276

[274] AA_I_1844_181

[275] AA_I_1844_180

[276] AA_III_1845_241

[277] AA I 1844, 181

[278] AMPF_1892_72

CHAPTER 7

The Île de France and Champagne

The towns close to Paris, with the best roads in the country (and then railways) radiating outward, generally lost their walls a couple of decades earlier than those further south, to accommodate not only the shibboleth of modernity, but also the requirements of industry. And although no towns were now first-class fortresses, the Génie was still much in evidence and, along with insouciant administrations, provided many opportunities for scholars to condemn them as crass and vandalistic. By the 1880s little Roman remained, obliterated under road works, or left to rot and then to be dismantled. For example, Chartres still had some ancient columns and capitals around Saint-Martin-en-Val,[1] their source unknown. The mediaeval streets "étaient bâties sans alignement bien arrêté,"[2] but by 1872 "le cordeau d'alignement novateur de la voirie munic-ipale" was imposing changes; and, after all, "l'on nous dit qu'il est juste que toute chose ait une fin."[3] Much of the ramparts of Château-Thierry survived into the 1880s, but were crumbling. The 19th century might have looked back to the 1616 by-law threatening prison and a fine for damaging the walls,[4] for by 1885 the question was whether neglect would bring them tumbling down, or whether sections would be classified as an historic monument.[5] Neglect won the day. The walls of Châlons-sur-Marne were dismantled in sections from 1742, and some stretches rented out, because they were recognised as "hors d'état de résister à une attaque sérieuse."[6] They had nearly all gone by 1850, but with some boulevards planned in 1874,[7] and the Génie retaining a grip on one section from 1876.[8] In the 18th century, the old town hall was demolished because it was gothic in style, even though "d'architecture infiniment plus riche que le bâtiment actuel."[9] It is suspected that antiquities went early into the lime kilns, or were re-cut, because "on n'a jamais trouvé traces d'un quel-conque grand monument (thermes, arènes, théâtre, temple) ni d'un forum," and only two stelai, of Dalmatian cavalrymen.[1]

---

1 Clause & Ravaux 1983, 17.

Beauvais

Beauvais[2] (Oise) is one of many French towns where mediaeval architecture dominates today, and which we do not associate with the Romans. The walls of Beauvais were similar to those of Soissons, and antiquities were retrieved in the 17th century.[10] But only scraps survived into the 19th century although they had been very extensive (and with several surviving towers) in the late 18th century. They were of petit appareil and brick, but the foundations courses were of spolia, and in the mid-19th century

> M. Capronnier, propriétaire de la maison dite de la belle image, adossée aux murs de l'enceinte gallo-romaine, en faisant percer une cave, les traversa sur une très grande épaisseur et trouva dans le massif un certain nombre de débris de colonnes, chapiteaux et sculptures antiques.[11]

Like other sites, the walls by the 1840s were a battleground between archaeologists and workmens' picks, as the enceinte came down.[12] The municipality was in favour of destruction, so that "le rempart une fois abattu, les maisons qu'il cachait s'embelliraient et offriraient bientôt de brillantes façades."[13] The walls were of course a tax on the town, and 140 surrounding villages also contributed to their upkeep. The mayor had begun their dismantling in 1804,[14] replacing them by promenades; but the work was lengthy, and one section was still standing in 1889.[15] The destruction was advanced and vigorous by 1842 and the Minister of the Interior, in spite of protests, decided it was pointless to stop the work.[16] In that year they were described as already a pretty walk:

> Ces remparts couverts d'arbres et entourés de fossés profonds, formaient une promenade d'où la vue dominait les environs. Inutiles â la défense de Beauvais depuis l'invention de l'artillerie, leur entretien constituait une des charges les plus onéreuses de la ville.[17]

Presumably because they were too difficult or too work-intensive to dismantle, the majority of the foundations survived.[18] At least the demolition allowed scholars to date them to Late Antiquity,[19] for they contained spolia such as sculpture, columns and even statues.[20] Work increased to a spurt for a few months in 1845:

---

2   Frézouls 1982, 109–176.

THE ÎLE DE FRANCE AND CHAMPAGNE

> On comprend l'immense tort fait à la ville ... Tandis que le conseil général souille, travestit, mutile et déshonore un évêché gothique, curieux monument de quatre époques différentes, le Conseil municipal arrache pierre à pierre des remparts gallo-romans qui imprimaient à la Cité un cachet original et pittoresque. Il y a rivalité de zèle pour les intérêts des administrés. Pauvre pays![21]

Some fragments and one tower were traceable throughout the town in 1861, especially in the cellars of later housing.[22] Yet so completely was the enceinte obliterated that (although short stretches of foundations kept coming to light) the Congrès archéologique of 1904 set tasks to be completed by local study for the congressists[23] – but there were no longer any walls, hence no related task. Yet papers were written on the walls in 1912, following digs. Some early houses were preserved.[24]

Outside the walls to the north-east was Mont-Capron, the site of a Roman temple,[25] and one of several fortifiable locations in the vicinity. In 1563, a local landowner uncovered antiquities here, "et la ville fit visiter le lieu pour sçavoir si ce avoit esté forteresse, chasteau ou aultre édifice."[26] In 1636, when the Spanish invaded Picardy, earth fortifications were raised here, and in the process more antiquities were uncovered.[27] The remains were taken to Beauvais, and re-used, the fortified position falling out of use:

> Plus tard, enfin, on planta la plate-forme et, en 1789, les remparts étaient devenus une espèce de promenade publique très fréquentée par les bourgeois et les Chevaliers du soleil du temps, pendant la semaine, et par les artisans, les dimanches et jours de fête. Les vieillards se disaient: "Allons faire un tour de remparts," comme ils se disent aujourd'hui: "Faisons un tour de boulevard."[28]

By the early 20th century, Mont-Capron was a town square. Excavations in 1896–1900 for the building of a reservoir there[29] recovered yet more material, matching blocks unearthed in the town itself, and suggesting that spolia from Mont-Capron had already gone into the Beauvais enceinte.[30]

Évreux

By 1835, Évreux was "une ville ouverte, qui a perdu presque tous ses monumens."[31] How did this happen? As an important Roman rown, it had been endowed with a citadel, walls and an aqueduct, as well as monuments.[32] The walls were pulled down starting in 1833, and spolia seen in the foundations;[33] sections were still being demolished in 1870, when the Congress met there.[34] This was a heavy task, for they were calculated to contain 45,000 cubic metres of masonry.[3] The Roman theatre was uncovered only in 1873, although the 17th-century naming of the location as "Chatel Sarrasin" and the later transformation of the structure into a fort might have been a sufficient clue.[35] The clue came up trumps in 1890 when the Town Hall was being rebuilt on the site, and in 1906, when "on retrouva des fondations constituées par des bas-reliefs, des fûts de colonnes et des chapiteaux."[36]

By 1845 the Abbaye de Saint-Sauveur at Évreux had become a barracks, and "on espère que le génie militaire respectera ce gracieux fragment,"[37] though congressists the following year feared its likely fate.[38] The town still possessed "many antique timber-framed houses, and on the Boulevards are traces of the walls which once defended it."[39] But in 1850, with a low population, and with few honourable exceptions, "le clergé, la magistrature et les membres de l'Université, se tiennent à l'écart du mouvement historique."[40] This nonchalance had a history: in 1652 ancient blocks and even statues had been re-cut into new slabs,[41] and soon the Cathedral was to be treated to restoration in the 1870s,[42] one of several "reconstruites partiellement et perdant leur cachet primitif pour prendre celui de M. Viollet-le-Duc et consorts," and "nulle part, toutefois, l'abus de pouvoir n'a été plus odieux qu'à Évreux."[43] This was indeed odious, for "démolir pour reconstruire, sous le prétexte de réparer, c'est le mot d'ordre de ces hommes, qui gaspillent les fonds du pays et défigurent à plaisir nos monuments les plus vénérables."[44] As the town modernised, in 1889 lime kilns as well as a large bronze were revealed when building the gas works.[45]

A few kilometres south-east of the town was Vieil Évreux, a small village, where the commune often dug for building stone. By 1839 it still had walls, the remains of an aqueduct,[46] and palace, circus and baths.[47] This site was enthusiastically dug, and yielded large quantities of antiquities, including bronze statues, as the 1850 publication of one excavator makes clear.[48] Here landowners were happy to have an archaeologist turn over the soil, "dont le terrain ne pouvait que s'améliorer par l'effet des fouilles."[49] The first dig was 1801–4, then 1842, then again 1911, 1933–49, and 1973–8.[4]

---

3   Follain 2005; Combet 2011, 48–50 for the calculated 45,000 cubic metres of large blocks at Périgueux, in the 950m enceinte.

4   Chiquet 1999.

Reims

Reims was a heritage site, where French kings were crowned, and the victim of German shelling in the First World War. The town was conscious of the importance of its monuments (which might have included a Roman castrum[50]) and sought to preserve them, including 16th century material,[51] as well as finds from the Roman cellars.[52] The Génie recorded in their archives a 1699 account of ancient monuments then surviving, including the triumphal arch,[53] which was embedded in the mediaeval walls until disengaged in the early 19th century. As was standard with so much earth-shifting, there were also finds of mosaic floors.[5] The town also recognised the support such a meeting of distinguished scholars could offer, and the 1845 congress held there included, for the first time, a special mass.[54] The Abbé Nanquette wrote in 1844:

> Depuis quelques années, les monuments historiques sont singulière-ment en faveur, et, grâce à la toute-puissance de l'opinion, leur conserva-tion est à peu près assurée. Il s'est formé entre l'Eglise et l'Etat, entre les sociétés savantes et tous ceux qui s'occupent d'art et d'histoire une espèce de sainte-alliance qui rendra désormais impossible le retour du vandalisme,

And he underlined the need to "rétablir, au moins sur le papier, ceux qui ont déjà disparu."[55] Such unanimity (scholars, municipality, Church, public opinion) was indeed unusual, contrasting with the relative lack of public interest in conservation, and was to make for some vigorous defences in the following decades. It was not always sweetness and light. The important church of Saint-Niçaise, with splendid architecture, was sold around 1798 to an entrepreneur; dismantling had started in 1791, and the structure was completely gone by 1844.[56] Although the tomb of its architect was transferred to the Cathedral of Notre-Dame,[57] the church and its stained-glass windows were not fully recorded. Its historiated mosaic floor (scenes from the Old Testament) was transferred to Notre-Dame (whose own labyrinth had been destroyed in 1778); but Saint-Rémi's floor went "à empierrer un chemin vicinal."[58] Much was thought to remain below ground, as reflected in one of several questions put

---

5   Boussinesq & Laurent 1933 I, 79–83; the arch had bas-reliefs and busts in roundels, now largely destroyed, and survives only because Duquenelle, a local archaeologist, got it classified. 93–6 for mosaics discovered 1650ff, toujours en place, en attendant qu'une occasion favorable permette de les recueillir.

by the Congrès here in 1845, "Donner autant que possible le plan de la ville gallo-romaine et de ses abords."[59] In 1848, as a way of providing employment, the administration ordered the demolition of part of the ramparts,[60] and the triumphal arch was in the way of the railway! The administration beat a retreat: "elle a bien compris que, si elle doit favoriser les développements de l'industrie, elle ne doit pas oublier que les études historiques comptent beaucoup de partisans."[61]

Laon

Laon was battered and besieged in 1814/15,[62] and promenades and antiquities were lost in their reworking and in the attacks,[63] although work in 1831 and 1836 brought to light other antique blocks.[64] Reworking the military esplanade in 1840 brought yet more to light, and portions of wall collapsed in the early 1850s.[65] The Génie made some repairs in 1853 which involved dismantling some of the Roman walls with gunpowder, At Laon, declassified in 1850, a dodge was used to maintain control of the town, for the tax-booths (the octroi, a longstanding reason for maintaining town walls) could make use of the old fortifications to control ingress and egress, meaning that they would be retained. In 1860 Demilly protested against this system in a 26-page pamphlet, mocking the desire for this new use for the (partial) walls,[66] the decrepit state of which he describes. He had bought a house in 1855, separated from a main street by a section of wall which, like Reagan of Berlin, he called on the Mayor to demolish. The walls were a brake on development:

> On ne peut que déplorer, au point de vue de l'intérêt général de la commune, la marche qui a été suivie en cette circonstance. Les obstacles qui ont été ainsi apportés à l'extension de la ville, à la facilité des communications, qui est le but des grands travaux publics de notre époque, nuisent à l'accroissement de la population et à tout développement inlustriel et commercial du chef-lieu du département.[67]

Archaeologists were active near the town as well, at Nizy-le-Comte in 1852–3, revealing a variety of antiquities,[68] and at Coucy in 1857, where stone cannonballs (conceivably cut from antiquities) were unearthed,[69] such projectiles being common not only in antiquity but also in the Middle Ages.[70] Huge quantities were fired, and many recovered, as at Thérouanne[71] and Amiens.[72]

THE ÎLE DE FRANCE AND CHAMPAGNE

Sens

Ce serait pour la ville un crime de lèse-archéologie et un acte de mauvaise administration de laisser par négligence perdre des trésors qui en sont à la fois l'histoire et l'honneur. Quand une ville a un musée romain qui se vient mettre à côté de ceux d'Arles, de Lyon, de Vienne et de Narbonne, elle se doit à elle-même de garder son rang. [1881][73]

Sens, "a large, ragged, ancient city,"[74] which nearly lost its cathedral during the Revolution,[75] began to lose some of the lower courses of its Gallo-Roman walls (the upper ones were mediaeval)[76] in the 1830s, when Caumont was distressed to see old blocks being sawn up for reuse.[77] Promenades were already planted on the line of the ditches in 1719, and an esplanade constructed from 1755. Work also proceeded with demolishing fortifications around the porte Saint-Didier. The Intendant would not allow the gate itself to be demolished, but the adjacent ditches were filled in 1791, and a new boulevard constructed,[78] while in 1801 the Conseil discussed getting rid of all the gates.[79] The early demolition work, the start of "une enceinte de délicieuses promenades" which Julliot describes in 1898,[80] together with the poor state of the ramparts as demonstrated by the 1814 siege,[81] show why in 1836 the enceinte was declassified, with the proviso that the antiquities therein be preserved. Inevitably, this condition was more honoured in the breach than in the observance. The municipality gave landowners the stretches adjacent to their property, and then sold surplus materials, including some decorated blocks from the foundation courses.[82] Thankfully, Caumont and Mérimée were able (temporarily) to halt this practice, so that Tastu could admire them in 1846, as well as the modern aspect of the town itself,[83] although others were disconcerted by what they saw as the low quality or unfinished state of some of the finds.[84]

In the early 1840s small sections between the St-Rémy and Dauphine Gates had been demolished, and Caumont expressed his delight at the finds revealed, in some cases only after getting a mason to remove the covering mortar. In other words, some stones would have been invisible because covered in hard mortar and, because the mortar was harder than the stone, needed professional masons to help get them cleaned, in this case to reveal architraves, a pedestal, etc.[85] The very use of hard mortar probably meant that large quantities of concealed sculpture were removed or destroyed without being recognised. In 1838 he had seen blocks pulled out and sawn up for reuse and, upon protesting, was informed that les architectes et inspecteurs officiels avaient vu toutes ces sculptures, qu'ils les avaient regardées avec indifférence, n'avaient fait aucune réclamation contre leur destruction, et qu'on avait conclu de là qu'elles n'avaient pas d'intérêt archéologique.[86]

The continuing loss of walls (a museum in themselves)[87] was reported in 1849:

Tout a été démoli, et les matériaux ont servi à de nouvelles et chétives bâtisses . . . la Société française pour la conservation des monuments historiques a témoigné ses regrets de ce qu'on ait laissé détruire l'une des murailles gallo-romaines qui offrait, en France, un des plus beaux exemples de l'architecture militaire antique.[88]

Indeed, by 1867 the museum contained only ten funerary monuments, eight bas-reliefs and a few inscriptions and architectural fragments[89] but, given what had already been retrieved from the walls, much more was to be expected. Abbé Fenel had known as much in 1736, "pourvu qu'on renverse la ville de fond-en-comble pour en retrouver toutes les pierres."[90] But when this was done (for the Roman level was at least 2m below the current one) retrieved antiquities such as mosaic floors, of which there were several, did not survive.[91] At least some of the blocks retrieved were drawn.[92] And in 1851 Caumont was complaining that the local administration provided funds only to transport the finds to Paris – quite the wrong thing to do with them: "c'est les détruire; autant vaudrait les jeter immédiatement dans l'Yonne."[93] This might have been an exaggeration, since in 1863 there were antiquities in the Town Hall courtyard, "mal défendus des intempéries par des hangars insuffisants, et condamnés, s'ils restent dans cet état, à une inévitable et prochaine destruction."[94] This was the beginnings of a lapidary museum, very much faute de mieux, the shelter being provided in 1848, and organisation delayed until 1864.[95]

For the large number of losses, and the poor state of the survivals, the finger was pointed at administrative indifference.[96] As Vaudin noted in 1882, referring back to destruction of the Archbishop's Chapel in 1793, the administration's vandalism was indeed incurable.[97] For Montaiglon in 1881, so much had already gone that the remainder must be preserved because, as we have seen, lack of protection would be the crime of "lèse-archéologie."[98] The lesson was evidently learned, for by the beginning of the next century the predominant advice was that the surviving remains of the walls together with their antiquities should be left in place, because extracting them would cause damage: "qu'on n'en tirera pas le plus souvent sans bien des chances de destruction."[99] And even if "la génération présente a vu disparaître, presque en totalité, la robuste enceinte de nos pères, remplacée de nos jours par des

THE ÎLE DE FRANCE AND CHAMPAGNE

jardins ensoleillés," the warlike remains of the town's past should nevertheless be preserved.[100] Although sections of wall were still being pulled down in 1910, such preservation was easier said than done, because the local Society was still chronically short of funds,[101] just as it had been thirty years previously.[102] In 1908 the Conseil Municipal came to a well-meaning decision to force speculators demolishing sections of wall to preserve any antiquities discovered; but blocks unearthed proved to be of little interest[103] – proof positive that the decision came nearly a century too late.

One kilometre south of the town walls were the remains of the Abbey of the Prémontrés, on a site known as the Motte-du-Ciar [conceivably César], and built with antiquities retrieved there. Substantial remains were above ground in the 18th century, but in 1844–6 the municipality sold the right to extract the remaining stones, to the alarm of the local Society. However, all they were able to do was to produce a plan, since the concessionnaire and surrounding proprietors were excavating as speedily as possible in the hope of selling the blocks to the railway company.[104] Varieties of marble had been found at the site, and as late as 1881 "cette Motte de Ciar a été et est encore une carrière pour Sens, où la pierre est rare et chère à cause du prix de transport."[105] The fact that two railway engineers at Sens were both members of the Society in the 1840s does not seem to have stopped the sell-off, any more than did municipal influence on the destruction of the town walls, being exploited as a stone-quarry by 1849.[106] Matters had certainly changed since 1518, when a citizen was fined and banished for filching stones from the walls.[107]

By the 19th century, little was left of the amphitheatre, supposedly systematically dismantled with some blocks perhaps making up the foundations of the town walls.[108] This was determined after desultory excavations in 1849),[109] when nothing decorative was discovered[110] – although this was scarcely surprising, given that funds were available for the employment of only two workmen. Further destruction of the town walls in 1910 to lay out the Boulevard du Mail produced stones probably re-used from the amphitheatre, which lay nearby.[111] Wooden houses fared no better than other antiquities. One such house, already repaired in 1540 (as declared in an inscription), lost its decorations in 1829: "Des artistes étrangers ont bien souvent dessiné ces figures qui ont été détruites récemment; mais qui embellissent aujourd'hui leur album."[112]

Soissons

The late Roman walls of Soissons, commanding the passage over the Aisne, covered only some 20ha, but with suburbs outside them[113] and a citadel within.[114] There was a mediaeval enceinte, but part of this was rendered

226   CHAPTER 7

superfluous by yet more walls which were added in 1414, and land cleared. With work by the Génie in the 1830s the fortifications, already well out of date by 1800, were brought up-to-date. This involved much digging over large stretches of ground,[115] not least because the town had been bombed by the Allies in 1814, forcing a capitulation after a month-long siege, and underlining the inadequacy of both walls and accommodation.[116] During this new work, significant antiquities were again unearthed,[117] part of the work being on the site of the Château d'Albâtre. Work on this site was renewed from 1841,[118] when the scholars were happy to have the Génie do the heavy lifting,[119] especially because of the large area the Château covered.[120] Their appetite had already been whetted by the unearthing in 1832 by the Génie of an important Niobid Group,[121] and finds in the area were still being made in the 1870s,[122] conceivably assisted by the ruination of part of the town in the 1870 bombardment.

A casualty was the site of the so-called Château (or Palais) d'Albâtre,[123] so rich in antiquities, and especially in rare marbles,[124] that it was believed to be a Gallo-Roman palace, although one author suggested the name derived from a Roman arms factory, the Balistaria.[125] This was dug for both antiquities and building materials at various times.[126] The buildings supposedly disappeared during the construction of the new walls, although a statue was found when fortifications were being dug in 1551, with contributions reluctantly made by the inhabitants.[127] (The 1551 fortifications included St-Jean-des-Vignes,[128] discussed below.) Accounts record the finding of marble, alabaster, jasper and porphyry in the area,[129] with more discoveries in the 1750s[130] as well as in 1762.[131]

However, all was not sweetness and light, for the Génie's work from 1826 dug and knocked down old walls, producing many finds; the administration was not interested, there was as yet no local archaeological society, and

> Les officiers du génie s'occupaient d'élever des murs de fortifications et de creuser des fossés; ils ne pensaient guère à constater l'existence de ces vieux murs qui revoyaient la lumière après tant de siècles d'enfouissement.[132]

In the early 19th century they also built into the new walls antiquities retrieved from the Château, and stored other antique débris in a garden they had appropriated.[133] As well as digging around the site of the Palais d'Albâtre, they also interfered with the Cathedral,[134] but only for their own purposes: "Des mosaïques se rencontraient partout... On fut obligé de faire sauter à la mine des masses de murailles dont l'épaisseur dépassait trois mètres."[135] Mosaic floors had been found since the 17th century, but destroyed.[136]

THE ÎLE DE FRANCE AND CHAMPAGNE

227

The important abbey of Saint-Jean-des-Vignes, within the 1551 walls, and already partly ravaged and dismantled as a result of the Revolution,[137] was largely destroyed by the military, although as late as 1837 "quelques réparations peu coûteuses suffiraient pour garantir longtemps encore la conservation des précieux restes."[138] Caumont had predicted as much three years before: "il ne reste plus que deux côtés qui seront probablement démolis par le génie militaire et vendus à la toise comme les deux cotés qui ont déjà disparu avec l'église de l'abbaye."[139] The Comité archéologique de Soissons was congratulated on drawing the church before the main body was pulled down,[140] leaving a magnificent façade which "sera heureusement conservée comme un monument d'architecture des plus remarquables de France."[141] Then came the 1870 bombardment, including the towers of this church,[142] following which there were more demolitions.[143] The bombardment had affected the small cloister, and "Le génie militaire, qui avait besoin de moellons pour réparer le corps d'habitation de ses officiers, en a détruit une partie, sous prétexte qu'elle menaçait de s'écrouler."[144] The façade still stands today, the gaps of the rose-window and doorways showing there is nothing but air behind it, and fragments of cloisters to the side. Such destruction proved to be pointless, for the town was declassified in 1885, roads and boulevards laid out where the fortifications had been, and some areas sold off for housing. Soissons

> deviendra une ville moderne, souriante, gaie, gracieuse, avec ses larges boulevards plantés d'arbres, ornés de villas coquettes où se trouve réuni tout ce que le génie industriel a inventé de plus confortable et de plus élégant.[145]

Soissons also possessed a very large Roman theatre, with seating for 22,000 spectators,[146] of which parts of the cavea survived into the 19th century. This sat in the gardens of the Great Seminary, and was unearthed by the Génie in 1836,[147] for non-archaeological reasons, a fact proved by their destruction of its walls to ground level a little later,[148] with some of its blocks doubtless incorporated into the defensive works they built near the site.[149] Characteristically, the Génie also tried in 1832 to block the purchase by the municipality of a building used as a Town Hall after the destruction by fire of an earlier structure: they wanted it for a barracks.[150]

Road-work within the town in the 1860s uncovered traces of Roman roads[151] – the same work which was straightening out the town's streets, to the detriment of her old brick-and-wood houses. One 15th-century specimen in rue St-Christophe was targeted for rescue in 1842, but was destroyed, the town council reckoning that the decorated wood ornaments were only of

228   CHAPTER 7

interest in the standing structure and, after all, think of the cost of purchase, and where were they to be housed? As a result, "Ils disparurent donc, et après avoir été offerts pour le prix ordinaire des bois de construction, ils finirent par être brûlés comme le bois le plus vulgaire."[152] The local scholars recognised their impotence in the face of such attitudes, and sometimes their inability to save even inscriptions: "quand les splendides monuments sont tombés, ces monceaux de gazon, ces quelques lettres échappées viennent relever un fait ignoré et qui allait retomber dans la nuit du temps."[153] They were also lugubrious about the "restoration of churches in their century, "livrées à des architectes, à des entrepreneurs, à des maçons, peu soucieux comme tout le monde alors, de l'art, de l'histoire et des monuments."[154]

What remained of the Roman or mediaeval town landscape after the waves of French modernisation? At Senlis (Lot), parts of the ancient towers (originally 29/30 in number) are still occupied as houses, although most of the walls went in the 19th century.[6] When the locals missed a trick, as at Senlis, it was to be strangers who undertook study of the ramparts.[155] Although most of the late Roman structure[156] had been demolished under Louis XI, "On en voit encore de précieux restes"[157] in the mid-18th century. There were plenty of antiquities found during 1805 demolitions,[158] and yet more remaining in 1866, namely "L'enceinte fortifiée, le vieux château, les arènes, le sol même de la cité sont autant de dépôts précieux où chaque jour amène de nouvelles découvertes,"[159] although relatively few sculpted blocks seems to have survived.[160] More of the surviving walls would have been visible had the houses set against them been demolished.[161]

Conclusion

The Île de France and Champagne were the richest parts of France, near the capital, more heavily populated than most other areas, and with good agricultural land. But because of these features these regions were denuded by wars and sieges and by the Revolution. The Génie, in the course of protecting such riches while town walls stood, did damage to many monuments. By the 19th century, as the walls came down, competition amongst themselves and

---

6 Durand & Bonnet-Laborderie 1995, 22–7 for gallo-roman and 28–35 for mediaeval walls. 28–9: Coqueret's 1811 plan shows the mediaeval walls partly intact, some sections coming down at the end of the 18th century; 33–35 for quarries, including Roman ones with vaults, under the town itself.

THE ÎLE DE FRANCE AND CHAMPAGNE

with the Capital meant that towns in this region were eager to be as up-to-date as Paris. They were generally uninterested in the past, and in the process of modernisation old centres were lost and town environs radically altered by new roads and railways. Prosperity and modernity, as well as providing funds to mangle standing religious monuments (the preservation-restoration dilemma), wreaked more destruction on ancient monuments than (in the current turn of phrase) the Saracens or Barbarians ever accomplished.

[1] CHA_1900_199
[2] BSA_Eure-et-Loire_I_1858_140
[3] BSA_Eure-et-Loire_V_1872_150
[4] Ann_Soc_Château-Thierry_1869_136
[5] BA_Comité_1885_185
[6] Grignon_1889_20–21
[7] Grignon_1889_214
[8] Grignon_1889_16
[9] Grignon_1889_147
[10] Mém_Oise_XVIII_1901_73–74
[11] Mém_Oise_XIV_1889_361
[12] BM_X_1844_340
[13] Barraud_1861_62
[14] Mém_Oise_XVIII_1901_503
[15] Mém_Oise_XIV_1889_362–363
[16] Barraud_1861_64
[17] Doyen_1842_84
[18] Labande_1892_3
[19] Barraud_1861_58
[20] Rép_Arch_France_Oise_1888_17
[21] Mém_Picardie_VIII_1845_320–321
[22] Barraud_1861_61–62
[23] Corresp_Hist_Archéol_XI_1904_122
[24] Guilbert_II_1845_136
[25] Barraud_1861_31

[26] Mém_Oise_XL_1880_449–450
[27] Barraud_1861_32
[28] Mém_Oise_XIV_1889_362
[29] Mém_Oise_XVIII_1901_61
[30] Mém_Oise_XVIII_1901_74
[31] Recueil_Soc_Ag_Eure_VI_1835_372
[32] Guilmeth_1835_7
[33] Schuermans_1877_79
[34] BM_XXXVI_1870_362
[35] BA_Comité_1901_222–223
[36] Blanchet_1907_38
[37] BM_XI_1845_621
[38] SG_XV_Falaise_1847_86
[39] Murray_1848_74
[40] Rogue_1850_VI
[41] Blanchet_1907_38
[42] SG_XLII_Chalons-sur-Marne_1875_451–452
[43] SG_XLII_Châlons-sur-Marne_1875_481
[44] SG_XLII_Châlons-sur-Marne_1875_452–453
[45] SG_LVI_Evreux_1889_258
[46] Panorama_Pittoresque_I_Paris_1839_10
[47] Malte-Brun_II_1881_14
[48] AA_X_1850_302

[49] Rever_1827_9
[50] Tarbé_1844_220
[51] Ann_Acad_Reims_II_1843–1844_270
[52] Tarbé_1844_37–38
[53] SHD_Génie_80/2
[54] AA_III_1845_129
[55] AA_Reims_II_1844_239
[56] AA_Reims_III_1843–1844_262–263
[57] AA_I_1844_145
[58] AA_Reims_II_1843–1844_252
[59] CS_France_XIII_1845_Reims_xxxii
[60] Anon_Reims_1864_64
[61] Anon_Reims_1864_149–150
[62] Martin_&_Jacob_I_1837_55
[63] Martin_&_Jacob_I_1837_63
[64] BSA_Laon_VII_1858_230
[65] Fleury_1877_197
[66] Demilly_1860_4
[67] Demilly_1860_5
[68] BSA_Laon_VI_1857_174
[69] BSA_Laon_VI_1857_276
[70] Mém_AIBL_II_série_VI_1888_65–66
[71] Enlart_1920_16
[72] Goze_1854_166
[73] Montaiglon_1881_18
[74] Thicknesse_1789_165

[75] Mém_Aube_XXXIII_1830_114–115

[76] BSA_Sens_1851_87

[77] BA_Comité_1910_129–130

[78] Tarbé_1838_350–407

[79] Julliot_1913_6–8

[80] Julliot_1898_28

[81] Perrin_1901_181

[82] BM_IV_1838_464–465

[83] Tastu_1846_14–15

[84] BSA_Sens_1852_27

[85] BM_XIII_1847_658–659

[86] Caumont_1851_150–151

[87] Montaiglon_1881_3

[88] BM_XV_1849_147–148

[89] BSA_Sens_IX_1867_286

[90] SG_XIV_Sens_1847_161

[91] Montaiglon_1881_3–4

[92] BM_XXVI_1860_112

[93] Caumont_1851_151

[94] BSS_Yonne_1863_XXXV

[95] Montaiglon_1881_4–5

[96] Vaudin_1882_240

[97] Vaudin_1882_194

[98] Montaiglon_1881_18

[99] BCA_Seine-Inférieure_XIII_1903–5_51

[100] Perrin_1901_4

[101] BA_Comité_1910_127–128

[102] BA_Comité_1884_270

[103] BA_Comité_1910_128

[104] SG_XIV_Sens_1847_50–52

[105] Montaiglon_1881_9

[106] BM_XV_1849_242

[107] BSA_Sens_1851_29

[108] BM_XV_1949_521

[109] BSA_Sens_1851_72

[110] BSA_Sens_1851_74

[111] BA_Comité_1910_37

[112] Tarbé_1838_135

[113] Leroux_1839_75

[114] Fleury_1877_196–197

[115] BSA_Soissons_V_1875_271

[116] Laurendeau_1868_145

[117] BSA_Soissons_VIII_1854_48–49

[118] SG_VIII_Caen_1841_64

[119] BSA_Soissons_VIII_1854_39

[120] BSA_Soissons_VIII_1854_29

[121] BICA_1832_145

[122] Fleury_1878_32

[123] Martin_&_Jacob_II_1837_286–287

[124] Martin_&_Jacob_1837_I_62

[125] Martin_&_Jacob_1837_I_61

[126] Leroux_1839_89–103

[127] BSA_Soissons_IX_1878_18

[128] BSA_Soissons_V_1875_282

[129] Leclercq_de_Laprairie_1854_20

[130] BSA_Soissons_XII_1881_140–141

[131] Fleury_1877_202

[132] BSA_Soissons_VIII_1854_45–46

[133] BSA_Soissons_XX_1892_120

[134] BSA_Soissons_VIII_1854_39

[135] BSA_Soissons_VIII_1854_48–49

[136] Martin_&_Jacob_1837_I_58–59

[137] BSA_Soissons_XVI_1861_74

[138] Martin_&_Jacob_II_1837_Appendix_39

[139] BM_I_1834_402

[140] AA_VIII_1848_232

[141] BM_III_1837_257

[142] BSA_Soissons_III_1872_234–235

[143] RFD_1872_11

[144] BSA_Soissons_IV_1875_94

[145] BSA_Soissons_VII_1897_1–2

[146] BSA_Soissons_VIII_1854_67

[147] BSA_Soissons_I_1847_86

[148] BSA_Soissons_I_1847_93

[149] BSA_Soissons_I_1847_109

[150] BSA_Soissons_V_1875_350

[151] BSA_Soissons_III_1862_143

[152] BSA_Soissons_VIII_1854_278–288

[153] BSA_Soissons_VI_1852_20

[154] BSA_Soissons_VII_1877_145–146

[155] Ann_Arch_Français_I_1877_62

[156] SG_XLIV_Senlis_1877_436–442

[157] Piganiol_I_1753_338

[158] Mém_Oise_XVIII_1901_75

[159] SG_XXXIII_Senlis_1866_26

[160] Espérandieu_XI_1938_8352

[161] SG_XXXIII_Senlis_1866_32–33

CHAPTER 8

Normandy, the North, Burgundy and Points East

Normandy and the Loire

Large amounts of Roman antiquities once survived in Normandy, only to be destroyed, mostly during the 19th century. At Bayeux, which retained some foundations from the gallo-roman walls in mid-century,[1] some scholars identified Roman antiquities in the Cathedral crypt,[2] and others had been identified in 1824 under S. Laurent,[3] which was on the site of baths.[4] Plenty of antiquities were found underground, such as column shafts and architectural elements visible in 1857 in the remains of its castrum.[5] Interest slackened in the 1870s,[6] but then picked up again.[7] Another important site was Lillebonne[1] (Seine-Inférieure) apparently little occupied beyond the 3rd century. It was neglected by scholars until details of its theatre were published in the mid-18th century, and then again until 1812 when some digging took place.[8] Just what treasures might once have existed is perhaps reflected in the finds around a lime kiln, including sections of a tomb, and sculptures.[9] It had a castrum, the site later occupied by the château[2] of the Dukes of Normandy, with more reused spolia,[10] so much that digging into the modern town revealed the Roman town beneath.[11] Three Roman bronzes were found in the enceinte of Lillebonne in 1870. Scholars were also slow in studying **Lisieux**, which had fortifications until the early 19th century.[12] However, although the subject of study in 1860,[13] no traces remained by 1900.[14] The theatre, discovered in 1762, had not been dug by 1911.[15] Many antiquities were revealed in the late 18th century, and cartloads carried away,[16] presumably as building stone.

Rouen

Just as freeing a town of the Army was described as a mania, so was the "fanatisme de la ligne droite," a juggernaut which destroyed everything in its

---

1 Lechevallier 1989, 47–78 for Roman monuments; 60–61 for dig of baths at place Félix-Faure; 76–7 for late castrum with reused blocks; the mediaeval château later took up the SE corner, and reused the retaining wall; 88–91 for plan of the castle hill from Caylus – but nothing on the 19th-century demolitions of walls etc.

2 Mesqui 2008, 117–168 for extracts from building accounts to demonstrate the building's afterlife; but containing no references to Roman blocks, presumably because their reuse was simply routine.

© KONINKLIJKE BRILL NV, LEIDEN, 2015 | DOI 10.1163/9789004293717_010

path[17] – and which in certain locations required the agreement of the Génie.[18] Thus in 1846 Rouen was already suffering from the Minister of Public Works' predilection for straight streets, and losing important buildings in the process.[19] Surely, wrote scholars of Rouen in 1859, some give-and-take was to be sought between the preservation of old structures and the needs of commerce?[20] The city was still complaining at the end of the century, noting that its old buildings were among the best in Europe,[21] and protesting against the authorities' ban on restoration of the structures they targeted, as they waited for them simply to fall down.[22] This destruction extended to Merovingian and earlier cemeteries outside the original walls, as towns expanded, as had already been the case for example at Angers in 1871[23] and at Nancy earlier in the century.[24]

Under the Empire, Rouen flourished behind her strong walls, but may have developed into just a military fortress by the 4th century,[3] and erected walls which one scholar believes remained unchanged into the mid-12th century.[4] Although she caught a new dose of the alignment-and-boulevard disease in the later 19th century, she stands out among the towns of northern France for the insistence with which her earlier monuments were protected by her scholars, generally struggling against the administration. The town had seen some destruction of old buildings in 1729,[25] and the dismantling of a fortress "dont l'utilité avait depuis longtemps été contestée."[26] Parts of the city had been modernised 1769–1785,[5] when the old 12th-century walls[27] were pulled down, boulevards put in their place (forming a feature remarked on by travellers,[28] and leaving several fragments in place[29]), street lighting introduced, and then houses numbered.[30] (Tours introduced paving, lighting, clean streets and water in the same period,[6] as did Reims).[7] Old structures were also destroyed in the early 19th century, because at this period "Rouen n'a pas la main heureuse en fait d'architectes municipaux,"[31] because

---

3 Esmonde Cleary 2013, 91: "It is interesting to note that the dux tractus Armoricani et Nervicani has listed among his installations Rouen, Avranches, Coutances, Vannes and Nantes, which under the early empire had been cities, but which, as we have seen in the case of Rouen, may by the fourth century have been more purely military."

4 Mollat 1979, 54; but little is known about its replacement.

5 Mollat 1979, 99–182: Changer la ville – security, hygiene (including moving cemeteries), water, and light.

6 Baumier 2007, 388–407.

7 Boussinesq & Laurent 1933 II, 149–214: La transformation de la ville de Reims au milieu du XVIIIᵉ siècle – lighting, paving, roadworks, water, fountains and promenades.

NORMANDY, THE NORTH, BURGUNDY AND POINTS EAST   233

le peuple s'était persuadé que l'art du moyen âge et de la Renaissance était hideux; on ne se bornait plus à supprimer ses œuvres quand des motifs d'utilité en fournissaient l'occasion...un vent de mauvais goût soufflait en tempête.[32]

Antiquities from the walls were being turned up in the mid-19th century,[33] and blocks from a substantial two-storey mausoleum were recovered from the ramparts in 1993; this section had been undermined and collapsed, probably in the 13th century, and conceivably in the search for blocks suitable for reuse.8 Luckily for earlier monuments, and in spite of an increase in population,9 the destruction now halted until the 1880s, with scholars and prefects following the same agenda, and the Prefect, Baron Kergariou, initiating the department's Commission des antiquités in 1818, and providing funds for digging.[34] The church of Saint-Georges de Boscherville was saved,[35] thanks to the Prefect, who congratulated himself in front of scholars in 1829 "d'avoir le premier donné l'impulsion à vos travaux, qui ont eux-mêmes contribué, sans doute, à propager dans le public le goût de l'archéologie."[36] This benevolence led to the discovery of Roman remains in the late 1820s[37] and, in its turn, to buttering up the next Prefect to maintain the same interest in the past, reporting that thanks to his help "quelques monuments remarquables ont été préservés d'une entière destruction."[38] In 1834 scholars wrote asking him to help save a gate, asking "pourquoi les souvenirs de notre ancienne France nous seraient-ils moins précieux que ceux d'Athènes et de Rome?[39] And in 1842 he was petitioned to clear the cluttered houses preventing clear views of St-Ouen, the best church in Rouen.[40] Discoveries had been made in the 18th century which might have been sections of the Roman walls,[41] but in 1839, at 4m below the surface, spolia-rich Roman foundation walls were found.[42]

Nor were later monuments neglected: by 1840 over 50 16th–18th-century tombstones were recovered, which by 1870 formed "au musée départemental un nécrologie monastique dont l'intérêt s'accroîtra avec les années."[43] In 1840 also, there was a successful plea to the Prefect to save the donjon of Philippe-Auguste,[44] renamed by some media-savvy and routinely dishonest politician the Tour Jeanne d'Arc. Even town improvements uncovered antiquities, as when in 1840 more sections of the ancient wall were uncovered,[45] and in 1846 the cutting of the new rue Impériale revealed a Roman house with wall paintings.[46] Punctiliously detailed lists were kept of antiquities uncovered,[47]

---

8   Delestre & Perin 1995, 11. 200 limestone blocks of the mausoleum were recovered, and a model made; Poirel 1995, 11–13 for the castrum, 28–29, 44–45 for reconstruction of the mausoleum.
9   Saupin 2002, 52–55 for figures.

234   CHAPTER 8

and a survey was published in 1860–61 on Rouen's archaeology.[48] Nor were
mediaeval and later houses and other structures neglected. It was here that
scholars could not see eye-to-eye with the administration, who were trying to
open the city for commerce but, of course, "les rues les plus pittoresques seront
presque toujours les moins saines, et dans des remaniements semblables à
ceux qui viennent d'être signalés, il ne peut manquer de s'offrir quelque sacrifice à faire pour l'archéologie."[49] Again, the Génie was in the forefront of
destruction, and the scholars had to negotiate to secure high-quality wood-
work,[50] even projecting in 1869 a museum for wood to match the existing one
for faïence.[51]

    Not that the museum was always alert to acquiring material from demoli-
tions, such as that of the church of Bonne-Nouvelle in 1885.[52] Parts of this
were from the time of William the Conqueror, but it was pulled down to
rebuild army barracks on the site; the façade was photographed, and officers of
the Génie made drawings.[53]

    But complete protectionism was not to work because, by the 1880s, Rouen
was an industrial city with a port, and mechanisation, so that "la modification profonde survenue depuis 1870 dans ses conditions d'existence se pour-
suit avec une rapidité extrême."[54] However, some were still alert to problems.
In 1894, when the Conseil Municipal proposed demolishing the 17th-century
chapel at the Lycée Corneille, a concerted protest campaign by scholarly societies and architects as far away as Paris saved the complex.[55] Rouen, indeed,
like other towns, pretended it had found a way of integrating the notable past
with the modernising present, noting in 1897 that the solution was "en ménag-
eant partout où il en est besoin de jolis îlots archéologiques qui rompent la
monotonie de la perspective et attirent l'œil des visiteurs."[56] Whistling in the
dark dated back to 1860, including the motto "Ville archéologique; ville-musée,
Rouen est également ville moderne."[57] But this was accommodation to a fait
accompli, and visitors might not have been satisfied by mere islets especially
when, at the beginning of the 20th century, the rue Jeanne-d'Arc, "la gloire de
Rouen," was mangled[58] and it was proposed to clear space around the cathedral – naturally by destroying old houses.[59] Parisian scholars deplored the
project and, while recognising that "les municipalités sont souvent d'accord
avec le mauvais goût du public," warned the Rouennais against "l'exemple
désastreux donné par les Parisiens, qui, après avoir créé un steppe devant la
façade Notre-Dame, ont écrasé l'abside de l'église par le voisinage d'immeubles
à cinq étages."[60] And even while providing funds for restoration of the cathedral, the Municipality declared poverty in the face of pleas from scholars and
from the Comité consultatif des Beaux-Arts to save an old house,[61] and also
managed to destroy any kind of historical aura at the square where Joan of Arc

NORMANDY, THE NORTH, BURGUNDY AND POINTS EAST

was burned at the stake in 1431, and marked with a cross on Baedeker's 1909 plan.[62]

Le Mans

This town in the Maine retains sections of an attractive set of walls, patterned in variously coloured stones and bricks (polychrome decoration also at Angers, Nantes and Rennes) and, like other towns, with large foundation blocks,[63] some of which bore sculptures.[64] However, only a minute part of the 4,500 cubic metres of the foundations have been recovered.[10] When the towers of the Place des Jacobins were pulled down during the 18th century, architectural elements were noted, but not preserved. As for servitudes, several towers have houses built into them, such as Tour du Vivier, des Ardents, de Tucé, and Madeleine. But as for walls, and old buildings in the town, "Nos édiles ont détruit tout cela,"[65] and damage to the walls "par les mains mercenaires de ses propres enfants" easily outpaced that which the Germans had caused in 1871.[66]

Jublains

At Jublains,[11] in Mayenne, a site which attracted interest from 1739,[12] the walls of the castrum still stand, enclosing an important sanctuary complex, and the baths part-survived because they were buried.[67] This complex was protected by an on-site guard in 1841,[68] and although much material remained, much had already disappeared because of the site's use as a quarry,[69] not least by the local church.[70] Jublains was a civitas capital, selected to control surrounding territory, "and had consisted essentially of a temple complex, baths and theatre/amphitheatre, the elements elsewhere characteristic of a major Gallic sanctuary complex, but here equipped with a street grid and a forum."[13] The grid was perhaps never fully developed, and the walls of an adjacent fort still stand; this was presumably built after the civil population declined or completely disappeared.

Tours

At Tours (Indre-et-Loire) most of the grid sections of the Roman town layout south of the Loire were no longer occupied by the end of 3rd century,

---

10   Guilleux 2000, 168.

11   Laurain 1928, 7–21 for excavations 1776ff, including the castle enceinte; 22–45 castellum; 45–55 temple; 56–62 baths, with church on top; 62–5 theatre, but not much dug.

12   Naveau 1996.

13   Esmonde Cleary 2013, 66.

236   CHAPTER 8

and the amphitheatre formed part of the walls, sections of which (others
had gone in 1680 and 1767[71]) were still in existence in 1853, with visible
foundations,[72] and contained an "énorme quantité de pierres taillées et cou-
vertes de sculptures."[73] The basilica of S. Cassius was decorated in marble,[74]
as was the important pilgrimage church of S. Martin,[75] entirely rebuilt in the
11th century[76] and at later dates.[77] The church was partly destroyed at the
Revolution, and the nave obliterated in 1802 in order to build the new rue des
Halles, so the imprecation "Impius at flammis haec dedit haereticus" on the
Saint's tomb[78] clearly had no effect. Indeed, as was well remembered even in
1910, "Elle fut détruite pour faire passer une rue!"[79] By 1861, when an engineer
from the Ponts et Chaussées directed a dig, there was no known plan of the
early state of the church, only one of the remains made in 1801 prior to selling
off what remained.[80] The plan was found in the archives, but a rich local had
to purchase houses around the apse before the dig could proceed.[81] There
were plenty of Roman remains to be found in 1847 under "un sol essentiellement romain qui recèle sans doute bien des richesses dans la profondeur
de ses entrailles."[82] In the 1850s, attention had turned to the castellum at
nearby Larçay, and scholars remarked how strange it was that archaeologists
had not yet studied the site,[83] which had antiquities in its foundations,[84]
part-built on "columns, sawn transversely and horizontally,"[85] and standing
towers.[86] But by the 1880s, others complained that plenty of Roman material at Tours itself, including sections of the walls,[87] still awaited study.[88]
Presumably the municipality was still as short of funds as it had been in the
previous century.[14] Sections remained into the 20th century, but these were
lime-washed (attracting the cry of vandalism),[89] and the amphitheatre had
completely disappeared.[90]

Angers

Angers (Maine-et-Loire), sections of whose aqueducts were still visible in
1814,[91] was transformed with "beaux boulevards."[92] The ramparts[15] were
demolished from 1808, and antiquities retrieved from them.[93] Alarm at the
speed with which the old town was disappearing was voiced in 1843,[94]
the ground terraced, and promenades developed. The church of S. Martin was
a woodstore by 1848, and some of its 12th-century columns rescued for the
museums.[95] Attention turned in 1847 to the nearby Camp de César, [96] perhaps as displacement therapy. Antiquities were still being recovered from
remains of one tower in the 1970s: five Ionic bases, three types of column shaft,

---

14   Baumier 2007, chap. V: Une pénurie financière permanente.
15   Prévost 1978, 133–148 for the ramparts.

NORMANDY, THE NORTH, BURGUNDY AND POINTS EAST   237

column sections, une inscription, and capitals composite, corinthian and tuscan, but apparently too disparate to rebuild into one funerary monument.[16]

Blois

Although Blois (Loir-et-Cher) might have had a Roman castrum,[97] and a water supply Roman in origin,[98] its main monument is the château, going back to Louis XII but, as already mentioned, in the hands of the Génie as a barracks since the Revolution: "Il n'y a aucune réclamation à faire à l'égard du château de Blois, aucune autorité à invoquer; le génie militaire y est seul maître et la troupe de ligne seul conservateur."[99] Although some restoration had been carried out by 1844,[100] and a section had been given to the town as a museum, important historical rooms remained with the military, one as a gymnasium.[101]

The North

Amiens

Today we associate Amiens[17] (Somme) with its cathedral, but it was also a splendid Roman city, with a large amphitheatre.[18] It shrank from the 3rd century (some insulae were abandoned), and the monuments were reused in her (4th century?) walls,[19] which incorporated forum and amphitheatre, the remains to be retrieved (along with pottery)[102] in the mid-19th century.[103] Amiens probably went from being a civilian town to contracting into mainly a military complex, the amphitheatre also later becoming a fortress. A Roman "palace" was demolished in the 15th and 16th centuries, leaving a few ruins, but "ils ont disparu, comme disparaissent peu à peu, tous les monuments qui attestent l'antiquité de notre ville, pour faire place à des constructions trop

---

16   Prévost 1980: tower in the rue Toussaint.

17   Bailly & Dupont for overview; 31–45 for Roman and subsequent city; 90–92 for 19th century urban change, including as the garrison town for II Corps from 1874.

18   Frézouls 1982, 9–106; Bayard & Massy 1983, 7–11 for 19th century, 73–108 for Roman monuments. But 73 Amiens, plus que les cités voisines de Reims ou de Paris, où subsistent des monuments hauts de plusieurs mètres, a ignoré jusqu'à une date récente ses richesses archéologiques encore enfouis dans le sol. 91 fig 32: amphitheatre and arcades dismantled in 1900; 85 fig.29, undated photo captioned les archéologues impuissants durant la destruction du forum au Logis-du-Roy, dug 1973–9.

19   Vasselle, François, & Will 1958, 480–482: L'enceinte du Bas-Empire et la formation de la ville médiévale; Esmonde Cleary 2013, 70–71: total fortified area of 20ha, whereas 140ha under the High Empire.

souvent mesquines, lourdes, ou sans goût."[104] Its original enceinte was replaced by an expanded one in the late 15th century, which in turn was superseded by the citadel designed by Errard under Henri IV.

The late walls were traced in the cellars of existing houses,[105] and on the site of the Augustins church, where new house foundations were being dug.[106] In addition, 26 cannonballs were retrieved, dating from Henri IV's 1597 siege of the town.[107] The mayor and échevins seemed keen on preserving their monuments, for example the Porte du grand Pont, repaired in 1461 because "ne voulant pas qu'elle fust à ruynes, considéré que c'estoit des plus anciennes portes de la ville." But it was nevertheless demolished in 1484.[108] Was it perhaps a gate made from antique columns and blocks, like the porte Saint-Pierre, demolished in 1831,[109] or the Tour du Géant?[110] After the Revolution in this town rich in religious buildings,[111] entrepreneurs took charge of demolition of the Couvent des Augustins,[112] and a long-lived Archbishop attracted the disdain of archaeologists by his own demolition work.[113] It was left to scholars, such as the architect Pinsard, to draw what was left or, "utilisant les quelques débris qu'offrent une maison à moitié démolie ou les restes d'une substruction, il reconstitue un monument ou une façade tels qu'ils étaient au jour de la splendeur."[114] But not much was left: the amphitheatre was discovered only in 1900, and its remains destroyed to build the town hall; sections of the forum followed in 1976.[20] In fact, local indifference had destroyed monuments well before World War II.[21]

Arlon

Arlon[22] in Belgium (province of Luxemburg, and never part of France) was a strategic site fortified by the Romans, and finds were also made in the vicinity.[115] It appears here because the Roman foundations of the town walls were rich in reused material, including tombstones.[116] Down the centuries warfare dealt much damage to them. Already in 1065 blocks were taken, then recut, to build a monastery, and the 17th century uncovered many more.[117]

---

20 Massy 1979, 26–7; 23 for the NE walls of the forum.

21 Vasselle & Will 1958, 469: Les monuments les plus vénérables de cette histoire ont été la victime, et cela bien avant 1940, de l'indifférence de la masse comme de l'impéité des édiles. Les restes du rempart antique, retrouvés au cours des années 1945–1952, étaient eux-mêmes trop peu importants pour ne pas céder aux exigences d'un urbanisme moderne.

22 Lejeune 2009, 53–205 from Republic to 476; 56ff for history of the dismantling of the rampart, and 64–5 for the walls of the castrum – followed by account of the blocks now in the museum.

NORMANDY, THE NORTH, BURGUNDY AND POINTS EAST

This site, rich in sculptures and inscriptions, was dubbed the "Panthéon de la Belgique."[118] The upper levels of the walls were destroyed (they were a strategic threat) in 1565,[119] and descriptions survive of what was found. Sculptures from these fortifications were taken to Palais Mansfield, at Clausen, to decorate the garden,[120] while what remained was flattened in 1671, with some blocks handed over to the locals (to pay them for dismantling work?) and others sold to merchants.

The East

Langres[23] (Haute-Marne)

Langres was a fortified region, and not just a town or citadel. It was still a fortress of the first class in 1909 (when its population was just under 10,000), and very important in the First World War. This town was planned as an entrenched camp under Vauban, as were Belfort, Verdun and Toul. The work was not done until the 1830s, but is an indication of its frontier importance, because such camps would house many more troops than would town garrisons. There are the fortified towns of Dampierre to the north, Chalindrey to the south, protected (in its later 19th century configuration) by a ring of forts. On a more general map, Langres is the back-stop to the west-south string of Verdun, Toul, Epinal, Belfort and Besancon.[24] The Franco-Prussian War ensured that the walls of Langres would be demolished later than at some other towns. Unfortunately the local military do not appear to have interested themselves in antiquities, hence the dearth of information in the archives.[25]

The ancient walls had already been part-dismantled and part-mangled as early as the 9th century,[26] and monuments were mostly known from literary sources.[27] The plethora of Roman remains was well known to Père Viguier in the 1660s;[121] he traced sections of the wall "composée de gros quarrées de belles pierres de taille, paroissant entierre et fort haute en beaucoup d'endroits

---

23 Journaux 2008, 39–66 for Langres romaine; 209–213 Les transformations du paysage urbain, mid-17th, including 18th century gardens and promenades.

24 Génie 1970, with plan of "L'ensemble fortifié de Langres."

25 SHD Génie Art.12.3, Croquis Carton 25: lots of military material on Langres, but nothing of antiquarian interest. All bastions and latrines again.

26 Rocolle 1972 I, 15: in 814 the Bishop of Langres received Imperial permission to raze all or part of the enceinte, in 817 ditto the Archbishop of Reims, presumably to build churches and other structures. Much the same happened at Frankfurt and Ratisbon in the early 9th century. At Beauvais, part of the enceinte was used to build the cathedral.

27 Frézouls 1988, 397–403.

240   CHAPTER 8

et d'une excellente maçonnerie,"[122] and noted other antiquities, including an aqueduct.[123] Sarcophagi and statues were also uncovered in the same period.[124] In 1835 Migneret provided details of 18th century retrievals, and averred that "il n'est pas une construction faite sur le sol langrois, à quelque époque que ce soit, qui n'ait révélé l'existence de bâtiments, de temples et de monuments romains, soit au-dedans, soit au-dehors de la ville."[125] Antiquities outside the town were sometimes recycled, for example to make a baptismal font,[126] or even a Christian altar.[127] A second, mediaeval wall was given to the Jesuits in 1745 to provide materials for a college,[128] and additional defences (exterior to the walls) had already been erected in the 16th century.[129]

Chef de Bataillon Richardot (Artillery), perhaps bearing in mind the site's military history,[130] assessed Langres in 1821 and recommended its further fortification, even though the taking of the Franche-Comté had placed the area behind the front line. The walls were in some parts in very bad condition, but he remarked on the visible antiquities encapsulated therein: "des tronçons de colonne, des portions d'Entablemens, des inscriptions, des figures en relief, etc; on y remarque surtout deux très beaux Arcs de triomphe Romains, dans le Mur en face de la route de Paris."[131] There may have been other "triumphal arches" (does he mean decorated gates?), for he gives chapter and verse for stones in the 17th century which might have belonged to them.[132] One was apparently demolished in 1655.[133]

The mayor of Langres in January 1822, namely Philippe de Rivière, explains in a letter to the Minister of War that the town, fortified at its own expense, could no longer afford to maintain the works, especially when the frontiers had moved. Hence the result: "elle a, comme toutes les villes à l'intérieur, cherché à tirer parti des terrains qu'elle avait acheté et des fortifications qu'elle avait fait construire."[134] In other words, blocks had been pilfered for other purposes, and the town did not wish to rebuild them. Thus the Army took over, but agreed with the municipality in 1832 that "Il sera fait remise à la ville de tous les objets d'arts et d'Antiquités qui seront détachés des murs dans lesquels ils se trouvent incrustés, il en sera de même de l'arc de triomphe situé près de la porte du marché, dans le cas ou le Génie militaire viendra à en ordonner la démolition"[135] – which it did not, this gate being blocked off and retained in the walls; it survives today.[136] Just how much material was to be saved we do not know, one author in 1838 reporting saving an inscription as it was about to be sawn down.[137]

In 1847 the municipality (with the permission of the Army) had a mediaeval gate demolished, advantageous "sous le double rapport de la salubrité de la rue des Moulins et de la facilité de la circulation."[138] They had done likewise in 1753, for the same reason.[139] The Army always had the Ministère de la Guerre

NORMANDY, THE NORTH, BURGUNDY AND POINTS EAST 241

to fall back on, as when a request against demolition of a wooden house outside the walls at Langres goes to the Minister himself![140] The townspeople did not like the impositions of the Génie from the 1830s, because their work impinged on properties near the walls which had been been private and undisturbed. Indeed, complaints against their high-handedness over property rights drag on for several years, and many pages, with army, ministry, mairie and offended individuals all involved. The walls had to be rebuilt to provide protection, for another 1836 remark was that they "sont presque nulles, considérées sous le rapport militaire."[141] To fortify the town, the Génie therefore rebuilt some sections, in the course of which they demolished the Longe-Porte,[142] leaving only one ancient gate.[143] Swings and roundabouts, of course: in the 17th century, the construction of bastions was no doubt destructive – but nevertheless threw up several antiquities.[144] Scholars bemoaned the town's fate:

> Vains regrets! Langres est devenue place de guerre, la science militaire moderne l'a décidé; espérons maintenant que ses interprètes distingués sauront nous conserver, dans son intégrité actuelle, notre plus précieux monument gallo-romain, la Porte antique du Marché.[145]

Perhaps in compensation, the Génie was still turning up spolia in 1892,[146] and at this date at least some inscriptions were saved.[147]

If the destruction noticed above was extensive, then also, according to Caumont, the antiquities of Langres were largely ignored until 1831. Then the walls, sections of which revealed plentiful blocks from earlier buildings,[148] including inscriptions and funerary reliefs,[149] were sold by the municipality to the Ministère de la Guerre. Scholars (they must have known the Génie's track-record) saw it was necessary to make an inventory of the material in the walls, because "le génie militaire pourrait désormais abattre d'un moment à l'autre."[150] 1836 also saw the foundation of the Société Archéologique de Langres, in order to save from destruction – "malgré les résistances de l'administration" – the blocks already unearthed.[151] By 1846, the little museum, founded because so much of the town's rich heritage had simply disappeared,[152] had retrieved 118 antique pieces, and 31 from the Middle Ages and the Renaissance.[153] In fact, the Génie then added to the haul in 1850, even offering "de dresser un plan exact de ces restes intéressants et d'en donner une description."[154] In 1858 they re-discovered a Gallo-Roman cemetery, already known about from 17th-century fortification work.[155] Their main work was to rebuild parts of the walls, and this provided yet more antiquities for the museum. But this presented a dilemma: the existing museum needed to be reorganised so the plan was put on hold, for how many more slabs would the

Génie uncover? Better to wait until their work was finished, so as the better to calculate what new museum premises would be needed.[156] The scale of the likely problem was already apparent in 1849, when the rebuilding of the Tourpiquante Bastion revealed a ten-metre length of the adjacent walls almost entirely built of spolia: "frises, chapiteaux, corniches, architraves, bas-reliefs, fûts et bases de colonnes s'y trouvaient entassés pêle-mêle, mais presque tous mutilés."[157]

Nancy

The "belles fortifications" of Nancy, acknowledged as merely decorative by the mid-18th century, gave way from 1731 to new suburbs,[158] while the coup de grâce to the "intéressants vestiges" was given in 1871, profiting from the absence of the Génie (since the Germans occupied the town),[159] for they had wished to preserve and occupy the citadel.[160] The Prefect was petitioned in 1849 to turn the remains of the Palais Ducal into a museum,[161] and this did indeed happen, although purists baulked at the reworking "à la romaine" of the chapel.[162] Remains of the Roman enceinte at Nevers,[163] under a later set,[28] attracted archaeologists in the 1860s.[164] It was given a second, larger enceinte in 1194 (rebuilt in 1398), with 15 towers.[29]

Metz

The population of the frontier town of Metz[30] declined in the 3rd century, the amphitheatre was fortified by an external ditch, and then walls were built, still enclosing a large area. Naturally, enceintes in such strategic locations were updated and even replaced by more substantial structures. Such was the case at Metz, frequently attacked and damaged,[165] where in the 16th century antiquarians were already excited by antiquities recovered from its walls,[166] and continued to be so in the 19th century,[167] with some standing remains in the early 17th century.[31] In the 1840s scholars asked the Génie to note any antiquities discovered in the course of their work in this important town.[168] They had already done so, discovering material to the north of the town in 1834,

---

28   Well illustrated in Le Hallé 1990, 165–170. Ibid., 177–182 for Autun, 206–209 for Auxerre; 209–212 for Avallon; 227–229 for Sens.

29   Frézouls 1997, 271–306 for the ancient town.

30   Frézouls 1982, 237–350; Thiriot 1970, 25–27 for 15th century defences, then 1550, 1730, and extensive outworks. 14 for remarks on the Gallo-Roman enceinte.

31   Le Moigne 1986, 21–65 for the enclosed Roman city, including figs 12 & 13, prints of the theatre/amphitheatre, and the grands thermes du nord, both by Claude Chastillon.

NORMANDY, THE NORTH, BURGUNDY AND POINTS EAST

and comparing their finds with Vigneulle's 1513 account.[169] Some digs in this ground rich in antiquities[170] were apparently enthusiastic rather than measured, and one made a mess of the amphitheatre remains to the south.[32] But pieces of exotic marble were to be seen around the town in 1837;[171] and antiquities once abounded throughout the region, many found near Thionville, 32km to the north.[172]

The descriptions of finds tail off in the later 19th century because Metz is refortified. It comes as no surprise that in 1870, after Marshal Bazaine surrendered his 160,000 troops at Metz after the two-month siege, and the Germans took over the town, they should modernise the fortress here and also at Thionville with a double ring of forts – a complex, the *Moselstellung*, which was not even attacked by the French in World War I, and took the American over two months to defeat in 1944. Such well-spread rings of forts were the new orthodoxy in fortification, built at distances sufficient to keep large-calibre shell-firing guns and howitzers well away from the target, in this case Metz itself. Following the Franco-Prussian War, then, it was clear to all (as it had been to some professionals for decades) that venerable town walls (Gallo-Roman or later) were no longer any defence, and could therefore be demolished, even though the Génie usually had to be fought for the privilege.

Burgundy (plus Points East and the Upper Rhône Valley)

Attempts from the 15th century to create a defensive frontier in Burgundy entailed strengthening Auxonne, Mâcon, Beane and Dijon, as well as Chalon, Autun, Langres, and Saint-Dizier. "These became more important with the loss of Franche-Comté in 1493 and the emergence of this region as the effective frontier... In Autumn 1546, Francis aimed to visit the frontier of Champagne and Burgundy, 'to see how effectively the fortifications he had ordered had been carried out.' "[33]

---

32   Esmonde Cleary 2013, 427: "Further up the Moselle at Metz, the evidence from the 'Grand Amphithéâtre' to the south-east of the walled area shows intense activity in the fifth century. Unfortunately, because of the early date of the excavations, it is not possible to be certain of the nature of this activity, whether it was domestic or whether there may have been a martyr church within the amphitheatre."

33   Potter 2008, 166.

Autun

Autun[34] (Saône-et-Loire) was another town negligent of its antiquities. Thanks perhaps to the Wars of Religion, the walls were already in a sorry state in 1580, "découronnées, rompues en cent endroits, exploitées comme une carrière,"[173] with large swathes of the town looking like a demolition site.[174] Edmé Thomas (d. 1660) described its glories, which included the Porte des Marbres, relating the "quantité de piliers, colonnes et corniches qui y ont été déterrés," conceivably when a later enceinte was being constructed in 1547–75.[175] He also noted the reuse of ancient materials to pave the parvis of a church;[176] remains of the Capitol (to be unearthed in the mid-19th century[177]) and ancient statues,[178] not to mention the Promenade des Marbres, supposedly on the site of a circus.[179] As elsewhere, any care was exercised by individual scholars. In 1710 Baudot admired the fine lettering on inscriptions he took from a tower in the walls.[180] By the 1830s, the collection of the librarian, M. Jovet, was to be visited; but his efforts to get the municipality, let alone the Société Éduenne to intervene to save an important mosaic were in vain – so he bought the land himself.[181] Stendhal in 1837 was anticipating fine ancient gates, because he remembered them illustrated by Montfaucon; but seeing them he had to conclude that "dans les ouvrages d'archéologie, les gravures méritent autant de confiance que les raisonnements."[182] Blocks from ancient monuments in the walls' foundations were uncovered when the prison was built in 1851.[183]

Millin formed a low opinion of the way the Autunois treated their monuments,[184] and Victor Hugo confirmed it.[185] Perhaps dismantling and reuse started very early.[186] Because of vandalism, Millin suggested Roman milestones should be collected together for study, and replaced by modern posts.[187] Parts of the amphitheatre were being sold off in the 1760s, and then other parts used in 1788 to build a church. Some of the vomitoria were accessible, and in 1807 Millin was quite clear that as much as possible should be left underground, since excavation would only provide more opportunities

---

34 Frézouls 1997, 1–172; Duval & Quoniam 1963. 1971–2, 10: after the barbarian invasions, the city contracts into the high part, the castrum, builds religious foundations, and consolidates the wall. S. Andoche goes against the roman rampart; aqueducts have been cut, so wells are dug instead. 11: la Porte des Marbres demolished only "vers le XIe siècle," and the Porte de Saint-Andoche went only in the 19th century, because transformed into a corps-de-garde. In the XIe siècle, stonecutters "retrouvent leurs ciseaux non seulement pour arracher les marbres des ruines romaines mais pour elever les murs de nouveaux sanctuaires." 14: By the Wars of Religion, the Roman walls are ruined, and another larger set is built, linking the upper and lower towns.

NORMANDY, THE NORTH, BURGUNDY AND POINTS EAST

for stone-robbing,[188] but this did not happen. Hence, inevitably, by the 1840s the whole structure had gone, although there were some walls of the theatre surviving, and standing to a height of more than 8 metres.[189] It was here that a house for a watchman was built, presumably to control any tourists. This was built largely of funerary antiquities – a veritable Musée Lapidaire on its own.[190]

And to plug a gap in the walls after an assault, parts of a Roman road were used.[191] This was no doubt because the granite blocks of which it was made caused shod beasts to slip, so their removal was some advance.[192] Plenty of material was available (perhaps still including some of the marble hymned by Gregory of Tours[193]), because the 19th-century town far from filled the Roman enceinte.[194] Indeed, it was in decline, with ruins all around, and "Autun a vu s'écrouler ses superbes basiliques et ses cloîtres majestueux."[195] What was retrieved from her monuments usually had no provenance,[196] and their occasional rescue was due to local aficionados.[197] But plenty of ancient blocks were available for reuse into the 1880s.[198]

Large sections of the late antique walls survived, but they were of hard cement and petit appareil, with no large blocks in evidence,[199] and therefore lacking the interest of blocks turning up at Dijon, Auxerre and other towns.[200] And in many places they were a mish-mash of various periods.[201] Their demolition no doubt required wood (for sapping and burning), saltpetre, and gunpowder, as it did elsewhere.[202] Restoration of the Porte Saint-André was given to Viollet-le-Duc, with predictable results.[203] Equally predictably, it was not the municipality but a society of scholars which, somewhat tardily, tried from 1861 to set up a Musée Lapidaire, and to cover its costs.[204] By the 1880s, with the museum working, it was a railway entrepreneur who presented it with significant items.[205] A glimpse of what was already lost was to be seen in the marble blocks collected here by 1877.[206] Digging was taking place by the 1860s, but again by entrepreneurs, and not for archaeology, thereby missing the opportunity to resurrect walls, some three metres high, which "constituaient la squelette d'un Pompéi gallo-romain."[207] The 19th century saw several attempts at the reuse of Roman aqueducts, but here this was apparently unsuccessful.[208] Outside the town, the "Temple of Janus" was already attracting too many visitors by 1807, trampling the wheat around it, so that its owner wished to demolish it. The locals helped by demolishing for reuse the stone covering on one side, and weather and rain then did its work,[209] so that only the inchoate concrete stump remains today.

As already narrated, the Congrès Archéologique de France, in its annual sessions, often set a questionnaire tailored to the location of the conference, to encourage members to provide local information. At Dijon in 1852, one task

246 CHAPTER 8

was to trace the influence of Roman architecture on that of Langres, Autun, Beaune and Dijon.[210] The responses demonstrated that the congressists were well aware that important centres such as Autun and Langres[211] (and Nîmes, and Trier) spread their influence like ripples throughout a pool.[212] Mérimée, as we might expect, had already made similar observations two decades earlier.[213] The town was still little-inhabited by 1900, one author estimating that the 15,000 population left three-quarters of the area within the walls taken up with fields and gardens.[214] By now, a large area near the Porte d'Arroux had been taken over by the army (the Caserne Changarnier), and a cavalry school placed on the Promenade des Marbres.[215]

Beaune

Noted today for its liquid attractions, Beaune (Côte-d'Or) was a Roman site, with 10,000 inhabitants in the mid-19th century (two-thirds that of Autun), and plentiful débris unearthed by the vignerons near the town[216] and also in surrounding communes. Nuits-Saint-Georges, for example, was "une mine inépuisable d'antiquités gauloises, romaines et même mérovingiennes."[217] Nonchalance toward the past was the common key, the church of Saint-Pierre demolished in 1804, together with Gallo-Roman sculptures which had decorated it.[218] Other sculptures had surfaced in the 17th and 18th centuries.[219] The walls, part-Roman but with later additions, survived into the 19th century, when pressure to destroy them and create boulevards began.[220] But the municipality could not demolish them because private properties had encroached; however, their destruction would have been very popular, because the inhabitants had caught modernisation: "La contagion de l'exemple, les destructions analogues accomplies dans la plupart des villes murées de la Bourgogne."[221] It was the new railway which brought congressists from Dijon in 1852, the station being conveniently just outside the walls – which were then ignored because of their mediaeval aspect.[222] By 1901 there were 14,000 inhabitants, most living outside the surviving walls, and enjoying the picturesque town, with its pleasant boulevards:

> L'édilité beaunoise a tiré un merveilleux parti de l'ancien caractère militaire de la ville. Les remparts découronnés, perdant tout aspect guerrier, ont été conservés comme promenades; leurs murs en bossage plongent encore dans les fossés souvent pleins d'eau. De grands arbres couronnent ces restes de défense, des boulevards élégants les enveloppent.[223]

Dijon (Côte-d'Or)

Many of Dijon's monuments, some described in the 6th century by Gregory of Tours, suffered in the course of the 19th century, including churches.[224]

NORMANDY, THE NORTH, BURGUNDY AND POINTS EAST

(But were older monuments standing in his day?).[225] Dijon expanded beyond the old walls, and a new set was begun in 1357, with work continuing on improvements for nearly a century, thereby rendering some of the Roman constructions superfluous.[226] Its modernisation meant that the Roman walls,[227] as well as later ones,[228] were dismantled in sections[229] from the beginning of the 19th century,[230] a task nearly done by the 1840s and completed in the 1860s,[231] leaving only a few fragments.[232] Some of the sculptures retrieved were of such quality that Caumont suggested moulding them for exchange with other societies.[233] The work destroyed the old-world look of the town,[234] and by 1900 this was no more than a memory.[235] The Sainte Chapelle was demolished with gunpowder in 1802,[236] and the Chartreuse and Rotunda of S. Bénigne[237] were two more complexes to be mangled,[238] the rout prompting the following question at the annual Congrès Archéologique in 1852: "quels seraient les moyens les plus efficaces pour éviter la destruction de ceux de ces monuments qui méritent d'être conservés?"[239] Very few, was the answer, since this town surrounded by quarries had itself been used as a quarry, and only débris remained.[240] Indeed, ragged dismantling of the château had occurred since the 1830s, thereby eradicating a symbol of Royal power and leaving the site a mess. The railway arrived in 1850, but only in 1865 was a concours for the eventual Place du Château launched.[35]

What happened to retrieved antiquities? Dijon's walls had been repaired and updated in the 1550s, and in the 17th century new squares and streets were laid out,[36] no doubt turning up antiquities in the process. Baudot, mayor in 1694, put into his courtyard those he found by demolishing a tower, and says others in the town also kept such antiquities.[241] Some at least of the workmen or the clients for new housing liked antiquities, Millin in 1807 praising one mason for setting an antique sculpture into the wall of the house he was building.[242] In 1767 Legouz de Gerland saved some blocks, and in 1781 Richard de Ruffey, President of the chambre des comptes de Bourgogne incorporated 42 fragments from yet another tower in his hôtel.[243] And then Count Vesvrotte, a member of the Société Française d'Archéologie, incorporated 19 pieces "trouvés dans des fouilles sur différents points de la ville" in the walls of his hôtel.[244] This annex, with its antiquities still in situ today, was built in 1854, and incorporated the best pieces found in the ruins of a tower in 1781.[245] Bas-reliefs were also incorporated in a house in the countryside near Dijon.[246]

---

35   Sautai-Dossin 2002; figs 8–10 for photos of the 1890s demolitions.

36   Farr 1989, 144: "In the private sector, Dijon's parlementaires increasingly poured capital into construction of stone hôtels to display their wealth and status."

248 CHAPTER 8

The Roman castrum,[37] with 18m-high walls,[247] and perhaps hurriedly erected,[248] was used for years as a quarry, and known to contain antiquities in its walls,[249] for the cellars of later constructions on top were visitable.[250] Its remains survived into the 1860s, but its walls were crumbling so, by standard bureaucratic reasoning, it was to be destroyed.[251] Surely, argued the archaeologists, who saw that there was pressure for new suburbs to be built, "On peut toujours mettre le neuf à côté du vieux, sans anéantir le vieux; il n'y a qu'à savoir s'y prendre."[252] Yet the castrum was destroyed, "malgré les protestations des archéologues et des artistes."[253] Although Claus Sluter completed his Puits de Moïse (1395–1405) well before we know Philippe le Bon authorised inhabitants to use the stones of the fortress in the construction of new buildings, it is tempting to wonder whether the sculptor took inspiration from antique spolia for his startlingly original faces, drapery and poses, which have more than a passing resemblance to late Roman draped portrait statues. It would also be tempting to suggest that the special alabaster-cutting saw ordered for work on the tomb of Philippe le Hardi meant that spolia were being used for it.[254] Certainly, the Dukes recycled plenty of materials (did these include antiquities?) in their numerous building projects.[38]

Some sections of the town were not interested in preserving the past, and the same Caumont struggled to piece together the fifth-century Tomb of Saint Andoche from Saulieu, which had been sold to a marbrier in Dijon for cutting up.[255] Speculators helped denude Dijon in the 1840s,[256] and it was contended that some wanted to make money by new building: "Ces hommes de progrès ont éventré la ville, à très-peu de distance du château, et ils ont un intérêt d'argent à créer, de ce côté, un quartier extra-muros."[257]

Lyon

Lyon (Rhône) matches Toulouse as a town which lost all her standing ancient monuments, some of which went into her walls.[258] This left remains often too indeterminate to identify,[259] provoking the wish "que la Société française pour la conservation des monuments soit définitivement constituée à Lyon, et qu'elle prenne l'initiative pour s'opposer aux actes de mauvais goût que l'on a souvent à déplorer en architecture."[260] She had aqueducts and spectacular

---

37 Fyot 1960, 445–51 for the castrum divionense, apparently c. 273 under Aurelian. Walls 9.5m high, with an external cladding averaging 1.5m and made from spolia, and moellons in the centre of about 1m; still in use after the erection of the enceinte begun in the 12th century; Frézouls 1988, 246–56.

38 Beck 2008.

NORMANDY, THE NORTH, BURGUNDY AND POINTS EAST

cisterns, but the line of her ancient walls remains obscure,[39] as indeed does what happened to most of their contents.[40] Monfalcon, her best 19th-century historian, is unclear about successive enceintes[261] until the 15th century set. He stated correctly that "il y a donc bien peu de chose à dire sur l'architecture de Lyon, du quatrième au neuvième siècle," his guess about the line of the Roman enceinte being just that, without supporting evidence,[262] even epigraphy.[263] Some arrived at the end of the century,[264] and much more in modern research.[41] So great was the confusion that Boitel, writing two decades earlier, believed that the Roman ramparts lasted to the time of François Ier.[265] We have a view of the walls dated to 1545/53, but although there are some very Roman-looking round-arched towers at Porte de la rue Neuve, no antiquities are visible.[42] It is easy to date the dismantling of the large monuments,[266] because of the reuse of the materials, such as large bossed limestone blocks in the Cathédrale Saint-Jean, especially the Romanesque apse and the whole of the north flank. The wall by the Jardin Archéologique of the cathedral was demolished in 1976, with inscribed blocks in its foundations.[43] And the late enceinte was methodically and not hurriedly erected, for the separation of erstwhile contiguous blocks in different sections of the wall shows that work went on in several stretches at once, with stones taken from a stockpile.[44] When the

---

39   Pelletier & Rossiaud 1990, 133ff. for water supply; ibid. 231ff., for any late-antique enceinte? The trajet by the Cathédrale Saint-Jean (down the hill) could have been just an enceinte for the episcopal material which dates from the correct period, namely 4th century: "A n'en pas douter, nous sommes en présence du nouveau centre monumental de la ville de Lyon."

40   Lyon: The archives possess a lot of documentation on the finances involved in building the new city walls in 1476–7 and 1513ff, but apparently without any references to antiuities therein, although Spon found at least one inscription in the city wall. Côtes are EE61–84, each with up to 100pp of paper or vellum.

41   Audin 1979, 30: in his table of important dates, puts at XIe and XIIe the destruction of the Imperial structures such as theatre, amphitheatre and odeon. 263: Fourvière abandoned 270/5, the latest money found there being of 249AD; monuments on Fourvière soon dismantled for building materials to be used at the bottom of the hill – i.e. in "old Lyon." 265–6: the large structures of theatres, forum, temples, were NOT reused in late antique wall, but "sauvegardés autant par la puissance de leurs structures que par le prestige attaché à des édifices encore utilisables. Il en allait autrement de la forêt des plus modestes monuments honorifiques... qui encombraient l'esplanade du sanctuaire fédéral."

42   Dureau, Jenna-Marie, Le plan de Lyon vers 1550, édition critique des 25 planches originales du plan conservé aux archives de la Ville de Lyon, Lyon 1990; plate 1 for other ruins.

43   Audin & Reynaud 1981. Authors' interest is in the content of the inscriptions, for "la destruction des grands monuments qui ont servi aux constructions des IVe et Ve siècles."

44   Audin & Reynaud 1981, 478–9.

façade of the odeon was uncovered in 1958, a lime kiln was found by the north stairway, and in it a few remains of the statues which had adorned theatre and odeon (including part of a caryatid). Also found were a host of various kinds of marble slabs, broken into manageable proportions for the kilns; tiles were also reused, and carefully cleaned of mortar; stone wall cladding also preserved for reuse, including some green cipollino for the doorway of the cathedral.[45]

But plenty of antique substructures were to be seen in cellars, as Mérimée noted,[267] and also in the walls of houses, as documented in the later 17th century by Spon, and there were so many figured spolia (Christian, pagan and modern) they must have been incorporated for decoration.[268] Seraucourt, writing in 1740, illustrates several antique monuments, including "4 tronçons sciez des deux Colonnes antiques qui flanquoient le Temple dédié à Rome et à Auguste, lesquelles soutiennent le Dôme de l'Eglise d'Enay." He also provides views of aqueducts, the amphitheatre (in the grounds of the Minimes), a cistern, very complicated; and an aedicular tomb, "monument antique que l'on appeloit le Tombeau des deux Amants, démoli en 1707."[269] Schneyder, writing in the mid-18th century, tells us how marble from the amphitheatre has been used:

> des marbriers de Lyon, de père en fils, employaient des marbres antiques dans les églises et autres bâtiments, jusque dans la Bourgogne. Nous voyons encore tous les jours des maçons vendre ceux qu'ils tirent des fondations dans les différents quartiers de la ville.[270]

Monfalcon's several attempts to elucidate the history of the antiquities of Lyon include his 1857 *Le Nouveau Spon. Manuel du bibliophile et de l'archéologue lyonnais*, which organises each bibliographical tranche by preceding it with a brief assessment of antiquities. The title indicates where a lot of spadework was done, namely by Jacob Spon, the 17th-century antiquary, in his *Recherches des antiquités de Lyon* (1675). The text emphasises how much has disappeared since Spon's day, for example on the site of the forum where were then discovered "au temps de Spon, quantité de fûts de colonnes en marbre et en pierre blanche, des chapiteaux, des briques portant le nom de Sévère."[271] By his own day, the ruins of the city had almost completely disappeared[272] and, as for the aqueducts, "l'antiquaire et l'historien assistent à cette destruction lente, mais régulière, d'un des chefs-d'œuvre de l'architecture romaine."[273] So how was knowledge of ancient Lyon to be captured? The only channel, he believed, was by epigraphy.[274] Indeed, scholars in the 1870s could look back on the

---

45   Audin 1979, 274ff.

discoveries quoted by scholars earlier in the century, as when old houses were demolished,[275] and on the "débris de palais et de temples" gathered at different periods, and forward to the fruits of modernisation, namely the railway: "Les travaux d'excavation, entrepris pour l'établissement de la gare du nouveau chemin de fer, dit la Ficelle de Saint-Just, ont donné d'abondantes récoltes de ces trésors archéologiques."[276] This must also have been the case as new roads were opened.[46]

In Lyon today,[47] the Musée Gallo-Romain is in a Parc Archéologique, with ancient shops and theatre. But the poverty of the remains of the latter show how thoroughly it has been robbed out, with no more than ten-metres-worth of column stump in all from the scenae frons in place, and no marble cladding in sight. The seats of the theatre are all rebuilt, or remade in place. As for the amphitheatre, under half the blocks remain.[48] After all, it was the easiest thing in the world simply to roll the blocks down the hill, for reuse by the rivers, which is why the Parc is largely denuded of interesting blocks. Place Wernet displays out of context Roman tombs, of a good size, well decorated and inscribed, moved down the hill (date unknown) from the Place de Trion. The centre tomb even has a damaged headless statue in front, and at the front is complete up to and including the cornice, some 5 metres high!

Valence

There were no late walls visible above ground at Valence (Drôme), but there was a mediaeval enceinte, and a citadel built by François Ier, dismantled in the mid-19th century, but without any significant spolia being unearthed.[277] They were then in perfect condition, as were the walls of Montélimar, further down the Rhône.[278] Valence was nevertheless of Roman origin, with a mosaic unearthed in 1873 by the citadel thanks to the Commandant du Génie.[279] Valence was a town which modernised early, and in 1741 the authorities "imposèrent des alignements et firent démolir les maisons qui menaçaient ruine. On rendit les rues plus droites, plus propres, plus accessibles à la circulation... On éleva de hautes et vastes habitations en pierres de taille, ayant grand air."[280] This was not universally popular for a commentator remarked in 1785: "nous fuyons ces quartiers qui sentent la moderne ville de province dans toute sa correction et sa banalité, nous préférons grimper à l'ombre des ruelles étroites ou prendre les pittoresques rues en escalier."[281] As late as 1899 the

---

46   Bonet & Dureau 1990 for the voirie 1789–1926, in AM serie O, 321WP.

47   Pelletier 1988, 88–109 for the best overview, including finds made digging the metro.

48   Pelletier 1988, 83: when the amphitheatre was dug in 1956, "a peine plus de la moitié" was found remaining – so presumably the rest went for building materials a long time ago.

252   CHAPTER 8

local Society was asked to intervene "auprès des entrepreneurs pour empêcher la destruction de toute œuvre d'art, inscription, sculpture, etc. existante dans les maisons qu'ils réparent ou démolissent," but it declined to do so.[282]

Vienne[49] (Isère)

Vienne, set in a countryside rich in villas,[50] was progressively abandoned during the third century on both sides of the Rhône, as evidence from houses and bath buildings demonstrates.[51] Her walls[52] and château were pulled down under the 1633 order by Louis XIII, and "La ville moderne a été construite plusieurs fois sur les ruines de l'ancienne; ainsi son sol a dû changer et nécessairement s'exhausser, comme les anciens monuments le prouvent."[283] Plentiful finds were appearing within the town in the 17th century, parts of "des bâtimens d'une extrême magnificence."[284] But they quickly disappeared, Charvet noting that "j'ai vu beaucoup de choses apparentes ou dans les fouilles des terres faites de mon temps, qu'on ne voit plus parce qu'elles ont été détruites ou recouvertes."[285] Schneyder, born 1733 and writing and excavating in the later 18th century, notes "les débris du luxe restés enfouis dans la terre, sur une quantité étonnante de mosaïques, de marbres, de médailles que l'on trouve dans quelque lieu que l'on fasse des fouilles."[286] By enumerating what he has found as fragments, conjures up the ancient glory of his town, where he founded the museum,[287] encouraging later writers to promote conservation.[288] Stendhal also remarked on plentiful fragments when he visited the town in 1837.[289]

Equally impressive in the 17th century were the ruins of the amphitheatre, with prodigious columns and statues, plus a bath nearby, but next century "Tout cela n'est plus dans Vienne."[290] Disappearance was to be the fate of yet more antiquities Charvet unearthed in the 18th century, for during a short absence unruly workmen either stole his finds, or built on top of them.[291] The discovery of a temple within the town (22 Attic bases, Corinthian capitals) included a multi-marble mosaic (which, from the description, might be opus sectile, as might pieces unearthed at Vieil-Évreux[292]), but the entrepreneurs had broken it up: "J'en tirai quelques morceaux. Ma plus grande douleur fut de n'avoir pas pu prendre le compartiment de ce beau et riche parquet."[293]

---

49 Pelletier 1982, Chap. X for waterworks, and Chap XI for housing; Pelletier 1988, 114–122, and 179–202 for the best survey of the town and area.

50 Ouzoulias 2010, 200–201 & fig. 5: 29 villas, yielding 306 inscriptions.

51 Esmonde Cleary 2013, 109.

52 Pelletier 1982, 103–10 for the enceinte.

NORMANDY, THE NORTH, BURGUNDY AND POINTS EAST

Such pavements have survived at Vienne.[53] Charvet also saw aqueducts destroyed, at the "maison des Canaux, ancien palais,"[294] but the town by the later 19th century was still using "les vestiges des aqueducs qui, grâce à quelques restaurations, alimentent encore la ville moderne d'eaux abondantes et d'excellente qualité."[295]

On the west bank of the Rhône, just across from Vienne, between Sainte-Colombe and Saint-Romain-en-Gal, were plentiful Roman remains. These were already well known in the 18th century: "Les massifs, les voûtes, les aque-ducs, les mosaïques et les marbres taillés qu'on y a trouvés ne permettent pas d'en douter."[296] The ruins, more fully described in 1837, yielded what were believed to have been exterior walls of glistening marble veneer – "tables de marbre...si nombreuses, qu'elles ont fait donner à l'enceinte qui les renferme le nom de Miroir, par les habitants."[297] The Palais du Miroir (in fact baths[54]) was in the middle of a vineyard. It had columns, friezes and capitals of white marble, and some of the decoration was in green marble.[298] Charvet found "des morceaux précieux, sciés pour le placage"[299] which, if he were not simply collecting a fragment fallen from the walls, might suggest that the building was never finished, that in late antique times blocks were being sawn up for veneer, or that this was French work from the 17th or 18th century, when marble veneer was particularly prized, for example at Versailles. Presumably it was the par-ticular soil conditions which maintained the gloss on the marble, giving the structure its name, but it is tempting to think of sheets of veneer in piles ready for fixing, or dismounted and for some reason abandoned (with might better preserve their shine) rather than fixed in place.

Schneyder[300] believed that the Palais du Miroir was a large public monu-ment, because the 22 collapsed columns stood on a marble floor; he kept one fragment, but the remainder "y compris les bases et les chapiteaux, a eu le sort des plus beaux monuments détruits dès qu'ils ont vu le jour."[301] Mérimée had seen the remains in 1835, by which date the proprietor had been conducting digs for several years,[302] and he noted "des tronçons de colonnes, de chapit-eaux, des fragments de corniches, et, ce qui est bien plus précieux, des statues en marbre blanc d'une grande proportion et d'un travail remarquable."[303] By the end of the century the structures had disappeared, but artefacts had been placed in museums and successive owners of the site also kept some finds in

---

53   Pelletier 1988, 177.

54   Pelletier 1982, 159–164, for excavation history; author believes the site was used in late antiquity as a refuge for pagan statues which once decorated the buildings of the town, and bemoans the fact that the site, still uncovered by later buildings, has never been the focus of methodical digs.

254 CHAPTER 8

a private collection. There were plenty, because although the only rooms left were in ruins undert the ground, "torses, pieds, mains et têtes se sont rencontrés par charretées."[304] But some of these sculptures were bought in 1922 by antique dealers in Paris. Michoud, a local landowner, opened his collection to the Congress in 1862, and this and the land itself, including the Palais du Miroir, had been bought by M. Jacquemet in the 1890s. The area was to become well known for its villas and mosaics, and already in the 1890s a local landowner had bought a mosaic to decorate his house.[305] The town museum was established in Vienne's look-alike Maison Carrée, the Temple of Augustus and Livia, the structure having been in the 1820s "a paltry-looking palais de justice."[306] Modernisation continued to take its toll, and the old town was declared to be sad and sordid, "d'étroites ruelles, mais, à travers ces tristes artères, on rencontre de beaux débris du passé."[307]

Conclusion

We can part-measure the survival of monuments by examining what various towns were able to offer to members of the Congrès Archéologique de France in the way of recently discovered antiquities. During the 1859 congress "promenades archéologiques ont eu lieu dans la ville de Rouen et dans les environs," while at the same meeting Metz was able to offer only a few finds from the vicinity; a session in Metz itself in 1846 asked "Quel a été l'état de l'art à Metz à l'époque gallo-romaine? A-t-on recueilli assez de fragments de sculpture pour s'en faire une juste idée?" receiving the answer: one significant torso. At Dijon in 1852, the destruction was reported of one of the most significant structures in France, at S. Bénigne: "une rotonde existait au-dessus de la crypte; cette rotonde... fut détruite en 1793, et ses derniers vestiges furent enlevés au commencement de ce siècle." Destruction was a frequent keynote throughout the whole of the region. At Vienne in 1879, one contributor looks back at what has disappeared since 1841:

> Mais que de monuments ont été recouverts ou détruits! Ici, c'est une construction romaine avec ses murs revêtus de marbres de différentes couleurs, ou portant des traces de peintures à fresque; là des mosaïques, des voies romaines, des portions d'égouts ou d'aqueducs.

The same question could be posed for other sites in this chapter, such as Autun or Angers, just as any investigation of Langres or Arlon, Tours or Amiens would necessarily dwell on what had been lost rather than on the few items which had managed to survive encroaching modernity.

[1] Caumont_1857_452–453

[2] BM_XVII_1851_207–208

[3] Mém_Normandie_1824_18–19

[4] Mém_Normandie_1824_36

[5] Caumont_III_1857_452

[6] SG_XXXVII_Lisieux_1870_40

[7] Malte-Brun_I_1881_14

[8] Précis_Rouen_1862_263

[9] BCA_Seine-Inférieure_V_1882

[10] Cochet_1871_133

[11] Malte-Brun_IV_1883_20

[12] Caumont_V_1867_197

[13] BM_XXVI_1860_24

[14] Blanchet_1907_39

[15] BA_Comité_1911_LXXIII

[16] BM_XXVI_1860_316

[17] AMPF_XV_1901_215

[18] Blanche_1869_37

[19] AA_IV_1846_53

[20] SG_XXVI_Strasbourg_1859_585

[21] BCA_Seine-Inférieure_XI_1898_387

[22] Bazin_1900_151

[23] SG_XXXVIII_Angers_1871_28

[24] B_Lorraine_II_1851_267

[25] BCA_Seine-Inférieure_IX_1894_134–135

[26] BCA_Seine-Inférieure_VII_1889_196–197

[27] Guilbert_V_1848_425

[28] Floyd_1859_21

[29] Cochet_1871_444

[30] Enlart_1906_11–12

[31] BM_XXVII_1861_181–182

[32] Enlart_1906_12–13

[33] SG_XXVI_Strasbourg_1859_519

[34] Guilbert_1848_391–392

[35] PV_Seine-Inférieure_I_1818–1848_48–49

[36] PV_Seine-Inférieure_I_1818–1849_107

[37] Cochet_1866_91

[38] PV_Seine-Inférieure_I_1818–1848_207–208

[39] PV_Seine-Inférieure_I_1818–1848_207–209

[40] PV_Seine-Inférieure_I_1818–1848_320

[41] Hugo_1835_III_137

[42] Cochet_1866_95

[43] RA_XXII_1870–71_322–323

[44] PV_Seine-Inférieure_I_1818–1848_286

[45] SG_IX_Bordeaux_1842_173

[46] Cochet_1866_93

[47] Cochet_1866_97

[48] Précis_Rouen_1860_177–225

[49] SG_XXVI_Strasbourg_1859_585

[50] BM_XXVII_1861_698–699

[51] BM_XXXV_1869_116

[52] BCA_Seine-Inférieure_VII_1889_53

[53] BCA_Seine-Inférieure_VII_1885–1887_155

[54] AD_Normandie-Orientale_1921_96–97

[55] CHA_I_1894_183

[56] BCA_Seine-Inférieure_X_1897_129

[57] Tour_du_Monde_1860_340

[58] Enlart_1906_14

[59] Enlart_1906_28

[60] AMPF_XV_1901_21–22

[61] L'Ami_des_monuments_XV_1901_14

[62] Enlart_1906, 14

[63] Schuermans_1877_79–80

[64] Caumont_I_1853_271

[65] Revue_Maine_I 1876_448

[66] Revue_Maine_IX_1881_110

[67] CS_France_XVI_1849_Rennes_78–9

[68] SG_VIII_Caen_1841_85

[69] Revue_Maine_X_1881_348

[70] SG_XLV_Le_Mans_1878_541–542

[71] Blanchet_1907_42

[72] Giraudet_1873_18–27

[73] Caumont_I_1853_269

[74] Gregory_of_Tours_I_1836_184

[75] RA_XIX_1869_313

[76] RA_X_1864_242

[77] Grandmaison_1879_46

[78] BSA_Touraine_V_1884_42

[79] AD_Touraine_Anjou_1910_127

[80] Grandmaison_1879_58

[81] Sorbonne_1861_171–172

[82] CS_France_XV_1847_Tours_75

[83] BM_XXII_1856_146

[84] BM_XXII_1856_315–316

[85] Roach_Smith_1855_10

[86] BM_XXII_1856_316

[87] BA_Comité_1883_126

[88] BSA_Touraine_V_1883_352

[89] Blanchet_1907_43

[90] AD_Touraine_Anjou_1910_127

[91] Pinkney_1814_244

[92] Baedeker_1884_219

[93] Bottin_1821_42

[94] Lachèse_1843_II

[95] Rép_Arch_Anjou_1866_98–99

[96] BM_XV_1849_459
[97] Guilbert_II_1845_680
[98] Pinkney_1814_316
[99] BM_IV_1838_275
[100] BM_X_1844_238
[101] RA_II_1845–1846_184–185
[102] Mém_Picardie_III_1840_123
[103] Goze_1854_10
[104] Dusevel_1848_10
[105] Goze_1854_13
[106] Mém_Picardie_I_1838_213
[107] Musée_Amiens_1845_76
[108] Dusevel_1848_48
[109] Dusevel_1848_135
[110] Dusevel_1848_11
[111] Whittington_1809_156
[112] MSA_Somme_I_1838_213
[113] SG_LX_Abbeville_1893_162
[114] SG_LX_Abbeville_1893_155–156
[115] Sibenaler_1905_99
[116] Sibenaler_1905_10–11
[117] Espérandieu_V_1913_211–212
[118] Sibenaler_1905_11–12
[119] Schuermans_1888_69–70
[120] Espérandieu_V_1913_301
[121] Vignier_1891_35
[122] Vignier_1891_31–2
[123] Vignier_1891_36
[124] Espérandieu_IV_1911_268
[125] Migneret_1835_40–41
[126] Saint-Fergeux_1836_393
[127] Saint-Fergeux_1836_293
[128] Migneret_1835_60
[129] Migneret_1835_180
[130] SHD_Génie_8.1_Langres

[131] SHD_Artillerie_XE512_Langres
[132] Saint-Fergeux_1836_70–71
[133] Macheret_1880_II_216
[134] SHD_Artillerie_XE512_Langres
[135] SHD_Artillerie_XE512_Langres
[136] Saint-Fergeux_1837_197–198
[137] Luquet_1838_132
[138] Mém_Langres_1847_2
[139] Migneret_1835_70
[140] SHD_Artillerie_XE_passim
[141] Saint-Fergeux_1836_314
[142] Migneret_1835_44
[143] Saint-Fergeux_1837_201–202
[144] Luquet_1838_325–6
[145] Mém_Langres_1847_141
[146] Mém_Langres_III_1892_41
[147] Mém_Langres_III_1892_33
[148] Saint-Fergeux_1836_317–318
[149] Migneret_1835_32
[150] BM_VI_1840_326–327
[151] Réunion_BA_1877_13
[152] Mém_Langres_I_1847–60_iii
[153] AA_IV_1846_255
[154] Mém_Langres_1847ff_2
[155] Mém_Langres_1847ff_17
[156] Mém_Langres_1847ff
[157] Mém_Langres_1847ff_9
[158] BSA_Lorraine_VIII_1858_6
[159] BM_XLIX_1883_26–27
[160] MSA_Lorraine_X_1860_248–250
[161] BSA_Lorraine_I_1849_95

[162] BSA_Lorraine_II_1851_237
[163] Tastu_1846_46
[164] BS_Nicernaise_I_1863_469
[165] Malte-Brun_V_1884_87
[166] SG_XIII_Metz_1846_225–227
[167] RA_1844–1845_493
[168] SG_XIII_Metz_1846_227
[169] SG_XXXI_Metz_1846_212–238
[170] Guilbert_IV_1845_444
[171] CS_France_V_1837_Metz_177
[172] BM_XI_1845_337
[173] Gaulthières_1883_5
[174] Gaulthières_1883_9
[175] Gaulthières_1883_35–36
[176] Thomas_1846_36
[177] Thomas_1846_133
[178] Thomas_1846_56
[179] Thomas_1846_209
[180] Baudot_1710_107–108
[181] Mérimée_1835_60–61
[182] Stendhal_1891_I_65
[183] Blanchet_1907_19–20
[184] Millin_I_1807_307–309
[185] Hugo_1835_III_81
[186] CS_France_VIII_1840_Besançon_121–2
[187] Millin_II_1807_109
[188] Millin_I_1807_309
[189] Tastu_1846_21–22
[190] Secrétaires_Autun_1848_124–127
[191] SG_XIII_Metz_1846_363–364
[192] Millin_I_1807_307
[193] Gregory_of_Tours_I_1836_86–87
[194] Baedeker_1884_92–93
[195] Histoire_Autun_1857_7

NORMANDY, THE NORTH, BURGUNDY AND POINTS EAST

[196] Secrétaires_Autun_
1848_175–297

[197] Secrétaires_Autun_
1848_175

[198] Mém_Éduenne_XII_
1883_97

[199] Secrétaires_Autun_
1848_141

[200] Mém_Éduenne_XX_
1892_343–344

[201] Mérimée_1835_59–60

[202] BSA_Drôme_XXVII_
1893_249–269

[203] Secrétaires_Autun_
1848_146

[204] Bulliot_1877_68–75

[205] Mém_Éduenne_XII_
1883_430

[206] Réunion_BA_1877_72

[207] Sorbonne_1867_146–147

[208] Secrétaires_Autun_
1848_166–167

[209] Millin_I_1807_313–314

[210] BM_XVIII_1852_214

[211] BM_XVII_1851_314

[212] BSA_Sens_1852_16–95

[213] Mérimée_1835_67

[214] AD_Basse-Bourgogne_
Sénonais_1901_72

[215] AD_Basse-Bourgogne_
Sénonais_1901_73

[216] Tastu_1846_79

[217] Foisset_&_Simonnet_
1872_Col 217

[218] Espérandieu_III_1910_
123

[219] Blanchet_1907_33

[220] AA_I_1844_93

[221] AA_I_1844_92–93

[222] SG_XIX_Dijon_1852_118

[223] AD_Haute-Bourgogne_
1901_109–110

[224] Gregory_of_Tours_II_
1860_427

[225] Goussard_1861_26

[226] Mém_Côte_d'Or_
1846–1847_IX

[227] AM_Dijon_H_
Fortifications_H131

[228] Jolimont_1830_9–15

[229] Dijon_AM_Gachet

[230] Millin_I_1807_244–245

[231] BM_XXVI_1860_455

[232] Foisset_&_Simonnet_
1872_3

[233] BM_XX_1854_626

[234] AD_Haute-Bourgogne_
1901_6

[235] AD_Haute-Bourgogne_
1901_2

[236] Mém_Comm_Côte-
d'Or_VI_1864_165–166

[237] Foisset_&_Simonnet_
1872_XLVI

[238] AA_XI_1851_124–125

[239] BM_XVIII_1852_213

[240] Goussard_1861_13–14

[241] Baudot_1710_7–8

[242] Millin_I_1807_
252–253

[243] Espérandieu_IV_
1911_371–372

[244] Goussard_1861_380

[245] Espérandieu_IV_1911_
371–372

[246] Millin_I_1807_263

[247] Goussard_1861_4–5

[248] Foisset_&_Simonnet_
1872_XLV

[249] Mém_Comm_Côte-
d'Or_III_1853_274

[250] Mém_Côte_d'Or_VI_
1864_LIII–LIV

[251] Goussard_1861_191

[252] AA_IV_1846_41–43

[253] AD_Haute-Bourgogne_
1901_7

[254] Prost_1913

[255] Mém_Côte_d'Or_III_
1853_V

[256] AA_III_1845_241–242

[257] AA_IV_1846_42

[258] Audin_&_Reynaud_
1981_460

[259] CS_France_IX_1841_
Lyon_425–6

[260] CS_France_IX_1841_
Lyon_353

[261] Monfalcon_1866_VI_11ff

[262] Monfalcon_1866_I_16off

[263] Monfalcon_1866_VII

[264] BA_Comité_1891_355

[265] Boitel_1843_II_483

[266] Allmer_&_Dissard_II_
1889_273–334

[267] Mérimée_1835_94

[268] Spon_1675_112

[269] Seraucourt_1740_22

[270] Schneyder_1880_52

[271] Monfalcon_1857_219

[272] Monfalcon_1857_
Avertissement

[273] Monfalcon_1857_240

[274] Monfalcon_1857_209

[275] Mém_Lyon_1879–81_
19–20

[276] Mém_Lyon_1876_476

[277] BSA_Drôme_XII_1878_
101–102

[278] Hughes_1822_94,
travelling 1819

[279] BSA_Drôme_VII_1873_
339

[280] BSA_Drôme_XXXI_
1897_342

[281] BSA_Drôme_XXXI_1897_
327

[282] BSA_Drôme_XXXIII_
1899_334

[283] Charvet_1869_124

[284] Chorier_1837_397

[285] Charvet_1869_57

[286] Schneyder_1880_28–29

[287] Schneyder_1880_21

[288] Chorier_1837_iii

[289] Stendhal_1891_I_188

[290] Charvet_1869_64

[291] Charvet_1869_60–61

[292] Rever_1827_56

[293] Charvet_1869_66–67

[294] Charvet_1869_184

[295] Année_Archéologique_1879_89

[296] Charvet_1869_57

[297] SG_XLVI_Vienne_1879_489

[298] Chorier_1837_161–162

[299] Charvet_1869_75

[300] Millin_II_1807_11–16

[301] Schneyder_1880_76

[302] Mérimée_1835_125

[303] SG_XLVI_Vienne_1879_108–109

[304] BA_Comité_1891_337

[305] BA_Comité_1894_227

[306] Hughes_1822_76–77

[307] AD_Région_Lyonnaise_1896_110

CHAPTER 9

Centre and West

Bourges

Bourges (Cher), capital of Aquitania, and an important town in the Renaissance, had a circuit of walls, their foundations of sculptured and inscribed blocks;[1] and sections of these, with gates, and some 4–5m in height,[2] were still to be seen in the mid-19th century,[3] with fragments of buildings surviving.[1] Their maintenance for defence was abandoned under Louis XIV,[4] but in 1754 they had been "presque tous entiers."[5] Several later buildings were raised on their foundations.[6] We may wonder whether the tomb of the early bishop, Félix, really was of Paros marble (because the term was frequently if loosely used to indicate precious marble[7]), and whether it came from the walls,[8] the extent of which also governed the lower stretches of the mediaeval cathedral.[9]

In Bourges, several structures were built on top of the Roman walls, including the Hôtel Jacques Coeur (1443–1453), which incorporated two of the towers;[10] many blocks appear to have been re-cut for their new destination.[11] Such hôtels (in effect palaces) were often built near old churches, and even built on top of Roman walls, as at Angers.[12] Decorated architectural blocks could be viewed in several more modern structures, writes Mérimée in 1838; he traced one wall for several hundred metres along the Séraucourt Promenade, and saw an antique structure in grand appareil near the Archbishop's Palace.[13] Many sculpted blocks in the Roman wall, however, were some 6m below the present ground level,[14] some of these actually below the foundations of Renaissance buildings, yet visitable.[15] The wall foundations were of five or six ranks of "fûts de colonnes, chapiteaux, frises, entablements, bas-reliefs, blocs couverts d'admirables sculptures ou à peine ébauchés, entassés pêle-mêle," but these, together with the 1705 enceinte, were disappearing by the mid-19th century.[16] This was when the new railway line, skirting the remains of the western ramparts, was built in the ditches. Ribault de Laugardière saw the walls being nibbled away in mid-century, and expressed the wish for

---

1 Meslé 1988, 27–29, 74–79, Les vestiges des monuments romains de Bourges; 271–281 Mutation dans le tissu urbain durant le XIXe siècle; 387–392, Archéologie urbain 1980–7, but nothing on the Roman walls in the 19th century.

© KONINKLIJKE BRILL NV, LEIDEN, 2015 | DOI 10.1163/9789004293717_011

ces débris vénérables être enfin conservés avec respect, et puissent les hommes de notre temps, renonçant à un déplorable vandalisme, se rappeler qu'au moyen-âge, ainsi que l'avait ordonné Louis VII, quiconque était accusé d'avoir détruit quoi que ce soit des murs gallo-romains de l'antique Cité, était tenu de réparer immédiatement le dommage, au jugement des Prud'hommes de la ville, et de plus devait payer soixante sols d'amende![17]

By the mid 19th century, however, it was judged that old Bourges was disappearing, in part because the town "tend à recouvrir ses vieilles murailles de la nouveauté parisienne."[18] Sections of the Hôtel Jacques Coeur were being degraded.[19] The amphitheatre, a rubbish-dump in the 16th century, was destroyed on the orders of the Prince de Condé in 1619, supposedly to make a fine square out of what was perceived as a mess.[20] Only fragments survived,[21] and Ribault suggested the 19th century should remember the losses, and try to conserve what was left.[22] There were still ruins, but the 1849 Congress had to descend 46 steps to find them.[23] And in 1860, sculptured blocks retrieved from the walls were deteriorating in the open, "malgré les promesses formelles faites à la Société française d'archéologie par le maire de cette cité."[24] These included sections of a large monument, but apparently no attempts were made to rebuild it.[25] The Hôtel Cujas, of 1515, was left without a roof for several years (a dodge surely even older than the late Roman Empire, to help buildings collapse), but was eventually restored and made into the museum.[26] Not before, however, a nasty standoff occurred between the local Society and the mayor, because they had nowhere to store or display recovered antiquities.[27]

Auxerre

Unlike Autun, but like Sens, Auxerre (Yonne)[2] did indeed build the foundations (and some lower courses?) of her walls with prestigious blocks, carved face inwards. These were extracted at various periods,[28] including the later 14th century from a suburban monastery,[29] and well described in 1850.[30] The walls survived into the 19th century (this was a small enceinte),[31] including some towers, no doubt because of the recalcitrant pebble and mortar mix which formed its nigh-indestructible core,[32] and because the upper sections

---

2 Rocher 1984, 38–51 for Gallo-Roman town, including enceinte, at least some of which had been levelled before 1600; 322–324 urbanism & architecture in 19th century; 349–355 Modernisation de la ville et transformations économiques.

CENTRE AND WEST 261

were evidently only of petit appareil.[33] Like Autun, there was a push in mid-century to found a museum, since it was feared that the blocks retrieved would go abroad.[34] The site was a rich one, prompting in 1848 an application to the Ministère de l'Intérieur for funds to conduct digs.[35] By 1852, a report on local investigations was ready, together with a map of Roman roads in the area,[36] sections of which were still being reported a decade later.[37] Outside the town, as the departmental yearbook wrote in 1853, "De charmantes villas furent sans nul doute établies dans la vallée où nous les voyons encore, le long des rives du ruisseau de Vallan, de beaux et grands jardins"[38] – but no trace of them survives. Pressure on the mediaeval monuments was also high, so that only a few mediaeval towers or spires survived.[39]

Orléans

In 1851 Orléans (Loiret) welcomed "ce parlement ambulatoire qu'on appelle un Congrès scientifique," perhaps regretting "d'avoir jeté bas la ceinture de ses murs, comblé ses fossés, déraciné ses grosses tours."[40] These walls and towers were once Roman,[3] with a later wall built on top,[41] so only fragments of the ancient walls survived into the 1880s, when attempts were made to preserve them.[42] A plan of the enceinte was started in the 1840s,[43] and plentiful antiquities were unearthed throughout the town.[44] Much of the old town also gave way to new boulevards;[45] old houses were demolished even if some façades were preserved, and these and other destructions, together with the dangers of radical town planning,[46] led the local scholars to pray that their town took some notice of its treasures,[47] since it was called more of a vandal than Paris itself.[48] This was due to the extensive reworking of the urban layout from 1750,[4] with the construction of boulevards in 1821 regretted by some for the destruction they caused.[49] A few local débris reached the museum[50] and, perhaps again as displacement therapy, the idea of an archaeological map of the region was floated.[51]

---

3 Vergnaud-Romagnési 1830, 3–9 for late antique enceinte, but nothing on blocks recovered; 9–21 for 2nd, 3rd & 4th enceintes; Debal 1983, 105–161 for the Roman city, including the late enceinte, with plan; Debal 1998, I 33–37 and cf. 73 for its survival into the 12th century; I 141–144 for La quatrième enceinte de la ville moderne, finished 1555.

4 Debal 1998 I 145–155 for new architectural styles, and II 58–61 for Les grands travaux d'urbanisme, with 112–119 for promenades and the railway, and then II 136–142 for the changes from 1870, with the ramparts just down

Limoges

The visitor to modern Limoges (Haute-Vienne) (no less than Mérimée[52] in 1838 and Caumont[53] in 1847) would be forgiven for thinking there had never been an antique city on the site, for there are no easily visible remains, and 19th-century doubt even about the existence of walls.[54] In fact, the prosperity of the mediaeval city obliterated them, the materials thoroughly re-used in mediaeval and later times. Thus the blocks discovered in 1700 near to the presbytery of Saint-Maurice, and the sculptures and frieze-blocks found in 1757 where the walls surrounding the Bishop's Palace were to be built, probably came from the enceinte.[5] Even the exact line of the ancient enceinte is in doubt, and its hypothetical path is deduced from the topography of the mediaeval city, but probably not to the full extent of the boulevards set up for the 13th century walls. Indeed, the late enceinte seems to have covered less than 3ha – minute in comparison with its Imperial extent of 150ha, and it was with reluctance in the mid-18th century that the townspeople dismantled the mediaeval enceinte, by then useless in its turn. As a result "La ville y gagnait en salubrité ce qu'elle perdait en pittoresque, et nos pères ne se doutaient point alors que leurs arrières-petits enfants éprouveraient un attrait de curiosité à exhumer quelques restes informes de ce qu'ils faisaient disparaître sans regrets."[55] What is more, the huge bath complex at the Place des Jacobins shows clear traces of systematic retrieval of material: vaults and even hypocausts were dismantled, sometimes at the cost of real sapping operations.[6] On the same site were discovered a load of limestone blocks which – like the similar pieces discovered at the Forum – probably escaped the kilns. So there were plenty of questions to be answered when the Congrès held its 1860 session at Limoges.[56]

Clermont-Ferrand

Little is known about the late enceinte of this town in the Puy-de-Dôme, although Caumont found parts of its grand appareil near the Cathedral,[57] and sections were still to be seen in the 1880s.[58] To believe Gregory of Tours (who had also remarked on the large blocks of the ramparts),[59] the town was rich in marble monuments, for example in S. Vénérand[60] and S. Namatius,[61] and sarcophagi (some in use as Christian altars) were still being broken up at the end of the 18th century.[62] And late in that century, the advice for a man wish-

---

5   Perrier 1964, 58f.
6   Loustaud 1980, 135.

CENTRE AND WEST

ing to build a barn and needing stone was not to buy it, but "de faire des fouilles et de profiter des pierres qu'il y trouverait enfouies."[63]

Périgueux[7]

Périgueux (Dordogne) had late antique walls, which left the forum outside their circuit, but included the amphitheatre (which might still have been operational) as part of the defences.[8] The walls were part-built with spolia, especially the foundation courses,[64] just like other walls in Gaul.[65] The débris they revealed were described by Beauménil in 1784,[66] and column drums were seen during dismantling in the 1820s;[67] sections of them survive today, but most of the antiquities have gone, eighty cartloads of stone being sold to entrepreneurs in 1784 alone,[68] although blocks were retrieved for the museum, created in 1835.[9] The church of Saint-Front had taken some, especially for the strange re-use of a variety of Roman columns in the bell-tower.[69] The site of St-Étienne was supposedly that of a temple, for large quantities of marble and granite were recovered when it was excavated in 1805;[70] and other recoveries suggest large and splendid buildings.[71] The Tour de Vésone also stands in part today, but stripped of its marble cladding.[72] This is the surviving cylinder of a circular temple, its peristyle and pronaos lost, and giving some idea of just how much marble from these elements was re-used elsewhere. The only survivals, imbricated column drums, and capitals, of limestone, twenty in all, were perhaps rejected. Blocks in the nearby gallo-roman wall could be from this temple, and a methodical dismantling could reveal more – but "ce serait une opération onéreuse, requérant des autorisations de multiples propriétaires" – the perennial problem.[10] Local antiquarians were sure, from the blocks seen, that there had indeed been other temples,[73] including one to Mars.[74] The Porte de Mars was dismantled and rebuilt in the 19th century. Baths were excavated in the early 19th century, but not published.[75] The degradation and destruction of

---

7   Combet 2011, 27–79: La ville antique, Ier-ve siècle, with plans, prints, photos and reconstructions of monuments.

8   Garmy & Maurin 1996, 128–154 Périgueux: tracé retained in MA, and called la Cité. In the 12th century the counts of Périgord built a tower "grande et forte" in the amphitheatre, using its materials; Girardy-Caillet 1998, 28–47 for visible remains, 48–57 for buried or vanished sites, and 22–7 for history of research.

9   Penisson 2005 for a well-illustrated catalogue of retrieved blocks; cf. Combet 2011, 175–211: 1788–1830, Bouleversements politiques d'une ville mobile.

10   Lauffray 1990 17, 123, and 74 for quote.

264   CHAPTER 9

this city's monuments were seen in a broad context in 1842, with the Tour de Vésone in danger, and "pierres druidiques" being used for road metal.[76]

In spite of the later finds mentioned above, the Gallo-Roman enceinte at Périgueux had largely disappeared by the fifteenth century,[11] probably because of the division of the population into two distinct sections. The Roman city had been down by the River Isle, on flat ground, and it was here that the enceinte was built; a rival settlement was built on the hill, to be known as the Puy-Saint-Front, and it was here that the cult of the saint, the cathedral and the thriving town, surrounded by its own ramparts, was to develop. The old enceinte was certainly insignificant in size: at 959 metres in length, and enclosing only 5.5 hectares, it was, with Antibes and Saintes, one of the smallest in Gaul. The walls were about 5m in breadth and 10m high, with 24 towers; and the amphitheatre (probably with its own three towers) was incorporated in the defences. The old name of Vesunna gave way to Civitas Petrucoriorum, and then just La Cité, with the church of Saint Etienne, which was the cathedral until 1669.[12]

The "birth-date" of its competitor is unknown, with the dates 1120, 1182 and 1204 being suggested for its walls. A natural and unfriendly rivalry quickly grew up between Puy and Cité.[13] An ambitious plan of 1240 to link the two settlements by a wall came to grief, although somewhat later (1250/69)[77] it was still planned that the area would be settled by "foreigners," induced to settle there by ten years of tax concessions. But the wall was never built: instead, in 1379 we find the Mayor and Consuls (that is, elected representatives) of the Puy complaining to their neighbours about the poor state of the Cité walls, which seems to have prepared the ground for an attempt by the Puy to have them demolished, for the Consuls of the Cité lodged an objection to this idea in 1389. Nevertheless, evidence suggests that the Cité walls were used for materials by the fourteenth century: a document of 1366/7 describes the construction of a staircase and crenellated wall, the materials coming both from quarries in the quarter of Limogeanne and at Saint-Martin – but also from the enceinte itself.[78] Consuls in 1414 objected to the demolition of their walls, which had been pulled down "a parte...de las arenas, inter turrim Basta et turrim de Volves" with a view to re-using the materials therein, mentioned as "quadros et scementa."[14] Similarly, the amphitheatre was used as a quarry: there survives a note of 1416 regarding the payment of 11 livres tournois for the working of three

---

11   Barrière 1930, 173ff.
12   Plans in Périgueux 1979, 30f.; Penaud 1983, 38, 113; & Higounet-Nadal 1984.
13   Penaud 1983, 73ff.
14   Higounet-Nadal 1978, 26.

CENTRE AND WEST

265

hundred baskets of stone done "en las arenas propi de la Ciptat," surely using the blocks of grand appareil from the structure.[79]

Perhaps some slight protection was given to the remains of the amphitheatre by the nuns of the Convent of the Visitation who, in 1644, were given permission to close within the walls of their nunnery the "grottes et amphithéâtres" belonging to the town. This they did, according to a 19th century account of their activities, building several chapels above the most complete grottoes, which they dedicated to the Mysteries of the Passion. They kept these well decorated, and often had processions to them;[80] a large grotto was dedicated to the Magdalene. The town Consuls allowed this occupation, it is suggested, because thereby the crimes committed there in honour of paganism were annulled.[15]

The demolition of the Gallo-Roman enceinte and amphitheatre clearly proceeded through the centuries, for we find Wlgrin de Taillefer noting that sculptures and bas-reliefs were still to be seen everywhere in and around Vésone, with several bas-reliefs are to be seen in the enceinte.[81] From the context, and from his lithographs, it is clear that these were not displayed but, in fact, revealed in the foundations and infill to the wall when the outer blocks were robbed for building purposes. Presumably such pilfering stopped only when the enceinte was classified as an historical monument, but this happened only in 1920. And long before that date, the coming of the railway had occasioned great changes in and around the town.[16]

Remnants of the Gallo-Roman enceinte still survive, and much surely remains to be discovered. Fragments filled with spolia are near the Porte Normande. Here decorated marble and stone slabs with their smooth verso used as facing blocks are to be found at the Maison Romaine (built directly on top of the enceinte which here, because of the drop to the river, has a height of about 12m), and the adjacent Château Barrière, also built on top of the Roman walls. By 1863, scholars could view Château and Tour de Vésone without leaving their train seats,[82] since the railway passed between them, and its construction might have been responsible for damage to both. Spolia have been used in the construction of the latter and some do indeed appear still displayed in its walls, just as others reportedly were; but, given its turbulent history, and its frequent and still obvious repairs, it seems impossible to date the work. In between the Château and the Maison Romaine are the remains of a very impressive round tower, of Roman date, some of the frieze blocks

---

15   Secret 1978, 276.

16   Combet 2011, 213–237, 1830–1870: Avant et après le chemin de fer, with 236–7 maps showing expansion 1800–50, 1850–1900, and 1900–1950.

forming the foundations of which have been laid decorated face outwards –
though presumably originally below ground level. Antiquities may also have
been displayed on Porte Romaine, a 19th century lithograph of which[83] shows
it with an inscription to the left of the gateway, a hooded niche above it, and a
square niche with entablature to the right. By analogy with the material still on
the gate to Saint-Bertrand-des-Comminges, there is no reason why they should
not be antique.

Apart from the material sold to entrepreneurs, what became of the spolia
extracted from the enceinte of the Cité? Plenty were still lying around in the
19th century – witness the drawing of the jardin Chambrin in mid-century,
with columns, capitals and blocks of frieze,[17] and many of these same pieces
are now to be seen in the central courtyard of the Musée du Périgord. And it
seems likely that many of the stones, recut and repolished, were used in the
construction of the new town, as Barrière remarks.[18] However, no evidence has
yet come to light to support this conclusion, beyond the payment for recutting stone from the amphitheatre, recorded above. Locally, the splendour of
ancient Vesone is seen as an example to artists, especially since several capitals
in Saint-Front are directly inspired by the antique.

Poitiers

Poitiers (Vienne) is one of the few centres where a mediaeval thirst for Roman
marble can be proved – thanks to the efforts of 19th century antiquarians,
rather than to those of 20th century builders of underground car-parks, which
have sometimes been the main engine driving archaeological excavation in
much of France. Presumably the large baths, discovered in the later 19th century, were also marble-veneered,[84] and these were dug over several years in
the 1870s and 1880s by R. P. de la Croix,[85] as were other sites around the town,
one of which required immediate demolition of Roman walls at the demand
of its owner.[86]

In spite of lobbying by scholars in the later 19th century to leave an important
part of its wall standing,[87] little survived of antique Poitiers except for a section of the late wall in the garden adjacent to the Palais des Ducs d'Aquitaine.[19]
The quality of the spolia herein testifies to the splendour of the Roman city,

---

17   Penaud 1983, 298.

18   Barrière 1930, 178.

19   Granger 1988 16 for gallo-roman ramparts, with photos of re-used blocks; good on the
      mediaeval walls, but nothing on 19th-century demolition.

CENTRE AND WEST 267

the construction of its walls traditionally (and wrongly) attributed to the Visigoths.[88] Further examples are on display in the museum. The foundation courses of the wall are largely made up of white marble blocks, some pilasters, and some decorated architectural members. In two places in this short stretch of less than 15m, blocks have been robbed out from the wall, leaving the courses above looking distinctly precarious. Indeed, town improvements meant that much of the rest of the wall disappeared between 1810 and 1820, to be replaced by a boulevard, with the railway appearing in 1851.[89] Parts of the wall's foundations survived, however, and a Roman house with wall paintings was discovered.[90]

However, what is the history of the late Roman wall? It is presumably uniform in date with other walls, and certainly provided the only protection for the shrunken city of the earlier Middle Ages: the enceinte left the amphitheatre 100m outside its protection (as happened to amphitheatres or theatres at Angers, le Mans, Bourges and Reims; whilst at Tours, Nîmes, Arles and Périgueux the amphitheatre was turned into a fortress). La Marsonnière states that material from the amphitheatre went to build the walls;[91] he is fixated on the idea that it was the Vandals who destroyed most of the amphitheatre at Poitiers, though he does try to link changes in structures to changes in laws.[92] By 1843, little was left of the amphitheatre, except for "les mesquines demeures qui se sont soudées à ses flancs comme des plantes parasites;" the structure was due for a clean-up by the local authorities.[93] The amphitheatre was occupied by private housing,[94] but it was hoped that the administration could take over the site and clear them out.[95]

The Gallo-Roman enceinte was apparently remade by Pepin in 766, but was attacked by the Normans in 845 and 857, and the city burned by them in 865. However, the sources are too vague to tell us what might have happened to the enceinte. A fortress at Saint Hilaire was raised circa 936, and is still mentioned in charters c. 1136 and in 1161, but was presumably by now outdated, for a new and larger enceinte had been constructed sometime in the earlier 12th century, although not yet in place in 1138. Favreau claims that the Gallo-Roman enceinte receives no further mention in documents after the 12th century.[20] The wall (evidently with its later additions) was still visible, being mentioned in a deed of 1393.[96] This enceinte was indeed a massive construction, with its walls usually 10m high and sometimes 6m in thickness, or even more near the Bishop's Palace; the towers were at intervals of about 25m. The foundations were, as stated above, of spolia, but the upper levels were of petit appareil. We can imagine these disappearing over the centuries because of their nuisance

---

20   Favreau 1978, 35, note 135.

value. However, we know what happened to the foundation courses, because Mangon de la Lande wrote a report on them in 1835 in which he describes a series of underground galleries: these are formed of walls eight or nine feet in height, and fifteen or twenty feet in width, with a flat ceiling. He followed one such gallery for a quarter of a league [1km], from beyond the Bishop's Palace to the rue des Filles-St-François. He also describes spolia piled up chaotically in the galleries.[97] With colleagues, he continued his explorations the following year by searching throughout the cellars of Poitiers on a line with the wall, and finding many more spolia still in place.[98] His description of the line he followed is given by reference to the street-names up above – so it is clear that much of the enceinte was by his day almost completely hollow.

What had happened to it? Had the Gallo-Roman enceinte always been hollow? The mystery is cleared up by Ledain, who greatly extended Mangon de la Lande's work by publishing plans of the surviving rampart together with a catalogue of interesting spolia. His work was commissioned in 1871 by the local antiquarian society. He dismissed Mangon's belief that the galleries or casemates might be Visigothic structures built against the Roman wall, and stated that they were the work of the Middle Ages, when the new and enlarged fortifications rendered the old enceinte useless.[99] The proof of this comes from two features: the first is that the floor level of the galleries sometimes drops beneath that of the Roman wall; and the second is that they found three small columns dateable to the 12th–13th centuries underneath some Roman blocks, and presumably placed there to give support to the wall above them; and also some more pillars and a mediaeval arch in a cellar near Saint-Simplicien – proof also that the dangers of indiscriminate sapping were recognised by those inhabitants of Poitiers lucky enough to have such splended proto-cellars on their property.

Precisely what became of the spolia extracted from the walls is not known. Ledain in 1871 can list only 53 pieces in his report – which is perhaps some indication of how thoroughly they were plundered. What is more, much of the spolia appears to have been marble, which must have been very rare in this part of France in the Middle Ages. Has anyone studied the types of marble used for figure sculpture in Romanesque Poitou? Could some of these be made from spolia? How frequently would it have been possible to detect such re-use? The town was described in 1754 as "des plus désertes & des plus ruinées par les guerres civiles,"[100] so perhaps spolia were absorbed into new building in the 19th century.

The Musée des antiquités de l'Ouest was in existence by 1820 and housed at first in the Temple Saint-Jean, but then because of lack of space moved in 1854 to the Faculty of Law and again in 1877 to the Hôtel de Ville and the Société des

CENTRE AND WEST

Antiquaires de l'Ouest.[101] Continuing destruction ensured that a 12th-century chapel built over a Roman tomb lost its storiated capitals not to the museum, but built into an entrepreneur's house.[102] The inscription from the Tomb of Claudia Varenilla, wrested with difficulty in 1823 from the house-owner who used it as a doorstop, and then tried to sell it on for slicing up, was rescued by scholars, and survived, no thanks to the local administration.[103] But items found in a cemetery in 1879 when the Génie were digging new barracks did not stay in Poitiers, being taken to Paris.[104] Conversely the church of Saint-Porchaire, slated for demolition in the 1840s, survived.[105]

Saintes

This, the important city of Mediolanum in Charente-Inférieure, boasted a range of prestigious buildings, and stands in a countryside rich in Roman remains, and very rich in fine Romanesque churches. Connections between the two periods have frequently been pointed out: the churches at Barret, Saint-Laurent-de-Cognac, and Chantillac sit directly over "magical" springs as does, probably, the Abbaye-aux-Dames at Saintes; at Thaims a Roman villa is incorporated into the church; the villa and bath-group at Talmost must have been very visible in the Middle Ages. The direct study of such antiquities is reflected in the re-use in Romanesque times of imbrication, fluting, rosettes and acanthus motifs.[21] Likewise, the city of Saintes was once rich in antiquities: it still has the "Arch of Germanicus",[22] albeit severely restored.[23] No population figures survive before 1813 (when there were but 10,300 inhabitants), but the dimensions of the Gallo-Roman enceinte suggest a very small community during the Middle Ages. There was, however, some growth of suburbs, and these did occasion the extension of the original rampart to the east (to bring it nearer to the river) and also to the south, where it came nearer to the line of the culvert draining the amphitheatre, apparently so that this could be used as a wet moat.[24]

But already in 1856 Caumont recognised that if steps were not taken "dans vingt ans... vous n'en trouverez plus de vestiges, ou vous n'aurez plus que

---

21   Crozet 1971, 18f., 119ff.; see also Crozet 1954, and Crozet 1956.

22   Dangibeaud 1933A, 29ff.

23   Maurin 1964–72, 264ff.; Maurin 1978 for the arch (71–81), forum (81–91), baths and aqueducts (93–105) and amphitheatre (105–109), but with only passing references to other survivals.

24   Thiebaud 1980, 42.

270 CHAPTER 9

des ruines informes."[106] Within the walls, imposing fragments of other civic buildings and of tombs are to be found in the museum,[25] which also housed débris removed from the ruins of the capitolium.[107] This structure, perhaps still part-antique, seems to have survived into the 14th century, and its remains (which apparently included marble architectural members) then mined again for improvements to the 16th-century walls.[108] The site was then reworked again in 1609 by having Henri IV's new citadel built on top of it,[109] when "de nombreux morceaux sculptés de monuments antiques" were found during the demolition of a "Roman" tower; these were reused in the new bastions.[110] The site eventually became part of the hospital, discussed below.[111]

The local Commission archéologique was praised in 1862 for its zeal, but that unfortunately "on a fait peu de cas de leurs avis et qu'on s'est même ingé- nié à exécuter le contraire de ce qu'elles avaient demandé."[112] Plus ça change, one might add. In any case, local landowners simply rode rough-shod over any antiquities on their land that they did not wish to preserve, one in 1853 build- ing on his land, with all that survived being mosaics fragments presented to the local museum.[113]

The late antique walls were built in part from earlier monuments, as were so many other enceintes.[114] Blocks from the late enceinte were again being re-used and, more importantly, displayed, in the new mediaeval ram- parts: for example, they made the Porte Aiguière (the water gate), next to which the remains of the Roman wall survived into the 19th century, and where one might see the débris of Roman monuments which had been used as materials.[26] But 1816 saw many sections of wall flattened as modernising improvements were made to the town;[115] and by the end of the 19th century most of the walls had gone, although fine pieces had been extracted from the retaining wall of the Hôpital Saint-Louis,[116] which was in the south-eastern corner of the late antique enceinte. Apparently, most of the blocks retrieved from the upper courses of this section of the town wall were used to repair the hospital.[117] Antiquities were recovered from the foundation courses of this same 500-metre stretch of three- or four-metre-thick town wall in the 1880s,[118] including inscriptions[119] and funerary monuments,[120] leading commenta- tors to ask what was to be done to preserve the amphitheatre and baths of the town.[121] Excavations of the hospital wall were still being urged in 1894,[122] and photographs of the discoveries were taken by the Bishop of Constantine and Hippo,[123] who would certainly have been conversant with the kinds of materi-

---

25   Dangibeaud 1933B.
26   Clouet 1949–63, 87: quoted from the notes of N. Moreau, Bibliothèque Municipale, Saintes.

CENTRE AND WEST

als likely to be retrieved. For Ledain in 1896, such retrievals allowed the "reconstruction" of the ancient city; "Grâce à eux, nous pouvons presque dire ce que fut la cité antique. Ces murs constituent de véritables archives, des documents inédits d'un intérêt capital."[124]

Saintes also once possessed a Doric temple, the remains of which were unearthed in 1815 or 1816 during the construction of a promenade.[125] These included six columns,[126] presumably destroyed with other sections of the temple during the driving of a new road immediately to its front.[127] Although a fragment of the temple frieze is preserved in the museum, most of the rich remains quickly vanished, presumably as road core.[128] Plentiful débris from the enceinte, including bronzes and rare marbles, were found underneath the hospital.[129] If local scholars were correct that this temple was Augustan, then its destruction is indeed a great loss, as was that of an inhabited house near the amphitheatre, declared to be Roman.[130]

The fate of such monuments tells a story all too common at Saintes, where modern excavators complain of the continuation of an easy-going vandalism. When in the 1970s Maurin carried out a rescue dig on a section of the Gallo-Roman wall at the Place du Marché Saint Pierre (for the inevitable underground parking), he seems to have got little help from anyone; but he published an eloquent series of photographs of Roman blocks being carted off to the municipal rubbish dump.[27] The following year a large hypocausted building complex was revealed, together with a mediaeval pottery or depot, with perhaps hundreds of intact pots: the building was destroyed, and somebody drove a mechanical shovel over the pots, breaking all of them except one.[28]

In the 19th century, the triumphal arch erected (AD 21) in honour of Germanicus sat in the middle of a bridge, rather than at one end, because the river had changed its course. When Millin saw it in 1811 it was in a bad state,[131] and in 1821 its decoration was described as "nearly obliterated."[132] The arch was to be moved, because it hindered fluvial navigation. It was brought down in part with gunpowder,[133] explained by one sarcastic commentator as the architect's best method of conserving it.[134] An 1845 report to the Minister of the Interior promised that the work was nearly complete,[135] and one commentator noted that "la démolition de ce monument romain est une honte véritable pour la France entière."[136] This had entailed demolishing the bridge, and work by the génie civil – "impitoyable comme les conclusions des sciences mathématiques" – who found many of the blocks so degraded that they could not be reused.[137] This may have been because the "dismantling"

---

27 Maurin 1976.

28 Maurin & Vienne 1977, 21f.

272   CHAPTER 9

using gunpowder had damaged many of the stones. One commentator protested against the whole exercise, because it would remove the arch from its context.[138] The Monuments Historiques had ordered its removal, but did not watch the process, arriving only in time to hear of some of the monument's stones knocked down in free-fall from 15m. It was not rebuilt on the shore for six years, and thanks to rough treatment and gunpowder, "Le nouvel édifice, plus rapproché du faubourg de quelques mètres, n'aura rien conservé de sa physionomie première."[139] It survives in its reconstructed state as one of the few antique glories of the town.

This tradition of almost wanton destruction (not to mention lack of study[29]) is unfortunate, for it underlines that the fragments now in the museum, although numerous and imposing, are but a fraction of what the city once possessed. The Génie naturally tried to help, wishing to destroy the church of Ste-Marie-des-Dames, which lay inside their barracks;[140] but the church survived their efforts. Furthermore, we cannot properly trace any interest in the Roman glories of the city during the Middle Ages, for research on the mediaeval city has been slight, thanks no doubt to the unfortunate destruction of the municipal archives in a fire at the Town Hall in 1871.

Other monuments also suffered badly. By the end of the 19th century the visible structures of both amphitheatre and baths were in a sorry state, as the following account demonstrates. In 1820 the baths were occupied by houses and gardens, and Chaudruc recommended a fence and guard as the only way to preserve the structure.[141] But inevitably it lost archaeological interest between 1820 and 1850, being stripped down to "quelques pans de murailles."[142] By midcentury, so little was visible of the amphitheatre that it could be seen only in the mind's eye, and "c'est que votre science a pu évoquer tout cela pour le plaisir de votre imagination."[143] In 1834, the Government offered funds for clearing the site, if the conseil municipal would also contribute, but they refused.[144] A partial change of heart came in the 1840s, when the local Society clubbed together with the administration to purchase sections of the amphitheatre site,[145] which was still occupied by some greedy proprietors who refused reasonable purchase offers, and planted trees there.[146] As Calvet remarked in 1844, "l'expropriation forcée pour cause de conservation des monuments est un moyen souvent utile et qui peut être employé,"[147] which is perhaps what happened. In any case, the whole site was in municipal control by 1866, and clearance and consolidation work began in 1880,[148] although excavation of the arena went slowly.[149] After a demolition scare,[150] excavation of the baths yielded some fine sculpture pieces by the 1890s.[151] Tourists would surely have

---

29   Clouet 1949–63, 83.

CENTRE AND WEST

been more plentiful had the town's heritage been protected during the 19th century.

Toulouse

> La Toulouse romaine et la Toulouse du moyen âge ont aujourd'hui entiè-
> rement disparu, et il est peu de grandes villes en France qui aient perdu
> aussi complètement toute trace de leurs plus anciens monuments.[152]
> [1881]

Old Toulouse (Tarn-et-Garonne) did indeed disappear, with a nonchalance that was perhaps traditional, earning the town in 1861 the appellation "métro-pole du vandalisme dans le midi de la France."[153] From the late 18th century, houses were still being built with "des débris de statues de saints, des inscrip-tions du moyen-age, des chapiteaux," prompting the comment that "ce qu'on a nommé le vandalisme est une vieille maladie qui existe encore de nos jours, et même avec une recrudescence qui afflige les amis des arts et ceux des vieilles gloires de la patrie."[154] Even in the 1870s, the proposals for reconstructing the Hôtel de Ville (which contained scant remains of the old Capitol)[155] and the work under way

> ne paraissent pas tenir un compte suffisant des monuments historiques;
> que celui qui a obtenu la préférence de l'autorité municipale ne remplit
> qu'en partie l'obligation de conserver les monuments classés,[156]

of which several remains were still in danger in 1872.[157] As for what was to be done with the remains, one recommendation was to preserve them within the Hôtel de Ville in place, rather than transport them elsewhere, pointing out that this was the cheaper option, and would add to the site's attractiveness.[158] A brave attempt was made to attribute earlier destruction to the usual suspects, the Visigoths, but the unanswerable question was whether the city was of no importance under the Romans, "parce qu'on ne voit plus dans son enceinte, ni temples, ni autels, ni statues, ni arcs de triomphe?"[159] (Yet they did exist, albeit in small quantities.[30]) And what was to happen to "ses antiques églises, ses vieilles maisons, garnies de sculptures qui sont la joie des archéologues"?[160]

---

30 Labrousse 1968, 237–290: L'enceinte gallo-romaine, i.e. the walls of the cité. 238–9 for various destructions of sections in the 13th century. NB use of petit appareil and brick (no stone in the area), but 276–281 the rempart de la Garonne does use spolia in its foundations.

The Château Narbonnais, next to one of the city gates, its blocks cramped and not mortared, came down in the mid-16th century,[161] including a splendid gateway decorated with a trophy, which Noguier illustrates in his 1556 book, writing of its "grosses pierres de taille."[162] He recognised that the blocks have "plus tôt apparoissance de dépouilles, reliques et vestiges des ruines d'anciens bastimens." But this was a clear-up job, and "les portes et les murs furent rasés pour l'embellissement de la ville. / Ainsi l'antiquité fut abolie pour l'urgence nécessaire,"[163] and sections of wall were re-found only when sewers were being laid at the end of the 19th century.[164]

The most interesting lost structure in Toulouse was the church of Notre Dame de la Daurade, which had "one of the richest and most elaborate programmes of decoration known anywhere in the West [in the 5th century], incorporating sculptures and gold mosaics."[31] Its cloister had splendid capitals, and its cemetery the tombs of the counts of Toulouse.[165] Destroyed in the later 18th century, the complex also incorporated pagan antiquities,[166] being constructed on ancient foundations,[167] and débris from it were already being collected by the early 19th century.[168] Luckily Alexandre Du Mège rescued many of the structure's sculptures, now in the Augustins museum,[169] and had free range collecting choice pieces from elsewhere in the town, "ce magnifique domaine de décoration architecturale provenant de la démolition de grands édifices religieux de Toulouse."[170]

Latterday Visigoths were at work in Toulouse, namely the "barbare Génie militaire," which had the convent and church of the Jacobins at their mercy for decades, after their capture of the complex in 1792.[171] Conservationists from the Société Archéologique du Midi de la France were still struggling with them in 1847 after getting "remodelling" work suspended: "mais, hélas! n'est-il pas à craindre que des ordres supérieurs ne viennent, avant que nos réclamations ne soient entendues, préscrire de continuer ces dévastations?"[172] But the Génie had already destroyed some sections, and the mayor of Toulouse was sent in 1847 as avenging fury because the town "demande le rétablissement des parties détruites, et elle ne demande en cela que ce qui est juste. Nous verrons si le Génie militaire taille et monte des meneaux aussi habilement qu'il sait les démolir."[173] Nothing had happened by 1851,[174] and degradation by "ce qu'on est convenu d'appeler le génie militaire" continued.[175] The Génie's method was to keep making promises, and continue with their expensive remodelling:

---

31   Esmonde Cleary 2013, 361–4.

CENTRE AND WEST

Qu'est devenu maintenant du mas enorme de pierres dentelées provenant de celle destruction, et qui devaient, nous disait-on alors être précieusement conservées?[176]

Conclusion

Many Roman towns in these areas, including Poitiers, Périgueux, Limoges and Saintes, probably shrank considerably during Late Antiquity, and monuments outside the new walls were lost as a consequence. The first three of these, plus Bourges, once protected the routes from Aquitaine to the North, but with shrinkage the monuments disappeared: blocks from the amphitheatre at Saintes went into the new walls, and at Périgueux the whole structure became part of the defences, while the forum and a main temple (the Tour de Vésone) lay outside and suffered much dismantling. Allowing such monuments to survive has been called "active maintenance,"[32] but an alternative explanation could be that there were no reusable materials left to justify knocking them down. Building churches on top of ruins (e.g. on the villa south of Poitiers, at Ligugé) was much more productive.

At Clermont-Ferrand, the small enceinte is little known, and even the site of the luxurious Temple of Mercury is unknown. When the Congress was held here in 1895, all that could be reported was a chance find a few years earlier: "on a découvert les restes d'un mur énorme ne pouvant provenir que du mur d'enceinte. Ses fondations reposaient sur de gros blocs de pierre de taille coulés dans du béton; sur l'un d'eux était gravé un oiseau, dû, sans doute, au ciseau de quelque ouvrier maçon, qui rêvait de devenir sculpteur." At Toulouse, the temple on the capitol was dismantled early, and systematically. But outside the enceinte, and just as they did at Bordeaux, the cemeteries disappeared as new suburbs were erected. A member of the Congrès Scientifique, which met here in 1852, commented: "on a détruit les cimetières gallo-romains et des premiers âges du christianisme. Lorsqu'on fait des fouilles sur ces emplacements, on trouve des quantités d'urnes et beaucoup de sarcophages en marbre blanc, couverts de figures et de feuillages en relief."

In all cases, the monuments had been used as quarries down the centuries, and what little was left was usually destroyed in favour of modernisation, as we have seen in the plentiful examples cited throughout this chapter.

---

32   Esmonde Cleary 2013, 121, 145.

[1] Gembloux_1840_326

[2] SG_XVI_Bourges_1849_105

[3] BM_V_1839_404–405

[4] Ribault_de_Laugardière_1858_20–21

[5] Piganiol_XI_1754_497

[6] Barral_1852_6

[7] Gregory_of_Tours_III_1862_87

[8] Gregory_of_Tours_III_1862_165

[9] V-le-Duc_II_1875_296

[10] BM_IV_1838_533

[11] BM_XXVII_1861_379–391

[12] BM_XXVIII_1862_13–14

[13] Mérimée_1838_2

[14] SG_XVII_Auxerre_1850_19

[15] BM_XXXIV_1868_228–229

[16] Ribault_de_Laugardière_1858_14

[17] Ribault_de_Laugardière_1858_14–15

[18] Gembloux_1840_258

[19] Gembloux_1840_267

[20] Sorbonne_1863_109

[21] AA_I_1844_267

[22] Ribault_de_Laugardière_1858_33–34

[23] SG_XVI_Bourges_1849_104–105

[24] BM_XXVI_1860_455

[25] BM_XXVII_1861_379–391

[26] SG_LV_Dax_1888_42

[27] BA_Comité_1888_213

[28] Caumont_II.2_1831_352

[29] BSS_Yonne_II_1848_505–506

[30] SG_XVII_Auxerre_1850_240–242

[31] CS_France_XXV_1859_Auxerre_216–7

[32] SG_XVII_Auxerre_1850_240–241

[33] Quantin_1884_10–11

[34] BSS_Yonne_IX_1855_267

[35] BSS_Yonne_II_1848_1–2

[36] BSS_Yonne_VI_1852_263–264

[37] BSS_Yonne_XVIII_1864_50

[38] Ann_Départ_Yonne_1853_243

[39] BSS_Yonne_II_1848_275

[40] CS_France_XVIII_1851_Orléans_216–7

[41] BSA_Orléanais_VII_1882_461

[42] BA_Comité_1883_171

[43] BM_XII_1846_413–414

[44] Caumont_I_1853_269–270

[45] Roach_Smith_1855_25

[46] BSA_Orléanais_IV_1863_130

[47] BSA_Orléanais_III_1862_91–92

[48] MSA_Orléans_III 1903_238–239

[49] Vergnaud-Romagnési_1830_20

[50] BSA_Orléanais_II_1859_102

[51] BSA_Orléanais_I_1854_129

[52] Mérimée_1838_97–98

[53] SG_XIV_Sens_1847_375

[54] Ducourtieux_1884_35

[55] BSAH_Limousin_XLVII_1899_501–502

[56] CS_France_XXVI_1860_Limoges_18–20

[57] SG_XVII_Auxerre_1850_142–143

[58] Malte-Brun_III_1882_16

[59] Gregory_of_Tours_I_1836_32

[60] Gregory_of_Tours_II_1860_411

[61] Gregory_of_Tours_I_1836_87

[62] Nouvelles_Archives_Art_français_VII_1879_295–6

[63] Laporte_1897_172–173

[64] Schuermans_1888_82–83

[65] Caumont_Cours_II.2_1831_359

[66] Taillefer_1826_155

[67] Taillefer_1826_141

[68] Jullian_1890_II_332

[69] Viollet-le-Duc_III_1868_290

[70] Caumont_Cours_III_1838

[71] Bull_Comm_Roy_Brussels_XXVII_1888_37–100

[72] CHA_I_1894_374

[73] Audierne_1859_251

[74] Audierne_1859_259

[75] Taillefer_1826_84

[76] SG_IX_Bordeaux_1842_89

[77] AM_Périgueux_AA33

[78] AM_Périgueux_AA32

[79] AM_Périgueux_CC772

[80] AM_Périgueux_BB15

[81] Taillefer_1826_398

[82] SG_XXX_Rodez_1863_2

[83] Taillefer_1826_pl_16.

[84] SG_XLV_Le-Mans_1878_397

[85] MSA_Ouest_II_1883_118–119

[86] MSA_Ouest_1883_14

[87] MSA_Ouest_IV_1889_59

[88] Guilbert_IV_1845_314

[89] Rollière_1907_18

CENTRE AND WEST

[90] SG_LX_Abbeville_1893_86

[91] La_Marsonnière_1858_30

[92] La_Marsonnière_1858_32

[93] BM_IX_1843_387–388

[94] Murray_1848_226

[95] SG_X_1843_Poitiers_28

[96] Ledain_1870–1_169

[97] Mangon_de_la_Lande_1835_51ff.

[98] Mangon_de_la_Lande_1836

[99] Ledain_1870–1_160

[100] Piganiol_VIII_1754_69–70

[101] Réunion_BA_XIV_1890_339

[102] Rollière_1907_296

[103] MSA_Ouest_IV_1889_513

[104] RA_XXXVIII_1879_46

[105] SG_X_Poitiers_1843_4

[106] CS_France_XXIII_1856_La_Rochelle_117

[107] Massiou_1834_178

[108] Massiou_1834_177

[109] Marion_1852_6–7

[110] Ledain_1896_196–197

[111] Marion_1852_6–7

[112] BM_XXVIII_1862_38

[113] CS_France_XX_1853_Arras_153

[114] Ledain_1896_193–194

[115] Chaudruc_1820_8

[116] Ledain_1896_194

[117] Chaudruc_1820_18–19

[118] BA_Comité_1887_210

[119] SG_LV_Dax_1888_43

[120] Chaudruc_1820_161

[121] SA_Bordeaux_XI_1886_LX

[122] SG_LXI_Saintes_1894_196–197

[123] SG_LXI_Saintes_1894_184

[124] Ledain_1896_200–201

[125] Chaudruc_1820_28

[126] BM_X_1844_502

[127] Chaudruc_1820_32

[128] Chaudruc_1820_32–33

[129] SG_LXI_Saintes_1894_187

[130] Chaudruc_de_Cazannes_1820_165–166

[131] Millin_IV_1811_672

[132] Berrian_1821_23

[133] AA_I_1844_87–88

[134] AA_I_1844_95

[135] BM_XI_1845_385

[136] AA_III_1845_65

[137] BM_XX_1854_246

[138] AA_I_1844_233

[139] Caumont, BM_XVI_1850_25

[140] BM_VI_1840_424–425

[141] Chaudruc_1820_87

[142] Marion_1852_5

[143] Moufflet_1845_21–22

[144] BM_I_1834_306–307

[145] BM_XXVII_1861_77

[146] SG_IX_Bordeaux_1842_51

[147] BM_X_1844_509

[148] SG_LXI_Saintes_1894_167

[149] MSA_Ouest_II_1880–1882_118

[150] SA_Bordeaux_XII_1887_XXIV

[151] SG_LXI_Saintes_1894_254

[152] Malte-Brun_II_1881_38–39

[153] AA_XXI_1861_255–256

[154] Mège_1862_242

[155] Merson_1865_308

[156] Du_Perrier_&_Barry_1872_185–186

[157] Du_Perrier_&_Barry_1872_186–187

[158] Du_Perrier_&_Barry_1872_188

[159] Cayla_&_Perrin-Paviot_1859_37–38

[160] BSS_Yonne_XLII_1888_36

[161] Noguier_1556_23

[162] Noguier_1556_24

[163] Noguier_1556_28

[164] Le_Temps_10_October_1897

[165] BSA_Midi_IV_1840–1841_6

[166] Mège_1835_140

[167] Lahondès_1920_111

[168] Mège_1835_11

[169] Mège_1835_140–141

[170] Vic_XVI_1904_110–111

[171] BSA_Midi_VII_1860_168–169

[172] AA_VI_1847_295–296

[173] AA_VI_1847_334–335

[174] BM_XVII_1851_180

[175] BM_XVII_1851_178–179

[176] BSA_Midi_VII_1860_150

CHAPTER 10

Centuries of Destruction: Narbonne and Nîmes

Narbonne

Introduction

The dismantling of late-Roman fortifications represented a great opportunity for local historians and archaeologists everywhere, assuming they were alert to the depradations of the entrepreneurs who did the work, and to the support or indifference of the local authority. The walls of Narbonne (Aude) provide a conspicuous and well-documented example of "managed dismantling" and monuments-proud municipality and scholars. They incorporated many Roman monuments, some of which local scholars believed were built into new walls erected for the first time in the 15th and 16th centuries, in part to protect against gunpowder cannon, and in part to decorate them by re-using antique fragments, as Caumont avers.[1] Some of the stone perhaps came from dismantling ancient monuments standing until that period,[2] although the recycling of parts of the old Gallo-Roman walls during the new building work is more likely:

> Au dedans, au dehors, partout, gisaient épars, mutilés, les restes des anciens édifices et des monuments funéraires que les Romains y avaient accumulés pendant près de six siècles. François Ier ordonna que ces restes fussent réunis, et les remparts furent achevés avec des matériaux de grandes dimensions et d'origines diverses. Alors les frises, les corniches, les chapiteaux, les colonnes, les trophées d'armes, les statues triomphales, les tombeaux, les inscriptions funéraires, les fragments de toute nature furent ramassés, coordonnés quelquefois, et placés en couronnement autour des nouveaux murs et auprès des portes qui furent édifiées.[3]

The recycling under François Ier, discussed below, was acknowledged as quite deliberate, for the engineers carefully chose ancient blocks with which to decorate their new constructions.[4] What is more, the later walls generally stood just outside the Gallo-Roman ones, but only a few metres from them,[5] so the transfer of blocks from one to another (this is an unprovable assumption) would have been easy. As yet more of the complex walls of the town

© KONINKLIJKE BRILL NV, LEIDEN, 2015 | DOI 10.1163/9789004293717_012

CENTURIES OF DESTRUCTION: NARBONNE AND NÎMES 279

were brought down over the centuries, so evidence of the earlier enceintes was revealed.[6]

The topography of Narbonne is well illustrated by Philippe Buache's plan of the city in 1760,[7] which shows the line of the François Ier enceinte. By the time those ramparts were erected, the defended town (the Cité up the hill, and the Bourg on the flat) was unified, although of course still cut in two by its waterway, La Robine.[8] In Roman and mediaeval times, however, only the Cité was defended by walls, and the Bourg apparently received proper defences only in the fourteenth century. In what follows, therefore, the term "City" refers to the walled area to the north of the dividing water, and "Bourg" to the unwalled area to its south.

Some scholars maintained that they had no interest in the walls themselves, but only in whatever antiquities they contained.[9] This town was the seat of an alert society, the Société Archéologique de Narbonne, founded in 1833, which produced a *Bulletin*. The Mayor petitioned the Emperor in 1865 to have the walls declassified.[10] Also mentioned were hygiene, the 1854 outbreak of cholera and, of course, the facts that the town had never been attacked "depuis des temps les plus reculés."[11] Caumont toured them after declassification, and reported to the Congrès Archéologique de France in 1868: "Ces murs, bâtis avec les pierres provenant de ses anciens monuments, attestent l'antique splendeur de la cité et sont un véritable musée en plein vent."[12] Dismantling began the following year, and so important were the likely finds considered to be that Duruy, Ministre de l'Instruction publique, asked to be kept informed of discoveries.[13] However, the walls, in some sections 6m thick, were now the prey of entrepreneurs, and they had to be restrained (by a petition to the Mayor) from using gunpowder to break them down, and of course any antiquities in the path of the explosions.[14] Unfortunately, local noses were put well out of joint when an outside scholar (from the AIBL, no less) reported on what was happening to unearthed antiquities:

> Il regrette, d'ailleurs, que M. Egger n'ait pas cru devoir faire connaître sa présence à Narbonne aux membres de la Commission, qui pouvaient seuls lui fournir, avec exactitude, tous les renseignements nécessaires à l'accomplissement de sa mission.[15]

The example of Narbonne provides, therefore, a rare combination of a rich legacy of antiquities, a documented re-use of that legacy in Renaissance times, and an active 19th-century body of scholars and town authorities. Four areas require investigation. The first is the date and nature of the walls surrounding

280   CHAPTER 10

Narbonne in the Middle Ages, and the possibility that antiquities were pulled out of them in the course of building work, especially for that on the new cathedral. The second is the status of the Capitol, its temple and surroundings, and the extent to which the remains survived and were used during the Middle Ages. The third concerns the origins of the palace (or rather palaces), parts of which incorporate antiquities in a manner which makes it clear that they were set up as tokens of civic pride. The fourth is the François Ier enceinte, with its reuse of antiquities. What follows is therefore an assessment of what antiquities were visible and available during the Middle Ages, and an attempt to disentangle the various hints in the archives which might throw light on a matter made much more confusing by the reuse of antiquities in the François Ier enceinte. Unfortunately, there are no mediaeval descriptions of the city, and no "quotations" survive from before the eighteenth century about its antiquities and the prestige they lend to the city, although in the later 18th century Bosquet sets out his plan to draw inscriptions and bas-reliefs in town and house walls.[16]

Narbonne from Roman Times to Mediaeval Walls

Narbonne was once a prosperous city and port, "devenue la seconde Rome, la première ville des Gaules,"[17] with a large amphitheatre,[18] located on an important trade-route, and with the area graced with monuments.[1] She was famous from the 18th century for her walls, of various dates, but first for her late Roman walls, which reduced the area of the town to 15–20ha. Indeed, it is not even known whether she had walls under the Early Empire: a vallum has been found, but not dated, and it has been surmised that a Republican rampart may have existed, though probably not of stone.[2] In its heyday, the approach to the city was splendid, and decorated with triumphal arches: 93 clusters of bas-relief trophies have been counted, diverse in style, and hence we can assume that there were several arches or other honorific monuments. Already in 1826 it was acknowledged that the walls "seuls formeraient un musée très-intéressant."[19] It had once been hymned by Ausonius,[20] but later the town presented to Sidonius a much more forlorn picture.[3]

---

1 Küpper-Böhm 1996.

2 Gayraud 1981, 281ff.

3 Frye 2003, 192: "Narbonne dazzles its onlookers with its walls, citizens, circuit, shops, gates, porticoes, forum, theater, shrines, capitol, mint, baths, arches, granaries, markets, meadows, fountains, islands, salt mines, ponds, river, merchandise, bridge, and brine ... Narbonne, we quickly surmise, is a rather unsightly place ... Narbonne's protective strongholds lie in ruin,

CENTURIES OF DESTRUCTION: NARBONNE AND NÎMES

With Saintes, Narbonne is perhaps the city in France from which most Roman material survives. This is an index of her importance as the second Roman colony (only Carthage is older), her key military position and, not least, her degradation in mediaeval times and very small population ever since. Given her antique splendour,[21] her fall was particularly sharp: taken by the Visigoths in 413, and wrested back, she was definitively captured in 462, and the Kings established here their capital. Indeed, Alaric had a palace here, and Amalaric chose Narbonne as the capital of his States in 511. In 719 the Saracens captured Narbonne, and held it until 759, when it was taken by Pépin le Bref, serving as a kind of southern capital for the Carolingian Empire. It was believed that many of its sumptuous marbles were taken to Córdoba at various times, to decorate the Mezquita.[22]

The mediaeval line of the walls seems to have followed exactly that of their Roman predecessors[4] – it being likely, as we shall see, that the walls in the Middle Ages were little more than refurbishments of the Roman ones. The line of the Roman (and mediaeval) wall was slightly smaller than that of the City side of the François Ier enceinte, and naturally had a river wall as well: this turned sharply north-west by the Archbishop's Palace and the Cathedral, the diagonal line of the wall rising up-hill towards the Capitol.[5] The Roman walls of Narbonne certainly contributed to the mediaeval prosperity of the city, for they continued to protect it. The thirteenth-century Chanson de Geste, *Aymeri de Narbonne*, describes (lines 261ff.) the rich galleys which reach it, on the sea water which fills the ditches: with its pont-levis raised, the city is secure against attack. The walls of the mediaeval city were to be an essential element in her importance, but this was of course not the case under the earlier Empire and before.

What indicators we have about the prosperity of Narbonne show that, from about 1320, the trend was inexorably downwards, and sealed by the disturbances of the mid-century. Even if was prosperous in mediaeval centuries, the town was failing commercially by the 14th century because of war, competition and poor management of her waterways, and especially the degradation of her port facilities.[23] Unfortunately, we have no censuses to help us: the population in Roman times and throughout the earlier Middle Ages is unknown, but there were probably no more than 3500 inhabitants in the fourteenth century, rising to about 9000 at the Revolution. Certainly, she had been prosperous in

---

and its walls, unprotected by heights, have been demolished in recent wars." Cf Sid. Carm. 23.51–87.

4 Cairou 1979A, 46f., plan 3.

5 Its line is shown in Solier 1979B, 37, and in Gayraud 1981, 289, where it is described, 286ff.

the thirteenth century, when the huge cathedral had been begun (but never finished), but then she was struck by local and regional disasters.

Sometime between 1320 and 1340, the course of the River Aude, the lifeline of her prosperity, changed dramatically, leaving the city a backwater, and changing it from a prosperous town of perhaps 3500 inhabitants into a small village. In 1320, the Jews were expelled, hastening a decline which was sealed by the competition from Aigues Mortes. Responses to requests for troops to fight in Flanders or Guyenne and Gascony tell much about the situation: on 14 March 1319, the Consuls of the Bourg sent only 75 footsoldiers to Flanders, and no cavalry at all; in response to a request of 20/23rd July, 1325, they pleaded disease and pirates and, a week later, stated that they could not deprive the city of its defenders, which suggests local difficulties; on 18 June, 1339, the Consuls protested that they had already supplied 100 crossbow-men for Gascony, and a subsidy of 1250 livres tournois, and could not go beyond this, pleading poor crops, floods and all the previous exactions.[24] The Consuls were a more recent institution than the Viscount, and first mentioned in 1132.

The walls (were any sections of the Gallo-Roman still visible?) were in bad shape by the mid-fourteenth century, and the consequences of this dilapidation for the discovery of antiquities will be discussed below. By this date, however, the problems of the city were multiple: funds were still short for the walls, and the great project to bring the Aude back to its ancient path required money from the Jews, as a memorandum of 25 September 1375 states – so their expulsion must have been partial or temporary. Yet still problems persisted with the ruling Viscount, who was traditionally in charge of the Bourg as the Archbishop of the City. For, on 9 December 1381, the Consuls protested to the King that they had at their own expense repaired a "turris, contigua porta palatii dicti domini vice comitis per se ipsam in parte cecidit et diruta fuit ad requestam ipsius domini vicecomitis" – which cost them 200 livres tournois. Continuing this policy, transactions of 6 July 1388 and 10 May 1389 rake over the various disagreements between the Consuls and the Viscount, and note a barbican built shortly before in front of the old bridge and before the entry to the Palace, as well as a gate 12 pans wide to help both him and the people get in and out of the town, all this being approved in letters from Charles VI dated 22 August 1388.[25]

In consequence of low population and prosperity, only a little town improvement took place in the 17th century.[26] As a once-important *place forte*, she was dead by 1659, when the Treaty of the Pyrenees secured Roussillon for Louis XIII. Closer to the now-Spanish border (some 80km from Narbonne) was the fortress of Salces/Salses, built in the 14th century, reworked by Charles V, and surrendered to the French in 1642. Inevitably, Narbonne's walls decayed,

CENTURIES OF DESTRUCTION: NARBONNE AND NÎMES   283

and were not reinforced for any of the King's military exploits. Inevitably, also, her port[6] and her waterways silted up for lack of maintenance, and efficiently constructed canals.[27] Navigation was described as feeble by 1837,[28] several stretches of the Roman canal (which gave access to quarries from which the ancient town was built)[29] were still visible at the end of the century.[30] Hence Narbonne, like Maguelonne,[31] was left stranded, although her port was still functioning in the 17th century.[32]

Various editions of stone ramparts protected the town, and in order to disentangle the history of their various spolia we need to know about their structural states and thus rebuildings.[7] One key to answering this question would seem to lie with the inscriptions and bas-reliefs thought to have formed part of this enceinte, and then re-used in the enceinte of François Ier, who liked the idea of decorating the fortifications with antiquities.[33] Attempts have been made on the basis of such spolia to date the walls to the fourth or fifth century, but Gayraud resists this, pointing out that with a few explicable exceptions the datable spolia are of the first and second centuries, with the latest dates ascertainable being coins of Maximian and a taurobolium of Iunia Balbina of 263, making it likely to have been constructed as a response to the invasions of 276/7, and therefore contemporary with the walls of nearby Béziers.[8] Grenier had given a similar dating, and Cairou[9] notes that this is uniform with the dating for the enceinte at Carcassonne. Tangential evidence that the wall was built for strictly military ends comes from Sidonius Apollinarius (c. 430–489; Carm. XXIII), who makes it clear that the enceinte was not honorific, built at great expense in peacetime, for there are no incrustations of gold, glass or ivory, and no gates decorated with gold or mosaic.

Whatever the date, the walls were exceptionally rich in spolia, one tower alone yielding 40 inscriptions and a large quantity of bas-reliefs.[34] One late-19th century author believed the sculptures and antiquities had been placed in the walls to hide them, because "On ne pouvait admettre que nos pères eussent méthodiquement détruit leurs temples et leurs tombeaux pour en enfouir les débris" – and in any case "il valait encore mieux les enfouir, que d'attendre qu'on les leur jetât à la tête sous forme de projectiles."[35] Certainly, there were some deposits of antiquities discovered around France, conceivably to protect

---

6   Cairou 1979B 120ff degradation of port facilities; 125ff creation of Aigues-Mortes.

7   Cairou 1979, 6–23 for gallo-roman enceinte; 32–53 enceinte from Middle Ages to 14th century and their layout, including now the bourg; 93–108 Une enceinte de plus en plus ruineuse et ruinée – huge costs; 108–115 Déclassement de l'enceinte from 1868.

8   Gayraud 1981, 286ff.

9   Cairou 1979A, 15ff.

284

CHAPTER 10

them; but it is fanciful to believe that hiding sculptures from marauders was the purpose of their incorporation in late antique walls.

All the above details form the essential preliminary to any understanding of the availability of antiquities in the later Middle Ages, and the background to another great struggle that the Consuls, the representatives of the townspeople, had to face in their attempts to maintain the wall, this time with the Archbishop – a struggle which provides plentiful bickering documents. Thus the Consuls were forced to point out (in an undated but 14th century document)[36] that the Archbishop "est caput civitatis solum in spiritualibus," but his assumed dominance showed in his thirst for materials first documented in 1176 and frequently thereafter.[37] The fourteenth-century difficulties surrounded the building of the new Cathedral, but already in 1218 some parts of the walls and of the (wooden and earthen?) defences of the Bourg had been pulled down on the orders of Prince Louis, son of Philippe Auguste, apparently in an attempt to diminish the powers of the Archbishop.[38] Simon de Montfort (who was thought to have pulled down the remaining Roman walls)[39] was successfully petitioned to allow rebuilding the same year, but the problems related above make it clear that the task was a large one. For his new building works, the Archbishop needed large quantities of stone, and this led to lengthy wrangles with the Consuls, who objected to his freebooting attempts to destroy parts of the City. He was to be stopped, as we shall see, from dismantling sections of both the Capitolium and the walls. His exact duties as regards the city seem to have been in doubt by this time: at nearby Agde, for example, the Consuls had to reach an agreement with the Bishop on 13 September 1332[40] concerning the contribution of the Bishop and Chapter to the repair of the walls of the town.

Dilapidated Mediaeval Walls

The great dilapidation (i.e. removal of stones) of the enceinte in the thirteenth century may be read into a statement of 15 March 1288 that the Consuls had a duty to demolish, repair or rebuild the walls of the town, as well as the ditches.[41] According to Cairou,[10] by the mid-fourteenth century the lawyer for the Consuls was obliged to admit that since time immemorial, the section of the walls from the Brown Gate (the Porte Saint Antoine) as far as the Porte

---

10   Cairou 1979, 36: in mid-14th century parts of the walls had to be demolished à cause de sa trop grande vétusté et des menaces de ruines. 37: the Avocat des Consuls admits que depuis un temps immémorial, les murs qui s'étendent de la porte appelé "Brune" [S. Antoine] jusqu'à la Porte Royale et de là jusqu'au Palais épiscopal, sont également démantelés et les débris de l'enceinte gisent dans les fossés.

CENTURIES OF DESTRUCTION: NARBONNE AND NÎMES

Royale, and from there as far as the Archbishop's Palace, were dismantled ("sont egalement démantelées"), leaving the debris of the enceinte in the ditches. Some sections were in such a bad state that they had to be demolished because of their great age, and because they were in danger of falling down.

Apparently, then, little was done to improve the enceinte between 1288 and the mid-fourteenth century – a time of great prosperity for the city when, perhaps, the walls were seen as an encumbrance to commerce. The Viscount had the Consuls make ditches around the walls in 1341, and then a wet moat using water from the Aude[11] – perhaps a reaction to the parlous state of the defences, and to the dangers of the times. His farsightedness was to be illustrated by the depradations of the Black Prince in 1355, who had devastated and burnt the Bourg but without, apparently, penetrating the walls of the City itself.

Already, however, in 1345, an injunction from Philip VI was needed to stop the Chapter and everyone else from demolishing the rampart of the city facing the church of Saint Just: they were not to touch this rampart for this or any other motive, and were constrained to repair any damage they might already have caused. And on the 17 October 1361, a transaction is recorded between the Consuls and the Chapter of Saint Just about the projected cloister, which would have leaned against the rampart of the city, thereby blocking an immemorial right of way, namely the walkway for the troops immediately behind the wall. The Chapter affirmed that the cloister was built on the very site of the old church, as one could see by its remains; and that the new cloister would leave the approach to the walls accessible through two gates. A compromise left an alley between it and the walls, and had it abut the new tower built by the Archbishop and containing the kitchens.[42] The 1345 reference suggesting that people other than the Archbishop were plundering the walls is strengthened by a document of 2 November 1357 complaining that citizens with houses against the walls had taken many stones, and that this must stop.[12] Did the Archbishop in fact dismantle parts of the Roman enceinte for his building? Very probably: for Pech[43] notes that the inscription beginning IMP: CAESARI: DIVI: ANTONINI was found on 29 December 1729 whilst demolishing an old wall of the Cathedral. Some index of the lack of interest in antiquities in this period is given by its reinterrment – in spite of the fact that its last two words are DECVMANI: NARBONENSES.

The campaigns of the Black Prince underlined such irresponsibility, and soon there began a campaign for the rebuilding of the city's walls. On 10 May 1356, the Consuls entrusted the care of the city's defences to a six-man

---

11   Cairou 1979A, 38.

12   Archives Nationales, coll. Doat, III, fol. 277.

commission, to deal with munitions as well. Then the King ordered the Consuls to demolish houses built against the walls, leaving a space of twelve paces between houses and ramparts. On 14 January, 1359, a letter arrived from the Count of Poitiers ordering the construction and repair, without delay, of the walls, ditches, fortresses and defensive walls of the Bourg, to be followed up on 27 March 1360 emphasising the need to fortify the city as well. The town found what may have been wide-ranging repairs difficult to fund for, following complaints by the Consuls, an order was issued on 17 March 1361 that those people who, during the recent unrest, had taken refuge within the town, should be obliged to contribute to the cost of the construction and repair of its walls.[44] Charles V ordered work on the fortifications on 27 August 1366, but nothing had been done by 20 January 1371, when a follow-up appeared, although some walls toward the Aude had been begun by 31 October 1373, when the Royal Procurator's letter mentioned difficulties created by the Viscount, who clearly did not like the idea of fortifications in the Bourg, and threw all the stones prepared for the work into the foundation trenches. This had been preceded in September 1373 by letters patent from Charles V curbing the Viscount, who had acted ultra vires by "arma sive signa sua depingi indebite [indebile?] fecerat in portali nostro barbacane antique civitatis, in capite pontis veteris dicte ville situato." By 19 May 1374 the barbican for the Bourg had been begun, but ten days later the Viscount was still protesting his opposition.[45] Most of the towers appear to have been built by 1377/9, and a document of 1370 mentions 42 towers for the city and 26 for the Bourg.[13]

Whatever walls stood in the Bourg were still, or once again, in a bad way by the late 17th century, when a theft of stone from them is recorded.[46] Indeed, in 1606 old structures were already being dismantled by entrepreneurs, such as the mas de Fontfroide (presumably part of the Abbey, which was to be sold to the town by the religious in 1702), as well as cut stone "la pierre de taille qui se trouve inutille aux murailles en l'endroict de la porte de vieux desseing, et aussi celle qu'ils pourront tirer des fondations des vieilles murailles de la ville."[47] Presumably the same source was meant when in 1635 entrepreneurs were allowed to take stone "provenant des travaux faits pour la fortification de la ville."[48] The walls continued as a source for thieves, the town council deliberating on the matter again in 1782, and swapping with the Pénitents blancs in 1784 "un bloc de marbre noir extrait des remparts."[49] Extensive star-shaped fieldworks (shown in the 1760 plan)[50] probably unearthed yet more antiquities from the surroundings. Certainly the local antiquarian, the Abbé Bosquet, writing from about 1783, shows in a highly whimsical plan of the Roman city

---

13   Cairou 1979A, 44.

CENTURIES OF DESTRUCTION: NARBONNE AND NÎMES

(dated 1776), that monuments were plentiful all around his town: for he marks the whole area (except for the roads) with them, and the legends "sepulchra in agris."[14]

A simplistic view would be that the Roman walls, patched and repaired, survived until François Ier pulled down their remains to build a new set, doubled in extent in order to take in the Bourg as well as the City, and larger in area over the City itself to allow, perhaps, better troop movement as well as a slightly expanded city population. Thus the antiquities prominently displayed in the new set would all have come out of the foundations of the Roman walls, and before that perhaps from necropoleis.[15] The implication of this is that antiquities were not available in earlier centuries, because they were buried at foundation level until the sixteenth century.

Hints in the archives may suggest that the great concern about the state of the walls in the later Middle Ages was because sections of them were in fact the Roman walls patched up without significant alteration, sometimes from the very foundations, for there are frequent complaints about stretches of wall lying collapsed in the ditches. That this must also have been the case with the François Ier enceinte can be inferred from a document of 1574 where it was noted that the Governor, M. de Rieulx, had protested several times that

> les murailles de la ville sont en beaucoup d'endroitz fort basses, lesquelles est nécessairement besoing faire repparer pour thuition et deffance d'icelle et garder à escalade, affin que les ennemys du roy ne s'en puissent emparer.[51]

And, he continued, it would be useful also to put water into the ditches, and repair everything as quickly as possible. Surely a new enceinte would not have become ruinous in such a short time. Indeed, nothing appears to have been done to remedy the situation, for Henry III wrote on 31 May 1579 relaying his and Rieulx' displeasure at the state of military unpreparedness of the city, and the need to repair the walls and ditches.[52]

The Capitol

The area at the top of the City was well known and much used during the Middle Ages, being in parts a prison and a quarry.[53] The Horreum, for

---

14   BM Narbonne MS 24, 1, prelims.

15   Solier 1979, 46: Pierre Garrigues' account of erection of the 16th century enceinte suggests that the antique pieces therein came from a late antique rampart, and thither from local necropoleis.

example, was known as "le Vieil Mazel" (viz. old market), and the western ends of the structure used for storage and habitation, as altered walls and floor levels testified. The name of "Old Market" was exact, for the ground lying directly above the Horreum was indeed the market area of the Roman city. Here also was the Capitolium, at the northern-most edge of the walls, which, indeed, appear to have been very close to the (by the 19th century) mound containing the remains; and it is possible that, as Perret surmises, the Capitol was already being dismantled by the fifth century in order to provide material for the new churches,[16] and was still being quarried in the 13th century.[54] He notes that the Spanish historian Rodericus of Toledo (in his *Historia Araborum*, ch. 20) says that the Arabs sacked the city in 719, and forced the inhabitants to transport their most beautiful marble columns to Córdoba for the Great Mosque. The wish here is father to the thought, let alone the deed, for the Mosque was only begun in the mid-century. Many of its columns are indubitably spolia (some of which certainly come from close at hand, from the palace at Medinet al Zahra); in any case, the great columns for the Capitolium at Narbonne were not monoliths, but in drums, and with a total height far too lofty for the needs of the mosque, for they measured about 18 metres.[17] So the citizens of Narbonne must have fed Córdoba with material from elsewhere. This, indeed, is certain, for the structure seems to have survived in some form into the fourteenth century, when it was known as Capduel, a corruption of Capitolium. The site may well have been a favourite of the Bishop's for, in 1277, Pierre de Montbrun, Archbishop from 1272, bought "de Guillaume du Capitole, toute la portion du Capitole que celui-ci possédoit dans la ville de Narbonne, dans la paroisse de Saint-Sebastien, avec les maisons dépendantes."[55] Since his predecessor had begun the new Cathedral in the 1260s, this must mean that he acquired parts of the site for their building materials. Certainly, a successor was raiding the same site in in 1344, when the Consuls won a case against him before the Royal Judge at Béziers, when the right to forbid demolition of buildings which embellished the city was maintained.

Perhaps because it was partly protected by the houses we have seen to be located there, knowledge of the Capitol itself survived, the locals retaining the memory of a Capitol on the Butte des Moulinasses.[18] We find the Abbé Bosquet in 1783 locating it accurately, and indeed stating that Archbishop Gaubert wished to knock down the Capitol tower in 1344 to repair the buildings of a prostitutes' refuge, but that the Consuls had a local official (the viguier

---

16   Perret 1955–6, 151, 175.
17   Solier 1979B, 43.
18   Gayraud 1981, 258ff.

CENTURIES OF DESTRUCTION: NARBONNE AND NÎMES   289

of Béziers) prevent this.[56] Excavation began only in 1877, when two courses of stone were still visible. Unfortunately the work, directed by Eugene Fil, was to be hampered by lack of money, and the opportunity to record fully what was discovered equally so by the stunning speed which drove them right down to pavement level, there to dig a trench, in under a fortnight. Notes were taken, however, and Fil remarks that only fragments of marble veneer, white and coloured, came to light, clear evidence that the site had been methodically robbed out.[57] Fil then affirms his desire for Narbonne to reveal some reminders of her great past.[58] More money was found, and huge blocks from a supposed temple complex were unearthed,[59] the searchers conscious that they needed quality results, and cheaply.[60]

The Palace

Another element in the mediaeval history of Narbonne was the Palais de la Vicomté, which stood on the very line of the Roman walls of the City, facing the river. Indeed, it is difficult for an eye accustomed to things Roman not to take the two rounded towers facing south-west as the towers of a Roman gate; until, that is, a glance at a plan shows them to be on different axes. After all, at Aix-en-Provence the palace of the later Empire was certainly fortified using the towers of the Porte d'Italie, and these survived in something like their original state until demolished in 1786.[19] Unfortunately, however, very little is known about the complex of structures which used to make up the Viscount's and Archbishop's palaces, and which are now the Hotel de Ville and the museums, for they have not been intensively studied[20] in spite of their evident interest and importance: few palaces, after all, stand on Gallo-Roman foundations. In 820, the Counts of Narbonne were replaced by Viscounts, and it is from this period that, according to Berthomieu, we must date the construction of the palace, which he maintains was built on the remains of an older fortress placed at this strategic defensive point of the City, facing the water.[21]

One problem in any modern investigation is that the area has been considerably tidied up, not only by Viollet-le-Duc when he produced the frontispiece for the Hotel de Ville, but also at the turn of the 20th century. In the 19th century, multi-storey houses covered much of the façade of the palace facing the modern rue de la République: these are clearly visible in drawings and paintings before Viollet-le-Duc's work, and reached as high as the balustrade he placed on the east façade. The houses were taken down about 1909,

---

19   Ambard 1984, 217, fig. 112.
20   Pradalier 1977, 63, pl. 3–4.
21   Berthomieu 1974, 89.

and the curtain wall between the great square tower and the round tower to the west cleaned up, surely with numbers of antique blocks removed. Carbonell-Lamothe's study of the south-facing façade shows that there may once have been arched openings, perhaps for the bays of a loggia, or even for the high arches which were on the eastern side even before Viollet-le-Duc's work.[22] If such work were datable, then we might be closer to suggesting a date for the display of antiquities in the same façade.

When we look for exact dating for the palace, the square tower of which now has several Gallo-Roman pieces set visibly in its south-facing wall, evidence is lacking. That the foundations to south and south-west are antique is not in doubt: indeed, this was shown when plumbing work for a WC on the first floor of the Donjon was linked with the sewers at about 4 metres underneath the paving slabs.[23] This tower is now called the Donjon Gilles Aycelin, after one of the city's archbishops, and is dated to 1290; there seems to be no firm documentary evidence for this dating, although a document of 1271 does note that several parts of the old palace needed rebuilding, and the rebuilding work on the Palace seems to have continued until 1346. Its much greater age is probably vouchsafed by its internal plan which, like the two adjacent towers, is circular. Carbonnel-Lamothe suggests that this is but the reflection of an earlier construction, reworked and encased in powerful defensive walls.[24] He supports this by pointing to the existence on the site, in the eleventh century, of the "castrum de Porta Aquaria," namely the Porte Aiguière or Water Gate of later documents; the foundations of this gate were still surviving in 1639.[61] There was a gate of the same name at Saintes, so called there because it supported an ancient aqueduct. Towers of the palace, such as the Tour Moresque/Mauresque, revealed plentiful antiquities in their foundations when they were demolished under Louis XIII,[62] as a gift from the King (who owned them) supposedly for a church nave.[63] The tower, believed at the time to contain débris from the Capitol,[64] was demolished to make the Place de la Cité, and Lafont notes that several important pieces (most of which have disappeared) were taken to the courtyard of the Archevêché, including a great altar affixed into a new wall, and another "attachée contre la muraille de la salle du synode."[65] Clearly, the Archbishop liked to display antiquities, including a two marble sarcophagi, and a stone with a victory on it, which he placed in his chapel; and he also collected them.[66] However, most retrieved materials were sold off for new building,[67] as also happened when more sections of the palace

---

22   Carbonell-Lamothe 1973, 229, figs. 7, 9.

23   Cairou 1979A, 24f., but he gives no further details.

24   Ibid. 223; and 219, fig. 1 bis.

CENTURIES OF DESTRUCTION: NARBONNE AND NÎMES 291

were demolished in the early 19th century.[68] These sell-offs were associated with road-widening around the Porte Connétable/de Perpignan, the antiquities from which were not preserved,[69] with the sculptors doing some of the work conceivably on the look-out for recyclable pieces.[70]

The François Ier enceinte

As already noted, the line of the Roman walls was followed almost exactly by the line of their mediaeval successors, up to the building of the François Ier enceinte.[25] This can be deduced from the antiquities discovered at various times in the towers which made up the Palace. A fourth century inscription survives which proclaims restorations to a bridge, aqueduct and city gates with the legend PONTEM – PORTAC – ACQUIDUCT. The re-use of this block as the base of the High Altar in the Chapelle Saint-Sauveur in the palace of the Viscount, built at the end of the twelfth century, gives proof that such antiquities were available and were, perhaps, carefully chosen: what more appropriate inscription, indeed, for a city whose prosperity depended on water and the sea?

Whatever defences the Bourg might have had in the years of the city's prosperity, it did not have a stone wall in Roman times; it is clear from various discoveries, however, that the area was rich in antiquities – antiquities of which the churches founded there made good use.[26] Now the François Ier walls enclosing the Bourg did indeed have antiquities incorporated in them (the only surviving fragment is in the Bourg), so these were either carted from the City or found on the spot. The François Ier enceinte was indeed slightly larger than its Roman and mediaeval predecessors, even on the City side, so it is perfectly conceivable that the older walls were dismantled right down to the very foundations in most places: nowhere, apparently, were the new walls built directly on top of the older ones although, as noted, they followed the same circuit. These have been catalogued and photographed, and were preserved in the city when these walls were dismantled after being declassified as a military installation in 1868. Photographs survive of just how the antiquities were re-used for the Portes de Béziers and de Perpignan, and a small stretch of wall has been left standing on the Blvd. Dr Lacroix, next to the Ecole Montmorency: this is nearly 5 metres high, with seven visible courses of large blocks, and a continuous frieze containing sculpted blocks and inscriptions; several of the lower blocks, which are of differing sizes, are also clearly spolia.[71]

The beginnings of the François Ier enceinte were due to military necessity[72] triggered by the erection of the great artillery fortress at Salses in the 1490s,

---

25 Gayraud 1981, 289; Chantal 2010a on the walls, their demolition and their antiquities.
26 Bonnery 1969, 5ff., 111ff., 137ff.

292   CHAPTER 10

which constituted a direct threat to French domains. The reactions are to be
seen in the acquisition of the Viscounty of Narbonne by Louis XII in 1507, and
fortification work there from 1510.[27] The work on this bastion for the protection of France's southern flank was, however, lengthy; and Pierre Garrigues,
the source of so much of our knowledge of the location of the antiquities displayed in the enceinte,[73] was still building the Porte de Perpignan in 1604.
Luckily, several antiquarians from the 16th century onward took an interest in
the walls, and drew and described the antique contents they found in a series
of surviving manuscripts, some of which were popular enough to be copied.[74]

The evidence of the few antiquities displayed in the mediaeval City make
it clear that not everthing was hidden. Nevertheless, the inscriptions in
the François Ier enceinte are funerary, strongly suggesting that these walls
were built with material from the late antique ones.[75] But the Roman walls
were evidently re-built or refurbished so thoroughly at various times, that we
have no records of what they might have looked like. Had we records such
as that provided by the stretch of antiquities-rich wall recently discovered at
Nîmes,[28] we could confirm that antiquities were indeed used only in the foundations of that wall, and not at all in its superstructure. But so complete was
the change wrought by the François Ier set, in part because it needed to protect against iron cannonballs,[29] that we cannot know the exact complexion
of the previous walls. For although we know that some material was found
within those walls, and reused in the François Ier enceinte, it is equally clear
that much else was not, and that plenty of antiquities were available uncon-
nected with them. Thus, on the one hand, according to G. Jallabert, writing
in 1832, Pierre Garrigues, the engineer in charge of the François Ier set, had a
fine cabinet of antiquities, and found "une superbe statue de Diane qu'il avait
trouvée dans les ruines des antiques fortifications."[76] On the other hand, the
Abbé Bosquet, writing about 1783, said specifically that his aim was to draw all
the inscriptions and bas-reliefs found in the walls, or in the houses of various
private persons; and his work, he says, builds upon that of Lafont,[77] Garrigues
and Renouard, as several blocks had been carried off or re-used since their
time. Only a hint of what might have been available comes from Bosquet's
account of the antiquities discovered while making the new road to Coursan

---

27   Potter 2008, 162.

28   Dedet 1981.

29   Cairou 1979, 53–81 for the 16th century enceinte. Work began in 1510. Fig. 5 for courtine of
     François Ier: 7 assises en gros appareil, la dernière formant une frise avec inscriptions et
     sculptures. NB frieze also visible to sides of the Porte du Roy, restored 1848 (Espérandieu's
     illustration).

CENTURIES OF DESTRUCTION: NARBONNE AND NÎMES

(on the way to Béziers) in 1783.[78] Some older writers such as Lafont are in no doubt that the surviving antiquities were spread all around the city, rather than in the earlier foundations:

> Le Roy François 1er... amateur et restaurateur des lettres et des anti-quitez, fit continuer et achever de fortifier Narbonne... il donna alors ses ordres exprès, en faisant démolir les restes des anciens édifices des Romains qui s'y estoient conservés, et ramasser toutes les antiqui-tés romaines qui s'y trouvaient et de les ranger comme une frise autour des murs continues et bastions qu'il y fit faire.[79]

This fine example, he maintains, was later followed under Charles IX, Henri IV and Louis XIII. Espérandieu, on the other hand, believes that the majority of pieces were pulled from the foundations of the Gallo-Roman walls of the city. Who is correct?

Availability of Antiquities

Although it is sometimes assumed that antiquities were displayed at Narbonne just because they were antiquities,[80] some might have been employed because they were of hard stone (this might have applied particularly to funer-ary pieces, always intended for the open air), and therefore especially suitable for walls which needed to be as strong as possible. We cannot know whether any prestige accrued by displaying sculptures was explicitly because they were antique, or because it was fashionable to decorate fortifications with sculp-tures. This applies to the François Ier enceinte: it was certainly decorated with sculptures – but then so so were the walls of Nancy, built between 1580 and 1624.[81] However, when Charles IX and Catherine de Médicis visited Narbonne in 1565, at the Porte Royale de la ville (the present Porte de Béziers, near the church of S. Sebastien):

> Au-dessus de cette porte de la ville n'y avoit autre chose que les seules armes du Roy; et n'y avoit on voulu mettre aucun enrichissement pour ne pas cacher ce beau trésor de l'Antiquité, qui est aux pierres de la même entrée, lesquelles furent fort regardées et admirées de tous.

This makes it clear that it is the antiquities which were admired, because the gate was not otherwise occluded by the traditional hangings or banners. The point is emphasised in the same contemporary narration as the royals actually walked around the walls: "Leurs Majestez employèrent tout le reste de ce jour, qui étoit la veille des Rois, à se promener et visiter les murailles et bastions de la ville."[82] And since the King was born only in 1550, it is unlikely that this was a tour prompted by fortification strategy rather than by the pride of the Narbonnais in their antiquities.

Thus when Pierre Garrigues, the Royal engineer,[83] was building the Porte Connétable (de Perpignan) at Narbonne, in 1604, and also introducing antiquities, this may have been because of local pride. The sentiment was catching, for he himself was specifically interested in them, drew a collection of them,[84] and also set some in the walls of his house, which were still there in 1832.[85] It is difficult to know what to make of large quantities of antiquities recovered in pieces in the later 19th century, presumably having been broken up for their reuse in the walls, but possibly long before Garrigues.[86] Again, his love of antiquities did not prevent one ancient altar being sawn in two in 1607 to make colonettes to flank the Royal coat-of-arms,[87] and at least one other block, in a 19th century assessment, broken before his eyes to serve in his decorated walls.[88] Nor does Garrigues appear to have done anything to protect a famous inscription found in 1566, the so-called Altar of Augustus, which sat against one of the towers of the archevêché for over a century, "siècle à l'admiration des érudits & aux outrages des enfants de la ville, qui le criblaient, après l'école, de projectiles variés."[89] An inscription which eventually found its place next to this altar had been retrieved from its use as a step in a church, and was then displayed prominently in the entrance to an abbey.[90] Altars were popular in fortifications because they were so solid; and there are examples at Narbonne, of which of course only one face could be known until the walls were dismantled.[91]

Plenty of antiquities seem already to have disappeared by 1700,[92] and others were sometimes freely reused in new building projects. As already mentioned, when the Tour Mauresque was dismantled in 1633/9 to make the Place de la Cité, inscriptions were found on the site. The stones were given by the King to the Carmelites for their new building work,[93] and the worked ones appear to have been displayed in their walls: this was even the case with altars which were plainly pagan. One altar, for instance, was prominently displayed in the street-facing wall of this convent. Incidentally, Pech voices what may have been a prevailing opinion, namely that the tower had been built by the Goths, "who had thrown in its foundations several Roman monuments in order to efface their memory."[30]

Other antiquities were preserved, such as a conglomerate of inscriptions still to be found in the walls of the Palace facing onto the present Jardin de l'Archevêché, and hence on two sides of a triangle the third of which is formed

---

30   E.g. Pech 1713, fols. 7, 9, 26–31.

CENTURIES OF DESTRUCTION: NARBONNE AND NÎMES

by the line of the Roman wall. Now this garden was certainly used in the eighteenth century as a collection point for the display of antiquities. Thus Pech mentions an altar with the inscription PACI: AUG being let into the wall of the Archbishopric courtyard in 1707. Even today there are two inscriptions let into the wall of the Palace looking onto the garden; many of the lower courses of which that wall is composed could well be Gallo-Roman; and it is likely that more are concealed underneath the two-metre-high plaster between the two round towers. As Cairou writes,[31] the wall is Gallo-Roman up to about three metres, with "matériaux de seconde main empruntés aux monuments romains détruits dont on distingue les trous de louve et les traces des crampons de scellement." These features, then, prove that the new work on the Palace (done sometime in the later thirteenth century) used spolia; and since we have documentary evidence of the Consuls ordering the Archbishop to keep his hands off the enceinte, and to repair any damage caused, it is reasonable to believe that at least some of the new Palace was built at the expense of that enceinte.

However, the area between the Palace and the walls was by no means as public as that between the river and the Porte Aiguière. Here, indeed, land was given by the Viscount to the Consuls on 13 June 1345 for a "portico sive mercato,"[94] to include a multitude of stone columns which might conceivably have been spolia. It was therefore on the most public face of the Donjon that antiquities were placed. There are at least ten pieces in the wall (plus one block with an indeterminate beast which, if a salamander, presumably relates to the François Ier period), and they are analagous to the blocks now stored in the lapidary depot, in the ex-church of Notre-Dame de la Mourgier.[95] The similarities are, of course, more than coincidence: clearly, at least some of the material on the Donjon came from the same monuments as that noted in the Lapidary Museum. But when were these antiquities incorporated in the Donjon Gilles Aycelin? We can dismiss the notion that, since the lowest courses of the tower appear to be Gallo-Roman, then the reliefs are of the same date. This is clearly not the case, for they are not built into the wall in regular courses: rather, the large blocks have been recut at some stage in order to accommodate them. This contrasts with, for example, the surviving stretch of the François Ier enceinte, where the antiquities form a continuous frieze. We are therefore left with two options: either absolutely all the spolia came from the Roman enceinte, which must therefore have been plundered at the time the Donjon was built or perhaps refaced; or Roman monuments were still standing into the later Middle Ages, and it was these which were used for both the Donjon and then for the François Ier enceinte. In terms of opportunity, however, it seems likely

---

31   Cairou 1979A, 26.

that plenty of antiquities were indeed available at the supposed build date of 1290 for the Donjon's superstructure, for we have already seen that Pierre de Montbrun was probably in search of building material at the Capitol in 1277. And since the city wall passes very near the Capitol, any antiquities displayed in the Donjon could just as easily have come from this northern location as from the wall adjacent to the new Palace.

From Open-Air Museum to Notre-Dame de la Mourgier

From the above, it is evident that at least some antiquities were collected together and displayed well before the sixteenth century, and that many must have come to light by chance from the walls (assuming that other sections of it were as rich as that under the Tour Mauresque). But it is far from clear just what the state of the Roman monuments was before the Renaissance, largely because of our lack of knowledge about the bas-reliefs, altars and other sculptures and inscriptions stored today at Narbonne. This statement may seem strange but, unfortunately, it is all too easily supported. At Saintes, attempts have been made to piece together the blocks taken from the walls, and campaigns of excavation have been consistent and strenuous; as a result, much is known about the complexion of the Roman city, and about the re-use of spolia in its walls. Narbonne, with more cubic metres of sculpture at its disposal, has been hampered not only by the confusion engendered by a second re-use in the François Ier enceinte, but also by the vicissitudes at Notre-Dame de la Mourgier where, even today, so much is stored that viewing conditions are very cramped.

Narbonne was well known throughout Europe for having antiquities in her walls (cf. Maffei's 1734 description,[96] from Italy), to view which, as Tastu remarked in 1846, the only way to compensate for the town's lack of complete monuments was to "regarder de près ses murailles, et reconnaître dans les matériaux dont elles sont construites quelque fragment d'une corniche, d'un chapiteau, etc."[97] In 1826 Artaud, Keeper of the Musée des Antiques at Lyon, noted that the town had not been attacked for a long time, but that the antiquities in the walls were weathering away,[98] making it the more regrettable that early illustrated catalogues of the inscriptions were often inaccurate.[99] We do not know if Lyon had designs on them, but Toulouse certainly did, for Narbonne in 1831 was fighting off attempts to appropriate antiquities from the enceinte, the mayor responding that

> Ces débris, ces fragmens de pierre que les siècles ont mutilés, nous plaisent tels qu'ils sont, nous les vénérons avec autant de respect qu'en avaient les païens pour leur sacrarium et les tombeaux de leurs pères.[100]

CENTURIES OF DESTRUCTION: NARBONNE AND NÎMES

When in the 1860s, Narbonne started the procedure for declassification and dismantling of her ramparts, population had doubled since the beginning of the century. She had her own Commission Archéologique,[32] and the arguments employed for dismantling were common. Her location was no longer strategic; the coming of the railway had nullified any defensive importance the walls once possessed; and their continuing presence was "un obstacle insurmontable au développement et à la prospérité de la ville."[101] In 1866, the Town Council painted a bleak picture of the town: the walls were "une cause de soufrances," and the town badly equipped:

> Elle a du acheter sa maison communale; pouvoir à une alimentation d'eau suffisante en engageant l'avenir. Elle n'a ni maison d'école, ni collège, ni théâtre, ni halle; nulle place publique, du moins suffisante; sa promenade publique, elle l'a emprunté au terrain militaire ... Le passé ne nous a rien transmis.[102]

There was to be street lighting by gas, and promenades built on the servitudes militaires. In 1867 the town fathers first authorised the mayor to buy the walls from the owner, the State, "l'achat de la fortification remise par le ministère de la guerre aux Domaines." They specified precisely what they were buying,[103] which of course involved much valuable land for the expanding town. They then faced the usual difficult problems. Who was to pay for the demolition? Would an entrepreneur undertake the task? And what was the value of the materials? Could the town simply re-apply the stone to new building projects?[104] Such large quantities of stone were recovered that 8,587 cubic metres were used to build the new boulevard, the rue du Luxembourg, at the same time it being stipulated that "tous objets d'art, statues, inscriptions, bas-reliefs, monnaies, médailles" found on land sold adjacent to the site of the walls belonged to the town, which would stand the expense of any necessary excavation. Indeed,

> toutes les pierres artistiques ou archéologiques qui font partie du rempart aliéné [sold off] seront réservées à la ville; qui celle-ci aura le droit de les prendre et même, si elle le juge convenable, de les fair enlever et ce, alors même que les acquéreurs s'abstiendraient de démolir la partie du rempart comprise dans leur lot.[105]

---

32   Alibert 2010, 92–110: La Commission archéologique de Narbonne et la sauvegarde patrimoniale, with some early photos of the walls and of ND de La Mourgier.

The stones were to go to Notre-Dame de la Mourgier, "qui servira di lieu de dépôt." This might at first have been intended as a temporary arrangement, since in October 1869 the church was reserved "en vue de la necessité où la ville pourrait se trouver un jour à raison de son agrandissement et de l'accroissment de sa population, d'acquérir cette église pour le service du culte ou pour tout autre usage."[106]

There does not seem to have been any calculation about the likely prestige, artistic or monetary value of antiquities to be recovered, presumably because they did not know at this date just how many blocks might be inside the walls. The 1868 proviso reserving antiquities for the town[107] was perhaps a common one. Certainly, Sens had stipulated similarly in 1836,[108] surely because there, too, the municipality did not know what materials would be found when the walls were demolished. At Narbonne, one driving force behind declassification and monument recovery was the mayor, Eugène Peyrusse, who had been on the Commission Archéologique since 1859. He kept a firm grasp on the recovered items and, like his fellow commissioners,

> il y avait pour nous un grand intérêt à hâter l'heure de leur chute pour grouper les débris des monuments antiques qui s'y trouvaient disséminés, pour rapprocher les uns des autres ceux qui provenaient du même monument, pour achever l'interprétation des inscriptions dont la position inaccessible rendait souvent la lecture malaisée, enfin pour mieux assurer leur conservation.[109]

He presumably kept a straight face and a resigned, far-away expression when he met the Emperor's representative in 1865, who promised "de chercher, de concert avec vous, quel serait le moyen de satisfaire aux vœux des habitants, sans trop sacrifier les intérêts militaires"[110] – for he knew that the town had lost any strategic importance in 1659. Nevertheless, the town had to face a counter-attack from the local Génie, who suggested in 1865 that, instead of knocking down the walls, the area of the enceinte be doubled.[111]

When the walls were dismantled, large quantities of antiquities were recovered, although some were soon lost.[112] These included the mosaic from a Roman house in the ditch to bastion 27,[113] and blocks from the bastions themselves,[114] which had to be strong as they housed artillery. So numerous were the retrievals that a running total was kept of inscriptions (not all blocks) which entered the museum. This reached 507 blocks by 1892.[115] Inscriptions were still coming out of the walls, and from buildings around the town, over a decade later.[116] There were large numbers of inscriptions in the Bastion Montmorency, and in adjacent courtines; many had been reused in staircases

CENTURIES OF DESTRUCTION: NARBONNE AND NÎMES 299

and as their steps, and others associated with churches, sometimes as altar tables, often as building materials. The museum profited.[33]

No buildings from ancient Narbonne survive, even in ruins, the standard explanation being that they were built in haste into fortifications,[117] with some figured reliefs hammered sufficiently flat to provide a tighter fit.[118] Indeed, some were completely reworked, and converted into Christian sculpture.[119] And although, as Espérandieu remarks, it was the ramparts of the city which constituted its true Lapidary Museum, with their destruction after 1868 few indications of Narbonne's ancient glory and importance were left visible about the city. It is only with the various rescue digs of post-war times that the richness of that city is being revealed, with finds of fine mosaic floors, of frescoes and glass, and of the Paleochristian basilica at the Clos de la Lombarde.[34]

Pride in the monumental blocks uncovered was widespread, but now came the problem: what was to be done with such immense quantities of antiquities? Reconstruction of monuments does not seem often to have been considered, because it was recognised how hypothetical such work would be.[120] Since here, according to one assessment of 1890, "Notre ville, après Rome, possède la collection la plus remarquable qui existe en Europe," the answer was to form a museum to contain what by 1890 amounted to "684 inscriptions intéressantes pour la science épigraphique et 1229 pièces ornées de sculptures, formant généralement des bas-reliefs ou des fragments d'architecture."[121] These figures for inscriptions are higher than those recorded above. We might note that it is inscriptions which seem to hold the greater interest; wonder what happened to the more than 150 inscriptions which apparently did not make it into the museum; and imagine the decisions needed to deal satisfactorily with the sculpted blocks. But apparently there were simply too many: by 1896 there were complaints about the deterioration of recovered blocks left in the open air, and the continuing degradation effected by unruly schoolchildren: surely the municipality should be approached, and then higher authority if nothing was done?[122] The problem, of course, was the sheer cubic metrage of often huge blocks, not many of which were of marble. Indeed, Narbonne had already faced flak from concerned scholars: two years earlier, in 1894, had been published an article entitled "Vandalisme, les Musées lapidaires du Midi," in which Momméja, of the Société Archéologique de Tarn-et-Garonne, at Montauban, and displaying the usual fraternal attitude to such rivals, had handled the Narbonne state of affairs very roughly, and even suggested a direct

---

33 Solier 1986. 19–23: L'histoire des recherches. Un musée d'antiquités en plein air. 113–124: Collections lapidaires de l'église Notre-Dame-de-Lamourguier.

34 Solier 1979B, 42, 5off.

approach to the municipality.[123] Fortunately and necessarily, a commission was already studying (since 1893) what to do with the antiquities, one possibility being a new room for the museum. But this was really in slow motion, since it had been obvious since the late 1860s that existing accommodation (including moving blocks from the Town Hall garden into the Museum) was insufficient[124] – and by then little of the walls had been dismantled, so it should have been easy to calculate quantities and start planning for their suitable reception.

Conclusion

We might reasonably ask, given the richness of her patrimony, why much more has not been made of the plentiful survivals from Narbonne, and why no larger and sheltered space was quickly found for her antiquities (for the church where they were stored was full by February 1877).[125] Unfortunately, and in spite of the importance of the survivals, little attempt has been made to place together blocks from the same monument – and none, apparently, to carry out a complete census even of material once in the François Ier enceinte. Espérandieu's *Recueil* is far from complete, for he deals only with figured work, and not with purely decorative friezes or inscriptions; and, as he admits for Narbonne, he has not included much of the material extracted by local antiquarians from the later walls. For example, the *Recueil* of the Chevalier de Viguier de Lestagnol,[126] however amateurish some of the drawings in its three large volumes might be, would bear collation against the survivals in Notre-Dame. He believed, for example, that he could identify parts of a Temple of Augustus from surviving friezes.[127] And even if he is wrong, it behoves our century to do better from the plentiful material at our disposal.

What a fine piece of work awaits a Ph.D student with a fork-lift truck, a camera, some imagination and a computer graphics program! Photographic maquettes could at least indicate the dimensions of some of Narbonne's ancient buildings; and an attentive examination of the blocks stored in the lapidary museum in the church might well reveal their use or lack of it during the mediaeval centuries. Some antiquities certainly survived all sets of walls, and by 1858 "Les ouvriers chargés des travaux du chemin de fer ont fait successivement, depuis plusieurs mois, quelques découvertes."[128] Many others followed, such as that found near the railway station, at a fruitful location where "on y trouvait depuis longtemps des aigles, des statues, des colonnes,"[129] or the large monument revealed in 1879 under fortification terracing "que l'on a pu, sans trop d'invraisemblance, attribuer au Temple provincial d'Auguste."[130]

CENTURIES OF DESTRUCTION: NARBONNE AND NÎMES   301

Ensérune

The area around Narbonne, and not just the town itself, was very rich in antiquities. Béziers, the nearest large town, followed the fortunes of Narbonne, but with less success: her soil was rich in antiquities into the nineteenth century and, like Narbonne, it had inscriptions built into its walls, especially near the Citadelle.[35] Little work appears to have been done, however, on the history of the city's antiquities, few of which survive.

Near to the Coursan-Béziers road stands the great hill-fort or Oppidum of Ensérune, famous in Gallic archaeology (along with Montlaures – even nearer Narbonne) as a Celtic site which imported good pottery (including fine Attic ware) from all over the Mediterranean. This entrepôt declined in importance with the establishment of the Roman arts of peace, but it may well be that its importance was not forgotten. Certainly, the mémoire sent from Béziers to the Académie Royale des Inscriptions et Belles-Lettres on 23 October 1829 by Dureau de la Malle writes of the neighbouring hill of Regimont ("à quelque pas" from the hill of Enserune) as Mons Regis:

> Le terrain de Regiment est semé des matériaux de marbres de diverses grandeurs, de vases, de briques Romaines, de Mozaïques, d'objets en bronze, et de fragments de statues.

He thought it to be a Roman palace "habité par leurs proconsuls," and also tells how crop marks caused a vineyard owner to dig deep, and discover a mosaic.[131]

Naturally, it is in the pre-Roman layers at Ensérune that attention focuses today – a site scattered with cisterns and other large underground storage vessels. Unusually, we know that the hill of Ensérune, and much of the land directly under the protection of the hill directly to its north, were thoroughly dug in the thirteenth century in the course of a spectacular and well-documented drainage scheme, which perhaps also uncovered Roman antiquities. The area to the north, called Malpas, was badly drained, and in 1248 the inhabitants got the permission of the Archbishop of Narbonne for a drainage scheme, receiving a charter for the work in 1270.[132] This involved retaining the depression responsible for the stagnant water, but making a virtue of its existence by making it the centre of a great "sunflower" pattern of fields (called today "le Soleil des Champs"), collecting all the run-off water at the centre, and then draining it off through an underground channel which pierced the hill of Ensérune itself.

---

35   BM Narbonne, MS 248, fol. 7v, 10v–12r.

302   CHAPTER 10

This is sophisticated water management – so why is there not more mediaeval attention paid to repairing ancient aqueducts?

Nîmes

Nîmes in Earlier Centuries

> Que sont devenus, en effet, tant de monumens qui attestaient la grandeur d'un peuple maître de l'univers, et dont nous n'avons fait qu'une énumération imparfaite? Il n'en est resté que des ruines dont l'examen a mis en défaut la sagacité des antiquaires ... à l'exception des Arènes.[133] [1831]

Although houses were abandoned earlier, the town centre of Nîmes (Gard) seems to have been occupied and maintained throughout the 3rd and into the 4th century, albeit with fewer mosaic floors. The majority of villas roundabout prospered during this period, and some were even working in the 6th century.[36] The city was sacked by the Vandals in 407/8, and besieged by Wamba in 673. Charles Martel, after the Battle of Poitiers, set about devastating Provence, which was a Saracen stronghold. He besieged Narbonne, supposedly burned the gates of Nîmes in 737, pulled down part of the walls and monuments, and attempted to do the same to the amphitheatre, "but the flames spared it."[134] Ménard claims that he dismantled the hillward walls – that is, the strong side, in order to weaken the city.[135] But precisely what damage the fury of Charles Martel caused to the amphitheatre is in doubt, because the signs of fire, popularly thought to be a result of his action, are only the soot from the fires of houses built inside and around it (although perhaps the site contained fortified towers, of wood, which he could easily destroy). Certainly Theodulphe, Bishop of Orléans, writing in 798 (in his *Paraenesis*, verse 116), describes Nîmes as a considerable and spacious city. The Normans pillaged it in 859. Some materials had gone by then, if we are to believe the Anianus *Annals* for 812, which state that Charlemagne, in rebuilding Maguelonne (also destroyed by Charles Martel), could find no columns or marble necessary for its construction on the spot, and so he ordered them to be brought with great care (*cum magna diligencia*) from the city of Nîmes.[37] Whether this is but another of the many stories focussing on Charlemagne the great builder (fully expressed, for example, in the Chanson de Geste entitled *Gestae Carolam Magnam ad Carcassonam*),

---

36   Esmonde Cleary 2013, 110, 446.

37   Mazauric 1934, 5.

CENTURIES OF DESTRUCTION: NARBONNE AND NÎMES

we cannot say; and other traditions hold that restoration work only began two hundred years later.[136]

Certainly, the local lime-burners helped in the destruction of antiquities, and their work was in a way indicative of population needs for, as a scholar remarked in 1897, "Le four à chaux est le baromètre de la santé publique."[137] A permission was accorded to the Templars by Viscount Bernard Aton V in 1151 to build a lime-kiln

> quod nulli liciat fornum edificare, nec publice, nec privatim, a via recta que discurrit a porteale beate Marie Magdalene per forum usque ad porta-rades, inferius usque ad vallatum arenarum et usque ad muros civitatis.[138]

This was a monopoly.[139] The area described must therefore have been their "beat" for unearthing marble for their kiln, which had exclusive right here, since the document further gives them permission to dismantle any "trespassing" kilns they may find. It cannot therefore be coincidental that Nîmes by the 19th century had a rue des Four-à-Chaux, that statues and other antiquities were still being unearthed there, nor that ancient mosaics were still in evidence in the area.[140] Unfortunately, given that white marble was the best material for lime-making, we may also imagine that some of the city's visible statuary disappeared into the kilns around this time of population expansion.

It may be as a result of such depradations (and of the introduction of inscriptions as building blocks in mediaeval churches,[141] including Saint-Baudile) that no temples except the Maison Carrée are known in Nîmes – nor yet their location. The façade of the cathedral is indeed inspired by antique example, but does not reuse antique blocks,[38] in spite of what Poldo believed.[142]

The interest of Renaissance scholars in her antiquities was extensive, and much remained to be discovered in later centuries, especially as the population expanded outside the lines of both the Roman and mediaeval walls, and as interest in antiquities arose from the 1530s.[39] This is made clear in Jacques Pineton's ode to the city, in Poldo d'Albenas' 1560 *Discours historial de l'antique et illustre cité de Nîsmes*, referring to "les vieux fragments / Des murailles magnifiques ... Tant de beaux marbres brisés,"[143] and by de Thou, visiting in 1582, who wrote of "les ruines de plusieurs monumens antiques, dont la magnificence et la majesté effacent encore aujourd'hui tous les bâtimens modernes."[144]

---

38   Lassalle 1975, 23, 25f.

39   Lemerle 2013, 75: it is the 1530s before interest is aroused – Albenas, Rulman, Peiresc.

Ménard, in the mid-18th century, logs "une quantité prodigieuse de tombeaux Romains"[145] and even statues, Nîmes being "comme d'un dépôt particulièrement destiné à les sauver du naufrage des temps et de la barbarie des peuples."[146] Tombs would have been discovered this late because the town was expanding beyond its original walls, and into areas which had been the domain of cemeteries. Poldo even asserted that Theoderic's interest in old monuments affected preservation at Nîmes.[147] Ménard believed that the baths by the Fountain of Diana (a complex of considerable interest to local scholars),[40] as well as the basilica of Plotinus and the Temple of Augustus, were destroyed early, by the Vandals.[148] Plenty survived to fuel local pride,[41] and investigation by men like Ménard and Séguier.[42] The mediaeval enceinte was indeed studied, and as late as the 17th century.[149]

Clearances such as were to be seen in the amphitheatre (below) were not followed by wholesale modernisation of the old town, which stayed much as it was, with developments well outside the centre.[150] But the evisceration of the old town was still a possibility in 1866, when one scholar wrote that

> Bientôt peut-être le marteau et la pioche pénétreront au cœur de la cité pour y ouvrir de larges voies de communication. Bien des maisons auxquelles se rattachent des souvenirs historiques, ou qui conservent quelques vestiges d'ancienne architecture, disparaîtront pour faire place à des contructions modernes. C'est le moment de recueillir ces souvenirs, de faire l'inventaire de ces restes du passé, avant que la démolition ait achevé son œuvre.[151]

Modernisation did indeed proceed in some sections into the 1880s, but the reduction in housing of about one third since the 16th century explains why Nîmes retained much earlier building stock.[152]

---

40   Veyrac 2006, 46–62 La source de la Fontaine. History of research for Bassin de la Source between Poldo d'Albenas (1559–60) and late 19th century. 45–46 In 9th century, after period of abandonment, a convent established on part of the Sanctuaire de la Fontaine.

41   Lassalle 1981.

42   Pugnière 2013, for Ménard at the Source de la Fontaine, and the work of Jean-Fr. Séguier.

CENTURIES OF DESTRUCTION: NARBONNE AND NÎMES   305

The Amphitheatre

We are badly informed about the monuments of Nîmes in mediaeval times,[43] except for the amphitheatre, and the continuing use of some aqueducts.[44] The amphitheatre is the best documented of all the remaining monuments, and enhanced the prestige not only of the city, but also of its inhabitants, for it was once used as a fortress. In its use for housing, perhaps from as early as the 5th century, it is no different from the structures at Arles or Lucca; but its "prestige" use as a "noble" fortress is more unusual, analogous to that of triumphal arches in Rome. It is not known exactly when it was transformed into a fortress, but this was probably under the Visigoths. Wamba the Visigoth, besieging the town in 673, found captured treasure there, so it was at least used as a strongroom; Mazauric states that Bishop Julian Toletanus (in his *Historia Wambae*) calls it Castrum Arenarum, and also that Visigothic material had been found there, together with inscriptions from nearby Roman monuments, as well as late Roman stelai.[45] He also complains how little note was taken of objects found during the clearance. One modern scholar is in no doubt of its importance: it was the residence of the Carolingian count, the focal point for the Comtat and its garrison; it was in front of the Castrum or one of its gates that the "mallus comtal" was held, so that the giving of justice took on the colour of a public demonstration.[46] It was used as a place of justice for the trying of pleas by the ninth century, for charters of 876 and 898 write of the *Castrum Arenae* and *in castro Arene*.[153] By 1097 there was a whole community living there, for an agreement between the Bishop of Nîmes and the Abbot of La Chaise Dieu refers to the churches of S. Martin and S. Pierre "dans le château qu'on appelle les Arènes."[154]

Throughout the Middle Ages, the amphitheatre was separated from the city by a ditch and, from about 1100 until the late fourteenth century, it was occupied by a group of knights, frequently referred to as the *milites castri Arenarum*. We know that the Bernard Aton family did indeed hold it from 956 to 1184, and

---

43   Gowon 1931, 1932, 1933 for summaries.

44   Veyrac 2006, 127–161 Aqueducts, Uzès to Nîmes, and Aqueduc de Valz – history of research. Comprehensive account, with some historical review of what happened to the system after Antiquity. Some of the water flow from the Source de la Fontaine was used to turn mills for paper and cloth. 49: Such mills may have been in operation by at least 1375.

45   Mazauric 1934, 29ff. for list.

46   Dupont 1968, 20.

306   CHAPTER 10

then the Counts of Toulouse until 1227.[47] Vassals of the Viscount of Nîmes, it is suggested,[155] lived there for security in an age of banditry, and their houses were probably also fortified. They are mentioned in twelfth-century deeds, and an oath administered to them c. 1100 also survives. They numbered 31 at the beginning of the twelfth century, 16 are named in 1148, 39 in 1163, about 50 in 1174, and about 100 in 1226. However, Royal power was established in 1226, and they were ordered out of the amphitheatre, to be replaced by Royal troops. At the same time, the Consulate was abolished. The move killed the knights' social status and, although the city successfully petitioned in 1270 for the revival of the Consulate, the bourgeoisie now had the upper hand politically, and the knight never regained their earlier power. The military prestige of the site was definitively weakened, it seems, when Charles VI built a fort near to the Porte des Carmes in 1391, and on the site of the old Porta Arelatensis which, according to Ménard, had already been fortified in the twelfth century.[156] When the knights moved out, ordinary people moved in, to an estimated number of some two thousand.[157]

To the west of the amphitheatre and the Maison Carrée was the area known as the Champ de Mars, and Poldo simply notes that he and his fellow-magistrates have seen the name while looking at old documents. He mentions no antiquities from the area, and his view shows only a few scattered houses between the amphitheatre and the Tour Magne outside the mediaeval water-filled ditch which appears to have been the only protection to that side until c. 1010, when a charter mentions a new wall to be built there; this took nearly a century to build. This section of the Roman wall was in ruins by 1194, as noted ("entièrement dégradée," writes Ménard)[158] in Raymond of Toulouse's permission then granted to build new ones. Following the 1207 revolt of the citizens against their overlord, the peace was signed the following year between Raymond V and the Consuls "in palatio suo quod situm est in castro Arenarum."[48] Raymond V certainly used some antiquities in his defences, for when these were demolished a gate was found with fixing holes for bronze letters.[159]

The clearing of the amphitheatre, housing as it did so many people, took place in stages, with a false start in 1647,[160] spurts in 1787 and 1809, and finished by the 1820s.[161] The idea had probably existed in the Renaissance, for a silver model of the Arènes had been presented to François Ier, who wanted to clean them up (just as he did the Maison Carrée, after Poldo supposedly explained its importance.[162] The provincial États thought likewise in 1647 on

---

47   Mazauric 1934, 44ff., suggests that, in earlier centuries, the site may have been held by the
      Counts of Nîmes; 192ff., 226ff.
48   Mazauric 1934, 291, 310.

prompting from the local bishop; but only in 1786 did the États vote money for the clearances, and evictions began.[163] Until the 1830s, we have details of the acquisition of buildings therein, followed by the restoration of the site: since the state was often engaged in buying the properties in one arcade at a time, it is easy to see why the relevant liasse[164] should be ten inches thick, why the Auberge de la Coquille was still in business in the amphitheatre in 1825, and why they should still be pricing the housing inside the arena in 1834.[165] Plans show how slow the process was, ground level when reached being 2m36 lower than the ground outside.[166] The purchases brought to light the damage caused by the inhabitants, including making free with the ancient stones, and cajoling letters were sent asking them to make repairs. Amongst this mournful reading is an 1808 report made to the Mayor by the Directeur des Travaux Publics, with a detailed description of just how the site had been adapted for habitation, how pleading letters to property owners therein had had little effect, and detailing the abstraction of stones from the structure.[167] After a certain amount of necessary refurbishment, the first bullfight was held in 1863.[49]

The Maison Carrée

Why was the Maison Carrée one of the few temples to survive in France? We might imagine that the civic pride of Nîmes in the prestige of their monuments could be measured, albeit tenuously, by whatever respect was shown for the Maison Carrée. However we should always remember that sturdy and watertight buildings would naturally be used when and where convenient; what is more, commentators were well aware that pride and negligence could alternate.[168] Yet the town did record several decisions that reflect a desire to conserve monuments. In 1643, the Consuls decided to improve the Porte de la Couronne, by enclosing it in "de murailles en forme de banquette, qui serviront de siege aux habitants qui se vont promener les soirs les dimanches, et de les décorer de quelques allées d'arbres." This was the origin of the Place de la Couronne. In the same year, the Consuls refused to allow the Jacobins (presumably in need of building stone) to demolish the two towers of the château, because they were an embellishment of the city. Likewise they pronounced against the destruction of local antiquities, "si considérables et d'une si haute réputation que les nations les plus étrangères viennent des lieux les plus reculés pour les voir et les admirer."[169] In 1748, work was undertaken at the Fontaine de Diane, "à remplir le triple but d'utiliser les monumens antiques, de conserver le volume des eaux, et de donner à la ville une promenade digne de l'importance qu'elle acquérait tous les jours."[170]

---

49   Soraluce Blond 2008, 151–152 for the clearing of the amphitheatre.

308   CHAPTER 10

However, the Maison Carrée had a very chequered history into the 19th century,[171] and one scholar reasonably suggested it survived only because the amphitheatre provided plenty of shelter, so there was no need to dismantle the temple for building materials.[172] In a document referring to the amphitheatre, of 1097, the church of S. Etienne is said to be near the Capitole. Poldo d'Albenas[173] says that local hearsay told him that it was once "la maison commune et des consuls de la ville," and here he was correct. For, although the Maison Carrée was never a Capitolium in Antiquity, it was indeed the mediaeval seat of government of the city. Brunel cites Giovanni Balbi's splendid thirteenth-century misinterpretation of the Capitol in Rome which, he maintained, was so called "quia ibi conveniebat Senatores, sicut in capitulo claustrales."[50] It is not clear when the building became a permanent seat of government, but Mazauric adduces a document to show that on 5 May 1898 a legal plea was heard "in ipso Capitolio," rather like the amphitheatre. In Toulouse, the Capitolum was already the place of assembly of their Capitouls in 1202. Poldo's view of Nîmes shows housing crowded around the temple in his day and, therefore, his plates of the building do not include the surrounding colonnade, which appears to have been unknown until the clearances. In an example of monumental chutzpah, the Duchess of Uzès tried to purchase the temple in 1576 as a mausoleum for her family.[174] It did not become a church until the 17th century, by which period it was supposedly in a state of collapse.[175] According to Ménard, Colbert wished to dismantle the structure and take it to Paris. In the 16th century, Pierre Boys had acquired it in exchange for a piece of land and a house in the quartier known as the Isle de la Colonne, "dont on fit un nouvel hôtel de ville." He built a house against the Maison as high as the volutes of the capitals, and fixed a staircase, "ce qui l'endommagea beaucoup." Next it was used as a stable by the seigneurs de S. Chatte, and then sold to the Augustins in 1670.[176]

The nineteenth-century vogue for restoration also affected the Maison Carrée which, conceivably, had had houses up against the temple and within the precinct for as long as had the amphitheatre. This can be only inferred, and then only from the period of the clearances, roughly between 1808 and 1838. Only the central part of the complex survived into the 19th century, and at first little seems to have been known about the surrounding colonnade, except that the whole area stood on a platform. This, indeed, the Municipality wished partly to demolish, in order to make the Place de la Comédie larger. The Engineer in Chief objected to such vandalism, and the plan failed, but nevertheless we cannot know whether the sales of materials from demol-

---

50   Brunel 1967, 26.

CENTURIES OF DESTRUCTION: NARBONNE AND NÎMES

ished houses in the vicinity included antique pieces.[177] By the 19th century antiquities were several feet underground,[178] so protected unless cellars and foundations were being dug. But by mid-century there seem to have been a sufficient quantity of identified pieces from the colonnade to make one wonder why there was then no push to have it re-erected.[179]

The Town Walls

The final element in the survival of antiquities in Nîmes were the city walls,[180] but we are very badly informed about both their history[51] and their possible contents,[181] except for the use of funerary monuments to repair damage,[182] and perhaps some elements of a temple.[183] They have never been properly studied,[52] and even their date is unknown, let alone that of the various changes in line. Much of the area covered by them was private property, and closed to the attention of scholars.[184] Excavation on the site of the old Maison d'Arrêt during work to extend the Palais de Justice revealed a length of wall put together with some very fine spolia,[53] none of which is later than the end of the second century. In 1734 Maffei gives a useful description not only of the lower courses "de deux lits de grosses & longues pierres," but also of the rest of the construction.[185] The excavators make no guesses about the original location of the spolia, but suggest that the wall might have been part of the "Castra Arenarum" mentioned in texts from the seventh century, none of which say that the fortress was restricted to the amphitheatre alone. This makes sense because the amphitheatre, for all its solidity, must have been well-nigh impossible for such a small company of knights to actually defend, given the special problems of dealing with a near-circular building.[186] Certainly, the position of this stretch of wall on the town side of the amphitheatre, and therefore well behind the Roman enceinte to its south, suggests some later fortifications connected with the "Castrum." It seems likely that A. N. Meusnier's finds of marble in the early nineteenth century, made as they were on the site of the new Palais de Justice, were from the same wall.

This late enceinte, then, whenever it was erected, was symptomatic of a shrinkage of population, together with delapidation of parts of the Roman walls, which originally formed an enceinte of 6km.[54] The earliest printed view of the whole site is in Poldo d'Albenas, and not only shows housing close

---

51 Varène 1992: no inscriptions or other antiquities in the first set of walls, because they are too early.

52 Cf. Varène 1981.

53 Dedet 1981, e.g. figs. 29–33, 35 & 49.

54 Dupont 1968, 11.

around the Maison Carrée, but also a water-filled ditch in front of the enceinte to the south. The same author notes various antiquities, including statues: one "sur le coing de la Maison d'Ageuillonat;" a clothed male atlante "près de la Trésorerie au front de la maison de Clappe;" and eagles on three houses, which he thinks must have come "de quelque frise d'edifice haultain." He discounts the local belief that all such works are headless because the Goths "les ayent tronquées et decapitees en opprobre des Romains." Not so, he avers, for reading the ancient authors proves them "n'avoir esté tant outrageus et insolens en leurs victoires que nous les disions communement, d'avoir ruîné tout le plus beau des edifices Romains, mais le contraire est la vérité."[187] The Roman walls from the amphitheatre to the Tour Magne, and then down the western side of the hill to join the mediaeval run of walls from the Château du Roy, are shown by Poldo as ruinous, and the eastern stretches even have windmills on them. The Château du Roy appears as two great round towers with a joining curtain wall, and give no hint that underneath is the Roman gate now known as the Porte d'Auguste. This structure, which bore comparison with Autun, came to light only in 1793,[188] having disappeared under a 14th-century fort.[189] Ménard, however, goes on to relate that the gate was also called "Roman Gate," and destroyed when the Royal fort was built on the site.[190] Does this hint suggest that the Roman gate itself might have been visible within the fortress, just as was, for example, that at Turin? As early as 1636, some of the wall ditches had collapsed and been part-allocated to the bishop, while

> les consuls profitèrent de leur emplacement pour y créer des promenades publiques: telle fut l'origine des deux anciens cours qui ont fait place aux boulevarts du nord; telle fut encore l'origine de l'Esplanade, resserrée d'abord entre la porte de la Couronne et les Arènes.[191]

The reduction in the area of the enceinte, together with the ruinous state of the Roman walls and the length of time needed to build new ones, meant that the city was protected only by small fortresses – namely the Tour Magne itself (defended and fortified on several occasions),[192] and the constructions at the Porte d'Espagne and the Porte d'Arles. Ruins were, of course, favourite sites for treasure-hunters, thus the Tour Magne was searched and badly damaged in the time of Henri IV.[193] Large treasures did indeed come to light, for example near the Roman walls, as Bazin reminds us for the later 19th century.[194] This was done by a local gardener, François Trancat, and was extensive: "cette excavation énorme, si bizarre dans son plan comme dans son élévation, et qui provoquera tôt ou tard la ruine totale de l'édifice."[195] Thanks to such devastation,

CENTURIES OF DESTRUCTION: NARBONNE AND NÎMES   311

restoration was required in 1844, which created "dans un monument antique un monument moderne."[196]

The demolition of the city walls was begun about 1774 and proceeded until 1790, the reasons given being that they were too weak to be a real defence, and that the inhabitants, crowded within them, needed clean air and new houses.[197] Their demolition caused water-supply problems.[198] Many arguments were advanced by scholars against demolition, but the beauty of the walls was not one of them. The Consuls expressed their enthusiasm for the task several times,[199] and they carefully planned to use the exercise to give work to the poor, as well as to use the materials recuperated for new public works, especially drainage.[200] Yet more reasons for the work are provided in their petition to the King of 1786.[201] Some of the stones from the ramparts were quickly put to work, when on 27 March 1788 permission was given to build a Salle des Spectacles near the amphitheatre.[202] Nevertheless, the Consuls were made aware that antiquities were probably going to be found in large quantities, for they received a memorandum from Sieur Pacotte in 1789, suggesting the Consuls should

> Ordonner... que tout les médailles, ornemens et instruments antiques qui seront découverts et trouvés dans les fouilles seront déposés et rassemblés dans un dépôt qui sera assigné par le maire et Consuls et appartiendront au Museum.

He goes on to advise forbidding the sale of similar antiquities found when digging on land sold to private individuals – clear evidence that the richness in antiquities of land adjacent to the walls was well known.[203] Fortunately, the richness and importance of Nîmes' classical past is now being realised, thanks to a series of digs that other cities might do well to imitate; nevertheless, as Pierre Garmy has it,[55] archaeology is still in its springtime, particularly at Nîmes.[56]

The Discovery and Display of Antiquities[57]

Poldo was frank about his reluctance to enumerate the loss of antiquities, because the process pained him, and his narrative would consist of "tristes élégies" for all the ruined structures, and

---

55   Garmy 1981, 57.

56   Nîmes 1990, 16–17 plan of 99 archaeological sites.

57   Pugnière 2010.

cest amour de la Patrie me cause en l'imagination vne semblable peine comme si je la voyois encor auiourdhuy, voire à toutes heures saccager, demolir, & rompre ces grands & magnifiques ouurages & bastiment de noz ancestres.[204]

Whereabouts in and around the city were antiquities found? Ménard notes that "il serait difficile de donner une juste idée du grand nombre d'antiques qui se sont trouvées depuis deux siècles sous les ruines de l'ancien Nîmes. On en a tiré toutes sortes de morceaux précieux, comme d'un dépôt particulièrement destiné à les sauver du naufrage du temps et de la barberie des peuples." Most of the finds he lists are recent, but he also features the statue of Dea Salus, found in 1622 in the excavation of the ditches of the bastion by the old Royal Fortress, near to the Porte des Carmes, while work was being carried out on the fortifications of the city.[205] Poldo notes a fragmentary mosaic floor in the Cathedral, which seems to have been antique; and also that François 1er took another (there were plenty to be found in the surrounding fields) back to Fontainebleau.[206] But usually Poldo's work is of little help, because of the vagueness of his references. He writes that epitaphs are known "par les antiques ruines, aussi de nostre ville, dont nous avons cy-après faict collection des plus élégantes et mémorables;" but he only gives the location of a few, and then unhelpfully, such as "près de la porte des Carmes, sur un montant de porte de jardin."[207] He does note, however, on the legend to his view of the city, "La Porte de la Couronne, avec son Boulevart, que mon père fait édifier, et y raporter tous les monumens antiques, que de présent y sont," the "boulevart" presumably being the area outside the gate, represented as a tall tower, and enclosed by a wall, where the moat was by that date paved over. Ménard dates these constructions to 1524, and notes that two caryatids were displayed there, one set into the enclosing wall, and the other into the external fabric of the same gate. If these were set up as trophies, then perhaps the other inscriptions recorded later were also so intended. For, indeed, as late as the 1760s, many antiquities were still here, as inscriptions collected by Séguier make clear; yet more were located at other gates, and near the amphitheatre.[208] Such display might have been common, the same author noting "anciennes inscriptions trouvées dans un champs près de l'église de Ste Perpetue et qu'on a affichées en 1780 au mur extérieur d'une maison."[58] Séguier, in the 1760s at Nîmes, also collected antiquities into his garden there, having extracted them from their find-sites,[209]

---

58   Nîmes 1987 for brief entries by date, on Poldo, Rulman, Guirau, Séguier, Maffei, Menard, Auguste Pelet, etc.

CENTURIES OF DESTRUCTION: NARBONNE AND NÎMES 313

where he was visited by scholars from all over Europe,[59] demonstrating that Nîmes was far from being a scholarly backwater in the 18th century.[60] Much of his collection survives in the Archaeological Museum at Nîmes.[61]

Discoveries could also be made outside the town, for example in 1778 at Saint-Baudile-hors-les-Murs, where a field was being prepared for vines, owned by a local druggist, M. Vache:

> On y a découvert plusieurs squelettes et quantité d'ossemens épars, plusieurs arcae recouvertes par des pierres plates, qui paroissent avoir servi aux payens, et sur lesquelles j'ai trouvé les inscriptions suivantes.[210]

They had hit part of a necropolis.[211] In 1784 the Consuls noted that "pierres curieuses par leur antiquité et par les formes et inscriptions dont elles étaient revêtues" were being found on the site, and deplored both the systematic digging of the area, and the stone being sold.[212] In 1735 the Baths had yielded "une statue colossale de marbre d'une beauté parfaite, quoique mutilée et brisée en plusieurs pièces qui étaient auprès du buste de cette statue" as well as column shafts; but what happened to these is not known.[213] Excavations in 1908 demonstrated their luxurious fittings.[214] And in 1797 a Roman gate was revealed under 14th-century walls, and its frieze blocks also discovered nearby were replaced.[215]

Conclusion

By the mid-19th century, Nîmes was an important industrial centre, especially for wines and spirits, and fabrics: denim is a twilled cotton cloth named from its source, "serge de Nimes." The town had an enceinte of only 6ha, and the 6,000 population in 1500 had grown to 50,000 in 1790, and to 80,000 by 1900, but most people then lived outside the walls, in straight 19th-century streets and boulevards, leaving the centre an elegant Renaissance-to-18th-century town, with only the amphitheatre and Maison Carrée left inside. Outside, few funerary antiquities could have survived the extensive 1629 star fortifications, which themselves took more space than did the town inside them, let alone the 19th-century urbanisation which was at least five times the spread of the old town nucleus. The "Temple de Diane," on the hill, was mutilated in the search for treasure.

---

59 Chapron 2008, 30–31 for maps showing visitors to his very popular cabinet, deriving from listings in his carnet de visiteurs, and carnet de connaissances.

60 Audisio & Pugnière 2005 for an overview of his work and influence.

61 Darde & Christol 2003. 86 items, with useful indications (where possible) of how and when they entered Séguier's collection.

Narbonne, in contrast, had been dead for centuries when her walls came down in the 1860s. She had little industry, a low population (28,000 by 1900), no commercial access to the sea, and poor inland communications until the arrival of the railway. Although boulevards were driven through part of the old town (Gambetta, Condorcet, Gambetta), much remained intact, and development took place outside the site of the walls, and in the Bourg.

Was either of these towns' councils intent on preserving their antiquities? The demolition of the walls ensured an overwhelming quantity of antiquities for Narbonne, which duly overwhelmed the municipality, so that the dépôt-museum at ND de la Mourgier is still in use, and still full. The Town Council in the 1860s realised they had to do something with blocks pulled out of the walls, but from their subsequent fate we might say that scholarly pressure had failed once again. In Nîmes the amphitheatre was indestructible, so simply cleared of houses; the Maison Carrée survived because its structure was also still useful – but it had lost its colonnade. Neither town preserved any other temple remains, and neither has seen intensive excavation over the past century: ancient Narbonne still lies under the mediaeval town, and any discoveries to be made at Nîmes will be well clear of the centre, near the Temple de Diane, or underneath her elegant inner streets. For the other outskirts have been destroyed (as already noted) by 17th-century fortifications and then 19th-century expansion. Narbonne lies well off the tourist trail, and Nîmes is happy with her triangle of Maison Carrée, amphitheatre and Temple de Diane. Everything else has long gone; while at Narbonne we may guess that much remains to be discovered. France is now drenched with museums, patrimaniacs and heritage identities, but few funds seem to be available for extensive excavations within such historic towns.

[1] Caumont_1838_255–256

[2] Tournal_1864_195

[3] Espérandieu_I_1907_355

[4] Millin_IV_1811_382–384

[5] SG_XXXVII_Lisieux_1870_70–71

[6] SG_XXXVII_Lisieux_1870_67–72

[7] Espérandieu_I_1907_358

[8] Dutens_I_1829_130–132

[9] BCA_Narbonne_IX_1906_256–257

[10] Ville_de_Narbonne_1888_3–4

[11] AM_Narbonne_H86

[12] SG_XXXV_Carcassonne_1868_274

[13] Tournal_1869_107

[14] PV_Comm_Archéol_Narbonne_1842–1889_257–258

[15] PV_Comm_Archéol_Narbonne_1842–1889_293

[16] Bosquet_1783_I_Avis

[17] Mounyès_1877_VII

[18] Mège_1840–1841_406

[19] Artaud_1826_254–255

[20] Mège_1840–1841_402

[21] Bosquet_1783_I_plan

[22] Mège_1840–1841_408

[23] Port_1854_161–205

[24] AM_Narbonne_EE_bydate

[25] AM_Narbonne_EE_FF_bydate

CENTURIES OF DESTRUCTION: NARBONNE AND NÎMES

[26] Favatier_1903_241

[27] Pigeonneau_II_1889_113

[28] BSA_Béziers_II_1837_228

[29] BCA_Narbonne_II_377

[30] BCA_Narbonne_III_1894_554

[31] Enlart_1920_38

[32] Mouynès_1872_672

[33] MDANE_VII_1826_255

[34] Thiers_1890_161

[35] Thiers_1890_158–159

[36] AM_Narbonne_FF_724

[37] Thiers_1890_164–169

[38] AM_Narbonne_JJ_13_fol_19

[39] Tournal_1864_194–195

[40] AM_Narbonne_II_1948

[41] AM_Narbonne_EE598

[42] AM_Narbonne_EE627

[43] AM_Narbonne_MS_27_fol_86

[44] AM_Narbonne_EE1647

[45] AM_Narbonne_EE1455

[46] Mouynès_1872_830

[47] Narbonne_Archives_Communales_1877_620–621

[48] Favatier_1903_260

[49] Mouynès_1877_409

[50] Espérandieu_I_1907_358

[51] AM_Narbonne_BB3_232

[52] AM_Narbonne_BB3 232

[53] BCA_Narbonne_1896_377

[54] SG_XXXVII_Lisieux_1870_74

[55] Devic_&_Vaissete_IV_1872_253

[56] AM_Narbonne_MS_24.1_179ff.

[57] Fil_1877_2

[58] Fil_1877_6

[59] PV_Comm_Archéol_Narbonne_1842–1889_462

[60] AM_Narbonne_MS_59_2r

[61] Devic_&_Vaissete_V_1875_540

[62] Devic_&_Vaissete_XV_1892_2

[63] BCA_Narbonne_1896

[64] AM_Narbonne_MS_26

[65] Lafont_1739_fol_9ff.

[66] Lafont_1739_fols_16–20

[67] Favatier_1903_267

[68] Acad_Toulouse_II.1_1830_11

[69] Favatier_1903_252

[70] Favatier_1903_252–253

[71] Espérandieu_I_1907_355–357

[72] Acad_Toulouse_XI_1858_105

[73] Roux_V_1823

[74] Devic_&_Vaissete_XV_1892_71

[75] SG_XXXVII_Lisieux_1870_72–73

[76] AM_Narbonne_MS_23_title

[77] Lafont_1890_89

[78] AM_Narbonne_MS_24_avis

[79] Lafont_1739_avis

[80] Roschach_1905_139–140

[81] BM_XLIX_1898_11

[82] Lafont_1890_96

[83] Devic_&_Vaissete_XV_1892_95

[84] Espérandieu_I_1907_356–357

[85] Devic_&_Vaissete_XV_1892_75

[86] Devic_&_Vaissete_XV_1892_ix–x

[87] Devic_&_Vaissete_XV_1892_171

[88] Devic_&_Vaissete_XV_1892_Narbonne_15.35

[89] Devic_&_Vaissete_XV_1892_6–7.23

[90] Devic_&_Vaissete_XV_1892_10.24

[91] Devic_&_Vaissete_XV_1892_Narbonne 1.3

[92] AM_Narbonne_MS_8_1739_341ff

[93] AM_Narbonne_MS_8_1739_fol_45ff

[94] AM_Narbonne_DD_773

[95] Tournal_1864_passim

[96] Maffei_1734_173

[97] Tastu_1846_183

[98] Artaud_1826_255

[99] Tournal_1864_66

[100] BCA_Narbonne_1892_135–152

[101] Tournal_1864_195

[102] AM_Narbonne_H86

[103] Ville_de_Narbonne_1888_135

[104] Ville_de_Narbonne_1888_141–142

[105] AM_Narbonne_H86_1868_fol_148r

[106] AM_Narbonne_H86_1869_fol_6v

[107] Ville_de_Narbonne_1888_172

[108] BSA_Sens_1851_34

[109] BCA_Narbonne_IX_1906

[110] Ville_de_Narbonne_1888_34

[111] AM_Narbonne_H86_1865_fol_94ff.

[112] Devic_&_Vaissete_XV_1892_4.16

[113] Tournal_1864_80

[114] BM_XXXVI_1870_95

[115] Devic_&_Vaissete_XV_ 1892_79

[116] BCA_Narbonne_1904_XX

[117] Thiers_1890_158–159

[118] BCA_Narbonne_III_ 1894_520–530

[119] Lafont_1739_fol_57r

[120] Roschach_1905_195

[121] BCA_Narbonne_I_1890_ 173–181

[122] BCA_Narbonne_1896_ LXVI

[123] BCA_Narbonne_III_ 1894_XXX

[124] SG_XXXV_Carcassonne_ 1868_258–259

[125] AM_Narbonne_H86_ 16_Feb_1877

[126] AM_Narbonne_MS_265

[127] AM_Narbonne_MS_265, 1, 123ff.

[128] Acad_Toulouse_XI_ 1858_105B

[129] BSA_Midi 1880–1881, 7

[130] Roschach_1905_198

[131] AM_Narbonne_MS_248

[132] Ginieis_1876_175

[133] Baragnon_I_1831_xxiv

[134] Devic_&_Vaissete_I_721f.

[135] Ménard_1750–58_VII_ 126

[136] Lenthéric_1876_333ff.

[137] Mém_Acad_Nîmes_XX_ 1897_144

[138] Ménard_1750–58_I_ Preuves_32

[139] Devic_&_Vaissete_VII_ 1879_187

[140] Mém_Gard_1875_34

[141] Germer-Durand_1893_ #52

[142] Poldo_d'Albenas_1560_ 69

[143] Poldo_d'Albenas_1560_ Preface

[144] Nouv_Coll_Mém_ Histoire_France_XI_1851_ 309

[145] Ménard_1750–58_VII_ 196–202

[146] Ménard_1750–58_VII_ 137ff

[147] Poldo_d'Albenas_1560_ 94

[148] Ménard_1750–58_I_57ff.

[149] Germer-Durand_1874_ 29–50.

[150] Berrian_1821_46

[151] PV_Acad_Gard_1866– 67_53–54

[152] Puech_1884_23–24

[153] Devic_&_Vaissete_III_ 1872_5

[154] Devic_&_Vaissete_V_ 1875_doc_327

[155] Michel_1909_4

[156] Ménard_1750–58_VII_ 79

[157] Pelet_1866_168–169

[158] Ménard_1750–58_I_ doc_31

[159] Millin_1811_IV_235

[160] Ménard_III_1832_14

[161] Woods_1828_152

[162] Poldo_d'Albenas_1560_ 75–76

[163] Balincourt_1896_13

[164] ADG_8T271

[165] ADG_8T250

[166] Pelet_1866_134–135

[167] ADG_8T270

[168] Pigault-Lebrun_&_ Augier_1827_161–162

[169] AM_LL21_445ff

[170] Baragnon_III_1832_ 313–4

[171] Soraluce_Blond_2008_ 123–125

[172] BCA_Narbonne_1890_ 37–53

[173] Poldo_d'Albenas_ 1560_75

[174] Durant_1853_XXI

[175] Baragnon_III_1832_91

[176] Ménard_1750–58_V_153ff.

[177] AM_8T340_20_Feb_1828

[178] Pigault-Lebrun_&_ Augier_1827_170–171

[179] Pelet_1854_65, cats 13–15

[180] Germer-Durand_1874_ 1–11

[181] Nîmes_AM_various

[182] Espérandieu_XI_1938_2

[183] Ménard_1838_105–106

[184] Ménard_III_1832_257

[185] Maffei_1734_169

[186] Balincourt_1896_7

[187] Poldo_d'Albenas_1560_ 26

[188] Ménard_1838_20–21

[189] Mém_Gard_1847–1848_ 43–66

[190] Ménard_1750–58_VII_ 120ff.

[191] Baragnon_II_1832_486

[192] Le_Bas_1845_plates_1_ &_13

[193] Mérimée_1835_368

[194] Bazin_1891_114

[195] MDANE_1837_114–115

[196] BM_X_1844_655

[197] AM_Nîmes_LL43

[198] Ménard_1835_IV_79

[199] AM Nîmes LL_44_fol_136

[200] AM_Nîmes LL_47_fols_ 88v–90r

[201] AM_OO_118

[202] AM_Nîmes_LL_47_ fol. 175v

CENTURIES OF DESTRUCTION: NARBONNE AND NÎMES

[203] AM_Nîmes_OO_118_ no_26

[204] Poldo_d'Albenas_1560_ 89

[205] Ménard_1750–58_VII_ 137ff.

[206] Poldo_d'Albenas_1560_ 59

[207] Poldo_d'Albenas_1560_ 148ff.

[208] BM_Nîmes_MS_109_ plates

[209] Devic_&_Vaissete_XV_ 1892_690.266

[210] BM_Nîmes_MS_110_ fol_113r

[211] Goiffon_1881_257

[212] Mém_Acad_Nîmes_ XXXVII_1914–15_173–181

[213] Bazin_1891_68–69

[214] Mém_Nîmes_ XXXI_1908_284

[215] Devic_&_Vaissete_ XV_1892_576

CHAPTER 11

Provence and the South: Monumental Losses

If Narbonne and Nîmes managed to retain moderately large quantities of antiquities, this was not always the case elsewhere in the south, as can be charted for several towns. Arles is dealt with at greatest length, because of her antique importance and the stock of buildings she managed to retain. Other towns suffered for a variety of reasons. Aix-en-Provence modernised early, with graceful boulevards and fountains. Avignon tried to do so, wishing to pull down her walls, but national clamour prevented complete destruction. Dax, a very small frontier town, also lost most of its walls in a bid for modernisation. So did the French Riviera (so named by the end of the 19th century), a once sensitive and fortress-rich territory which we now know as a playground. Fréjus, much shrunken over the centuries, survived almost as a village, with antiquities taken for the railway which was to connect with the Italian border, eventually turning Antibes and the rest from frontier strongholds into tourist resorts. Even Cassis once boasted antique inscriptions.[1] In the Rhône valley, Orange retained monuments because her small population did not need to recycle them; and Vaison, even smaller (with about 2,000 by 1900) retained sufficient monuments to be given as its modern name, Vaison-la-Romaine.

Arles

Introduction
In the 4th century Arles was an important town, housing imperial administration, including the Praetorian Prefect of the Gauls and other officials, and perhaps an imperial palace.[1] According to Theodulf of Orleans, it was still important in the Carolingian period (Urbs Arelas, aliis quae pluribus urbibus extat / Prima gradu tamen est, Narbo, secunda tibi). But her subsequent decline was steep, with transformations documented by modern research.[2]

---

1 Esmonde Cleary 2013, 210–212 for the archaeology.
2 Heijmans & Sintes 1994, Fig. 6 for plan of ancient town; 158–9 for 5–6th century, showing late wall touching S exterior of the theatre and then curving along to the river; 162–3 for details of the enceinte and what has recently been found. 160: 5th century coins found in the amphitheatre, so many that it must have been inhabited by then. The theatre beginning to be systematically pillaged by the mid-5th century.

© KONINKLIJKE BRILL NV, LEIDEN, 2015 | DOI 10.1163/9789004293717_013

PROVENCE AND THE SOUTH: MONUMENTAL LOSSES

She was one of several towns which developed new uses for their monumental architecture, following maintenance of their buildings throughout the 3rd and 4th centururies, as at Aix and Nîmes.[3] Sections of the forum (not identified until the eighteenth century) were dismantled only in the 5th century, with some earlier houses surviving until that period; the circus, subject to flooding, lasted in some form until the later 6th century, when it was abandoned and dismantled. The amphitheatre had various successive uses.[4] Large cemeteries, from the 5th century, both around Arles itself and over the river at Trinquetaille, suggest some continuing prosperity, as at Bordeaux and elsewhere.[5] Of these, the Alyscamps was one of the most famous cemeteries in Christendom. Whether this was a matter of decline, change or transformation is in part a nice etymological point.[6]

By the 5th century, many erstwhile inhabitants of Gaul would not have recognised their towns: for example, parts of Amiens were abandoned by the mid-3rd century, and others such as Lillebonne and Tours were largely abandoned by the same date; yet more, such as Aix-en-Provence, Arles, Nîmes and Vienne had shrunk in population well before any wall circuits were constructed,[7] with monuments broken up for reuse in the 6th century,[8] although some gates survived.[9] The whole of southern Gaul was far from secure in the earlier Middle Ages, and Arles was no exception. Between 427 and 587 the Visigoths

---

3 Esmonde Cleary 2013, 114: "Further west, at towns such as Bordeaux and Périgueux, the construction of the new wall circuits left the forum area outside the defences, but one cannot assume that the complexes ceased to function ... does not support the idea of a systematic abandonment of the centres of civic political identity until late in our period, and it suggests that these cities still had a concept of municipal government and of public life through the fourth century."

4 Soraluce Blond 2008, 152–153 for uses and reclamation.

5 Halsall 2007, 347 for prosperity in 5th century Arles, Marseilles and Bordeaux, and general christianisation of towns.

6 Esmonde Cleary 2013, 405–408; 117–118 for overview and bibliography on late Roman cities, and the changing etymologies of decline and transformation.

7 Esmonde Cleary 2013, 107–108.

8 Sintes 1994, 185: several mausolea converted into houses, their marble sarcophagi broken up, their limestone ones sawn up. The whole lot, including the circus, was destroyed in the second half of the 6th century. No trace of circus materials on site, leading G. Hallier to propose official organisation for reusing its materials for the remaking of the city ramparts.

9 Stouff 1985, 239: Porta Lutosa was a Roman triumphal arch which becomes a gate in the mediaeval enciente, as "L'Arc Admirable." Also, the preserved Porte de la Redoute (twin round towers) was a castellum in the Middle Ages, but it had been the ancient gate guarding the decumanus. Fornasier 1994: Evidence for these triumphal arches comes from spolia recovered from the SE bastion of the late Porte de la Redoubte. Author mentions that other

were the ruling force; the Normans pillaged the city in 859; and the Saracens, after a first alert in 734, plundered Arles in 842, 850 and 883. The consequence of such instability was to accentuate the militarism of much of the urban life of South-East Gaul, in which the ancient monuments played a convenient part.

In spite of so much destruction, Arles has retained a higher proportion of her monuments than Nîmes or Narbonne, which is the result of a sequence of circumstances. The remains were first inhabited for protection in dangerous times; the importance of the city as a Christian centre then comes to the fore, enhanced by the trade which was a result of her key position on the river Rhône. Finally, the precocious prosperity and prominence of Arles (which developed much earlier than adjacent centres) did not last, the apogee being between the years 1200 and 1340. And as Aix, Avignon and Montpellier developed, Arles stagnated; so that, by the mid-fourteenth century, she was only a marginal town. Had the Popes chosen Arles rather than Avignon, things might have been different. Had the King of Aragon, then Count Raymond Beranger IV, chosen Arles as his capital instead of Aix, then prosperity and political prestige might have continued.

For our theme, however, the result was beneficial: for whereas Avignon, which was of importance in Antiquity, lost all her remains with her new-found prosperity and the building work it entailed, Arles retains several of her monuments to this day. The prosperity of the earlier Middle Ages had caused an almost continuous suburb to grow up outside the walls, later called the "Tour de Ville;" texts indicate that this was in place by the eleventh century, but it had declined almost to nothing by the end of the fourteenth century. The Bourg indeed, was as distinct from the Cité as were the two parts of Narbonne, and this received ramparts of its own: Stouff believes that the process was under way by 1190, and perhaps nearly completed by then.[10] Because of a low population, some cemeteries were disaffected, and even turned into vineyards. Indeed, the parish of Notre Dame de Beaulieu, to the south of the walls, was without a church by 1365, for it had been destroyed. Because of the dangerous times, there now occurred a repetition of that relocation of religious establishments intra muros already seen several centuries earlier, leaving the remaining antiquities outside the walls relatively undisturbed until modern times. Although we know little of any concern for the past in earlier centuries, some finds were recorded, for example in the Monastery of S. Caesar in 1587,[2] and at the Couvent des Minimes during the 17th century.[3]

---

relief sections were retrieved from bastions erected in the 8th century or 9th century – so presumably the monument still stood then?

10   Stouff 1979, 60–61, 64, 71ff.

PROVENCE AND THE SOUTH: MONUMENTAL LOSSES

By the early 18th century the ditches of the town walls were full of rubbish (a likely pointer to dilapidation of the walls), and the Archbishop's 1706 interest in the walls was to ask for a bastion as his garden.[4] Like Nîmes, Arles possessed triumphal arches, but what was apparently the best, still standing under Louis XIII, disappeared for the usual reason – in 1743 the consuls wished to widen the street.[5] There were remains of aqueducts in the vicinity;[11] and in the town were evidently antiquities, "all the parts of these that are known, are occupied as cellars, and make no appearance above ground."[6] One reason for this was that antiquities, discovered for example when excavating the foundations for the Hôtel de Ville, went straight away into new building.[7] This is presumably what happened to the circus, of which nothing except for the (transplanted) obelisk was above-ground: evidently "il a été détruit dans les guerres du moyen âge, et prouvé que les débris ont servi à réparer les remparts de la cité."[8] Ironically, in 1814 Veran, appointed the previous year Conservateur des antiques, suggested the new town hall as a suitable location for the museum, with sarcophagi between the columns. His stolen motto was "Arelas quanta fuit, istae Ruinae Docent."[9]

In the early 19th century, because Arles was on a river, her antiquities continued to be plundered, some as gifts to Paris, others by entrepreneurs to Marseille,[10] sometimes in the face of successful local opposition.[11] Millin described her "extreme decadence" in 1810,[12] and noted the Museum Arelatense set up in the Alyscamps in 1784–5, which was little more than a pile of blocks: "on ne sait cependant comment on a pu décorer du nom de musée cette nef en ruine et ces monumens amoncelés."[13] The "museum" actually started like this, Thicknesse in 1789 noting "an infinite number of Pagan and Christian monuments, all lying thick upon the surface, in the utmost disorder and confusion."[14] When a proper Musée Lapidaire was founded, (before 1789), some of the best material was taken from Renaissance and later houses about the town, into which marble blocks had been built.[15] Antiquities also appeared when the Porte Ste Etienne of the Archbishop's Palace was demolished early in 1810, and Roman remains discovered:

> présenta une masse de pierres, la plus part d'une grosseur extraordinaire, presque toutes placées sans ordre, sans liaison et sans mortier. On trouva bientôt épars des fustes, des tronçons de colonnes, des socles, ds bases, de chapiteaux, de frises, d'architraves, de corniches, d'impostes etc. etc.

---

11   Servonat 1999, 33 for plan of the aqueducts. 101: reckons the aqueducts continued working "et probablement sans entretien" until destroyed by Charles Martel in 736.

322   CHAPTER 11

This gateway was thought by Veran to stand on a Roman one, set in the town walls, and the jumbled antiquities to be placed in a hurry "à la veille de quelque siege ... personne ne déterminait l'époque de cette construction." But the excavation went down less than two metres; the municipality could not get funds from the prefect; the contractor got fed up of waiting, and filled in the hole.[16]

Unlike many other towns, Arles did not see the centre much modernised and refurbished in the 19th century. This happened only outside the remains of the ramparts, which still contained visible spolia in 1876,[17] and more of which were revealed as parts of the walls were demolished at the turn of the century.[18] Arles had retained standing monuments, in a dilapidated condition, and "des débris de temples, de palais, d'édifices de toute espèce, sont répandus çà et là sur tous les points de la ville."[19] The town itself was still shrunken and scruffy in the 1840s, and its mediaeval monuments especially neglected:

> ces édifices religieux d'Arles associés aux ruines, à demi exhumés de ses places publiques, et ces tronçons de colonnes servant de bornes, et dégradés par de plus vils usages, contribuaient à cette mélancolie d'une ville si dépeuplée relativement à son étendue.[20]

Unfortunately, standing ruins were not looked after or promoted, one author claiming in 1837 that the amphitheatre was little known.[21] One triumphal arch had become so dangerous that the Consuls had it demolished, "on ne sait précisément à quelle époque."[22] At least two such arches were destroyed,[23] one perhaps being used for late repairs to the enceinte;[12] and other monuments of which we have no knowledge were presumably stripped to clad churches in marble.[24] The "Palais de la Trouille" [perhaps from *Trullum*, the name for the palace at Constantinople] (de Constantine) stood to cornice level, with some piping intact, and

> Les fragmens de statues, de colonnes de granit et de marbre, de corniches, de frises, les restes de mosaïques, les portions de tuyaux de plomb, la quantité excessive de pierres froides, bien polies et d'une grosseur prodigieuse, qui ont été trouvées dans cette enceinte, sont des preuves évidentes de

---

12   Fornasier 1994. Evidence for these comes from spolia recovered from the SE bastion of the late Porte de la Redoubte. Author mentions that other relief sections were retrieved from bastions erected in the 8th century or 9th century – so presumably the monument still stood then?

PROVENCE AND THE SOUTH: MONUMENTAL LOSSES

la magnificence de ce palais, dont les ravages des temps, la superstition, l'avarice et la méchanceté des hommes, ont causé la destruction.[25]

In 1811, Millin thought that the local marble-workers had destroyed more antiquities than the Visigoths, Saracens and revolutionary armies combined, and deplored the state of Arles' monuments, as well as the "méchanceté, le besoin de nuire, de détruire."[26] Because there had been so much destruction and neglect, the question of restoration grew in importance in the course of the 19th century. The picturesque was invoked in 1837: "Laissons aux ruines la majesté de leur vieillesse, leur caractère triste et solennel."[27] This was not practical, and Estrangin in 1838 believed Parliament should contribute, "non seulement pour les intérêts matériels du pays, mais encore pour la conserva-tion de ses monuments historiques, qui font partie de ses illustrations et de sa gloire."[28]

Town Walls

The first mention of the walls is in a letter of Theodoric in the winter of 508/9, referring to their restoration (Cassiodorus *Variae* 3.44, in PL69). The same letter also says that "ad cultum reducere antiqua moenia festinemus," which suggests a deliberate policy of using suitable monuments as churches. Texts of the ninth and tenth century refer to the wall and its gates: the Porta Lutosa is still there to the north, and the walls follow the rocky ledge to the east; but from the Tour de Morgues, the circuit has apparently shrunk slightly in size since Antiquity, for it now passes close to the theatre. Stouff believes this change may date from the ninth century, when Archbishop Rolland built the eponymous tower above the Porte de Laure. He notes that the hinge of the problem (which is insoluble) is whether the tomb of Saint Cesaire was inside the city walls, and therefore whether it was these or some other walls which held out the Saracens.

There are always great difficulties in deciding exactly what documentary mentions of changes to town walls actually mean. When we read a statement in the *Gesta Comitum Barcinonensium*, for example, that the Count of Provence destroyed the walls of Arles in 1161, it is impossible to know what walls are indicated, and whether the whole circuit is intended. Sparse texts which get over-interpreted and then form the basis of unproved and unprovable state-ments tend to attract misguided followings – such as the general belief that a completely new enceinte was built in 1263, based on the "fact" of the 1161 destruction. On the contrary, there are very few examples anywhere of city walls being so completely razed that they cannot be reconstructed; and hence all documents should be treated with care. Of course, such difficulties as are

324   CHAPTER 11

encountered at Arles are compounded by the lack of excavation: consequently, the references to a "murum antiquum" in an act of 1152, as well as to three towers in the length of the rue de Mejan in 1293 and 1333 cannot be linked to any surviving remains.[13]

Like many other walls in Gaul, those of Arles, although altered by 16th-century fortification,[14] yielded many spolia when sections of them were demolished at various dates. They were perhaps complete in 1805,[29] and sections were still standing in 1885, and were photographed.[30] This would have been well known to earlier centuries as well: Lantelme de Romieu, for example, writing of the myriad antiquities to be seen around the city, also notes that parts of the walls and towers are built with similar stones. And in his chapter on the epitaphs of the city, he notes that

> en fondements d'une vieille Tour, qu'on abbatit pres du portal de Laure, quelques epitaphes anciens, en des pierres moult belles, et bien entieres: desquels j'en ay mis ici trois des plus correctz et plus notables[31]

– that is, three figured stelai, one of a woman,[32] another which he perhaps misinterprets by showing as two women holding hands (a married couple), and the third of a couple who look at each other. These finds, which he says were made "not long ago," might indicate that the flow of antiquities from the old city walls was both of good quality material, and plentiful. Indeed, the fact that the towers constructed at the theatre, and the houses within, were made at least in part from antiquities taken from the cemeteries outside the walls can be checked by the funerary altars retrieved in more recent years from the the theatre itself.[33] This suggests either that sections of the original wall were demolished when the enceinte was drawn in to the line of the theatre or, more likely, that funerary antiquities were generally available outside that enceinte in the Middle Ages. Certainly, the towers were targetted in 1561 by the municipality as likely sources of "de gros cartiers de pierre" which could be reused for repairing the Portail de la Cavallerie, the argument being that the work could include refurbishing that section of the walls.[34]

---

13   Stouff 1979, 63, from AD BDR III G 16, fols. 17v–18r.

14   Potter 2008, 163–164 in the 1530s "The first fully bastioned fortress was begun at Saint-Paul de Vence, possibly by Jean de Saint-Rémy in 1537, to cover the invasion route by land from Nice, while Arles, Avignon, Beaucaire, Gap, Marseille, Sisteron and Tarascon were all provided with bastions in this period."

PROVENCE AND THE SOUTH: MONUMENTAL LOSSES

Amphitheatre and Theatre

Both these structures survived as fortresses and housing; or, to be more precise, they formed a small but secure walled village, protected in the case of the theatre by towers, within which life might proceed in dangerous times. In order to learn any more about ruins below the ground, the modern houses built on top would have to be demolished.[35]

The first mediaeval date for the occupation of the amphitheatre is 734 when, amidst the uncertainty of the wars between Charles Martel and the Saracens, the inhabitants of Arles abandoned their invaded town to take refuge in the amphitheatre, taking with them the relics of Saint Genes from the Aliscamps.[15] Like its almost identical fellow at Nîmes, this amphitheatre was also used for housing (it had streets,[36] with "ses ruelles étroites et ses escaliers tortueux").[37] The earliest informative view is perhaps the etching by I. Peytret of 1686 which, as well as houses in the arena itself, also shows several houses in the outer arcades, and several more backed onto those arcades and extending further out. This is included in Séguin's book of 1687, where there is an account[38] describing the structure's sorry state:

> Nous vîmes neantmoins la face du second et du troisième êtage environnée de colomnes, avec leurs bases et leurs chapiteaux, ou paroit une corniche richement travaillée, le tout d'un ordre italique et composée.

Part of the reason for the mess was that in 1664 the stage area of the theatre became part of a convent.[39] Today, the theatre's features are very dilapidated indeed, and many have been heavily restored or, indeed, replaced with modern copies. Clearly, therefore, the degradation has been heavy since the seventeenth century, if we believe the accuracy of Séguin's account; this perhaps we should do, since he also includes a plate of the amphitheatre "as it once was."

According to Romieu, François Ier was most impressed by the structure: "grand amateur de belles choses, lorsqu'il fut voir nostre ville, s'en montra fasché, jusques à reprendre ceux qui avaient permis telle faute et n'avaient pas respecté ce lieu là."[40] As at Nîmes, the amphitheatre took time to clear, and only by 1830 had 183 of the 213 houses[41] been removed – a task which François Ier, Henri IV[42] and then Napoléon had ordered without result, although Napoléon did get the obelisk moved.[43]

Except for the basic structure, by the 19th century little was left inside the amphitheatre[44] because, as in the theatre, the inhabitants had caused so much damage.[45] The Mayor wished to clear out the modern constructions and to

---

15   Michel 1909, 3, note 1.

execute digs: "Ce magistrat a à cœur de dégager et de restaurer un monument qui ne peut manquer d'attirer les curieux, et il compte avec raison sur le concours du gouvernement pour y parvenir."[46] The interior of the amphitheatre was to be cleared in the earlier 19th century, although the exterior took longer to free.[47] Certainly, sections were now difficult to recognise let alone reassemble, and statue fragments lay among the débris.[48] In the early 1820s, parts of the theatre were cleared, and antiquities recovered,[49] the work continuing into the 1830s[50] and then the 1840s, because of last-ditch resistance from some of the residents,[51] against whom Mérimée recommended to the Minister the application of the law on appropriation.[52] Sufficient was reclaimed relating to the scenae frons to know how lavishly decorated it had been, but there were insufficient remains even to contemplate a re-build.[53]

The *Life of S. Hilaire of Arles* (Bishop 426–449) states that Cyril the Levite had the theatre stripped of its marble, and suffered as a result.[54] Destroying such a large structure would be difficult as well as dangerous, and we may imagine that the fragments found at various times, and supposedly deliberatey smashed,[55] were simply united with the standard narrative of saints as destroyers of pagan monuments. Séguin comments that the destruction of the edifice was completed

> à l'occasion des Guerres sanglantes, ou par les Ennemis, ou même par les Habitans de cette ville, pour se servir des pierres toutes taillées, et fort propres à fermer les brèches, dans les pressantes nécessitez.[56]

This is interesting: for, like Lantelme de Romieu, he has noticed the re-used blocks in the city walls, but has concluded that these constitute repairs rather than parts of the original construction. Whether such blocks were "displayed" (perhaps including decorated pieces) we cannot of course say. The fortification of the theatre may date from the ninth century, by which time the wall of the theatre cavea had become part of the line of the ramparts, and when Archbishop Rolland built his tower above one of the arcades. This, the Porte de l'Aura, was still used as a gate at the end of the Middle Ages: as with other gates the name of which has a similar stem, the appellation might be a contraction of "aurea" – particularly if we parallel its construction from antique blocks with the more highly decorated Arch of Trajan at Benevento, incorporated into the walls of that city and also called the Golden Gate.

Nor was the fortification of Arles restricted to theatre and amphitheatre for, by 1150 the Porta Lutosa of the city had become the castrum de Portaldosa, held by the de Baux family. This was demolished in the fourteenth or fifteenth century, leaving only the Roman triumphal arch known as the "arc admirable."

PROVENCE AND THE SOUTH: MONUMENTAL LOSSES

In other words, an arch had been used as the basis for a small fort – as happened at Orange, and so often at Rome. Furthermore the "capitole," which was presumably the area around the Temple of Augustus, was also somehow fortified. Two of its columns were still standing in 1336, when they were the subject of a dispute between two proprietors, solved by the urban magistrates giving one column to each.[16]

Cemeteries and Roads

In the Middle Ages, Arles was famous for her cemeteries, for three interconnected reasons. The first was that they housed famous relics. The second was position, for the town lay on the route from Italy towards Spain, which was to be the Via Tolosana, one of the great pilgrimage routes leading in stages and via great churches and relic-collections to Santiago da Compostella. The third was the complex of epics in which her monuments, and particularly her cemeteries, appear, as heroic explanations for the masses of impressive sarcophagi. Different versions of the *Chanson de Roland* (11th century in its present version) have the dead knights, including Roland and Oliver, buried on the way from Blaye to Roncevaux, while others on the road from Roncevaux to Saint-Gilles and Arles. From this we may conclude that prestigious sarcophagi were already to be found there, some perhaps antique. In the same fashion, one of the Charlemagne legends has him fighting the Saracens near Arles, upon which a multitude of tombs miraculously emerged from the earth to receive the dead from the battle; another has Charlemagne and Turpin carrying their dead companions to the Aliscamps, and a third has Charlemagne besiege the Saracens within the city, and defeat them by diverting a subterranean aqueduct which feeds the city (presumably an antique one, and perhaps even the one remains of which were still visible in the seventeenth century).[57] The Middle Ages therefore knew something of Roman aqueducts: this was hardly surprising, since many would have been large enough for at least a child to crawl along.

The popularity of the Aliscamps through the Chansons de Geste and pilgrimages led to a great demand for burial space, and therefore to yet more spectacular sarcophagi. Already in the thirteenth century, writing of the church of Saint Geniès in Trinquetaille, *Le Guide du pèlerin de Saint Jacques* noted that

> nulle part ailleurs, on ne pourrait trouver un ancien cimetière tant de tombes de marbre, ni de si grandes, alignées sur la terre. Elles sont d'un travail varié, portant d'antiques inscriptions sculptés en lettres latines;

---

16   Stouff 1979, 48–49.

> mais dans une langue inintelligible. Plus on regarde de loin, plus on voit s'allonger la file des sarcophages.[17]

In spite of Renaissance depradations, many more survived into the seventeenth century[58] than are visible today, because so many of the finest decorated marble vessels were given away or taken.[59] The eventual decline in interest in the Aliscamps probably aided the preservation of at least some of its less attractive tombs; thus Stouff calculates a declining percentage of the wills of citizens requesting burial there: for the period 1376–1400: 56.9%; 1401–25: 40.7%; 1426–50: 34.6%; 1451–75: 22.9%. Occasionally, the requests were specific, such as that of Johan Boye to be buried "in tumulo sive sepulcro antiquo"[18] – though how old we cannot tell.

The Alyscamps were already a mess in the 18th century, when gunpowder was used to blast a track into them from the walls, the same work uncovering an aqueduct, its channel completely furred up.[60] But modernity came to Arles with a vengeance in 1846, with the cutting of the Arles-Marseille railway line right through the cemetery.[61] The juggernaut could not be stopped, the antiquities would often be destroyed, although some grave goods were preserved,[62] so drawing was the only answer: "c'est de décrire et de figurer tout ce qui sera mis au jour dans les fouilles, ou ce qui sera en danger de périr par suite des changements qui vont s'opérer dans cette partie du territoire de l'antique cité."[63] In the 1860s it was the Arles-Lunel branch line that uncovered sections of the then scarcely inhabited Roman town across the river, at Trinquetaille.[64] The destruction was deplored by Ramé in 1851, explaining that whereas Saint-Trophîme was echoed in Saint-Gilles-du-Gard, the cemetery was indeed unique, and wondering why no alternative route could be found for the railway.[65] In the same year Didron Aîné, Editor of the *Annales Archéologiques*, disputed that amphitheatres and cathedrals had had their day, and that funding should now go into railways:

> Nous croyons donc que l'on peut fort bien, d'une main bâtir des embarcadères et aligner des chemins de fer, et de l'autre consolider les cathédrales anciennes ou même bâtir des cathédrales nouvelles.[66]

Indeed, by the end of the century neary all the cemetery was gone, for Arlesians had destroyed it,[67] and the railway had helped mightily in the destruction.[19]

---

17 Vieillard 1969, 37.

18 Stouff 1979, 49, citing AD BDR 404 E 97, for 15 June 1398.

19 Servonat 1999, 80 for plan of the railway layout in 1844 and how it obliterated antiquities.

PROVENCE AND THE SOUTH: MONUMENTAL LOSSES

If the Aliscamps retained their popularity as a burial place into the fifteenth century (and their fame as a source of high-quality sarcophagi for at least two centuries thereafter), the cemetery across the river, in the suburb of Trinquetaille, was apparently already abandoned by the later Middle Ages. In Lantelme's day, the 1570s, the area was

> ores quasi déserte, au regard du passé, ne s'y trouvent bonement quertes plus de quatre vingts ou cent maisons, neanmoins il appert avoir esté grand chose autrefois... voyant mesmement plusieurs ruines, qui vont bien avant dans la Camargue, ou se trouvent souvent des pierres antiques gravées, et grande quantité de medailles.[68]

When Séguin wrote in 1687, that side of the river was still not much inhabited:

> Cette partie étoit autrefois considérable, étant à bien près, la moitié de la Ville d'Arles comme on le voit par les ruines des Tours et des murailles qui estoient d'un grand Circuit, parmi lesquelles on déterre tous les jours de grands quartiers de pierre, des médailles antiques, des Urnes, des pavez à la mosaïque.[69]

The water level must have risen since ancient times for, when the Rhône fell periodically, there were uncovered the remains of a pagan necropolis, of house walls, docks and the bridge linking Arles with Nîmes across the Petit Rhône. The whole area was, of course, surrounded by a comprehensive network of Roman roads which appear frequently as boundary and land markers in documents of the thirteenth and fourteenth centuries. Two examples will serve. The first is an inquest dated 1268.[70]

The second is from a description of the bounds of the Crau d'Arles in January 1430, mentioning the same markers: "trium peyronorum in quo sunt littere sculpte juxta quod legitur" at the frontier between the territories of Arles and Aureille, and on an antique road "quandam viam antiquam apparatam."[20]

As for roads, Devic & Vaissete catalogue well over 200 milestones around the Narbonnaise because, of course, so many were erected and so many survived, since they were a popular element in wall-building,[71] as Ménard describes for Nîmes and surroundings.[72] Their original location is nearly always known, and the entries place them – "87th on the Domitia, Narbonne to Nîmes," and so on. They are easily transportable, because they can be rolled or, if necessary, dragged by men or animals. Those looking for building materials also

---

20   Stouff 1979, 45, note 197.

330   CHAPTER 11

knew where to find them (and at what intervals). They were reused as church columns (six in Saint-Martin de Quart (Gard) to hold up the vaulting), one of them transported to a private property after the church collapsed, another as a bollard in the same village. Another served as a step in a vineyard, another as a scrubbing-board for washerwomen, largely erasing the inscription, another as a notice-board in front of a château and then a Protestant church. Yet another was sliced up to make rollers, and for building into a wall.[73]

Other Ancient Monuments

If the purpose of the theatre and amphitheatre was hard to mistake, there were other monuments the original use of which was not clear. One was the cryptoporticus (the exact purpose of which is, indeed, still unclear). Lantelme de Romieu writes that this was used as cellars by the inhabitants of the Parish of Saint Lucien: above ground were

> les fragments d'un Capitole très ancien, fait en dos d'âne, avec corniches et frontispice, comme celuy de Nismes, qu'on appelle la Maison quarrée, et orné de belles colonnes, avec bases, et chappitaux, qui sont ores quasi toutes cachées, ou démolies, parmi les maisons de certains particuliers.[74]

The cryptoporticus began at the aforesaid church, and went as far as the Great Clock Tower, and several inhabitants used the structure in various places "selon la commodité de leurs maisons prochaines," each one having taken a section according to his need, but always with the permission and licence of the Consuls. Séguin, writing in 1687, believes they formed part of the baths, being "une double galerie qui servit à se promener, devant ou après le bain." Further misunderstandings surrounded the actual Baths, known throughout the Middle Ages and later as the Palace of Constantine. This misunderstanding stemmed partly from the desire to link the city's famous son with a surviving monument, but largely from its use as a palace by the counts: it is so listed in documents of the thirteenth and fourteenth centuries. Thus Charles of Anjou possessed "domum seu palatium que vocatur Trullia ubi sunt multe domus."[21] By the fifteenth century, the palace might well have probably gone, as the terrier of 1437 declares that several people have houses, courtyards, stables and cellars there.[22] Lantelme de Romieu confirms that there were indeed houses there in his day, noting that

---

21   Baratier & Villard 1966, 402.
22   Stouff 1979, 47.

PROVENCE AND THE SOUTH: MONUMENTAL LOSSES

> encore se voit là, derrière un vieil bâtiment de briques, fort grand et espais, soustenu par le devant d'arcs et colonnes, qui sont ores quasi toutes abbatues, ou couchées par les nouveaux édifices de certains particuliers, lequel on présume avoir esté jadis le palais des roys d'Arles.

But they still perhaps formed a "prestige" site, for they belonged to "Messieurs les Commandeurs de Sainte Luce,"[75] a religious and social confraternity. In Séguin's time, large columns of granite and white marble, together with pieces of cornice, were still to be found in nearby houses; and still visible (apparently also re-used in the same houses) were "quantité de grandes pierres froides, d'une largeur prodigieuse, et d'une polissime incroyable, qui seroient au pavé de la basse Cour de ce château."[76] Clearly, Séguin thought the structure was once a strongold – in spite of mentioning the large quantities of lead pipes still to be found on the site.

Discoveries in the area continued into the 19th century.[77] Arles also possessed a circus, the outline of which may have remained visible well into modern times, judging by the fact that an obelisk decorating the spina was apparently never buried. Not that it was recognised as such: for Gervase of Tilbury, writing in the early 13th century, stated that it had belonged to a temple where human sacrifices had been made. Not surprisingly, this gory tale remained popular, and Lantelme de Romieu identified the very altar, "dressé sur deux très hautes colonnes," where the actual sacrifices had taken place. (The story was even being retailed at the end of the eighteenth century, in Dumont's 1789 *Description des anciens monuments d'Arles*.) By Lantelme's day, the obelisk may have been partly hidden, perhaps by vegetation, for he notes that it "fut descouvert entièrement et visité par la Reine Mère de France, laquelle fut ici à Arles avec le Roi Charles neuf." Lantelme adopted the general Renaissance belief that obelisks were connected with death and commemmoration,

> ayant à la sommite d'iceluy un trou assez grand, et est d'une pierre fort dure, melée de chaire, rouge et noir, comme jaspée, lequel à mon jugement peut avoir servy par le passé pour le mausole ou monument de quelque prince Romain.[78]

Prompted, perhaps, by the Royal visit, he records that the city fathers intended to move it to the Place du Marché, "pour Mémoire de son Antiquité."

As for temples, Arles certainly once possessed a number: but where were they located? Etienne Dumont, towards the end of the eighteenth century, knew of none: "C'est ce qui est enseveli dans des ténèbres presque inpénétrables." Séguin, however, a century earlier, thought he could detect the remains

332   CHAPTER 11

of a Temple of Diana from pieces of column, and cornices, "qui sont au long des murailles, vers la porte de Laure dans la Ville."[79] Lantelme de Romieu was perhaps confused by the crush of houses in the theatre, for he interpreted remains of what might have been the double frieze decorating the north arcade of the theatre[80] as

> le reste de la ruine d'un temple magnifique ... contenant plusieures arcs triomphants, voire sur l'entrée en y a encore trois, l'un sous l'autre, ornes de frises et frontispices, ou sont gravés les disques et testes des thoreaux, qui significent selon les anciens, que ca esté un lien destiné pour les sacrifices.[81]

In compensation, as it were, at least one church near the town seems to have been built on and of Roman remains, as Mérimée recognised.[82]

Civic Pride and the Monuments

From their survival, we may conclude that the town was proud of its monuments. As Stouff says of mediaeval Arles, the emphasis is on continuity, with Rome emphasised in the Chansons de Geste, and her pilgrims. When the pilgrims and poetry dried to a trickle, she was left with her monuments, and gradually developed a broader interest in them, partly, perhaps, as a reflex against her declining prosperity. From the sixteenth century, her streets and soil were plundered by collectors, and what little remained was bought gradually from private ownership for the prestige of the town. We cannot at this remove judge how richly she was endowed before such incursions, but Lantelme, the local antiquarian, noted that

> Bref, il n'y a guère rues, maisons, ou eglises dans nostre ville qui ne soient décorez de quelques bases, chapiteaux et tronçons de colomnes antiques, ça et la disposées: ce que demonstre évidemment y avoir en icy par le passé plusieurs bastiments magnifiques, autant en plus qu'en ville qui soit de ça les Montz, desquelles pierres encor une partie de nos murailles et tourz en sont basties.[83]

He prefaces his account with two sonnets, very much modelled on Joachim Du Bellay's collection called *Les Antiquitez de Rome*, and hymning "ses superbes Arènes, / Son obélisque aussi, et ses vieils monuments, / engravés tout au tour de vers doctes et graves."[84] Lantelme's pride did not stop at writing in the best modern "Roman heroic" vein, for another sonnet prefacing his manuscript concentrates on the great figures who visited the city.[85] Romieu is disgusted

PROVENCE AND THE SOUTH: MONUMENTAL LOSSES   333

by the damage wrought on the Arènes, which "semble avoir esté aucunement ruiné, et rebastiz de tous costez par plusieurs particuliers, qui se sont là de long temps accomodez et accagés par une trop facile licence, qui est certes grandement préjudiciable à telle memorable antiquité."[86]

The buoyant tone here may be poetic licence; but a century later, Brunet's hommage to I. Séguin, printed in the Preface to his *Les Antiquitéz d'Arles* of 1687, is much more downcast, perhaps reflecting a diminution of available antiquities and perhaps an impoverishment of the population which was certainly in effect by 1800. Part of his poem reads:

> De cent Antiquitéz les beautez effacées.
> Arles n'avoit plus rien de sa grandeur première,
> Ce n'étoit qu'un amas de funestes débris,
> Sa gloire comme sa matière,
> Confondue avec la poussière,
> Se perdroit pour jamais, sans tes scavans écrits.

Lantelme, over-enthusiastically linking his town with great names (Orange tried to do the same), then suggests that the toponym "Camargue" is a corruption of "Campus Marii", named after the Consul Caius Marius, who fought the Cymbri tribe. He would have been disappointed to learn that the suffix is probably from "agger," meaning a field or a ditch. What is more, he included the surroundings of the city in her glory, writing on the triumphal arch at Saint Chamas, and quite correctly calling the arch and mausoleum at Saint Rémy "le plus excellent qui sont deça les Monts, pour la memoire des Romains."[87]

The Downside of Civic Pride

We may assume that the municipality was powerless to prevent remains being filched, which went against their developing awareness of the prestige of local antiquities, formalised from the seventeenth century by the widespread convention of gathering important works in the main square or in the Town Hall. The circus obelisk was raised in 1676 with the help of eight large ship's masts, and placed in the square, the happy conjunction of obelisk and Sun King being more than a coincidence. A statue of Mithras was found in 1598 outside the Porte de la Roquette, on the site of the circus; but this was only taken to the staircase of the Hotel de Ville in 1723, having been bought by the Consuls; and the altar to the Bona Dea, found in July 1758 while working on the great door of Notre Dame de la Major, was placed there immediately.[88] Perhaps the taste for antiquities, so evident at Arles in the Renaissance, was growing again. For example, it was only in the 1730s that the Council decided against allowing the rebuilding of a ruinous house in the Arènes "parce que par là on a défiguré un vieux monument de l'Antiquité."[89]

Unfortunately, however, the very fame of Arles and her surviving antiquities worked against the interests of her citizens, for it led only to further depletion of her antiquities, by commissioners with an eye to quality. If her monuments were so famous, and hymned in poetry, then others would wish to acquire the best of them. Thus Lantelme records[90] that the church of La Major had eight porphyry columns, which Charles IX carried off in 1564 "au grand regret des citoyens." These were indeed a fine haul, for individual porphyry columns are rare in France (assuming they were true porphyry, and not from a French quarry),[91] let alone a matched suite of eight. At the same time the Queen Mother took marble decorations from in front of the presbyterium of Saint Honoré: these were two marble heads, each paired (presumably representations of Janus). She also took "quelques beaux monuments de marbre antiques, tous ouvrez" from the façade of the same church. Lantelme contents himself that there are plenty left, and that the Queen Mother cannot get at the "notables antiquitez en pierres de marbre figurées," which are built into walls, some of which resemble those in Rome, in the collection of cardinal Cesi. And in his discussion of antique statues in the town, he says that a statue of Hadrian was given by the Seigneur de Beyners to François of Lorraine, Grand Prieur de France, when he visited Arles; this was taken off to Marseilles.[92] Amongst many other examples of expropriation was the sarcophagus which, in 1521, stood to the right of the entrance to Saint-Honorat on the Aliscamps: this was also taken to Marseilles, this time on the orders of another Grand Prieur, Henri d'Angoulême.[93] On at least one occasion, such robbery failed: for when Charles Emmanuel, Duke of Savoy, visited Arles in 1593, and wished to carry off a vessel from the same church, the cart could not get out of the cemetery (divine intervention?); and it did not reach Marseille until 1803.[94]

More was to go in the seventeenth century. The head of the famous Venus of Arles came to light in 1651, when a priest named Bon dug a well in his house, located in front of the two columns (which still survive) of the theatre's scenae frons: "La beauté de la tête, trouvée la première à six pieds et plus de profondeur, décida les Consuls à faire continuer et agrandir la fouille à leurs frais, pour se procurer, s'il étoit possible, le reste de la figure"[95] – which they did for the most part, presenting the work in 1683 to Louis XIV, who was then collecting material for Versailles.[96] Astutely, Dumont observed that the state of the Venus indicated that it must have fallen from some high niche for, had it been hammered and then deliberately buried, the traces of such treatment would have been clearly visible.

PROVENCE AND THE SOUTH: MONUMENTAL LOSSES   335

Nor did such robberies cease in later centuries: Jean-Julien Estrangin, writing in 1837, complained that

> Il fut un temps où le Musée d'Arles occupait tout l'espace de la cité et se trouvait partout; dans les rues, dans les places, dans les églises, dans les maisons et jusque dans les champs; mais qu'en est-il résulté? L'enlèvement ou la dégradation des monuments. De 1804 à 1808, des forbans en antiquités ont enlevé à la face du soleil, de nos rues et de nos places, les marbres et les granites pour les transporter par la voie de mer à Marseille, par celle du Rhône à Lyon, pour en trafiquer.[97]

Aix-en-Provence

Aix[23] (Bouches-du-Rhône) was a prosperous town under the earlier Empire, with houses built outside its Augustan walls, but which declined in the third century,[24] perhaps reviving in the late 5th century under Christianity, with its amphitheatre used for housing. It built an impressive baptistery, with thirty-foot marble columns, perhaps from some of the remains of the forum.[98] Some more impressive columns were retrieved at the end of the 16th century[99] and, in 1809, by which date its walls were in ruins, "un vaste bassin et de plusieurs bases de colonnes."[100] The Duc d'Epernon, besieging Aix in 1590, perhaps faced fortifications already in bad shape because of bad building practices.[101] He built a series of forts, one of which, the tour d'Entremont, was made from Roman blocks,[102] some of which were retrieved in 1817,[103] others of which were reused in modern buildings during the course of the century.[104] Another Roman monument also fared badly, namely a multi-stage mausoleum which, during its dismantling for reuse in the rebuilding of the Palais Comtal and the Tribunal in the 18th century,[105] revealed three funerary urns.[106] In fact, no fewer than three Roman towers were to disappear almost completely during this building work.[25] To destroy such monuments, it was asserted, was

---

23   Clerc 1916 370–453 for surviving monuments, including the antique towers incorporated in the Palais des Comtes de Provence, destroyed in 1786; 459–481 recherches sur le tracé de l'enceinte. Pradalié 2008 f or overview; 27–45 for Roman and late antiquity.

24   Ambard 1984, 155ff: La cité réduite. Esmonde Cleary 2013, 109: "a number of large, well-appointed houses. Through the course of the third century, these houses on the periphery were progressively abandoned and demolished."

25   Ambard 1984, 193–213: the mausoleum (Tour de l'Horloge), and the Tours du Trésor et du Chaperon. Louis XVI signed letters patent for the reconstruction of the palace in 1786,

to obliterate "ses Archives les plus glorieuses, & la preuve incontestable de l'antique noblesse de son origine."[107] The inevitable question was how it came about that "the Barbarians" preserved them, and the modern inhabitants destroyed them?[108] These need not have been destroyed, and work on the new palais de justice which replaced them could at least have given the opportunity to refurbish and make operational aqueducts at the site; but this did not happen;[109] indeed, the remains of Roman baths and their piping were blocked off.[110] Aix lost her walls in the 19th century when they no longer served for defence,[26] and when workers needed to be kept from starving.[111] This did not mean that dismantled buildings were necessarily preserved: a poster of 1874 announced the selling off of materials from the Porte Notre-Dame.[27] Part of the town's modernity was expressed in the avenues some of which replaced the walls, others of which joined the old town to the new.[28]

Avignon

Avignon (Vaucluse), where some Roman remains survived into the 19th century,[112] had a late, perhaps mid-4th century wall, with large spolia blocks, the secondary reuse of which Mérimée detected scattered through the town;[113] but the walls visible in the 19th century were built in 1350–68, with later alterations.[29] In 1789, the town was "all shut in with the most beautiful ancient fortification walls I ever beheld, which are in perfect repair,"[114] and remained "in perfect beauty and preservation" when Pinkney visited in 1814[115] and when Hughes saw them in 1822.[116]

In 1836 one commentator noted that the walls were famous throughout Europe, but conceded that "avec les progrès toujours croissants de ces terribles moyens de destruction qu'emploie le génie militaire moderne, nos remparts

---

26 Lam & Galland 2006, 24, Aix: L'Empire, ses guerres, et les troubles de 1830 s'éloignent, l'enceinte n'a plus aucune fonction défensive et ne délimite plus qu'un espace fiscal et une communauté – and 1848 problems a plongé les ouvriers dans la misère et la démolition des remparts donne travail et dignité. Carpentras' walls go at the same period.

27 Lam & Galland 2006, 6–8, Aix, chronology 1819–1991, and plan. In 1976–7 parts go for the Parking Bellegarde.

28 Benedict 1989, 34: "Between 1583 and 1646, Aix-en-Provence witnessed the development of three new quarters that more than doubled that city's size. The last expansion also permitted the construction through the center of town of a broad avenue (today's Cours Mirabeau) lined with aristocratic *hôtels* and wide enough for the city's leading residents to drive up and down it in that new means of conveyance, the carriage."

29 Clap & Huet 2005, 23–34 for alterations etc. from 15th century; 38–53 Le XIXe, siècle de tous les dangers, with 46–53 Percer, Détruire, Restaurer.

PROVENCE AND THE SOUTH: MONUMENTAL LOSSES 337

ne sont plus qu'un ornement."[117] Herein lay the problem: why preserve use-less walls? The municipality, countered by historians and archaeologists, was to spend decades arguing for their destruction, and standing by while churches such as the Cordeliers were degraded.[118] Across the river, Villeneuve had also suffered vandalism, but not by 1834 the "vandalisme des réparateurs."[119] Destruction within the town was also of long standing, as Loudon lamented in 1842.[120]

The first attack on the walls was from the railway in 1846. At first this was intended to follow the bend of the river, which ate away at the land, and to require embankments which in one plan would replace the walls.[121] But in the hope of one scholar such embankments would protect them.[122] Municipal strategy seems to have been to nibble at them bit by bit, Caumont complain-ing in 1855 that sections had already been destroyed.[123] The railway, wrote one observer in 1860, had stripped the town of her commercial importance, and it was the Musée Calvet that was paying for the restoration of the Palais des Papes and the ramparts.[124]

The second attack on the monuments of Avignon was on the Palais des Papes. This had suffered during the Revolution, being by 1822 "little more than a damp bare shell, filled with the broken remains of monumental figures."[125] In 1847 Caumont warned that "Le génie militaire s'en est emparé, et avec le zèle anti-archéologique qui n'appartient malheuseusement pas qu'à cette institu-tion, il dénature le plus qu'il peut ce magnifique monument."[126] This had hap-pened by 1839, when a "jeune industriel" wrote to Montalembert protesting against the depradations of "cette froide barbarie."[127] Paintings had already disappeared under plaster, "grâce au zèle éclairé d'une commission du conseil municipal de 1820,"[128] and the barracks were sure to degrade it further. The municipality refused to maintain the building, claiming in 1850 that it was State property.[129] And what were the army doing here, since "Avignon, d'ailleurs, n'était pas, à proprement parler, une place de guerre"?[130] Napoleon III, pass-ing through in 1860, provided one answer: build a barracks elsewhere in the town.[131] They did so, in the old Couvent des Célestins, after it had been a military hospital, prison and store, their possession requiring an amount of demolition "pour permettre au régiment de s'aligner entièrement."[132] These same town-council vandals, it was suggested in 1896, would surely demolish the Palais des Papes (entry to which required Génie permission)[133] if they got a good price for the stone.[134] The Palais survived.

The spotlight was turned on Avignon when the Congrès Archéologique met here in 1882, and asked for information on Roman remains in the area;[135] and, from that date, scholars bombarded the learned periodicals with com-plaints about the destruction and disappearance of ancient remains.[136] In 1894 the municipality voted to demolish a section of the ramparts;[137] they had

338   CHAPTER 11

demanded permission of the Commission (for the walls were already classified as an historical monument) in order to improve traffic. But they were refused,

> les conseillers municipaux votèrent ab irato la démolition de tous les remparts d'Avignon qui ne bordent pas le Rhône, et les plus acharnés allèrent jusqu'à proposer que cette seconde moitié elle-même, qui pourtant constitue un décor admirable, cher à tout le Midi, ne fût pas plus épargnée que l'autre.[138]

The near-perfect Porte Imbert was then demolished,[139] and the municipality next made ready to pull down the south ramparts, peculation included. "On sait, en effet, qu'elle [the municipality] favorisait une certaine société formée pour la construction d'immeubles à la place des anciennes murailles." This was against the protests that the walls were indeed the property of the State, "acte de vandalisme accompli au mépris de tout droit, de toute règle de jurisprudence et d'administration."[140] Across the Channel, amazement was the reaction.[141]

State property or not,[142] the mayor returned to the charge in 1901 and agreed to leave the rest of the walls alone if only he could demolish 700 metres of them.[143] The following year the mayor made two new breaches, one within the section being restorated by Viollet-le-Duc![144] In effect the mayor won, at least in part, Baedeker summarising the result in 1914:

> The Ramparts, skirting the boulevards and the railway ... of late largely restored ... There were once ten gates, but the Porte d'Imbert was demolished in 1896, and the Porte de l'Oulle in 1900 ... Several openings have also been made to make way for new streets. The best-preserved part is near the Porte St-Lazare.[145]

Dax

Protected by an early château, the walls of Dax[30] (Landes) were of petit appareil, but with large blocks for the gates,[146] and sculpted blocks in the foundations.[147] These important survivals of the early town were dismantled, having already been mangled by the army Génie:[148]

> Jusqu'au milieu du xixe siècle, Dax présentait un pittoresque tableau par son enceinte gallo-romaine demeurée intacte et qui était le plus curieux

---

30   Garmy & Maurin 1996, 82–125 ramparts of Dax, including demolition and fragments.

PROVENCE AND THE SOUTH: MONUMENTAL LOSSES

spécimen d'ouvrage militaire de ce passé lointain que nous possédions en France. On a jeté bas ces remparts vingt fois séculaires pour donner de l'air à la cité qui étouffait dans son enceinte. L'hygiène y a gagné, l'archéologie a perdu et aussi le paysage.[149]

Like other better-known centres, Dax promoted itself toward the end of the 19th century as a tourist resort with thermal baths and casino. "On the site of the old walls adjoining the Adour now lies the pretty Promenade des Remparts, and in the old moat are the Bains St-Pierre," wrote Baedeker in 1914, having observed in 1895 that "In spite of its antiquity this town has no noteworthy monuments." Yet the Roman elements were much in evidence in the mid-18th century,[150] and the walls ready for defence from the time of Colbert.[151] Murray's Guide in 1848 had written that "Near the bridge are portions of the old fortifications; and Roman masonry may, it is said, be discovered in their substructions." In the following half-century this important set of Roman walls, and no doubt many other monuments from the Roman capital and ancient thermal establishment (Aquae = Dax), were demolished. This puzzled a commentator in 1868, who wondered why the inhabitants wanted to flatten out the town and get rid of shade-giving trees; he suspected "quelque entrepreneur de démolitions derrière les hommes sans goût et sans patriotisme, qui réclament des travaux aussi dispendieux que déplorables et improductifs."[152]

The walls were still intact in 1845, as was "toute sa vieille physionomie militaire."[153] It was "une des villes les plus intéressantes du midi de la France, et c'est peut-être la seule ville qui possède encore entière son enceinte gallo-romaine."[154] But its hot springs were little patronised, and other monuments had already gone.[155] The trigger for urban change at Dax was its declassification in the 1850s as no longer of military importance. Yet in 1856 Dax was still a listed fortress and, apart from covering the walls (very badly, and not completely) with plaster, the Génie committed no crimes here.[156] For indeed, the scholars were watching the town closely, and marked the fall of the walls with detailed and indignant protests. One of the first came in 1856 from Léo Drouyn, Inspecteur des Monuments de la Gironde, who noted not only that the Municipality wished to destroy them "sous prétexte d'embellissement," but also that one who voted was a member of the Comité des arts et monuments.[157] Caumont attributed the developing disaster to the spinelessness of the responsible administrator.[158] A campaign was organised; Roach Smith came over from England to lend his support, and stirred up the newspapers when he returned home. Naturally, the French bridled at his intervention.[159] But all to no effect,[160] in spite of the authority and prestige of Chaudruc de Crazannes, Inspecteur-Conservateur des Monumens d'Antiquité de la Charente Inférieure.[161] Countersigned by scholars and a cardinal, a petition went to the Emperor in 1859 "car, de par la volonté impériale, tout ce qui reste de l'antique enceinte romaine sera sauvegardé."[162] But it was not, and indeed were already being pulled down, because the Municipality said that "il faut que tout change dans ce monde, et il ne veut pas être ganalisé."[163] Caumont in 1860, as a congressist addressing the questions posed annually, selected one on preservation, focussed on Dax, and opined that "On peut dire que la France, qui avait des monuments si intéressants, est le pays dans lequel on parle le plus de conservation, mais aussi un de ceux où l'on conserve le moins."[164]

By 1865 parts of the walls were down, and all the gates, for stupidity trumped reason:

> Certains habitants de Dax se sont persuadé, a dit M. de Caumont, que ce qui fait l'unique intérêt de leur ville, les murs romains, est ce qui empêche le commerce de se développer. Pourquoi n'avons-nous pas d'industrie? disent-ils gravement; parce que nous avons des murs romains.[165]

One consolation was that vandalism at Dax got a bad press, a Bayonne newspaper recalling the funds available from the Government for conservation, with Paris and Bordeaux trying to keep monuments – but "A Dax, on travaille à renverser!!!"[166] And the struggle did not go unnoticed, for in 1869 the Société française d'archéologie presented a medal to "M. de Lobit de Monval, de Dax, en récompense de la défense courageuse qu'il a opposée au projet de destruction des murs romains de Dax."[167] A small section of the walls was apparently still standing in 1888, although it was remarked how few of the works discovered during demolition ("briques sigillées, tuiles à rebords, monnaies, débris de statues en marbre blanc, groupes en marbre, inscriptions, autels votifs, etc") ended up in a museum.[168] The château-fort was also dismantled during these years. Its lower courses were Roman blocks,[169] and the foundations had to come out in 1891 (revealing an inscription), because this was to be the site of "le futur établissement de Dax-Salin-Thermal,"[170] advertised at the 1895 XIIIe Exposition de Bordeaux as "une station unique qui prend son essor. L'avenir lui appartient."[171]

St-Lizier

In the Ariège, this town in the Conserans is described in Baedeker in 1914 as "a decayed little town, pictuesquely situated ... still has a large part of its Roman walls." It apparently began as a military encampment rather than a civilian

PROVENCE AND THE SOUTH: MONUMENTAL LOSSES   341

town; it was only a stone's throw from St-Girons. St-Lizier retains large sections of her late antique walls, and has a splendid 12th–13th-century cloister and church, the apse of which was built in part with large antique blocks and frieze sections,[172] believed to originate as two defensive towers, with mediaeval courses on top.[173] The enceinte, with twelve towers, is considered one of the best-preserved in France.[174] Inside the 19th-century saw "les débris de tombeaux antiques, les ruines de temples de marbre, les restes de monuments."[175] This was naturally a site for the congressists to visit in 1884; the walls were mediaeval on top of Roman petit appareil,[176] and the town had plenty of other antiquities.[177]

Béziers

Béziers, in the Hérault, lost some of its Roman walls and citadel (itself built with spolia)[178] in 1632, although the site of the amphitheatre (with "débris informes et presque introuvables"),[179] still visible in 1841, contained a garden,[180] and was explored.[181] The walls' foundations, some of them visible from the public promenade, gave up antiquities throughout the century,[182] and so complete was the destruction (in spite of random discoveries of its alignment during the century)[183] that even the layout of the enceinte was uncertain by 1907,[184] and a plan of 1628 had to be consulted to trace them.[185] However, plenty of antiquities were uncovered from below ground.[186] Antiquities were plentiful in the surroundings, at Murviel, where in 1825 "on dirait que c'est une ville qui vient d'être renversée,"[187] and near Sète.[188] At Poussin, château and walls incorporated Roman material.[189] Not far away is Ensérune, discussed under Narbonne in Chapter Ten.

Perpignan[31]

Sited in the Pyrénées-Orientales, Perpignan was an important stronghold on the frontier with Aragon, and was annexed to France under Richelieu. In the mid-18th century one could tour the ramparts in a coach, and between them and the New Town "en a fait une esplanade capable de tenir cinq ou six mille hommes en bataille, & y à faire planter des allées d'arbres."[190] At the Congrès

---

31   Roux 1996, 46ff for the first late 12th century enceinte, then 64ff for the Mayorcan late
       13th century walls; figs 1–31 to the large quantity of land which was ploughed up for forti-
       fications over the centuries.

342   CHAPTER 11

Archéologique de France in 1868, Caumont argued for the then declassified walls to be left in place. The mayor offered to store recovered spolia, but space was wanting,[191] so the ramparts disappeared and, by 1914, "the well-built new quarters occupy the site of the old ramparts ... The old town consists of a labyrinth of narrow streets."[192] Nor was this the only destruction, for by 1835 the Génie had damaged the church of the Dominicans, and established its workshops there,[193] and continued the destruction two years later, selling off some of the arcades of the cloister.[194] The Génie also owned the monastery of the Cordeliers, and demolished its church in 1849 to extend the adjacent military hospital, with only one tombstone noticed, as an indication of how much of interest might have been destroyed.[195]

Fréjus – Cannes – Antibes – Villefranche

Several antique settlements spread east along the Côte d'Azur. After Actium, Augustus founded a colony of veterans at Fréjus, and established an important port.[196] Eventually it was given a large enceinte (of which the later town occupied only a section), and a wide range of public buildings,[32] including public baths abandoned by the end of the 3rd century (although part of an aqueduct was thought viable in the 18th century).[197] Just when the pagan monuments were degrading or were reused is difficult to determine,[33] although finds underline how rich was the town in sculpture.[34] The mediaeval and later town occupied only one-twelfth of the area of the ancient city,[198] and reused so many monuments that little survived by 1900.[35] Elements of the port were identifiable in the 18th century,[199] as was the paved road down to it.[200] Fragments remain today, but much was destroyed for local reuse in the 19th century, partly because of the dearth of suitable building stone in the surroundings,[201] some of the ruins obviously being reused in the buildings of the town.[202]

Drawings from 1808 show plenty of monuments standing tall.[203] The Roman walls were "assez bien conservés" in 1803 and still in 1829, with the modern town nestling in their western section,[204] and the 16th-century walls

---

32   Philip 2008, 14–23, with a maquette of the Roman port, and two photos of the enceinte;
      75–79 Les traces de la ville antique, with the Porte Dorée now an undecorated wreck;
      88–93: amphitheatre.

33   Carle 2011 ranges over Africa, the Orient, Egypt as well as Gaul.

34   Lemoine 2011 for the large numbers of statues and bas-reliefs reclaimed. 183 for find-
      sites – 246 in all. 188–190 for reuse.

35   Sautel & Imbert 1929, 18–27.

PROVENCE AND THE SOUTH: MONUMENTAL LOSSES 343

survived in parts into the 20th century.[205] Yet in 1804 the amphitheatre was a sump for stagnant water, and the port similarly "un marais infect"[206] – and "stagnant" was the epithet applied to the whole town in 1822.[207] In 1835 Mérimée described what he thought were some of the port dependencies,[208] of which the ruins were extensive.[209] In the mid-century, ruins lay all around, including a mistaken Golden Gate ("la porte Dorée" – really the Porte d'Orée, leading to the shore),[210] and already partly and pointlessly dismantled in 1744.[211] Texier had made a small (and official) dig in 1828, but the statue fragments he found in the baths were left uncared-for in a heap, open to the elements and surrounded by rubbish, in a corridor next to the town hall.

So why, by 1845, were there not visiting archaeologists to explore the remains of the town's marble pavements?[212] Until the Toulon-Nice railway arrived in 1861, there were no good roads to the town, which was more easily approachable from the sea, and then over tracks on mule-back. Thus Fréjus preserved some of the white and coloured marbles with which it has been decorated, "et les restes que l'on trouve dans la ville font partie des constructions modernes."[213] Luckily, the scholarly societies talked up the town and its monuments.[214] In 1864, Petit visited the site, using the Abbé Girardin's text of 1729 to help him – more than help, since much of his own text simply repeats the earlier one, perhaps an indication of how much less remained on the surface.[215] Sections of the walls survived, with modern structures "bâtis pauvrement sur l'ancien quartier romain."[216] This included housing in the amphitheatre, with cellars,[217] and no doubt much destruction of a "marble building" when foundations were dug for the hospital.[218] Yet in 1882 M. Aubenas, of the Société Archéologique de Fréjus, who found mosaics and other antiquities at the site,[219] thought much more needed to be done, in studying the important system of fortification, and the port.[220] Too late, as usual, thanks (again, as usual) to the arrival of the railway in 1861, when important inscriptions were broken up for building materials.[221] Fortunately, these had already been copied.[222] But this was not the only problem, since structures around the port were being plundered by this date,[223] and much material was needed for railway works.[224] The amphitheatre had largely been stripped of its marble at some earlier period, for Texier found a marble workshop within it.[225] By the 20th century, the main structure still lay under several metres of earth and débris.[226]

Further east along the Côte d'Azur are settlements few remember today as antique, but which were indeed of Roman origin. These were on or near the French frontier – Saint-Tropez, Cannes, Antibes, and Villefranche-sur-Mer (east of Nice).[227] At Vallauris, near Antibes (which itself had revealed many Roman remains),[228] "on se trouve tout-à-coup en présence de véritables fortifications écroulées: débris de colonnes, grandes pierres taillées, murs énormes, et alignements considérables de ruines,"[229] presumably all antique in date. There were Roman remains and discoveries all around the region (with a Roman theatre at Ventimiglia). The remains of an aqueduct feeding Nice survived, but her Roman walls did not, having been replaced in the Middle Ages; however, her citadel did contain several antique inscriptions, and was levelled in 1706.[230]

Military necessity and then tourism development made short shrift of such old remains. Digs at Saint-Tropez at various times uncovered columns, bronzes, sarcophagi and mosaics.[231] Antibes once had 350m length of Roman walls, with towers,[232] which yielded some inscriptions, and was still a first-class French Place de Guerre in 1869 (when the citadel of Saint-Tropez was only third class). The amphitheatre at Antibes went in 1691, to build an artillery park[233] and new walls,[234] although one of her two aqueducts, restored in 1786, survived,[235] plus a distribution point.[236] Cisterns, and gates and towers of the ramparts, together with the remains of the amphitheatre, were drawn in 1808,[237] and many of these relicts were admired by the Congrès Scientifique de France, when its members visited in 1878.[238] Much of the theatre might have gone into the new town walls, begun in 1691.[239] It was because they were made from Roman spolia (some bearing inscriptions) that these were so strong.[240] When they came down at the end of the century, walls which had been "le boulevard de la France jusqu'à l'annexion du comté de Nice" (this occured in 1860) now gave way to broad streets and hotels.[241] The scholars naturally deplored that this was often done with dynamite, thereby obliterating any inscribed or sculpted blocks,[242] or with other unspecified "engins violents."[243] The Génie also got into the act, with Vauban starting the expropriations; the Army placed their arsenal in the old Couvent des Cordeliers, and the caserne Clerici, before the Revolution, was the Bernadine Couvent S. Joseph.[36] But most people were looking forward to a new era of prosperity, already in progress elsewhere on the Riviera.[244]

---

36   Froissard 2002, 35–6 for Vauban and the servitudes he created. From 1860 no longer a ville frontière; déclassement is 1872, but the necessary law appears only in 1889 for le dérasement de toutes les vieilleries désormais inutiles. Inevitably, the town was broke, so an entrepreneur did the work.

Orange

Annexed to France only with the Peace of Utrecht in 1713, this important Roman colony (Vaucluse) had a large early enceinte,[245] still traceable in parts in the early 19th century, but no late walls with spolia. The theatre appears to have been in use to the end of the 4th century, just like its amphitheatre, and also the circus at Arles and the theatre at Aix.[37] In 1807 Auguste Caristie, who was to restore the Orange Arch, reported it as being mired in débris from the 13th century,[246] when the Princes of Orange made it their fortress, and covered some of the bas-reliefs with plaster.[247] It was these defensive works established around the arch[248] that Caristie had to remove before he could start work. On one of the trophies could be read the word MARIO, adding incorrectly to the structure's fame.[249] (Such adventurious etymology was common.)[250] But much of the sculpture had been removed or was badly deteriorated, due to the poor quality of the stone. Artaud formed a collection of antiquities here, and the town took charge of it in 1838 but, apart from some which went to Lyon (where he was curator), the exhibits seem to have vanished.[38]

The post-mediaeval town was built on and near the gymnasium, and "On ne peut marcher ici sans fouler aux pieds quelque chose qui ait appartenu aux Romains" – witness mosaic floors to be seen in basements, for later detritus meant that the ancient town lay metres below the present one.[251] As was often the case here, the mosaics did not survive.[252] Supposedly the gymnasium (sometimes considered to have been a circus) was demolished only in 1621, by Maurice de Nassau for materials for his fortress on the hill.[253] But this did not last long, itself being demolished in 1673, because it was considered by Louis XIV "une menace pour la tranquillité du Midi," for which reason he had fortified Marseille.[254] However, fragments of its granite columns were still strewn all around town in 1815.[255] The circus was indeed much stronger than the defences built around the Arch in the 13th century,[256] but presumably too large to be fortified. Gasparin claimed with some fanfare in 1810 to have (re-)discovered the circus,[257] but a "circus" was noted in the mid-18th century: this was possibly a reference to the theatre,[258] to part of which the circus was apparently attached.[259]

By the 19th century the theatre was in a poor state, devoid of its marble except for fragments too difficult to extract from the scenae frons.[260] It sheltered the town prison, and several shops,[261] as well as hovels and what had

---

37   Esmonde Cleary 2013, 118.
38   Bruyère & Lavagne 1992. With Héron de Villefosse (writing in 1905), the authors deplore the lack of a museum at Orange: one was created only in 1928.

346   CHAPTER 11

once been the armoried houses of the gentry.[262] It was, nevertheless, declared in 1846 to be "le seul théâtre romain, assure-t-on, dont la France ait gardé des ruines appréciables"[263] – a reflection of just how much has been destroyed in a land once rich in Roman monuments. Because of such depradations, it was theatre and circus which "ont fourni la plus grande partie des matériaux de la ville moderne, qui paraît à peine garder le souvenir de sa grandeur passée."[264]

Orange had no museum even by the beginning of the 20th century, and most of her antiquities had been "expatriées ou perdues,"[265] with inscriptions degraded because they were on poor stone, or taken for building if they were of good stone.[266] A few antique fragments were housed in the theatre;[267] they had been there since the 1830s,[268] and were piled up higgledy-piggledy. Héron de Villefosse railed in 1905 against such poor treatment of some interesting pieces,[269] noting that the local administration seemed indifferent to Orange's past. He claimed that objects unearthed got channeled through the hands of dealers when they should go to a local museum.[270] This was a common call from scholars.[271] Over a century earlier, Quatremère de Quincy had suggested that Arles and Orange should be dug, and the finds placed in some local monument. Nothing happened, any more than did his 1817 prompting the Académie des Inscriptions to take over Grivaud de la Vincelle's *Recueil des Monuments antiques de l'Ancienne Gaule* (2 vols, Paris 1817).[272]

Near to the town is the necropolis of Fourches-Vieilles, the recent study of which demonstrates just how thorough some dismantling of monuments could be. First the metal was taken, then stone blocks, and finally even the rubble and mortar from the walls of the various monuments.[39]

Vaison-la-Romaine[40]

Due to the uncertainties of the times, mediaeval Vaison (Vaucluse) was clustered on the opposite side of the river Ouvèze, on the precipitous hill overlooking the Roman site, where it could be protected by the castle. The Roman site was effectively abandoned until the 19th century: a cadastre dated 1821 in the Archives Municipales shows the Haute Ville still very populous, and the rest circumscribed to the West by the Chemin des Dominicains, and stretching as far as the Place du Marché to the NE. The old Cathedral is completely off the sheet, although the cadastre of 1826 shows the area, which is known

---

39   Mignon 2008.

40   Bezin 1999 for a pictorial survey with reconstructions; 81: chevet of the Cathedral, perhaps 6th century, with ancient column drums as foundations.

as La Grande Eglise; between it and the Chemin des Dominicains is an area containing a group of buildings called La Villasse. Antiquities abounded, with inscriptions in modern walls, and tombstones as thresholds,[273] plus cadastre markings on marble blocks, and a pavement in opus sectile.[41]

We know almost nothing about Vaison in the Middle Ages, for the subject has not been studied: and the Abbé Sautel, the hero of the Roman excavations, never bothered to record the mediaeval layers when he dug down to the Roman levels. However, the availability of antique architectural and decorative members to the mediaeval centuries is not in doubt here, for they were used both as straightforward building spolia, and for close imitation. Near the Cathedral, for example, antique marble and stone are in re-use for wall-building, just as column shafts, capitals and bases are used in the foundations of the Cathedral itself. And the Chapel of Saint Quentin, although clearly Romanesque of the later twelfth century, has a very antiquarian east end.[42]

Antique statues and funerary spolia were also in evidence (including a Diadoumenos secured for the British Museum). On 5 December 1638, the Town Council authorised the Bishop to remove the statue of Saint Neble (presumably some altered pagan statue) from the city gate, replacing it with a statue of the Virgin Mary.[274] The Bishop was Josph-Marie de Suarez (appointed 1633), and he collected some of the riches of the city:

> La quantité de monuments antiques dont on voit de précieux restes, plusiers inscriptions et une infinité de statues... Les derniers évêques ont fait transporter dans leur palais épiscopal quelques cippes et quelques pierres de marbre... un plus grand nombre fut transporté à Rome dans le palais Barberini, par ordre de l'évêque J-M de Suarès.[275]

Neither the council minutes nor Fornery, the author of the *Histoire du Comté Venaissin*, says why this was done, but two conflicting clues come from other minutes. On 16 August 1605, the Bishop had a marble statue removed from the Queiras Quarter, where it was giving rise to superstitious practices, and had it placed near to the cross by the access to the Roman bridge; a stone head was added – presumably thereby converting it from a pagan into a saint.[276] But on 15 July 1756, we find the Town Council objecting to a local landowner, Dominique Siffrein Audibert, who attempted to enfief an area including Notre Dame de Nazareth, because it was 14 centuries old, worthy of

---

41   Goudineau & Kisch 1991, 36, 68; a good survey, but little on the history of the excavations; Goudineau 2007, 21–25.

42   Dumoulin 1980, 58ff., 65ff.

348   CHAPTER 11

respect, and possibly founded on a pagan temple.[277] Here, therefore, we find
the Council objecting to a private individual taking over the Chapel of Saint
Quentin, because it was worthy of town honour and protection on account of
its great age.

Such interest in antiquities may have been first stimulated by Bishop
Suarez, perhaps the first to gather suitable material into his Palace. Other cler-
ics followed, such as the Abbé Saint-Véran who, in the 1770s or 1780s, noted the
existence of underground channels, lead pipes, and antique houses, painted in
fresco and decorated with columns and mosaics.[278] As Louis Anselme Boyer
had written in 1731,[279] the site was very rich in antiquities, and statues were
found which the ignorant regarded as saints:

> parmi ces anciens monuments, on a trouvé des colonnes d'une grosseur
> extraordinaire, des grands Simulachres ou Dieux des Gentils, ou peut-
> être des statues de ces hommes puissants, et fameux dans l'Antiquité que
> les Chrétiens ignorants prenoient même de nos jours pour des figures
> de quelques Saints, trompez par une certaine forme d'habit majestueux
> que l'habile main des Sculpteurs leur avoit fait, mais qui n'était pas ni du
> siècles passé, ni du présent.

In this telling the Bishop,

> aussi sçavant dans la science des Saints que de l'Antiquité profane,
> connoissant par cette forme d'habit ce qu'étoient véritablement ces sta-
> tues, les fit transporter dans son Palais Episcopal, afin dôter au peuple
> grossier toute occasion d'erreur, et d'Idolatrie.

Note that Suarez (saving the plebs from error) did not have the works destroyed,
any more than did Bishop Henry of Winchester in the 12th century, who used
exactly the same excuse for taking statues from Rome to England.

Conclusion

More antiquities survive in Provence than in the rest of France, but this is due
to the relative economic backwardness of the region in the 19th century, in
contrast to the modernising developments further north. These proceeded
outwards from Paris, and involved much destruction, as we have seen in previous chapters. Down the Rhône, it was the railway which brought modern life,
and nearly lost Avignon all of her splendid mediaeval walls. In the south east,

PROVENCE AND THE SOUTH: MONUMENTAL LOSSES

now called the Riviera, fortresses and antiquities also fell. But it was also the railway which opened up the region, taking materials from Fréjus, and turning a wild and hilly countryside from a set of Roman settlements with later frontier forts into a tourists' playground. Modernity embraced tourism which, as we have seen, is a natural extension of railways; and, in the inevitable irony, such development destroyed monuments which might have further deepened the enjoyment of tourists, so that any questionnaire in Avignon or on the Côte d'Azur today would reveal that the majority do not know what is missing. To remind them what survives, Vaison changed its name to Vaison-la-Romaine early in the 20th century.

[1] Barbier_1855_90
[2] BMA_MS_746_55ff.
[3] BMA_MS_166_ 65–88
[4] SHD_Génie_Art.8_PA_ Arles
[5] Lenthéric_1878_223
[6] Woods_1828_157
[7] Lalauzière_1808_29
[8] Estrangin_1838_106
[9] Veran_BMA_MS_722
[10] Estrangin_1838_114
[11] BA_Comité_1885_95
[12] Millin_III_1808_480
[13] Millin_III_1808_558–583
[14] Thicknesse_1789_26
[15] Bull_Archéol_ Arles_1889_VI_81–83
[16] Veran_BMA_MS_767_4–7
[17] Viollet-le-Duc_I_1876_314
[18] Peyre_1910_75–76
[19] Clair_1837_90–91
[20] Guilbert_I_1844_581
[21] MSRAF_XIII_1837_1–47
[22] Lalauzière_1808_40
[23] Clair_1837_84
[24] Perrot_1840_31
[25] Millin_III_1808_620–621

[26] Millin_IV_1811_130–131
[27] Clair_1837_72
[28] Estrangin_1838_25
[29] BMA_MS_734
[30] BMA_MS_1443
[31] Lantelme_de_Romieu_ 1574_fols_5v_38vff.
[32] Espérandieu_I_1907_ 198
[33] Espérandieu_I_1907_ 138–40
[34] BMA_MS_217_anno_ 1561
[35] Estrangin_1838_74
[36] Millin_III_1808_615–616
[37] Lenthéric_1878_224
[38] Séguin_1687_41ff.
[39] Lenthéric_1878_241
[40] BM_Arles_MS_240_ fol. 3r
[41] Fabre_I_1833_176
[42] Sommerard_1876_40
[43] Millin_III_1808_617
[44] Estrangin_1838_10–11
[45] Perrot_1840_250
[46] MSRAF_VII_1826_LIII– LIV
[47] Estrangin_1838_12–13
[48] Estrangin_1838_46
[49] Penchaud_1826_225–226

[50] MDANE_III_1837_49
[51] Mérimée_1843_7–8
[52] Sommerard_1876_345
[53] Caumont_III_1838_ 416–417
[54] Séguin_1687_35
[55] Clair_1837_40–41
[56] Séguin_1687_35
[57] Séguin_1687_Part_2_ 35f.
[58] Séguin_1687_Part_2_ 1ff.
[59] Woods_1828_158
[60] Estrangin_1838_78–79
[61] BM_XII_1846_63
[62] RA_XXXIII_1877_393
[63] BM_XIII_1847_125
[64] SG_XXXIII_Senlis_ 1866_232
[65] AA_XI_1851_32
[66] AA_XI_1851_186
[67] Rance_1890_253
[68] Lantelme_de_Romieu_ 1574_fol_7v
[69] Séguin_1687_Part_2_38f.
[70] AM_Arles_FF156_ inquest_1268
[71] MSA_Ouest_XIII_1891_ 47
[72] Ménard_1750–58_VII_ 429ff

[73] Devic_&_Vaissete_XV_1892_599.156

[74] Lantelme_de_Romieu_1574_fol_3

[75] Lantelme_de_Romieu_1574_fol_6

[76] Séguin_1687_49ff.

[77] Estrangin_1838_83

[78] Lantelme_de_Romieu_1574_fol_4r

[79] Séguin_1687_37ff.

[80] Espérandieu_I_1907_no_206

[81] Lantelme_de_Romieu_1574_fol_3v

[82] Mérimée_1835_417

[83] Lantelme_de_Romieu_1574_fol_5r

[84] Du Bellay 1558

[85] Lantelme_de_Romieu_1574_Preface

[86] Lantelme_de_Romieu_1574_fol_3r

[87] Lantelme_de_Romieu_1574_fols_34v_38v

[88] Dumont_1789_51

[89] Arles_AC_BB47_1731–35

[90] Lantelme_de_Romieu_1574_fol_4r

[91] Garcin_I_1835_459

[92] Lantelme_de_Romieu_1574_fol_4

[93] Espérandieu_I_1907_no._167

[94] Espérandieu_I_1907_no_184

[95] Dumont_1789_19.

[96] Rance_1890_358

[97] Espérandieu_I_1907_114

[98] Pinkney_1809_278

[99] Rouard_1841_7

[100] Rouard_1841_9

[101] APC_VII_1874_289–290

[102] Recueil_Mémoires_Aix_I_1819_204

[103] Recueil_Mémoires_Aix_1819_194–211

[104] Mém_Acad_Aix_VI_1845_367–368

[105] SG_XXXIII_Senlis_1866_263

[106] Mém_AIBL_IX_1831_94–95

[107] Achard_1787_41–43

[108] Garcin_I_1835_26–27

[109] Achard_1787_157

[110] Garcin_I_1835_27

[111] Rouard_1841_6

[112] Garcin_I_1835_20

[113] Mérimée_1835_132–133

[114] Thicknesse_1789_58

[115] Pinkney_1814_442

[116] Hughes_1822_136

[117] Rastou_de_Mongeot_1836_150–151

[118] Frossard_1854_129

[119] Frossard_1834_4

[120] Loudon_1842_454–455

[121] AA_IV_1846_56

[122] AA_IV_1846_56–57

[123] SG_XXII_Châlons-sur-Marne_1855_433

[124] BSA_Orléanais_III_1859–1861_134

[125] Hughes_1822_145

[126] BM_XIII_1847_581

[127] Montalembert_1839_16–17

[128] SG_XLII_Châlons-sur-Marne_1855_500–501

[129] Sommerand_1876_242

[130] Sommerard_1876_226–241

[131] Sommerand_1876_240

[132] CHA_1902_153B

[133] SG_LXIV_Nîmes_1897_114

[134] AMPF_X_1896_166–167

[135] SG_XLIX_Avignon_1882_62

[136] Annales_Midi_II_1890_470–471

[137] Corresp_Hist_Archéol_I_1894_299

[138] AMPF_IX_1895_304

[139] Corresp_Hist_Archéol_III_1896_216

[140] Corresp_Hist_Archéol_III_1896_216–217

[141] Brown_1905_33

[142] CHA_VIII_1901_211

[143] AMPF_XV_1901_113–115

[144] CHA_1902_153

[145] Baedeker_1914_504

[146] Merson_1865_44–45

[147] BM_XXII_1856_587

[148] BM_XXII_1856_572–589

[149] AD_Gascogne_1903_201

[150] Piganiol_VII_1754_312

[151] Clément_V_1868_111

[152] BM_XXXIV_1868_475–476

[153] Guilbert_II_1845_477

[154] BM_XXII_1856_212–225

[155] Greppo_1846_97

[156] BM_XXII_1856_584–585

[157] BM_XXII_1856_213

[158] BM_XXII_1856_588

[159] CS_France_XXVI_1859_Limoges_431–2

[160] Revue_Aquitaine_III_1859_238–239

[161] BCHA_Auch_III_1862_491–503

[162] Revue_Aquitaine_III_1859_351

[163] Revue_Aquitaine_III_1859_93

[164] BM_XXVI_1860_454–455

[165] Merson_1865_43

PROVENCE AND THE SOUTH: MONUMENTAL LOSSES

[166] BM_XXXIV_1868_474–475
[167] BM_XXXV_1869_216
[168] SG_LV_Dax_1888_181
[169] Société_Borda_Dax_XVI_1891_LXXXVII
[170] Société_Borda_Dax_XVI_1891_233
[171] Société_Borda_Dax_XX_1895_140
[172] BA_Comité_1896_460
[173] BSA_Midi 1889, 86
[174] Revue_Comminges_IX_1894_195–193
[175] Malte-Brun_I_1881_20
[176] SG_LI_Pamiers_1884_171
[177] BCA_Narbonne_1896_115–130
[178] BSA_Béziers_II_1837_187–188
[179] Hugo_II_1835_77
[180] BSA_Béziers_IV_1841_143
[181] BSA_Béziers_IV_1841_83
[182] BSHA_Philologie_XIII_1829_52–53
[183] Bonnet_1905_170–171
[184] Blanchet_1907_205
[185] Bonnet_1905_171–172
[186] Vilback_1825_335–336
[187] Vilback_1825_591
[188] Vilback_1825_599
[189] Mérimée_1835_388
[190] Piganiol_XIII_1754_310
[191] BM_XXXIV_1868_914–91
[192] Baedeker_1914_188
[193] Mérimée_1835_406
[194] BA_Comité_1892_614
[195] BCH_Jan_1849_120
[196] Mém_AIBL_II_1849_169–277
[197] Petit_1864_575
[198] SG_L_Caen_1883_18

[199] Acad_Delphinale_1868_389
[200] Maffei_1734_172
[201] Mém_AIBL_II_1849_253
[202] Héron_de_Villefosse_&_Thédenat_1884_17–18
[203] Millin_III_1808_30–31
[204] Aubenas_1881_387
[205] Dunlop-Wallace-Goodbody_1904_298
[206] Recueil_Tvx_Soc_Agri_Agen_I_1804_96
[207] Hughes_1822_259–260
[208] Mérimée_1835_253
[209] Perrot_1840_178
[210] Guilbert_I_1844_650–651
[211] Dunlop-Wallace-Goodbody_1904_188
[212] BM_XI_1845_527
[213] Mém_AIBL II_1849_181–182
[214] BM_XIX_1853_489
[215] Petit_1864_570
[216] Petit_1864_702
[217] SG_XXXIII_Senlis_1867_280
[218] Mém_AIBL_II_1849_257
[219] Aubenas_1881_481–482
[220] BA_Comité_1882_156
[221] Gentleman's_Mag_CCXCVII_1904_189
[222] Héron_de_Villefosse_&_Thédenat_1884_35
[223] Aubenas_1881_499–500
[224] Aubenas_1881_629–630
[225] Dunlop-Wallace-Goodbody_1904_186
[226] Dunlop-Wallace-Goodbody_1904_183
[227] De_Bourcet_1801_7
[228] Garcin_I_1835_49–50

[229] Thierry_de_Ville_d'Avray_1909_12
[230] ASL_Alpes-Maritimes_XX_1907_134
[231] Guilbert_1844_I_652
[232] Thierry_de_Ville-d'Avray_1909_84–85
[233] Thierry_de_Ville_d'Avray_1909_201
[234] Guilbert_1844_656
[235] BSA_Midi_IV_1841_396
[236] ASL_Alpes-Maritimes_v_1878_205
[237] Millin_III_1808_30–31
[238] RA_XXXV_1878_196
[239] ASL_Alpes-Maritimes_v_1878_204
[240] SG_L_Caen_1883_24–25
[241] AD_Provence_Maritime_1898_215
[242] BA_Comité_1897_LIV
[243] SG_LXIV_Nîmes_1897_40
[244] AD_Provence_Maritime_1898_315
[245] Guilbert_IV_1845_102
[246] Mém_Acad_Nîmes_XX_1897_24
[247] Frossard_1854_156
[248] Mérimée_1835_170
[249] Nouv_Coll_Mém_Histoire_France_XI_311
[250] Lantelme_de_Romieu_1574_fol_8r
[251] Pigault-Lebrun_&_Augier_1827_38–39
[252] Gasparin_1815_121–122
[253] SG_XLIX_1882_Avignon_598–621
[254] Michel_1879_45
[255] Gasparin_1815_124–125
[256] Malte-Brun_v_1884_26
[257] Tvx_Acad_Gard_1811_166

[258] Piganiol_IV_1753_394

[259] SG_XXII_1855_Châlons-sur-Marne_413

[260] Gasparin_1815_81–82

[261] Woods_1828_146

[262] Gasparin_1815_76

[263] Tastu_1846_115

[264] Lenthéric_1878_246–247

[265] Espérandieu_I_1907_182

[266] Gasparin_1815_126

[267] Baedeker_1914_500

[268] BM_I_1834_220

[269] BSN_Antiq_France_1905_295

[270] BSN_Antiq_France_1905_295–296

[271] BSA_Drôme_VII_1873_350

[272] Schneider_1910_237–238

[273] Mérimée_1835_174

[274] Vaison_AM_Register_BB20

[275] Fornery_III_nd_589

[276] Vaison_AM_Register_BB14

[277] Vaison_AM_BB29_fols_697v–698v

[278] Carpentras_BM_MS_1721_104–106

[279] Boyer_1731_3

Conclusion: Heritage? What Heritage?
The Transformation of Townscape and Landscape

> Les monuments anciens sont pour les pays ce que sont les ossemans des aieux pour les individus; aussi c'est un précieux devoir pour toute contrée, d'honorer les ruines et de préserver de dégradation les moindres édifices, auxquelles se rattachent des souvenirs historiques ou qui ont été consacrés par la vénération des siècles.[1] [1813]

This book has studied nineteenth-century French attitudes toward its past, detailing a chronicle of destruction and of largely ineffectual attempts to salvage at least some vestiges of their heritage. The survivals are sparse because of the lure of modernization, the juggernaut of the centralized State, and the usually spurious demands of national defence, executed thanks to the destructive energy of the French army engineering corps. If scholars fought and wrote passionately to try and salvage monuments, general indifference to the past was widespread, allowing the local pressures of mayors and contractors to expand and "improve" their towns. Over the long term, scholars and archeologists placed objects in museums to "save" them, but the separation of artefacts from their sites usually doomed the latter to neglect or redevelopment. There is both irony and contradiction in the dismal fact that attempts to save France's archeological heritage by housing it in museums thereby condemned so many sites to obliteration and redevelopment. Thus well-meaning solicitude sometimes proved to be almost as destructive as the vandalism of builders and military engineers.

We may sometimes picture France as an efficient state governed from Paris, with the provinces all dancing to the same tune, but this was far from the case in the 19th century, because of communication problems and the inevitable campanilismo. As the Chinese proverb has it, "The mountains are high and the emperor far away." And if the protection of monuments and the establishment of museums increased as communications improved throughout the country, few heeded the homily of Veran, cited above. It was the remoteness of town councils from the policy-forming, questionnaire-issuing centre of Paris which rendered easy and without retribution the destruction of France's heritage on an enormous scale. Regional learned societies hoped they had influence, but their concern for the past was shared by few others. The detailed accounts throughout this book offer an essential antidote to the official narrative, which proclaims that France generally treasured and conserved her important

© KONINKLIJKE BRILL NV, LEIDEN, 2015 | DOI 10.1163/9789004293717_014

monuments. The Wars of Religion and the Revolution often appear as an alibi or excuse for whatever was lost, yet the destruction they wrought was minor in comparison with later losses.

19th-century France did not always treasure surviving monuments – but why not? There are several answers. Central authority did not know exactly what monuments France possessed, and even when protection was desirable was in any case leery of encroaching on the touchy question of private ownership. Attempts to discover just what was out there were weakened by psephological puerility, and the inability of most administrators central and local to grasp the extent of the cataloguing problem (a moving target), let alone to conceive of who could possibly answer the quirkish questions posed in floods of questionnaires.

We might even surmise that, as France became more democratic, it became less interested in its past as opposed to its future. With such debates over modernity, the preservationists would nearly always be on the losing side, and their movement was largely ineffective in deflecting the new modernist orientation to the future. The unsatisfactory results of "preservationism" underline that, centralised bureaucracy though France might be, nobody seemed to believe that the various questionnaires issued from Paris should be answered by people known to be qualified and directed from the centre of government. And who might these be? Certainly, the few inspectors of monuments. But then? The proceedings of local societies contain much information about the work to be done; but there was apparently no official attempt to place all the work of cataloguing in the hands of such qualified people, even though they evidently combined organisation, knowledge and publishing ability, and their publications were sometimes accompanied by illustrations (engravings, lithographs, photographs, maps).

One index of the uncertain nature of cataloguing, documentation and conservation was the lack of any nation-wide plan for what to do with conserved monuments and, especially, extensive sites. Bylaws stipulating what towns and railway companies should do when they came across antiquities simply did not exist (although they did in Asia Minor during the same period). There was no planning for discoveries, and no uniform policy for the establishment of museums to hold finds, this being left to local initiatives. In other words, the concept of national heritage, while enunciated here and there by local societies, and echoed by authorities, did not occasion a national policy (or funding) for such protective institutions, let alone any clearly defined steps to be taken from discovery to protection of monuments and their antiquities.

The thirst for modernity was, as we have seen, part of the problem, because to most people the new was more attractive than the old. But the benefits of

CONCLUSION: HERITAGE? WHAT HERITAGE? 355

modernity (road and rail, new building types, the periodical press) could all have been invoked to plan for the retention of some monuments and provide for the means to visit them. Certainly, this was the point of the lists of protected historic monuments; but how many monuments were destroyed by the push for modernity without ever having a chance to get included in such a list? A great many, as the above pages make clear. The problem was perennial, Lafont complaining from Narbonne in the 18th century that he included in his writing antiquities "qu'on ne trouve plus à Narbonne, que nos anciens antiquaires avaient autrefois recueillis, qui ont péry par l'injure du temps et le marteau, ou qui ont été données, vendues et transférées ailleurs."[2] Destruction continued into the 20th century, with autoroutes now a force for vandalism.[1] Recent decades have seen attempts to redress such destruction, by studying how remaining fortifications (among other survivals) can be preserved and integrated into modern life.[2] But too late! Towns negligent of their antiquities (such as Orange and Avignon) spent considerable energy attracting tourists (via the railway, of course) to come and admire whatever relicts their improvidence had allowed to survive.

The general conclusion is inevitably that down the centuries neither the governors nor the governed, preferring to be up-to-date with the advantages that conferred, were much interested in the monuments of the past, at least not enough to protect many of them. The public recognised the disadvantages of old structures and the all-mod-cons aspect of new ones, some of which proclaimed the convenience of modernity: railway stations, banks, theatres, and various public utility structures. As a result many old buildings suffered from neglect benign or malign, sometimes being whittled away to serve as materials for new building projects. In spite of the warnings and outrage of the scholars in those supposedly enlightened days, little changed during the 19th century, with the greatest number of destroyed monuments to its debit. The restoration movement, certainly a reaction to monumental decay and neglect, was the result of a targeted interest in the past informed by over-confident architects wishing to re-make buildings which had never existed but which, like Turner's imaginary sunset, should have done. Arguably, this dealt almost as much

---

1 Demoule & Stiegler 2008, 223–45: L'archéologie de la France: un refoulement national? See 227: Comme on le sait, tout le réseau autoroutier construit jusqu'au milieu des années 1980 n'a été précédé d'aucune fouille préventive.

2 Polonovski 1995, with discussions revealing the same restoration/preservation/cost dilemmas as the 19th century; Fouret 2007.

destruction to an accurate representation of the past as civic indifference and barbarian entrepreneurs did to the fabric of so many towns and their environs.[3]

The contribution of the Génie to the destruction of old France was substantial. This unforgiving force with a government remit was detested by many citizens, because they had force majeure arguments with which to demolish houses and even burn crops. It was an irony that their main duty was to achieve the means to defend the land of France – but could apparently only do so by degrading or demolishing so many of her treasures.

Today's force majeure comes from cars, roads and urban transport, and a large book is waiting to be written on underground carparks as a trigger for urban archaeology, plus new roads and motorways for discoveries in the countryside. This is the ironical mirror-image of the change to 19th century towns, more interesting because foundations go deeper, and of course are more destructive. Rescue archaeology is a potent PC shibboleth, but it tends to record rather than save what it finds. As for how 19th-century attitudes to the past might have affected the course of French archaeology in the following century, this is not the place for such an inquiry, although scholars from other countries may sometimes be critical.[3]

Certainly, some of the authors discussed above, and writing for the various scholarly societies, took liberties with the evidence, and let imagination, their reading and sometimes national pride overtake mature judgment. But then, they probably had not read the warning in an 17th-century manuscript:

> On ne doit écrire qu'en maître,
> Il en coûte trop au bonheur;
> Le titre trop cher d'autheur
> Ne vaud pas la peine de l'être.[4]

---

3 Cf. Marxist critiques of environmental movements as essentially by-products of the very capitalist forces they ostensibly seek to critique if not turn back. A necessary antithesis?

[1] BMA_MS_243_frotispiece   [3] Murray 2001, 522–535   [4] Carpentras_BM_MS_1721_
[2] Lafont_1739_avis   fol.169

Appendix
Questionnaires, Laws and Circulars

What was the point of the many archaeo-historical questionnaires sent out in the 19th century, and where is it stated? Of course, in general terms, central government (or a particular département) was trying to gather information but, as will be clear from the excerpts below, they were framed by different people with differing knowledge and interests, let alone estimates of what was necessary or even feasible in the time allowed. There is frequent duplication, lack of precision or clarity, with the later questionnaires sometimes trying to rectify such mistakes in the earlier ones. Many of them ask for judgment, but there seems little evidence that the framers knew of who might be competent to provide judicious and knowledgeable replies. Why were the interrogators apparently fixated on stories and legends? Answer: because the various congresses seem to have been as well.[1] As we know in our psephology-conscious times, the nature of the answer depends in various ways on the complexion of the question. What follows offers only one side of the question: a good PhD topic would be an examination of returns, and any action provoked by those which escaped the circular filing cabinet. As for laws, only a few excerpts are included below, to highlight the business of questionnaires.[1] But it was clear to many (and has been pointed out repeatedly throughout this book) that laws were necessary, just as they were found to be in the British Isles.[2]

Instructions were sometimes provided, for example by Mérimée/Lenoir/Lenormant for the 1839 *Instructions sur l'architecture gallo-romaine*,[2] or by Prosper Mérimée, Alexandre Lenoir & August Leprévost for the 1839–43 *Architecture du Moyen Âge*.[3] A classic of interrogatory grandeur is provided by Paul-Arthur Nouail de la Villegille's 1853 *Instructions sur l'archéologie*, this section's task being defined as

> de rechercher et de proposer la publication des documents inédits relatifs à l'histoire des arts de la France; d'inventorier les monuments religieux, militaires ou civils; de conserver, pour les temps à venir, au moyen du dessin ou de la gravure, les œuvres remarquables d'architecture, de peinture, de sculpture en pierre, en marbre et en bois; de préparer, enfin, les matériaux d'une histoire complète de l'art en France.[4]

---

1 Andrieux 1997, 239–243, Chronologie des principaux textes sur les monuments historiques et naturels en France – 1887–1997 laws.

2 Boulting 1976 for conservationist legislation across the Channel.

© KONINKLIJKE BRILL NV, LEIDEN, 2015 | DOI 10.1163/9789004293717_015

358 APPENDIX

This task would suit a well-staffed and well-funded university department today as a twenty-year project.

In what follows, a few of many phrases have been *emboldened* to highlight just how vague, sweeping, or even impossible to answer are some of the questions in these modern versions of something like the Domesday Book. Setting bad questionnaires is easy; answering them in any coherent fashion would have been from difficult to impossible, especially since the answering was apparently unfunded. Where were the staff and/or expertise to be found to complete such tasks? How many of the questions had been satisfactorily answered even a century after they were posed? Many of the questions call for judgment, asking respondants to make an assessment of age, state of repair (relative to other monuments), urgency of need for repair, or interest. Other call simply for details of all monuments, so that a form of stamp-collecting replaces any exercise of judgment. And would respondants in one département have similar judgment to those in another? Of course not. Tinkering with the questions from circular to circular emphasises cumulative echoes and reworkings of existing questions. Also included are a few extracts from local societies to show how circulars were received and commented.[3]

1810

Charmes_1886. See I_CXXI: Dès le mois de mai 1810, le Ministre de l'intérieur, comte de Montalivet, posait cette question aux préfets, dans une circulaire que nous croyons devoir reproduire.

Anciens Monumens. / Paris, 10 mai 1810. / Le Ministre de l'Intérieur [comte de Montalivet] aux Préfets.

J'ai besoin de renseignemens exacts sur les monumens français et principalement sur les anciens châteaux qui ont existé et qui existent encore dans votre département: ces renseignemens seront déposés au bureau de la statistique, où ils pourront être consultés, au besoin. / Je vous invite donc à vouloir bien m'adresser tous ceux qu'il vous sera possible de rassembler. Les questions suivantes vous feront connoître les objets sur lesquels vos recherches doivent porter plus particulièrement: / Quels sont les châteaux intéressans, soit par des faits historiques ou des traditions populaires, soit

---

3 Bercé 1979, 401–423 for Les enquêtes de 1810 à 1840, i.e. the antecedants of the Commission, with some of the departmental responses in various archives, and in those of the Monuments Historiques, des copies anciennes de ces réponses, parfois disparus ultérieurement (401). These are noted only in outline, without any indication of their length. Mayer 1980 for an indication of the sheer quantities of information later requested, in this case for Basse Normandie.

APPENDIX

par la forme de leur architecture? en quel état se trouvent-ils? dans quelles communes sont-ils situés? / Quelles sont les anciennes abbayes qui existent encore dans le département? où sont-elles situées? dans quel état sont-elles? à quoi servent-elles maintenant? / Que sont devenus, où ont été transportés les différens tombeaux, ornemens ou débris curieux qui existoient, au moment de la Révolution, dans chacun des châteaux ou abbayes?

Est-il quelque personne dans le département avec laquelle on puisse correspondre sur ces différens objets? / Il faudroit que les réponses à chacune de ces questions fussent assez détaillées pour qu'on eût une idée de l'intérêt que chacun des lieux peut présenter par son origine, par son importance dans l'histoire, ou par l'époque de l'art qu'il retrace. / Cette circulaire présente d'autant plus d'intérêt qu'on y voit déjà se dessiner le cadre d'une organisation de recherches scientifiques semblable à celle que Moreau avait conçue et que M. Guizot devait créer plus tard.

1819

Mém_Institut_VII_1824_8–10 Circular 18, 8 April 1819, stating that "La France avait pu être considérée autrefois comme le pays le plus riche en monuments de tous les âges" – the "autrefois" presumably pointing to the Revolution as the alibi for the present state of the monuments. A four-page list of questions was now provided:
Rechercher et décrire dans chaque département:

1   Tous les monuments en pierres...connus du vulgaire...sous les noms de pierres aux fées, de pierres levées, etc;
2   Tumuli...
3   Les vestiges de toutes les routes anciennes ou du Moyen Âge, soit même des routes moins anciennes qui auraient été depuis longtemps;
4   Toutes les bornes milliaires antiques qui existent encore ou qui ont été trouvées autrefois (again the "autrefois" alibi);
5   Tous les monumens, édifices, colonnes, fondations, murs de villes...Dans les murs qui passent pour être de construction romaine, examiner attentivement s'ils ne sont pas fondés sur des substructions plus anciennes, gauloises peut-être, ou grecques dans les villes du midi (and give details of changes of line, especially pre-10th century);
6   Indiquer exactement tous les emplacemens où l'on a trouvé, à différentes époques, des *antiquités quelconques, et la nature de ces antiquités*;
7   Roman Inscriptions (with instructions for making facsimiles);
8   Châteaux;
9   Abbayes;

360 APPENDIX

10 Later Inscriptions;

11 Toponymic indicators of antiquities;

12 Charts, chronicles, mémoires, etc;

Mém_Institut_VII_1824_12–14: La totalité des mémoires envoyés par le Ministre remplit deux cartons, dont il a été fait un examen attentif. Il en résulte que, *sur les quatre-vingt-six départemens qui composent aujourd'hui la France, quarante-un ont fourni des renseignemens complets*, six ont seulement répondu sommairement, et trente-neuf n'ont absolument rien envoyé . . . Tous ces mémoires ne sont pas également intéressans: on voit même que la plupart sortit des compilations, dont les auteurs ont seulement évité d'indiquer les sources. Il seroit convenable, si ce travail devoit se continuer, d'inviter les personnes qui s'en occuperont, à s'attacher sur-tout à donner des détails matériels sur les édifices, à recueillir toutes les notions locales, et en quelque sorte populaires, qui auroient rapport à leur état et aux changemens qu'ils ont éprouvés, et, lorsqu'elles voudront y joindre *des recherches plus étendues, de choisir les notices inédites, les chartes manuscrites*, de préférence aux ouvrages déjà imprimés sur les provinces.

1824

Rapport_1824: Instruction jointe au Rapport de la Commission des mémoires et des antiquités de la France: Rechercher et décrire dans chaque département,

1. Tous les monumens en pierres simplement posées ou superposées, connus du vulgaire, dans divers endroits, sous les noms de pierres aux fées, de pierres levées, &c., et auxquels on a attribué la dénomination de monumens Celtiques;

2. Toutes les éminences ou terres rapportées, connues sous le nom de tumuli; indiquer ceux qui n'ont pas été fouillés, et les objets qu'on a trouvés dans les fouilles;

3. Les vestiges de toutes les routes anciennes ou du moyen âge, soit même des routes moins anciennes qui auroient été abandonnées depuis long-temps: citer les lieux par où elles passent, et dresser une carte de ces routes; indiquer exactement les villages, ou même les édifices, ponts ou autres constructions qui se trouvoient sur ces routes *et qui n'existent plus*; donner les *détails les plus circonstanciés* sur ces lieux ou ces édifices, lorsqu'ils n'auront pas été décrits dans quelque ouvrage imprimé; s'ils ont été décrits, donner le titre de ces ouvrages et indiquer les pages où se trouve la description; se contenter ensuite de décrire leur état actuel; et s'ils appartiennent à des particuliers, faire connoître le nom des propriétaires;

4. Toutes les bornes milliaires antiques qui existent encore, ou qui ont été trouvées autrefois: faire connoître par des cartes dressées ad hoc, ou par une distance donnée à un lieu marqué sur les cartes gravées, *l'emplacement précis* où elles ont été trouvées,

APPENDIX 361

et indiquer ce que sont devenues celles qui ont été déplacées; donner les titres des ouvrages où elles ont été décrites, et indiquer les pages où se trouvent ces descriptions;

5. *Tous les monumens*, édifices, colonnes, fondations et murs de villes: il faut sur-tout remarquer dans ces murs de villes ceux qui attestent diverses époques par des constructions différentes; savoir, avec ou sans ciment, en pierres grandes ou petites, carrées, parallélogrammes, ou en losange; décrire les tours rondes ou carrées et les portes.

Dans les murs qui passent pour être de construction Romaine, examiner attentivement s'ils ne sont pas fondés sur des substructions plus anciennes, Gauloises peut-être, ou Grecques dans les villes du midi.

Remarquer encore s'il n'existe pas de monumens de leurs agrandissemens successifs; remarquer toutes les constructions antiques ou du moyen âge, toutes celles qu'on croit antérieures au Xe siècle; indiquer bien exactement leur emplacement, et faire connoître la configuration du terrain qui les environne; donner des dessins et des descriptions détaillées de celles qui seroient inconnues; et pour celles qui auroient déjà été décrites, indiquer le titre des ouvrages qui en font mention, et citer les pages qui contiennent tout ce qui leur est relatif;

6. *Indiquer exactement tous les emplacemens* où l'on a trouvé, *à différences époques*, des antiquités quelconques, et la nature de ces antiquités; faire connoître les traditions relatives à ces lieux, et les ouvrages qui en ont parlé;

7. Rechercher et dessiner *toutes les inscriptions ou fragmens d'inscriptions*, soit Grecques, soit Latines, soit du moyen âge, qu'on croit antérieures au Xe siècle, et qui se trouveroient dans le département. Indiquer tous les ouvrages où les inscriptions seroient déjà rapportées, et les pages de ces ouvrages où elles se trouvent relatées;

8. Rechercher et décrire toutes les anciennes abbayes, tous les anciens châteaux, et toutes les constructions faites depuis le commencement du Xe siècle jusqu'à la fin du xive; donner des dessins de celles qui sont *suffisamment conservées*; faire connoître les ouvrages où elles sont décrites, et citer les pages où se trouvent ces descriptions;

9. Les châteaux, abbayes ou autres constructions depuis la fin du XIVe siècle jusqu'à nos jours, qui se font remarquer, *soit par les formes de leur architecture, soit par des traditions populaires*. Faire connoître celles qui ont été détruites, la destination actuelle de celles qui existent; dire ce que sont devenus et où ont été transportés les tombeaux, ornemens ou débris curieux qui y existoient; donner les titres des ouvrages qui en auroient parlé;

10. Rechercher les épitaphes ou inscriptions les plus remarquables qui pourroient être utiles pour l'histoire, et qui se trouvent sur tous les *monumens modernes*;

11. Rechercher particulièrement, parmi les titres, *les noms que les différens lieux ont portés*, soit en latin, soit en français ancien ou en dialecte vulgaire, et étendre ces recherches jusqu'aux petits lieux ou hameaux qui pourroient dépendre d'une commune;

362   APPENDIX

12. Donner *la liste des anciennes chartes, des anciens titres, des anciennes chroniques, des mémoires, des vies de personnages célèbres, et enfin de tous les documens manuscrits,* utiles pour l'histoire, qui existent dans le département, soit dans des bibliothèques ou dépôts publics, soit entre les mains des particuliers; et, lorsqu'il sera possible, faire dresser, des plus intéressans, des notices plus ou moins étendues.

Bull_Sciences_Historiques_I_1824_308, on the above: D'après ces instructions et les ordres de S. Exc. le ministre de l'intérieur, chaque préfet chargea une on plusieurs personnes de la description des antiquités de son département; le ministre et l'académie activèrent ce travail de tous leurs moyens, et *il en est résulté aujourd'hui une collection très-considérable de mémoires, plans et dessins, qui forment les véritables archives monumentales de la France.* Le projet de publier convenablement ces importans matériaux n'a pas été perdu de vue, comme la seule manière de faire jouir les savans et le public du fruit de tant de recherches; il est arrivé aussi quelquefois que les autorités locales, devançant le vœu du gouvernement, ont fait imprimer sur les liens quelques-nus de ces mémoires généraux ou particuliers. L'ouvrage que nous annonçons est de ce nombre, M. le comte de Castéja, préfet de la Haute-Vienne, et le conseil général de ce département ayant encouragé l'auteur de leur autorité et de leurs moyens.

1837

Sommerard_1876_291–292, Concours des communes et des départements ponr la restauration. – Nature du concours apporté par le Gouvernement pour la conservation des monuments historiques. – Commission des monuments historiques, 1837, letter to prefects: Monsieur le Préfet, *le culte des souvenirs* qui se rattachent à l'histoire des arts ou aux annales du pays est malheureusement trop négligé dans les départements; on laisse en oubli des monuments précieux; on passe avec indifférence devant des vestiges qui attestent la grandeur des peuples de l'antiquité; on cherche en vain les murs qui ont vu naître des grands hommes dont s'honore la patrie, ou les tombes qui ont recueilli leurs restes; et cependant *tous ces souvenirs, tous ces débris vivants des temps qui ne sont plus, font partie du patrimoine national et du trésor intellectuel de la France*...Il importe de mettre un terme à cette insouciance. Le Gouvernement et les Chambres viennent de donner à cet égard une nouvelle preuve de leur sollicitude: le fonds destiné aux monuments historiques a été augmenté, mais ce fonds ne peut être considéré que comme un encouragement au zèle des communes et des départements; ils doivent comprendre que la conservation des anciens monuments les intéresse autant qu'elle les honore, en *offrant un attrait de plus aux méditations de l'historien ou à la curiosité du voyageur.*

Je vous invite donc, Monsieur le Préfet, *à recueillir tous les documents propres à me faire connaître les anciens monuments qui existent dans votre département,* l'époque de

APPENDIX

363

leur fondation, le caractère de leur architecture et les souvenirs historiques qui s'y rapportent. *Vous les classerez dans leur ordre d'importance*, et vous indiquerez les sommes qui seraient nécessaires pour les conserver ou remettre en bon état, sans oublier que les secours que je puis donner ne sont qu'une prime au généreux empressement du conseil général et des conseils municipaux.

1838

Comité_Travaux_II_1886_81–82: Circulaire relative à l'envoi d'un questionnaire archéologique / 30 novembre 1838.

Aux Correspondants du Ministère. / Monsieur, voulant fournir au Comité historique des arts et monuments, établi près du Ministère de l'instruction publique, de nouveaux moyens de recueillir tous les documents relatifs à nos antiquités nationales, j'ai cru devoir adresser à chacun des correspondants la série de questions ci-jointe. / Je réclame votre active collaboration pour une œuvre si digne de tout votre intérêt.

J'ai pensé qu'il *pourrait être utile d'associer à ce travail d'exploration les inspecteurs des écoles primaires*. Par la nature de leurs fonctions, ils sont en mesure de donner des renseignements prédeux sur les monuments qui existent dans un grand nombre de communes. Vous jugerez sans doute convenable d'entrer en communication avec eux et de mettre à profit leur coopération.

Vous voudrez bien consigner sur le cadre préparé par le Comité le résultat de vos recherches, et inadresser tous les documents que vous aurez recueillis. / Recevez, etc. / Salvandy.

Followed by a list of questions Gauloises (20 questions), Roman (15), Middle Ages (39), and nothing later. Each question is on the left of the page – and space for réponse on the right, so evidently they are not expecting long answers.

Comité_Travaux_II_1886_91, Circulaire demandant aux inspecteurs primaires quels monuments historiques existent dans les communes de leur circonscription, 1838.

1839

Documents_Inédits_1839_331–359, Gasparin, le Comte de, Président du comité historique des arts et monuments, "Rapport sur les travaux du Comité Historique des Arts et des Monuments." 332: Le comité a choisi des correspondants dans cette classe de la societé qui peut le plus pour la conservation des églises, ces monuments si nombreux et si importants de notre pays; il a désigné à votre nomination *plusieurs ecclésiastiques connus par des travaux d'archéologie*, ou réputés pour le zèle dont ils ont fait preuve a l'égard des edifices dont ils sont les usufruitiers. Ainsi, là où le comité a des correspondants du clergé, *il n'y a plus à craindre désormais ni le badigeon qui salit et dénature un monument, ni la pioche qui l'entaille, ni l'ignorance qui aliéne à vil prix* des reliquaires, des statues, des boiseries, des vitraux précieux.

334: Pour que le comité central, qui siége a Paris, fasse participer les départements au mouvement historique et archéologique si prononcé dans la capitale, il a, en vertu de votre arrêté de décembre dernier, présenté à votre nomination, comme membres non résidants, les quinze plus célèbres antiquaires de nos provinces.

336: La mission du comité est, en effet, *de fouiller notre France monumentale; de cataloguer, décrire et dessiner tous les objets d'art dissemines sur notre sol; de dresser enfin un cadastre archéologique, assez succinct pour que les monuments de tout âge et de toute nature* y soient mentionnés, assez étendu pour que chaque oeuvre d'art y obtienne une place proportionnée à sa valeur esthétique ou historique.

337: II a donc paru *indispensable d'arrêter un plan uniforme de travaux*, et d'y ramener invariablement tout ce qui se ferait par la suite au dedans comme au dehors du comité. / Deux moyens se sont présentés pour atteindre ce resultat; tous deux ont été adoptés. D'abord on offrira des monographies et des statistiques modèles auxquelles se conformeront, pour le plan scientifique comme pour l'exécution matérielle, toutes les statistiques et monographies qui se feront ultérieurement. Ensuite on adressera des instructions à tous les correspondants, *à tous les antiquaires de la France*, pour indiquer le plan d'après lequel les recherches devront être faites, pour déterminer les expressions qui devront être consacrées dans la description d'un monument et les signes caractéristiques qui servent à classer les oeuvres d'art et à determiner leur âge.

344: Le comité a cru que le meilleur moyen pour procéder immediatement et à peu de frais à cette reconnaissance monumentale de toute la France était de dresser un tableau qui comprendrait *des questions très-succinctes et très-précises* sur les antiquités gauloises, romaines et du moyen âge. A toutes les questions posées, il n'y aura qu'à répondre oui ou non. *Ce tableau sera tiré à 36,000 exemplaires, autant qu'il y a de communes en France*; car il n'existe pas de commune qui n'ait ou une église, ou un château, ou une maison ancienne, ou quelques débris de peinture et de sculpture. Ce questionnaire sera adressé, par l'entremise de MM. les recteurs, à tous les inspecteurs des écoles primaires, que leurs fonctions obligent à parcourir toutes les communes; et que leur éducation met à même de repondre à ce genre de questions; il sera adressé, en outre, à tous les correspondants du comité, pour que les correspondents et les inspecteurs s'aident et s'eclairent réciproquement. Le tableau proposé par M. Lenormant et rédigé par M. Vitet est imprimé; il se tire d'abord à six mille exemplaires, qu'on va envoyer comme essai dans une douzaine de départements. Renvoyés au comité avec les réponses, ces tableaux apprendront ce que nous possédons de monuments, leur gisement et leur valeur.

350: Un des membres du comité, M. Léon de Laborde, a proposé de sceller sur tous les monuments de la France, au lieu le plus apparent, *une inscription en métal* qui

APPENDIX   365

dirait 1'âge du monument, sa valeur esthétique, son interet historique, qui relaterait tous les faits interessants accomplis autour ou au dedans de l'édifice. *On aurait ainsi un immense musée monumental classé, annoté, utile aux voyageurs et aux antiquaires.*

BA_Comité_II_1886_92, Circulaire demandant communication des inscriptions romaines existant en France, 1er mars 1839.

1840

Sommerard_1876_345, Mérimée's 1840 report to the Minister: La Commission s'est occupée d'un règlement que vous avez revêtu de votre approbation, pour fixer les honoraires des architectes employés par votre département; obligée de se renfermer dans les limites d'une sévère économie, elle a pensé qu'il convenait de donner à des artistes estimables un témoignage honorifique de la satisfaction du Gouvernement, pour les soins et le zèle qu'ils apportent à des travaux toujours longs et pénibles et dont les honoraires sont souvent insignifiants. Vous avez bien voulu, sur sa proposition, accorder à quelques architectes une médaille spéciale.

La même distinction était due aux correspondants qui, par des mémoires archéologiques ou par des renseignements utiles qu'ils adressent journellement à votre ministère, ont le plus contribué à faire connaître ou à conserver des édifices remarquables.

Enfin cette médaille sera décernée également aux personnes qui, par des sacrifices généreux, ont sauvé de la destruction des monuments dignes d'intérêt.

La Commission tous a proposé d'accorder vingt-trois médailles seulement; car elle a cru que cette récompense acquerrait un nouveau prix par sa rareté et par les titres incontestables des artistes et des savants qui l'obtiendraient.

1841

Mérimée_1842_25–26, circular on conservation: Paris, le 19 février 1841... Pour qu'une affaire puisse être mise utilement sous les yeux de la Commission des monuments historiques, il est nécessaire de m'adresser les pièces suivantes:

1°   Un exposé des besoins du monument et de son état actuel;
2°   Une notice historique et une description;
3°   Des plans, coupes, dessins, ou du moins des croquis et un plan avec des mesures;
4°   Un devis rédigé par un architecte, aussi détaillé que possible des travaux projetés.

Ces travaux seront divisés en trois catégories: La première comprend *les travaux très-urgents*, qui ont pour objet la consolidation immédiate de l'édifice; La seconde, *les*

368   APPENDIX

travaux moins urgents qui concernent la conservation; La troisième, *ceux qui peuvent toujours être différés* et qui doivent en compléter la restauration. On devra enfin indiquer dans le même devis les dépenses qui ne peuvent être divisées en raison de la nature des travaux, ou de toutes autres circonstances.

Mérimée_1842_14, circular: Paris, le 1er octobre 1841.

Monsieur le Préfet, / Je vous adresse la liste des monuments historiques qui ont été provisoirement classés dans le département d... par la Commission attachée au Ministère de l'intérieur pour délibérer sur toutes les affaires qui dépendent de ce service. Veuillez vous entendre avec les correspondants du Ministère de l'intérieur, les sociétés savantes et les architectes du département, *pour y proposer les rectifications et les additions que vous jugerez convenables*. Ces modifications devront être accompagnées des pièces réclamées par ma circulaire du 19 février dernier. Elles seront examinées par la Commission, et, sur son avis, j'arrêterai définitivement une liste à laquelle ne pourront être ajoutés que des édifices dont l'intérêt jusqu'alors méconnu me serait signalé par la suite.

Mém_Côte_d'Or_1_1841, prints as appendix Instruction du Ministre de l'Intérieur sur les recherches des Antiquités de la France, adressée à MM. les Préfets pour les Commissions départmentales d'Antiquités. NB repeats many of the categories and much of the wording of circulars of 1819 and 1824.

Rechercher et décrire dans chaque département:

1   Tous les monuments en pierre (Pierres aux Fées, etc.);
2   Toutes les éminences... Tumuli;
3   Les vestiges de toutes les routes anciennes ou du moyen âge;
4   Toutes les bornes milliaires;
5   *Tous les monumens*, édifices, colonnes, fondations, murs de villes;
6   Indiquer exactement tous les emplacemens où l'on a trouvé à différentes époques des antiquités quelconques, et la nature de ces antiquités;
7   Rechercher et décrire *toutes les inscriptions*;

And then on to abbeys, châteaux, epitaphes, and

12. Lists of ancient charters, chronicles, memoires, soit dans les bibliothèques ou dépôts public, *soit entre les mains des particuliers*.

1843

Documents_Inédits_1843, "Instructions du Comité Historique des Arts et Monuments," includes "Musique," "Monuments Fixes, Civilisation Chrétienne," "Architecture Militaire au Moyen Âge," all separately paginated. Starts with prehistoric material,

APPENDIX

with plentiful illustrations, but often (for Roman architecture) takes examples from Italian sites.

4: Letter from the Minister to the correspondant responsible for work related to the history of France, repeated in 1857: Il n'y a pas encore longtemps qu'on a reconnu combien les études historiques doivent emprunter de secours à l'étude des monuments. Les hommes laborieux des deux derniers siècles, qui ont sauvé d'une destruction inévitable un si grand nombre de chartes et de pièces manuscrites en les faisant revivre par leurs patientes transcriptions, ont laissé se dégrader et s'écrouler sous leurs yeux cette innombrable variété de monuments que les siècles passés avaient entassés sur tous les points du royaume. *Si des dessins et des descriptions fidèles* nous en avaient reproduit les formes et les dimensions, *si seulement un relevé exact* nous en donnait le dénombrement, que de problèmes pourraient être résolus! que de lumières sur des questions à jamais douteuses!

Il est trop tard pour réparer ce déplorable oubli; mais plus nos regrets sont vifs, plus rigoureux est le devoir de ne pas mériter à notre tour les reproches des siècles à venir. *Nos richesses monumentales, quoique décimées depuis cinquante ans,* égalent encore en beauté et surpassent en variété celles de tous les autres pays de l'Europe. Notre premier soin, assurément, doit être de travailler à leur conservation, de les entourer de respect et de prolonger leur durée. Mais, quoi que nous fassions, ces pierres sont périssables, et le jour viendra où la postérité en cherchera vainement la poussière. Qu'il en reste au moins une image, un souvenir. Que partout où un monument existe aujourd'hui on sache à jamais qu'il a existé; que ses proportions, sa figure, son importance, sa destination, soient religieusement conservées, et que les historiens futurs puissent en retrouver dans tous les temps une trace impérissable.

C'est pour accomplir cette œuvre difficile, ce travail tout nouveau, qu'on fait appel à la patience et aux efforts de MM. les correspondants. Il s'agit de dresser la carte monumentale de la France. Les 37,200 communes devront être visitées, explorées en tous sens. *Il ne faut pas qu'il existe un seul monument, un seul fragment de ruine, à quelque siècle, à quelque civilisation qu'il appartienne, sans qu'il en soit fait mention, ne fût-ce que pour constater qu'il ne mérite pas qu'on l'étudie.*

5: J'ai l'honneur de vous transmettre dès aujourd'hui la première partie des instructions adoptées par le comité, savoir: celles qui se rapportent aux monuments élevés en France avant l'établissement definitif du christianisme, soit par les Gaulois, soit par les Grecs et les Romains, et celles qui concernent les monuments chrétiens. M. Albert Lenoir a rédigé la partie de ces instructions qui est relative aux monuments religieux et civils des Gaulois, des Grecs, des Romains et des chrétiens, jusqu'au x^{ie} siècle; M. P. Mérimée s'est charge des voies et des camps; à M. Ch. Lenormant appartiennent les instructions sur les monuments meublés: armes, poteries, ustensiles et monnaies. Ultérieurement seront publiées les instructions relatives aux monuments chrétiens du x^{ie} au xv^{ie} siècle.

368 APPENDIX

17–21: Colonisation grecque. In their instructions on Gallo-Roman fortifications (32–33), which they characterise accurately and reckon were built in haste (33: et d'ordinaire on remarque que les murailles sont bâties avec les débris de grands édifices, comme si on les avait sacrifiés pour en tirer des matériaux à l'approche du danger), there are no instructions about getting the monuments out of such enceintes and doing anything with them, or any sentiment that such walls should indeed be pulled down. Indeed, all the "instructions" read like a first-year undergraduate summary of the monuments' characteristics.

1845

Mém_Picardie_VIII_1845_38: Il serait à désirer que l'exemple donné par M. Darcy [inventorying archives] fût suivi par tous les maires, *que chaque commune possédât un inventaire régulier de ses archives*, que ces titres, à la conservation desquels sont souvent attachés de précieux intérêts, fussent mis à l'abri du pillage et de la destruction.

Une circulaire de M. le Préfet a dernièrement appelé l'attention des maires sur cette partie si importante de leur devoir; elle fera cesser, nous n'en doutons pas, *une incurie* aussi préjudiciable aux intérêts de l'histoire qu'aux intérêts matériels des communes et des particuliers.

1859

Charmes_III_1886_471–479, dated 1859: Chaboullet, Instructions sur le répertoire archéologique de la France, with a full specimen "answer" (prehistoric onwards for one canton of the Arrondissement de l'Orient, which takes up four closely packed pages).

471: Comme le titre l'indique, ce sera le répertoire des monuments de tous genres et de tous âges, disséminés dans toutes les parties de l'empire; en un mot, ce livre sera un guide, à la fois pratique et scientifique, de l'archéologue en France. Bien qu'au premier abord ce projet paraisse immense, un examen sérieux et la lecture du programme démontreront *qu'il est facilement réalisable*, "il ne s'agit pas," comme la très judicieusement fait observer un membre du Comité, dans la discussion qui suivît l'exposé du projet, "*il ne s'agit pas de rédiger des descriptions minutieuses de tous les monuments répandus sur la surface de la France*, mais bien de composer un guide archéologique qui fasse connaître l'existence des monuments de chaque localité, en renvoyant aux ouvrages spéciaux où ces monuments sont décrits plus amplement."

APPENDIX

1860

BM_XXVI_1860_186–187: Congrès central des Académies, session de 1860. Le Congrès des délégués des Académies est convoqué à Paris, comme les années précédentes, pour le lundi de Pâques, 9 avril 1860. D'importantes questions d'organisation académique figureront cette année au programme, et toutes les Sociétés savantes de France ont un immense intérêt à se faire représenter par plusieurs membres à cette conférence, qui se réunit depuis douze années.

Voici quelques-unes des questions, purement archéologiques, que nous avons remarquées dans le programme:

Quelles mesures devrait-on prendre pour la conservation des monuments romains partout où il en existe en France?

Le théâtre romain de Champlieu a-t-il été réparé sous les Mérovingiens, comme l'ont avancé quelques savants contradictoirement à d'autres archéologues? Quelle opinion doit être décidément adoptée?

Les découvertes qui ont eu lieu en France depuis quelques années n'ont-elles pas produit des faits nouveaux pour l'histoire de la céramique? Indiquer sommairement ces faits.

Quelles sont les découvertes les plus importantes faites en France depuis l'année dernière?

La rotonde de St-Bénigne, à Dijon, ne devrait-elle pas être réparée? Ce type des églises rondes, si nombreuses avant le XIIIe siècle, pourrait-il être, dans certains cas, adopté avec avantage pour les églises contemporaines?

Quels ont été, en 1859, les efforts tentés pour l'avancement des études, et les publications les plus intéressantes sur le moyen-âge?

1873

BSA_Vendômois_XII_1873_211: Nous avons reçu du Ministère des Beaux-Arts la circulaire suivante en communication: Monsieur le Préfet,

La Commission des Monuments historiques s'occupe en ce moment de réunir tous les documents nécessaires pour dresser une liste définitive des édifices dont la conservation présente un véritable intérêt au point de vue de l'art. Sur cette liste les Monuments seront inscrits dans un ordre de classement méthodique, c'est-à-dire que ceux qui représentent le point de départ ou le complet développement d'une école d'architecture figureront en première ligne, tandis que ceux qui ne sont, par rapport aux précédents, que des dérivés, seront classés en seconde ou troisième ligne, suivant leur intérêt relatif.

Vous pouvez, Monsieur le Préfet, apporter un utile concours à la préparation de cet important travail *en me signalant les édifices de votre département qui vous paraîtraient susceptibles d'être classés, bien qu'ils ne figurent pas sur la liste actuelle des Monuments historiques*, que j'ai l'honneur de remettre sous vos yeux.

Afin que la Commission pût statuer utilement sur les propositions que vous croirez devoir m'adresser à ce sujet, il conviendrait d'y joindre des photographies des Monuments dont vous demanderez le classement.

Je vous recommande. Monsieur le Préfet, de ne pas perdre de vue l'objet de la présente communication. Il s'agit, en quelque sorte, de *dresser l'inventaire des richesses architecturales de la France*, et je ne doute pas que vous soyez heureux d'apporter à cette œuvre le concours de votre zèle éclairé.

1882

Mém_Éduenne_XII_1883_459, circular from Paris, 20 March 1882, addressed to president of the Commission de la géographie historique de l'ancienne France: La Commission désirerait établir *l'inventaire de toutes les inscriptions antiques qui existent sur le sol de l'ancienne Gaule.*

Cette statistique présenterait un double intérêt. D'abord elle permettrait de savoir où trouver un certain nombre de textes qu'il serait utile d'étudier; ensuite les épigraphistes seraient fixés sur les inscriptions restées inédites ou mal interprétées jusqu'à ce jour. *Il sera facile, une fois ce travail fait et centralisé, de vérifier, à l'avenir, les textes nouvellement découverts et, probablement, de retrouver des monuments connus par des publications déjà anciennes et considérés depuis comme disparus.*

Le travail préparatoire que la Commission demande à ses collaborateurs est assez simple. Il consiste à copier, pour chaque inscription déjà publiée, les premières lignes, et à indiquer très exactement la dimension du monument, hauteur, longueur et épaisseur, ainsi que les provenances et le lieu où il est déposé aujourd'hui. Plus tard, la Commission aura à demander des estampages, lorsque l'intérêt de la science l'exigera.

1886

BSA_Orléanais_VIII_1886_566–571, round-robin from Tranchau, Inspecteur d'Académie honoraire du département du Loiret, with list of 44 questions for their preparation of a carte archéologique, addressed to all communes, answers to be sent in within three months. Items 12–44 are Renaissance to modern times; 6–11 Gallo-Roman. Some of the questions:

APPENDIX

1–5. Monuments primitifs:

6. Y a-t-il trace de chaussée ou de chemin pavé dénommé voie romaine, chemin de César ou autrement?

7. Remarque-t-on des terrains entourés de fossés ou de talus et connus sous le nom de camp romain, camp de César, etc.?

8. Y a-t-il des restes de pont? de gué pavé? des débris de murailles en pierres de grandeur égale et d'un appareil régulier? des vestiges de substructions? de thermes? d'aqueducs? d'amphithéâtre?

9. Rencontre-t-on des bornes milliaires? Portent-elles des lettres ou des figures?

10. A-t-on trouvé des tombes? monolithes ou maçonnées? Leur forme? Que contenaient-elles?

11. A-t-on découvert des fragments de mosaïque, de marbres, des tuiles à rebord, de la poterie rouge ou grise, des verroteries, des armes, des médailles, des objets de mobilier, etc.?

12. *L'église est-elle ancienne?* Connaît-on un titre authentique de sa fondation? Où se trouve-t-il mentionné? Si elle est de construction récente, de quelle date était l'ancienne?

Préciser l'emplacement des découvertes.

The round-robin includes: "La Société voudrait tout d'abord dresser une Carte archéologique du Loiret, qui pût permettre de retrouver facilement, et d'embrasser comme d'un coup d'œil, au moyen de signes conventionnels, les divers monuments ou vestiges antiques dont notre région est abondamment pourvue" – and they include a list of no fewer than 51 such signs.

Réunion_BA_X_1886, speech by the Ministre de l'Instruction Publique, René Goblet, 53: Bien souvent le vœu avait été exprimé de voir adopter par les Chambres des dispositions législatives capables de garantir les objets mobiliers on les immeubles que leur mérite artistique ou leur valeur historique commandent de soustraire à la destruction et à l'oubli.

L'intervention de la Commission des monuments historiques ne suffisait pas, il y fallait le secours de la loi. L'Institut, la Société des antiquaires de France, la plupart des sociétés elles-mêmes l'avaient réclamé à maintes reprises. Je vous avais annoncé l'intention de reprendre l'étude de la question et de soumettre de nouveau au Parlement un projet de loi antérieurement préparé dans ce dessein par un de mes honorables prédécesseurs.

Aujourd'hui j'ai la satisfaction de vous annoncer que la loi est faite ou à peu près. Votée sans discussion par la Chambre, elle n'a subi devant le Sénat que de très-légères modifications, et nous avons l'assurance qu'elle sera définitivement adoptée dès la rentrée prochaine. M. le sous-secrétaire d'État aux Beaux-Arts, qui en a suivi la discussion, tient à honneur de la faire promptement aboutir.

372 APPENDIX

Désormais, grâce à des dispositions aussi sages qu'efficaces, non-seulement les monuments, les inscriptions, mais les objets mobiliers, statues, meubles, bijoux, pierres sculptées, trésors enfermés dans les vieux châteaux ou les vieilles églises, et aussi les découvertes à provenir des fouilles qui pourraient être entreprises soit sur le territoire de la France, soit en Algérie et dans les pays soumis à notre protectorat, pourront être classés *s'ils présentent un intérêt sérieux au point de vue de l'art ou de l'histoire.*

Il en sera ainsi même pour les immeubles appartenant à des particuliers ou pour les fouilles entreprises sur leurs terrains, au moyen de l'expropriation étendue à ces divers cas.

Si l'intérêt matériel, quand il concerne des collectivités, autorise une semblable atteinte au droit de propriété, combien n'est-elle pas plus légitime encore quand il s'agit de l'intérêt des souvenirs et des traditions et des richesses artistiques ou historiques qui forment une part si précieuse du patrimoine national!

SG_LIII_Nantes_1886_35–36, presaging the 1887 law: Depuis deux ans, un grand mouvement s'est produit au sein de l'Institut et des Sociétés savantes afin d'obtenir une loi vraiment protectrice des monuments historiques. Toutes les Sociétés françaises se sont unies dans ce but. Après la Chambre des Députés, le Sénat a voté un projet, dont il est difficile d'apprécier dès aujourd'hui les résultats futurs, mais qui fixe enfin une législation pour la conservation des monuments historiques, et *consacre le principe de l'expropriation pour cause d'utilité publique*, en matière de monuments historiques. Diverses dispositions sont aussi applicables aux objets d'art mobiliers appartenant aux départements, aux communes et aux fabriques.

Sans entrer dans l'examen détaillé de la loi, nous pouvons dire que, sagement appliquée, elle crée un progrès réel. / *Malheureusement, en attendant son vote définitif, les monuments disparaissent chaque jour, par suite de l'indifférence, de l'incurie ou du mauvais vouloir.* Nous ne voudrions pas en citer d'exemples, mais on nous permettra de rappeler cependant la destruction presque systématique des monuments romains de Tunisie où, en moins de trois ans, plus de dégâts ont été commis par des gens éclairés que les Arabes n'en avaient fait pendant dix siècles.

1887

Loi pour la conservation des monuments, 30 march 1887,[5] Art. 4. *L'immeuble classé ne pourra être détruit, même en partie, ni être l'objet d'un travail de restauration. de réparation ou de modification quelconque*, si le ministre de l'instruction publique et des beaux-arts n'y a donné son consentement.

L'expropriation pour cause d'utilité publique d'un immeuble classé ne pourra être poursuivie qu'après que le ministre de l'instruction publique et des beaux-arts aura été appelé à présenter ses observations.

APPENDIX

373

Les servitudes d'alignement et autres qui pourraient causer la dégradation des monuments ne sont pas applicables aux immeubles classés.

Art. 14. Lorsque, par suite de fouilles, de travaux ou d'un fait quelconque, on aura découvert des monuments, des ruines, des inscriptions ou des objets pouvant intéresser l'archéologie, l'histoire ou l'art, sur des terrains appartenant à l'État, à un département, à une commune, à une fabrique ou autre établissement public, le maire de la commune devra assurer la conservation provisoire des objets découvert, et aviser immédiatement le préfet du département des mesures qui auront été prises.

Le préfet en référera, dans le plus bref délai, au ministre de l'instruction publique et des beaux-arts, qui statuera sur les mesures définitives à prendre.

Si la découverte a eu lieu sur le terrain d'un particulier, le maire en avisera le préfet. Sur le rapport du préfet et après avis de la commission des monuments historiques, le ministre de l'instruction publique et des beaux-arts pourra poursuivre l'expropriation dudit terrain en tout ou en partie pour cause d'utilité publique, suivant les formes de la loi du 3 mai 1841.

Art. 15. Les décisions prises par le ministre de l'instruction publique et des beaux-arts, en exécution de la présente loi seront rendues après avis de la commission des monuments historiques.[6]

1903

AMPF_XVII_1904_27, Chambre des Députés, Proposition de Loi ayant pour objet de protéger les sites pittoresques historiques ou légendaires de la France, 5 February 1903:

Art. 2. Lorsqu'une propriété, autre que celles appartenant à l'Etat, aura été classée par la Commission, *le propriétaire sera invité à prendre l'engagement* de ne détruire ni modifier les lieux ou leur aspect sans autorisation du Préfet, après avis de la Commission.

Si l'engagement est donné, la Commission en prendra acte et il deviendra définitif et perpétuel, en quelque main que passe l'immeuble.

Si l'engagement est refusé, la Commission notifiera le refus au département et aux communes sur le territoire desquels la propriété est située.

Art. 23: Dans chaque département est constituée une Commission présidée par le Préfet et composée de fonctionnaires, de conseillers généraux, de conseillers d'arrondissement, de conseillers municipaux et enfin d'artistes, d'amateurs d'art, d'hygiénistes, etc. Cette Commission, en tout ou partie, classe les propriétés foncières qui dans le département offrent un intérêt général au point de vue pittoresque, historique, légendaire ou scientifique.

Cette sorte d'inventaire une fois terminée, l'Administration *invitera le propriétaire à prendre l'engagement* "de ne détruire ni modifier les lieux ou leur aspect" sans une autorisation du Préfet, après avis de la Commission.

Art. 24: *Il y aura des propriétaires récalcitrants* et qui ne voudront pas souscrire à cette atténuation du jus utendi et abutendi.

Voici la double procédure que nous ouvrons dans ce cas-là au département ou à la commune sur le territoire desquels la propriété est située: 1° *l'expropriation pour cause d'utilité publique* (dans ce cas, l'acquéreur, département ou commune, pourra ou bien garder l'immeuble ou bien le revendre grevé de la servitude "de ne détruire ni modifier les lieux ou leur aspect;" 2° *l'établissement pur et simple de la servitude* ... La servitude sera constituée en vertu d'un arrêté préfectoral. Bien entendu, le propriétaire aura droit à une indemnité équivalant à la moins-value que subira l'immeuble par l'établissement de la servitude.

---

[1] SG_XIX_Dijon_1852_133

[2] Charmes_1886_III_3–59

[3] Charmes_1886_III_60–231

[4] Charmes_1886_III_335–359

[5] Brown_1905_85–90

[6] SG_LIII_1886_Nantes_93–99

Bibliography: Sources

Although this book contains an amount of 16–18th-century documentation, the great majority is from the 19th century, the one witnessing the devastation of monuments which is the theme of the book. It also saw the establishment of large numbers of scholarly societies in many of the towns and departments of France, and their papers, reports and discussions form the meat of the endnotes (whereas modern scholarship appears in footnotes). For most citations (which are abbreviated according to the key immediately below) the 19th-century authors are not named, unless they are well-known, important or especially active, in which case they will appear in the A–Z listing below. Where relevant, their affiliations, useful descriptions and qualifications are given as they appear on the title page; and of course, these change over the years. Sometimes my own comments are added, to aid assessment of the text. Conversely, there are occasions when throughout the literature only the author's surname is used, and therefore known.

In many cases, periodicals are listed only by date, since the numbering of the various series (and even their dating) is far from consistent and often confusing: thus the Bulletin Monumental for 1860, on the title page as "3e série, tome 6e, 26e vol. de la collection," is given the overall volume number, in this case 26. They also change their titles from time to time, and do not necessarily publish annually: the *Mémoires de la Société des Sciences naturelles et archéologiques de la Creuse*, for example, published only five volumes 1847–1886; while the *Société historique et archéologique de Langres* produced only six volumes of bulletins and mémoires 1847–1892. The SG (Séances Générales, Congrès Archéologique de France) often took place in more than one location, of which only the first is given in the notes.

Abbreviations (with start dates where appropriate):

AA	1844 Annales Archéologiques
Acad_Toulouse	1782 Histoire et mémoires de l'Académie royale des sciences, inscriptions et belles-lettres de Toulouse.
ADG	Archives du Gard
AHL_Nord	1831 Archives Historiques et Littéraires du Nord de la France
AIBL	1663 Académie des Inscriptions et Belles-Lettres
AM	Archives Municipales/Communales
AMPF	1887 Amis des Monuments (et des Arts) Parisiens (et Français)
APC	1831 Annales des Ponts et Chaussées

ASA_Château-Thierry	1864 Annales de la Société Archéologique et Historique de Château-Thierry
ASL_Alpes-Maritimes	1865 Annales de la Société des lettres, sciences et arts des Alpes-Maritimes
B_Lorraine	1849 Bulletin mensuel de la Société d'archéologie lorraine et du Musée historique
BA_Comité	1838 Bulletin Archéologique du Comité des Travaux Historiques et Scientifiques
BA_Comité_Bibliographie	1835 Bulletin Archéologique du Comité des Travaux Historiques et Scientifiques—bibiography
BCA_Narbonne	1876-7 Bulletin de la Commission Archéologique et Littéraire de l'Arrondissement de Narbonne
BCA_Seine-Inférieure	1867 Bulletin de la Commisssion des Antiquités de la Seine-Inférieure
BM Bulletin Monumental	1834 [or Bibliothèque Municipale according to context]
BMA	Bibliothèque Municipale, Arles
BSA_Abbeville	1833 Mémoires de la Société [Royale; Impériale] d'Émulation d'Abbeville
BSA_Drôme	1866 Bulletin de la Société d'archéologie et de statistique de la Drôme
BSA_Midi	1832 [Mémoires] 1869 Bulletin de la Société Archéologique du Midi de la France
BSA_Béziers	1836 Bulletin de la Société Archéologique de Béziers
BSA_Eure-et-Loire	1864 Bulletin/Mémoires de la Société archéologique d'Eure-et-Loire
BSA_Laon	1852 Bulletin de la Société académique de Laon
BSAH_Limousin	1846 Bulletin de la Société Archéologique et Historique du Limousin
BSA_Orléanais	1851 Bulletin de la Société Archéologique de l'Orléanais
BSA_Ouest	1836 Bulletin de la Société des Antiquaires de l'Ouest
BSA_Provence	1904 Bulletin de la Société Archéologique de Provence
BSA_Seine-et-Marne	1861 Bulletin de la Société Archéologique de Seine-et-Marne
BSA_Sens	1846 Bulletin de la Société Archéologique de Sens
BSA_Soissons	1847 Bulletin de la Société archéologique, historique et scientifique de Soissons
BSA_Touraine	1842 [Mémoires] 1869 Bulletin trimestriel de la Société Archéologique de Touraine
BSA_Vendômois	1862 Bulletin de la Société archéologique, scientifique et littéraire du Vendômois
BSH_Paris	1874 Bulletin de la Société Historique de Paris et de l'Île-de-France

BIBLIOGRAPHY: SOURCES

BSS_Yonne	1847 Bulletin de la Société des Sciences Historiques et Naturelles de l'Yonne
CHA	1893 La Correspondance Historique et Archéologique
CS	Congrès Scientifique de France
MAS_Marseille	1803 Mémoires de l'Académie des Sciences de Marseille
MDANE	1817 Mémoires et Dissertations sur les Antiquités Nationales et Étrangères
Mém_AIBL	1815 Mémoires … de l'Académie des Inscriptions et Belles-Lettres
Mém_Angers	1831 Memoires de la Société Agriculturale d'Angers
Mém_Aube	1822 Mémoires de la Société académique d'agriculture, des sciences, arts et belles-lettres du département de l'Aube
Mém_Beaune	1874 Mémoires Société d'histoire, d'archéologie et de littérature de l'arrondissement de Beaune
Mém_Côte_d'Or	1841 Mémoires de la Commission des Antiquités du Département de la Côte d'Or
Mém_Doubs	1841 Mémoires de la Société d'émulation du Doubs
Mém_Éduenne	1872 Mémoires de la Société Éduenne
Mém_Gard	1835 Mémoires de l'Académie du Gard [+ Procès-verbaux]
Mém_Langres	1847 Mémoires [Bulletin 1872] de la Société Historique et Archéologique de Langres
Mém_Lorraine	1849 [Bulletin] 1859 Mémoires de la Société d'archéologie lorraine et du Musée historique lorrain
Mém_Lyon	1860 Mémoires de la Société Littéraire, Historique et Archéologique de Lyon
Mém_Nîmes	1805 Mémoires de l'Académie de Nîmes
Mém_Normandie	1825 Mémoires de la Société des Antiquaires de la Normandie
Mém_Oise	1847 Mémoires de la Société Académique du Département de l'Oise
Mém_Picardie	1838 Mémoires de la Société des Antiquaires de la Picardie
Mém_Pontoise	1879 Mémoires de la Société Historique et Archéologique de Pontoise et du Vexin
Mém_Senlis	1862 Comité Archéologique de Senlis, Comptes-Rendus et Mémoires
MSA/BSA_France	1817 [Mémoires] 1857 Bulletin de la Société des Antiquaires de France
MSA_Ouest	1835 Mémoires [Bulletin 1836] de la Société des Antiquaires de l'Ouest
MS	Manuscript
MSRAF	1817 Mémoires de la Société Royale des Antiquaires de France

Précis_Rouen	1744 Précis analytique des travaux de l'Académie des sciences, belles-lettres et arts de Rouen
PV	Procès Verbaux
PV_Seine-Inférieure	1818 Procès Verbaux de la Commisssion des Antiquités de la Seine-Inférieure
RA	1844 Revue Archéologique
Réunion_BA	1877 Réunion des Sociétés des Beaux-Arts des Départements
Revue_Maine	1876 Revue historique et archéologique du Maine
SA_Saint-Quentin	1831 Société Académique de Saint-Quentin
SA_Bordeaux	1874 Société Archéologique de Bordeaux
SAH_Charente	1845 Société archéologique et historique de la Charente
SG_session_place_date	1833 Congrès Archéologique de France, Séances Générales
Sorbonne	1861 Mémoires lus à la Sorbonne: Archéologie

Académie Delphinale, *Documents inédits relatifs au Dauphiné* III, Grenoble 1868.

Achard, Amédée, *Description historique, géographique et topographique des villes ... de la provence ancienne et moderne*, Aix 1787.

Allmer, Auguste, & Dissard, Paul, *Musée de Lyon: inscriptions antiques*, Lyon, 5 vols, 1888–93.

Anderson, Joseph, "Our national monuments," in *AR* I 1888, 186–191.

Annuaire de l'Institut des Provinces et des Congrès Scientifiques, Paris 1850. De Caumont was Director-General, and this volume gives a good summary of the Institute's activities, and the names of the various departmental learned societies; so the volume is a kind of clearing-house for reports on meetings around the country. See also VIII, Paris 1856, and *Annuaire* X, Paris 1858.

(Anon), *Histoire de la ville d'Autun et de la foire S-Ladre*, Mâcon 1857.

(Anon), *Histoire de la ville de Reims*, Reims 1864. Entered as Anon_Reims_1864.

Appert, Allart & Leclère, M.M., *Démolition des murs de ronde et déplacement de l'enceinte de l'octroi, présenté au Conseil Municipal 5 novembre 1884*, Reims 1884.

Artaud, F., Conservateur du musée des antiques à Lyon, "Lettre de Sextus Fadius, gravée sur un monument découvert à Narbonne," in *MSRAF* VII 1826, 244–256.

Archives historiques et littéraires du Nord de la France, Valenciennes 1842.

Aubenas, J.-A., *Histoire de Fréjus, Forum Julii, ses antiquités, son port*, Fréjus 1881.

Audierne, Abbé, Inspecteur des Monuments Historiques, *Périgueux. Ses monuments antiques et modernes. Guide monumental II*, Périgueux 1859.

Ausonius, *Works*, White, Hugh G. Evelyn, ed., 2 vols, London & New York 1919 & 1921.

Babeau, Albert, *Le village sous l'ancien régime*, Paris 1878.

———, *La ville sous l'ancien régime*, Paris 1880.

———, *La vie militaire sous l'ancien régime: les soldats*, Paris 1889.

BIBLIOGRAPHY: SOURCES

————, *La Province sous l'Ancien Régime* II, 1894, 119–129 for L'Administration Militaire; 168–193 Les Travaux Publics.

Baedeker, Karl, *Le Nord de la France*, Leipzig/Paris 1884.

————, *Southern France*, Leipzig etc 1914.

Balincourt, E. de, "L'ancienne ville des Arènes," in *Revue du Midi* 19, 1896, 1, 5–24.

Barbier, Jean, *Itinéraire historique et descriptif de l'Algérie, avec un vocabulaire français-arabe des mots les plus usités et un résumé historique des guerres d'Afrique*, Paris 1855.

Baragnon, P. L., père, *Abrégé de l'histoire de Nismes, de Ménard, continué jusqu'à nos jours*, 4 vols, Nîmes 1831–5.

Barral, Octave de, *Notice sur les murs d'enceinte de la ville de Bourges*, Bourges 1852, illustrated with lithographs, from a MS of General Vicomte de Barral, Prefect of the Cher.

Bard, Joseph, *L'Algérie en 1854. Itinéraire général de Tunis à Tangier*, Paris 1854.

Barelli, Hervé, "Le château de Nice vu par lers historiens et mémorialistes (XVIe–XVIIe siècles)," in Bouiron 2013, 195–235.

Barker, Edward Harrison (1851–1919), *Wanderings by southern waters: Eastern Aquitaine*, London 1893.

Barraud, L'abbé, "Beauvais et ses monuments pendant l'ère gallo-romaine et sous la domination franque, in *BM* 1861, 29–64, 217–237. With plenty on the cemeteries and monuments discovered therein, including sarcophagi.

Baudel, M.-J., *Un An à Alger, excursions et souvenirs*, Paris 1887.

Baudot, François. *Lettres en forme de dissertation sur l'ancienneté de la ville d'Autun et sur l'origine de celle de Dijon*, Dijon 1710.

Bazin, Hippolyte, *Les monuments de Paris. Souvenirs de vingt siècles*, Paris 1902.

————, *Nîmes gallo-romain*, Nîmes 1891.

————, "Lyon Gallo-Romaine," in *BA* 1891, 354–378.

————, *Arles Gallo-Romain*, Paris 1896.

————, *Une vielle cité de France: Reims, monuments et histoire*, Reims 1900.

Bernadau, *Le Viographe Bordelais*, Bordeaux 1844.

Berrian, Rev. William, *Travels in France and Italy in 1817 and 1818*, New York 1821.

Bertillon, Jacques (1851–1922). *La dépopulation de la France: ses conséquences, ses causes, mesures à prendre pour la combattre*, Paris 1911.

Bertrand, Louis, *Histoire de Philippeville*, Philippeville 1903.

Bescherelle, Louis-Nicolas (1802–1883). *Monuments élevés à la gloire militaire par les Romains et les Français*, Paris 1851.

Bibliographie annuelle des travaux historiques et archéologiques publiés par les sociétés savantes de la France, 1902–1903, Paris 1905.

Bitard, Adolphe, *Dictionnaire de biographie contemporaine française et étrangère*, Paris 1886.

Blanche, Raymond. *Places de guerre, étude sur les servitudes militaires*, Caen 1869.

Blanchet, Adrien, *Les enceintes romaines de la Gaule; étude sur l'origine d'un grand nombre de villes françaises*, Paris 1907.

———, *Recherches sur les aquéducs et cloaques de la Gaule Romaine*, Paris 1908.

Block, Maurice, *Annuaire de l'administration française, première année*, Paris/ Strasbourg 1858 – for all departments of France. But no entry for fortifications, places de guerre, etc. – presumably because these were centrally administered by the Ministère de la Guerre.

Boitel, Léon, *Lyon ancien et moderne*, 2 vols, Lyon 1843.

Bonnald, Monseigneur de, "Extrait de la circulaire adressée à MM. les curés de son diocèse, par Monseigneur De Bonnald, Évêque du Puy, Conservateur des Monuments historiques de la Haute-Loire," in *BM* V 1839, 228–236. On "archéologie chrétienne."

Bonnard, Louis. *La Gaule thermale: sources et stations thermales et minérales de la Gaule à l'époque gallo-romaine avec la collaboration médicale du Dr Percepied*, Paris 1908.

Bonnardot, Alfred, *Dissertations archéologiques sur les anciennes enceintes de Paris, suivies de recherchés sur les portes fortifiées qui dépendaient de ces enceintes. Ouvrage formant le complément de celui intitulé Etudes archéologiques sur les anciens plans de Paris*, Paris 1852, with a list of plans as an appendix, Paris 1877. A thorough account, and with illustrations, but it is not clear just how many of the towers and wall-lengths he illustrates actually survived and had been seen, or been excavated.

Bonnet, Émile, *Antiquités et monuments du Département de l'Hérault*, Montpellier 1905.

Bonnin, T., "Notice sur un tombeau celtique découvert à Saint-Étienne-du-Vauvray," in *SG* LIII Nantes 1856, 340–351.

Bosquet, l'Abbé, *Antiquités Romaines de la Ville de Narbonne*, MS 24, Bibliothèque Municipale, Narbonne, 3 vols. 1783ff (no dates, but the "Avis" says it was begun in 1783).

Bottin, S., chevalier de l'ordre royal de la Légion-d'Honneur, secrétaire général, "Rapport sur les travaux de la Société royale des Antiquaires de France, lu à la séance publique du 2 juillet 1820," in *MDANE* III 1821, 15–123. Includes antiquities chronologically, then ethnography – myths, marriage and funeral customs, popular beliefs, feasts, dances etc. – showing how broad are the interests of antiquaries.

Bouiron, Marc, ed., *Nice, la colline du château. Histoire millénaire d'une place forte*, Nice 2013.

Bourassé, Abbé J.-J., *Archéologie chrétienne, ou précis de l'histoire des monuments religieux du moyen âge*, Tours 1841.

Bourges, anon, *Catalogue du Musée Lapidaire de Bourges*, Bourges 1873. Entered as Bourges_lapidaire.

Boyer, Victor, *La cité de Carcassonne*, Paris 1884.

Breuillac, Henri-Georges, *Le soldat et le domaine militaire devant la loi*, thèse pour le doctorat soutenue le 24 juin 1870, Poitiers 1870.

BIBLIOGRAPHY: SOURCES

Brutails, J.-A., *L'archéologie du Moyen-Âge et ses méthodes. Étude critiques*, Paris 1900.

Bulliot, J.-G., *Essai sur le système défensif des Romains dans le pays Éduen*, Paris/Autun 1856.

———, "Société Éduenne des Lettres, Sciences et Arts," in *Réunion BA* 1877, 68–75.

Bureaux-Pusy, J. X., *Rapport sur la conservation et le classement des Places de Guerre et Postes militaires...fait à l'Assemblée Nationale*, le 24 mai 1791.

Cambry, Jacques, *Monuments celtiques, ou recherches sur le culte des pierres*, Paris 1805.

La Campagne du nord. Opérations de l'armée française du nord (1870–1871). Avec cartes d'ensemble et plans de bataille (25 février 1873), Paris 1873.

Candas & Yveri, Entrepreneurs de travaux publics, *Travaux du Génie Militaire, Procès en dénonciation calomnieux*, Paris 1881, p. 106.

Carnot, M., *De la défense des places fortes*, Paris 1812.

Cartailhac, Émile, *La France préhistorique d'après les sépultures et les monuments*, Paris 1903.

Catalogue du Musée départemental et communal d'antiquités, fondé à Amiens en 1836, par la société des antiquaires de Picardie, Amiens 1845.

Catalogue du musée fondé et administré la la Société Historique et Archéologique de Langres, Langres 1886.

Caumont, Arcisse de (1801–1873), *Cours d'antiquités monumentales: histoire de l'art dans l'Ouest de la France, depuis les temps les plus reculés jusqu'au XVIIe siècle, professé à Caen*, 6 vols, Paris 1830–1841.

———, *Caumont_Cours_1830, Avertissement, separately published p. 8*.

———, *Statistique monumentale du Calvados* 5 vols, Caen 1846–1867.

———, *Abécédaire ou Rudiments d'Archéologie* I, 1853.

———, *Catalogue du musée plastique de la société française d'archéologie à Caen*, Caen 1860.

———, "Sculptures antiques découvertes dans les murs de Sens," in *BM* 1851, 150–153; and describes and illustrates the blocks.

Cayla, J.-M., & Perrin-Paviot, *Histoire de la ville de Toulouse*, Toulouse 1859.

Caylus, Comte de, *Recueil d'antiquités egyptiennes, etrusques, grecques et romaines*, II, Paris 1766; IV, Paris 1761.

Chardon, Olivier-Jacques, *Histoire de la ville d'Auxerre II*, Auxerre 1835.

Charmes, Xavier, *Le Comité des Travaux Historiques et Scientifiques: histoire et documents*, 3 vols, Paris 1886.

Charvet, Claude [a priest, 1715–1772], *Fastes de la Ville de Vienne*, Manuscrit inédit, Vienne 1869, Savigné, E.-J., ed. Charvet deals with what he has seen: he keeps writing "j'ai vu."

Chaudruc de Crazannes, Baron, Inspecteur-Conservateur des Monumens d'Antiquité de la Charente Inférieure, *Antiquités de la Ville de Saintes*, Paris 1820.

Cherbonneau, Auguste (1813–1882), "Constantine et ses antiquités," from the *Nouvelles Annales des Voyages*, Février 1857.

Chevalier, Michel, *Des Intérêts matériels en France. Travaux publics. Routes. Canaux. Chemins de Fer*, 3rd edn., Paris 1838.

Chévrier, Jules, *Chalon-sur-Saône pittoresque et démoli*, Paris 1883.

Chorier, Nicolas, *Recherches sur les antiquités de la ville de Vienne*, Lyon 1846. First published 1658 (some examples 1659).

Circulars of Information of the Bureau of Education, 1 1881: Education in France, Washington 1881.

Clair, H., *Les monumens d'Arles antique et moderne*, Arles 1837. His report to the Commission archéologique d'Arles.

Clemen, Paul, *Die Denkmalpflege in Frankreich*, Berlin, 1898.

Clément, Pierre, ed., *Lettres, instruction et mémoires de Colbert*, V, Paris 1868.

Cochet, L'abbé, (1812–1875), *La Seine Inférieure, historique et archéologique, époques Gauloise, Romaine et Franque*, 2nd edn., Paris 1866.

———, *Répertoire Archéologique du Département de la Seine-Inférieure*, Paris 1871.

Collection de documents inédits sur l'histoire de France publiés par ordre du Roi et par les soins du Ministre de l'Instruction Publique: Rapports au Ministre, Paris 1839. Entered as Documents-Inédits.

Cook's practical guide to Algeria and Tunisia, Algiers 1908. Entered as Cook_1908.

Corbun, Jean-Marie, deputy for the Gironde, *Observations sur les projets de vente ou d'aliénation du Château-Trompette et la destruction entière de la place, que le Conseil des Cinq-Cents a adoptés d'après des plans proposés, et qu'aurait contredits Corbun*, (nd, surely late 18th century).

Cottier, F-R-J-C, *Recueil de Divers Titres ... dont jouit la ville de Carpentras*, Carpentras 1782.

Courajod, Louis, *Alexandre Lenoir, son journal et le Musée des Monuments Français*, 2 vols Paris 1878 & 1880.

Courtin, M., Secrétaire général de la Direction générale des Ponts-et-Chaussées, *Travaux des Ponts-et-Chaussées depuis 1800, ou tableau des constructions neuves*, Paris 1812.

Daremberg, Charles, & Saglio, Edmond, *Dictionnaire des antiquités grecques et romaines*, I.2, Paris 1887.

De Bourcet, Lieutenant-Général P.-J., *Mémoires militaires sur les frontières de la France, du Piémont et de la Savoie*, Berlin 1801.

Decombe, Lucien, *Trésor du Jardin de la préfecture à Rennes, époque gallo-romaine*, Rennes 1882.

De la Noë, Colonel G., *Principes de la fortification antique*, Paris 1888.

Delorme, T.-C., *Dissertation sur l'enceinte fortifiée de Vienne sous les Romains*, Vienne 1842.

BIBLIOGRAPHY: SOURCES

Demilly, Chef de division à la Préfecture de l'Aisne, membre du Conseil des bâtiments civils et de la Société académique de Laon, etc., *De la Prétendue enceinte de la ville de Laon et de son illégalité au point de vue de l'octroi*, Laon 1860.

Despois, Eugène, *Le vandalisme révolutionnaire*, Paris 1868. With sticker on the front cover: *Ouvrage approuvé par le Ministère de l'Instruction Publique pour les bibliothèques populaires & scolaires*.

Devic, Dom Claude, & Vaissete, Dom Joseph, *Histoire générale de Languedoc*, 15 vols, Toulouse 1872–92. Originally 5 vols, Paris 1730–1745, but extended to 15 and re-edited. Vol. 15 contains the inscriptions, divided by editors into type; herein only page and then inscription numbers are cited. Vol. XVI is by Ernest Roschach, q.v.

Dictionnaire Universel de la France, Paris 1771.

Direction des Beaux-Arts, Monuments Historiques. *Loi et Décrets relatifs à la conservation des monuments historiques. Liste des monuments classés*, Paris, Imprimerie Nationale, 1889.

Dochier, M., *Mémoires sur la ville de Romans*, Valence 1812.

Doyen, C.-L., *Histoire de la ville de Beauvais depuis le 14ᵉ siècle* II, Beauvais 1842.

Du Camp, Maxime, *Paris: ses organes, ses fonctions et sa vie dans la seconde moitié du XIXᵉ siècle*, 5th edn., Paris 1875.

Dumont, le père Etienne, *Description des anciens monuments d'Arles*, Arles 1789.

Du Perrier, Baron, & Barry, Edward, "Rapport de la Commission nommée par la Société Archéologique du Midi de la France à l'occasion du projet de reconstruction du Capitole. De la conservation et de la restauration des monuments historiques renfermés dans le périmètre de l'hôtel de ville de Toulouse," in *BSA_Midi* IX 1866–1871, 185–190.

Dunlop-Wallace-Goodbody, F. G., "All that Remains of Forum Julii (Fréjus)," in *Gentleman's Magazine* CCXCVII 1904, 170–194, 284–304. Describes remains of the port, and has evidently walked around it.

Durant, Simon, et al., *Album archéologique et description des monuments historiques du Gard*, Nîmes 1853.

Dusevel, H., *Histoire de la ville d'Amiens depuis les Gaulois jusqu'à nos jours*, 2nd edn., Amiens 1848.

Dussieux, L., *Géographie historique de la France*, Paris 1843.

Dutens, J., *Histoire de la navigation intérieure de la France, avec une exposition des canaux à entreprendre pour en compléter le système*, I, Paris 1829.

Encyclopaedia Britannica, 11th edn., Cambridge 1910–1911. Entered as EB_vol_entry.

Enlart, Camille, *Manuel d'archéologie française*, I, architecture religieuse, Paris 1902.

———, *Manuel d'archéologie française* I: architecture, II, architecture civile et militaire, Paris 1904.

———, *Rouen*, Paris 1906.

———, *Villes mortes du Moyen Âge*, Paris 1920.

384 BIBLIOGRAPHY: SOURCES

Espérandieu, Émile, *Recueil général des bas-reliefs de la Gaule romaine*, 11 vols., Paris 1907–1938.

Estrangin, Jean-Julien, Avocat à Arles, *Le Musée lapidaire de la ville d'Arles*, Marseille 1837.

———, *Études archéologiques, historiques et statistiques sur Arles, contenant la description des monuments antiques et modernes ainsi que des notes sur le territoire*, Aix 1838.

Fabre, Augustin, *Histoire de Provence*, 4 vols. Marseille 1833–1834–1834–1835.

Favard de Langlade, le Baron, *Répertoire de la nouvelle législation civile, commerciale et administrative*, IV, Paris 1825.

Favatier, Léonce, *La vie municipale à Narbonne au XVIIᵉ siècle*, II, Narbonne 1903.

Fil, E., *Rapport adressé à MM. les Membres de la Commission Archéologique (sur les fouilles de la Butte des Moulins)*, dated 11 September, 1877. BM Narbonne, MS 58.

Flammermont, Jules, "Histoire des institutions municipales de Senlis," in *Bibl. École Hautes Études* XLV, Paris 1881. But only goes up to the early 17th century.

Fleury, Édouard, *Antiquités et monuments du Département de l'Aisne*, I & II, Paris 1877–8.

Floyd, Rev. M., *Travels in France and the British Islands*, Philadelphia 1859. In spite of its title, largely confined to Paris and Normandy.

Foisset, Paul (1831–1885), and Simonnet, Jules (1824–1875). *Voies romaines du département de la Côte-d'Or et répertoire archéologique des arrondissements de Dijon et de Beaune publiés par la Commission des antiquités du département de la Côte d'Or*, Dijon & Paris 1872. The Répertoire does each commune by date, "Ép. Celtique . . . Ép. romaine . . . Ép.moyen-âge" etc.

Fornery, J. (1675–1756), *Histoire du Comté Venaissin* III, nd, MS Vaison la Romaine (other copies are in Carpentras & Avignon).

Franklin, Alfred (1830–1917), *Les Sources de l'histoire de France, notices biographiques et analytiques des inventaires et des recueils de documents relatifs à l'histoire de France*, Paris 1877.

Frossard, Émilien, *Tableau pittoresque, scientifique et moral de Nîmes* I, Nîmes 1834.

Garcin, E., *Dictionnaire historique de la Provence ancienne et moderne* I, Draguignan 1835. With plentiful information on the whole variety of Roman remains.

Garrigues, P., *Recherches historiques sur les Antiquités de la France X: Aude: Antiquités de Narbonne*, dated Reims 1823. BM Narbonne, MS 25. (This is an autograph copy of parts of Garrigues' work, now at Chatsworth: cf. Espérandieu I 360).

Gasparin, Adrien-Étienne-Pierre, comte de, ainé, *Histoire de la ville d'Orange, et de ses antiquités*, Orange 1815.

Gaulthières, Dom Nicole de, Les grandes et admirables merveilles descouvertes au Duché de Bourgogne près la ville d'Authun au lieu dict la Caverne aux Fées," in *Mém Éduenne* XII 1883, 1–39, Fontenay, Harold de, ed., dated 1580, printed 1582.

BIBLIOGRAPHY: SOURCES

Gembloux, Pierquin de, *Notices historiques, archéologiques et philologiques sur Bourges et le Département du Cher*, Bourges 1840.

Germain, A., *Notice sur le manuscrit original de l'Histoire de la Ville de Montpellier du Chanoine Charles de Grefeuille*, Montpellier 1869.

Germer-Durand, E., *Promenades d'un curieux dans Nîmes*, Nîmes 1874.

———, et al., *Inscriptions antiques de Nîmes*, Toulouse 1893. Find-spots given where known; majority extracted from building in town and suburbs, mostly mid-18th century to date.

Gerstner, F. de, *Mémoire sur les grandes routes, les chemins de fer et les canaux de navigation*, Paris 1827.

Ginieis, L'Abbé, "L'étang de Montady et les percées du Malpas," in *L'Hérault Historique Illustré*, ed. A. & P. Fabre, 1876, 168–82.

Girault de Saint-Fargeau, Eusèbe, *Guide pittoresque, portatif et complet du voyageur en France: contenant les relais de poste, dont la distance a été convertie en kilomètres*, 3rd edn., Paris 1842.

Goiffon, l'Abbé, *Dictionnaire topographique statistique et historique du Diocèse de Nîmes*, Nîmes 1881.

Goussard, J., *Nouveau guide pittoresque du voyageur à Dijon*, 3rd edn., Dijon 1861.

Goze, A., *Les enceintes successives d'Amiens*, Amiens 1854 (overstamped 1853).

Grandmaison, Charles de, Archiviste d'Indre et Loire, *Tours archéologique*, 1879.

"Graves" (no other name), *Notice archéologique sur le Département de l'Oise, comprenant la liste des monumens de l'époque celtique, de l'époque gallo-romaine et du moyen-âge qui subsistent dans l'étendu du pays, et l'indication de ceux dont on retrouve encore les vestiges*, Beauvais 1839 – title says it all. Extract from the Annuaire du département de l'Oise for 1839, pp. 236 including index of places. This is a very interesting, detailed and evidently useful compilation; various people wrote in to help compile the lists – see. vi–vii.

Gregory of Tours, *Histoire Ecclésiastique des Francs*, 2 vols, Guadet, J., & Taranne, eds., Paris 1836 & 1838.

———, *Les livres des miracles et autres opuscules*, Bordier, H. L. ed., 3 vols, Paris 1857, 1860, 1862.

Greppo, J. G. H., *Études archéologiques sur les eaux thermales ou minérales de la Gaule à l'époque romaine*, Paris 1846.

Grignon, Louis, *Topographie historique de la ville de Châlons-sur-Marne*, Châlons 1889.

Grille de Beuzelin, Ernest, *Rapport à M. le Ministre de l'Instruction Publique sur les monuments historiques des arrondissements de Nancy et de Toul, accompagné de cartes, plans et dessins*, Paris 1837. Ouvrage faisant partie de la Collection de documents inédits publiés par les soins du Ministre de l'instruction publique.

Gsell, Stéphane, *Les Monuments antiques de l'Algérie* I, Paris 1901.

Guibert, Aristide, *Histoire des villes de France*, I 1844, II–III–IV 1845, V–VI 1848, all Paris.

386 BIBLIOGRAPHY: SOURCES

Guillaumot, Georges, *L'organisation des chemins de fer en France*, Paris 1899.

Guilmeth, Alexandre-Auguste. *Notices historiques sur la ville d'Évreux et ses environs: le bourg de Gaillon, le Château-Gaillard et le bourg d'Écouis, près Andelys*, Paris 1835.

———, *Notice historique sur la ville et les environs d'Évreux*, Rouen 1849.

Hamerton, Philip G. (English artist), *The mount. Narrative of a visit to the site of a Gaulish city on Mont Beuvray with a description of the neighboring city of Autun*, Boston 1897.

M. Henry, "Notice sur l'amphithéâtre d'Arles," in *MSRAF* XIII 1837, 1–47.

Hérisson, Maurice d'Irisson (1839–1893), *Relation d'une mission archéologique en Tunisie*, Paris 1881.

Héron de Villefosse, A., & Thédenat, H., *Inscriptions romaines de Fréjus*, Tours & Paris 1884.

Hughes, Rev. W., *A Tour Through Several of the Midland and Western Departments of France*, 1803.

Hugo, Abel, *France pittoresque*, 3 vols. 1835. Gives population, administration, and military town by town.

Hugo, Victor, "Guerre aux démolisseurs," in *RDM* 1 March 1832, 607–622.

Hunnewell, James, F., *The historical monuments of France*, Boston & New York 1898.

Inventaire général des richesses d'art de la France; archives du Musée des Monuments Français I, Paris 1883, etc. etc.

Jablonski, Ludovic, *L'armée française à travers les âges* II, Paris/Limoges 1891.

Jacobs, Alfred, *Géographie de Grégoire de Tours de Frédégaire et de leurs continuateurs*, Paris 1861.

Jolimont, T. de, *Description historique et vues pittoresques des monuments les plus remarquables de Dijon*, Paris 1830.

Joulin, L., *Les établissements gallo-romaines de la plaine de Martres-Tolosanes*, Paris 1901.

Jousselin, Joseph, *Traité des servitudes d'utilité publique ou des modifications apportées par les lois et par les règlements à la propriété immobilière en faveur de l'utilité publique*, II, Paris 1850.

Jullian, Camille, *Inscriptions romaines de Bordeaux* II, Bordeaux 1890.

———, *Gallia. Tableau sommaire de la Gaule sous la domination romaine*, 2nd edn., Paris 1902.

———, *Histoire de la Gaule V, La civilisation gallo-romaine*, Paris 1920.

Julliot, Gustave (1829–1903). *Inscriptions et monuments du Musée gallo-romain de Sens: descriptions et interprétations*, Sens 1898.

———, *Essai sur l'enceinte de la ville de Sens*, Sens 1913. Excellent piece, with plenty of quotes and references to the archives.

Kersaint, Armand-Guy, *Discours sur les monuments publics, prononcé au Conseil du Département de Paris, le 15 Décembre 1791*, Paris 1792.

BIBLIOGRAPHY: SOURCES

Kirkman, Marshall M., *The science of railways: Economy of rates. Private versus government control*, Chicago 1894.

Labande, Léon-Honoré, *Histoire de Beauvais et de ses institutions communales jusqu'au commencement du XVe siècle*, Paris 1892.

———, *Étude historique et archéologique sur Saint-Trophîme d'Arles du IVe au XIIIe siècle*, Caen 1904.

Labédollière, Émile de, *Histoire des environs du nouveau Paris*, Paris 1860.

Lachèse, Elisciu, *Angers pittoresque*, Angers 1843.

Lacombe, Ferdinand de, "Le siége de Toul en 1870," extrait de *L'Abeille de Fontainebleau*, Fontainebleau 1874.

Lafaye, Georges, & Blanchet, Adrien, *Inventaire des mosaïques de la Gaule et de l'Afrique*, I, Gaule, Paris 1909.

Laferrière, Firmin Julien (Louis-Firmin), *Cours de droit public et administratif, mis en rapport avec les lois nouvelles et précédé d'une introduction historique*, 5e edn., Paris 1860.

Lafforgue, P., *Histoire de la ville d'Auch depuis les Romains jusqu'en 1789*, II, Auch 1851.

Lafont, Guillaume, *Les antiquitez de Narbonne, contenant les inscriptions, tombeaux et epitaphes romaines, qui se trouvent en divers endroits de la dite ville ensemble les demy-reliefs et reliefs des Romains qui sont en icelle ville*, Narbonne AM Ms 8vo, 1700, but modern note has 1739.

Lafont, P., "Charles IX et Catherine de Médicis à Narbonne," in *BCA Narbonne* 1890, 88–96, 147–157.

Lagrèze-Fossat, A., lawyer at Moissac, and Inspecteur des Monuments Historiques for Tarn-et-Garonne, *Etudes historiques sur Moissac*, 3 vols, Paris, 1874.

Lahondès, Jules de, *Les Monuments de Toulouse, histoire, archéologie, beaux-arts*, Toulouse 1920.

Lalaure, M., *Traité des servitudes réeles*, rev. Pailliet, Paris 1827. Comprehensive treatment in 905 pages, also explaining how various towns (such as Toulouse, Toul, Reims, Noyon, Lyon) got their servitudes.

Lalauzière, de Noble, *Abrégé chronologique de l'histoire d'Arles*, Arles 1808.

La Marsonnière, Jules-Levieil de (1818–1901), *Étude historique sur les textes de lois romaines expliquant la destruction des monuments dans les derniers temps de l'Empire d'Occident*, Poitiers 1858, extract from *MSA Ouest* XXIV 1857.

Laporte, Adolphe, architecte à Clermont-Ferrand, "Quelques mots sur Augusto-Nemetum [Clermont]," in *SG* LXII 1895 Clermont-Ferrand 161–176.

La Scava; or, some account of an excavation of a Roman town on the hill of Chatelet, in Champagne, between St. Dizier and Joinville, discovered in the year 1772, by the author of "Letters from Paris in 1791–2" etc., London 1818.

388   BIBLIOGRAPHY: SOURCES

Lasteyrie, Robert-Charles de, et al., *Bibliographie Générale des Travaux Historiques et Archéologiques publiés par les Sociétés savantes de la France, dressées sous les auspices du Ministère de l'Instruction Publique*, 3 vols, Paris 1888–1901, and then New Series 1901ff. Divided by department, and then by societies within each one.

Laurendeau, Maxime. *Les Sièges de Soissons en 1814, ou dissertation sur le récit de la campagne de France, en ce qui concerne la ville de Soissons*, Soissons 1868.

Leclercq de Laprairie, Jules, *Notice sur le château d'albâtre ou palais gallo-romain de Soissons*, Laon 1854.

Le Bas, Philippe, *Dictionnaire encyclopédique de la France*, Paris 1845.

Lebègue, A., Professeur à la Faculté de Toulouse, "Notice sur les fouilles de Martres-Tolosanes," in *BA* 1891, 396–423.

Ledain, B., 1870–1 "Mémoire sur l'enceinte gallo-romaine de Poitiers," in *MSA* Ouest 35_1870, 157–224.

Ledain, B., "Notice sur l'enceinte romaine de Saintes," in *SG* LXI 1894 Saintes 193–210.

Lehugeur, Paul, *Histoire de l'armée française*, Paris 1884.

Lenormant, Charles, "Rapport fait à l'Académie Royale des Inscriptions et Belles-Lettres, au nom de la Commission des Antiquités de la France, lu à la séance publique du 9 Août 1844," in *Revue Archéologique, ou recueil de documents et de mémoires relatifs à l'étude des monuments et à la philologie de l'antiquité et du Moyen Âge*, Première Partie 1844, 363–377. Entered as Lenormant 1844B.

Lestiboudois, Dr. Thémistocle, *Voyage en Algérie, ou Études sur la colonisation de l'Afrique française*, Lille 1853.

Levasseur, E., *Histoire du commerce de la France II, De 1789 à nos jours*, Paris 1912.

Lhuillier, L., "La Société Archéologique et son influence en Touraine," in *BSA* Touraine V 1884, 414–428 – thumbnail sketches of working members.

Loriquet, Charles, *La mosaïque des promenades et autres trouvées à Reims*, Reims 1862.

Leroux, M., *Histoire de la ville de Soissons I*, Soissons 1839.

Lorain, Prosper, *Histoire de l'Abbaye de Cluny, depuis sa fondation jusqu'à sa destruction à l'époque de la Révolution française*, 2nd edn., Paris 1845.

Lottin, D., *Recherches historiques sur la ville d'Orléans depuis Aurélien, l'an 274, jusqu'en 1789*, II, Orléans 1837.

Loudon, J.-B.-M., *Avignon, son histoire, ses papes, ses monumens*, Avignon 1842.

Lucas, Félix, *Etude historique et statistique sur les voies de communication de la France d'après les documents officiels*, Paris 1873.

Luquet, J. F. O., *Antiquités de Langres*, Langres 1838.

Macgibbon, David, *The architecture of Provence and the Riviera*, Edinburgh 1888.

Clement Macheret, *Journal de ce qui a passé de mémorable à Langres et aux environs depuis 1628 jusqu'en 1658*, 4 fasciscules, Langres 1880.

Maffei, Scipione, *Galliae Antiquitates quaedam selectae*, Verona 1734.

Maître, Léon, "Le théâtre de Coussol en Petit-Mars," in *BA* 1885, 57–60.

BIBLIOGRAPHY: SOURCES

Malte-Brun, V.-A., *La France illustré*, 5 vols. Paris 1881–4.

Mangon de la Lande, C.-F.-J., "Rapport sur les galeries souterrains de la ville de Poitiers," in *MSA Ouest* I 1835, 49–58.

Mangon de la Lande, C.-F.-J., "Rapport sur les galeries souterrains, ou l'antique enceinte de la ville de Poitiers," in *MSA Ouest* II 1836, 344–54.

Manuel des lois du batiment élaboré par la Société centrale des architectes. [...] Suivi du: Recueil des lois, ordonnances et arrêtés concernant la voirie ayant trait aux Constructions, Paris 1863.

Marion, Jules, *Notes d'un voyage archéologique dans le sud-ouest de la France*, Paris 1852.

Marmottan, Paul, "De la conservation des anciens hôtels historiques: Rapport présenté au Comité de la Société des Monuments parisiens," in *AMPF* V 1891, 14–23.

Martin, Henry, & Jacob, Paul-L., *Histoire de Soissons depuis les temps les plus reculés jusqu'à nos jours, d'après les sources originales*, 2 vols, Soissons 1837.

Massé, M., *Mémoire sur les vestiges de l'ancienne Ville de Thérouanne [Pas-de-Calais], et l'Etat qu'elle étoit en 1730*, Paris 1730.

Massiou, Léon, "Sur les Monumens romains de la ville de Saintes," in *BM* I 1834, 173–186.

Mège, Alexandre du (1780–1862), *Description du Musée des Antiques de Toulouse*, Toulouse 1835.

———, *Archéologie pyrénéenne, antiquités religieuses, historiques, militaires, artistiques, domestiques et sépulcrales d'une portion de la Narbonnaise, et de l'Aquitaine, nommée plus tard Novempopulanie, ou Monuments authentiques de l'histoire du sud-ouest de la France, depuis les plus anciennes époques*, III.1, Toulouse 1862.

Mège, Chevalier Alexandre du, officier du génie, "Sur l'amphithéâtre de Narbonne," in *BSA Midi* IV 1840–1841, 401–408.

Melleville, Maximilien, *Histoire de la ville de Laon*, 2 vols, Laon/Paris 1846.

Mémoires et documents inédits pour servir à l'histoire de la Franche-Comté I, Besançon 1838. Entered as Mémoires_Franche-Comté.

Ménard, L., *Histoire civile écclesiastique et littéraire de la ville de Nîmes*, 7 vols, Paris 1750–58.

———, *Histoire des antiquités de la ville de Nismes et de ses environs, septième édition, par Perrot*, Nîmes 1838.

Mérimée, Prosper, *Notes d'un voyage dans le Midi de la France*, Paris 1835.

———, *Notes d'un voyage dans l'ouest de la France, extrait d'un rapport addressé à M. le Ministre de l'Intérieur*, Paris 1836.

———, *Notes d'un voyage en Auvergne, extrait d'un rapport addressé à M. le Ministre de l'Intérieur*, Paris 1838.

———, *Monuments Historiques. Rapport au Ministre de l'Intérieur*, Paris 1843. Viz for their work in 1842.

Merruau, Charles, *Souvenirs de l'Hôtel de Ville de Paris, 1848–1852*, Paris 1875.

Merson, Ernest, *Journal d'un journaliste en voyage*, Paris 1865.

Michaelis, Adolf, *Ancient marbles in Great Britain*, Cambridge 1882.

Michel, Adolphe, *L'ancienne Auvergne et le Vélay* III, Moulins 1847.

Michel, Georges, *Histoire de Vauban*, Paris 1879.

Michel, R., "Les chevaliers du Château des Arènes de Nîmes au XIIe et XIIIe siècles," in *Revue Historique* 102, 1909, 3–19.

Migne, L'Abbé, *Nouvelle Encyclopédie théologique* XXX, Paris 1852.

Migneret, S., avocat, *Précis de l'histoire de Langres*, Langres 1835.

Millénaire de Cluny: Congrès d'histoire et d'archéologie, 2 vols, Mâcon 1910. Entered as Millénaire.

Millin, Aubin-Louis, *Voyage dans les Départemens du Midi de la France*, 5 vols., Paris 1807–1811.

Miln, James, *Excavations at Carnac (Brittany). A record of archaeological researches in the Bossenno and the Mont Saint Michel*, Edinburgh 1877.

Ministère de l'Instruction Publique et des Cultes, *Répertoire des Travaux Historiques* I, 1882.

Ministère des Travaux Publics, *Documents relatifs aux canaux*, Paris 1840.

Moliner-Violle. *Thamugas, ses fouilles et ses découvertes... par Moliner-Violle, (15 septembre 1890.)*, Batna 1891.

Momméja, J., "Dom Bernard de Montfaucon et l'archéologie préhistorique," in *Revue de Gascogne* 39, 1898, 5–22, 73–88.

Moncaut, Cénac, *Voyage archéologique et historique dans le Pays Basque et le Guypuscoa*, Tarbes/Paris 1857.

Montaiglon, Anatole de, *Antiquités et curiosités de la ville de Sens*, Paris 1881.

Montalembert, Charles Forbes, le comte de, *Du vandalisme et du catholicisme dans l'art (fragmens)*, Paris 1839, with 1–69 his letter 1833 to Victor Hugo, "Du vandalisme en France," with many flatulent generalities.

Monfalcon, Jean-Baptiste (1792–1874), *Le Nouveau Spon. Manuel du bibliophile et de l'archéologue lyonnais*, Paris 1857.

———, *Histoire monumentale de la Ville de Lyon*, 6 vols, Paris 1866.

Moreau, Inspecteur des monuments historiques de la Charente Inférieure, "Rapport," in *SG* VIII 1841, 116–120.

Mortet, V., *Recueil de textes relatifs à l'histoire de l'architecture en France au Moyen Age*, 2 vols, Paris 1911 (XI–XIIe siècles) and 1929 (XIIe–XIIIe siècles).

Moufflet, Principal du Collège à Saintes, vice-président de la Société archéologique de Saintes "Rapport sur l'amphithéâtre de Saintes," in *BM* 1845, 18–30.

Mouynès, Germain, *Ville de Narbonne: Inventaire des archives communales antérieures à 1790*, II, Narbonne 1877.

Murcier, Arthur, *La sépulture chrétien en France d'après les monuemts du XIe au XVIe siècle*, Paris 1855.

BIBLIOGRAPHY: SOURCES 391

Murray, David, *Museums, their history and their use*, 3 vols. Glasgow 1904. Useful for its bibliography and list of museums, neither restricted to the UK. Good on early collectors (I, 13–101).

Murray, John, *Handbook for travellers in France, being a guide to Normandy, Brittany etc.*, 3rd edn., London 1848.

Narbonne, *Archives Communales antérieurs à 1790, Série BB*, II, Narbonne 1877.

Normand, Charles, "Histoire de la découverte des Arènes et de la lutte contre le vandalisme," in *AMPF* VIII 1894, 49–126.

Normand, Charles, "Les fouilles d'Yzeures (Indre-et-Loire) et la Gigantomachie inédite récemment découverte," in *AMPF* X 1896, 293–311. Normand was director of this review.

Nouvelles Annales de la Construction, publication rapide et économique des documents les plus récents et les plus intéressants relatifs à la construction française et étrangère, I, Paris 1855.

Panorama pittoresque de la France, Paris 1839.

Paté, Lucien, *L'état et les monuments historiques, conférence faite au Palais du Trocadéro le jeudi 9 août 1900*, Paris 1900.

Pech, Canon, *Inscriptions et bas-reliefs qui sont a Narbonne*, BM Narbonne MS 27, 1713; taken from the work of Guillaume Lafont, Les Antiquitez de Narbonne. Cf. Espérandieu I 360.

Pelet, Auguste, *Catalogue du Musée de Nîmes, Notice historique sur la Maison Carrée*, Nîmes 1854.

———, *Description de l'amphithéâtre de Nîmes*, 3rd edn., Nîmes 1866.

———, "Fouilles à la Porte d'Auguste à Nîmes (1849)," in *Mém Gard 1847–1848*, 1849, 43–66.

Penchaud, Michel-Robert, architecte départmentale, Conservateur des monumens du département des Bouches-du-Rhône, "Fouilles du Théâtre d'Arles," in *Mémoires et Dissertations sur les Antiquités Nationales et Étrangers publiés par la Société Royale de France* VII, Paris 1826, 225–231.

Penjon, A., *Cluny, La ville et l'abbaye*, Cluny 1884.

Perrot, J. F. A., Antiquaire ancien Conducteur des Fouilles, *Lettres sur Nismes et le Midi, et description des monumens antiques du Midi de la France*, Nîmes 1840.

Perrot, Henri de, et al., *L'église romane de Saint-Sulpice (Vaud) et sa restauration*, Lausanne 1888.

Perrot, G., "Rapport [to the Minister] sur les fouilles de Martres," in *RA* 1891, 56–73. They spent a week, divided between examining finds in the museum, and three days at the site. The 1826–30 dig, by Dumège, brought most sculpture to light, the 1842 one fewer.

Pesquidoux, Léonce Dubose de, *Voyage artistique en France; études sur les musées d'Angers etc. etc.*, Paris 1857.

Petit, Victor, "Esquisses des monuments romains de Fréjus," in *BM* 1864, 569–612, 681–704, 761–794.

Petitjean, Narcisse-Nicolas, *Les grands travaux de Paris: l'exposition de 1900, le métropolitain, la démolition des remparts, la nouvelle enceinte, le tout-à-l'égout*, 3rd edn., Paris 1895.

Peyronny, Charles, & Delamarre, Emmanuel, *Commentaire théorique et pratique des lois d'expropriation pour cause d'utilité publique*, Paris 1859.

Peyre, Roger, *Nîmes, Arles, Orange, Saint-Rémy*, 2nd edn., Paris 1910.

Picard, Albert, *Les chemins de fer, aperçu historique*, Paris 1918.

Piépape, Léonce de, *Histoire militaire du pays de Langres et du Bassigny*, Langres & Paris 1884.

Piesse, Louis, *Itinéraire historique et descriptif de l'Algérie*, Paris 1862.

Pieyre, Adolphe, *Histoire de la ville de Nîmes*, II, Nîmes 1887, III Nîmes 1888.

Piganiol de la Force, *Nouvelle description de la France*, 3rd edn., 13 vols, Paris 1753–4. Pays considerable attention to describing town fortifications and their environs.

Pigault-Lebrun, Charles-Antoine-Guillaume, and Augier, Victor, avocat, *Voyage dans le Midi de la France*, Paris 1827.

Pigeonneau, H., *Histoire du commerce de la France* II, Paris 1889.

Pihan, L'Abbé L., *Beauvais, sa cathédrale, ses principaux monuments*, Beauvais 1885.

Pillet-Will, Michel Frédéric, *De la dépense et du produit des canaux et des chemins de fer*, Paris 1837.

Pingaud, Léonce, *Choiseul-Gouffier: la France en Orient sous Louis XVI*, Paris 1887.

Pinkney, Lieut-Col. Nathan, of the North-American Native Rangers, *Travels through the south of France and in the interior of the provinces of Provence and Languedoc in the years 1807 and 1808*, London 1809; 2nd edn. 1814.

Polonceau, A. R., *Observations sur les routes, suivies de propositions sur leur amélioration et sur leur entretien*, Paris 1829.

Poldo d'Albenas, Jean, *Discours historial de l'antique et illustre cité de Nîsmes*, Lyon 1560.

Port, Célestin, *Essai sur l'histoire du commerce maritime de Narbonne*, Paris 1854.

Postel, Raoul, *En Tunisie et au Maroc*, Paris 1885.

Prost, Bernard, *Inventaires mobiliers et extrait des comptes des Ducs de Bourgogne de la maison de Valois 1363–1477*, II, Paris 1913.

Proust, Antonin, *Rapport fait au nom de la Commission chargée d'examiner le projet de loi adopté par le Sénat pour la Conservation des Monuments et objets d'art*, Paris, Chambre des Députés 1887.

Puech, Albert, *Une ville au temps jadis: Nîmes à la fin du XVIᵉ siècle*, Nîmes 1884.

Quantin, Maximilien (1814–1891), *Catalogue raisonné du musée d'Auxerre. ıre division: monuments lapidaires*, Auxerre 1884.

Quatremère de Quincy, Antoine Chrysostome, *Considérations morales sur la destination des ouvrages de l'art*, Paris 1815.

BIBLIOGRAPHY: SOURCES

393

Rance, A-J., *L'Académie d'Arles au XVIIᵉ siècle d'après les documents originaux*, III, Paris 1890.

Rapport de la Commission chargée de l'examen des mémoires relatifs aux antiquités de la France, envoyés à l'Académie par son Exc. Le Ministre de l'Intérieur. Signed by Walckenaer, Petit-Radel and Laborde, in *Mém AIBL* VII 1824. Entered as Rapport 1824.

Rastoul de Mongeot, Alphonse, *Tableau d'Avignon*, Avignon 1836.

Reclus, Onésime (1837–1916), *À la France: sites et monuments, Pyrénées Orientales, etc.*, Paris 1903.

Reinach, Salomon, and other members of the Commission de l'Afrique, *Instructions adressées par le Comité des Travaux Historiques et Scientifiques aux correspondants du Ministère de l'Instruction Publique: Recherches des antiquités dans le nord de l'Afrique, Conseils aux archéologues et aux voyageurs*, Paris 1890.

Réunion des officiers, *Les défenseurs des forteresses et subsidairement la réorganisation de l'Artillerie et du Génie*, Paris 1873.

Rever, François, *Mémoire sur les ruines du Vieil-Évreux*, Évreux etc. 1827.

M. Rey, "Plan d'un ouvrage intitulé: Histoire du Vandalisme en France, depuis le XVIᵉ siècle, communiqué à la Société Française pour la conservation des Monuments, dans la séance du 24 janvier 1839," in *BM* V 1839, 223–228.

R.F.D., *Observations sur le siège de Soissons en 1870 et sur l'avis du conseil d'enquête*, (signé: R.F.D.), Versailles 1872.

Ribault de Laugardière, Charles. *Notes historiques sur la ville de Bourges, son origine, ses fortifications, ses monuments gallo-romains civils*, Bourges 1858.

Roach Smith, Charles, *Notes on the antiquities of France made during a fortnight's excursion in the summer of 1854*, London 1855.

Rogue, Nicolas-Pierre-Christophe, *Souvenirs et journal d'un bourgeois d'Évreux, 1740–1830*, Évreux 1850.

Rollière, Brothier de, *Nouveau guide du voyageur à Poitiers*, Poitiers 1907.

Romieu, Lantelme de, *Histoire des Antiquitez d'Arles, avec plusieurs écrits et épitaphes antiques, trouvés la-mesmes, et en autres lieux*, MS 240 of the Bibliothèque Municipale, Arles, dated 1574 and in a transcription of 1776; the library at Carpentras has a 16th century version, MS 608.

Roschach, Ernest, *Histoire graphique de l'ancienne Province de Languedoc* XVI, Toulouse 1905.

Rouard, E., *Rapports sur les fouilles d'antiquités faites à Aix (Bouches-du-Bhône), en 1841, 1842, 1843, 1844*, Aix 1841–844. With considerable finds – rooms, mosaics, hypocausts, inscriptions, statues, coins, etc.

Rouvière, F., *Mercredis révolutionnaires*, Nîmes 1901.

Roux, Antoine, *Recherches historiques sur les Antiquités de la France. Vol X: Aude: Antiquités de Narbonne*, Reims 1823.

Rupin, Ernest, *L'abbaye et les cloîtres de Moissac*, Paris 1897.

Sageret, P. F., *Almanach et annuaire des bâtiments, des travaux publics et de l'industrie*, Paris 1841.

Saint-Fergeux, Pistolet de, *Recherches historiques et statistiques sur les principales communes de l'arrondissement de Langres*, Langres 1836. Antique inscriptions noted in many communes.

———, "Notice sur deux arcs de triomphe romains, à Langres," in *MSRAF* III 1837, 197–202.

———, "Anciennes fortifications de Langres," in *Mém Langres* II 1862–77, 231–252.

Saint-Mandé, Ville de, *Déclassement des fortifications et annexion à la ville de Paris des terrains de la zône des servitudes militaires*, Saint-Mandé 1913. In full: *Déclassement des fortifications et annexion à la ville de Paris des terrains de la zône des servitudes militaires. Requête présentée par la Ville de Saint-Mandé. Modification au projet de convention entre l'État et la Ville de Paris, relatif au déclassement des fortifications et à l'annexion de la zone militaire. Requête présentée par la ville de Saint-Mandé... pour obtenir une modification au projet de convention...*, Paris 1913.

Saint-Paul, Anthyme, *Viollet-le-Duc, ses travaux d'art et son système archéologique*, Paris 1881.

Samazeuilh, J.-F., "Mémoire sur les fouilles de Nérac," in *Revue d'Aquitaine* IX 1865, 263–278, 345–356, 429–455.

Sansas, Pierre, "Vestiges d'aqueduc de l'époque Gallo-Romaine signalés sur différents points de la ville Bordeaux," in *SA Bordeaux* I 1874, 55–58.

———, "Notes archéologiques sur les fouilles exécutées à Bordeaux de 1863 à 1876," in *SA Bordeaux* V 1878, 123 130 and *SA Bordeaux* IX 1878, 102–108.

Schayes, A.-G.-B., *Les Pays-Bas avant et durant la domination romaine* II, Brussels 1838.

Scheler, Auguste, *Dictionnaire d'etymologie française*, 3rd edn., Brussels / Paris 1888.

Schmit, Jean-Philippe. *Nouveau manuel complet de l'architecte des monuments religieux, ou Traité d'application pratique de l'archéologie chrétienne à la construction, à l'entretien, à la restauration et à la décoration des églises*, Paris 1859.

Schneyder, Pierre [b. 1733], *Histoire des antiquités de la ville de Vienne*, Vienne 1880.

Schneider, René, *Quatremère de Quincy et son intervention dans les arts (1788–1830)*, Paris 1910.

Shuermans, Henri, "Remparts d'Arlon et de Tongres," in *Bull. Comm. Bruxelles* XVI 1877, 451, 502; XXVII 1888, 37–100; XXVIII 1889, 77–124; XXIX 1890, 35–94.

Les secrétaires de la Société Éduenne et de la Commission des Antiquités d'Autun, *Autun Archéologique*, Autun 1848. Very well illustrated, and with detailed descriptive text. Entered as Secrétaires Autun 1848.

Séguin, Joseph, *Les antiquitez d'Arles, traitées en manière d'entretien, et d'itinéraire, où sont décrites plusieurs nouvelles Découvertes qui n'ont pas encore veu le jour*, Arles 1687.

BIBLIOGRAPHY: SOURCES

Séguier, Jean-François, *Inscriptions relevées par l'Abbé Séguier à Nîmes et aux environs de cette ville*, bearing dates of 17 Aug. 1768 and 21 March 1765; BM Nîmes MS 109.

Seraucourt, Claude, *Plan géométral de la ville de Lyon*, Lyon 1740.

Sibenaler, J.-B., *Guide illustré du musée lapidaire-romain d'Arlon: contenant de nombreuses photogravures des monuments romains expliqués et décrits*, Arlon 1905.

Soil, E.-J., *Tournai archéologique en 1895*, Tournai 1895. A good description of the town, noting and briefly describing all the impressive houses still standing.

Sommerard, E. du, *Les monuments historiques de France à l'Exposition Universelle de Vienne*, Paris 1876.

Sopwith, T., *Notes of a visit to Egypt, by Paris, Lyons, Nismes, Marseilles and Toulon*, London 1857.

Spon, Jacob, *Recherche des antiquités et curiosites de la ville de Lyon*, Lyon 1675.

Stendhal, *Mémoires d'un touriste*, 2 vols, Paris 1891. Travelling in 1837.

Taillefer, comte Wulgrin de, *Antiquités de Vésone, cité gauloise, remplacée par la ville actuelle de Périgueux*, II, Périgueux 1826.

Tarbé, Gratien-Théodore, *Recherches historiques et anecdotiques sur la ville de Sens*, Sens 1838.

Tarbé, Prosper, *Reims, ses rues et ses monuments*, Reims 1844.

Tastu, Mme Amable, *Voyage en France*, Tours 1846. Excellent and sometimes detailed descriptions of monuments.

Terninck, Auguste, *Arras, histoire de l'architecture et des beaux-arts dans cette ville depuis les temps les plus reculés jusqu'à la fin du XVIIIe siècle*, Arras 1879.

Tétreau, Louis, *Législation relative aux monuments et objets d'art dont la conservation présente un intérêt national au point de vue de l'histoire ou de l'art*, thèse pour le doctorat, Faculté de droit de Paris, Paris 1896.

Thicknesse, Philip, *A year's journey through France and part of Spain*, 3rd edn., II, London 1789.

Thierry de Ville d'Avray, H., *Histoire de Cannes* I, Cannes 1909.

Thiers, F.-P., "Notes sur l'enceinte pré-wisigothique de Narbonne," in BCA Narbonne 1890, 158–169.

Thomas, Edmé, *Histoire de l'antique cité d'Autun, par Edmé Thomas, mort en 1660*, Autun 1846. Annotée par la Société éduenne.

Thorode, Louis-Michel, *Notes sur la ville d'Angers*, Angers 1897, composed 1772.

Tournal, Paul, *Catalogue du Musée de Narbonne*, Narbonne & Paris 1864.

———, "Travaux et découvertes à Narbonne," in BM 1869, 107.

Trélis, *Notice des travaux de l'Académie du Gard pendant l'année 1811*, Nîmes 1813.

Trumet de Fontarce, Armand. *Souvenirs d'Afrique. Algérie, Tunisie. Mission officielle, journal de voyage*, Bar-sur-Seine 1896.

Vasseur, Charles, "Quelques réflexions sur le tracé de l'enceinte gallo-romaine de Lisieux," in BM II 1860, 315–322. With a plan of the site.

Vaudin, Eugène, *Fastes de la Sénonie*, Auxerre/Paris 1882.

(Vaux), L'Église Saint-Sulpice de Vaux et sa restauration, Lausanne 1888.

Veaugeois, "Notice abrégée d'un voyage archéologique et géologique, fait, en 1820, dans les Alpes de la Savoie et dans les départemens méridionaux de la France," in *MSRAF* III 1821, 370–390.

Veran, Pierre, *Démolition d'une partie du ci-devant Palais de l'archévêque d'Arles, appelé l'arc de l'archevêché, et courte dissertation sur les ruines antiques qu'on a trouvées*, 1810, BMA Arles MS 767.

————, *Musée projeté dans la ville d'Arles*, 1814, BMA Arles MS 722.

Verdier, Aymar, & Cattois, Dr. F., *Architecture civile et domestique au moyen âge et à la renaissance*, 2 vols, Paris 1857.

Vergnaud-Romagnési, C. F., *Histoire de la ville d'Orléans*, Orléan 1830.

Vignier, Jacques, *Chronicon Lingonense*, Langres 1665. Links Langres just about to the whole of western history from BC onwards. Affirming that the city was founded shortly after the Flood, and Babylon!

————, *Decade historique du diocèse de Langres*, 2 vols, Langres 1891 & 1894.

Viguier de Lestagnol, le Chevalier, *Débris d'anciens monumens. Les Antiquités narbonnoises ou debris des édifices élevés par les Romains dans l'ancienne Narbonne*, BM Narbonne MS 265, 3 vols.

Vilback, Renaud de, *Voyages dans les départemens formés de l'ancienne province de Languedoc*, Paris 1825.

Villacrose, A., *Vingt ans en Algérie, ou Tribulations d'un colon racontées par lui-même: la colonisation en 1874, le régime militaire et l'administration civile, moeurs, coutumes, institutions des indigènes, ce qui est fait, ce qui est à faire*, Paris 1875.

Ville de Narbonne, *Documents rélatifs au déclassement de la ville de Narbonne*, Narbonne 1888.

Viollet-le-Duc, Eugène-Emmanuel, *Dictionnaire raisonné de l'architecture francaise du XIᵉ au XVIᵉ siècle*, 10 vols, Paris 1854–68.

Whittington, Rev. G. D., travelling 1802–3, *An historical survey of the ecclesiastical antiquities of France*, London 1809.

Woods, Joseph, *Letters of an architect, from France, Italy and Greece*, 2 vols, London 1828. Travelling in France in 1816. Very sensible: interested in working out the dates of buildings.

Young, Arthur, *Travels in France during the years 1787, 1788, 1789*, 3rd edn., London 1890.

Zônes militaires de la ville de Paris et des forts. Destruction des propriétés par le génie pour la défense nationale, Paris 1872.

Bibliography: Modern Scholars

Books and Papers with Useful Bibliographies are Preceded by *B.*

Albanese, Ralph, "Republican School Discourse and the Construction of French Cultural Identity: La Fontaine and Corneille as Case Studies," in Chaitin 2008, 64–82.

Alibert, Chantal et al., *Narbonne et le Narbonnais. Regards sur un patrimoine*, Portet-sur-Garonne 2010.

———, "Les antiquaires narbonnais à l'origine de la politique patrimoniale de Narbonne," in Krings & Valenti 2010, 87–96.

Al-Tikriti, Nabal, "Negligent mnemocide and the shattering of Iraqi collective memory," in Baker, Raymond W. et al., eds, *Cultural cleansing in Iraq. Why museums were looted, libraries burned and academics murdered*, London & New York 2010, 93–115.

Ambard, R., *Aix Romaine. Nouvelles observations sur la topographie d'Aquae Sextiae*, Aix-en-Provence 1984.

B Anderson, James C., *Roman architecture in Provence*, Cambridge 2013.

B Andrieux, Jean-Yves, *Patrimoine et histoire*, Paris 1997. The most interesting, subtle and best-referenced work on the topic, with extensive quotes throughout the text, and a large bibliography.

———, *B* ed., *Patrimoine: sources et paradoxes de l'identité*, congrès 2008, Rennes 2011. These papers are culturally much richer than those in *The Ashgate research companion*.

———, "L'architecture de la République en France au XIXᵉ siècle: comment les nations fabriquent-elles les habits de l'identité," in Andrieux 2011, 71–95.

B Anheier, Helmut, & Raj Isar, Yudhishthir, eds., *Heritage, memory and identity*, London etc. 2011. Very broad, with little on the terms' historical dimension.

Ardouin-Dumazet, Victor-Eugène, *Voyage en France*, Paris 1897–1907, in over 40 volumes, region by region. These are detailed and up-to-date guide books, with useful maps, and an emphasis on old towns as well as on modernity. Entered as AD region date page.

Audin, A., *Lyon miroir de Rome*, Paris 1979.

Audin, A., & Reynaud, J.-F., "Le mur des bords de Saône et ses inscriptions antiques," in *Bull. Musées et Monuments Lyonnais* VI, 1981.2, 457–79.

B Audisio, Gabriel, & Pugnière, François, eds., *J.-F. Séguier. Un Nîmois dans l'Europe des lumières*, Aix-en-Provence 2005.

Bailly, Xavier, & Dupont, Bernard, eds., *Histoire d'une ville: Amiens*, Amiens 2014. Well-illustrated overview.

Balmelle, C., *Les demeures aristocratiques d'Aquitaine. Société et culture de l'Antiquité tardive dans le Sud-Ouest de la Gaule* (Aquitania Supplément 10) Bordeaux 2001.

Baratier, E. & Villard, M, *Archives Départmentales des Bouches du Rhône. Répertoire de la série H 56 H*, Marseille 1966.

Barbanera, Marcello, "Tra visionarietà e osservazione: la riproduzione dei monument antichi nel XVIII secolo e le origini della moderna topografia classica," in D'Achille 2011, 189–203.

B Bardet, J.-P., *Rouen aux XVIIe et XVIIIe siècles. Les mutations d'un espace social*, Paris 1983, with a separate volume of documents, photos, graphs, plans, tables.

Barret-Kriegel, Blandine, *Les académies de l'histoire*, Paris 1988. Useful for setting the scene for the 19th century.

Barrière, P., *Vesunna petrucoriorum. Histoire d'une petite ville è l'époque gallo-romaine*, Périgueux 1930.

Barros, Martin, *Les fortifications en Île-de-France 1792–1944*, 3rd edn., Paris 2005.

B Baumier, Béatrice, *Tours entre Lumières et Roi. Pouvoir municipal et métamorphoses d'une ville (1764–1792)*, Rennes 2007.

Baxter, Douglas, *Servants of the Sword: French Military Intendants of the Army, 1630–1670*, Urbana ILL 1976.

B Bayard, Didier, & Massy, Jean-Luc, *Amiens romain*, Amiens 1983.

Bayrou, Lucien, *Languedoc-Roussillon Gothique, L'architecture militaire de Carcassonne à Perpignan*, Paris 2013.

Beck, Patrice, "Le remploi sur les chantiers de construction du domaine ducal de Bourgogne dans la seconde moitié du XIVe siècle," in Bernard 2008, 517–522.

B Bedon, Robert et al., *Architecture et urbanisme en Gaule romaine. I: L'architecture et les villes en Gaule romaine; II: L'urbanisme en Gaule romaine*, Paris 1988. With excellent atlas detailing each town's site, foundation, enceinte, hydraulics, cemeteries, etc.

Bellanca, Calogero, "Recupero, riciclo, uso del reimpiego fra dottrina e attuazione," in Bernard 2008, 219–228.

Benedict, Philip, ed., *Cities and Social Change in Early Modern France*, London/New York 1989. Includes 22–23 tables of urban population trends 1500–1790.

———, "French cities from the sixteenth century to the Revolution: an overview," in Benedict 1989, 6–61.

Bercé, Françoise, *Les premiers travaux de la Commission des monuments historiques, 1837–48, procès-verbaux et relevés d'architectes*, Paris 1979. Of the 177 relevés illustrated, only 3 are Roman, the majority being mediaeval churches, some châteaux, and a few houses.

———, "Arcisse de Caumont et les sociétés savantes," in Nora, Pierre, ed., *Les lieux de mémoire* II Paris 1986, 532–67.

———, *B* *Des Monuments Historiques au patrimoine, du XVIIIe siècle à nos jours*, Paris 2000.

BIBLIOGRAPHY: MODERN SCHOLARS

———, *B* *La correspondance Mérimée-Viollet-le-Duc*, Paris 2001.

———, "Mérimée et les monuments antiques du Midi," in Glaudes 2008, 155–170.

———, *B* *Viollet-le-Duc*, Paris 2013a.

———, "Restaurer au XIXe siècle?" in Krings & Pugnière 2013, 249–266.

Bernard, Honoré, *Arras, ville fortifiée*, Arras 1993.

Bernard, Jean-François et al., eds, *Il reimpiego in architettura. Recupero, trasformazione, uso*, conference Rome 2007, Rome 2008.

Bernardi, Philippe, "Le bâti ancien comme source de profits. Une facette du rapport entre architecture et économie," in Bernard 2008, 503–516.

Berthomieu, Maurice, "Le Palais Vicomtal de Narbonne," in *BCA Narbonne* 36, 1974, 89–97.

Bezin, Christine, *Vaison la Romaine*, Aix-en-Provence 1999.

Billard, Cyrille, ed., *Une histoire des campagnes aux portes de Bayeux. Recherches archéologiques menées dans le cadre de la déviation de la RN13*, exhibition, Caen 2002.

Bilsel, S. M. Can, *Architecture in the museum: displacement, reconstruction and reproduction of the monuments of antiquity in Berlin's Pergamon Museum*, PhD, Princeton 2003.

Blanchard-Lemée, M., "Mosaïques tardives et survie des villas en Gaule moyenne à l'èpoque mérovingienne", in *Mosaïque. Recueil d'hommages à Henri Stern*, Paris 1982, 75–80.

Bogard, P., ed., *La maison urbaine d'époque romain: atlas des maisons de Gaule Narbonnaise*, 2 vols, Avignon 1996.

Bonet, F., & Dureau, J.-M., *Inventaire de la voirie urbaine: ouverture, élargissement et prolongement des rues 1789–1926*, 226 pages, Lyon 1990, in Lyon, Archives, serie O, 321WP.

Bonnery, A., *Le Suburbium de Saint Paul de Narbonne à la fin de l'époque romaine. Mémoire pour la Maitrise d'Enseignement d'Histoire, Université de Toulouse*, October 1969 (typescript, Bibliothèque Municipale de Narbonne, FL 494).

Bonnet, Corinne et al., *Connaître l'antiquité. Individus, réseaux, stratégies du XVIIIe au XXIe siècle*, Rennes 2010.

Boulting, Nikolaus, "The law's delays: conservationist legislation in the British Isles," in Fawcett 1976, 9–33.

Boussinesq, Georges, & Laurent, Gustave, *Histoire de Reims depuis les origines jusqu'à nos jours*, 2 vols, Reims 1933. Well illustrated.

Brown, Frederick, *For the soul of France. Culture Wars In the Age of Dreyfus*, New York 2010.

Brown, G. Baldwin, *The care of ancient monuments. An account of the legislative and other measures adopted in European countries for protecting ancient monuments and objects and scenes of natural beauty, and for preserving the aspect of historical cities,* Cambridge 1905.

Bruyère, Gérard, & Lavagne, Henri, "François Artaud et la collection du premier musée d'Orange," in Laurens & Pomian 1992, 145–154.

Buffat, Loïc, "Fermes et villas en Gaule Narbonnaise," in Ouzoulias & Tranoy 2010, 177–188.

B Buisseret, David, *Ingénieurs et fortifications avant Vauban. L'organisation d'un service royal aux XVIe–XVIIe siècles*, Paris 2000. Excellent text, and very well illustrated.

B Burdeau, François, *Histoire de l'administration française du 18e au 20e siècle*, 2nd edn., Paris 1996.

Butler, Beverley, *Return to Alexandria. An ethnography of cultural heritage revivalism and museum memory*, Walnut Creek CA 2007.

Cabanel, Patrick, "Introduction: patrimoine et identité: des inventions du XIXe siècle?" in Andrieux 2008, 11–20.

Cairou, R., *Narbonne: vingt siècles de fortifications*, Narbonne 1979A.

———, *Narbonne dans le renouveau économique des XIIe et XIIIe siècles*, Commission Archéologique de Narbonne, roneo, 1979B.

Cameron, Averil, *The Mediterranean world in late antiquity, AD 395–600*, London & New York 1993.

Capelle, Guy, et al., *Villes fortifiées du Nord. Augustin Boutique photographe 1862–1944*, Douai 1994.

Carbonell-Lamothe, Y., "Recherches sur la construction du Palais Neuf des Archévêques de Narbonne," in *Narbonne: archéologie et histoire*, 3 vols, Montpellier 1973.

Carcassonne, *De la place forte au monument. La restauration de la cité de Carcassonne au XIXe siècle*, Exposition permanente à partir du 4 mars 2000, Paris 2000.

Carle, Jacques, "Destructions ou conservation des monuments païens: des textes disponibles offrent-ils des perspectives d'interprétation pour Fréjus?" in Pasqualini 2011, 193–201.

Carvais, Robert, "Redivivus. Qui est de rechief mis en besogne comme s'il estoit tout neuf. Le réemploi des matériaux de construction à Paris sous l'ancien régime," in Bernard 2008, 531–547.

B Caseau, Béatrice, "Religious intolerance and pagan statuary," in Lavan & Mulryan 2011, 479–502.

Castillo, Alicia, ed., *Archaeological Dimension of World Heritage. From Prevention to Social Implications*, New York 1994.

Chaitin, Gilbert D., "The Politics of Culture," in Chaitin, Gilbert D., ed., *Culture wars and literature in the French Third Republic*, Newcastle upon Tyne 2008, 1–19.

B Chaline, Jean-Pierre, *Sociabilité et érudition. Les sociétés savantes en France*, Paris 1995.

BIBLIOGRAPHY: MODERN SCHOLARS

Chanet, Jean-François, *Vers l'armée nouvelle. République conservatrice et réforme militaire 1871–1879*, Rennes 2006.

B Chapron, Emmanuelle, *L'Europe à Nîmes: les carnets de Jean-François Séguier (1732–1783)*, Avignon 2008.

Chevallier, R., ed., *Présence de l'architecture et de l'urbanisme romains. Hommage à Paul Dufournet*, Paris 1983. 30 papers, only two of which deal with France.

B Chevallier, R., ed., *Les eaux thermales et les cultes des eaux en Gaule et dans les provinces voisines*, colloque Aix-les-Bains 1990, Tours 1992. Nothing on the later use of the same springs.

B Chiquet, Dominique, et al., *Le vieil Évreux. Un vaste site gallo-romain*, Évreux 1999. Excellent account, with much on 19th-century activity; but bibliography largely 20th century.

Choay, Françoise, *Le patrimoine en questions. Anthologie pour un combat*, Paris 2009. From Suger, through Spon, Millin, Quatremère, and Viollet to Malraux and UNESCO.

Citron, Suzanne, *Le mythe nationale. L'histoire de France revisitée*, Paris 2008. First pub'd 1987.

Clap, Sylvestre, & Huet, Olivier, *Les remparts d'Avignon*, Avignon 2005.

Clause, Georges, & Ravaux, Jean-Pierre, *Histoire de Châlons sur Marne*, Roanne le Coteau 1983.

Clerc, Michel, *Aquae Sextiae. Histoire d'Aix-en-Provence dans l'antiquité*, Aix 1916.

Clouet, M., "Au village des Arènes de Thénac, près Saintes," and "Le castrum gallo-romain de Saintes," in *Recueil de la Société d'Archéologie et l'Histoire de la Charente Maritime* 23, 1949–63, 116–26, 83–102.

Coffyn, André, ed., *Aux origines de l'archéologie en Gironde. François Daleau (1845–1927)*, Bordeaux 1990.

Combet, Michel et al., eds., *Histoire de Périgueux*, Périgueux 2011.

Cooper, Richard, *Roman Antiquities in Renaissance France, 1515–65*, Farnham 2013.

Costa Guix, Francesc Xavier, *Viollet-le-Duc's restoration of the cité of Carcassonne: a 19th century architectural monument*, MSc U. Pennsylvania, 1988.

Coulon, Gérard, & Golvin, Jean-Claude, *Voyage en Gaule romaine*, 3rd edn., Paris 2011. Divided by type, no photographs, exclusively reconstruction drawings, with plenty of quotes. Valuable for an overview of the evidence for what once existed.

Crozet, R., *L'art roman en Saintonge*, Paris 1971.

———, "Survivances antiques dans l'architecture romane du Poitou, de l'Angoumois et de la Saintonge," in *MSA France* 3, 1954, 193–202.

———, "Survivances antiques dans le décor roman du Poitou, de l'Angoumois et de la Saintonge," in *BM* 1956, 7–33.

D'Achille, Anna Maria et al., eds., *Aubin-Louis Millin (1759–1818) tra Francia e Italia*, Rome 2011.

Dangibeaud, C., *Mediolanum Santonum: le Municipe*, Saintes 1933A.

———, *Mediolanum Santonum: les ruines (le musée)*, Saintes 1933B.

Darde, Dominique, & Christol, Michel, *La collection Séguier au Musée Archéologique de Nîmes*, Nîmes 2003.

Debal, Jacques, *Histoire d'Orléans et de son terroir, 1, Origines à la fin du XVIᵉ siècle*, Roanne Le Coteau 1983.

———, B* *Orléans, une ville, une histoire*, 2 vols, Orléans 1998. Beautifully done, well-illustrated, but brief.

Decamps, Jean-Claude, & Guillemin, Jack, *Maubeuge: les pierres des pensées. Le déman-tèlement des fortifications, projets et réalisations, 1679–1963*, Maubeuge 1992.

Dedet, B. et al., "Découverte d'une enceinte de l'Antiquité tardive ou du Haut Moyen Age à Nîmes," in *Ecole Antique de Nîmes* NS 16, 1981, 147–63.

Delestre, Xavier, & Perin, Patrick, *Le mausolée antique de Rouen. Fouilles de l'espace du palais*, Seine-Maritime 1995.

Demoule, Jean-Paul, *La France archéologique. Vingt ans d'aménagements et de décou-vertes*, Paris 2004. Excellent illustrated survey, with lots of rescue archaeology, in sites all over France.

———, *On a retrouvé l'histoire de France. Comment l'archéologie raconte notre passé*, Paris 2012.

Demoule, Jean-Paul, & Stiegler, Bernard, eds., *L'avenir du passé. Modernité de l'archéo-logie*, Paris 2008.

B Demoule, Jean-Paul, & Landes, Christian, *La fabrique de l'archéologie en France*, Paris 2009. Useful on rescue archaeology, and on the political angle.

Den Boer, Pim, "Historical Writing in France, 1800–1914," in Macintyre, Stuart, et al., eds., *The Oxford history of historical writing 1800–1945*, Oxford 2011, 184–203.

Desvallées, André, "A l'origine du mot 'patrimoine'," in Poulot 1998, 89–105.

B Dey, Hendrik W., *The Afterlife of the Roman City: Architecture and Ceremony in Late Antiquity and the Early Middle Ages*, New York 2015.

B Díaz-Andreu, Margarita, *A world history of nineteenth-century archaeology. Nationalism, colonialism and the past*, Oxford 2007.

Diaz-Andreu, Margarita, and Champion, T., *Nationalism and Archaeology in Europe*, Boulder 1996.

Dietler, Michael, "Our Ancestors the Gauls: Archaeology, Ethnic Nationalism, and the Manipulation of Celtic Identity in Modern Europe," in *American Anthropologist* 96.3 1994, 584–605, 587–593 for "French Nationalism and Celtic Identity."

Direction des Travaux du Génie de Lyon, *La Défense de Lyon*, exhibition catalogue, Lyon 1986, well illustrated and wide-ranging, but mostly 19th century.

Dolphin, Freddy, ed., *Septentrion. Villes fortes entre Mer du Nord et Meuse, Patrimoine urbain et projets durables*, Paris 2007.

BIBLIOGRAPHY: MODERN SCHOLARS

Drinkwater, John, and Elton, Hugh, eds., *Fifth-Century Gaul: A Crisis of Identity?* Cambridge, 1992.

Dubled, H., *Carpentras: capitale du Comtat Venaissin*, Marseille 1975.

Ducourtieux, P., *Histoire de Limoges*, Paris 1925. 1884. Very good on the demolition of walls, towers and forts.

B Durand, Isabelle, *La conservation des monuments antiques*, Rennes 2000.

Durand, Marc, & Bonnet-Laborderie, Philippe, *Senlis et son patrimoine. La ville en ses forêts*, Beauvais 1995. Very well illustrated pp. 151 folio.

Duval, P. M., & Quoniam, P., "Relevés inédits des monuments antiques d'Autun," in *Gallia* XXI 1963, 155–89.

B Dyson, Stephen L., *In Pursuit of Ancient Pasts. A History of Classical Archaeology in the Nineteenth and Twentieth Centuries*, New Haven & London 2006.

Ennen, E., "Les différents types de formation des villes européennes," in *Le Moyen Age* 62, 1956, 397–41.

B Erder, Cevat, *Our architectural heritage: from consciousness to conservation*, Paris 1986.

Escher, Katchin, *Les sites de la France préroman. Hauts lieux du premier Moyen Âge* (*v^e–xe siècles*), Lacapelle-Marival 2013.

Esmonde Cleary, Simon, *The Roman West, AD 200–500. An archaeological study*, Cambridge 2013. Blanchet 1907 would be a useful addition to his bibliography.

Esperou, Jean Luc, et al., *L'aqueduc romain de Béziers. Les sources et l'alimentation en eau de la cité au haut-empire*, Servian 2009.

Eychart, Paul, *La destruction d'un site majeur: Gergovie*, Brioude 1994, p. 77.

Farr, James R., "Consumers, commerce and the craftsmen of Dijon," in Benedict 1989, 131–170.

Faucherre, Nicolas, et al., *Les plans en relief des places du Roy*, Paris 2007. i.e. the Galerie des Plans-Reliefs, now mostly in the Musée de la Guerre.

———, *Places fortes: bastions du pouvoir*, Paris 2011.

———, "Des villes libres au pré carré. Genèse de l'état monarchique en France," in Picon 1996, 65–87.

Favreau, R., *La ville de Poitiers à la fin du Moyen Age. Une capitale régionale*, 2 vols, Poitiers 1978.

———, "Le Palais de Poitiers au Moyen Age: étude historique," in *MSA Ouest* 11, 1971, 35–65.

Fawcett, Jane, ed., *The future of the past. Attitudes to conservation 1174–1974*, London 1976.

———, "A restoration tragedy: cathedrals in the eighteenth and nineteenth centuries," in Fawcett 1976, 74–115.

Feyel, Christophe, "Jean-Antoine Letronne (1787–1848) et l'archéologie de son temps," in Perrin-Saminadayar 2001, 160–179.

Fichtl, Stephan, *Les premières villes de la Gaule. Le temps des oppida*, Lacapelle-Marival 2012.

Flavigny, Laurence, "L'abbé Cochet, un champion de l'archéologie nationale, 1812–1875," in Laurens & Pomian 1992, 241–249.

Flutsch, Laurent, & Hauser, Pierre, "Les mausolées d'Avenches-en-Chaplix: mythologie et démolition," in Moretti, Jean-Charles, & Tardy, Dominique, eds., *L'architecture funéraire monumentale: la Gaule dans l'Empire romain*, colloque 2001, Paris 2006, 407–18.

Flutsch, Laurent, & Fontannaz, Didier, *Le pillage du patrimoine archéologique. Des razzias coloniales au marché d'art, un désastre culturel*, Paris 2010. Largely 20th century–21st century.

Follain, Éric, *Évreux: guide du rempart gallo-romain*, Évreux 2005. Well illustrated with plans and photos.

Forero-Mendoza, Sabine, *Le temps des ruines. L'éveil de la conscience historique à la Renaissance*, Seyssel 2002. Broad, and focussed on Italy.

Fornasier, Bruno, "Les arcs de triomphe d'Arles," in *Histoire de l'Art* 27, Oct. 1994, 19–29.

Fouret, Claude, "Démantèlement et urbanisme, esquisse d'une réflexion," in Dolphin 2007, 121–135.

Fournier, Laurent Sébastien, et al., eds., *Patrimoine et désirs d'identité*, Paris 2012. Very broad.

Fraïsse, Chantal, *Moissac, histoire d'un abbaye*, Cahors 2006.

Frangne, Pierre-Henry, "Patrimoine, identité et culture. L'éclairage de la philosophie et de l'esthétique," in Andrieux 2011, 265–282.

B Frézouls, Edmund, ed., *Les villes antiques de la France, Belgique I*, Strasburg 1982.

———, *B* *Les villes antiques de la France, Germanie Supérieure I, Besançon, Dijon, Langres, Mandeure*, Strasburg 1988.

———, *B* *Les villes antiques de la France, Lyonnaise I: Autun, Chartres, Nevers*, Paris 1997. The focus in both Frézouls' volumes is indeed on the antique plan and monuments, and not on later dismantling.

Froissard, Michelle et al., *Antibes: grandeur et servitudes d'une place forte, XVIe–XIXe siècle*, exhibition, Antibes 1995, 2nd edn., 2002.

B Frye, David, "Aristocratic responses to Late Roman urban change: the examples of Ausonius and Sidonius in Gaul," in *The Classical World* 96, 2003, 185–96.

Fyot, Eugène, *Dijon: son passe évoqué par ses rues*, Dijon 1960.

Gaggadis-Robin, Vassiliki, et al., eds, *Les ateliers de sculpture régionaux: techniques, styles et iconographie*, Colloque Arles/Aix 2007, Arles 2009.

B Gaillard, Hervé, *Carte archéologique de la Gaule: la Dordogne 24/1*, Paris 1997.

Galinié, H., "Archéologie et topographie historique de Tours – 4e–11e siècle," in *Zeitschrift für Archäologie des Mittelalters* 6 1978, 33–56.

BIBLIOGRAPHY: MODERN SCHOLARS 405

Gamboni, Dario, *The Destruction of Art: Iconoclasm and Vandalism since the French Revolution*, Chicago 1997.

Gannier, Odile, "Des ruines aux monuments historiques: les notes de voyage de l'inspecteur Mérimée," in Goyot & Massol 2003, 181–199.

Garmy, Pierre, "L'Archéologie à Nîmes," in *Histoire et Archéologie: les Dossiers* 55, 1981, 52–7.

Garmy, Pierre, & Maurin, Louis, eds., *Enceintes romaines d'Aquitaine, Bordeaux, Dax, Périgueux, Bazas*, Paris 1996.

Gayraud, M., *Narbonne antique des origines à la fin du IIIᵉ siècle* (*Revue Archéologique de Narbonnaise*, Supplement 8), Paris 1981.

Geary, Patrick J. *Before France and Germany: The Creation and Transformation of the Merovingian World*, New York, 1988.

Génie, "Le fort de Dampierre" (by the Direction des Travaux du Génie de Châlons-sur-Marne) in *Les Cahiers d'Histoire Militaire* 2, Jan. 1970, 37–48.

B Gerrard, James, "Demolishing Roman Britain," in Rakoczy 2008, 176–194.

Gillet, Louis (1876–1943), *Le trésor des musées de province: Le Midi*, Paris 1934.

Girardy-Caillet, Claudine, *Périgueux antique*, Paris 1998.

Giraudet, Eugène, *Histoire de la ville de Tours, I, Des origines au XVIᵉ siècle*, 1873, republished Cressé 2012.

Glaudes, Pierre, ed., *Mérimée et le bon usage du savoir*, Toulouse 2008.

B Glendinning, Miles, *The conservation movement: a history of architectural preservation, antiquity to modernity*, London & NY 2013. Excellent but broad.

Godet, Olivier, *Patrimoine reconverti du militaire au civil*, Paris 2007, but most reconversions are from 19th–20th new-built military installations.

Goodman, Penelope J., *The Roman City and Its Periphery from Rome to Gaul*, Abingdon etc. 2007.

———, *B* "Temples in late antique Gaul," in Lavan & Mulryan 2011, 165–193.

Goudineau, Christian, *Promenades archéologiques en survolant la Gaule*, Paris 2007.

B Goudineau, Christian, & Guilaine, Jean, eds., *De Lascaux au Grand Louvre. Archéologie et histoire en France*, 2nd edn., Paris 1991, but nothing on what has been lost.

Goudineau, Christian, & Kisch, Yves de., *Vaison la Romaine*, Paris 1991.

Gowon, M., "Nîmes pendant le Haut Moyen-Age," in *Ecole Antique de Nîmes* 12, 1931, 79–94; 13, 1932, 119–38; 14, 1933, 90–106.

B Graham, Brian & Howard, Peter, eds., *The Ashgate research companion to heritage and identity*, Aldershot 2008. The problem is that the terms are so broad that they can mean anything to anyone wishing to employ them.

Gran-Aymerich, Eve, *Naissance de l'archéologie moderne, 1798–1945*, Paris 1998.

Gran-Aymerich, Jean, "Visions de la Gaule indépendante au XIXe siècle. Mythe historique et réalité archéologique", in *Le monde des images en Gaule et dans les provinces voisines*, colloque Paris, ENS, 1987, *Caesarodunum* 23, Paris 1988, 109–119.

Granger, Michel, *Poitiers et ses remparts*, Poitiers 1988. Very well illustrated folio of p. 174.

B Gravagnuolo, Benedetto, *La progettazione urbana in Europa. 1750–1960. Storia e teorie*, Bari 1994.

Greenhalgh, Elizabeth, *The French army and the First World War*, Cambridge 2014.

B Greenhalgh, Michael, *The survival of Roman antiquities in the Middle Ages*, London 1989. 250–281 for bibliography.

———, *B* *The military and colonial destruction of the Roman landscape of North Africa, 1830–1900*, Leiden & Boston 2014.

Gros, Pierre, "Moenia: aspects défensif et aspects représentatifs des fortifications," in Van de Maele, S. & Forsse, J. M. eds, *Fortificationes antiquae*, Amsterdam 1992, 211–25.

———, *B* "L'architecture romaine du début du IIIe siècle av. J. C. à la fin du Haut-Empire, I, les monuments publics," Paris 2002. Divided by type (enceintes 26–55; arches 56–94 etc.) and well illustrated.

Gucht, Daniel Vander, *Ecce Homo Touristicus. Identité, mémoire et patrimoine à l'ère de la muséalisation du monde*, Lovernal 2006. The title says it all.

Guilleux, Joseph, *L'enceinte romaine du Mans*, Saint-Jean-d'Angély 2000, pamphlet with fold-out map for visit, and excellent colour photos.

Goyot, Alain, & Massol, Chantal, eds., *Voyager en France au temps du romantisme*, Grenoble 2003.

Grell, Chantal, *Le dix-huitième siècle et l'antiquité en France, 1689–1789*, 2 vols, Oxford 1995, from a doctorate.

Hadjiminaglou, G., "Le grand appareil dans les églises des IXe–XIIe siècles de la Grèce du Sud," in *BCH* 118, 1994, 161–97.

Hartmann-Virnich, Andreas, "Le rôle des matériaux antiques en réemploi dans la sculpture monumentale antiquisante en Provence romane: l'exemple d'Arles et de Saint-Gilles-du-Gard," in *Revue archéologique de Narbonnaise* 33, 2000, 288–292.

Heers, Jacques, *L'histoire assassiné: les pièges de la mémoire*, Versailles 2006. A sour and accurate account of what he believes to be the current state and range of the study and consumption of history.

Heijmans, M., & C. Sintes, "L'evolution de la topographie de l'Arles antique. Un état de la question," in *Gallia* 51, 1994, 135–70.

Hellmann, Marie-Christine, ed., *Paris, Rome, Athènes: le voyage en Grèce des architectes français aux XIXe et XXe siècles*, exhibition catalogue, Paris 1982.

B Henigfeld, Yves, & Masquilier, Amaury, *Archéologie des enceintes urbaines et de leurs abords en Lorraine et en Alsace (XIIe–XVe siècle)*, Revue Archéologique de l'Est, Supp. 26, Dijon 2008.

BIBLIOGRAPHY: MODERN SCHOLARS 407

Hermant, Daniel. "Destructions et vandalisme pendant la Révolution française," in *Annales ESC* 33, 1978, 703–19.

Higounet-Nadal, A., *Périgueux aux XIVᵉ et XVᵉ siècles. Etude de démographie historique*, Bordeaux 1978.

———, *Périgueux*, in the series *Atlas Historique des Villes de France*, Paris 1984.

Hobsbawm, Eric, "Mass-producing traditions: Europe 1870–1914," in Hobsbawm, Eric, & Ranger, Terence, *The invention of tradition*, Cambridge 1992, 263–307.

Horn, Jeff, *Economic development in early modern France. The privilege of liberty, 1650–1820*, Cambridge 2015.

Jean Hubert, "L'abbé Cochet et l'avènement d'une science de l'archéologie," in *Centenaire de l'abbé Cochet, 1975: Actes du colloque international d'archéologie* (Rouen 1975) Rouen 1978, 13–17.

B Hurley, Cecilia, *Monuments for the people. Aubin-Louis Millin's Antiquités Nationales*, Turnhout 2013.

———, Les Antiquités Nationales d'Aubin-Louis Millin: un voyageur autour du patrimoine," in D'Achille 2011, 111–122.

(ICOVIL, M Visteaux, President), *Dijon: histoire urbaine*, Dijon 2000. Good photographic summary, with illustrations of *La Ville des Grands Ducs d'Occident* at pp. 18–19, and their fortress with its four round towers.

Johnson, S., *Late Roman Fortifications*, London 1983.

B Jokilehto, Jukka, *A History of Architectural Conservation*, Oxford 1999.

B Journaux, André, *Histoire de Langres des origines à nos jours*, 3rd edn., Langres 2008.

Keylor, William R., *Academy and Community: The Foundation of the French Historical Profession*, Cambridge MA 1975.

Knight, J., *Roman France: an archaeological field guide*, Stroud 2001.

B Krings, Véronique, & Pugnière, François, eds., *Nîmes et ses antiquités. Un passé présent XVIᵉ–XIXᵉ siècle*, Bordeaux 2013.

B Krings, Véronique, & Valenti, Catherine, *Les antiquaires du Midi. Savoirs et mémoires XVIᵉ–XIXᵉ siècle*, Paris 2010.

Kulikowski, Michael, *Late Roman Spain and its cities*, Baltimore 2004.

Küpper-Böhm, A., *Die römischen Bogenmonumente der Gallia Narbonensis in ihrem urbanen Context. Kölner Studien zur Archäologie der römischen Provinzen, 3* Espelkamp 1996.

B Labrousse, Michel, *Toulouse antique des origines à l'établissement des Wisigoths*, Paris 1968, doctorat, Paris. With good indices, and bibliography divided by monument (e.g. enceinte urbaine, temples, aqueducts).

Lagarde, Pierre de, *La mémoire des pierres*, Paris 1979, with annexes on post-war preservation and restoration efforts.

Lam, Brigitte, & Galland, Anna, *Portes et remparts à Aix. Chronologie d'une disparition*, Aix 2006.

408 BIBLIOGRAPHY: MODERN SCHOLARS

Laming-Emperaire, Annette, *Origines de l'archéologie préhistorique en France: Des superstitions médiévales à la découverte de l'homme fossile*, Paris 1964.

Landes, Christian, "Amateurs et sociétés savantes," in Demoule & Landes 2009, 54–66.

Lange, Santino, *L'Héritage roman: la maison en pierre d'Europe occidentale*, Milan 1988.

B Langins, Janis, *Conserving the enlightenment. French military engineering from Vauban to the Revolution*, Cambridge MA & London 2004.

Lassalle, V., "Note sur la façade romane de la Cathédrale de Nîmes," in *Ecole Antique de Nîmes*, NS 10, 1975, 21–37.

————, "Les monuments romains de Nîmes à travers les siècles," in *Histoire et Archéologie: les Dossiers*, 55, 1981, 80–88.

————, L'héritage de l'antiquité dans l'architecture nîmoise de la Renaissance et de l'époque classique," in Krings & Pugnière 2013, 89–118.

Lauffray, Jean, *La Tour de Vésone à Périgueux*, Gallia supp 49, Paris 1990. Concentrates on the seven digs 1965–9.

Laurain, E., *Les ruines gallo-romaines de Jublains*, Laval 1928.

Laurens, Annie-France, & Pomian, Krzysztof, eds., *L'anticomanie. La collection d'antiquités aux 18e et 19e siècles*, Paris 1992. Europe-wide.

Lavagne, Henri, "Le nouvel Espérandieu, recueil général des sculptures sur pierre de la Gaule, état de la question," in Gaggadis-Robin et al., 2009, 8129–821.

B Lavan, Luke, "The political topography of the late antique city: activity spaces in practice," in Lavan & Bowden 2003, 314–337. On neglect and redevelopment.

Lavan, Luke, & Bowden, William, eds., *Theory and practice in late antique archaeology*, Leiden & Boston 2003.

Lavan, Luke, & Mulryan, Michael, eds., *The archaeology of late antique paganism*, Late Antique Archaeology 7, 2009, Leiden & Boston 2011.

B Lazzeretti, Luciana, & Cinti, Tommaso, *La valorizzazione economica del patrimonio artistico delle città d'arte: il restauro artistico a Firenze*, Florence 2001.

Lechevallier, Claude, et al., *Lillebonne des origines à nous jours*, Saint-Georges-de-Luzençon 1989.

Le Hallé, Guy, *Histoire des fortifications en Bourgogne*, Amiens 1990.

Lehmann, Stephan, "Die Heraklesreliefs aus der Villa von Chiragan. Mythologische Prachtreliefs des ausgehenden 3 Jahrhunderts," in Gaggadis-Robin et al., 2007, 125–134. NOT late antique from Aphrodisias.

Lejeune, Louis, ed., *Le musée archéologique luxembourgeois*, Arlon 2009.

Le Maho, Jacques. "La réutilisation funéraire des édifices antiques en Normandie au cours du haut moyen âge," in Fixot, Michel, & Zadora-Rio, Elisabeth, eds., *L'environnement des églises et la topographie religieuse des campagnes médievales*, Actes du IIIe congrés international d'archéologie médiévale, Aix-en-Provence 1989, Paris 1994, 121–134.

BIBLIOGRAPHY: MODERN SCHOLARS

Lemerle, Frédérique, "L'entablement dorique du théâtre d'Arles et la diffusion du modèle dans l'architecture de la renaissance," in *BM* 154-IV, 1996, 297–306.

———, "Premiers témoignages sur les antiquités de la Gaule (1494–1520) des voyageurs d'Europe du Nord aux diplomates et marchands italiens," in Bondeau, Chrystèle, & Jacob, Marie, eds., *L'Antiquité entre Moyen Âge et Renaissance. L'antiquité dans les livres produits au Nord des Alpes entre 1350 et 1520*, Paris 2011, 111–123.

———, "La réception des antiquités nîmoises (1500–1600)," in Krings & Pugnière 2013, 73–88.

Le Moigne, François-Yves, ed., *Histoire de Metz*, Toulouse 1986.

Lemoine, Yvonne, "Les sculptures antiques de Forum Julii et de son territoire: découvertes en contexte archéologique et remplois," in Pasqualini 2011, 181–191.

B Léon, Paul, *Les monuments historiques, conservation, restauration*, Paris 1917. He was Director of the Monuments Historiques for 10 years; cites archives, 31 periodicals, and has large bibliography.

———, *La vie des monuments français: destruction, restauration*, Paris 1951. Excellent and detailed p. 584, profusely illustrated, with notes to contemporary documents.

Le Rouzic, Zacharie, *The megalithic monuments of Karnac and Locmariaquer: their purpose and age*, Eng.trans 1908.

———, "Les monuments mégalithiques du Morbihan: causes de leur ruine et origine de leur restauration," in *Bull. Soc. préhistorique de France* 36, 1939, 234–251.

Liebeschuetz, W., "The end of the ancient city," in Rich, J. ed., *The City in Late Antiquity*, London and New York 1992.

Loew, Sebastian, *Modern architecture in historic cities. Policy, planning and building in contemporary France*, London & New York 1998. Straightforward account of "The history of planning and heritage protection in France," 17–44.

Loustaud, J.-P., *Limoges gallo-romain*, Limoges 1980.

B Lowenthal, David, *The heritage crusade and the spoils of history*, Cambridge 1998 (first published in 1968 as *Possessed by the past: The heritage crusade and the spoils of history*). A splendidly sceptical, well-read and well-referenced overview.

———, "La fabrication d'un héritage," in Poulot 1998, 107–127. Suitably cynical.

Loyer, François, & Schmuckle-Molard, Chrisiane, eds., *Façadisme et identité urbaine*, colloque 1999, Paris 2001.

B Maffi, Irène, *Pratiques du patrimoine et politiques de la mémoire en Jordanie*, Lausanne 2004, from a PhD.

Malinowski, Jacques, *Liste des différents objets dispersés dans Cahors et dans les autres endroits du Département du Lot qu'il serait facile de réunir au Musée*, BM Cahors, MS 322(2), Collection Greil, c. 1880.

Massy, Jean-Luc, *Amiens gallo-romain*, Amiens 1979, summary of PhD, well illustrated with photos and plans.

——, *B* Les agglomérations secondaires de la Lorraine romaine, Paris 1997. Includes histoire de recherches for some sites.

Maurin, L., "L'arc de triomphe de Germanicus sur le pont de Saintes," in *Recueil de la Société d'Archéologie et l'Histoire de la Charente Maritime* 24, 1964–72, 255–72.

——, B* *Saintes antique*, Saintes 1978, dedicated "à tous les archéologues du dimanche."

Maurin, L., & Vienne, G., *Fouilles gallo-romaines à Saintes en 1977*, Saintes 1977.

Maurin, L., ed., *Villes et agglomérations urbaines antiques du Sud-ouest de la Gaule. Histoire et archéologie, Aquitania* Supplement 6, Bordeaux 1992.

Maurin, Louis, et al., *Inscriptions latines d'Aquitaine*, Bordeaux 2010.

Mayer, Janine, *Catalogue des plans et dessins des archives de la Commission des Monuments Historiques, I, Basse Normandie: Calvados, Manche et Orne*, Caen 1980. Contains an enormous number of documents without historical framework, analysis, let alone organisation by date of building – just lists.

Mazauric, F., *Histoire du Château des Arènes de Nîmes*, Nîmes 1934.

McClellan, Andrew. *Inventing the Louvre: art, politics, and the origin of the modern museum in 18th Century Paris*, 1994.

McDowell, Sara, "Heritage, memory and identity," in Graham & Howard 2008, 37–53.

McGowan, Margaret, *The Vision of Rome in Late Renaissance France*, New Haven 2000.

MacGregor, A., "Antiquity Inventoried: Museums and 'National Antiquities' in the Mid-Nineteenth Century," in Brand, V., ed., *The Study of the Past in the Victorian Age*, Oxford 1998, 125–138.

Méaux, Danièle, "La 'Mission Héliographique' entre inventaire et archéologie," in Goyot & Massol 2003, 359–373.

Mérimée Inspecteur Général des Monuments Historiques, exhibition catalogue, in *Les Monuments historiques de la France* NS XVI. 3 July–Sept. 1970. 270 commented exhibits, profusely illustrated, quotations from M's writings and archival materials. Essential reading.

Meslé, Emile, *Histoire de Bourges*, Roanne Le Coteau 1988.

Mesqui, Jean, *Le château de Lillebonne des ducs de Normandie aux ducs d'Harcourt*, Caen 2008.

Meynen, Nicolas, ed., *Valoriser les patrimoines militaires. Théories et actions*, Rennes 2010.

Meyran, Régis, *Le mythe de l'identité nationale*, Paris 2009. Contemporary issues, and the politics of race and identity.

Mignon, Jean-Marc, "Destruction et pillage des mausolées antiques de Fourches-Vieilles à Orange (France)," in Bernard 2008, 273–283.

Miller, Peter N., ed., *Momigliano and Antiquarianism. Foundations of the Modern Cultural Sciences*, Toronto 2007.

BIBLIOGRAPHY: MODERN SCHOLARS 411

B Mintzker, Yair, *The defortification of the German city, 1689–1866*, Cambridge etc. 2012.

Mollat, Michel, ed., *Histoire de Rouen*, Toulouse 1979. Excellent, but sociological rather than architectural.

Montclos, Claude de, *La mémoire des ruines. Anthologie des monuments disparus en France*, Paris 1992.

Moore, Michael E., *A sacred kingdom, Bishops and the Rise of Frankish Kingship, 300–850*, Washington DC 2011.

Moreau, Hughes, *Les remparts d'Angoulême*, Angoulême 1997, p. 16, illus.

Murphy, Kevin D., *Memory and Modernity: Viollet-le-Duc at Vézelay*, University Park, PA, 2000.

Murray, Tim, *Encyclopaedia of archaeology*, Santa Barbara CA, 2001.

Narboux, Roland, *Bourges mystérieux, vestiges antiques, grottes…*, Issoudun 2003.

Naveau, Jacques, "Jublains, un site urbain dans l'ouest de la Lyonnaise," in Bedon, Robert, ed., *Les villes de la Gaule Lyonnaise*, Caesarodunum XXX, Limoges 1996, 113–131.

Nîmes, Musée Archéologique, *L'Épigraphie à Nîmes du XVIᵉ siècle à nos jours*, exhibition 1987.

———, *Archéologie à Nîmes. Bilan de 40 ans de recherches et découvertes 1950–1990*, exhibition 1990.

B Noble, Thomas F. X., ed., *From Roman provinces to medieval kingdoms*, in the series *Rewriting histories*, London & New York 2006.

O'Byrne, Johann, "L'identité culturelle dans l'histoire de l'Europe," in Zuppinger 1997, 21–46.

O'Donnell, James J., *The ruin of the Roman Empire. A new history*, New York 2008.

Omont, Henri, *Missions archéologiques françaises en Orient au XVII et XVIII siècles*, 2 vols, Paris 1902.

Ouzoulias, Pierre, "Les campagnes gallo-romaines: quelle place pour la villa?" in Ouzoulias & Tranoy 2010, 189–211.

B Ouzoulias, Pierre, & Tranoy, Lawrence, eds., *Comment les Gaules devinrent romaines*, Paris 2010.

B Ozouf-Marignier, Marie-Vic, *La formation des départements. La représentation du territoire français à la fin du 18ᵉ siècle*, Paris 1992.

Pailler, Jean-Marie, "Voyages en archéologie. Mérimée et la Gaule," in Glaudes 2008, 137–154.

Paquot, Thierry, *Les faiseurs de villes, 1850–1950*, Gollion 2010. Critical assessments of mostly 20th century planners.

Parisel, Reynaud, "Perpignan, place forte espagnole au XVIᵉ siècle: adaptation de l'enceinte urbaine au progrès de l'artillerie," in Blieck, Gilles, et al., eds., *Les enceintes urbaines (XIII–XVIᵉ siècle)*, congress, Nice 1996, Paris 1999, 243–259.

412 BIBLIOGRAPHY: MODERN SCHOLARS

*B*Parsis-Barubé, Odile, *La province antiquaire. L'invention de l'histoire locale en France* (*1800–1870*), Paris 2011.

——, "Mutations du statut des "antiquités" dans la culture historienne en France des Lumières au romantisme," in Krings & Pugnière 2013, 53–70.

B Pasqualini, Michel, ed., *Fréjus romaine. La ville et son territoire, 8e colloque historique de Fréjus 2010*, Antibes 2011.

Patton, Mark, *Statements in stone. Monuments and society in megalithic Brittany*, London & New York 1993.

B Payot, Jean-Pierre, *La guerre des ruines. Archéologie et géopolitique*, Paris 2010. A broad overview.

Pelletier, André, *Vienne antique*, Le Coteau-Roanne 1982.

——, *Histoire et archéologie de la France ancienne: Rhône-Alpes*, Le Cateau 1988. Excellent & well-illustrated survey of these 8 departments, with introduction (5–78) then gazetteer.

Pelletier, A., & Rossiaud, J., *Histoire de Lyon, I, Antiquité et Moyen-Age*, Le Cateau 1990.

Penaud, G., *Histoire de Périgueux des origines à nos jours*, Périgueux 1983.

Pénisson, Elisabeth, "Le décor architectonique de Vésone et les collections du Musée gallo-romain," in *B* Tardy, Dominique, *Le décor architectonique de Vesunna* (*Périgueux antique*), Aquitania supp. 12, Bordeaux 2005.

Périgueux, Musée du Périgord, *Vésone, cité bimillénaire*, Exhibition catalogue, Périgueux, 1979.

Périn, Patrick. "À propos des cryptes de Jouarre," in *Documenta archeologia: Paris, foyer d'art au moyen âge* 3, 1973, 114–27.

Pernot, J.-F., & Thomassin, Luc, eds., *Le patrimoine militaire de Paris*, Paris 2005.

Perret, V., "Le Capitole de Narbonne," in BCA *Narbonne* 24, 1955–6, 148–76.

Perrier, J., *Carte Archéologique de la Gaule Romaine: Département de la Haute-Vienne*, Paris 1964.

Perrin-Saminadayar, Eric, ed., *Rêver l'archéologie au XIXe siècle: de la science à l'imaginaire*, Saint-Etienne 2001.

——, "Les résistances des institutions scientifiques et universitaires à l'émergence de l'archéologie comme science," in Perrin-Saminadayar 2001, 47–64.

Pertué, Michel, ed., *L'administration territoriale de la France (1750–1940)*, 1993 colloque, Orléans 1998. A narrower time-spread would have made for more useful papers.

Pevsner, Nikolaus, "Scrape and anti-scrape," in Fawcett 1976, 34–53.

Philip, Benjamin, ed., *Fréjus, musées, monuments, promenades*, Paris 2008. Surely a bad sign when museums appear before monuments in a title?

B Picon, Antoine, *La ville et la guerre*, Besançon 1996. Produced by the Génie, and illustrated mostly with material from the SHD.

Pierrevelcin, Gilles, *Les plus grands sites gaulois. Atlas des oppida*, Lacapelle-Marival 2012. Excellent picture-book, with plans.

BIBLIOGRAPHY: MODERN SCHOLARS 413

Pinon, Pierre, "Réutilisations anciennes et dégagements modernes de monuments antiques: Arles, Nîmes, Orange et Trèves", Cæsarodunum supp. 31, Tours 1978.

———, "Les réutilisations architecturales dans l'histoire", in Catalogue de l'exposition Pratiques de la réutilisation. CNMHS, *Les Cahiers de la réutilisation* 1, 1985.

———, *La Gaule retrouvée*, Paris 1991. Potted overview of antiquarianism, profusely illustrated, with apposite contemporary quotes – and of course ends with Astérix. Highly recommended as fundamental reading.

———, "Les pratiques de l'archéologie et les circonstances des découvertes au XVIe et au début du XIXe siècle," in Demoule & Landes 2009, 54–66.

———, *B* *Paris détruit du vandalisme architectural aux grandes opérations d'urbanisme*, Paris 2011. Pp. 317 of useful if general text, no footnotes, very well illustrated.

Poirel, Evelyne, et al., *Le mausolée antique de Rouen, Fouilles de l'espace du palais*, Rouen 1995.

Poisson, Olivier, "Prosper Mérimée et l'archéologie monumentale," in Glaudes 2008, 39–53.

Polonovski, Max, ed., *Quel avenir pour le patrimoine fortifié?* Paris 1995.

Pomian, K., "Franks and Gauls," in P. Nora (ed.), *Realms of Memory: Rethinking the French Past I: Conflicts and Divisions*, New York 1996, 27–76.

Potofsky, Allan, *Constructing Paris in the age of Revolution*, Basingstoke 2009.

B Potter, David, *Renaissance France at war. Armies, culture and society, c. 1480–1560*, Woodbridge 2008.

Pouille, Dominique, ed., *Rennes antique*, Rennes 2008.

Poulot, Dominique, ed., *Patrimoine et modernité*, Paris 1998. Co-editor of a series entitled *Patrimoines et sociétés*.

———, "Le patrimoine et les aventures de la modernité," in Poulot 1998, 7–67.

———, *B* *Une histoire des musées en France*, Paris 2008. Pp. 195 8vo, so not much space for detail.

Pradalié, Laurent, ed., *Histoire d'une ville: Aix-en-Provence*, Marseille 2008. Well-illustrated overview.

Prendergast, Christopher, *The Classic. Sainte-Beuve and the nineteenth-century culture wars*, Oxford 2007.

Prost, Philippe, "La ville et la guerre de Vauban à Napoléon Ier," in Picon 1996, 89–121.

Prévost, Michel, *Angers gallo-romain, naissance d'une cité*, Angers 1978. Summary of his PhD.

———, Une tour dans l'enceinte gallo-romaine d'Angers," in *Gallia* XXXVIII 1980, 97–116.

Pugnière, François, "Antiquaires et antiquités à Nîmes de la Renaissance aux lumières," in Krings & Valenti 2010, 13–29.

Rakoczy, Lila, ed., *Archaeology of destruction*, Newcastle on Tyne 2008.

Réau, Louis, *Histoire du vandalisme. Les monuments détruits de l'art français*, Paris 1959; édition augmentée, Fleury, Michel, & Leproux, Guy-Michel, eds., Paris 1994.

Reinach, Salomon, "Esquisse d'une histoire de l'archéologie de la Gaule des origins à 1895," in *Amalthea* 3, 1931, 407–44.

Rigby, Brian, *Popular culture in modern France. A study of cultural discourse*, London & New York 1991.

B Robb, Graham, *The discovery of France*, London 2007. Cf H-France Review 8, 2008, 237–242, condemned for putting academic noses out of joint, and for its sins of popularity, lack of scholarship and "anti-modernist green progressivism."

Rocher, Jean-Pierre, ed., *Histoire d'Auxerre des origines à nos jours*, Le Coteau Roanne 1984.

Rocolle, Colonel Pierre, *2000 ans de fortification francaise*, Limoges/Paris 1972. Overview with his own sketches. 2nd edn., 1989.

Roslanowski, T., "Trèves au début du moyen âge (3/4–10 siècles). Contribution au problème de la continuité des villes en Europe occidentale," in *Archeologia* 16, 1965, 94–108.

Rouche, Michel, *L'Aquitaine des Wisigoths aux Arabes 418–781: Naissance d'une région*, Paris 1979.

Roux, Antoine de, *Perpignan de la place forte à la ville ouverte, X–XXᵉ siècles*, Perpignan 1996.

B Rush, Laurie, ed., *Archaeology, cultural property and the military*, Woodbridge 2010.

B Salamagne, Alain, *Construire au moyen âge. Les chantiers de fortification dc Douai*, Villeneuve-d'Ascq 2001.

Salch, Charles-Laurent, ed., *Atlas des villes et villages fortifiés en France (Moyen Âge)*, Strasburg 1978. Well illustrated, including old prints and maps, with the basic information for hundreds of towns and villages which have preserved all or part of their ramparts. The 14 maps underline that it is poorer locations, or frontiers, which have preserved such walls.

Samson, R., "The Merovingian nobleman's house. Castle or villa?" in *Journal of Medieval History* 13, 1987, 287–315.

Sardain, Marie-France, "Les servitudes militaires autour des fortifications au XIXᵉ siècle," in *Revue Historique des Armées* 274, 2014, 3–14.

B Saupin, Guy, *Les villes en France à l'époque moderne (XVIᵉ–XVIIIᵉ siècles)*, Paris 2002.

Sautel, Abbé, & Imbert, L., *La Provence Romaine, histoire, art, monuments*, Avignon 1929.

Sautai-Dossin, Anne-Véronique, "Dijon, le débastionnement à travers la presse et les publications locales et régionales," in Blieck, Gilles, et al., ed., *Le château et la ville. Conjonction, opposition, juxtaposition (XIᵉ–XVIIIᵉ siècle)*, Paris 2002, 369–83.

BIBLIOGRAPHY: MODERN SCHOLARS 415

Scheidegger, F., *Aus der Geschichte der Bautechnik, 1: Grundlagen*, Basle etc. 1990. *II: Anwendungen*, Basle etc. 1992.

Schnapp, Alain, "French Archaeology: Between National Identity and Cultural Identity," in Díaz-Andreu & Champion 1996, 48–67.

———, Antiquaires et archéologues: ressemblances et dissemblances," in Krings & Valenti 2010, 184–190.

Schnitzler, Bernadette, *La passion de l'antiquité. Six siècles de recherches archéologiques en Alsace*, Strasburg 1998.

Sear, Frank, *Roman theatres. An architectural study*, Oxford 2006.

Secret, J., "Sur un plan de l'amphithéâtre de Vésune levé en 1821 par de Mourcin," in *BSHA Périgord* 105, 1978, 270–7.

Seigel, Jerrold, *Modernity and Bourgeois Life. Society, Politics, and Culture in England, France, and Germany since 1750*, Cambridge 2012.

Servonat, Jean, *Arles, territoire antique et aqueducs romains*, Arles 1999.

Shaw, Wendy, "The rise of the Hittite sun. A deconstruction of Western civilization from the margin," in Kohl, Philip L., et al., editors, *Selective remembrances: archaeology in the construction, commemoration, and consecration of national pasts*, Chicago & London 2008, 163–184.

Sintes, C., "La réutilisation des espaces public à Arles: un témoignage de la fin de l'Antiquité," in *Antiquité Tardive* 2, 1994, 181–92.

Solier, Yves, *Narbonne, Les monuments antiques et médiévaux. Le Musée Archéologique et le Musée Lapidaire*, Paris 1986.

———, "Narbonne antique va-t-elle renaître?" in *Archeologia* 133, August 1979, 36–49.

Solier, Yves, & Sabrié, M. & R., "Découvertes récentes à Narbonne," in *Archeologia* 133, August 1979, 50–59. Entered as Solier 1979B.

B Soraluce Blond, José Ramón, *Historia de la arquitectura restaurada*, Corunna 2008. Interesting and well illustrated, and could easily be twice as long.

Spencer, N., "Heroic time: monuments and the past in Messenia, Southwest Greece," in *Oxford Journal of Archaeology*, 14.3 1995, 277–292.

Stirling, Lea, *The learned collector. Mythological statuettes and classical taste in late antique Gaul*, Ann Arbor 2005.

Stouff, L., *La Ville d'Arles à la fin du Moyen Age*. Doctorat, Université de Provence, 2 vols, Aix-en-Provence 1979.

———, "Murs et portes de l'Arles mediévale," in Heers, J., ed., *Fortifications, portes de villes, places publiques, dans le monde mediterraneen* (Collections et Civilizations mediévales IV), Paris 1985, 237–53.

Takeda, Junko Thérèse, *Between Crown and Commerce: Marseille and the Early Modern Mediterranean*, Baltimore 2011.

Tardy, Dominique, *Le décor architectonique de Saintes antique. Les chapiteaux et bases*, Aquitania supp. 5, Paris/Bordeaux 1989.

416   BIBLIOGRAPHY: MODERN SCHOLARS

————, *Le décor architectonique de Saintes antique, II, Les entablements*, Aquitania supp. 7, Bordeaux 1995.

B Tatlioglu, Timur, "Destruction, identity and dynasty: the rôle of martial architecture in 18th century designed landscapes," in Rakoczy 2008, 69–89.

B Tauber, Christine, *Bilderstürme des Französische Revolution. Die Vandalismus-Berichte des Abbé Grégoire*, Freiburg etc. 2009.

Thiebaud, B., et al., *Saintes. 2000 ans d'histoire en images*, Saintes 1980.

Thiriot, Jean, *Portes, tours et murailles de la cité de Metz. Une évocation de l'enceinte urbaine aux XVIe et XVIIe siècles*, Metz 1970.

Torrejon, Nathalie, & Canet, Paul, eds., *Bastides en Aquitaine. Repères d'urbanités. Patrimoine et modernité*, Billère 2008.

Van Andringa, William, "Camille Jullian et l'archéologie de la Gaule," in Perrin-Saminadayar 2001, 180–196.

Van Ossel, P., & Ouzoulias, P., "Rural settlement economy in northern Gaul in the late empire: an overview," in *JRA* 13, 2000, 133–160.

B Varène, Pierre, *L'enceinte gallo-romain de Nîmes. Les murs et les tours*, Gallia supp. 53, 1992.

Vasselle, François, & Will, Ernest, "L'enceinte du Bas-Empire et l'histoire de la ville d'Amiens," in *Revue du Nord* XL, Oct.–Déc. 1958, 467–482.

Vergnolle, Eliane, "La pierre de taille dans l'architecture religieuse de la premiere moitie du XIe siècle," in *Bulletin Monumental* 154-III, 1996, 229–34.

Veyrac, Alain, *Nîmes romaine et l'eau*, Paris 2006. Gallia supp. 57.

Vieillard, J., *Le Guide du pèlerin de Saint Jacques*, 4th edn., Mâcon 1969.

Vuillemot, G., *Regards sur 19 siècles d'urbanisme autunois*, exposition temporaire de documents, Musee Rolin, Autun, 1971–2.

B Ward, Stephen V., *Selling places. The marketing and promotion of towns and cities 1850–2000*, London 1998.

Wawro, Geoffrey, *The Franco-Prussian war. The German conquest of France in 1870–1871*, Cambridge 2003.

Weber, Eugen, *Peasants into Frenchmen. The modernisation of rural France 1870–1914*, Stanford CA 1976.

B Weerd, H. van de, "Enceintes et vieux murs de Tongres," in *Revue belge de philologie et d'histoire*, Tome 9 fasc. 1, 1930. pp. 95–119. Suggests Grande Enceinte is High Empire, because there are no spolia in it.

Wenzler, C. *Architecture Gallo-Romaine*, Rennes 2002.

Westermann-Angerhausen, Hiltrud, "Spolie und Umfeld in Egberts Trier," in *Zeitschrift für Kunstgeschichte* 50, 1987, 305–36.

Wickham, Chris, "Studying long-term change in the West, AD 400–800," in Lavan & Bowden 2003, 385–403.

Wolfe, Michael, *Walled towns and the shaping of France from the medieval to the early modern era*, New York 2009.

Wright, Thomas. "On Antiquarian Excavations and Researches in the Middle Ages," *Archaeologia* 30, 1844, 438–57.

Zeller, Gaston, *L'organisation défensive des frontières du Nord et de l'Est au XVIIᵉ siècle*, Paris 1928.

Zuppinger, Renaud, ed., *Représentations du passé. Patrimoine, musées, problématiques identitaires et culturelles en Europe*, Paris 1997.

Index

Abbeville 89, 104, 158, 200

abbeys & monasteries 3–4, 8, 30–1, 53, 57–8, 62–7, 82, 88, 115, 121, 135–6, 138, 220, 225, 227

administration 9, 11, 85, 129–30, 132–7, 139, 150–1, 158, 160, 166, 168, 195, 197, 211, 222–3

   central government 7, 12, 102–3, 106, 134–6, 139, 141–3, 168, 171, 178, 180–1, 209–10, 308, 354, 356–7

   clergy & antiquities 160, 238–9, 259, 281–2, 284–5, 288, 290, 295, 301, 321

   intendants 135, 205, 223

   local 2, 63, 319

      consuls 264, 282, 284–6, 288, 295, 306–7, 311, 313, 322, 330, 333–4

      modernising 27, 80, 135, 158, 270, 354

      town councils 6, 16, 134, 139, 143, 178, 227, 297, 314, 347, 353

   ministers & ministries 20, 22, 107, 114, 136, 140, 150, 152, 164–5, 167–8, 172–6, 180, 200–201, 240–1, 366–7

   monuments historiques: lists 65–6, 128

   prefects 12, 29, 67, 114, 123, 134–7, 154–5, 158, 168, 172, 174, 176, 210, 233, 242

   questionnaires 168, 171, 173–4, 177, 245, 349, 354, 357–8

Agde 284

AIBL (Académie des Inscriptions et Belles-Lettres), 9, 18, 33, 36, 175, 279

Aigues-Mortes 13, 57, 96, 282–3

Aix-en-Provence 32, 62, 76, 289, 318–20, 335–6, 345

Alésia 110

altars 31, 40, 58–9, 112, 114, 157, 170, 205, 290, 294–6, 324, 331, 333, 340

Amiens 3, 32, 62, 137, 190, 200, 222, 237, 254, 319

amphitheatres 32–3, 43–5, 47, 68, 209–10, 235–8, 242–4, 249–52, 263–7, 269–72, 302, 304–14, 325–6, 332–5, 341–5

   Dugga 45

   Lucca 45, 305

Angers 2, 37, 63, 82, 96, 168, 188, 197, 200, 232, 235–6, 254, 259, 267

Angoulême 78, 96, 168, 334

Antibes 43, 97, 141, 264, 318, 342–4

antiquarians 1, 4, 6, 22–4, 26, 35, 107, 111, 122–3, 180–1, 263, 269, 286, 292, 300

antiquities 14, 18, 22–6, 111, 114–15, 233, 237, 240, 268, 274, 293, 299, 334, 339, 348

   and agriculture 40, 46, 52

   buried 47, 94, 121, 219, 233, 279

   conservation 49, 52, 61–2, 67, 131, 136–7, 141, 154, 156, 159–60, 177, 180, 185, 271, 273–4

   dismantling 89, 192, 198, 247

   and money 4, 19, 49, 60, 65, 77, 117, 126, 128, 132, 141–5, 166, 248–9, 282, 289

   recovered 54, 107, 134, 145, 203, 205–6, 224, 247, 260–1, 290

   Roman 25, 40, 94, 97, 111, 157, 198, 231

      buried 14, 301

   survivals 32–3, 52, 54, 56, 58, 106–7, 130, 154–5, 157, 172–3, 261, 263, 300, 332, 334

aqueducts 45–6, 111–12, 130, 219–20, 236, 244–5, 248, 250, 253–4, 290–1, 305, 321, 327–8, 342, 344

archaeologists 17–18, 22–4, 26, 46, 52, 104, 106–9, 111–12, 114–15, 124, 126, 148–50, 153–4, 192–4, 248

archaeology 11, 17–18, 22–4, 43–4, 76–7, 90, 110, 133, 148–9, 151–4, 166–8, 188–9, 233–4, 244–5, 339–40

   congresses 65–9, 111, 137, 139, 149, 151–2, 168–9, 171, 219–22, 245–7, 254, 260, 262, 275, 340–1

   discoveries 24, 46–7, 49–51, 70, 90–1, 94, 111–12, 169–71, 206–7, 233, 251–2, 311, 313–14, 354, 356

   excavation 47, 49–51, 86–7, 109, 143–4, 150, 166, 219–20, 225–6, 243–4, 251–3, 272, 309–14, 321–2, 346–7

   fieldwork 202

Argentan 152

Argenton 68

Arles 22, 24, 43–6, 52–4, 57–9, 64, 76–7, 105–6, 132–3, 139, 141, 318–29, 331, 333–4, 345–6

   Saint-Honorat 334

   Saint-Trophîme 328

   Trinquetaille 319, 327–9

INDEX

Arlon   160, 238, 254
Arras   39, 55, 90, 201
artillery   2, 78–9, 86, 197, 278, 291
   gunpowder   46, 66, 102, 211, 222, 245, 247,
     271–2, 279, 328
   large-calibre   79–80, 85–6, 91–2, 199, 243
Asia Minor   43, 49–50, 64, 69, 95, 118, 143,
   162, 176, 354
Ausonius   42, 50, 76, 280
Autun   44, 46–7, 49, 53–4, 64, 96, 114, 136,
   175, 191–2, 196, 242–6, 254, 260–1, 310
Auxerre   61, 96, 114, 193, 200, 242, 245, 260
Auxonne   3–4, 243
Avesnes   89
Aveyron   64, 83
Avignon   77, 82, 87, 89, 97, 105–6, 116, 127,
   136, 318, 320, 324, 336–8, 349, 355
   Musée Calvet   337

Bagnols   39
baths   42–3, 45–7, 49, 52–3, 61, 179, 231, 235,
   252–3, 262–3, 269–70, 272, 330, 336,
   342–3
   bathing 19thC
     Aix-les-Bains   46
     Amélie-les-Bains   46
     Arles-les-Bains   46
     Dax   339
     Evaux-les-Bains   46
     Néris-les-Bains   46
     Vichy-les-Bains   46
   bathing post-antique
     Bourbon-Lancy   47
     Bourbon-l'Archambault   47, 211
Beaucaire   54, 64, 68, 324
Beaune   97, 122, 198, 246
Beauvais   58, 67, 82, 96, 168, 194, 218–19, 239
Belgium   77, 80, 160, 200, 238
Bergerac   197
Besançon   4, 55, 78, 82, 90, 104, 127
Béziers   64, 77–8, 81, 161, 175, 283, 288–9,
   291, 293, 301, 341
Blois   83, 86–7, 237
Bordeaux   32–3, 42, 45, 59, 62, 66–7, 96, 134,
   137, 185–6, 202, 204–5, 207, 319, 340
   Château Trompette   202–5
   Fort d'Hâ   202–4
   Fort Saint Louis   203
   Piliers de Tutelle   202–3, 205
Bosquet, Abbé   286, 288, 292

Boulogne   30, 85, 107, 143, 193
Bourges   30, 55, 82, 96, 126, 159, 259–60, 267,
   275
   blocks stockpiled   160, 186
   Hôtel Jacques Coeur   259–60
bridges   36, 44, 46, 48, 94, 101, 113, 115, 155,
   271, 280, 282, 291, 339, 347
Brittany   35, 37, 43, 93
Brive-la-Gaillarde   199
building
   engineers   24, 35, 153, 155
     civil   36, 115
     military   84, 110, 353
     royal   294
   lifting equipment   30, 34, 107, 226
   manpower   76, 121, 168, 187
   new construction   66–7, 91, 93–4, 193,
     202–3, 205, 226, 228, 248, 264–7, 286,
     289–90, 309–10, 312, 326
buildings in wood   17, 32, 42, 59–60, 62, 92,
   113, 144, 164, 193, 228, 234, 284, 302
building stones   30–3, 35–6, 44–6, 57–61,
   94–5, 114–15, 126–7, 223–5, 263, 265–6,
   272–3, 284–6, 293–4, 296–8, 345–7
   alabaster   53, 226
   blocks   97–8, 160–2, 169–70, 206–7,
     223–5, 227, 238–41, 244–5, 251, 261–3,
     265–7, 270–1, 274–5, 294–6, 298–300
     foundation   34, 96, 223, 235, 263,
       267–8, 270, 287
   columns   24, 29–31, 44, 47, 54, 203, 205,
     263, 266, 268, 271, 288, 327, 331–2, 334
     capitals   58–9, 65–6, 102, 105, 205,
       207–8, 217–18, 220, 228–9, 253, 259,
       266, 273–4, 281, 320–1
     granite   345
     porphyry   30
   decorated   34, 161, 223
   friezes   40, 43, 108, 189, 242, 253, 259, 262,
     265–6, 291–2, 295, 300, 313, 321–2, 332
   granite   29, 245, 263, 331
   inscriptions   22–3, 40–1, 76–8, 165–6,
     174–5, 203, 205–7, 224–5, 239–41, 249,
     291–2, 294–301, 312–13, 343–4, 346–7
   kilns   69, 107, 217, 220, 231, 250, 262, 303
   limestone   29, 35, 86, 233, 249, 262–3,
     319, 336
   marble   51, 53, 58, 244, 246, 250, 252–4,
     301, 303, 322, 327, 331, 340–1, 343, 347
     blocks   31, 245, 253, 267, 321, 343, 347

420 INDEX

building stones (cont.)
  marble (cont.)
    decorative 265, 334
    structural 53
    exotic 49, 53, 250
    floors 253
    veneers 30, 44–5, 53, 60, 251, 253, 263, 289
    workshop 343
  porphyry 226, 334
  re-erecting 33
  re-used 76, 266, 326
Burgundy 64, 231, 233, 235, 237, 239, 241, 243, 245, 247, 249, 251, 253, 255, 257

Caen 82, 89, 92, 113, 134, 136, 151, 171, 199–200
  Saint-Étienne 136
canals 11, 24, 101, 113, 115, 151, 187–8, 190, 283
Cannes 342–3
Carcassonne 30, 77, 96–7, 127, 130, 180, 283
Carnac 36–8, 61, 178
cartography & surveying
  archaeological 109, 111–12, 261, 370–1
  Cassini 26, 109, 111–12
  Dépôt de la Guerre 110–12
  Ingénieurs Géographes 109
  Ordnance Survey 109
  topography 26, 109, 158, 262, 279
    cadastres 109, 111, 346–7
cathedrals 54, 56, 64–5, 86, 88, 137, 141–2, 160–1, 220–1, 234, 249–50, 264, 280–2, 284–5, 346–7
Caumont, Arcisse de 9, 17–18, 36–7, 58, 60, 139–41, 143, 149, 167, 170–2, 223–4, 247–8, 262, 337, 339–40
Cavaillon 31, 193
Caylus, Comte de 8–9, 18, 24–5, 38, 69, 141, 174, 231
cemeteries 53–5, 57–9, 76, 86, 90, 104, 106–8, 175, 232, 269, 274–5, 319–20, 324, 327–9, 334
Châlons-sur-Marne 3, 69, 82, 217
Chalon-sur-Saône 3, 58, 96, 189
Champagne 217, 219, 221, 223, 225, 227–9, 243
Champlieu 39
Charlemagne 57, 63, 106, 302, 327
Chartres 55, 64, 88, 92, 142, 161, 188, 217

Château-Thierry 122, 124, 142–3, 217
châteaux 61, 63, 68–9, 82–3, 86–8, 106, 131, 203, 226, 237, 247–8, 265, 310, 330–1, 340–1
  Château-Gaillard 131
  Chaumont 3, 88
  dismantling 3
  St-Maixent 88
  Uzès 64, 305, 308
Chazeaux 52
Cherchel 53, 94, 175, 196
churches 57–65, 67, 87–9, 124–6, 128–9, 153–4, 164–5, 169, 221, 227–8, 233–6, 269, 298–300, 334, 341–2
  baptisteries 46, 58–9, 161, 335
  chapels 45, 89, 155, 224, 242, 265, 290, 347–8
  12th-century 269
  17th-century 234
  deconsecrated 63, 161
  ruined 30, 88, 113, 143
Ciar 225
circuses 39, 210, 220, 244, 319, 321, 325, 331, 333, 345–6
Clermont-Ferrand 33, 50, 200, 262, 275
Cluny 66, 121
Colbert, Jean Baptiste 68, 203, 308, 339
columns, honorific 83
commissions 9, 13, 18, 21, 112, 116, 123, 155, 158, 166–7, 169–72, 174, 180, 208–10, 337–8
  archaeological 122, 124, 270, 297–8
  Commission des Monuments Historiques (CMH), 9, 13, 38, 70, 116, 123, 125, 169–71, 362, 365, 369, 371, 373
  departmental 125, 136, 233, 366
  historical 170
  local 18, 176
Condom 150, 188
Córdoba 281, 288
Coucy 222
Creil, Saint-Evremont 160
Crussol 131

Dax 3, 87, 96, 318, 338–40
  château 338
Dijon 13, 18, 54, 59, 89, 102, 144, 161, 165, 168, 198, 243, 245–8, 254

INDEX

Sainte Chapelle   247
S. Bénigne   54, 59, 247, 254

England   1, 31, 42, 101–2, 109, 128, 151, 157,
 174, 177
 British Museum   157, 162, 347
 monuments   168
 scholarship   18, 131
 visitors to France   68, 108, 137–8
Ensérune   301, 341
entrepreneurs   32–3, 36–7, 85, 115, 133–4,
 141, 143–5, 166, 169–70, 252, 263, 266,
 278–9, 286, 321–2
Espérandieu   8, 207, 292–3, 299–300
Évaux   47
Évreux   43, 96, 108, 113, 137, 142, 163, 200,
 219–20

Fenel, Abbé   224
Fère-en-Tardenois   36, 59
Ferté-Milon   3, 69
Fontainebleau   165, 312
Fontevrault   158
fortifications   2–3, 31–3, 76–81, 85–6, 90–3,
 95–7, 197–203, 222–4, 226–8, 237–40,
 242–4, 259–71, 283–7, 291–6, 341–3
 17th century   3, 79, 241, 313–14
 bastides   42, 115, 187
 bastions   32, 86, 92, 96, 192, 194, 211,
  239, 241, 270, 292–3, 298, 312, 319–22,
  324
 demolished   205, 223, 344
 fortresses   232, 237
 mediaeval   78, 96, 211, 225, 240, 251, 262,
  304, 319
 Renaissance   88, 198, 203, 292
 towers   69, 88, 174–5, 209, 212, 235–6,
  242, 247, 259–61, 264–5, 285–6, 289–91,
  294–5, 324–6, 344
 Vauban   3, 39, 78, 91, 197, 239, 344
fortresses   39, 43, 77, 79–81, 88, 127–8, 131,
 202–5, 239, 243, 267, 305–6, 309–10,
 325–8, 345
 royal   211, 312
France
 19thC transformations   24, 32, 41, 114, 118,
  158, 163, 185, 189, 197, 202, 208, 232, 239,
  318 19

defence of   27, 76–7, 79, 81, 83–5, 87, 89,
 91, 93, 95, 97, 99, 199, 240, 243
education   2, 10, 12, 20–1, 117, 133, 148, 151,
 156–8, 162, 164
 universities   117, 151, 156
First World War   12, 221, 239
nationalism   8, 11–12, 24, 150, 156, 354
and North Africa   31, 43, 61, 77, 84, 89,
 93–4, 115, 144, 175–6
patrimony   21–2, 26, 129, 205, 210
picturesque   23, 62, 97, 103, 152, 159,
 194–6, 323
 costumes   192
 sites   91, 159, 340
politics   11, 62, 109–10, 121, 129, 140, 156,
 185
Revolution   4, 130, 135, 140
and war   2, 4, 80, 83–4, 86, 89, 91, 94,
 110–12, 180–1, 210–11, 240–1, 321, 326,
 336–7
 Franco-Prussian War   79–82, 93, 104,
  156–7, 187, 210, 239, 243
François 1er 165, 249, 251, 278–81, 283, 287,
 291–3, 295–6, 300, 306, 312, 325
Fréjus   12, 14, 43, 45, 62, 70, 96–7, 106–7, 112,
 126, 318, 342–3, 349
French architecture   6, 42, 176
 architects   25, 32–3, 123–4, 128–30, 132,
  136, 149, 152–4, 162, 171, 221, 224, 228,
  232, 234
 demolition   42–3, 63, 67–9, 123–5, 127,
  131–3, 141–3, 198, 200–204, 206–11,
  240–1, 264–6, 269–71, 311, 336–8
 dismantling   31, 34–5, 65–6, 80–1, 87–8,
  116, 193, 197–9, 203–5, 218, 221–2, 263,
  278–9, 297, 308
 education   130
 façades   54, 58, 65, 128, 161, 165–6, 196,
  218, 227, 234, 238, 250, 261, 289–90, 303
 restoration   9, 13, 15–16, 18, 58, 63, 65,
  122–30, 132, 134–5, 137, 152–5, 177,
  307–8, 323
 ruins   23, 30, 33, 39, 47, 49–52, 66, 127–8,
  198, 200, 245, 247, 250, 252–3, 342–3
French army   1–3, 5, 29–30, 39, 80–2, 84–91,
 93–4, 96–7, 108–10, 179, 181, 199, 231–2,
 239–41, 282–3
 Africa   89, 93–4, 342

INDEX

French army (cont.)

Algeria   17, 39, 41, 85, 89, 93–5, 102, 107, 115, 122, 128, 145, 180, 196

artillery   5, 39, 50, 59, 78, 80, 87, 127, 131, 140, 240, 344

barracks   81–3, 86–9, 93–4, 122, 127, 131, 187–8, 192, 199, 204, 220, 227, 269, 272, 337

building projects   81, 83, 89, 291

garrisons   76, 81, 96, 101, 143, 192, 237, 239, 305

génie   79–80, 83–91, 93–4, 103–4, 107–8, 110–11, 199, 220–2, 226–8, 234, 236–7, 239–43, 271–2, 274, 336–7

hospitals   47, 337, 342

frescoes   8, 51, 53, 60, 89, 166, 209, 254, 299, 348

Gard   24, 31, 46, 68, 111, 115, 117, 154–5, 174, 302, 330

Garrigues, Pierre   287, 292, 294

Gaul   4, 25–6, 31–2, 35, 42–3, 45, 47–8, 50, 55, 57–8, 76–7, 168, 263–4, 318–19, 324

Gergovia   36

Germany & Germans   12, 43, 79–80, 87, 118, 125, 156–7, 162, 177, 197, 235, 242–3

Berlin, Pergamon Altar   118, 162

Germigny   60

Gironde   149, 177, 197, 206–7, 339

Greece   17–18, 32, 152, 156, 163, 175

Athens   69, 142, 151–2, 162, 187, 195, 233

Grégoire, Abbé   5–6, 140

Grenoble   52, 55, 59, 77–8, 88, 97, 160

guidebooks   129

Ardouin-Dumazet   185

Baedeker   81, 103, 212, 235, 338–40

Murray   107, 129, 339

Guizot, François   63, 111, 135, 159, 167, 172

Guyenne   205, 282

Haussmann, Georges-Eugène   6, 29, 126, 161, 188–9, 195–6, 208, 210–13

Henri III   142, 287

Henri IV   97, 131, 190, 238, 270, 293, 310, 325

heritage   1, 4, 6, 8, 10–12, 14, 16, 19–20, 22, 26, 51, 121, 131, 185–6, 353–6

local   273

neglect   5, 17, 41, 70, 125, 142, 180, 186, 217, 223, 323, 353, 355

patrimony   11, 17, 19–22, 26, 83, 156, 177, 187, 300

sites   20, 221

heritage & identity

identity   1–28, 58, 150, 152, 156

local   11, 32, 111, 199

and modernisation   11

national   10–11, 19–20

political   319

souvenirs   51

housing   6, 10, 32, 43, 54, 101, 164, 197, 202, 205, 227, 304–9, 325, 335, 343

demolishing   159, 166, 286, 356

hôtels   106, 108, 189, 193, 198, 205, 211, 247, 259, 268, 273, 289, 333, 336, 344

houses   42–3, 45, 52–5, 66, 92–4, 165–7, 189, 206, 234–5, 247, 250–2, 308, 324–5, 330–2, 334–5

owners   36–8, 42–3, 46, 50, 62, 69, 131, 133, 142–5, 172, 177–9, 195, 198–9, 201, 253

timber-framed   6, 158–9, 165–6, 196, 220, 225, 241

industrialisation   10, 21, 24, 80, 101, 191, 197

industry   7, 65, 67, 101–2, 104, 152, 160, 186–8, 190, 196, 200, 212, 217, 222, 313–14

inscriptions   14, 26, 40, 156, 174, 249–50, 299, 312–13, 324, 347, 370

bronze   144

Italy   15, 18, 25, 29, 52, 54, 56–7, 59, 61, 78, 88, 109, 131, 157, 296

Rome   17–18, 25, 30, 32, 90, 126, 151–2, 156, 299, 305, 308, 327, 332, 334, 347–8

Jublains   64, 70, 136, 235

Langres   2, 24, 55, 63–4, 81–2, 86, 91, 96, 126, 130, 142, 239–41, 243, 246, 254

Lantelme de Romieu   324–6, 329–34

Lanuejols   54

Laon   86, 88, 96, 144, 188, 222

Larçay   236

Lectoure   165

legislation & laws

Code Napoléon   84, 180

lawyers   135, 178, 191, 284

Le Mans   33, 64, 82, 96, 107, 111, 114, 122, 235, 267

INDEX 423

Lenoir, Alexandre 139, 161, 357
  museum 132, 156, 161–2
Lenormant, Charles 17–18, 23, 357
Lillebonne 45, 58, 144, 231, 319
Limoges 32, 43–4, 115, 165, 168, 185, 195, 198, 200, 262, 275
Limousin 37, 49–50, 93, 205
Lisieux 33, 113, 143, 231
Louis VIII 88
Louis XI 2, 63, 228
Louis XII 237, 292
Louis XIII 252, 282, 290, 293, 321
Louis XIV 3, 30, 53, 78, 81, 93, 97, 139, 142, 202–3, 206, 212, 259, 334, 345
Louis XV 139
Louis XVI 205, 335
Lyon 43, 46, 49, 52, 55, 57–8, 78, 81, 88, 115–17, 130–1, 142, 144, 248–51, 296
  Musée Gallo-Romain 251

Mabillon 9, 174
Mâcon 3, 47, 194, 243
Maguelonne 56–7, 283
Marseille 45, 62, 64, 67–8, 117, 133, 191–3, 196, 205, 319, 321, 324, 334
  Saint-Maximin 67
Martres-Tolosane 49–50, 144
mausolea 143, 233, 308, 333, 335
Melun 104, 108
Mérimée, Prosper 9, 13, 44, 86–7, 102, 129, 131, 135–6, 169, 171–2, 250, 253, 259, 262, 357
Merovingians 109, 246
  architecture 58–9, 131
  cemeteries 55, 59, 108, 166
  sarcophagi 59
  sites 57
Metz 33, 46, 55, 76, 80, 82, 86, 242–3, 254
  Saint-Pierre-aux-Nonnains 46
Michelet, Jules 21, 172
Middle Ages 29–32, 46, 48, 53–4, 57, 59, 154–5, 176, 267–9, 280–1, 283–4, 287, 319–20, 326–7, 329–30
Millin, Aubin-Louis 8, 52, 125, 134, 136, 151, 162, 175, 191, 244, 247, 271, 321, 323
modernisation 6–9, 11, 15, 17, 62, 66, 180–1, 185–9, 191–2, 198–9, 204–5, 212–13, 228–9, 246–7, 304

architectural consequences 185, 187, 189, 191, 193, 195, 197, 199, 201, 203, 205, 207, 209, 211, 213
Moissac 63, 67
Montpellier 53, 57, 81, 87, 194, 198, 200, 320
monuments 14, 23, 25, 111, 135, 170, 219, 252, 273, 279, 331, 348
  in cellars 48, 51, 160, 219, 238, 248, 250, 268, 309, 321, 330, 343
  classified 134, 169–71, 173, 177, 180–1
  conservation 19, 21–2, 67, 123, 125–6, 129–30, 136–7, 140–2, 166–7, 170–2, 177, 221, 298, 340, 354
  destruction 4–9, 14–16, 35–7, 65–7, 82–4, 121–3, 128–36, 138–42, 158–60, 208–10, 224–5, 232–4, 271–3, 340–3, 353–6
  funerary 54, 159, 206, 224, 237, 270, 309
  inspectors of 62, 124, 135, 168, 354
  large 35, 217, 249, 253, 260, 300
  losses 318–19, 321, 323, 325, 327, 329, 331, 333, 335, 337, 339, 341, 343, 345, 347
  preservation 9, 50, 58, 62, 130, 158
  protection 15, 21, 29, 52, 60, 92, 118, 125, 163, 177, 180, 265, 267, 348, 354
  rebuilding 2, 44, 56, 62, 78, 200, 206–7, 210, 220, 236, 241–2, 251, 263, 272, 290
  reconstructions 159, 263, 299
  Roman 29, 44, 125, 154, 202, 210, 250, 259, 336
    fragments 44, 50–1, 63–4, 67, 161, 170–1, 175, 206–7, 224, 247, 252–4, 259–61, 270–3, 298–9, 345–7
  sapping 46, 131, 245, 262, 268
  survivals 3, 5, 16, 45, 67, 98, 138, 221, 224, 259, 290, 324
  threatened 14, 150, 171, 176, 353
mosaics 40, 45, 47–8, 50–3, 105, 107, 133, 165–6, 221, 226, 251–4, 298–9, 301–3, 343–5, 347–8
museums
  catalogues 47, 163, 167–8, 174, 177, 209, 268
  Europe 157
  France 3–4, 50, 55, 67, 105, 116, 156, 158–63, 165–6, 206, 266, 268, 296, 299, 321
    municipal rubbish dump 271
    sculpture 161, 163, 165, 224, 245, 295, 299–300, 321

424 INDEX

Nancy 55, 159, 175, 232, 242, 293
Nantes 13, 54, 64, 114, 142, 159–60, 235
Napoleon III 26, 201, 208, 337
Narbonne 42–3, 68–9, 81, 89–90, 127, 161–2,
    168–9, 199, 201–2, 278–83, 287–9, 291–
    301, 313–15, 317–18, 320
  Cathedral 62
  Horreum 287–8
  la Robine 279
  Tour Moresque 290, 294, 296
Nérac 44, 48, 150
Nîmes 43–6, 76–7, 81–3, 107–8, 154–5,
    165–6, 186–8, 198, 200, 278–9, 291–3,
    301–9, 311–15, 317–21, 329
  Maison Carrée 61, 154–5, 254, 303,
    306–8, 310, 313–14
  Tour Magne 108, 306, 310

Orange 33, 44–5, 58, 68, 77, 126, 132, 139, 141,
    160, 318, 327, 333, 345–6, 355
Orléans 13, 43–4, 58, 64, 82, 106–7, 113, 115,
    127, 166, 175, 188, 190, 196, 261

palaces 49, 53, 59, 154, 159, 226, 253–4,
    280–2, 288–91, 294–6, 301, 309, 330,
    335, 337
Paris 15, 17, 24–5, 45–7, 57–8, 78–80, 93,
    104–6, 116–17, 126–8, 139–40, 185–7,
    195–6, 208–12, 353–4
  apartment buildings 211
  heritage 211
  imitating 188
  monuments
    Arc de triomphe 212
    Bastille 198
    Eiffel Tower 212
    Vieux Paris 209–10, 213
  museums
    Gare d'Orsay 105
    history museum 211
    Louvre 87, 105, 116, 156, 162, 195, 209
  scholars 17, 180, 234
  transport 105
Patte, Pierre 6
Périgueux 32, 53, 61, 83, 96, 202, 220, 263–4,
    267, 275, 319
  Saint-Front 263, 266
  Tour de Vésone 53, 61, 83, 263–5, 275

Perpignan 2, 191, 291–2, 294, 341
Philippeville 94–5
photography 46, 50, 97, 116–17, 125, 189, 195,
    197, 206, 211, 263, 266, 270–1, 291, 297
Poitiers 32, 54, 63, 83, 96, 107, 110, 124, 161,
    168, 266–9, 275, 302
Poldo d'Albenas 303–4, 306, 308–12
Pompeii 49, 245
Pont-Audemer 107
Ponts et Chaussées 36–7, 44, 101, 115, 155,
    236
population 1–2, 14, 43, 76–7, 101–2, 121–2,
    200–201, 220, 222, 233, 281–2, 297–8,
    303, 313–14, 318–20
  diminished 31, 43
pottery 55, 107, 166, 237, 301
Prehistoric monuments 26–7, 34–7, 111, 130,
    156, 368
  Bronze Age 114
  dolmens 35, 37–8, 110–11, 169, 171
  druidic 110, 112
  megaliths 16, 32, 35–8, 43, 96, 139
  menhirs 35–6, 38, 61
  pierres druidiques 9, 61, 264
  sites 177
  stone tools 36
  tumuli 35, 37–8, 40, 171, 288, 359
Provence 186, 318–19, 321, 323, 325, 327, 329,
    331, 333, 335, 337, 339, 341, 343, 347–9

quarries & quarrying 30, 36, 39, 45, 53, 57,
    141, 145, 228, 235, 247–8, 264, 275, 283,
    287
  Saint-Béat 53
Quatremère de Quincy, Antoine
    Chrysostome 21, 129, 159, 161, 346

railways 1, 7, 10–11, 79–80, 93, 101–8, 115,
    117–18, 187–8, 190–2, 196, 265, 328,
    337–8, 348–9
  companies 80, 101, 108, 225, 245, 354
  construction 48, 104–7, 113, 187
  engineers 105, 107, 225
  excursions 105, 108, 117, 196, 265
  lines
    Arles-Lunel 328
    Arles-Marseille 328
    Avignon-Marseilles 117

INDEX   425

Bordeaux-Toulouse   67
Dijon-Châlon   117
Lyon-Aix   102
Orléans railway   50
Paris-Aix   102
Paris-Avignon   117
Paris-Bordeaux   117
Paris-Lyon   102
Paris-Mantes   108
Paris-Tours   117
Saint-Just   55, 251
Sens-Langres   51
Toulon-Nice   343
network   104, 117, 135, 199
stations   4, 47, 52, 96, 101–6, 118, 143, 159,
    162, 188, 195–6, 199, 212, 251, 300
timetables   103
workmen   300
Reims   52, 54–5, 58, 64, 66–7, 102, 104, 106,
    194, 196, 198, 221, 232, 237, 239
    Cathedral   133
    Saint Niçaise   67, 221
Reinach, Salomon   115, 159
Rennes   96–7, 160, 175, 198, 235
Revolution, French   4, 6, 8–9, 11, 45, 47, 62,
    65, 67, 82, 135, 143, 156–8, 227–8, 236–8
Rhône   24, 39, 52, 82, 102, 248, 251–3, 318,
    329, 338, 348
Richelieu, Duc de   47, 68–9, 88, 139, 179,
    198, 341
roads   10–11, 46, 48, 101–3, 105, 113–15, 117–18,
    130–1, 173, 175, 187, 189–90, 327, 342–3,
    355–6
    reusing antiquities   35–7, 46, 59, 65–6,
        106, 114, 264, 271
    Roman   39–40, 110, 113–14, 227, 245, 261,
        329
        milestones   54, 112–13, 244, 329, 359
Rouen   67, 96, 103, 109, 122, 136, 138, 159, 190,
    196, 198, 231–4, 254

Saint-Bertrand-de-Comminges   31–2, 44–5,
    266
Saint Chamas   333
Sainte-Beuve   4, 26, 185
Saintes   32–3, 40, 43, 45–6, 68, 87, 153, 161,
    168, 264, 269–71, 275, 281, 290, 296
    Abbaye-aux-Dames   269

Saint-Gaudens   13
Saint-Germain-en-Laye
    museum   26, 40, 105, 107, 313
Saint-Gilles-du-Gard   53, 165, 327–8
Saint-Lizier   143, 340–1
Saint-Loup   198
Saint-Macaire   194
Saint-Martial   43
Saint-Maximin   65
Saint-Paul-Trois-Châteaux   39, 107, 160
Saint-Porchaire   269
Saint-Quentin   53, 108, 137, 200, 347–8
Saint Rémy   333
Saint-Riquier   13
Saint-Romain-en-Gal   43, 52, 253
Saintt-Nazaire-de-Valentane   137
Saint-Tropez   343–4
Saint-Wandrille   66
Saint-Yrieix   165
Salses/Salces   88, 282, 291
Sanxay   131, 142, 150
Saracens   14, 40, 56, 112, 229, 281, 320, 323,
    325, 327
sarcophagi   31, 40, 54, 57–9, 105, 133, 155,
    240, 262, 275, 319, 321, 327–9, 334, 344
Sarrebourg   83
Saumur   37, 86, 169
Scève, Maurice   144
Schneyder, Pierre   52, 250, 252–3
scholarly societies   7, 9, 17–18, 21–2, 106–7,
    111–12, 136–7, 149, 151, 167–72, 180–1, 209,
    224–5, 244–5, 247–8
    archaeological   62, 112, 160, 169, 180–1,
        241, 274, 279, 299, 343
    local   5, 50, 83, 106, 123, 142, 208, 225, 252,
        260, 268, 272, 354, 358
    national   107, 149
        Académie Celtique   35
scholars & scholarship   16–17, 35–40, 48–51,
    60–3, 103–7, 111–16, 123–7, 129–31, 140–3,
    148–51, 157–69, 173–81, 209–11, 231–4,
    278–9
    research   9, 23, 116, 150, 155, 160, 250, 299,
        335, 366
sculpture   23, 47, 49–50, 52, 56, 58, 218,
    223–4, 235–6, 239, 246–7, 254, 259–60,
    283–4, 292–3
    bas-reliefs   32

426 INDEX

sculpture (cont.)
  bronzes 231
  statues 193, 334, 347
    bronze 220
Séguier, Abbé Jean-François 304, 312–13
Séguin, Joseph 325–6, 329–31, 333
Senlis 45, 64, 96, 127, 160, 197, 228
Sens 96, 113–14, 122, 126–7, 131, 145, 178, 223, 225, 242, 260, 298
Seraucourt, Claude 250, 259
Sluter, Claus 248
Soissons 43, 51, 58, 62, 64, 86–8, 90, 112, 138, 148, 168, 180, 218, 225, 227
  St-Jean-des-Vignes 88, 226
speculators 5, 63, 67, 94, 137, 141, 143–4, 150, 204, 248
spolia 29–30, 32, 53–5, 97–8, 202, 218–20, 241–2, 248, 265–8, 283, 295–6, 309, 322, 341–2, 344–5
Spon, Jacob 249–50
Strasburg 80, 96, 199

technology 27, 30, 60, 79, 91, 101–3, 105, 107, 109, 111, 113, 115–17, 159, 186–7, 196
telegraph 7, 101, 188, 196
temples 42, 46–7, 61–2, 169–70, 202–3, 235, 251–2, 263, 271, 275, 300, 303–4, 307–9, 314, 331–2
  sites 62
theatres 43–5, 47, 92, 94, 110, 112, 139, 179, 203–4, 231, 235, 249–51, 323–6, 332, 344–6
tombs 8, 206, 248, 250–1, 283, 296, 304, 341
tombstones 40, 59, 64, 89, 233, 238, 342, 347
Toulouse 44, 50, 52, 83, 88, 90, 139, 145, 188, 193, 196, 200, 273–5, 306, 308
  Augustins 50, 88, 238, 274, 308
  ND de la Daurade 274
tourism 20, 24, 47, 51–2, 103, 105, 108, 116–18, 159, 163–4, 187–9, 192, 314, 318, 349
Tourny, Marquis de 204–5, 212
Tours 54–5, 57–8, 64, 82, 88, 96, 175, 179, 232, 235–6, 245–6, 262, 267, 329, 335
town layouts 1, 7, 11, 41, 79, 101, 155, 227, 232, 235, 297, 353
  alignment 10, 35–6, 61–2, 164–6, 194–7, 200, 217, 227, 313, 341

boulevards 34, 81, 91–3, 188–9, 193–4, 199, 217, 219–20, 223, 225, 227, 246, 261–2, 310, 312–14
Champs Élysées 59, 106, 188, 212
esplanades 92, 193, 223, 249, 310, 341
expanding 121, 297
gardens 34, 160, 170, 194, 226–7, 239, 246, 266, 272, 295, 312, 321, 341
gates 78, 126–7, 200, 202, 223, 280, 282–3, 285, 290, 305–6, 310, 312, 319, 326, 338
  ancient 241, 244
  decorated 240
improvements 6, 10, 34, 43, 97, 107, 135, 142, 191, 195, 198, 205–6, 212, 261, 267
lighting 6, 187–8, 212, 232, 297
modernisation 38, 62, 212, 231, 272, 304–5, 307–8
picturesque 91, 189, 207, 219, 234, 262
promenades 34, 92, 97, 190, 192–4, 196–9, 202, 204, 207, 209, 218–19, 222–3, 244, 246, 297
servitudes militaires 5, 80, 85–6, 91, 181, 195, 201, 210, 235, 297
squares 6, 62, 106, 190, 196, 198, 204, 219, 234, 247, 260, 333
street names 138, 193, 268
streets 2, 4, 54, 94, 97, 159, 164, 196, 199–200, 204, 321, 325, 332, 338, 344
unimproved 6, 42, 101, 196, 198, 212, 342
towns
  finances 2, 4, 16, 30, 40–1, 65, 103, 137, 141, 143, 163, 199, 204, 282–3, 286
  frontier 242, 318
  inhabitants 3, 6, 199–200, 207, 210, 212, 246, 268–9, 281–2, 301, 305, 307, 311, 325, 330
  mayors 12, 14, 134, 136–7, 139, 143, 201, 207–8, 218, 222, 238, 240, 279, 296–8, 338
  museums 4–5, 52–3, 69–70, 107, 117–18, 122–7, 129–31, 148–9, 155–67, 236–8, 241–2, 260–1, 269–72, 298–300, 353–4
  Roman 55–7, 237, 242, 261, 264, 266, 286, 288, 296
  taxes 2–3, 68, 135, 178, 218
  town councils 4–5, 7, 85, 87, 142, 144, 163, 200, 221, 225, 234, 240–1, 244–6, 298–300, 337–40

INDEX

town halls   101, 144, 217, 220, 224, 227, 238, 272, 300, 321, 333, 343
town walls   3–4, 39–41, 88–90, 92–3, 105–7, 192–4, 197–200, 202–3, 225, 238–9, 261–2, 285–6, 322–3, 337–8, 341–2
   11th-century   97
   12th-century   232
   13th-century   115
   14th-century   2, 97, 313
   16th-century   270, 342
   declassification   22, 85–6, 89, 143, 181, 193, 195, 199–201, 279, 283, 297–8, 339, 342, 344
   dismantling   2, 68, 82, 84, 90, 127, 143, 195, 197–200, 234, 239, 245–7, 284–5, 307–8, 337–8
   Gallo-Roman   87–8, 169, 171, 204–6, 243–4, 259, 265–8, 270, 280–2, 287, 289–92, 295, 309–10, 339–42, 344
   maintainenance   222
   mediaeval   55, 106, 221, 228, 240, 266, 280, 284, 303, 348
   as museums   159, 245, 280
   useless   2, 80, 82, 85, 198, 243, 337
travelling & travellers   14, 29, 94, 101–2, 113, 115, 117–18, 172, 176, 188, 190, 199, 204, 224–5, 232
treasure & treasure-hunting   37, 143, 179, 305, 310, 313
Trie-Château   189, 200
Trier   55, 77, 246
triumphal arches & victory monuments   77, 87, 90–1, 106, 153, 157, 159, 196, 221–2, 271, 280, 319, 321–2, 326, 333
Troyes   96, 127, 143, 168, 198
Tunisia   192

Vaison-la-Romaine   14, 30, 43, 45, 51, 58, 318, 346–7, 349
Valcabrère   54
Valence   58, 77, 82, 90, 131, 137, 160, 166, 200, 251
Valognes   54, 179
vandalism   5–6, 12–13, 17, 60, 62–3, 65–7, 84, 105–7, 121–3, 127–31, 133–41, 143, 158, 207, 273

by administration   137, 339
by archeolatry   163
by the army   217
by the church   154
by modernisation   185
by negligence   69, 115, 122
by reconstruction   140
by repair   337
by Revolution   140
Verdun   57, 76, 88, 239
Vernaison   82
Verneuil   189
Versailles   30, 53, 126, 253, 334
Vézelay   87, 191
Vieil-Évreux   51, 220, 252
Vienne   43–6, 52–3, 57, 61, 63–4, 76–7, 81, 86, 107, 110, 131, 143, 157, 177, 252–4
   museum   254
   Palais du Miroir   53, 253–4
villas   39–40, 42, 44, 46–52, 56, 76, 107, 114, 179, 202, 252, 254, 269, 302
   Antone   49–50
   Chiragan   49–51
   Ligugé   275
   Serquigny   50
   St-Georges-de-Montagne   50
   Thaims   269
Villefranche   342
Vincennes   86, 89, 93, 139, 211
Vinet , Élie   205
Viollet-le-Duc   15, 88, 116, 123–4, 126–30, 149, 154, 187, 191, 220, 245, 289, 338
Visigoths   56, 268, 305
Vitet, Ludovic   87, 124, 129, 131, 168, 172, 175

water supply & management   46, 130, 188, 232, 249, 279, 285, 287, 289, 291, 305
   cisterns   249–50, 301, 344
workmen   24, 26, 50–2, 64–5, 67, 69–70, 103, 107, 114, 131, 133–4, 154, 247, 252, 336
   masons   248, 250
   sawn blocks   64, 223, 236, 240, 250, 253, 294, 319

Young, Arthur   204

Illustrations

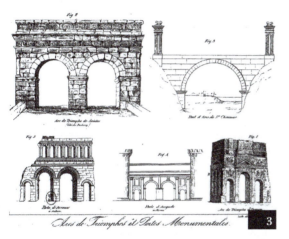

Ancient Arches & Gates *survived because towns always needed closable gates for security and tax purposes. 1. Langres: a triumphal arch, much degraded, was still built into the walls in the mid-19thC, and not considered of any importance. 2. Besançon: town gate in 1825. 3. Millin in 1838 shows several gates, including Autun. 4. At Cavaillon, little was left of the arch, which had been built into the Archbishop's palace. 5. At Autun, the gate is seen across ruins outside the walls.*

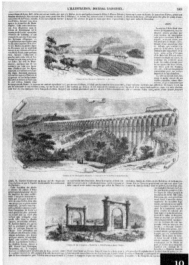

Ancient structures. Gunpowder used along with mines (6–7) to demolish fortifications in 1847 at Bapaume: even with gunpowder, mines and artillery, the task took three weeks, watched by four Belgian, three British, one Spanish and one Prussian officer – presumably dismantling fortifications was a hot topic. Also used to help construct the boulevards of Paris (here, 8, Blvd des Italiens), and to excavate for railway track, seen here (10, from L'Illustration, 1846–8) illustrating the sites on the Avignon-Marseille section that rail made accessible. 9. The arch on the bridge at Saintes in 1845, partly dismantled with gunpowder, and moved. Use of gunpowder sometimes equates with lack of expertise, or to save manpower on large jobs, such as building railway cuttings.

Retrieved antiquities. *If only a few buildings survived, many smaller antiquities were dug up and collected together, some to be preserved in museums. 11. Avignon: fragments from the Roman city. 12. Nîmes: a collection of antiquities retrieved around the town in a print of 1840. 13. Vienne: what happened to the antiquities illustrated here, including the colossal torso? 14. Bourbon-Lancy: Roman fragments found while excavating the baths. 15. Langres: Some evidently high-class antiquities were retrieved from its late antique walls.*

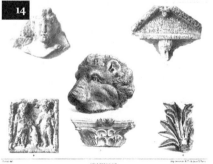

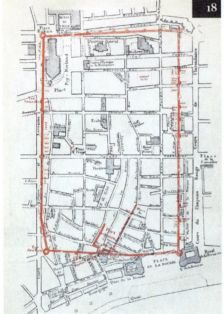
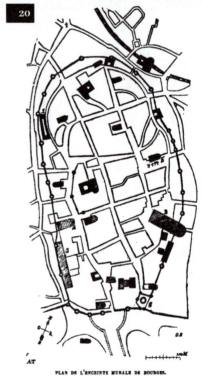

PLAN DE L'ENCEINTE MURALE DE BOURGES.

Les ruines romaines sous le palais du duc Jean, indiqué n°. 3 sur le plan, suivent l'alignement de la muraille militaire.

LE MUR ROMAIN, COURS D'ALSACE-ET-LORRAINE.

Walls and Antiquities. Late antique town walls in France and Spain contained large quantities of antiquities, the retrieval of which could have given the 19th century a veritable bonanza of archaeological knowledge – unfortunately largely missed. The walls survive at Lugo, 16–17, but many of the antiquities (largely funerary) are in the local museum. 18. Bordeaux: plan of the Roman walls (including towers) drawn in 1890. 19. The Roman wall in 1890, in the Cours d'Alsace-et-Lorraine. 20. Bourges: plan of the Roman enceinte.

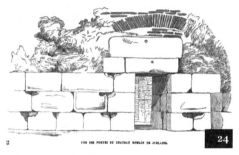

Walls and Antiquities. 21–22. The walls of Dax, still standing in 1856, and a sally-port constructed from large Roman blocks. 23. Périgueux: view of the late antique walls from the Antiquités de Vésone. 24–25. Jublains: castellum in a view of 1854, and a sally-port of large blocks, their excavated corners suggesting they were held in place by lead, and robbed out later by scavengers seeking this popular metal.

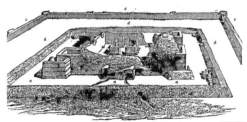

Walls and Antiquities at Dijon. Many of Dijon's monuments, some described in the 6th century by Gregory of Tours, suffered in the course of the 19th century, including churches. Its modernisation meant that the Roman walls as well as later ones, were dismantled in sections from the beginning of the 19th century. 26. Plan, published 1581. 27. Funerary antiquities retrieved from the walls during the demolitions of the 19th century, and now in the museum. 28. Roman pilasters retrieved from the substructures of the palace in 1856.

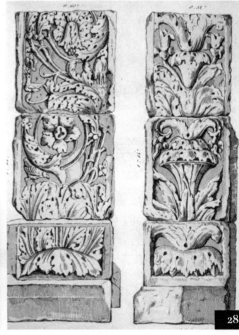

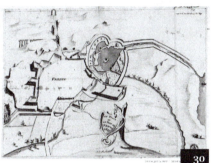

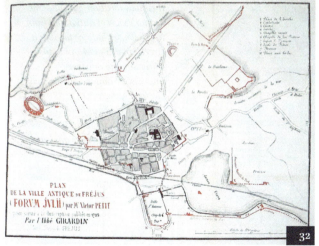

Fréjus was eviscerated by modernisation and the railway, and its heritage lost. 29. The town walls in Meunier's watercolour of 1793. 30. The town and port in a plan of 1647, and in one of 1727 (32) showing the outlying Roman monuments. These were in bad condition, structures such as the amphitheatre (31) stripped down to the concrete, and the prestigious cladding and other marble elements reused about the town.

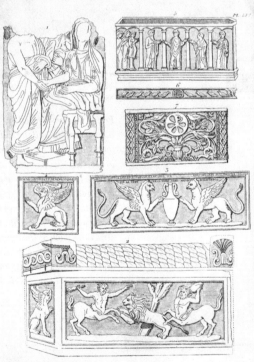

Antiquities in Provence.
33. Fréjus, in Millin's 1807 atlas, with his misunderstanding of the baptistery as a "temple antique servant de baptistère à la paroisse," whereas in fact the eight columns were moved to their new location. 34. The same author's view of antiquities from Marseille, including (top left) a Greek funerary stele, plus one Christian and one (very impressive) pagan sarcophagus. Naturally, there is a preponderance of funerary antiquities – stelai and sarcophagi – because ancient cemeteries outside towns were dug up as population expanded.

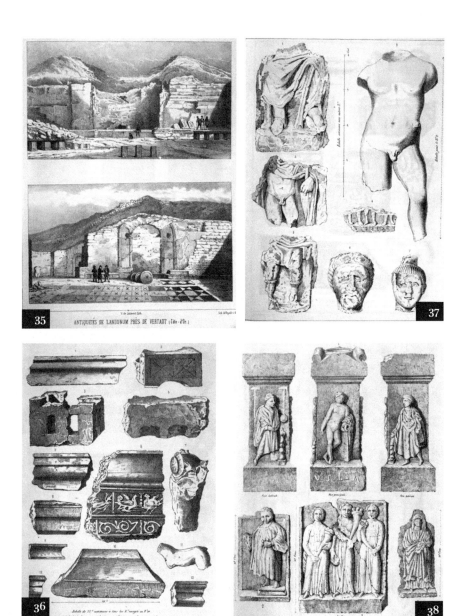

Landunum *(near Vertaut, Côte-d'Or), an important ruined town, discovered in 1849. As one scholar reported in 1850, "Rues, édifices, temples, bains, tout y est reconnaissable et d'une belle conservation." It was visited by the Congress in 1856, one of whose members reported on a bath: "Les nombreux vestiges de peintures sur enduits et les fragments de placage en marbre qu'on a rencontrés... Notre grand regret, en terminant cette partie de notre travail, est de n'avoir pu, par des fouilles suffisantes, trouver le château d'eaux vives qui entretenait les thermes et toute la cité." Fragments from the frescoed architecture are illustrated, together with sculpture and altars.*

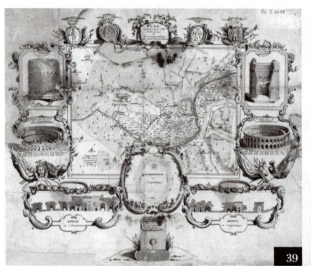

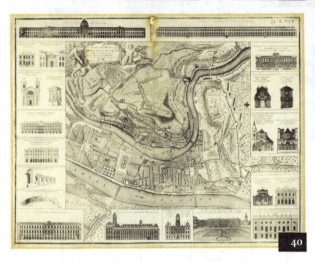

Proclaiming the old and the new. Could the old survive along with the new? Périgueux does have antiquities to display; but Lyon, an important industrial town, does not. Did antiquities go into the extensive fortifications on its northern flank? 39. The 1811 plan of Périgueux shows the amphitheatre in glory, and only its ruins below. 40. The 1801 plan of Lyon does show a funerary monument, and ruins of aqueduct and theatre, but also displays the new alignments between the rivers. 41. Another way of incorporating the old in the new is seen at Arles, where an obelisk from the circus was transferred (with great difficulty) to the square adjacent to S. Trophîme and the Town Hall.

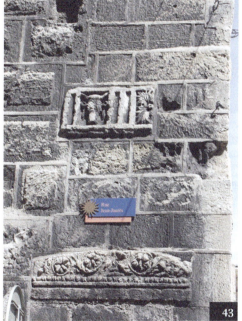

Narbonne's *decline from fortified frontier town to provincial backwater allowed the survival and preservation of more antiquities than even Bordeaux, a much larger settlement. 42. A sarcophagus used as a lintel in the church of S. Paul. 43. Antiquities built into the Archbishop's Palace. 44. The basalt cannonballs were used as a frieze on top of the 16th-century walls, making one wonder whether this was where Boullée got his ideas from. The Porte de Perpignan (45) and the Porte de Béziers (46), with the antiquities built into them. Not all the rich antiquities displayed here survived to find a place in the museum.*

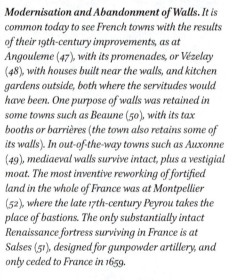

Modernisation and Abandonment of Walls. *It is common today to see French towns with the results of their 19th-century improvements, as at Angouleme (47), with its promenades, or Vézelay (48), with houses built near the walls, and kitchen gardens outside, both where the servitudes would have been. One purpose of walls was retained in some towns such as Beaune (50), with its tax booths or barrières (the town also retains some of its walls). In out-of-the-way towns such as Auxonne (49), mediaeval walls survive intact, plus a vestigial moat. The most inventive reworking of fortified land in the whole of France was at Montpellier (52), where the late 17th-century Peyrou takes the place of bastions. The only substantially intact Renaissance fortress surviving in France is at Salses (51), designed for gunpowder artillery, and only ceded to France in 1659.*

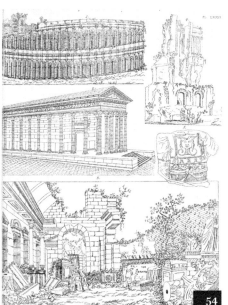

Nîmes. 53. Poldo d'Arenas' plan dates from 1560, and shows the walls. He writes in verse: La belle ville, je dis, Non pas celle qui est ores, Mais celle qui fut jadis, Dont les reliques encores, Les tours, et les vieux fragments Des murailles magnifiques, De la grandeur des antiques Donnent certains argumens... Tant d'épitaphes gravés, Et tailles en pierre dure, Et tant de riches pavez, Trouvez aux champs d'aventure, Tant de beaux marbres brisés, Colonnes, chapiteaux, bases. 54. Millin's 1807 views of the amphitheatre, Maison Carrée, Tour Magne, and nymphaeum (Temple de Diane), plus the military torso of a (colossal?) statue. The temple is already being used as an al fresco museum. 55. The amphitheatre being cleared out in 1867. 56. The Porte d'Auguste.

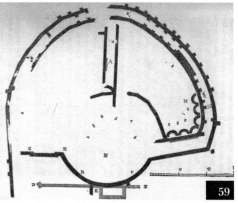

Theatres. *Like amphitheatres, these were sturdy structures easily adapted for housing and/or defence, but not used for their built purpose since late antiquity. 57. Orange: interior of the theatre in 1835. 58. Plan of the theatre at Orange in 1835, showing the 45 private properties to be acquired "pour son complet déblaiement et isolement." 59. By 1853, when it was dug, the theatre at Vieux (Calvados) was little more than a collection of walls flush with the ground. 60. Millin's 1807 views of theatre and arch at Orange, the latter once a fort, and considerably more damaged than its present-day "restored" appearance.*

MAISONS ANCIENNES DÉMOLIES A ORLÉANS EN 1888
Vis-à-vis la maison dite « A LA COQUILLE ».
Photographie d'Alfred Normand, membre de l'Institut.

LE VANDALISME A ROUEN

LE QUARTIER DE JEANNE D'ARC OU RUE SAINT-ROMAIN QU'ON VEUT DÉMOLIR
EN ABATTANT LA MAISON AB ET SES VOISINES.

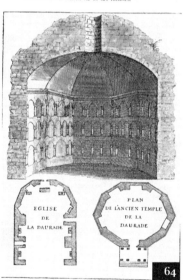

Modernisation, Houses and Churches. *Although some towns retain groups of old houses because they were too poor to modernise, one big problem with modernisation was what to do with housing when new roads were cut, or old roads widened or straightened. The usual response was to demolish wooden houses, in some cases retaining decorative features for the local museum. The fate of stone houses, some dating to the later Middle Ages, was a lottery: Paris demolished them, Lyon and other towns retained many. 61. Orleans: houses demolished in 1888. 62. Rouen: houses in the Quartier Jeanne d'Arc, about to be demolished in 1901. 63. At Toulouse, modernisation destroyed churches (here the Carmelites, 1808–9, from the 1885 publication* Le Vieux Toulouse Disparu), *by which date the sense of loss was widespread. 64. The greatest architectural loss was the Daurade.*

Paris: 65. 1892 Protest against a railway station near the Invalides, with the comment "Quand il n'y aura plus dans Paris, que des rues, des gares et des cimetières, Paris sera devenu inhabitable." NB the workmen destroying Paris' crown are toffs in top hats – the entrepreneurs. 66. The saving of the Paris amphitheatre required private money. 67. Labédollière's Nouveau Paris, of 1860, with illustrations by Gustave Doré. He writes (p. 32) "De 1848 à 1860, Paris a pris une physionomie toute nouvelle: nous allons essayer de la dépeindre en parcourant tour à tour les vingt arrondissements. Nous recueillerons pieusement les souvenirs qui se rattachent aux pierres dispersées, en même temps que nous ferons la description des monuments nouveaux qui s'élèvent." Doré's frontispiece, with a gothick typography that drips antiquitiy if not menace, shows Haussmann, like God the Father (with a map of Paris) directing the destruction below.

When digging trenches for the railway lines near the Invalides in 1896, what should they find but one of Ledoux' barrières: (68) but unfortunately for destruction, not urban archaeology!

Prehistoric monuments were popular and plentiful in many regions of France, but survive in large numbers only in less-developed (less modernised) regions. 69. Carnac in Cambry's view of 1805, and 70. Avebury in a print of 1845. Both are incorrect: some of the Carnac stones are 4.5m high, but the drawing adds several metres; the Avebury rings are too perfect, and the village in and around them is omitted. 71. The Dolmen de Kerlan, near Carnac, has been Christianised, helping ensure its protection. 72. 1845 print of monoliths at Dol (near Rennes: La Pierre du Champ-Dolent) and at Joinville (near Chaumont, called La Haute-borne), by the Roman road.

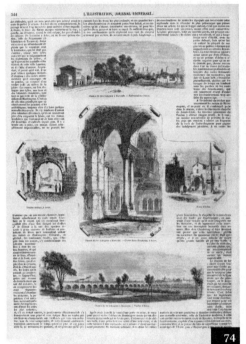

Rail travel in L'Illustration. *Pictures of goods trains invigorating the French economy had no mass appeal, but views of monuments visitable conveniently only by rail certainly did. Nearly all issues of* L'Illustration *pictured the attractions of rail travel. 73. The railway bridge crossing the river at Tarascon. 74. The Avignon-Marseilles line shows some of the monuments of Arles, plus the station and viaduct (1847–8): "aussi est-ce avec un vif sentiment que le voyageur sent la locomotive, qui ne doit pas s'arrêter, courir vers Arles aussi vite qui lui permettent les règlements de police, et qu'il aperçoit les murailles et les édifices de cette ville fameuse, où il a hâte d'arriver." Speed sold railway tickets, and then motor cars. How many monuments survived or were restored because they were on rail routes? How many mouldered and collapsed because they were not? 75. Similarly, the Paris-Tours railway shows tourists the sights they will pass on their journey (1846).*

CARCASSONNE, BEFORE THE RESTORATION.

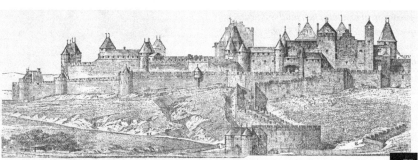
CARCASSONNE, THE NORTHERN END, POSTERN, AND CASTLE, RESTORED.

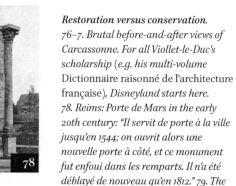

Restoration versus conservation.
76–7. Brutal before-and-after views of Carcassonne. For all Viollet-le-Duc's scholarship (e.g. his multi-volume Dictionnaire raisonné de l'architecture française), *Disneyland starts here.*
78. Reims: Porte de Mars in the early 20th century: "Il servit de porte à la ville jusqu'en 1544; on ouvrit alors une nouvelle porte à côté, et ce monument fut enfoui dans les remparts. Il n'a été déblayé de nouveau qu'en 1812." 79. The print shows how little of the Gate is original. None of it would have survived had the railway followed its first intended track.

Modernisation. 80. Angers: illustrating the problem of restoring old buildings, such as these picturesque wrecks. 81. Façadism in action. When land was scarce, whole complexes were destroyed, as at S. Jean des Vignes at Soissons, leaving just the façade and towers. Caumont had predicted in 1834: "il ne reste plus que deux côtés qui seront probablement démolis par le génie militaire et vendus à la toise comme les deux cotés qui ont déjà disparu avec l'église de l'abbaye." 82. Orleans in 1836, with the ramparts replaced (or just disguised?) by tree-shaded promenades.

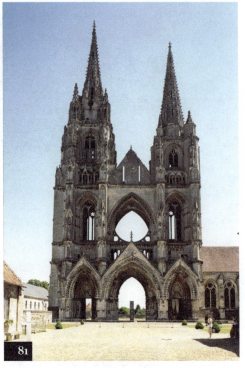

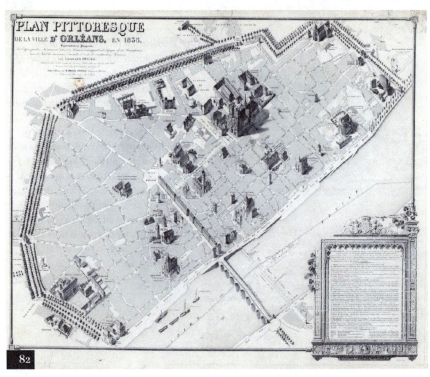

Modernisation and alignments. 83. Poitiers in 1568, with amphitheatre centre-left, some of its blocks no doubt reused in adjacent town walls and houses. 84. Plan of 1786, with "les améliorations, alignemens et nouvelles Rues." As for Antiquity, "l'on pourrait encore juger de ses imposantes Fortifications." Most of the old streets have gone, probably taking antiquities with them, and the walls have now given way to tree-punctuated boulevards. 85. Plan of Moissac, where we can still admire the smaller cloister. The larger one, indicated by "K" on the plan, was bulldozed along with the fortifications ("L") to make place in 1845 for the railway. This is another example of the 19th century being willing to preserve fragments, but not the whole complex. This was a pity: fortified mediaeval monasteries are rare.

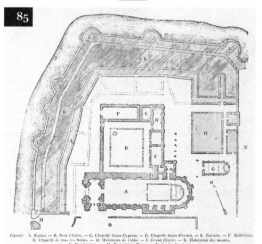

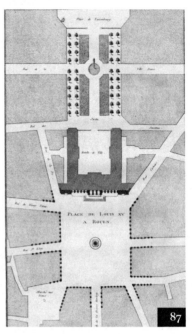
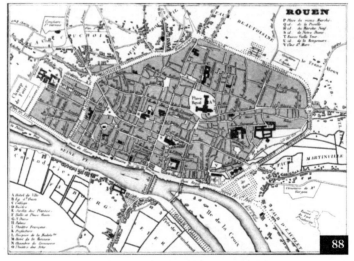

Modernisation at Rouen. *86. The Quartier Jeanne d'Arc, scheduled for demolition at the end of the century. 87. Patte designed a square for King Louis XV but, as was explained in 1881, "comme il s'agissait de dépenser un million pour tous ces projets d'embellissement, les Rouennais reculèrent devant les frais. Les travaux furent abandonnés, et Louis XV dut se contenter de faire couler en bronze le modèle de sa statue." 88. In the town plan of 1835, the city retains its old layout, but only temporarily. As Baedeker comments in 1909: "the construction within the last forty years of handsome streets like those of Paris has swept away a large number of the quaint old houses."*

89. Maisons près de la Cathédrale. (XVIe Siècle.)

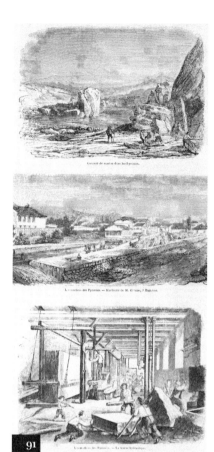
91.

90. DÉTAILS des MAISONS en BOIS.

Effects of Modernisation. *89. Troyes in the* Voyage Archéologique et Pittoresque *of 1837, and (90) wooden ornaments from such houses from the same publication. One of these houses nests against the cathedral – just the kind of pot-pourri the modernisers determined to destroy, and quaintness and the picturesque with it, the better (they believed) to present large churches uncluttered. Hence most of France's church or cathedral squares became "steppes" – waste-lands without character or any sense of architectural development through time. 91. The three woodcuts from* L'Illustration *(1847–8) shows that marble from the Pyrenees could now be quarried and cut on an industrial scale; Louis XIV had opened the quarries (and the Romans before him) – but transport in the 19thC was now so much easier than in the 17thC. Certainly, from the 17th century onwards there was insufficient surviving spolia marble to ornament any large projects.*

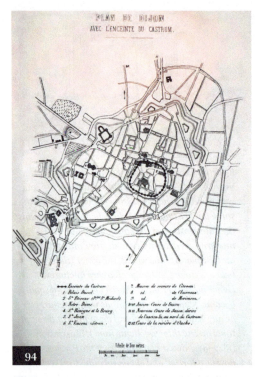

Later Fortifications. *The 17th century saw the further development of bastioned and star-shaped fortifications, which took up huge amounts of ground, as can be seen here. 92. Soissons in a view of 1747. 93. Plan of Senlis in 1815. 94. Dijon in 1856 showing the castrum and the 17thC fortifications. 95. Langres, an importants frontier town. We can only guess how many antiquities (especially funerary ones) such extensive earth- and stone-works displaced and destroyed outside erstwhile Roman towns and over their cemeteries, for no reports are known. Such building work involved the greatest turnover of soil since the Romans, and before the laying of railway tracks.*

Amphitheatres. 96. Saintes: the amphitheatre in 1845, the area largely private property. 97. Autun: an optimistic view of the amphitheatre (including sculptures!) of 1802. 98. Périgueux: amphitheatre in a view of the early 1820s, from the Antiquités de Vésone, showing how little survived above ground. 99. Angers: illustrating the problem with restoring old buildings; the amphitheatre, in another optimistic view, of 1843 (the remains went in the 1860s as the rue des Arènes was laid out). 100. Arles: the amphitheatre with its housing in a view of 1666; the structure survives in such good condition not because it was in or near a town (as were all on this page), but because it was inhabited – and private property!

Funerary Antiquities: *101. Arles: The Champs Elysées in the early 19thC, showing how little survived of this famous cemetery, which once had large and prestigious sarcophagi. As Estringin wrote in 1837, "où sont les statues de nos anciens dieux grecs et romains? dispersés dans les Musées de Paris, de Lyon, de Marseille, ou perdus dans des collections particulières." 102. At Sens, the walls were of brick and stone, and many funerary stelai were recovered from them. Espérandieu comments (IV.3), "Le Musée gallo-romain de Sens provient presque en entier des assises inférieures de l'ancien mur d'enceinte de la ville." 103. Beauvais: surviving sections of a funerary monument. 104. Millin's 1807 views of monuments at S. Rémy de Provence. It is astonishing that so few architectural funerary monuments survived in France, those at S. Rémy doing so perhaps because they were nearly 2km from the town.*

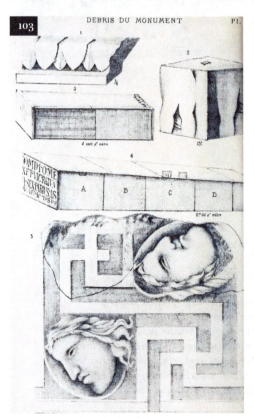

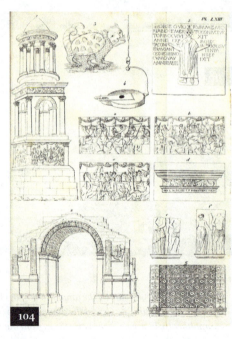

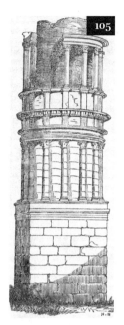

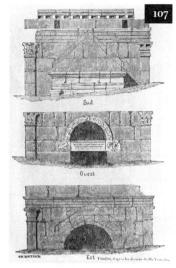

Funerary Antiquities. *105. Aix-en-Provence: mausoleum, which disappeared in the late 1780s, and 106, sarcophagi set up as fountains. 107. Lanuéjols is one of the few Roman funerary complexes to part-survive into the 19th century, with many of its blocks already reused in the village houses. But there were surely hundreds of such monumental tombs which have completely disappeared. 108. A stele retrieved from the walls of Boulogne in 1896. 109. La Grande Cheminée, a Roman funerary monument near Valogne, Normandy, in 1845. Here were also baths, and their owner "chercha à les détruire par la sappe et la mine; il fit casser en 1773, avec des masses de fer, la piscine et les petits fourneaux qui étaient dessous."*

Temples. All Roman towns had temples, but most disappeared because their architectural elements could not be conveniently reused except in some sections of mediaeval churches. 110. Bordeaux: les Piliers de Tutelle, destroyed in 1677. 111. Périgueux: the Belleforest view of 1575 shows the amphitheatre (D) as a substantial standing structure, and the Tour de Vésone (A) below it, already apparently devoid of cladding or columned peristyle. 112. Vienne: LeBas' view of the Temple of Augustus. 113. Peristyle of the temple at Riez, drawn in 1845; the town also has a baptistery. 114. Vernegues (N of Aix): temple, the subject of a question for the congressists in 1876: "A qui était-il dédié et quelle est l'époque de sa construction?"

***Reuse.** 115. Autun: house built with tomb monuments, and these are clearly intended to be decorative. 116, 117. Two views of a Roman tomb at Vaison-la-Romaine, taken over as a house. 118. Arles, theatre: in 1839, the interior had still not been cleared: plan with the numbers "des maisons qui restent à acquérir." In other words, it was still largely private property and, like the amphitheatre survived in reasonable condition. 119. In Dijon antiquities found during urban development were used to decorate several town houses, such as the Hotel du Comte de Vesvrotte in 1854. 120. Poitiers: the amphitheatre in 1699.*

Reuse. 121. Senlis: an 1877 view of houses still on top of the gallo-roman walls. 122. At Sens: 31 blocks came from the façade of the baths (reconstructed here), demonstrating how some ¾ of the ensemble has been lost, presumably for local housing, or burned for lime. Photography is now a useful substitute for physical survival. 123. At Saint-Gilles-du-Gard, reused columns are in evidence, but figural sculpture, bas reliefs and veneers are also cut from spolia, since there was no marble quarrying in France when the church was built. 124. Vienne: section of a Roman road near the town. Such relics survived, and were still in use, in remote and mountainous areas where the moderns did not themselves wish to build roads. 125. La Turbie in 1845 appears with its crumbling mediaeval fortifications, and little sign that it was a victory monument. Some of its sculptures were by 1865 in the palace of the Governor General at Monaco.

Reuse. *126. Arles: remains of the 'Palace of Constantine" in 1845, incorporated into a later building. 127. Vienne, view of what Lemaître in 1845 calls the theatre portico. 128. The Roman spring building at Les Fumades (Gard) in 1908, where "plusieurs des petits monuments extraits du puits sont enchassés dans la rocaille. 129. In Autun, the Mausoleum of Saint Lazare (1140–50) was adorned with coloured marbles, which must have been scavenged from Roman monuments, of which there were once plenty in and around the town. Some ornamented other churches such as S. Martin, "ornée des plus beaux marbres antiques." 130. In Algeria in the 1840s, the walls of Constantine still stood, reinforced with columns and other antiquities, while some house doorways (131) in the town were supported by fragments of inscriptions, and columns. All these spolia have now disappeared.*

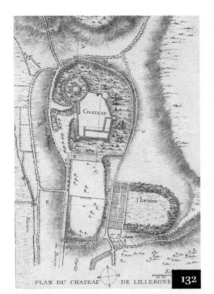

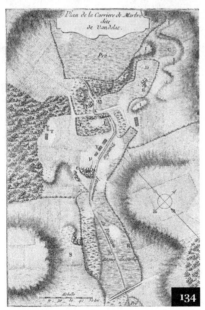

Caylus' Recueil d'Antiquités. This was the largest and best-illustrated compendium of antiquities of the later 18th century although Caylus did not at first focus on Roman Gaul. 132. Plan of Lillebonne (Recueil VI, 393ff) was drawn for him by M. Duchesne, Sous-Ingénieur des Ponts et Chaussées at Rouen. The plans in his Recueil are often the best information we have for the state of antiquities in the later 18thC. 133. The Tombeaux des Deux Amants (Recueil II, 357), at Vaise, near Lyon, the occupying statues long gone. 134. The Roman quarries at Vandelat, near the Loire (Recueil VI, 353–5); Caylus deduces, correctly, that the Romans did not import all their marbles; and he was sure the quarry was not used under Louis XIV and later because no traces of gunpowder were found! 135. Amphitheatre at Tintignac, near Tulle (from vol VI); this, by 1838, "ne se distingue plus au milieu des champs cultivés que par une élévation régulière qui en accuse le périmètre, et par quelques massif en opus incertum qui percent la terre çà et là." A perusal of Caylus' highly illustrated volumes will emphasise just how much has disappeared since the later 18th century.